Principles, Construction and Application of Multilingual Wordnets

Proceeding of the 5th Global Wordnet Conference

Principles, Construction and Application of Multilingual Wordnets

Proceeding of the 5th Global Wordnet Conference

Editors

Pushpak Bhattacharyya
Christiane Fellbaum
Piek Vossen

Narosa Publishing House
New Delhi   Chennai   Mumbai   Kolkata

Editors
Pushpak Bhattacharyya
Department of Computer Science and Engineering
Indian Institute of Technology Bombay
Powai, Mumbai
Maharashtra, India

Christiane Fellbaum
Computer Science Department
Princeton University
35 Olden Street
Princeton, New Jersey
USA

Piek Vossen
Professor of Computational Lexicology
Faculteit dre Letteren
VU University Amsterdam
De Boelelaan 1105
1081 HV Amsterdam
Netherlands

Copyright © 2010, Narosa Publishing House Pvt. Ltd.

NAROSA PUBLISHING HOUSE PVT. LTD.

22 Delhi Medical Association Road, Daryaganj, New Delhi 110 002
35-36 Greams Road, Thousand Lights, Chennai 600 006
306 Shiv Centre, Sector 17, Vashi, Navi Mumbai 400 703
2F-2G Shivam Chambers, 53 Syed Amir Ali Avenue, Kolkata 700 019

www.narosa.com

All rights reserved. No part of this publication may be reproduced, stored in a retrieval system, or transmitted in any form or by any means, electronic, mechanical, photocopying, recording or otherwise, without prior written permission of the publisher.

All export rights for this book vest exclusively with Narosa Publishing House Pvt. Ltd. Unauthorised export is a violation of terms of sale and is subject to legal action.

Typesetting
Camera-ready by Arun Karthikeyan Karra, Salil Rajeev Joshi, Saurabh Sohoney and Anup Kulkarni from sources files provided by authors.

Cover page design
Sam Vossen

Acknowledgement for using copyright images
Paul De Koninck, Laval University, www.greenspine.ca
Christopher Collins, Faculty of Science, University of Ontario Institute of Technology, http://www.christophercollins.ca

Printed from the camera-ready copy provided by the Editors

ISBN 978-81-8487-083-1

Published by N.K. Mehra for Narosa Publishing House Pvt. Ltd.,
22 Delhi Medical Association Road, Daryaganj, New Delhi 110 002

Printed in India

Preface

This is the Fifth International WordNet conference and the second to be held in India, a country with twenty-four official and hundreds of unofficial languages and thus a befitting host. It is also the tenth anniversary of the Global WordNet Association. The growth of the worldwide community of wordnets is reflected in the program, which includes presentations with data from twenty-seven languages in addition to reports on Indian and Asian wordnets, each covering multiple regional languages. The increase in the number of wordnets necessarily grants a wider perspective and generates new proposals for the structure of wordnets and ways of representing lexical and semantic information both for linguistic investigation and applications.

The keywords of the presentations hint at the breadth of the topics and promise an exciting and stimulating meeting with humour and a story that may involve circles and squares, where images float by while emotions are detected, where friends divide the labour, a python is crawling through the crowd and an adventure concludes it all.

Our thanks go to all participants for sharing their work, to the program committee for their thoughtful reviews and to the local organizers for their hard work.

Mumbai

Christiane Fellbaum
Pushpak Bhattacharyya
Piek Vossen

Organization

The fifth Global WordNet Conference is organized by Indian Institute of Technology Bombay, Center for Indian languages Technology, at Department of Computer Science and Engineering in co-operation with the Global WordNet Association.

The conference home page can be found at http://www.globalwordnet-iitb2010.in

PROGRAMME COMMITTEE

Program Chairs

Christiane Fellbaum (Princeton University, New Jersey, USA)
Piek Vossen (VU University Amsterdam, Netherlands)

Area Chairs

German Rigau (EHU, San Sebastian, Spain), Dominique Dutoit (Memodata, Caen, France), Adam Kilgarriff (Sussex University, UK), Adam Pease (Articulate Software, San Francisco, US), Ales Horak (Masaryk University, Brno, Czech Republic), Darja Fiser (University of Ljubljana, Slovenia), Bernado Magnini (ITC-Irst, *Trento, Italy*. Trento, Italy), Shu-kai Hsieh (NTNU, Taipei, Taiwan), William Black (University of Manchester, UK), Gloria Vasquez (Barcelona, Spain), Ana Fernandez (Barcelona, Spain), Piek Vossen (VU University Amsterdam, Netherlands), Roxane Segers (VU University Amsterdam, Netherlands), Pushpak Bhattacharyya (IIT Bombay, India), Christiane Fellbaum (Princeton University, New Jersey, USA), Hitoshi Isahara (National Institute of Information and Communications Technology, Kyoto, Japan), Eneko Agirre (University of Basque, Spain), Karel Pala (Masaryk University, Brno, Czech Republic), Kyoko Kanzaki (National Institute of Information and Communications Technology, Kyoto, Japan), Ted Pedersen (University of Minnesota, Duluth), Francis Bond (Nanyang Technological University, Singapore), Monica Monachini (CNR-ILC, Pisa, Italy), Claudia Soria (CNR-ILC, Pisa, Italy), Andrea Marchetti (CNR-IIT, Pisa, Italy), Maurizio Tesconi (CNR-IIT, Pisa, Italy), Francesco Ronzano (CNR-IIT, Pisa, Italy), Wauter Bosma, (Vrije Universiteit, Amsterdam, Netherlands) Bolette Pedersen (University of *Copenhagen, Denmark,*) Jordan Boyd-Graber (Princeton University, Princeton, NJ, USA), Horacio Rodriguez (Universitat Politècnica de Catalunya, Barcelona Spain), Axel Herold (Berlin-Brandenburg Academy of Sciences, Germany), Thomas Pfuhl (Berlin-Brandenburg Academy of Sciences, Germany), Amanda Hicks (Berlin-Brandenburg Academy of Sciences, Germany), Yannick Mathieu (Paris, France), B. Mallikarjun (CIIL Mysore, India), Sudeshna Sarkar (IIT Kharagpur), S. Arulmozi (Dravidian University, Kuppam, India), Girish Nath Jha (Jawaharlal Nehru University, New Delhi, India), S.Rajendran (Tamil University, Thanjavur, India), Prabhakar Pandey (IIT Bombay, India), Rajat Mohanty (AOL, Bangalore, India), Dipti Mishra Sharma (IIIT Hyderabad, India)

ORGANIZING COMMITTEE

Organizing Chair

Prof. Pushpak Bhattacharyya

Members

Malhar Kulkarni, Vasant G. Zende, Rupash Modak, Arun Karthikeyan Karra, Mitesh Khapra, Prabhakar Pandey, Deepak Jagtap, Madhu Prasad Sharma

Contents

Preface	v
Organization	vii
Crowdsourcing WordNet	1
Chris Biemann and Valerie Nygaard	
Why Wikipedia Needs to Make Friends with WordNet	9
Kow Kuroda, Francis Bond and Kentaro Torisawa	
WordNets for Indian Languages: Some Issues	17
Panchanan Mohanty	
On Polysemy in Tamil and other Indian Languages	22
Panchanan Mohanty and S. Arulmozi	
Interactions of South African Languages: Case Study of Tsotsitaal	29
Karolina Brook	
Contrastive Polysemy in Concept Space: Implications for Multilingual Semantic Lexicons	34
Somsukla Banerjee, Achla Raina and Harish Karnick	
Generating Domain-specific Ontology from Common-sense Semantic Network for Target-specific Sentiment Analysis	39
Ashish Sureka, Vikram Goyal, Denzil Correa and Anirban Mondal	
Domain-specific Word Sense Disambiguation Combining Corpus based and Wordnet based Parameters	47
Mitesh M. Khapra, Sapan Shah, Piyush Kedia and Pushpak Bhattacharyya	
Finding Humour in the Blogosphere: The Role of WordNet Resources	56
Antonio Reyes, Paolo Rosso and Davide Buscaldi	
Exploring Hindi WordNet as a Lexical Interface and Subject Headings Tool in Library OPAC	62
B. A. Sharada	
Verbs of Emotion in French and English	70
Yvette Yannick Mathieu and Christiane Fellbaum	
Classification of Verbs—Towards Developing Bengali Verb Subcategorization Lexicon	76
Somnath Banerjee, Dipankar Das and Sivaji Bandyopadhyay	
Representing Compound Verbs in Indo WordNet	84
Soma Paul	
Unification of Universal Word Dictionaries using WordNet Ontology and Similarity Measures	92
Sangharsh Boudhh and Pushpak Bhattacharyya	
Semantic Services in FreeLing 2.1: WordNet and UKB	99
Lluís Padró, Samuel Reese, Eneko Agirre and Aitor Soroa	
Weighted Edge: A New Method to Measure the Semantic Similarity of Words based on WordNet	106
Liang Dong, Pradip K. Srimani and James Z. Wang	
LOOK4: Enhancement of Web Search Results with Universal Words and WordNet	111
Aram Avetisyan and Vahan Avetisyan	
Similarity, Comparability and Analogy in WordNet: Squaring the Analogical Circle with *Mondrian*	116
Tony Veale and Mourad el Moueddeb	
Challenges in Multilingual Domain-specific Sense-marking	123
Jaya Saraswati, Rajita Shukla, Sonal Pathade, Tina Solanki and Pushpak Bhattacharyya	

Hindi Semantic Category Labeling using Semantic Relatedness Measures   131
Siva Reddy, Abhilash Inumella, Navjyoti Singh and Rajeev Sangal

An Intelligent Framework for Reasoning on Story Plots using WordNet   135
A. Jaya and G. V. Uma

Exploring the Integration of WordNet and FrameNet   141
Egoitz Laparra, German Rigau and Montse Cuadros

Towards Universal Multilingual Knowledge Bases   149
Gerard de Melo and Gerhard Weikum

Division of Semantic Labor in the Global Wordnet Grid   157
Piek Vossen and German Rigau

Using DEB Services for Knowledge Representation within the KYOTO Project   165
Aleš Horák and Adam Rambousek

Developing the Persian WordNet of Verbs: Issues of Compound Verbs and Building the Editor   171
Masoud Rouhizadeh, Mahsa A. Yarmohammadi and Mehrnoush Shamsfard

sloWNet: Construction and Corpus Annotation   177
Darja Fišer and Tomaž Erjavec

Semi Automatic Development of FarsNet: The Persian WordNet   184
Mehrnoush Shamsfard, Akbar Hesabi, Hakimeh Fadaei, Niloofar Mansoory, Ali Famian, Somayeh Bagherbeigi, Elham Fekri, Maliheh Monshizadeh and S. Mostafa Assi

Experiences in Building the Konkani WordNet using the Expansion Approach   192
Shantaram Walawalikar, Shilpa Desai, Ramdas Karmali, Sushant Naik, Damodar Ghanekar, Chandralekha D'Souza and Jyoti Pawar

Growth and Revision of Estonian WordNet   198
Kadri Kerner, Heili Orav and Sirli Parm

French WordNet Progress and Structured Concepts Embodiment Inside Wordnet   203
Dominique Dutoit, Patrick de Torcy and Yann Picand

Domain Specific WordNet on Customs Law   211
Zoltán Alexin, János Csirik, Attila Almási and Veronika Vincze

Hierarchy of Perceptional Adjectives in RussNet   216
Irina Azarova and Maria Yavorskaya

Modeling Attitude, Polarity and Subjectivity in Wordnet   224
Isa Maks and Piek Vossen

WNMS: Connecting the Distributed WordNet in the Case of Asian WordNet   232
Kergrit Robkop, Sareewan Thoongsup, Thatsanee Charoenporn, Virach Sornlertlamvanich and Hitoshi Isahara

Linking CoreNet to WordNet - Some Aspects and Interim Consideration   239
In-Su Kang, Sin-Jae Kang, Se-Jin Nam and Key-Sun Choi

A WordNet for Tulu   243
B. S. Shivakumar

Building a WordNet for Dravidian Languages   250
S. Rajendran, G. Shivapratap, V. Dhanalakshmi and K. P. Soman

Tamil WordNet   255
S. Rajendran

Telugu WordNet   259
S. Arulmozi

Toward plWordNet 2.0   263
Maciej Piasecki, Stanisław Szpakowicz and Bartosz Broda

Representation of Complex Predicates in WordNet   271
Uma Maheshwar Rao Garapati and Rajyarama Koppaka

The Representation of Idioms in WordNet	277
Anne Osherson and Christiane Fellbaum	
Enriching the Romanian WordNet using Semi-automatically Identified Hyponymic Patterns	282
Verginica Barbu Mititelu, Dan Ştefănescu and Alexandru Ceauşu	
Introducing Sanskrit Wordnet	287
Malhar Kulkarni, Chaitali Dangarikar, Irawati Kulkarni, Abhishek Nanda and Pushpak Bhattacharyya	
A Wordnet for Bodo Language: Structure and Development	295
Shikhar Kr. Sarma, Biswajit Brahma, Moromi Gogoi and Mane Bala Ramchiary	
Experiences in Building the Nepali Wordnet - Insights and Challenges	299
Alok Chakrabarty, Bipul Syam Purkayastha and Arindam Roy	
Introducing Filipino WordNet	306
Allan Borra, Adam Pease, Rachel Edita.O. Roxas and Shirley Dita	
Foundation and Structure of Developing an Assamese WordNet	311
Shikhar Kr. Sarma, Rakesh Medhi, Moromi Gogoi and Utpal Saikia	
Collaborative Management of KYOTO Multilingual Knowledge Base: The Wikyoto Knowledge Editor	316
Francesco Ronzano, Maurizio Tesconi, Salvatore Minutoli and Andrea Marchetti	
Resources for Extending the PolNet-Polish WordNet with a Verbal Component	325
Zygmunt Vetulani and Tomasz Obrêbski	
Rejuvenating the Italian WordNet: Upgrading, Standardising, Extending	331
Antonio Toral, Stefania Bracale, Monica Monachini and Claudia Soria	
The Need for Amharic WordNet	338
Tessema Mindaye, Meron Sahlemariam and Teshome Kassie	
Wordventure - Developing WordNet in Wikipedia-like Style	342
Julian Szymañski	
Adding Information to a Terminological Database by Means of Image Files	347
Rita Marinelli, Giovanni Spadoni and Sebastiana Cucurullo	
Online Multilingual Amarakośa: The Relational Lexical Database	354
Girish Nath Jha, R. Chandrashekar, Umesh Kumar Singh, Vibhuti Nath Jha, Satyendra Pandey, Surjit Kumar Singh and Mukesh Kumar Mishra	
Eurown: An Euro WordNet Module for Python	360
Neeme Kahusk	

Crowdsourcing WordNet

Chris Biemann
Powerset, a Microsoft Company
475 Brannan St 330
San Francisco, CA 94107, USA
cbiemann@microsoft.com

Valerie Nygaard
Powerset, a Microsoft Company
475 Brannan St 330
San Francisco, CA 94107, USA
vnygaard@microsoft.com

Abstract

This paper describes an experiment in using Amazon Mechanical Turk to collaboratively create a sense inventory. In a bootstrapping process with massive collaborative input, substitutions for target words in context are elicited and clustered by sense; then more contexts are collected. Contexts that cannot be assigned to a current target word's sense inventory re-enter the loop and get a supply of substitutions. This process provides a sense inventory with its granularity determined by common substitutions rather than by psychologically motivated concepts. Evaluation shows that the process is robust against noise from the crowd, yields a less fine-grained inventory than WordNet and provides a rich body of high precision substitution data at a low cost.

1 Introduction

Disappointing progress in Word Sense Disambiguation (WSD) competitions has often been attributed to problems with WordNet (Miller et al., 1990). While a valuable resource to the NLP community, WordNet was not originally designed for WSD. Still being the best option available, it became the standard resource in Senseval and Semeval competitions. High WSD performance scores using WordNet suffer from the extremly fine-grained distinctions that characterize the resource and by the relatively little available data for senses in contexts (cf. e.g. (Agirre and Edmonds, 2006)) . For example, of the eight noun senses of "hook", four refer to a *bent, curvy object*. However, in the entire SemCor (Mihalcea, 1998) there is only one occurrence recorded for this sense altogether, so for most of the senses the only data available are the glosses and the relations to other synsets. Even if some fine-grained classes are combined by clustering WordNet senses (Mihalcea and Moldovan, 2001), alignment of the sense inventory and the target domain or application remains a problem. Using WordNet, or any predefined inventory, for WSD may result in a mismatch with the target domain of the application. If it does not fit well, domain adaptation will be required, a costly endeavor that will likely have to be repeated. Corpus-based word sense acquisition, on the other hand, guarantees a match between inventory and target domain.

A major potential application of WSD is to supply correct substitutions in context for ambiguous words. The ability to make the right substitutions, in turn, gives rise to fuzzy semantic matching in Information Retrieval. However, as (Sanderson, 1994) estimated, at least 90% accuracy is required before the benefits of WSD-supplied substitutions or term expansions outweigh the drawbacks from errors.

Since semantic annotation tasks are notoriously difficult and low inter-annotator agreement goes hand in hand with low WSD scores, the OntoNotes project (Hovy et al., 2006) aimed at high agreement through word sense grouping to mitigate the problems above. In (Hovy et al., 2006) it was shown that enforcing more than 90% inter-annotator agreement and more coarse-grained sense groupings in fact can ensure accuracy levels close to 90%. However, manual methods of sense reduction such as those used in OntoNotes are costly and may not be scalable due to their dependence on highly trained annotators working for extended periods to learn the annotation protocols.

In this work, we pursue another path: we set up a bootstrapping process that relies on redundant

human input to crystallize a word sense inventory for given target words and a target corpus. Instructions are kept short and tasks are kept simple. Because some degree of noisy input is tolerated in this method, naiive annotators can be used, and data can be produced quickly, at low cost and without access to a full in-house annotation staff.
As a crowdsourcing platform, we use Amazon Mechanical Turk (AMT). AMT allows requesters to post arbitrary tasks, which are done for pay by a large pool of annotators. AMT allows to specify the number of annotators per task item, as well as to restrict the annotator pool by various criteria. The quality of annotations from AMT has been shown to be comparable to a professional annotators when answers from four or more different annotators are combined, see (Snow et al., 2008).

The remainder of this paper is organized as follows. First, we describe the three different crowdsourcing tasks in detail. Then, we lay out an overall system that connects these steps in a bootstrapping cycle carefully motivating our design decisions.
Finally, we lay out an experiment we conducted with this system, provide a quantitative and a qualitative analysis and evaluation and describe the resource resulting from this experiment.

2 Three Turker Tasks

This section is devoted to three elementary tasks given to annotators whom we will refer to as *turkers* in the AMT platform. The nature of crowdsourcing makes it necessary to follow some guidelines when designing tasks: (1) Both tasks and instruction sets for those tasks must be simple to hold training to a minimum, (2) redundancy is necessary to assure quality. The inherent noisiness of the process requires that only answers supplied multiple times by different turkers should be accepted. Requiring redundancy in answers is also important in identifying deliberate scammers.

2.1 Task 1: Finding Substitutions

The rationale behind this task is to be able to identify word senses by the differences in possible substitutions. For information retrieval applications, we find this substitution-based definition of senses desirable. Here, WSD is input for determining which lexical expansions should be used for matching, so the concept of substitutability is central.

In this task, turkers are presented with a sentence containing a target word emphasized in bold. They are asked to supply possible substitutions for the bolded word in the specific sentential context. Turkers must supply at least one, and up to a maximum of five substitutions. This task is very similar to the task used in (McCarthy and Navigli, 2007). In addition, turkers are asked to state whether the sentence is a good or acceptable representative of the target word meaning. When turkers indicate that assigning a sense to the target is hard or impossible, part-of-speech violations and insufficient contexts are potential culprits.

2.2 Task 2: Aligning Senses

This task measures how similar the senses of two usages of the same word are. The rationale behind this task is to measure closeness of senses and to be able to merge senses in cases where they are identical. Turkers are shown a pair of sentences that contain the same emphasized target word. They are then asked whether the meaning of this target word in the two sentences is identical, similar, different or impossible to determine.

2.3 Task 3: Match the Meaning

This task presents a sentence with a bolded target word and requires turkers to align usages of the target word to a given inventory: they are asked to choose one of a set of sentences containing the target word in different meanings representing the current sense inventory. They also can state that the sense is not covered by the current inventory, or label the sense as impossible to determine. To make the task more efficient and easier, this assignment contains ten of these questions for the same word using the same inventory, so the annotator has to understand the inventory choice only once.

3 Bootstrapping a Word Sense Inventory

This section describes how a word sense inventory is constructed using the tasks in Section 2. Figure 1 provides a schematic overview of how the three tasks are executed in sequence. Note that each target word is processed separately, and that the process is described for a single target word. We will use the noun target "station" for exemplifying the steps.

When using untrained turkers, the process that distills their raw responses to usable data must be formulated in a way that uses redundant answers and is robust against noise. Various thresholds described below have been introduced for these reasons. When trained, professional annotators are used, most of these constraints could be relaxed.

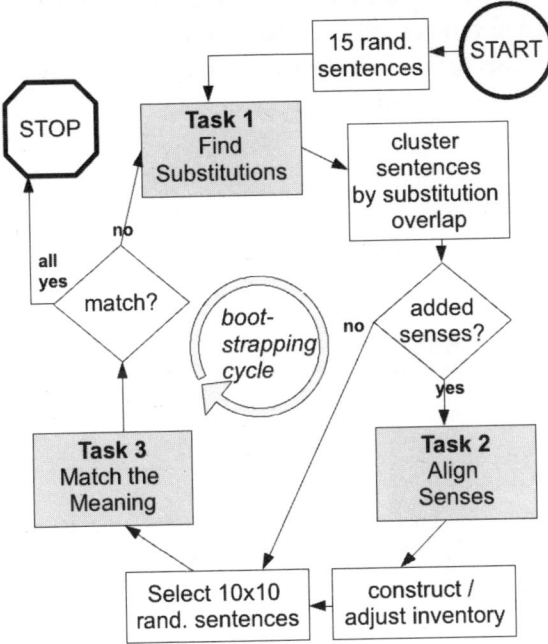

Figure 1: Bootstrapping process with Turker tasks

3.1 From Start to Task 1

For the target word, 15 random sentences are selected from a corpus resource. While 15 sentences is a somewhat arbitrary number, we have found that it ensures that the major senses of the target word are usually covered. These sentences are seeds to initiate the cycle, and need not cover all the senses in the corpus or final inventory.

In our experiments, we select by lemma and part-of-speech, so e.g. for the noun target "station" we would select sentences where "station" or "stations" were tagged as a noun. These sentences are presented in Task 1. We will use these three sentences as an example:

- **A:** The train left the *station*.
- **B:** This radio *station* broadcasts news at five.
- **C:** Five miles from the *station*, the railway tracks end.

These were assigned the following substitutions (multiplicity in brackets):

- **A:** terminal(5), railway station(3), rail facility(1), stop(1)
- **B:** radio station(4), network(3), channel(2)
- **C:** terminal(3), stop(2), train depot(2), railway station(1)

3.2 From Task 1 to Task 2

Having obtained a set of substitutions from the crowd, we compute a weighted similarity graph with the sentences as nodes. Edge weights are given by the amount of overlap in the substitutions of sentences. If two sentences share at least 3 different keywords, then their similarity is given by the sum of the common keywords they share. In the example, sentences A and C would get a score of 8 (terminal) + 4 (railway station) + 3 (stop) = 15. We only use sentences that are good or acceptable representatives for this task (as judged by turkers).

Using Chinese Whispers (Biemann, 2006), we apply graph clustering on this graph to group sentences that have a high similarity assuming that they contain the target word in the same meaning. We have chosen Chinese Whispers because it has been shown to be useful in sense clustering before (by e.g. (Klapaftis and Manandhar, 2008)) and has the property of finding the number of clusters automatically. This is crucial since we do not know the number of senses a priori. Note, however, that we do not use the outcome of the clustering directly, but ask turkers to validate it as part of the next step in the cycle, as described in the next section.

We exclude clusters consisting of singleton sentences. For each cluster, we select as the most prototypical representative sentence, the sentence that has the highest edge weight sum within the cluster. Ties are broken by evaluating difficulty and length (shorter is better). This sentence plus the substitutions of the cluster serves as sense inventory entry. In case this steps adds no senses to the inventory or the clustering resulted in only one sense, we continue with Task 3, otherwise, we validate the inventory.

3.3 From Task 2 to Task 3

The danger of clustering is either that two senses are merged or one sense is split into two entries. While merging merely results in more bootstrapping cycles, to ensure that the lost meaning not represented by the prototypical sentence is recovered, avoiding multiple entries per sense is more serious and must be dealt with directly. This is why we present all possible pairs of prototypical sentences in Task 2. If the majority of turkers judge that two sentences have identical meanings, we merge the entries, choosing the representative sentence at random.

Then we retrieve 100 random sentences containing our target word, group them in sets of ten and present them in Task 3.

3.4 Closing the loop

All sentences that could be matched to the inventory by the majority of turkers are added to the resource. Sentences for which the sense of the target word could not be determined due to disagreement are set aside. Sentences that are marked as uncovered by the current inventory re-enter the loop and we retrieve substitutions for them in Task 1. In our example, these might be sentences like

- **D:** The mid-level *station* is situated at 12400ft altitude.

- **E:** They were desperately looking for a gas *station*.

Those sentences will probably display a high overlap in substitutions with other sentences of the current or previous iterations. In this way, additional senses are identified and verified against the current inventory.

Only if almost none (we use a threshold of three) of the 100 sentences are marked as uncovered, we estimate that the vast majority of the senses in the corpus are represented in our inventory, and the process terminates for the target word.

4 Experiment

4.1 Experimental Setup

The choice of the underlying corpus was determined by our target application, a semantic search on Wikipedia. We used a sentence-broken, POS-tagged version of English Wikipedia (dump from January 3rd, 2008) and applied a few filters to ensure complete sentences of reasonable length. Due to its diversity in topics, Wikipedia works well as a corpus for word sense acquisition. We ran the bootstrapping acquisition cycle on the 397 most frequent nouns, implementing the crowdsourcing part with Amazon Turk. During the annotation process of the first 50 words, the data supplied by five turkers per task was heavily curated and scammers were identified and blocked manually.

The most productive and reliable ten turkers were then invited to perform the annotation of the remaining 347 words with virtually no curation or manual intervention. With these trusted turkers, a redundancy of three assignments per task was shown to be sufficient. With the current set of trusted turkers, we were able to reach a speed of 8 words per day for the overall process. The speed can be increased by simply adding more annotators.

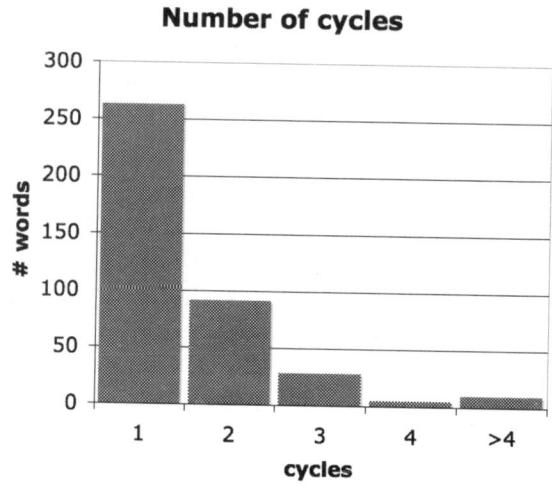

Figure 2: Distribution: words per number of cycles until convergence. On average, a word needed 1.56 cycles to converge.

4.2 Quantitative Analysis

Figure 2 shows the distribution of the number of cycles the words needed to converge. About two thirds of all words need only one cycle to complete, only ten words entered the cycle more than four times. The run for two words was finally terminated after ten iterations (see Section 5.3)..

Taking a look at the granularity of the inventory, Figure 3 shows the distribution of the number of words per number of senses. Even when using the highest frequencies nouns, almost half of the words are assigned only one sense, and over 90% of words have fewer than five senses.

For learning approaches to word sense disambiguation it is important to know how much data is available per sense. Figure 4 provides the distribution of sentences per sense in the resource. Minor

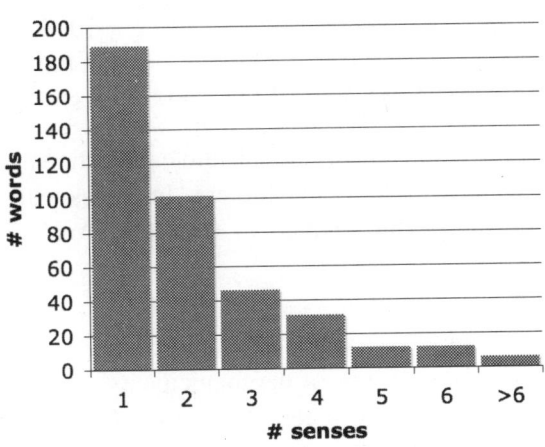
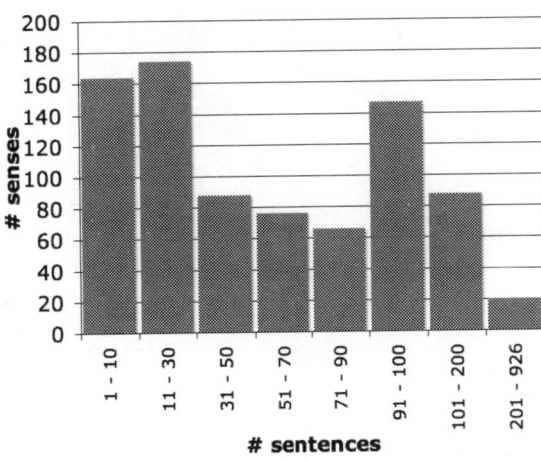

Figure 3: Distribution: number of words per number of senses. There are three words with seven senses, two words with nine senses and one word with ten senses. The average is 2.1 senses per word.

Figure 4: Distribution: number of senses per number of sentences interval. Only 5 senses have collected more than 300 sentences, at an average of 62.9 sentences per sense.

senses have a low number of sentences. Targets with only one sense have almost 100 sample sentences, resulting from the 100 sentences presented per iteration in Task 3. The experiment yielded a total of 51,736 sentences with a single sense-labeled target word. It is therefore built into our method to create a substantial corpus that could be used for training or evaluating WSD systems, complete with a level of frequency distribution among the senses, which is valuable in its own right. We collected substitutions for a total 8,771 sentences in Task 1. On average, a target word received 17 substitutions that were provided two or more times, and 4.5 substitutions with a frequency of ten or more. Manual inspection reveals that substitution frequencies over four are very reliable and virtually error-free.

5 Evaluation

Having characterized the results of our experiment quantitatively, we now turn to assessing the quality of the results and compare the granularity of the results with WordNet.

5.1 Quantitive Comparison with WordNet

Since we developed this resource in order to overcome the excessive splitting of WordNet terms into senses, we now compare the granularity of our sense inventory with WordNet. For our 397 target words, WordNet 2.1 lists 2,448 senses (excluding named entity instances), an average of 6.17 senses per target and almost three times as many senses as listed in our inventory (average number of senses: 2.1). Looking at the data reveals that most fine-grained WordNet distinctions have been conflated into coarser-grained senses. Also, obscure WordNet senses have not been included in our inventory. On some occasions, our inventory lists more senses, e.g. the WordNet sense *station#n#1* includes both railway stations and gas stations, whereas the crowdsourcing process distinguishes these. Figure 5 provides a 3D-plot of the number of targets for most of the combinations of number of senses in WordNet and in our inventory. There is a direct correlation between the number of senses: words with a large number of WordNet senses also tend to be assigned a high number of senses in the crowdsourcing inventory.

5.2 Qualitative Evaluation

We now turn to the quality of the data obtained by our acquisition cycle. Since the goal of this resource is to provide sense labels and their substitutions, we are interested in how often the substitution assigned via the sense label is acceptable. Note that we only asked for substitutes on context for 8,771 sentences in Task 1, but project these substitutions via aggregation (clustering), inventory checking (Task 2) and matching the meaning (Task 3) to our full set of 51,736 sentences, which do not overlap with the sentences presented

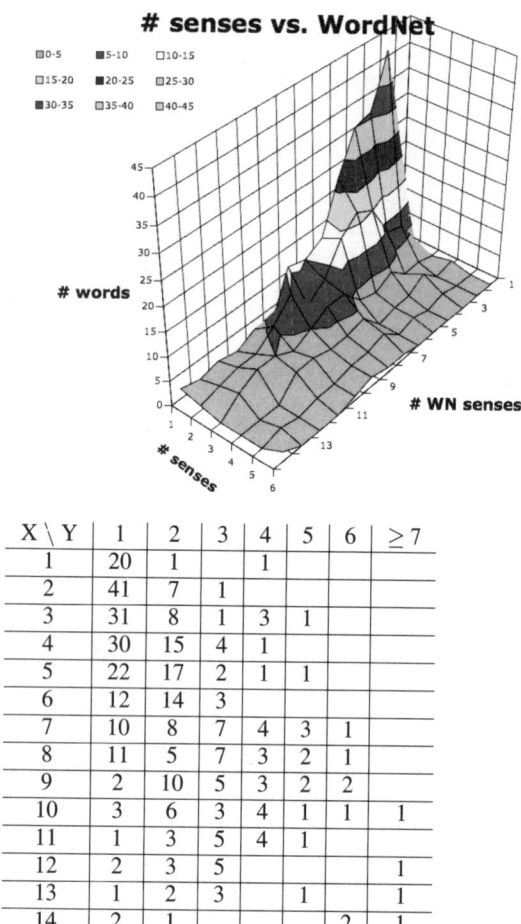

		System	
		Projection	Random
Vote	YES	469 (93.8%)	10 (2%)
	NO	14 (2.8%)	481 (96.2%)
	SOMEWHAT	17 (3.4%)	9 (1.8%)

Table 1: Evaluation of the substitute projection using majority vote on five turkers. Instances without majority are counted in the SOMEWHAT class.

X \ Y	1	2	3	4	5	6	≥ 7
1	20	1		1			
2	41	7	1				
3	31	8	1	3	1		
4	30	15	4	1			
5	22	17	2	1	1		
6	12	14	3				
7	10	8	7	4	3	1	
8	11	5	7	3	2	1	
9	2	10	5	3	2	2	
10	3	6	3	4	1	1	1
11	1	3	5	4	1		
12	2	3	5				1
13	1	2	3		1		1
14	2	1				2	1
≥ 15			1	3	4	5	2

Figure 5: Number of words that have X WordNet senses vs. Y senses in this inventory. 14 targets have 15 or more WordNet senses and are omitted.

in Task 1. This section describes an experiment to estimate the error rate of this projection. We selected the most frequent substitution per sense and added the second and third-ranked substitution in case their frequency was three or more. This produced three substitutions for most senses and one or two substitutions for minor senses. From our full list of sentences, we randomly sampled 500 sentences and set up an AMT task where we presented the sentence with the target word in bold along with a) the substitutions from this projection and b) random substitutions from the set of substitutions in separate tasks. Turkers were asked whether the substitutions matched the target word, matched the target word somewhat, do did match the target or the task was impossible for some reason. Table 1 shows the confusion matrix and the percentages of judgments, obtained by majority vote on five turkers. Manual checking of the positive answers for random substitutions revealed that these were in fact valid substitutions. For example, the substitutions of the municipality sense of "community" were randomly selected for a sentence containing the municipality sense of "city" as target.

Closer examination of the undecided and negative judgments for the projected substitutions showed that most of the negative judgments contained many judgments for "somewhat matching" (whereas NO answers for randomly supplied substitutions where mostly unanimous). Other sources of negative judgments included minor senses that had only substitutions with frequency one. Given that less than 3% of projected substitutions were unanimously judged as not matching, while random substitutions were judged as not matching in over 96% of cases, we concluded that the data produced by our process is of very high quality and is suitable for both evaluation and training Word Sense Disambiguation systems.

5.3 Error Analysis

In this section we report findings on analyzing the bootstrapping process for a total of 100 target words. Systematic errors of the process can serve as indicators for improvements in later versions of out acquisition cycle.

For the 100 targets, we observed the following problems (multitude shown in brackets):

- (4) Overlap or containment of one sense in the other leads to matching with two classes. This can be sorted out by taking into consideration the confusion matrix of meaning matching (Task 3) and the similarity of senses as measured in Task 2. An indicator of this is the number of set aside sentences in Task 3.

- (3) Systematic part-of speech tagger errors. Especially prevalent with targets that are more frequent in the non-noun reading, such as "back". Turkers did not consistently mark POS errors as impossible (although instructed). However, they reliably distinguished among senses. For example, "back in time" and "back in the yard" received separate inventory entries.

- (3) Conflation of senses. Despite differences in meaning, two senses (as perceived by us) had sufficient overlap in their substitutions to not get clustered apart, as it happened for "relationship" in the business and personal sense. This was detected by repeatedly getting a lot of "uncovered" judgments in Task 3 yet no new senses via the substitution step in the cycle.

- (2) Oscillation of senses. Differences in the subjective judgment of turkers caused the sense inventory to oscillate between grouping and distinguishing senses, such as "over the centuries" vs. "the 16th century". With a larger team of trusted turkers this oscillation became less of an issue since a more diverse crowd drove the process in one direction or another.

In total, we observed a successful process for about 90% of targets, with minor problems in the remainder that seldom led to noise in the data. The following issues relate to the power-law nature of word sense distributions (cf. (Kilgarriff, 2004)), which results in many minor senses:

- Minor senses in set aside sentences. When sampling a set of 100 sentences for Task 3, minor senses are likely to be set aside or not taken up by the clustering for lack of support. We observed this in eight targets in our analysis. While a larger sample mitigates this problem, for most applications, we are not interested in minor senses because of their low incidence and we thus do not view this as a problem. Inevitably, some minor senses in the domain did not make it into the sense inventory; however, the cases never represented more than 4% of sample sentences.

- Few substitutions for minor senses. Of the 834 senses distinguished in our experiment, 41 did not get any substitution with frequency ≥ 2 and 142 senses did not record a substitution frequency of four or more. A way to overcome few substitutions for minor senses is to simply ask for more substitutions in the style of Task 1 for the inventory sentence or for the matched sentences for a sense in question.

6 Conclusion and Future Work

In this paper we have demonstrated how to create a high quality semantic resource from scratch. Using Amazon Turk as a crowdsourcing platform and breaking down the problem of substitution and word sense inventory acquisition into three simple tasks, we were able to produce a rich semantic resource for semantic indexing for a comparatively low cost. Further contributions of this work are the definition of word senses along substitutability and the usage of a bootstrapping process on human input.

Compared to WordNet, which is the most commonly used inventory for word sense disambiguation, our resource has a much richer set of sample usages, a larger set of substitutions, fewer fine-grained distinctions and provides a corpus-based estimate on word sense distribution. Our method does not need pre-processing other than lemmatizing and POS tagging and can be directly applied to other domains or languages.

We have run a pilot study for verb sense acquisition with equally encouraging results. Further work can proceed along two lines: On the one hand, one can explore how to enrich the resource itself, e.g. by expanding the target set, acquisition of hypernyms or other relations in Task 1 style, for example, or by creating synsets of senses with the same substitutions that can substitute for each other. However, we are mainly interested in whether this resource is better suited to serve as a sense and substitution inventory for search applications.

Some sample data will be made available for download by the time of publication and is available at request.

Acknowledgements

We would like to thank Julian Richardson for fruitful discussions and the evaluation of initial experiments. We are indebted to thank our team of trusted turkers for performing our tasks so diligently. Thanks goes to Livia Polanyi for valuable comments on an earlier version of the paper.

References

Eneko Agirre and Philip Edmonds, editors. 2006. *Word Sense Disambiguation: Algorithms and Applications*, volume 33 of *Text, Speech and Language Technology*. Springer, July.

Chris Biemann. 2006. Chinese whispers - an efficient graph clustering algorithm and its application to natural language processing problems. In *Proceedings of the HLT-NAACL-06 Workshop on Textgraphs-06*, New York, USA.

Eduard Hovy, Mitchell Marcus, Martha Palmer, Lance Ramshaw, and Ralph Weischedel. 2006. OntoNotes: The 90% solution. In *Proceedings of HLT-NAACL 2006*, pages 57–60.

Adam Kilgarriff. 2004. How dominant is the commonest sense of a word. In *In Proceedings of Text, Speech, Dialogue*, pages 1–9. Springer-Verlag.

Ioannis P. Klapaftis and Suresh Manandhar. 2008. Word sense induction using graphs of collocations. In *Proceedings of the 18th European Conference On Artificial Intelligence (ECAI-2008)*, Patras, Greece, July. IOS Press.

Diana McCarthy and Roberto Navigli. 2007. SemEval-2007 task 10: English lexical substitution task. In *Proceedings of the Fourth International Workshop on Semantic Evaluations (SemEval-2007)*, pages 48–53, Prague, Czech Republic, June. Association for Computational Linguistics.

Rada Mihalcea and Dan Moldovan. 2001. Automatic generation of a coarse grained WordNet. In *Proceedings of the NAACL worshop on WordNet and Other Lexical Resources*, Pittsburg, USA.

Rada Mihalcea. 1998. SEMCOR semantically tagged corpus. unpublished manuscript.

George A. Miller, Richard Beckwith, Christiane Fellbaum, Derek Gross, and Katherine Miller. 1990. WordNet: An on-line lexical database. *International Journal of Lexicography*, 3:235–244.

Mark Sanderson. 1994. Word sense disambiguation and information retrieval. In *Proceedings of the 17th Annual International ACM-SIGIR Conference on Research and Development in Information Retrieval. Dublin, Ireland, 3-6 July 1994 (Special Issue of the SIGIR Forum)*, pages 142–151. ACM/Springer.

Rion Snow, Brendan O'Connor, Daniel Jurafsky, and Andrew Y. Ng. 2008. Cheap and fast - but is it good? evaluating non-expert annotations for natural language tasks. In *Conference on Empirical Methods in Natural Language Processing, EMNLP 2008, Proceedings of the Conference, 25-27 October 2008, Honolulu, Hawaii, USA*, pages 254–263.

Why Wikipedia Needs to Make Friends with WordNet

Kow Kuroda,* Francis Bond,**,* Kentaro Torisawa*
kuroda@nict.go.jp bond@ieee.org torisawa@nict.go.jp
*National Institute of Information and Communications Technology (NICT), Japan
3-5 Hikari-dai, Seika-cho, Sooraku-gun, Kyoto, 619-, Japan
**Linguistics and Multilingual Studies, Nanyang Technological University, Singapore

Abstract

This paper describes the compilation of hypernym hierachies from the Japanese Wikipedia (Sumida et al., 2008). It then compares the Wikipedia-derived hypernyms and the lemmas from the Japanese WordNet (Bond et al., 2008; Bond et al., 2009) by determining how many matches there are at which levels. The results show that the two data sources contain different information. This means that the Wikipedia-derived data and manually crafted data like WordNet (Fellbaum, 1998) are best understood as complementary to each other.

1 Does Wikipedia dispense with the need for WordNet?— Introduction

Data of various kinds acquired from Wikipedia[1] is gaining popularity in NLP and related areas of research. One reason for this is that Wikipedia provides us with broad coverage. No other freely available linguistic resource can match its breadth. It is often claimed that this is evidence for the triumph of "collective intelligence."

Radical enthusiasts of Wikipedia even go on to claim that researchers in NLP and SemanticWeb no longer need WordNet (WN) (Fellbaum, 1998).[2] They allude to the superiority of Wikipedia-derived data over manually crafted data like WN in terms of development ease, speed, and cost as well as coverage. WN comes with precision endorsed by psychological reality that most WWW-derived data lacks, but some people also tend to criticize the subjective nature of the word senses that WN specify, no matter how fine-grained its sense distinctions are. All in all, they seem to try to dismiss WN-like lexical resources by suggesting that they are outdated in the age of WWW. And here comes the crucial question, *Does Wikipedia dispense with the need for WordNet?*

In this paper, we argue that the answer is *No*, suggesting that we should make a good compromise. We show that lexical hierarchies derived from the Japanese Wikipedia are not as well articulated as the upper ontology of Japanese WordNet. This allows us to presume that the hypernym set of language L obtained from the Wikipedia of L is poor compared to the WN of L. Under this assumption, the WN and the Wikipedia of language L are best understood to be complementary in the following way: The WN of L specifies the mapping between an upper ontology to lexical items, $w_1, w_2, \ldots, w_n$, of L. The conceptual hierarchies distilled from the Wikipedia written in L specify links to named entities described in $w_1, w_2, \ldots, w_n$ of L.

Organization

This paper is organized as follows. In §2 we describe how we processed the hypernym-hyponym pairs acquired from the Japanese Wikipedia by Sumida et al. (2008). In §3, we show how the hypernyms obtained in the way specified in §2 were linked to lemmas of Japanese WordNet (WN-Ja) (Bond et al., 2008; Bond et al., 2009). In §4 we discuss the implications. Finally, in §5, we state tentative conclusions

2 Acquiring taxonomic hierarchies from Wikipedia hypernyms

Recently, we finished the manual cleaning of approximately 67,000 Japanese hypernym hierarchies paired with roughly 900,000 hyponyms. We show some details of this process in §2.4. The original data, comprising roughly 2,400,000 hypernym-hyponym pairs, was automatically compiled from the Japanese Wikipedia (Sumida

---

[1] *Wikipedia: The Free Encyclopedia*, http://wikipedia.org/.

[2] In http://www.mkbergman.com/417/99-wikipedia-sources-aiding-the-semantic-web/ (retrieved on 2009/12/01) for example, you can find a bold claim like: "Wikipedia has arguably replaced WordNet as the leading lexicon for concepts and relations. Because of its scope and popularity, many argue that Wikipedia is emerging as the de facto structure for classifying and organizing knowledge in the 21st century.".

et al., 2008). They used Support Vector Machines (Vapnik, 1995) to classify the acquired data. The hypernym-hyponym pairs extracted by Sumida et al. (2008) consist not only of links between Wikipedia entries, but also consider noun phrases extracted from the text of the Wikipedia entries themselves.

While the data thus acquired has an impressive coverage, it is noisy and unreliable at least two ways: First, both hypernyms and hyponyms can be misparsed phrases, due to the low performances of a Japanese tokenizer[3]. Second, even correctly parsed phases can have hypernyms that are themselves relational nouns (such as *kind*, *member*): they suffer from **semantic unsaturatedness** in the sense of Kuroda et al. (2009) and fail to serve as good hypernyms.

2.1 Extracting base hypernyms

The data we processed resemble the following, where h is the hypernym and I is the instance (or hyponym):[4]

(1)   a. h: famous British rock singer
         I: Peter Gabriel

     b. h: former member of Pink Floyd
         I: Syd Barrett

The set of hypernyms extracted form Wikipedia consist mainly of complex NPs like *famous British rock singer* and *former member of Pink Floyd*. Clearly, terms like these are not ideal hypernyms. Thus, we tried to extract **base** hypernyms by gradually removing modifiers from the complex NPs. In this way, the two pairs in (1) are converted into the following hierarchies:

(2)   a. h_1: singer
         h_2: rock singer
         h_3: British rock singer
         h_4: famous British rock singer
         I: Peter Gabriel

     b. h_1: member
         h_2: former member
         h_3: former member of Floyd
         h_4: former member of Pink Floyd
         I: Syd Barrett

---

[3] The precision of Japanese tokenizers at the state-of-the-art come close to 98% against newspaper articles, but they show much lower precision against open text such as Wikipedia.

[4] Although we work on Japanese data, we present the English translations in this paper as the semantic phenomena are not language specific.

The pairs $(H; I)$, where $H = h_1, \ldots, h_n$, are automatically generated from such pairs $(h_{max}; I)$. We refer to H as the **hypernym path** for I,[5] and to units like $h_1, h_2, \ldots, h_n$ as the **path elements** of H. A hypernym path may contain: (i) bare nouns (e.g., *singer*), (ii) modified nouns (e.g., *famous British rock singer*, *former member*), or (iii) noun phrases.

We are able to create these paths in this way because we are looking specifically at hypernym relations. Removing a modifier broadens the denotation, and thus gives a hypernym of the more restricted term.

2.2 Problems with automation

Paths like the ones above were constructed by automatically removing modifiers from h_n (in Japanese) one by one. This operation is not error-free. Manual cleaning was performed to eliminate unconventional and/or unacceptable units like *former member of Floyd*, h_4 of (2b) which was produced by the automatic simplification. We could not use a Named Entity tagger for this task as it performed too poorly on the isolated noun phrases.

2.3 What terms make good hypernyms?: Effect of semantic saturatedness

During the manual process of cleaning, it also became apparent that checking for the conventionality of path elements alone was not effective. We also needed a systematic treatment of composite units like *former member* to take care of the function of modifiers. However, **lexical** databases like WordNet are not guaranteed to contain composite phrasal units like *former X* ($X=\{$ member, president, ... $\}$). This means that we cannot rely on lexical resources to distinguish valid phrases from invalid ones which are only theoretically possible.

This was a problem because raters we hired showed confusion as to the conventionality of such terms and disagreed in their ratings. To them, terms like *member* made good terms even if they were presented in isolation, but terms like *former member* did not. When they were presented in isolation, most raters hesitated to rate them as good hypernyms.

Part of the reason for this disturbance can be attributed to the semantic unsaturatedness of units like *former member*, but the situation seems more

---

[5] For both practical and theoretical purposes, we did not distinguish between **instance** and **hyponym** relations.

complex. Interestingly, raters showed little disagreement on the goodness of *member*, which is also a semantically unsaturated noun. So, the real reason for rater's trouble in classification is not a term's semantic unsaturatedness alone. Consequent research suggests that frequency has an effect on this: frequent semantically unsaturated nouns tend to be classified as saturated nouns.

In passing, it deserves a brief mention that most linguists' tacit assumption that relational nouns are relatively rare and exceptional, and that their set is closed seems far from well grounded. The assumption would be true of simple nouns, but it is not true of composite nouns with modifiers. The source of unsaturatedness of composite nouns are their modifiers. For example, *former* caused the effect in the example above. It is easy to provide similar examples: the unsaturatedness in *sister city* comes from a metaphorical sense of *sister*: *city* is arguably a saturated noun, but *sister city* is unsaturated because *sister* adds unsaturatedness to it. This is why it is possible to say "X and Y are *sister cities*" or "X is the/a *sister city* of Y."

We can add examples with more complexity. For example, *disciple* is a semantically unsaturated noun. In the combination *fellow disciple(s)*, *fellow* adds further unsaturatedness. This is why it is possible to say "X and Y are *fellow disciples* under Z" or "X is the/a *fellow disciple* of Y (?under Z)" and why we infer that both X and Y have a common master, Z when we hear such expressions.

Notably, the unsaturatedness for *fellow* and *disciple* can co-exist.[6] Cases like this show that unsaturatedness accumulates through modification.

Another class of cases show that unsaturatedness is composable, allowing the unsaturatedness of one noun to get **bridged** to another. In cases like *secretary of the Minister (of Foreign Affairs)*, unsaturatedness is reduced through variable-binding, because *secretary of X*, X is bound to *the Minister (of Y)*, and when Y is bound to *Foreign Affairs* (with the aid of *of*), it gets saturated; otherwise, it stays unsaturated.

Examples of the sort briefly mentioned above strongly suggest that the semantics of modifiers is rather complex and needs serious investigation. It is not guaranteed that proper analysis of modifiers is possible within a natural extension of the semantics of individual words, partly because analogy, metaphor and metonymy play a crucial role. Note that modifiers undergo (often very subtle) semantic extensions: at least, *sister* is not used in its literal sense in *sister cit(y|ies)*.[7] With this fact in mind, it would be safe to assume that semantic unsaturatedness becomes more serious at the level of composite nouns or noun phrases. In fact, they posed a challenge in the cleaning process to be explained below.

2.4 Path element cleaning in some detail

We give an outline of the cleaning procedure below.

Step 1: Fully automatic generation of hypernym paths

First, all hypernyms were morphologically analyzed with a morphological analyzer/tokenizer for Japanese.[8] This gave us a set of paths consisting of a series of morphemes coupled with part-of-speech (POS) and other information. Based on the POS information thus provided, we generate a series of terms that serve as a hypernym path.[9]

During this process we excluded some problematic hypernyms. However, hypernyms with disjunctive semantics were not excluded.

Step 2: Manual evaluation of path elements

We asked four raters to evaluate each of the path elements for their conventionality and/or semantic saturatedness. The criteria used were:

(3) a. If a path element X is felt to be fully conventional and saturated, it should be classified as G[ood].

---

[6] Note here that a mutuality interpretation of relational nouns (Eschenbach, 1993) seems to have an interesting effect on the construction and interpretation of *sister cit(y|ies)* and *fellow disciple(s)*.

[7] For the case of *fellow disciples*, the meaning of *fellow* can be literal. We can say that two disciples of Z, X and Y, are in the relation of FELLOW-OF-THE-OTHER(X, Y). But this is not true of *sister cities*. We can only say that two cities, X and Y, are in **some relation analogous to the relation** of *sister-of-the-other* rather than they are properly in the relation of SISTER-OF-THE-OTHER(X, Y).

[8] We used MeCab 0.95 (http:///mecab.sourceforge.net/) with its default dictionary IPA Dic. While our pilot study showed that the combination of MeCab with UniDic (http://www.tokuteicorpus.jp/dist/) developed by the National Institute for Japanese Language provided better results we could not in the end use it due to its restrictive license.

[9] We are afraid the the same automation would not be possible for nonhead-final languages because the criteria used are specific to modifiers that appear before the head noun.

b. If *X* is felt to be incomplete for less conventionality or strong unsaturatedness, it should be classified as L[ess Good].

c. If *X* is felt not to be rather unconventional but the rater cannot be sure if it is really a nonword, it should be classified as D[ubious].

d. If *X* is felt to be fully unconventional and nonsensical, it should be classified as B[ad].

We collected the ratings thus created and selected the most appropriate class.[10] Admittedly, L and D are mixtures of different subclasses. But we did not attempt to create proper labels for subclasses.[11]

Step 3: Automatic reconstruction of hypernym paths and finalization

Because relevant information is distributed over different paths, they are reconstructed from scratch for canonicalization. After this, the first author edited the results based on his intuition. He edited the paths and even added missing intermediate terms and some abstract (super)hypernyms with D status at the root (such as 者*, 手*, and 校* to be discussed in §3.3).

In the process of this cleaning, the original set of roughly 95,000 hypernyms was reduced to the set of 67,000.

3 Linking Wikipedia hypernyms to WordNet

In this section, we describe how compared the hypernym hierarchies constructed in the method above with the Japanese lemmas in the Japanese WordNet (WN-Ja) (Bond et al., 2008; Bond et al., 2009).

3.1 Nature of hypernyms and hyponyms in Wikipedia

Recall that we processed hypernym-hyponym pairs automatically acquired from the Japanese Wikipedia. The data consists of roughly 67,000 hypernym hierarchies paired with roughly 900,000 hyponyms.

We cleaned up all the hypernyms of the data, but we did not process the hyponyms for the following reason: nearly 2/3 of the hyponyms are proper names or named entities. The amount of knowledge required to determine if such pairings are valid or not goes well beyond the personal knowledge of an average person. At the time we started the cleaning, it was unclear how to deal with them.

This, on the other hand, suggests an interesting possibility: if pairings of cleaned-up hypernyms with hyponyms turn out to be valid, the huge database of such pairings should complement traditional thesauri as WordNet (Fellbaum, 1998) which mainly consist of upper level concepts (by its very design). With this hypothetical mapping between coarse-grained concepts in the upper ontology and finer-grained concepts in the lower ontology, we can specify the linkage from named entities to upper ontology. If this is possible, it is very promising.

With his hope in mind, we linked the roots of the hypernym hierarchies cleaned in the way illustrated above to nodes in the WN-Ja.

WN-Ja is a Japanese translation of WordNet 3.0 developed and maintained at the National Institute for Information and Communications Technology (NICT). After the first public release in 2009, WN-Ja underwent several updates. We used versions 0.80 and 0.90 for this study.

3.2 Current status

Currently, 95% of the hypernym hierarchies are linked to WN-Ja. Crude statistics are given in Table 1. A sample of matches are shown in (4).

(4) shows sample matches of WN-Ja lemmas (in bold) against Wikipedia hypernym path elements (all in Japanese): Terms are separated by ":" and matched terms are underlined.

(4) a. **校**: **学校**: **大学**: 締結大学: 協定締結大学: 交換留学協定締結大学: 国内交換留学協定締結大学

b. **機**: コミューター機

c. **ジャーナリスト**: 経済ジャーナリスト

d. **病**: 消化器病

e. **大会**: 選手権大会: 日本選手権大会

f. **船**: 艦船: 海軍の艦船: イギリス海軍の艦船

---

[10] The final class selection was done by the first author on the basis of their intuition guided by the information about distribution. This means that the winners were not always the ones that had acquired the most votes. One reason for this was that some of the raters committed systematic errors.

[11] The agreement rate in terms of Fleiss' kappa against a sample of 2000 cases was 0.492 under the distinction among G, L, D, and B. This is not so good, but it increased to 0.759 if class L was discarded, and it increased up to 0.916 if classes L and D were unified as one. This suggests that rater's classification is highly stable over the identification of G and B, and that raters were confused between L and D.

g. 地理: 府の地理: 京都府の地理
h. 違反: 交通違反
i. 手: 選手: スポーツ選手: グルジアのスポーツ選手
j. 遺産: 世界遺産: ベトナムの世界遺産
k. 企業: 親密な企業: グループと親密な企業: 三井グループと親密な企業
l. シングル: 未歩のシングル: 小松未歩のシングル
m. 員: 委員: 専門委員
n. ソフト: 書き換えソフト: ニンテンドウパワー書き換えソフト

Table 1: Number and ratio of matches of WN-Ja lemmas over Wikipedia-derived hypernym

Depth	# of Covered	Ratio	# of Types
1	64,412	0.9592	3,272
2	24,554	0.3657	2,447
3	2,804	0.0418	465
4	53	0.0008	30

Depth in Table 1 refers to the levels of hypernym hierarchy (measured from the root) at which WN-Ja lemmas have matches. For example, 64,400 root hypernyms out of 67,000 (tokens) have matches with WN-Ja, consisting of 3,272 unique types.

In this linkage process, however, we did not take into account the effect of word sense disambiguation. This suggests that we have fewer correct matches than the figures in Table 1 indicate.

As Table 1 suggests, WN-Ja hypernyms and Wikipedia-derived hypernyms have matches at very shallow levels (the average is nearly 3). More specifically, lower level nodes of WN-Ja match the upper level nodes of Wikipedia-derived hypernyms. This forms the strongest support for our suggestion that Wikipedia-derived hypernyms cannot do without WN. Rather, the two kinds of resource enhance each other.

3.3 Details of the hypernym paths

In Table 2, we show some examples with relevant details. The most common 12 root hypernyms were picked with example paths. In most cases, the lowermost elements of the hypernym paths are hypernyms for named entities. This tendency is obvious when they are at the bottoms of the long paths with more than one modifiers. All in all, the result suggests that the structure of modification needs to be carefully examined to have effective links between named entities and categories/classes of upper ontology.

3.4 Prospects for sense matches

In the example above, the hypernym matches against WN-Ja are simple string-matches and are not sense-matches, because sense disambiguation is not performed on any of the path elements.

This is regrettable. Fortunately, the co-occurrence information required for sense disambiguation on the upper-ontological elements, which have WN-Ja matches, is already available in the paths as long as they are long enough. Actually, it is intuitively obvious that the terms with WN-Ja matches have sufficiently specific senses, unless they are too short. For example, 手 in 手:選手:スポーツ選手:グルジアのスポーツ選手 of (4i) corresponds to agent-denoting suffix -er of English, though it means "hand" when it is used us an independent word. For, the English translation of the path would be: *-er: player: sport(s) player: Georgian sport(s) player*.[12] This can be contrasted with cases like 手:禁じ手:相撲の禁じ手 which can be translated into *technique(s): prohibited technique(s): prohibited technique(s) in Sumo wrestling*.

In Japanese analysis, recognition of sub-lexical units like 手 in 選手 and 機 in コミューター機 is unavoidable, because they are bound morphemes that play a role in basic word-formation. To our great annoyance, they are not always properly recognized in the analysis using Japanese tokenizers because they tend to treat them as single units when combinations become conventional. For example, there is no tokenizer that separates 手 from 選手.[13]

This implies that comparison of daughter terms on the WN-Ja side would enable sense matches; and that sense disambiguation is easy to do if (i) enough positive examples of specific senses are provided in composite form and (ii) similarity of a target term against the composite positive examples can be calculated. Thus, the only barrier is

---

[12] Incidentally, 手 is not the only morpheme that corresponds to -er. 者 and 人 are other major possibilities.

[13] Another complication for composite terminology is obvious here. The most appropriate English translation of コミューター機 of (4b) would be "commuter type" (of aircraft) or "commuter model" (of aircraft) rather than "commuter apparatus" or "commuter machine" even if the most straightforward translation of 機 would be "apparatus" or "machine."

Table 2: Most common 12 path elements (including unsaturated (L) and dubious (D) ones): terms with asterisk (e.g., 者*, 品*, 社*, 家*) are bound morphemes whose hypernym status are dubious.

Rank	Term	Count	Sample Hypernym Path(s)
1	者*	2,396	者* (person): 首謀者 (mastermind): 直接首謀者 (active mastermind): 事件の直接首謀者 (active mastermind of (the) affair): 爆破事件の直接首謀者 (active mastermind of (the) bombing affair)
2	品*	2,115	(1) 品* (item): 製品 (product): ドイツの製品 (products of Germany) (2) 品 (item): 用品 (item(s) for …): 園芸用品 (gardening supply)
3	社*	1,973	(1) 社* (company): 出版社 (publisher): 音楽出版社 (music publisher): 日本の音楽出版社 (music publisher in Japan) (2) 社* (place for sacred activity): 神社 (shrine): 市の神社 (shrine of (a) city): 鎌倉市の神社 (shrine of Kamakura City)
4	会社	1,881	社* (company): 会社 (company): 食品会社 (food company): 大手食品会社 (major food company)
5	番組	1,758	番組 (program): 音楽番組 (music program): クラシック音楽番組 (classical music program)
6	作品	1,630	品* (item): 作品 ((piece of) work): 題材にした作品 ((piece of) work on …): 吸血鬼を題材にした作品 ((piece of) work on vampires)
7	家*	1,615	(1) 家* (family): 五家 ((major) five schools): 禅宗五家 ((major) five schools of Zen): 中国禅宗五家 ((major) five schools of Chinese Zen) (2) 家* (-ist): 運動家 (activist): フェミニズム運動家 (feminism activist)
8	人*	1,496	人* (person): 料理人 (cook): フランス料理人 (French cook)
9	校*	1,482	校* (school): 学校 (school): 高校 (high school): 女子高校 (girl's high school): 公立女子高校 (public girl's high school)
10	手*	1,425	(1) 手* (-er): 騎手 (jockey): イギリスの騎手 (British jockey) (2) 手 (technique(s)): 禁じ手 (prohibited technique(s), foul): 相撲の禁じ手 (prohibited technique(s) in Sumo wrestling)
11	人物	1,356	人物 (person): 長寿人物 (longevity person): 最長寿人物 (the oldest person): 世界最長寿人物 (world's oldest person): 元世界最長寿人物 (former world's oldest person)
12	選手	1,242	手* (-er): 選手 (player): 野球選手 (baseball player): プエルトリコの野球選手 (baseball player of Puerto Rico)

that we do not have enough positive examples for word senses in composite forms, arguing for the building of sense tagged data with broad coverage. In other words, if we build sense tagged data based on Wikipedia, it would be quite beneficial. We will try on this in future using the method described in Toral et al. (2009).

4 Discussion

The WN-Ja coverage over the original hypernym-hyponym pairs was only 8%: that is 8% of the extracted pairs were already found within the Japanese WordNet.[14] This means that most of the pairs extracted in §2.4 are new additions to WordNet. We are adding a great deal of new information to the Japanese WordNet.

Looking at named entities specified as hyponyms in the Wikipedia data and entities in WN-Ja, there are a lot of **missing links** with which various intermediate concepts can be specified. Our impression is that these intermediate, concrete enough concepts are exactly the concepts that people use to conceptualize the world around them. For example, *famous rock singer* (of a country) and *former member* (of a group) in (1). We may assume that they are building blocks in their mental models. If this is correct, filling the missing links would be very rewarding for NLP applications and related fields such as the SemanticWeb. Admittedly, it needs more research to validate this hypothesis.

Hypernym-hyponym pairs automatically acquired from Wikipedia cannot be linked fully automatically. We required manual processing for the hypernym cleaning. With current extraction techniques lexical hierarchy data constructed fully automatically from Wikipedia is very unlikely to be as precise as WordNet's synset hierarchies.

Finally, we would like to also note that the kind of upper ontology specified in the form of WordNet and similar lexical resources would not be enough to cover the incredible variety of ontological entities that appear in Wikipedia. In particular, it contains quite a lot of imaginary entities — most notably, a full range of characters that appear in books, movies, legends, and folk tales. It is understandable, however, that they are not just components of people's fantasies but are actual elements of people's realities. Sometimes, it becomes quite hard to tell if they are real or unreal.

---

[14] This comparison was made using WN-Ja 0.8.

Lexical resources like WordNet do not currently provide a proper place to hold them all. We may need to broaden the standard upper ontologies to meet the specification requirements by Wikipedia that seems to describe people's realities without categorically distinguishing between fact and fictions, between true and untrue facts, and between scientific and unscientific knowledge. Wikipedia can be a challenge for scientific categorization because pieces of knowledge of all kinds are mixed in it together. It would not be surprising if no single upper ontology can successfully handle it.

There has been much work on linking the English Wikipedia to WordNet, with YAGO (Suchanek et al., 2007) being a good example. Our work differs in several ways. Trivially, we are looking at Japanese, rather than English. More interestingly, we only consider only hypernym relations, while YAGO considers a wide range of relations, such as `BornInYear` and `LocatedIn`. On the other hand, we consider a wider range of possible entities: YAGO only looks at Wikipedia entries and their categories while Sumida et al. (2008) considers the text within the entry. Because of this, there is no guarantee that the terms we link are unambiguous entities, in fact we collapse even Wikipedia disambiguation pages. In future work, we hope to disambiguate these again, perhaps using automatic methods such as Toral et al. (2009).

In future work, we hope to extend these links to English, exploiting the multilingual links in both WordNet and Wikipedia, in cooperation with on-going work on hyponymy extraction in both languages (Oh et al., 2009).

5 Conclusion

This paper described base hypernym extraction from the hypernym-hyponym pairs automatically acquired from the Japanese Wikipedia. It then compared Wikipedia-derived hypernyms and the lemmas of WordNet-Ja by determining how many matches there are at which levels. The results suggest that neither of the two data sources are redundant. This means that we cannot fully dispense with WordNet-like, manually developed high-precision lexical resources even if we have Wikipedia. Thus, the two kinds of resources are best understood as complementary to each other. In fact, if they are successfully coupled, we can finally have links from named entities to abstract entities in the upper ontology. The links help to form the set of all encompassing, all inclusive hierarchies that we long for.

References

Francis Bond, Hitoshi Isahara, Kyoko Kanzaki, and Kiyotaka Uchimoto. 2008. Boot-strapping a WordNet using multiple existing WordNets. In *Proceedings of the 6th International Conference on Language Resources and Evaluation (LREC-2008)*.

Francis Bond, Hitoshi Isahara, Sanae Fujita, Kiyotaka Uchimoto, Takayuki Kuribayashi, and Kyoko Kanzaki. 2009. Enhancing the Japanese WordNet. In *The 7th Workshop on Asian Language Resources*, pages 1–8, Singapore. ACL-IJCNLP 2009.

P. Eschenbach. 1993. Semantics of number. *Journal of Semantics*, 10(1):1–31.

Christiane Fellbaum, editor. 1998. *WordNet: An Electronic Lexical Database*. MIT Press.

Kow Kuroda, Masaki Murata, and Kentaro Torisawa. 2009. When nouns need co-arguments: A case study of semantically unsaturated nouns. In *Proceedings of the 5th International Workshop on Generatvei Approaches to the Lexicon, Sep. 17-19, 2009, Pisa, Italy*, pages 193–200.

Jong-Hoon Oh, Kiyotaka Uchimoto, and Kentaro Torisawa. 2009. Bilingual co-training for monolingual hyponymy-relation acquisition. In *Joint Conference of the 47th Annual Meeting of the Association for Computational Linguistics and the 4th International Joint Conference on NLP of the Asian Federation of NLP*, Singapore.

F. M. Suchanek, G. Kasneci, and G. Weikum. 2007. Yago: A Core of Semantic Knowledge. In *Proceedings of the 16th International World Wide Web Conference (WWW 2007)*, New York, NY, USA. ACM Press.

Asuka Sumida, N. Yoshinaga, and Kentaro Torisawa. 2008. Boosting precision and recall of hyponymy relation acquisition from hierarchical layouts in Wikipedia. In *Proceedings of the 6th International Conference on Language Resources and Evaluation (LREC-2008)*.

A. Toral, Ó. Ferrández, E. Agirre, and R. Muñoz. 2009. A study on linking Wikipedia categories to Wordnet synsets using text similarity. In *RANLP 2009*.

V. N. Vapnik. 1995. *The Nature of Statistical Learning Theory*. Springer.

WordNets for Indian Languages: Some Issues

Panchanan Mohanty
Centre for ALTS
University of Hyderabad
Hyderabad 500046, India
panchanan_mohanty@yahoo.com

Abstract

The WordNet experiment still remains an experiment even after two decades though a lot of progress has been made and a number of new horizons in this area unknown at that time have been discovered since then. It is, in fact, a good sign that indicates that the field has been growing gradually. The present paper aims to discuss some specific issues in building WordNets for Indian languages and argue that inclusion of corpus analysis data is necessary for creating better synsets.

1 Introduction

Creation of the Hindi WordNet is a pioneering effort by the Indian Institute of Technology Bombay NLP group (Chakrabarti et al. 2002), and it has become the model for building WordNets in other Indian languages. In fact, the WordNet groups of various Indian languages are following the Hindi WordNet, mostly translating the Hindi synsets with additions and deletions, wherever necessary.

With the sole exception of the Tamil, no other Indian language seems to have a large-sized corpus-based dictionary. Hence, conventional dictionaries have been used to find synsets in Hindi and the strengths and weaknesses of the Hindi WordNet are being transferred to other Indian languages. This paper looks at the synonyms of selected Hindi synsets along with entries in the dictionaries of certain Indian languages, i.e. Hindi, Oriya, Bangla, and discusses the problems involved in depending on such dictionaries.

2 Hindi, Oriya and Bangla : A Brief Note

Hindi, Oriya and Bangla- all these languages belong to the Indo-Aryan group of the Indo-European family of languages and have SOV as the unmarked word order along with other common morpho-syntactic characteristics of the verb-final languages. But Oriya and Bangla have assimilated a significant amount of Dravidian vocabulary as well as grammatical features due to their close contact with Dravidan for millennia. (Chatterji 1970, Mohanty 2008). Hindi shows less of these features for obvious reasons.

3 Semantics of Simple and Conjunct Verbs in Indian Languages

Verbs form more or less a closed set in every language and therefore, unlike nouns, their number is always limited. For this reason, verbs are more polysemous than nouns in almost all languages. Fellbaum (1998b:99) mentions: "A relational analysis of English verbs has revealed some striking ways in which verbs differ from nouns. The semantics of verbs are generally more complex." It means the same principles should not govern the creation of NounNets and VerbNets. In other words, creation of a VerbNet in a language should follow certain principles that may be different from the ones followed in the creation of a NounNet. But it does not seem to be practised in the Indian language WordNets because of the dependence on the available conventional dictionaries.

Verbs can be divided into three categories, and let me illustrate these with example from Hindi:

a) Simple verbs: These consist of single verb roots, e.g. /ja:/ 'to go', /kha:/ 'to eat'.

b) Compound verbs: These consist of two or more verb roots, e.g. /kha: le-/ 'to eat up', /gir paR-/ 'to fall down'.

c) Conjunct verbs: These consist of a noun or an adjective followed by a verb root. Though a group of verb roots can be used in this slot, /kar-/ 'to do' and /ho-/ 'to be' are the most common ones, e.g. /sapha: kar-/ 'to clean', /band he-/ 'to be closed' in Oriya.

It is worthwhile to note that Sanskrit did not have compound verbs and it was quite possible in it to substitute a simple verb for a conjunct verb in a sentence without significantly affecting its meaning. In fact, creation of conjunct verbs by adding the verb root √kr̥ 'to do' to a noun is a very productive process in Sanskrit. The following examples are illustrative:

1) ra:mah ka:vyam paThati
   Ram poetry reads

2) ra:mah ka:vyam paThanam karoti
   Ram poetry reading does
   'Ram reads poetry.'

Most probably under the influence of Sanskrit, the same trend has been followed by the lexicographers of Neo Indo-Aryan (henceforth NIA) languages. I must point out here that there are many simple verbs in Indian languages, especially the so-called *deshaja* or native ones, for which conjunct equivalents are not available. The following Oriya examples will drive home the point:

3) dhaka:iba: 'to gasp'
4) ba:Rhiba: 'to serve (food)'

We cannot substituts conjunct verbs for these simple ones in Oriya. There are also concepts, though very few in number, which are expressed through only conjunct verbs and simple verbs are non-existent in such cases. Let us take the concepts 'to work' and 'to love' in English. A conjunct verb is used to express each of these concepts in all the major Indian languages. For example, for 'to work' we have /ka:m kar-/ in Hindi, /ka:ma kar-/ in Oriya, /ka:j kar-/ in Bangla, /pani cey-/ in Telugu. It can be glossed as 'to work-do'. Then 'to love' can be rendered as /pya:r kar-/ in Hindi, /bhala pa:-/ in Oriya, /prem kar-/ in Bangla. This concept can be glossed as 'to love-do'. None of these Indian languages uses a single verb to express any of these concepts.

However, if we look at the head entries of simple verbs in various NIA language dictionaries, we find that conjunct verbs are the preferred synonyms in most cases. Consider the following examples:

Oriya

5) paRiba: = patita heba 'to fall'
6) dhariba: = dha:raNa kariba: 'to hold'

Bangla

7) kha:wa: = bhakkhaN kara:, pa:n kara:
8) dhara: = dha:raN kara:

Hindi

9) kha:na: = bhojan karna:, bhakSan karna:
10) ja:na: = prastha:n karna:, gaman karna:

Before discussing these, I should metion that conjunct verbs can be of two types: synthetic and analytic. A synthetic conjunct verb is one in which both the constituents form an inseparable whole from the semantic point of view. In other words, it is almost like a frozen expression that is semantically non-compositional in nature. On the other hand, an analytic conjunct verb is semantically compositional, and it is the result of a productive process. But, interestingly and surprisingly, these analytic conjunct verb synonyms are not appropriate in meaning to their simple counterparts in many cases. For example, consider the following Oriya and Hindi simple verbs along with their conjunct synonyms in order to see how they are inappropriate in various contexts:

Oriya

11) dhariba: = dha:raNa kariba: 'to catch, hold'
11a) se bahut ma:cha dharila:/*dha:raNa kala:
     he/she many fish caught
     'He/she caught a lot of fish.'
11b) ta:ku thaNDa: dharichi/*dha:raNa karichi
     to him/her cold has caught
     'He/she has caught cold.'

Hindi

12) kha:na: = bhojan karna:/bhakhshaN karna:
12a) usne   ma:r   kha:ya:/*bhojan kiya:/*bhakhshaN kiya:
     he/she beating ate
     'He was beaten up.'
12b) usne samosa: kha:ya:/ ??bhojan kiya:/ ??bhakhshaN kiya:
     he/she *samosa:* ate

'He/she ate a *samosa:*.'

All these examples clearly show that a conjunct verb need not as a rule be a synonym of a simple verb. But this is what is found in the Hindi synsets. For example, /rona:, rudan karna:, krandan karna:/ 'to shed tears from eyes' (ID No. 235), /pi:na:, pa:n karna:/ 'to drink' (ID No. 6855), /joDna:, jama: karna:, sancit karna:, ikaT-Tha: karna:, ekatrit karna:/ 'to put together' (ID No. 7674), /sunna:, shravaN karna:/, 'to hear' (ID No. 8334), /paDhna:, adhyayan karna:/ 'to read' (ID No. 11727), /kha:na:, ji:mna:, bhojan karna:/ 'to eat' (ID No. 13868), etc.

Use of a simple verb in the place of a conjunct verb also poses similar problems. Consider the following examples from Oriya in which substitution of a conjunct verb, i.e. /dha:raNa kari/ by the corresponding a simple verb, i.e. /dhari/ makes the sentence unacceptable:

13a) hari kappa:Lare tiLaka <u>dha:raNa kari</u> mandiraku gala:
   Hari forehead-on sacred mark having put temple-to went
   'Hari went to the temple with the sacred mark on his forehead.'

13b) * hari kappa:Lare tiLaka <u>dhari</u> mandiraku gala:
   Hari forehead-on sacred mark having put temple-to went
   'Hari went to the temple with the sacred mark on his forehead.'

These examples demonstrate that the collocational or selectional restrictions of simple and conjunct verbs are different. Fellbaum (1998b:73) states: "We have generally avoided placing verbs that differ significantly with respect to their selectional restrictions into the same synset." For these reasons, the Indo-WordNet community has to examine the facts thoroughly and decide whether a conjunct verb should usually be given as a synonym for a simple verb or vice-versa.

There is another issue that demands our attention. According to Fellbaum (1998a:2), "Linguistic theories attempt to model human grammar, or linguistic competence, but often these theories rely on data that are not well documented in actual use." WordNet is no exception to it. If a WordNet has to be an analogue of the lexical knowledge of its speakers, then it must be organised accordingly. I should mention here Lakoff's (1987) emphasis on prototypes for deciding the most unmarked representative of a concept. If we agree with Lakoff (1987), then a prototype is the best example of a concept. It follows from it that ordering of the responses obtained form the speakers of a language with reference to a concept is indicative of their cognitive organisation of different signifiers of a signified. Let us again consider the synset /kha:na:, ji:mna:, bhojan karna:/ 'to eat' (ID No. 13868). It has /ji:mna:/ listed in the second position; but its occurrence is extremely rare. On the other hand, /bhojan karna:/ that is listed last is more commonly used than /ji:mna:/ and this is reflected in the Hindi corpus also.

All these clearly indicate that conventional dictionaries are not the best resources for determining synsets and therefore, corpus data may be considered as an aditional and reliable resource for this purpose.

4 Adjectives in the Hindi WordNet

The other concern is efficacy of the Hindi synsets. We will concentrate only on three issues which are demonstrated below by taking the following examples from the category of adjectives. The first concept under consideration is /jo a:ya: hua: ho/ (ID No. 7) 'one who has come', and there are only two synsets given in Hindi, i.e. /a:gat, sama:gat/. But a careful scrutiny shows that /a:ya: hua:, a:ye hue/ are very well used in Hindi and hence, should be listed as equivalents in the synsets. These two synonyms also occur in the DoE Hindi corpus. For example:

13) citpa:wan bra:hmaN a:rya nahi:M haiM, mishr se <u>a:e hue</u> yahu:di: haiM.
'The Chitpawan Brahmins are not Aryans, they are Jews who came from Egypt.'

The second concept is /jo yogya na ho/ (ID No. 23) 'one that is not fit' for which ten synonyms have been given, i.e./ayogya, anupayukta, na:qa:bil, na:ka:bil, anarha, na:la:yak, na:-la:yak, anal:yak, apa:rag, aprabhu/. Among these, the occurrence of /aprabhu/ is extremely rare and it is not found in even in some celebrated Hindi Dictionaries, like Ram Chandra Varma's (n.d.) *ma:nak hindi: kosh*. Then, /anal:yak/ is used only in poetry (ibid.:93) and the occurrence of /anarha/ is found mostly in formal Hindi.

The third concept under consideration is /bina: na:mka: ya: jiska: koi: na:m na ho/ 'without a name or one who does not have a name.' The three synonyms given for it are listed in this order: /ana:m, bena:m, na:mhi:n/. When I looked at the frequency of occurrences of these three words in the Hindi corpus, I found that each one of these occurred only once. Therefore, I asked some native speakers of Hindi who preferred the following order based on their intuition: /na:mhi:n, bena:m, ana:m/. It is just the reverse of the order given in the Hindi WordNet. Therefore, a detailed corpus analysis is necessary. Not only that, such an analysis will also reveal very interesting aspects of the meaning of a word. Let us take a fascinating example. Earlier, the meaning of the English phrasal verb 'to set in' was given as follows: 'to begin, to become prevalent, to run landwards' (Macdonald 1972:1239) and 'appear and gradually increase, flow, become settled' (Garmonsway 1987:661). But after a careful scrutiny of The Bank of English corpus, Sinclair (1991:73-75) has discovered its hidden meaning: "The most striking feature of this phrasal verb is the nature of the subjects. In general, they refer to unpleasant states of affairs." Since then its meaning has been changed to refer to something unpleasant to begin and continue CCELD:1323).

Again, a corpus analysis of the use of 'got' and 'gotten', the two irregular forms of the verb 'to get' in American English, shows that the former does not usually express a perfective meaning (e.g. He hasn't got an examination tomorrow) whereas the latter almost always does that (e.g. He has gotten his salary today) (Biber et al. 1995:398-399). These examples make it evident that inclusion of corpus analysis in the development of a WordNet will bring about a qualitative change in it.

5 Conclusion

To sum up, the following points have been highlighted in this paper:

(i) Though simple verbs and their conjunct counterparts are synonymous in Sanskrit, the same is not always true in the NIA languages. That is why, Indo WordNet developers must be very careful while giving a conjunct verb as a synonym for a simple verb.

(ii) The Hindi WordNet, which is quite elaborate and exhaustive, is based primarily on conventional Hindi dictionaries. Though these lexicographers were great scholars, they did not have a corpus to fall back on. Therefore, along with these dictionaries corpus data have to be taken into account while creating synsets in Hindi as well as in other Indian languages.

(iii) Some of the given synonyms are either very rare or register-specific. Therefore, trying to find equivalents for such words in other Indian languages is not only very difficult, but also not desirable.

(iv) Some synonyms, thought quite commonly used, do not find a place in certain synsets.

(v) Synonyms in the Hindi synsets may be arranged according to their frequency of occurrence in the corpus and the same should be followed in the case of other Indian languages. It will facilitate a cross-lingual comparison of the semantics of a lexical item in the languages concerned whose outcome can be used for various purposes.

Before closing let me quote from Miller (1998: xix), who states: "We have always considered WordNet to be an experiment, not a product." Let us listen to the leader.

References

Biber, Douglas, Stig Johansson, Geoffrey Leech, Susan Conrad & Edward Finegan 1995. *Longman Grammar of Spoken and Written English*. Harlow: Pearson Education Limited.

CCELD = Collins Cobuild English Language Dictionary 1987. London, Glasgow: Collins.

Chakrabarti, Debasri, Dipak Kumar Narayan, Prabhakar Pandey, & Pushpak Bhattacharyya 2002. Experiences in building the Indo WordNet: a WordNet for Hindi. In, *Proceedings of the First Global WordNet Conference*. Central Institute of Indian Languages, Mysore, pp. 57-64.

Chatterji, Suniti Kumar 1970. *The Origin an Development of the Bengali Language*. George Allen and Unwin, London. (first published in 1926)

Das, Gyanendramohan 1986. *ba:ngla: bha:Sa:r abhidha:n*. Sahitya Sansad, Calcutta. (2nd edition)

Fellbaum, Christiane. (ed.) 1998. *WordNet: An Electronic Lexical Database*. MIT Press, Cambridge, Mass.

Fellbaum, Christiane. 1998a. Introduction. In, Fellbaum (ed.), pp. 3-19.

Fellbaum, Christiane. 1998b. A semantic network of English verbs. In, Fellbaum (ed.), pp.69-104.

Garmonsway, G. N. 1987. *The Modern English Dictionary*. Leicester: Galley Press.

Hindi WordNet. Indian Institute of Technology Bombay, Mumbai. (available at CALTS, University of Hyderabad, Hydrabad).

Lakoff, George 1987. *Women, Fire and Dangerous Things: What Categories Reveal about the Mind*. University of Chicago Press, Chicago.

Macdonald, A. M. 1972. *Chambers Twentieth Century Dictionary*. Bombay: Allied Publishers. (new edition)

Mohanty, Panchanan 2008. Dravidian Substratum and Indo-Aryan Languages. *International Journal of Dravidian Linguistics*. Vol. XXXVII, No. 1, pp.1-20.

Miller, George A. 1998. Foreword. In, Fellbaum (ed.), pp. xv-xxii.

Nanda Sharma, Gopinath. 2008. *shabdatattwabodha abhidha:na*. Friends' Publishers, Cuttack. (reprint)

Sinclair, John 1991. *Corpus, Concordance, Collocation*. Oxford: Oxford University Press.

Varma, Ram Chandra n.d. *ma:nak hindi: kosh*, Vols. 1 & 2. Hindi Sahitya Sammelan, Prayag.

On Polysemy in Tamil and other Indian Languages

Panchanan Mohanty
Centre for ALTS
University of Hyderabad
Hyderabad 500046, India
panchananmohanty@gmail.com

S. Arulmozi
Dept. of DCL
Dravidian University
Kuppam 517425, India
arulmozi@gmail.com

Abstract

Scholars (e.g. Burrow 1968:300) have expressed surprise regarding the very small number of borrowed words from Sanskrit in Tamil as opposed to the other three major literary Dravidian languages, i.e. Telugu, Kannada, and Malayalam. But there is no detailed discussion as to why it has happened in Tamil when other Dravidian languages possess a lot of Sanskrit borrowings. We want to argue here that the small number of consonant letters in Tamil alphabet is responsible for it. And its natural outcome is that other Dravidian languages have borrowed from Sanskrit whenever necessary whereas Tamil has managed its situation by developing polysemy. In other words, Tamil is more polysemous compared to its sister languages. In fact, we want to propose that if a language has a smaller alphabet than others, it has to be more polysemous than the latter. In this paper, we will demonstrate it with examples from Tamil vis-a-vis their cognates in Telugu.

1 Introduction

Lexical ambiguity is one of the most difficult problems in language processing studies, and not surprisingly, is at the core of lexical semantics research. It is true that most words in a language have more than one meaning, but the ways in which words carry multiple meanings can vary (Pustejovsky & Boguraev 1995).

Therefore, it is not surprising that most words inherited from proto-Dravidian by the extant Dravidian languages are polysemous. Burrow (1968:300) has expressed surprise regarding the presence of a few Sanskrit borrowings in Tamil as opposed to their abundance in the other three major literary Dravidian languages, i.e. Telugu, Kannada, and Malayalam. With reference to this, Mohanty (2008:17-18) has argued that "...the contact between Tamil and Sanskrit was predominantly literary and that the structure of Tamil was such that it could not have borrowed freely from Sanskrit. Therefore, writing Sanskrit words with less number of letters, with the restriction of not using /r/ and /l/ word-initially, and without consonant clusters, was certainly an unmanageable task for the literate Tamilians at that time. All these naturally lead us to believe that Tamil has less synchronic variation and more polysemy." Thus, Tamil is believed to be more polysemous than the other three major Dravidian languages, viz. Telugu, Kannada and Malayalam. In order to test this hypothesis, we would like to compare the meanings of some randomly selected Tamil words with the corresponding cognates from Telugu, which has a more elaborate alphabet.

Most words derived from the proto-Dravidian that are available in Tamil and Telugu are polysemous. But Tamil is more polysemous compared to Telugu and other major Dravidian languages. The reason we propose is that if a language has a smaller alphabet (such as Tamil) than others, it has to be more polysemous than the latter.

1.1 The Tamil language

Tamil is a South Dravidian language of the Dravidian family of languages. Tamil alphabet is descended from the Southern Brahmi script and has 12 vowels, 18 consonants and one *aytam* in addition to five Grantha letters (mainly used to write consonants borrowed from Sanskrit).

1.2 The Telugu language

Among the other major Dravidian languages, Telugu belongs to the South Central Dravidian subgroup, the other two Kannada and Malayalam falling under the South Dravidian subgroup. Telugu is a highly Sanskritised language, but it has a unique feature that all its words end with a vowel sound.

The Telugu alphabet is also a descendent of the Southern Brahmi script. Telugu has 16 vowels and 36 consonants, which are more in number than those of Tamil.

2 Polysemy

Polysemy plays a major role in the historical development of word meanings because lexemes continually shift their meanings and develop new meaning variants (Lobner, 2002). In Tamil, the word *poTu* has over a period of time developed numerous meanings (29 senses to 54 senses between 1998 to 2008)[1]. But in the case of Telugu, it is not the same because of the influence of Sanskrit. That is, Tamil uses the same word to represent different senses whereas Telugu has the option of falling back on Sanskrit to provide different words for different senses. One can get a clear picture about this from the examples given in 2.1 below.

Among the 3000 and odd verbs in Tamil, about 1185 exhibit more than one sense, 525 with 2 senses, 243 with 3 senses, 290 words with 4-6 senses, 55 words with 7-10 senses; 25 words have 10-54 senses; and so on. Out of the 2500 odd Telugu verbs, only 1427 have more than 1 distinctly different sense. This proves the point that we proposed earlier with regard to the less number of letters in an alphabet giving rise to polysemy.

In what follows, we present the data taken from the Tamil and Telugu dictionaries for demonstrating the senses in both the languages. We also provide the etyma for the words selected from the revised edition of the Dravidian Etymological Dictionary (DEDR).

2.1 Tamil and their cognates in Telugu

I. DEDR

Tamil: *accu*, n: mould, type.
Telugu: *accu*, n: stamp, impression, print, mould

---

[1] CreA. 1998, 2008. taRkaalat tamil akarati. Dictionary of Modern Tamil. CreA, Chennai.

Tamil: அச்சு, accu, n
1. type in printing
2. printing
3. printed form; impression
4. in print; under print
5. mould
6. exact likeness
7. a kitchen gadget

Telugu: అచ్చు, accu, n
1. a stamp, a type, a printing press
3. a mould
4. the handle of hand mill,
5. an image or picture

In the above example, both Tamil and Telugu retain the proto form *accu*.

II. DEDR

Tamil: *aTakkam*, n: submission, patience, repose
Telugu: *aDakuva*, n: humility, modesty, submissiveness

Tamil: அடக்கம், aTakkam, n
1. humility; modesty; unobtrusive behavior
2. inconspicuousness
3. (of size and use) compactness; handiness
4. being inclusive
5. burial
6. cost of production; cost price

Telugu: అడకువ, aDakuva
1. submission, obedience, politeness.
2. humility

In this case, *aDakuva* is the Telugu form for the Tamil *aTakkam*. But *aDakuva* has become obsolete and the following words are used in the present day Telugu: *namrata, vinayamu, vidheyata, anakuva, nigarvam* for submission, obedience, humility and *mariyAda* and *sanmAnamu* for politeness.

III. DEDR

Tamil: *atir*, v: to shake, quake, tremble (as by an earthquake, the fall of a tree, the rolling of chariots), be scartled, alrmed, resound (as thunder), reverberate, sound (as a drum), roar (as beasts)
Telugu: *adaru*, v: to tremble, shake, quake, shiver

Tamil: அதிர், atir, v
1. vibrate; shake
2. (of drums) be sounded
3. be shaken (by the sudden impact of an event, situation)

Telugu: అదరు/అదురు, adaru/aduru
1. To tremble, shake, quake, shiver

IV. DEDR

Tamil: *ATTam*, n: motion, vibration, swinging, play, game, one's turn in a game
Telugu: *ATa*, n: play, game, dancing, acting on the stage, jest, gambling

Tamil: ஆட்டம், ATTam, n
1. jerking movement
2. dance
3. game; play
4. (in games) one's turn
5. (in a movie theatre) show
6. unrestrained behavior (generally not approved by others)

Telugu: ఆట, ATa
1. play, sport, a game
2. a dance, acting or stage performance
3. jest, joke, gambling

V. DEDR

Tamil: *ATu*, v: to move; wave, swing, shake, dance, act a part or play, play, sport, cohabit, fight, go, wander about, say, do, enjoy
Telugu: *Adu*, v: play, sport, act on the stage, dance, mover, shake, totter, vibrate, throb

Tamil: ஆடு, ATu, v
1. move in a swaying motion; move to and fro
2. (of body) shiver; tremble
3. vibrate
4. shake
5. (of a swing or one in a swing) go forward and backward; swing
6. perform (a dance, drama)
7. dance or move as if dancing
8. play (a game)
9. dance to the tune of
10. behave without restraint; have an intemperate life-style

Telugu: ఆడు, ADu v
1. to play, dance work, act, do move, ply
2. to shake, totter, wag
3. to beat, as the pulse
4. to speak, say

VI. DEDR

Tamil: *Avi*, n: breath, sigh soul, steam, vapour, smoke
Telugu: *Avi*, n: steam, vapour, heat

Tamil: ஆவி, Avi, n
1. (hot) vapour (from boiled water or hot drinks); mist (from ice); vapour (from petrol, etc. when exposed to air)
2. breath (as a sign of life)
3. spirit of the dead (believed to be wandering or existing somewhere); ghost

Telugu: ఆవి, Avi
1. steam, vapour

For the 2 and 3 senses, Telugu uses the word *Upiri* instead of *Avi/Aviri*.

VII. DEDR

Tamil: *iTam*, n: place, room, spot, opportunity
Telugu: *eDa*. n: place, spot

Tamil: இடம், iTam, n
1. spot (on a part of a person's body or a thing); part or area (of a region, town, etc.)
2. context or situation (in a story, play, etc.)
3. space (occupied by people or objects); room
4. seat (in a vehicle, etc.)
5. admission (in a college, etc. to study a course)
6. post; situation vacant (in an office, etc.)
7. seat (contested by a candidate in an election)
8. room (for speculation, happening, etc)
9. grade; rank; place (due to admissibility)
10. place; status
11. (particular or specified) situation
12. (in grammar) person
13. word used as a locative sign; `with'

Telugu: ఎడ, eDa
1. place, distance

Telugu uses *choTTu, sthAnam, sthAyi, sthalam* to represent the senses expressed by *iTam* in Tamil.

VIII. DEDR

Tamil: *iTu*, v: to place, deposit, put in, keep, throw, cast away, discharge (as arrows) give, pour (as rain), put on (as a bangle), compare, bury, lay (as an egg)
Telugu: *iDu*, v: to place, put, lay, give, offer

Tamil: இடு, iTu, v
1. put (food, flour, into a vessel, etc.); place
2. lay (egg)
3. put on (sacred ash, on the forehead); smear
4. put (garland on s.o.) garland; put on (pieces of jewellery)
5. put (a line, dot, etc. on a surface); make (border on one end of the saree, etc.)
6. set up; erect (a fence, etc.)
7. make; prepare (papad)
8. make (plans)
9. give (s.o. a name); name
10. issue (order, etc.)
11. pronounce (curse)

Telugu: ఇడు, iDu
1. to give, offer, place, put, lay, plant

Even though Telugu has *iDu* in usage, words such as *vEyu* and *peTTu* are predominantly used to represent the senses exhibited by Tamil.

IX. DEDR

Tamil: *izhu*, v: to draw, pull, drag along the ground, attract (as a magnet), wheedle, draw out, stretch out, draw into (as a whirlpool), engulf, absorb; have convulsions, gasp for breath
Telugu: *Iducu, Idcu*, v: to pull, haul, drag, draw, attract

Tamil: இழு, izhu, v
1. pull (s.o. or sth. Causing to follow or drawing towards oneself); draw
2. (of limbs) have spasmodic jerks; get convulsed
3. pull (sth. to a desired place or position); draw
4. drag out (a person); take (a person compelling him to come)
5. drag (s.o. into sth); involve
6. leave (what one has started saying) unfinished; drag on
7. protract
8. gasp (for breath)
9. take in; take a drag
10. attract; draw close
11. draw (water)
12. draw (a line)
13. make (into a wire or fibre)

Telugu: ఈడ్చు /ఈడు చు IDcu/IDucu
1. to pull, haul, drag

Idcu in Telugu is mostly replaced by *lAgu* to represent the senses expressed in Tamil.

X. DEDR

Tamil *iRangku*, v: to descend, alight, fall (as rain), disembark, settle into place, halt, abase (as poison, small-pox, etc.) bow respectfully, fall from a high state
Telugu: *eragu*, v: to descend, bow or make obeisance, prostrate oneself.

Tamil: இறங்கு, iRangku, v
1. come down; get down; climb down
2. filter through in drops; trickle; drip
3. get off (a vehicle); get down
4. (of price) come down
5. (of fever, temperature) come down; subside
6. (of voice) become low; become faint
7. begin to get busy with (an activity); get down to
8. get into (the water of a river, etc.)
9. (of a nail, wheel of a cart) go into
10. arrive (at a destination or place)
11. (of food) go down
12. (of venom) be removed; be counteracted
13. (in cards) play (at one's turn)
14. (in cricket) go in (to bat)
15. be reduced; be deflated

Telugu: ఎరగు, eragu, v
1. to descend
2. to salute, to make a bow, to bow down to, to prostrate oneself

Telugu mostly uses *digu* for the senses expressed in Tamil.

XI. DEDR

Tamil *OTu*, v: to run, flee, sail, operate (as the mind), happen, be defeated
Telugu: *ODu*, v: to run, be defeated, fail, be afraid, flow, trickle

Tamil: ஓடு, OTu, v
1. run
2. run; ply
3. (of watches, clock) go; run
4. (of breath) move in and out (of the lungs)
5. (of water, blood, etc.) flow
6. (of root, vein in the body) run
7. (of grey hair) show up in streaks
8. (of film) run; (of work) proceed; progress
9. (of good) get sold
10. (of time) pass (quickly)
11. function (normally)

Telugu: ఓడు , ODu
1. to fail, lose, to be defeated or worsted
2. to flow or be lost, as blood
3. to shrink, hesitate, fall back
4. to be frightened
5. to rush, as a flood

Even though, *ODu* is in usage, it is rarely used. Instead, Telugu uses *parigettu, ADu,etc.* for the senses expressed in Tamil

XII. DEDR

Tamil *OTu*, n: shell (of egg, tortoise, crab), tile, potsherd, earthen vessel, skull
Telugu: *ODu billa*, n: a roofing tile

Tamil: ஓடு, OTu, n
1. tile (for roofing)
2. broken piece of earthenware; potsherd
3. (of a tortoise, etc.) shell; hard outer cover (of certain fruits, e.g. almonds)

Telugu: ఓడు, ODu
1. roofing tile, a pantile

XIII. DEDR

Tamil *kaTTu*, v: to tie, fasten, build, wear, put on, bind by spells, marry, shut up, store, hug, compare with, be equal

Telugu: *kaTTu*, v: to tie, bind, wear (clothes), build, bewitch, obstruct.

Tamil: கட்டு, kaTTu,v
1. construct (a house, bridge, etc)/(of birds) build (a nest)
2. inlay (stones in ornaments)/have a denture fixed
3. compose (a song)
4. build (ship, coach, etc)
5. heap up earth at the base (of a plant) as support
6. (of a book) make (page)
7. fasten (s.o. with sth.); tie (sth.) up; tie (a packet, etc. with a string); pack (sth.)
8. bandage (the injured part of the body)
9. wear (a saree, dhoti, etc.); tie (a piece of cloth around the head, waist, etc.)
10. wear (wrist watch, talisman, etc.)
11. blindfold
12. tie a know (as when getting married)
13. yoke (oxen to a cart, plough, etc.)
14. string up (flowers); make (a garland)
15. fold (hands across the chest or around the knees)
16. marry
17. dam (up water)/stagnate
18. (of phlegm, blood) accumulate; clot
19. (of price, rent, charges) be reasonable
20. pay (fees, interest, etc.)
21. bet (in a horse, race)
22. play (a part in a stage play, film)
23. brand (s.o.); label
24. counteract venom (as an antidote)
25. (of stools) become hard/harden (the stools)

Telugu: కట్టు, kaTTu, v
1. to tie, bind
2. to wear, as clothes
3. to connect, affix, attach
4. to store up, to lay by
5. to build, erect
6. to fascinate, charm, bewitch
7. to fabricate, compose, or put a story together
8. to impute a sin or offence
9. to find fault with, to lay blame on
10. to gird up the loins or be prepared
11. to water a garden
12. to dress a wound
13. to get ready a carriage
14. to pay money
15. to restrain the appetite

XIV. DEDR

Tamil *vai*,v: to put, place, seat, lay by, store up, possess, keep, create, set up

Telugu: *vEyu*,v: to place, put, put on (as a dress)

Tamil: வை ,vai, v
1. put or place (sth. in or on sth.)
2. place
3. put (flowers) on; place (sth. decoratively)
4. place (sth.on view)
5. plant
6. put (full stop, comma, seal); mark; stamp
7. set (fire)/light (a lamp)
8. give (a blow)
9. take (a step)
10. provide (sth. as food)
11. place (a bomb)
12. provide with
13. bring one's hand to forehead (as in salute)
14. make; prepare (food)
15. make (offering)
16. erect (a statue); establish (an institution)
17. have or run (a shop)
18. have; employ (s.o.)
19. set up (a home after one's marriage)
20. grow (beard, moustache)
21. prescribe (rules, regulations); follow; have
22. have (evidence, details)
23. keep
24. keep (in memory)
25. conduct; hold (an event)
26. arrange
27. play (radio, record)
28. give (as pledge, security)
29. set (sth. apart)
30. keep (in an account)
31. apportion; portion (sth.) out
32. keep; maintain
33. have (affection, love for s.o); place (one's trust in s.o.)
34. establish; maintain (friendship, contact)
35. prescribe (a text for study)
36. look after; take care of
37. put forth; present
38. cast a spell (on)
39. put on flesh

Telugu: వేయు , vEyu, v
1. to throw, cast, or fling
2. to discharge a missile or fire arms
3. to let drop
4. to place, put or put on, as a dress
5. to put a lid on
6. to make the carriage ready
7. to saddle a horse
8. to ask a question
9. to build a hut
10. to light torches
11. to give fodder
12. to give a cry
13. to shut up
14. to to draw out
15. to pluck up or out
16. to push away
17. to draw out
18. to write off
19. to give away

In addition to *vEyu,* Telugu uses *peTTu* to represent the senses expressed in Tamil.

From the above data, it is clear that Tamil, which has less letters in its alphabet, exhibits more polysemy examples than Telugu that has more letters in its alphabet and hence uses different words including borrowings for representing various senses.

3 Conclusion

To conclude, based on our argument that less number of letters in the alphabet of a language will discourage borrowing from other languages if the contact between them is primarily literary, we have demonstrated that Tamil is more polysemous than Telugu. It strengthens our hypothesis that words in a language that has a smaller alphabet will be more polysemous than that which has an elaborate alphabet.

References

Apresjan, J. D. 1973. *Regular Polysemy.* Mouton, The Hague.

Burrow, T. and Emeneau, M. B. 1984. *Dravidian Etymological Dictionary.* Munshiram Manoharlal Publishers, New Delhi. (revised edition)

Brown C. P. 1903. *A Telugu English Dictionary.* Language. Christian Knowledge Society's Press, Madras.
http://dsal.uchicago.edu/dictionaries/brown/

Burrow, T. 1968. *Collected Papers on Dravidian Linguistics.* Annamalai University, Annamalai Nagar.

CreaA. 1998/2008. *taRkaalat tamizh akarati*. CreA, Chennai.

Cruse, D.A. 1986. *Lexical Semantics*. Cambridge University Press, Cambridge.

Gywnn, J.P.L. 1991. *A Telugu-English Dictionary*. Oxford University Press, New Delhi. http://dsal.uchicago.edu/dictionaries/gwynn/

Krishnamurti, Bh. 1961. *Telugu Verbal Bases*. University of California Press, Berkeley.

Lobner, S. 2002. *Understanding Semantics*. Arnold Publishers, London.

Miller, G.A. 1995.` WordNet: A Lexical Database for English', *Communications of the ACM*. Vol.38, No.11.

Mohanty, P. 2008 Dravidian Substratum and Indo-Aryan Languages. *International Journal of Dravidian Linguistics*. 37:1, 1-20.

Pustejovsky, J. 1991. `The Generative Lexicon', *Computational Linguistics* 17:4, 409-41.

Pustejovsky, J. and Boguraev, B. 1995. Lexical Semantics in Context, *Journal of Semantics*. 12:1-14.

Ravin, Y and Leacock, L. 2000. `Polysemy: An Overview', Y.Ravin and C. Leacock. eds. *Polysemy: Theoretical and Computational Issues*. Oxford University Press, Oxford.

Reddy, G. N. 1990. *Dictionary of Synonyms in Telugu*. Pratibha Publications, Hyderabad.

Interactions of South African Languages: Case Study of Tsotsitaal

Karolina Brook
Princeton University
Program in Linguistics
`kbrook@princeton.edu`

Abstract

South Africa, viewed to be one of the most multilingual countries in the world, recognizes eleven official languages. This paper represents a sociolinguistic analysis of Tsotsitaal, an unofficial creole language that formed as an amalgamation of Afrikaans and isiZulu. Today, Tsotsitaal has evolved into a collection of distinct yet mutually understandable languages projected from the speaker's native language. It is marked by a high degree of codeswitching and overlexicalisation. I discuss the challenges that these properties present in developing a WordNet for a creole such as Tsotsitaal.

1 Introduction: The birth of Tsotsitaal

South Africa is viewed to be one of the most multilingual countries in the world, recognizing eleven official languages (van der Merwe and van der Merwe 2006:2). In addition to the officially-recognized languages, Tsotsitaal is a creole not recognized in official censes (Mesthrie 2002:12; Makhudu 2002:399). Creole languages are defined as being young dynamic languages, only one to three centuries old (see McWhorter 2005 for a review of creoles).

Tsotsitaal is integrally tied with its birthplace and subsequent area of development. The language developed largely among racially segregated residential areas, located in Johannesburg around the gold reef (consult Molamu 2003:xviii for map of area). Despite the attitude to segregate races, in particular blacks from whites, these three communities shared extensive social interactions and came to develop some sense of overarching community (xviii-xix). The subculture that developed was vibrant, dynamic and distinctive, characterized by dance parties, music, alcohol and escalating violence (xx). During the 1950s black people were relocated during forced removals to provide housing for working white people. The exact origin of Tsotsitaal is largely unclear, although it is possible that Tsotsitaal developed (and continues to be associated with) various criminal gangs that were active on the Witwatersrand in the early to mid 1900s (Slabbert and Myers-Scotton 1996:321), although it is also believed that Tsotsitaal came into fruition around the 1950s and 60s (Motshegoa 2005:1). The language developed for several intertwined reasons: it was born as a language of creativity and passion as well as an expression of the sadness, anger and resentment felt by these people dislocated from their sense of identity; it acted as a bridge among young segregated communities that spoke several distinct languages (Molamu 2003:xxi, xiii); it functioned as the *lingua franca* of male social interactions (Slabbert and Myers-Scotton 1996:322); and finally, it served as a means to organize illicit activities yet remain unintelligible to police who could not speak the language (Motshegoa 2005:1).

The 'culture' of Tsotsitaal was characterized by wearing clothes of particular labels, oftentimes flamboyantly expensive (Motshegoa 2005:1-2). In this essentially macho culture, knowing Tsotsitaal separated boys from men, and was a means to show streetwise character (1). This is exemplified by the alternate name for Tsotsitaal, namely Flaai- or Fly Taal, which would denote someone who is slick and citywise (Makhudu 2002:402). Additionally, a breed of music was born that came to be known as Kwaito, or 'bubble gum music' (Motshegoa 2005:3). An integral part of the beliefs of Tsotsitaal speakers was characterized by an interest in crime and violence. Tsotsitaal was largely used as a means of communication among those interested in crime-related activities (Molamu 2003:xiii, xxii). The derivation 'tsotsi' as part of the name describing this language is descriptive of this function of the language; today, the word has largely come to refer to a hooligan, thug or gangster (xxii-xxiii). In response to the oppression enforced on the black communities by the Afrikaners, Tsotsitaal was largely a secret language that was used as a means of rejection of Afrikaans, but also to ensure Afrikaans-speakers, particularly the police and other law-enforcers, did not understand the activities the youths were organizing (Molamu 2003:xiii, Motshegoa 2005:2). Afrikaans indeed formed the basis of Tsotsitaal, retaining some grammatical rules of Afrikaans while completely violating other grammatical constructions (Molamu 2003:xxv). The derivation *taal*, comprises the second part of Tsotsitaal, and is the Afrikaans word meaning 'language' (xxii). Thus, Tsotsitaal lay in the middle ground between these two separate worlds: the Afrikaans people who forced their language on this oppressed group, and the ensuing world of crime and violence.

2 The nature of Tsotsitaal today

The slang or street language that emerged from this political and social melting pot came to transcend the physical segregation of the original three communities in which the language developed, and today spans areas and townships around Johannesburg (Molamu 2003:xxii, Makhudu 2002:399). In these areas, Tsotsitaal may also go by different names, but confusion has arisen in the literature whether these are different languages or in fact the same language (refer to Ntshangase 1995, Makhudu 2002, and Molamu 2003 for opposing arguments). Mesthrie (2008: 95-109) recently proposed a unified account of Tsotsitaal, describing it as a 'slang lexis' which incorporates all of its varieties including Tsotsitaal associated with crime (as discussed) to simply street speech spoken by urban youth today, thereby including the Tsotsitaal based on Afrikaans, Zulu, Sotho and Xhosa, and even an English Tsotsitaal that Mesthrie proposes (see 103-108) as existing among Indians and Coloureds living in KwaZulu Natal.

In clarifying this issue, I will first discuss the aspects of the dependence of Tsotsitaal on the speaker's native language (L1), as well as the property of code switching inherent in this language, before moving to discuss my own fieldwork and conclusions.

2.1 L1-dependence of Tsotsitaal

The individuals who responded to my search for Tsotsitaal speakers had mother tongues including Zulu, Xhosa, Sotho, Tswana and English. What I discovered was that these native speakers all spoke a different version of Tsotsitaal that appeared to depend on the speaker's native language, while incorporating lexicon from Afrikaans as well as isiZulu and isiXhosa, and, to lesser degrees, Sesotho, Setswana, Sepedi, Tshivenda and Xitsonga. In addition to this dependence on the speaker's native language, the Tsotsitaal spoken also seemed to depend on the speaker's main residential area (which in turn is related to the major language spoken in that area) as well as the speaker's age, with older-generation Tsotsitaal speakers being more familiar with the 'original' Afrikaans-based Tsotsitaal.

A consequence of this is that the same sentence spoken in Tsotsitaal can differ depending on the speaker's L1. For instance, 'Let's talk' can be said in Tsotsitaal as the Afrikaans-based *Let's wiet*, or as the Sotho-based *Let's qamtha*. As one speaker told me, 'There is an own Tsotsitaal [sic] in every place – as many as there are beds'. But what is even more astounding is that, as confirmed by my speakers, all these versions of Tsotsitaal are mutually understandable.

2.2 Code switching in Tsotsitaal

Code switching and code mixing are two separate phenomena, the former more specifically referring to 'the alternation of elements longer than one word, from two languages or dialects', while the latter referring to 'the alternation ... of shorter elements, often just single words' (McCormick 1995:194-195; Gough 1996:69; see Slabbert and Finlayson 2002 for a review of code switching in South African townships). In this paper, I will refer to both as 'code switching'.

In a country where most speakers are multilingual, code switching has become prevalent in slang use among the youth of South Africa. Slang is an idiosyncratic method by which the youth in South Africa express their identity, in a city 'characterized by a high degree of language diversity' (Bembe and Beukes 2007:464). Code switching is often used in the township environments, where there is no one single *lingua franca*. Practically, people living together in the townships in South Africa speak a variety of languages, and in order to communicate effectively, it is imperative to be able to speak several languages and be able to swop from one language to another, as this quote (taken from Slabbert and Finlayson 2000:124) illustrates (emphasis changed from the original):

' ... *[L]et's take for instance,* ngikhuluma isiZulu lesi, lesi, lesi; *and* wena ungumPedi, fanele, *we must communicate,* sizo*communicate*a kanjani? Fanele ngi *compromise,* ngi*mixe with your language* ukuthi uzongizwisisa, uyabona.'

... [L]et's take it that I am speaking Zulu and you are a Pedi, it is imperative that we communicate – how will we do that? I will have to compromise and mix my language with yours so that you can understand me, you see.'

2.3 Selected sentences in Tsotsitaal

Follows are sentences taken from my fieldwork provided by native speakers of Tsotsitaal. They serve to illustrate the L1-dependence of Tsotsitaal, as well as the high degree of code switching present in the spoken language.

2.3.1 Zulu-based Tsotsitaal

Bengi vaye ne-mpinshi
1sg go.PAST with-friends
yami si-yozama i-leve ejozi.
3sg-looking for.life in.town
'I went with my friends looking for life in town.'

2.3.2 Afrikaans-based Tsotsitaal

Sharota is 'n lekker mshoza.
PROP.N is INDEF nice woman.
'Sharota is a pretty woman.'

2.3.3 Tswana-based Tsotsitaal

Bafwetho arevayeng re
Guys let's go (to many people) to
tuba die gamula nyoko.
take/rob DEF rich.man money.
'Guys, let's go rob the rich man of his money.'

2.3.4 Sotho-based Tsotsitaal

If ore haona yona
(If) 2sg.said 2sg.NEG have it
ngaye fife yanga ke
give.to.1sg five (5) 50-cent so
elo baya toss.
1sg.can buy matches.
'If you said you don't have it give me 5 50-cent coins so I can buy matches.'

2.4 Tsotsitaal: one language or several?

These characteristics of Tsotsitaal present two problems relevant to WordNet. Firstly, the same concept can be expressed in Tsotsitaal using different words solely based on a different L1. Should such lexemes be considered synonymous? Or should we categorize the lexicon as entirely separate languages, i.e. Afrikaans Tsotsitaal, Zulu Tsotsitaal, etc? Should the fact that the speakers claim the different versions to be mutually understandable be taken into account?

Secondly, the issue of code switching represents an interesting dilemma for the definition of this language. Is Tsotsitaal a language that possesses a high degree of code switching as a fundamental property? Or rather, should we view it as a code switching phenomenon present in a large body of languages – rather than a language in its own right? How will a decision on this matter affect Tsotsitaal's representation within WordNet?

3 Tsotsitaal lexicon

In this section, I present several examples of lexical items that have been documented in Tsotsitaal. The speakers also confirmed their use in Tsotsitaal.

3.1 Selected lexical items in Tsotsitaal

tsotsi [tsɒtsi][4]: *n* In general, the word refers to a 'violent, usually young criminal who usually lives by his wits ... [and has] broadened to incorporate an entire youth gang subculture'[5]. The connotations vary between a criminal who steals and kills to just a hooligan (as opposed to a 'thug'). The exact origin is unknown, and several possibilities exist: 1) it originates from the **zoot suits** that were worn by Americans in the 1940s, and their stereotype is that tsotsis play the part of the zoot-suiter: '[t]hey are street-corner dandies, lounging in the doorways of vacant stores, idling in the train stations and bus terminals, giving passersby the hard eye'[5]; 2) it has been argued that the word was used to describe the stove-pipe trousers that were in fashion in the 1940s and as such may be derived from the Afrikaans word **stof-pipe** that described these tight-fitting trousers, or from **tso(lo)**, which meant the trousers they wore were sharp (fine or nice)[5]; 3) it could possibly originate from South Sotho **ho tsotsa**, a verb to engage in crime and thuggery, or **tsotsana** which means 'to fight' in Sesotho[5], although it has been contended that while the word has 'a Sotho phonemic structure, it is not a Sotho lexical item'[2]; 4) the !Kung San, an ethnic group in southern Africa, refer to non-San people as **zo si**, which refers to dangerous animals, and consequently they refer to such people as angry or dangerous[5]; 5) the reputation of **Tutsi** warriors in Rwanda and Burundi, who were involved in vicious and brutal crimes in the 1930s/40s, came to be known in the South African townships and came to refer to gangsters who were extremely physically violent[5]. **Tsitso** is a nickname that is modified from the word **tsotsi**; **tsotsigeid** (or similarly, **tsotsi-ism** or **tsot-**

sism[2]) uses the Afrikaans **–geid** suffix that is equivalent to **–ness** in English in order to mean 'thuggery', the criminal acts that are carried out by tsotsis[5], or just the lifestyle and behaviours of the tsotsis[2].

kwaito [kwʌItəʊ[4]] *n* Popular township dance music 'featuring rhythmically recited vocals over an instrumental backing with strong bass lines'[4], or alternatively slowed-down US/UK house music with added African vibes[6]. The style of music emerged during the time of apartheid in the townships, and was a creative outlet during an economically-depressed time. Kwaito continues to be popular today with artists such as Mandoza or Zola. The noun can also possibly be used to refer to boys who sing in the streets. The word originates from **Amakwaito,** purportedly a group of gangsters in Sophiatown[1], or **amakwaitosi**, which supposedly means 'gangster'; this in turn derives from the word **kwaai** [kwaI[1,2]] (alternatives: **kwaad, kwaaje, kwaat, kw(a)i, quaai, quei**). Kwaai is a modern-day Afrikaans word that refers to something bad-tempered or angry, as in ' ... the lions on the opposite side were more <u>kwaad</u> ... than those where we now were'[2]. Kwaai also has slang usage to refer to something that is great or fantastic, as in, 'The music is <u>kwaai</u> but nobody wants to [dance]'[2]. This connection seems apt, particularly since the music was a form of expressing the township dwellers' anger and frustration during their oppression.

malalapipe [mala:lapaIp/məlɑləpaIp[2]]: *n* Literally refers to someone who sleeps in drainage pipes, or more generally, someone who sleeps rough or on the streets[5], though possibly specifically referring to a homeless child[2] (which is supported by the related word **malunde,** which is a term used to refer to sleeping out without parental permission[5]), as a result of being chased away from home and having nowhere else to stay. Possibly, the person's intent may be to ambush someone or perform a criminal act. It is possible the word originates from the isiZulu **umalalepayipini,** meaning 'homeless child', which can be broken down into **uma-** = one who + **lala** = sleeps + **epayipini** = in a drain, which itself may be derived from the English word **pipe**[2]. Pipe, in addition to referring to a tubular piece of metal or plastic, also may have connotations of referring to a vagabond[5], which may be through the use of the word to refer to the instrument for smoking drugs and the sexual connotations associated with the word[3]. Another possibility is that the word is a combination of the isiZulu word **ukulala**, which means to sleep, plus **pipe.**

chicken murder: *adj* a person having a relationship with a younger person[5]. This 'relationship' varied in nuance, from an older man sleeping with a younger woman, or even rape. 'chicken' is possibly used in reference to a younger, more innocent person; perhaps the relationship is viewed as taking away the innocence of a younger person. This expression would be equivalent to the American expression 'cradle robber' or 'cradle snatcher'[6]. There might be a relation between this expression and that of **chicken run,** an expression that was used to describe the exodus of white people and businesses from Zimbabwe and South Africa for fear of their future in the country[1,2,4].

3.2 Overlexicalisation in Tsotsitaal

Overlexicalisation, refers to the enormous number of words that can be used to refer to the same thing, and can be subdivided into two types: words that differ based on their language of origin, and words that differ based on their region of use, although these are not necessarily mutually exclusive (Makhudu 2002:402-403).

The examples presented were obtained from cross-referencing dictionary [5]. The prevalence, from highest to lowest, was determined from the speakers I interviewed.

girlfriend/woman:cherie/cheriekie/cherietjire, mathara, mshoza, tlakadula, tletletle, baby, rwatla, show, giedieng, tlakawibit, wherrie, charowibits, wibit.

young (streetwise) male: jieta, ma-Gents, ma-G-men autie, clever/klevaa, mfo, mri/mrio, deaden/laaities basie, bap,b[r]oer, (vaal)japie, ducktail, juba.

money: bucks, nyoko, miering, zak, chien, smackers, magegeba, kuneining, tsang, dummy, koezat.

3.3 Lexical issues for WordNet

This sampling of lexical items suggests further potential issues of Tsotsitaal for WordNet. Firstly, as a hybrid language, spellings in Tsotsitaal have not been officially finalized, and thus numerous variations of a word, even more than the ones provided here, exist.

Secondly, in keeping with the original purpose of the language, the majority of the words pertain to crime, sex and violence. The lexicon also includes concepts and words not present in other languages. Thirdly, the enormity of overlexicalisation presents a unique problem for WordNet. It is difficult to assess the synonymity of the overlexicalised items: while they seemed broadly similar, I did detect slight differences in the connotations of the words. It would be necessary to confirm that these connotations are widespread among Tsotsitaal speakers.

On the other hand, while Tsotsitaal is lexically rich in these concepts, it may be lacking in others. For instance, 'sun', 'moon', 'grass', 'dog', 'to dream', and 'to give birth', are just a few words that simply do not exist (Mesthrie 2008:102).

4 Conclusion

While WordNets are being developed for so-called "official" languages, creoles such as Tsotsitaal should also be studied and integrated into the Global WordNet Grid. The variable nature of Tsotsitaal does however present interesting challenges to the development of a Tsotsitaal WordNet. These issues can be summarized as follows: 1) how do we view synonymity that depends on the speaker's L1?; 2) how do we define the language based on code switching?; 3) how do we handle the high variability in spelling?; 4) we must be aware that the language will be lexically rich in some concepts, while poor in others; and 5) we must be careful in deciding whether over-lexicalised items are truly synonymous.

Acknowledgements

The author would like to thank both J.T.Katz and C.Fellbaum of Princeton University for their guidance, advice and support in the writing of this manuscript. Field research was funded through the Fred Fox 1939 Grant. This paper would not have been possible without the language input from the native speakers, to whom the author extends her gratitude. Finally, thanks go to my parents for helping me locate native Tsotsitaal speakers while so far from home

References

Please note: The works preceded by bracketed numerals ([1], [2], etc) were used in the various dictionary sections for clarity.

Bembe, Magdeline Princess, and Beukes, Anne-Marie. 2007. The use of slang by black youth in Gauteng. *Southern African Linguistics and Applied Language Studies*. 25:4, 463-472.

[1] Dictionary of South African English (DSAE). 1987. Third Edition. Oxford: Oxford University Press.

[2] Dictionary of South African English on Historical Principles (DSAE-HP). 1996. Oxford: Oxford University Press.

Gough, David. 1996. Black English in South Africa in Varieties of English Around the World: Focus on South Africa. Ed. de Klerk, Vivian. Amsterdam: John Benjamins Publishing Company. 15, 53-78

Makhudu, K.D.P. 2002. An Introduction to Flaaitaal (or Tsotsitaal) in Language in South Africa. Ed. Mesthrie, Rajend. University of Cape Town, Cambridge University Press. 398-406.

McCormick, K. 1995. Code-switching, Code-mixing and Convergence in Cape Town in Language and Social History. Ed. Mesthrie, Rajend. Cape Town & Johannesburg, David Philip. 193-208.

McWhorter, John H. 2005. Defining Creole. Oxford, University Press.

Mesthrie, Rajend. 2002. South Africa: A Sociolinguistic Overview in Language in South Africa. Ed. Mesthrie, Rajend. University of Cape Town, Cambridge University Press. 11-26.

---. 2008. 'I've been speaking Tsotsitaal all my life without knowing it' – towards a unified account of tsotsitaals in South Africa in Social lives in language--sociolinguistics and multilingual speech communities : celebrating the work of Gillian Sankoff. Meyerhoff, M., Nagy, N (ed). Philadelphia: John Benjamins.

[5] Molamu, Louis. 2003. Tsotsi-Taal: A Dictionary of the Language of Sophiatown. Pretoria, University of South Africa.

Motshegoa, Lebo. 2005. Township Talk: The language, the culture, the people. The A-Z Dictionary of South Africa's Township Lingo. Cape Town, Double Storey Books.

Ntshangase, Dumisani Krushchev. 1995. Indaba yami i-straight: Language and Language Practices in Soweto in Language and Social History. Ed. Mesthrie, Rajend. Cape Town & Johannesburg, David Philip. 291-297.

[3] Oxford English Dictionary (OED). 2008. Oxford: Oxford University Press. Accessed from http://www.oed.com/

Slabbert, Sarah and Finlayson, Rosalie. 2000. 'I'm a cleva!': The Linguistic Makeup of Identity in a South African Urban Environment in Language and Ethnicity in the New South Africa. Ed. Kamwangamalu, Nkonko M. *International Journal of the Sociology of Language*. 144, 119-135.

---. 2002. Code-switching in South African Townships in Language in South Africa. Ed. Mesthrie, Rajend. University of Cape Town, Cambridge University Press. 235-257.

Slabbert, Sarah and Myers-Scotton, Carol. 1996. The Structure of Tsotsitaal and Iscamtho: Code Switching and In-Group Identity in South African Townships. *Linguistics*. 34:2, 317-342.

[4] South African Concise Oxford Dictionary. 2002. Ed. The Dictionary Unit for South African English. Cape Town, South Africa, Oxford University Press Southern Africa.

[6] Urban dictionary. Accessed from www.urbandictionary.com

van der Merwe, I.J. and van der Merwe, JH (ed). 2006. Linguistic Atlas of South Africa: Language in Space and Time. Stellenbosch: SUN PReSS.

Contrastive Polysemy in Concept Space: Implications for Multilingual Semantic Lexicons

Somsukla Banerjee
Centre for Applied Linguistics and Translation Studies
University of Hyderabad
somsukla2005@gmail.com

Achla Raina
Humanities and Social Sciences
Indian Institute of Technology Kanpur
achla@iitk.ac.in

Harish Karnick
Department of Computer Science and Engineering
Technology Kanpur
hk@iitk.ac.in

Abstract

We propose a model of polysemy within a larger framework *Concept Space* accounting for the organization and generation of concepts in the human cognitive architecture. The predictions of the model about the bilingual user's resolution of contrastive polysemy are worked out taking a subset of verbal polysemies from English and Hindi and crosslinguistic interrelationships in a semantically rich lexicon are modeled along the lines of the *Concept Space* framework. Computational implications of the present work are outlined.

1 Introduction

The phenomenon of polysemy has, in the recent years, emerged as the focus of attention of lexical semanticists primarily for the implications it has for cognitive and computational modeling of natural language. Polysemy refers to multiple senses for a given word. However, polysemous words often show interesting crosslinguistic distributional parallels and contrasts with synonym sets in another language. The word *walk* in English, for example, is polysemous between self-motion and cause-motion senses (e.g., `John walked` as against `John walked the dog`). In Hindi, these two distinct but related word senses are expressed through different, though morphologically related verbs, `chal` and `chalaa`. On the other hand, the verb `see` in English is polysemous between perceive-through-sight and perceive-mentally, and its synonym in Hindi, `dekh`, parallels these word senses. These crosslinguistic parallels and contrasts in lexical polysemy have significant implications for bilingual processing of natural language, some of which are being explored in the present study. When we consider a pair of languages, we often come across words which have more than one senses in one language but these different senses are realized as separate lexical units in the other. This is an instance of contrastive polysemy (CP) across languages: polysemous words in L-1 map into different words into L-2 and vice versa (Boas, 2001). Like many other issues in lexical semantics, contrastive polysemy is of interest from the twin perspectives of computational and cognitive modeling of natural language. In the domain of computational modeling, the study of CP could be useful in domains like computational lexicography and natural language understanding and generation systems. In the domain of cognitive modeling on the other hand, CP emerges as an important issue in crosslinguistic lexical processing in the bilingual mind.

In this paper, we begin with an outline of the preliminaries of the *Concept Space* model which accounts for generation and organization of concepts in the human mind and their subsequent mappings to linguistic expressions. Thereafter we present a description of how polysemy and contrastive polysemy is handled in the *Concept Space* considering instances of contrastive polysemy English and Hindi with their mappings in the other language. We also look into a set of polysemous verbs from Hindi, and their English equivalents. The contrasts are examined in terms of the various operations such as *addition, removal, widening narrowing, abstraction* and *projection* of attributes and *addition* and *removal* of functions apply on concepts to derive concepts corresponding to polysemous words in question. We conclude the paper with some observations regarding the implications of the present work for multilingual machine readable lexical databases.

2 Concept Space

Concepts in the proposed model are autonomous and prelinguistic. The *Concept*

Space CS consists of the pair (C, O) where C denotes a set of concepts and O is a finite set of operations on concepts. The set of attributes and functions present in a concept form its *representational structure*. An attribute is a three tuple <name, type, value. An attribute is a static feature whereas a function is dynamic in nature consisting of the three tuple <argument, process, returned value>. A function has typed formal arguments. When the values are passed for these arguments, an operation is undertaken and a value, which can be a reference to another concept, is optionally returned after the completion of the operation. A function can change the values of its arguments or of attributes in the concept.

The *Concept Space* is endowed with the potential to generate infinitely many concepts using a finite set of operations. With these operations, the human cognitive processor is able to perform a variety of tasks in *the Concept Space* which includes *addition* or *removal* of attributes, *projection* of attributes to form a new concept, *widening* or *narrowing* of attribute types and invocation of functions that may lead to the formation of new concepts.

Apart from other attributes such as physical extension, countability etc., we introduce the attribute *derivation_account* which captures the derivational history associated with a particular concept. Assuming that it is possible to derive new concepts from the existing ones by the use of a set of operations, the *derivation_account* includes details about the specific operation/s through which the concept has been derived. The *derivation_account* is a generalization of the traditional hierarchical structure.

We consider words and other visual signs as a part of the conceptual system. We refer to these as w*ord concepts*. A w*ord concept* has an attribute called the *conceptual_referent* and this attribute acts as a reference to the conceptual entity that a word stands for. Similarly, a concept has an attribute known as the *linguistic_referent* which is a pointer to the *word concept* which is its linguistic representation. Knowing the meaning of a word involves establishing the link between the relevant *word concept* and its corresponding concept through the *conceptual_referent*.

In C*oncept Space,* there are concepts that have only attributes. We refer to these concepts as *entity_concepts* and these can be distinguished on the basis of attributes such as *physical_extension*, *countability* etc. There are concepts which include both attributes and functions in their *representational structure.* We refer to these concepts as *event_concepts.* A concept such as GIVE may be viewed in terms of an operation involving an act of TRANSFER of an object from one entity to another. It is not possible to conceptualize the event GIVE without the entities that take part in it. We refer to such entities as *participating entities* of an *event_concept* and they are present as attributes in the *representational structure* of the concept. An *event_concept* is always instantiated in a particular context. The function takes the context as an argument and creates a new concept which is derivationally related to the earlier concept.

The instantiation of an *event_concept* invokes the embedded function. The *event_concept* is always instantiated in a particular context and the function takes the context as its argument(s) and creates a new concept. The tense and aspectual properties of events are derived procedurally by the function when an *event_concept* is instantiated.

We propose the following operations in the *Concept Space:*

1. **add_attribute** (*a*) adds attribute *a* in concept *C*.
2. **remove_attribute**(*a*) eliminates an attribute *a* from concept *C*.
3. **add_function**(*f*) inserta function *f* in concept *C*.
4. **remove_function**(*f*) eliminates function f from concept *C*. The function *f* includes the signature so there is no ambiguity regarding the function in question.
5. **widen_attribute** (*a, t*) widens the type of attribute *a* to *t* in concept *C*.
6. **narrow_attribute**(*a* ,*t*) narrows the type of attribute *a* to *t* in concept *C*.
7. **project_attribute**(S_a, S_f) projects a set of attributes S_a and /or functions S_f from concept *C* to form a new concept.
8. **reify**(*C*) applies all the derivations in concept *C* to produce a fully specified concept with an empty derivation.

9. ***abstract***(<$C_1, C_2, ..., C_n$>) produces an abstract concept with only the common attributes in the sequence of concepts of $C_1, C_2, ..., C_n$.

The list of operations is indicative and not exhaustive. The derivational history of a concept is stored in the attribute *derivation_account*. Clearly, a derivation can model a hierarchy, so we do not explicitly organize concepts in a hierarchy.

3 Word Concepts and Polysemy

Words as well as visuo-motor signs which stand for concepts are concepts in their own right in the *Concept Space*. The *linguistic_referent* of a concept may contain more than a single value pointing to multiple *word concepts*, as is the case with synonyms. Conversely, the *conceptual_referent* of a particular *word concept* may be linked to multiple concepts, thus yielding polysemies.

We would now consider derivations of a few *event_concepts* as our discussion here concentrate on verbal polysemies in Hindi and English. By now we know that *event_concepts* have an embedded function which takes the context as argument and derives a new concept. Let us consider the derivational mechanisms for a set of verbal polysemies. The representational structures of the concepts corresponding to the polysemous *word concept* 'walk' as illustrated in (1a-b):

(1) a. Ram **walked** in the park
 b. Ram **walked** the dog in the park.

(1) WALK$_1$
 1. <participating_entity1, Human, ram>
 2. <participating_entity3, Place, park>
 3. < event type, Processive_event, process_instance>

function(walk)
 4. <derivation_account, Derivation, null>
 5. <linguistic_ referent, Word concept, walk>
 --Tense(procedure_time) : past
 --Aspect (procedure_aspect) :activity

(2) WALK$_2$

 1. <participating_entity1, Human, Ram>
 2. <participating _entity 2, Animate, dog>
 3. <participating_ entity3, Place, park>
 4. < event type, Processive_event, process_instance>

function(walk)

 5.<derivation_account, Derivation, add_attribute < participating_entity, Animate, dog>
 6. <linguistic_referent, Word concept, walk>
 --Tense(procedure_time) : past
 --Aspect (procedure_aspect):activity

One can derive WALK$_2$ from WALK$_1$ by the operation *add_attribute* which inserts an additional *participating_entity* in the representation of WALK$_1$. Both are *event_concepts* where WALK$_1$ involves a *participating_entity* undertaking the process and WALK$_2$, where one of the *participating_entities* causes another to undertake this process. Similarly it is possible to derive WALK$_1$ from WALK$_2$ by the operation *remove_attribute*.

4 Contrastive Polysemy

We have mentioned in the introduction about the existence of contrastive polysemy across languages. We now consider set of verbs in English and Hindi that demonstrate contrastive polysemy. The data in (2-3) illustrate a range of senses expressed by the English verbs *'run'*, and *'raise'*

(2) a. Maya **ran** on the road.
 b. Maya **ran** the dog off the road.

The verb *'run'* in both (2a) and (2b) corresponds to *processive_events*. If we look at the Hindi equivalent of (2), as given in (3), we find that Hindi uses distinct *word concepts* to express the different meanings of each of these events. In Hindi the corresponding *event_concepts* are bhag and bhagaa respectively.

We now present examples of Hindi polysemous verbs which are realized as distinct word concepts in English. The Hindi verb mil is polysemous and it has two distinct *conceptual_ reference* links, FIND and MEET.

This will be clear from the examples from Hindi given below.

(3) a. use ek kitaab **milii**.
     He-dat one book find-past-png
     (He found a book.)

   b. vaha tumse **milaa** thaa.
      he   you-acc meet be-past-png
      (He met you.)

The polysemous *word concept* mil corresponding to the *stative_event* concepts FIND and MEET can be derived by the operations *widen* or *narrow_attribute*. The *participating_entities* of MEET are HUMAN and from this concept one can derive FIND by the operation *widen_attribute* which expands the type of *participating_entities* that can be passed as the argument of the function.

So far we have seen that the various concepts that correspond to the multiple senses of the polysemous *word_concepts* can be derived from one another by the use of the various operations that exist in *Concept Space*. In the next section we discuss the implications of the present approach for bilingual machine readable lexicons.

5 Computational Implications

The framework of *Concept Space* through which we have dealt with the issue of contrastive polysemy that we have presented so far is of particular relevance to WordNet and other such databases that aim to store cross linguistic lexical semantic information. Conceptual and lexical representation is two essential elements of language processing. Multilingual representation of lexical knowledge which links a concept to its linguistic mappings in different languages will enable language processing in multiple languages. Though a large amount of work has been done in word sense disambiguation for the purposes of machine translation, the need for semantically rich bilingual lexicons still remains. If some of the principles *Concept Space* framework is employed for organizing large bilingual databases, significant crosslinguistic lexical information can be captured in an economical and efficient way. A semantically rich bilingual lexicon will have applications in various domains of natural language like semantics-driven translation, multilingual natural language understanding systems and other semantic analysis tools. Recently there has been a move towards constructing bilingual concept MRDs. However it is reasonably difficult to build such a lexicon for as one has to consider two ontologies and also the fact that the evolution of such a lexicon is quite challenging. The issue of contrastive polysemy is very crucial in multilingual lexical resources where one has to list the multiple senses of a word and link it to the appropriate mappings in the other language. Describing a polysmous word concept in terms of its various attributes and functions and participating entities in case of event and property concepts will enable a productive description.

In the last decade, there has been considerable emphasis on research related to bilingual cognitive processing. A question that is often posed in this context concerns the relationship between the conceptual and linguistic structures, or more specifically, whether conceptual representations in the bilingual are unitary or language specific.

6 Conclusion

In this paper we have outlined the *Concept Space* model and described how this framework handles the issue of polysemy in general and contrastive polysemy in particular. We have analyzed a fragment of Hindi English contrastive polysemies drawing upon a concept space based representation of these units. We have further suggested that some of these Concept Space based structures are crucial to bilingual processing of language and should be incorporated in the construction of a bilingual MRD.

References:

Hans C. Boas, .2001. Frame-semantics as a Framework for Describing Polysemy and Syntactic Structures of English and German Motion Verbs in Contrastive Computational Lexicography, P. Rayson, et al., (eds.), *Proceedings of the Corpus Linguistics 2001, Technical Papers,* 13, University Centre for Computer Corpus Research on Language.

Somsukla Banerjee. 2008. *Modelling Concept Space: An Investigation into Bilingual Language*

Processing, Unpublished PhD Dissertation, IIT Kanpur.

Yael Ravin and Claudia Leacock (eds.),2000. *Polysemy: Theoretical and Computational Approaches,* Oxford University Press, USA.

Generating Domain-specific Ontology from Common-sense Semantic Network for Target-specific Sentiment Analysis

Ashish Sureka
IIIT Delhi
New Delhi, India
ashish@iiitd.ac.in

Vikram Goyal
IIIT Delhi
New Delhi, India
vikram@iiitd.ac.in

Denzil Correa
IIIT Delhi
New Delhi, India
denzilc@iiitd.ac.in

Anirban Mondal
IIIT Delhi
New Delhi, India
anirban@iiitd.ac.in

Abstract

Target or feature specific sentiment classification of a product review consists of extracting opinion or sentiment expressing phrases, extracting the targets (features in a product domain), computing the semantic orientation of the sentiment expressing phrase and assigning the sentiment expression to the product feature it targets. Each of the tasks is fundamental to the problem of target-specific sentiment analysis. In this paper, we present an algorithm to automatically build a domain-specific ontology (a graph consisting of product features and semantic relations between them) which can be used as a lexical resource for performing target-specific sentiment analysis in real-time. We use ConceptNet (a large semantic network of commonsense knowledge) for extracting domain-specific ontology. We evaluate our approach on publicly available pre-annotated dataset from *phone* and *camera* domain. The advantages of our approach are that it uses a resource which is created by volunteers on the Internet and not by trained or specialized knowledge engineers. Another advantage is the product feature lexicon that is created is in the form of semantically rich domain ontology rather than a flat list of phrases. We investigate the usefulness of commonsense knowledge for generating domain-specific ontology for feature extraction task in sentiment analysis application and conclude that the approach is feasible.

1 Introduction

Opinion mining and sentiment analysis is a subtopic of natural language processing and text mining that deals with the automated discovery and extraction of knowledge about people's sentiments, evaluation and opinions from textual data such as personal blogs, review websites and customer feedback forms. Opinion mining and sentiment analysis is an area that has received significant interest in recent times because of its practical usage and application in today's environment. One example usage of sentiment analysis systems is user opinion summarization and sentiment extraction for a particular model or brand of digital camera and its various features based on reviews posted on an e-commerce website. Another example is summarizing the general opinion of people on policy decisions made by a political leader based on user generated content on the Web. Such analysis is quite useful to product manufacturers who want to get insight into the voice of the customer, for buyers who want to make purchase decisions based on the experience of others who have used the same product and also companies or governments who want to get feedback on what people think about their company or a policy. There has been a surge in research activity on opinion mining and several commercial products are now available in the market. A detailed survey on opinion mining and sentiment analysis is provided by Pang et al. and a chapter on sentiment analysis is written by Liu in Handbook of Natural Language Processing (Liu et al., 2010) (Pang et al., 2008). Feature-based (also referred as aspect-based or target-specific) opinion analysis consists of a fine-grained analysis with respect to the attributes, features or aspects of an object (a product, an organization or a person) commented on by reviewers. In the context of a product domain, the problem of feature-based sentiment classification can be decomposed into the following four main tasks:

1. Product feature extraction (for example battery life, image quality and resolution in a camera domain and seating comfort, maximum speed, wheels and steering in a car domain).

2. Opinion and sentiment expressing phrase extraction (for example extremely comfortable,

not smooth, quite heavy, good and bad).

3. Polarity classification or semantic orientation determination of sentiment expressing phrases (for example the word denotes a positive sentiment and the word bad denotes a negative sentiment or evaluation).

4. Intensity or strength determination of sentiment expressing phrases (the word excellent is a strong positive word whereas the word good is a weak positive word).

The focus of the work presented in this paper is on automatic product feature extraction from customer reviews.

1.1 Related Work

Automatic product feature extraction (a sub-problem of target-specific sentiment analysis) is an important problem as the numbers of product domains are huge and it is hard to manually create and maintain a comprehensive product feature lexicon for all domains (manual approach is not scalable). Product feature extraction is fundamental to the problem of target-specific sentiment analysis and forms a building block of a larger system. Product feature extraction from customer reviews is a challenging problem and has thus received a great deal of interest in recent times. In this section, we provide an overview of the related work by presenting the main idea behind traditional approaches. To the best of our knowledge, the paper by Chih-Ping Wei et al. is the most recent paper specifically on the problem of product feature extraction (Wei et al., 2009). Chih-Ping Wei et al. provide a comprehensive literature survey and classify existing product feature extraction techniques into supervised and unsupervised techniques (Wei et al., 2009). The work done by Wong et al. (Wong et al., 2005) (Wong et al., 2008) falls into the category of supervised learning approach (requiring pre-annotated training dataset) as they employ Hidden Markov Models and Conditional Random Fields as the underlying learning method for extracting product features. The technique proposed by Hu et al. (Hu et al., 2004) (Hu et al., 2004b) falls into the category of unsupervised learning as their techniques not require pre-annotated training dataset. The main features of the approach by Hu et al. is the application of association rule mining algorithm to discover product features (nouns and noun-phrases in a review represented as item-sets). The approach by Wei et al. is an improvement over the approach by Hu et al. (Wei at al., 2009) which introduces an additional step of semantic-based refinement that leverages subjective adjectives from General Inquirer. Another class of solution for solving the problem of product feature extraction is based on information extraction techniques (tagging specific pieces of information from a free-form text based in hand-crafted rules or models induced by applying machine learning techniques). The approaches proposed by Popescu et al. (Popescu et al., 2005) and Kobayashi et al. (Kobayashi et al., 2004) falls into the category of information-extraction based techniques. Ferreira et al. (Ferreira et al., 2008) presents a comparative study of feature extraction algorithms in customer reviews and provides an overview of related work on product feature extraction. The paper by Ferreira et al. and Chih-Ping Wei et al. provides a comprehensive overview of product feature extraction algorithms based on various techniques and approaches like: supervised learning methods like Hidden Markov Models and Conditional Random Fields, application of information extraction, application of association rule mining, creation of pre-build databases, application of Point-wise Mutual Information and usage of General Enquirer. Ferreira et al. systematically compares two feature extraction algorithms: an approach by Nasukawa et al. (Nasukawa et al., 2003) which consists of identifying candidate features by applying a set of POS patterns and pruning the candidate set based on the Log Likelihood Ratio test and the other approach by Hu et al. (Hu et al., 2004b) which consists of performing noun-phrase extraction and then applying association rule mining for identifying frequent features.

1.2 Paper Contributions

In this section, we present the main idea behind our solution and list the advantages of our solution over traditional approaches. The key difference between the proposed solution in this paper and previous approaches is that we employ a semantic network of common-sense knowledge-base (ConceptNet) for automatically creating a domain specific ontology of product features and attributes. Previous approaches create a flat list of product features whereas we create ontology where product features are concepts or nodes in a semantic network connected to other nodes using multiple types of semantic relationship. Thus, the product ontology and lexicon created from our approach is semantically richer than the lexicon created from previous approaches. Creating ontology from ConceptNet gives the ability to perform reasoning and inferences (i.e. if direct knowledge is not available one can exploit the network of semantically related knowledge to make inferences). The types of semantic relations in ConceptNet are more than in WordNet. For example, we not only make use of semantic relationships like *IsA* and *HasA* but also other relationships like *CreatedBy*, *MadeOf*, *PartOf*, *DesireOf* and *DefinedAs*. Another difference is that the nodes in ConceptNet can be higher level concepts (compound concepts) such as "battery life", "read book" and "eat food" which are useful to us for solving the problem at hand. ConceptNet knowledge is also informal as unlike WordNet it is not handcrafted by experts and knowledge engineers but contributed by thousands of ordinary people as volunteers on the Internet. The scope of ConceptNet is general world knowledge and not limited to a specific domain. The concepts in ConceptNet are informal in nature which is useful for the task of extracting product features from user comments. ConceptNet has redundant concepts and multiple ways of expressing the same concept which is useful for the problem at hand (A camera is used for: photography, record images, making fotos, take photographs, take pictures). To the best of our knowledge, the application of ConceptNet for solving sub-problems in sentiment analysis and opinion mining is an unexplored area and this work is a step in the direction of our research motivation on investigating the usefulness of ConceptNet for opinion mining applications. The contributions of this paper are as follows:

1. A novel use of common-sense knowledge-base (ConceptNet) for automatically constructing product domain ontology for target-specific sentiment analysis. The product domain ontology is represented as a directed and labeled graph which is semantically richer than a lexicon consisting of a flat list of product features for a particular domain.

2. An algorithm to extract product features from customer reviews using text chunking and then pruning based on the product domain ontology created using common-sense knowledge-base. The extracted product feature is connected to the product domain by finding all paths from the product feature node to the product domain node in a directed and labeled graph representing the product domain ontology.

2 Solution Approach

We leverage ConceptNet (which is machine-interpretable semantic network representing common-sense knowledge) for creating a domain specific ontology. The common-sense knowledge present in ConceptNet is collected from volunteers on the Internet since the year 2000 and represents facts that ordinary people knows about the world (Havasi et al., 2007). The data present in ConceptNet is contributed by ordinary people unlike lexical resources such as WordNet and FrameNet which are mainly created by trained and specialized knowledge engineers. As ConceptNet is a semantic network, it consists of nodes connected by edges. The nodes represent the concepts and the edges represent predicates. Predicates express semantic relationships between two concepts. Some relationships between concepts in the ConceptNet semantic network are: IsA, MadeOf, UsedFor, CapableOf, DesireOf, CreatedBy, InstanceOf, PartOf, PropertyOf and EffectOf (Havasi et al., 2007). The relation types are grouped into various thematic such as: Things (IsA, PropertyOf, PartOf, MadeOf, DefinedAs), Agents (CapableOf), Events (PrerequisiteEventOf, FirstSubeventOf, SubeventOf, LastSubeventOf), Spatial (LocationOf), Causal (EffectOf, DesirousEffectOf), Functional (UsedFor, CapableOfReceivingAction) and Affective (MotivationOf, DesireOf) (Liu et al., 2004),(Liu et al., 2004B). In ConceptNet, an assertion is uniquely defined by five properties: language, relation, concept1, concept2 and frequency. The Language property defines the language an assertion is expressed in (such as English). The Relation property defines the relation or the name of the predicate that connects the two concepts in the assertion (such as IsA, PartOf). Concept 1 and Concept 2 defines the first and the second argument of the relation (words and phrases). The Frequency property expresses how often the given concepts would be related by the given relation, ranging from never to always. Also for each assertion, there is a field which defines the

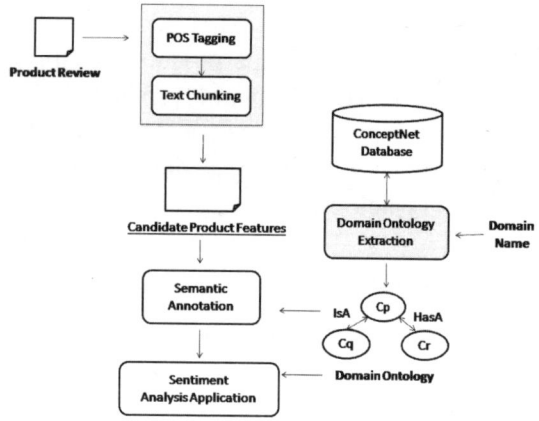

Figure 1: Architecture diagram of the product ontology and product feature extraction system

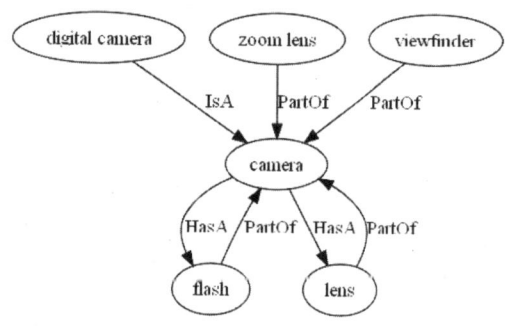

Figure 3: Snapshot of Camera product-domain ontology derived from ConceptNet

assertion type. The value of the assertion type is +1 if the assertion makes a positive statement (such as Diamonds are pretty) and -1 if it makes a negative statement (such as a person doesn't want anxiety). The process fo creating a domain specific ontology is a multi-step process which exploits certain types of relations and connection between words.

Figure 1 presents the proposed multi-step process for automatically creating a domain specific ontology from ConceptNet and then using it for extracting product-features from customer reviews. The domain ontology is created automatically from the product domain name (for example *camera* or *telephone*). Given a domain name (for example, *camera* or *telephone* which exists as a concept in ConceptNet), we first extract all assertions (forward as well as reverse) where the domain name is one of the concept in the assertion. We add only those assertions in the domain ontology which satisfies any one of the rule. One rule consists of forward assertions (i.e., the concept searched occurs as concept1 in the assertion)

where the relationship is of type *IsA*, *HasA*, *DefinedAs*, *MadeOf* and *CreatedBy* and the assertion type is positive. The other rule consists of reverse assertions (i.e., the concept searched occurs as concept2 in the assertion) where the relationship is of type *IsA*, *part of* and *DefinedAs* and the assertion type is positive. We create a directed labeled graph from the extracted assertions. The vertices in the graph represents the concepts (concept1 and concept2) present in the assertion, the direction of the arc in the graph corresponds to the direction (forward or reverse) of the assertion (between concept1 and concept2) and the label of the graph corresponds to the semantic relation (such as *IsA*, *HasA*, *MadeOf*, *PartOf*). In the first step of ontology creation, we expand only the domain name (the seed) to one level. We apply the same procedure two more times: one for the first level nodes connected to the domain name and the second time to the second level nodes connected to the domain name. Figure 2 and 3 illustrates a snapshot (and not the complete ontology) of product ontology automatically extracted for the *telephone* and the *camera* domain. We chose to present an ontology (for the *telephone* domain) which is big enough to fit one complete page inorder to showcase the richness of the ontology that can be derived. Automatic creation of product domain ontology is one aspect of the proposed solution. The other aspect is to extract candidate product features from the product review and assign it to the nodes in the ontology for further analysis. As shown in Figure 1, product domain ontology is constructed offline and product feature extraction is performed for each customer review. To identify candidate product features, we apply a technique called as text *chunking* wherein non-overlapping multi-sequence tokens (for example noun-phrases) are extracted from a sentence. *Chunking* is a commonly used pre-processing step for natural language processing tasks such as named-entity extraction, information extraction and syntactic parsing of text. We perform sentence segmentation on each product review (a review is basically a sequence of sentences) and then recognize the chunks that consists of contiguous sequence of nouns within each sentence. We used Natural Language Toolkit (NLTK)[1] in our research and development for performing Natural Language Processing (NLP) tasks such as sentence segmentation,

---
[1] http://www.nltk.org/

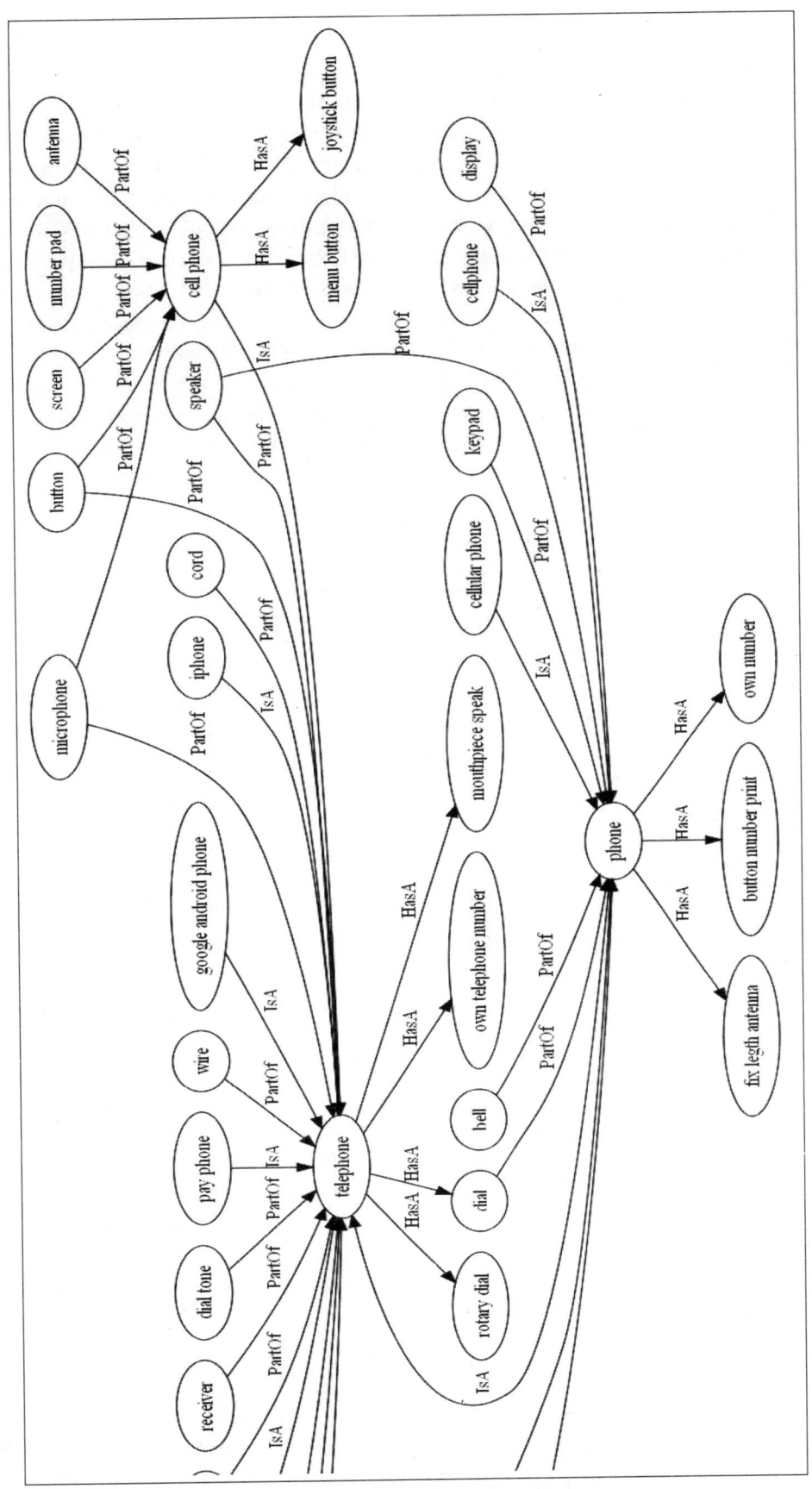

Figure 2: Snapshot of Telephone product-domain ontology derived from ConceptNet

part-of-speech tagging and text chunking (Bird et al., 2004). The chunk grammar (regular expression or linguistic rules that specify how sentences should be chunked) consists of one or more contiguous sequences of noun forms such as Singular Noun, Plural Noun, Proper Singular Noun and Proper Plural Noun. The output of this step is a set of chunks which is pruned in later steps to identify the chunks representing product features and eliminating chunks that are not product features. The text chunks extracted consists of a large number of chunks some of which may not be product features and thus needs to be pruned. We compute a text similarity analysis between the candidate product features (text chunks extracted) and the nodes in the domain ontology. We consider two strings (one from the set of candidate product features and the other from the set of nodes in the product domain ontology) as a match if their Levenshtein distance (also called as edit distance) is less than or equal to two or if there is a common token between the two strings. Since the concepts in ConceptNet are natural language fragments and the candidate phrases extracted from the customer review can have typos, short-forms and informal notations, we apply a fuzzy string matching function. The matched string from the candidate product feature is assigned to the appropriate node in the product domain ontology and the un-matched strings present in the set of candidate product features are omitted. Only the strings in the candidate product features that matched one of the nodes in the product domain ontology is tagged as the final product feature that is extracted from the customer review.

3 Empirical Evaluation

The evaluation dataset for our experiments consists of publicly available (at University of Illinois at Chicago website) annotated customer reviews of consumer electronics products [2]. The annotated reviews were from amazon.com and has been used in the paper by Hu et a. (Hu et al., 2004) and other papers (Ferreira et al., 2008),(Wei et al., 2009). We used the annotated reviews for two products: Canon G3 digital camera and Nokia 6610 cellular phone. We parsed the input data files and computed the number of manually tagged unique product features as well as the total number of product features tagged. The Nokia Phone dataset has 112 manually tagged product feature whereas the total number of product features tagged is 340 (including duplicates as several product features were mentioned in multiple reviews). The Canon Camera dataset has 105 manually tagged product feature whereas the total number of product features tagged is 286. The first step of text chunking (extracting non-overlapping multi-sequence tokens consisting of various noun forms) for the Nokia cellular-phone dataset resulted in a set of 868 chunks which constitutes the candidate feature set. We observed that from the 112 manually annotated product features in the experimental dataset for Nokia phone, 73 phrases were present in the candidate feature set and 39 phrases were not present in the candidate feature set. This amounts to a recall of $73/112 = 65.17\%$. We investigated the part-of-speech tagging results and noticed that phrases like bluetooth, infrared, key lock, pc cable, screensaver, software, vibrate setting, voice dialing and wallpaper which are manually tagged as product features in the experimental dataset were not recognized as candidate features because the constituents words were assigned a non-noun lexical category. For example, bluetooth was assigned a lexical category of Determiner, infrared as Past Participle, key lock as adjective and Noun, pc cable as noun and adjective, screensaver as Adverb, vibrate setting as noun and Gerund, vibrate as infinitive, dialing as Gerund and voice-activated dialing as Adjective and Gerund. In the experimental dataset, Hu et al. (Hu et al., 2004) have provided annotations for product features on which the user has stated an opinion or evaluated the respective product feature. Hu et al. have not manually annotated product features on which no sentiment has been expressed. This issue has also been noted by Ferreira et al. (Ferreira et al., 2008) and hence we notice many product features that are present in the candidate feature set but are not present in the set of manually annotated features in the experimental dataset. There were several product features extracted by the text chunking process but are not part of the manually annotated dataset such as: aol instant messenger software, appearance, audio quality, background wallpaper, battery power, bluetooth functionality, buttons, camera attachment, cdma tri-band, color screens, data kit, display, extra features, family plan, fm radio option, games, signal strength, speaker qual-

---

[2]http://www.cs.uic.edu/liub/FBS/sentimentanalysis.html

	Telephone	Camera
Nodes in Ontology	433	26
Edges in Ontology	466	27
Targets (Annotated Dataset)	112	105
Targets Extracted from Ontology	43	20
Candidate Targets (Noun Phrases)	868	1032
Targets Extracted from Candidates	219	96

Table 1: Recall results for product feature extraction for telephone and camera domain.

ity, stereo headphones, speakerphone feature, usb, voice recognition and wap browser. We observed that from the 105 manually annotated product features in the experimental dataset for Nokia phone, 70 phrases were present in the candidate feature set and 35 phrases were not present in the candidate feature set. This amounts to a recall of $70/105 = 66.67\%$. Similar to the cellular-phone dataset, there were several product features extracted by the text chunking process in the camera dataset which are not part of the manually annotated product features such as: accessories, add-on flash unit, adjustability, aperture priority, auto exposure settings, autofocus delay, backup battery, battery duration, battery power, buttons, close-up photos, compact flash, control panel, default settings, digital pictures, durability, exposure settings, flash photography, focus range, knobs, lcd panel, lcd viewfinder, lens protector, megapixels, photographs, pictures, remote control, resolution, sharpness, shutter button, user-interface and zoom lens unit.

Table 1 presents experimental result on the publicly available *camera* and *telephone* customer review dataset. The number of nodes (representing features and attributes of the object) and edges (representing semantic relations between the nodes) in the product ontology for the *telephone* object or domain were 433 and 466 respectively. The number of nodes and edges in the product domain ontology for *camera* were 26 and 27 respectively. We noticed that the number of assertions in ConceptNet related to *camera* domain were much less than the *telephone* domain. The overall quality of the product domain ontology is dependent on the amount of data present in ConceptNet for that particular domain. The quality of the ontology affects the performance of our product feature extraction system as only those candidate phrases that are similar (fuzzy similarity) to the nodes in the ontology are extracted. The number of product features that were manually tagged in the evaluation dataset for the *camera* and *telephone* were 105 and 112 respectively. Our system was able to recall 20 and 43 product features respectively. This amounts to a recall of 19.04% and 38.39% respectively. Table 1 presents the number of candidate product features extracted from the corpus of *camera* and *telephone* customer reviews. The number of product features extracted from the candidate phrases (i.e., the candidate phrases that matched at-least one node in the domain ontology) for the *camera* and *telephone* domain were 96 and 219 respectively. Notice that the number 96 and 219 are not unique product features (the same product feature such as *lens* or *battery* can be mentioned multiple times in the customer review corpus) as it is also important for the analyst to capture the frequency of the mention of each product feature. The number of times a product feature is talked about in customer reviews is useful information for the business analyst. Also, a single noun phrase can map to multiple nodes in the domain ontology. This is due to the fuzzy string matching technique employed in our system (for example *zoom lens* and *camera lens* and *lens* candidate phrases extracted from the customer reviews will all map to the node *lens* in the domain ontology). Since, we extract product domain ontology from ConceptNet semantic network and model the extracted ontology as a directed labeled graph, we can apply graph operations on the extracted ontology or graph. This is a useful feature for the business analyst as he can print all paths from an extracted product feature to the root node (the name of the domain). The limitations of our approach are that currently the recall is not high as the extracted product domain ontology does not contain many important concepts (attributes and features of the product) present in the customer review. Any candidate phrase (which is a true positive) which does not match with any one of the nodes in the product ontology is omitted.

4 Conclusions

This paper investigates the usefulness of common-sense knowledge for extracting product features from customer reviews and constructing a domain ontology for target-specific sentiment analysis. Evaluation on test data consisting of publicly available pre-annotated customer reviews shows that leveraging common-sense knowledge that is shared by the vast majority of people for the task of product feature extraction and domain ontology construction is feasible. Certain types of relationships between concepts and the connection between words and concepts in a semantic network like ConceptNet can be exploited to build a product domain ontology consisting of product features and semantic relations. The accuracy and coverage of the words is a function of the number of concepts, assertions, relations and quality of data in the common-sense knowledge-base.

References

Ana-Maria Popescu, and Oren Etzioni. 2005. *Extracting product features and opinions from reviews* Human Language Technology and Empirical Methods in Natural Language Processing, 339–346

Bing Liu. 2010. *Sentiment Analysis and Subjectivity,* , Second Edition Handbook of Natural Language Processing, (editors: N. Indurkhya and F. J. Damerau),

Bo Pang, and Lillian Lee, 2008. *Opinion mining and sentiment analysis,* Foundations and Trends in Information Retrieval, 2(1-2):1135

Catherine Havasi, Robert Speer and Henry Lieberman, 2007. *ConceptNet 3: A Flexible Multilingual Semantic Network for Common Sense Knowledge,* Recent Advances in Natural Langues Processing

Chih-Ping Wei, Yen-Ming Chen, Chin-Sheng Yang, and Christopher C. Yang. 2009. *Understanding what concerns consumers: a semantic approach to product feature extraction from consumer reviews*, Information Systems and E-Business Management

Guang Qiu, Bing Liu, Jiajun Bu and Chun Chen, 2009. *Expanding Domain Sentiment Lexicon through Double Propagation,* 21st International Joint Conference on Artificial Intelligence (IJCAI), Pasadena

Hugo Liu and Push Singh, 2004. *Commonsense Reasoning in and over Natural Language, International Conference on Knowledge-Based Intelligent Information and Engineering Systems (KES)*, Wellington

Hugo Liu and Push Singh, 2004. *ConceptNet: A Practical Commonsense Reasoning Toolkit, BT Technology Journal*, Volume 22 Kluwer Academic Publishers

J. Yi, T. Nasukawa, R. Bunescu, and W. Niblack 2003. *Sentiment analyzer: Extracting sentiments about a given topic using natural language processing techniques,* 3rd IEEE International Conference on Data Mining, 427–434

Liliana Ferreira, Niklas Jakob, and Iryna Gurevych, 2008. *A Comparative Study of Feature Extraction Algorithms in Customer Reviews,* IEEE International Conference on Semantic Computing, 144–151

Minqing Hu and Bing Liu, 2004. *Mining and summarizing customer reviews,* International Conference on Knowledge Discovery and Data Mining (KDD), Seattle, Washington.

Minqing Hu and Bing Liu, 2004. *Mining opinion features in customer reviews,* International Proceedings of American association for artificial intelligence (AAAI) conference, 755–760

Nozomi Kobayashi, Ryu Iida, Kentaro Inui, and Yuji Matsumoto, 2004. *Opinion extraction using a learning-based anaphora resolution technique,* International joint conference on natural language processing, Jeju Island, 173–178

Stefano Baccianella, Andrea Esuli, and Fabrizio Sebastiani, 2009. *Multi-facet Rating of Product Reviews, 31st European Conference on IR Research on Advances in Information Retrieval,* 461–472

Steven Bird, and Edward Loper, 2004. *NLTK: the natural language toolkit, Proceedings of the ACL demonstration session*, Barcelona, 214–217

Tak-Lam Wong, and Wai Lam, 2008. *Learning to extract and summarize hot item features from multiple auction Web sites,* Knowl Inf Syst, 14(2):143–160

Tak-Lam Wong, and Wai Lam, 2005. *Hot item mining and summarization from multiple auction Web sites,* IEEE International conference on data mining, Houston

Domain-specific Work Sense Disambiguation Combining Corpus based and WordNet based Paramenters

Mitesh M. Khapra   Sapan Shah   Piyush Kedia   Pushpak Bhattacharyya

Department of Computer Science and Engineering
Indian Institute of Technology, Bombay
Powai, Mumbai – 400076,
Maharashtra, India.
{miteshk,sapan,charasi,pb}@cse.iitb.ac.in

Abstract

We present here an algorithm for domain specific all-words WSD. The scoring function to rank the senses is inspired by the quadratic energy expression of Hopfield network, a well studied expression in neural networks. The scoring function is employed by a greedy iterative disambiguation algorithm that uses only the *words-disambiguated-so-far* to disambiguate the current word in focus. The combination of the algorithm and the scoring function seems to perform well in two ways: (i) the algorithm beats the domain corpus baseline which is typically hard to beat, and (ii) the algorithm is a good balance between efficiency and performance. The latter fact is established by comparing the iterative algorithm with a PageRank like disambiguation algorithm and an exhaustive sense graph search algorithm. The accuracy values of approximately 69% (F1-score) in two different domains- where the domain corpus baseline stands at 65%- compares very well with the state of the art.

1 Introduction

Sense distributions of words are highly skewed (Kilgarriff, 2004) and depend heavily on the domain (Magnini *et. al.*, 2002) at hand. This fact makes it very difficult for WSD approaches to *beat the corpus baseline*, as the common parlance goes. To disambiguate a word, simply pick the most frequent sense of that word in the corpus, *independent of the context*.

One could live with this situation, were the baseline performance good enough for most applications. But as an embedded module, *e.g.*, in a pipelined machine translation system, WSD should happen with very high precision and recall for lexical substitution to work effectively, and corpus baseline level performance is hardly adequate for this. For high accuracy disambiguation it is imperative to accumulate and use the context evidence.

The difficulty of beating the corpus baseline was brought home by the task of evaluating a number of WSD systems for the English all-words task in SENSEVAL-3 (Snyder and Palmer, 2004). It was observed that only 5 out of the 26 systems were able to outperform the most frequent corpus sense heuristic derived from SemCor[1].

Our work reported here, we admit, is on a beaten track. What is the need for yet another WSD algorithm? However, the demands of a large MT task described in the next para, coupled with the discussion on existing work will show that no final word has yet been said on the important problem of *all-word-domain-specific-WSD,* and the task will need all ingenuity and investment in methodology, tools and resources to obtain satisfactory solutions.

Large scale strictly result-oriented efforts are on in India to translate from English to Indian languages. The approach is essentially rule based, SMT being infeasible due to lack of large quantities of parallel corpora. WSD forms a critical component in this, influencing lexical substitution. The domains of interest are tourism and health and languages involved are *Hindi, Marathi, Punjabi, Bengali, Tamil, Kannada* and *Telugu.* The speaker population of each of these languages is hundreds of millions, with Hindi leading the pack at approximately 500 millions.

The organization of the paper is as follows: section 2 is on literature survey. Section 3 describes the parameters used in our scoring function for disambiguation. The description and the rationale behind the scoring function follow in section 4. Section 5 presents the three algorithms used by us for WSD, *viz.*, greedy and iterative, PageRank based and exhaustive search based. Section 6 discusses the results obtained. Section

---
[1] http://multisemcor.itc.it/semcor.php

7 gives a qualitative comparison of the three algorithms. Conclusions and future work are presented in section 8.

2 Literature survey

Knowledge based approaches to WSD such as Lesk's algorithm (Michael Lesk, 1986), Walker's algorithm (Walker D. & Amsler R., 1986), conceptual density (Agirre Eneko & German Rigau, 1996) and random walk algorithm (Mihalcea Rada, 2005) essentially do Machine Readable Dictionary lookup. However, these are fundamentally *overlap based* algorithms which suffer from overlap sparsity, dictionary definitions being generally small in length. Further, these algorithms completely ignore the domain specific sense distributions of a word as they do not rely on any training data.

Supervised learning algorithms for WSD are mostly word specific classifiers, *e.g.*, WSD using SVM (Lee et al., 2004), Exemplar based WSD (Ng Hwee T. & Hian B. Lee., 1996) and decision list based algorithm (Yarowsky, 1994). To the best of our knowledge none of these algorithms have been adapted to the task of domain-specific all-words disambiguation.

Semi-supervised and unsupervised algorithms do not need large amount of annotated corpora, but are again word specific classifiers, *e.g.*, semi-supervised decision list algorithm (Yarowsky, 1995) and Hyperlex (Véronis Jean, 2004). Hybrid approaches like WSD using Structural Semantic Interconnections (Roberto Navigli & Paolo Velardi, 2005) use combinations of more than one knowledge sources (wordnet as well as a small amount of tagged corpora). This allows them to capture important information encoded in wordnet (Fellbaum, 1998) as well as draw syntactic generalizations from minimally tagged corpora. *These methods which combine evidence from several resources seem to be most suitable in building all-words disambiguation engines* and are the motivation for our work.

Previous attempts at domain specific WSD have emphasized the correlation between domain and sense distributions (Magnini *et. al.*, 2002) and have focused on learning the distributions of a small set of high frequency words in an unsupervised (Agirre et. al., 2009) or supervised manner (Koeling *et. al.*, 2005; Agirre and Lopez, 2008; Agirre et. al., 2009). In this paper we emphasize the importance of other factors dependent on the sentential context and show that combining these with the domain specific sense distributions can help to beat corpus baseline.

3 Parameters essential for domain-specific WSD

We discuss a number of parameters that play a crucial role in WSD. To appreciate this, consider the following example:

The river flows through this region to meet the sea.

The word *sea* is ambiguous and has three senses as given in the Princeton Wordnet (PWN):

S1: (n) sea (a division of an ocean or a large body of salt water partially enclosed by land)
S2: (n) ocean, sea (anything apparently limitless in quantity or volume)
S3: (n) sea (turbulent water with swells of considerable size) "heavy seas"

Our first parameter is obtained from **Domain specific sense distributions.** In the above example, the first sense is more frequent in the tourism domain (verified from manually sense marked tourism corpora). Domain specific sense distribution information should be harnessed in the WSD task.

The second parameter arises from the ***dominance of senses in the domain.*** Senses are expressed by synsets, and we define a dominant sense as follows:

> A synset node in the wordnet hypernymy hierarchy is called *Dominant* if the synsets in the sub-tree below the synset are frequently occurring in the domain corpora.

A few dominant senses in the Tourism domain are *{place, country, city, area}*, *{body of water}*, *{flora, fauna}*, *{mode of transport}* and *{fine arts}*. In disambiguating a word, that sense which belongs to the sub-tree of a domain-specific dominant sense should be given a higher score than other senses. The value of this parameter (θ) is decided as follows:

$\theta = 1$; if the candidate synset is a dominant synset

$\theta = 0.5$; if the candidate synset belongs to the sub-tree of a dominant synset

$\theta = 0.001$; if the candidate synset is neither a dominant synset nor belongs to the sub-tree of a dominant synset.

Our third parameter comes from **Corpus co-occurrence**. Co-occurring monosemous words as well as *already disambiguated words* in the context help in disambiguation. For example, the word *river* appearing in the context of *sea* is a monosemous word. The frequency of co-occurrence of *river* with the "water body" sense of *sea* is high in the tourism domain.

Our fourth parameter is based on the **semantic distance** between any pair of synsets in terms of the shortest path length between two synsets in the wordnet graph. An edge in the shortest path can be any semantic relation from the wordnet relation repository (*e.g., hypernymy, hyponymy, meronymy, holonymy, troponymy etc.*).

For nouns we do something additional over and above the semantic distance. We take advantage of the deeper hierarchy of noun senses in the wordnet structure. This gives rise to our fifth and final parameter which arises out of the **conceptual distance** between a pair of senses. Conceptual distance between two synsets S_1 and S_2 is calculated using Equation (1), motivated by Agirre Eneko & German Rigau (1996).

$$\text{Conceptual Distance}(S1, S2) = \frac{\text{Length of the path between (S1, S2) in terms of hypernymy hierarchy}}{\text{Height of the lowest common ancestor of S1 and S2 in the wordnet hierarchy}} \quad (1)$$

The conceptual distance is proportional to the path length between the synsets, as it should be. The distance is also inversely proportional to the height of the common ancestor of two sense nodes, because as the common ancestor becomes more and more general the conceptual relatedness tends to get vacuous (e.g., two nodes being related through *entity* which is the common ancestor of EVERYTHING, does not really say anything about the relatedness).

To summarize, our various parameters used for domain-specific WSD are:

Wordnet-dependent parameters
- *belongingness-to-dominant-concept*
- *conceptual-distance*
- *semantic-distance*

Corpus-dependent parameters
- *sense distributions*
- *corpus co-occurrences*.

4 Our scoring function

We desired a scoring function which:
(1) Uses the strong clues for disambiguation provided by the monosemous words and also the already disambiguated words.
(2) Uses sense distributions learnt from a sense tagged corpus.
(3) Captures the effect of dominant concepts within a domain.
(4) Captures the interaction of a candidate synset with others synsets in the sentence.

We have been motivated by the Energy expression in Hopfield network (Hopfield, 1982) in formulating a scoring function for ranking the senses. Hopfield Network is a fully connected bidirectional symmetric network of bi-polar (0/1 or +1/-1) neurons. We consider the asynchronous Hopfield Network. At any instant, a randomly chosen neuron (a) examines the weighted sum of the input, (b) compares this value with a threshold and (c) gets to the state of 1 or 0, depending on whether the input is greater than or less than or equal to the threshold. The assembly of 0/1 states of individual neurons defines a state of the whole network. Each state has associated with it an energy, E, given by the following expression

$$E = \theta_i V_i - \sum_{i=1}^{N} \sum_{j>i}^{N} W_{ij} V_i V_j \quad (2)$$

where, N is the total number of neurons in the network, V_i and V_j are the activations of neurons i and j respectively and W_{ij} is the weight of the connection between neurons i and j. Energy is a fundamental property of Hopfield networks, providing the necessary machinery for discussing convergence, stability and such other considerations.

The energy expression as given above cleanly separates the influence of self-activations of neurons and that of interactions amongst neurons to the global macroscopic property of energy of the network. This fact has been the primary insight for equation (3) which was proposed to score the most appropriate synset in the given context. The correspondences are as follows:

Neuron → *Synset*
Self-activation → *Corpus Sense Distribution*
Weight as a function of

| Weight of connection between two neurons | → | corpus co-occurrence and Wordnet distance measures between synsets |

$$S^* = \underset{i}{\arg\max} \left(\theta_i * V_i + \sum_{j \in J} W_{ij} * V_i * V_j \right) \quad (3)$$

where,
$J = Set\ of\ disambiguated\ Words$
$\theta_i = BelongingnessToDominantConcept\ (S_i)$
$V_i = P(S_i\ |\ word)$
$W_{ij} = CorpusCooccurences\ (S_i, S_j)$
    $* 1/WNConceptualDistance(S_i, S_j)$
    $* 1/WNSemanticGraphDistance(S_i, S_j)$

The component $\theta_i * V_i$ is the energy due to the self activation of a neuron and can be compared to the corpus specific sense of a word in a domain. The other component $w_{ij} * V_i * V_j$ coming from the interaction of activations can be compared to the score of a sense due to its interaction in the form of corpus co-occurrence, conceptual distance, and wordnet-based semantic distance with other words in the sentence. The first component thus captures the rather *static corpus sense*, whereas the second expression brings in the sentential context.

5 Our algorithms for WSD

We present three algorithms which combine the parameters described above to arrive at sense decisions, viz., (i) a greedy iterative algorithm (ii) an exhaustive graph search algorithm and (iii) a modified PageRank algorithm.

5.1 Algorithm-1: Iterative WSD (IWSD)

Algorithm 1: *performIterativeWSD(sentence)*

1. Tag all monosemous words in the sentence.
2. Iteratively disambiguate the remaining words in the sentence in increasing order of their degree of polysemy.
3. At each stage select that sense for a word which maximizes the score given by Equation (3)

Algorithm1: Iterative WSD

Monosemous words are used as the seed input for the algorithm. Note that they are left out of consideration while calculating the precision and recall values. In case there are no monosemous words in the sentence, the disambiguation will be started with the first term in the formula which represents the corpus bias (the second term will not be active as there are no previously disambiguated words). The least polysemous word thus disambiguated will then act as the seed input to the algorithm.

IWSD is clearly greedy. It bases its decisions on already disambiguated words, and ignores completely words with higher degree of polysemy. As shown in Figure 1, $Word_3$ is the current polysemous word being disambiguated. The algorithm only considers the interaction of its candidate senses with previously disambiguated and monosemous words in the context (shown in dark circles). $Word_4$ (which is more polysemous than $Word_3$) does not come into picture.

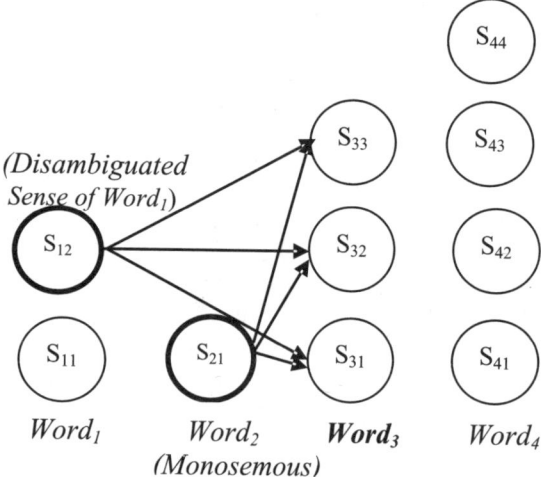

Figure 1: Greedy operation of IWSD.

5.2 Algorithm-2: Exhaustive graph search algorithm

Suppose there are n words $W_1, W_2, W_3, ... W_n$ in a sentence with $m_1, m_2, m_3, ..., m_n$ senses. WSD can then be viewed as the task of finding the best possible combination of senses from the possible $m_1 * m_2 * m_3 * ... * m_n$ combinations.

Each of these combinations can be assigned a score, and the combination with the highest score gets selected. The score of each node in the combination can be calculated using Equation (4).

$$score(node_i) = \theta_i * V_i + \sum_{\substack{j \in all\ Words \\ j \neq i}} W_{ij} * V_i * V_j \quad (4)$$

The terms on the RHS have the same meaning as in equation (3). Note that the summation in the second term is performed over all words as opposed to IWSD where the summation was performed only over previously disambiguated words. Thus unlike IWSD, this algorithm allows *all* the words, already disambiguated or otherwise, to influence the decision for the current polysemous word.

The score of a combination is simply the sum of the scores of the individual nodes in the combination.

$$score(combination)$$
$$= \sum_{j \in C} \theta_i * V_i + 0.5 * \sum_{j \in C} \sum_{\substack{i \in C \\ i \neq j}} W_{ij} * V_i * V_j \quad (5)$$

where,
  C = all words in the context

Note: The second term is multiplied by half to account for the fact that each term in the summation is added twice.

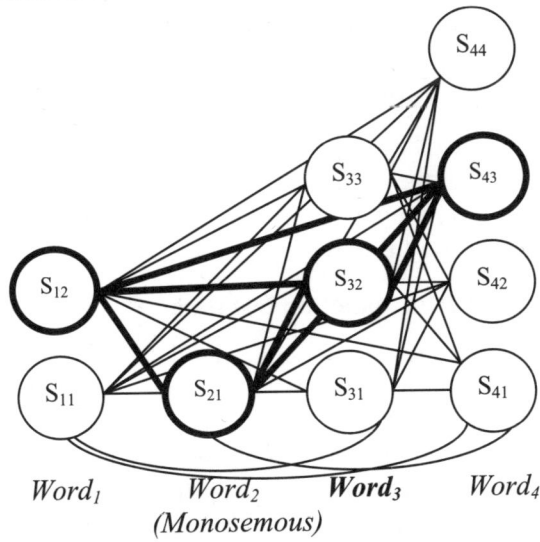

Figure 2: Exhaustive operation of graph search method.

As shown in Figure 2, there is an edge between every sense of every word and every sense of every other word which means that every word influences the sense decision for every other word. Contrast this with IWSD where $Word_4$ had no say in the disambiguation of $Word_3$. Also the objective here is to select the best combination at one go as compared to IWSD which disambiguates only one word at a time. Note that each combination **must** contain at most and at least one sense node corresponding to every word. A possible best combination along with the connecting edges is highlighted in Figure 2.

This is definitely not a practical approach as it searches all the possible $m_1 * m_2 * m_3 ... * m_n$ combinations to find the best combination and hence has exponential time complexity. However, we still present it for the purpose of comparison.

5.3 Modifying PageRank to handle domain-specificity

Rada Mihalcea (2005) proposed the idea of using PageRank algorithm to find the best combination of senses in a sense graph. PageRank is a Random Walk algorithm used to find the importance of a vertex in a graph. It uses the idea of voting or recommendation. When one vertex links to another vertex it is basically casting a vote for that vertex (something like *"This synset is semantically related to me, hence I am linking to it"*). The nodes in a sense graph correspond to the senses of all the words in a sentence and the edges depict the strength of interaction between senses. The score of each node in the graph is then calculated using the following recursive formula:

$$score(S_i) =$$
$$(1-d) + d * \sum_{S_j \in In(S_i)} \frac{W_{ij}}{\sum_{S_k \in Out(S_j)} W_{jk}} * Score(S_j)$$

Instead of calculating W_{ij} based on the overlap between the definition of senses S_i and S_j as proposed by Rada Mihalcea (2005), we calculate the edge weights using the following formula:

$$W_{ij} = CorpusCooccurences(S_i, S_j)$$
$$* 1/WNConceptualDistance(S_i, S_j)$$
$$* 1/WNSemanticGraphDistance(S_i, S_j)$$
$$* P(S_i | word_x)$$
$$* P(S_j | word_y)$$
$$* \theta_i$$

d = *damping factor* (*typically* 0.85)

This formula helps capture the edge weights in terms of the corpus bias as well as the interaction between the senses in the corpus and wordnet. Just like exhaustive graph search, PageRank allows every word to influence the sense decision for every other word. Also the algorithm aims to select the overall best *combination* in the graph as opposed to IWSD where the aim is to disambiguate one word at a time. Even though PageRank and the graph search method look similar there is a subtle difference in the scoring functions used. PageRank uses a recursive scoring function, where the score of every node is updated in every iteration, whereas the graph search method uses a static formula which calculates the score of each node only once. Following Rada Mihalcea (2005), even we set the value of d as 0.85

Algorithm	Tourism Domain			Health Domain		
	P %	R %	F %	P %	R %	F %
Iterative WSD	72.08	67.33	**69.67**	78.74	72.15	**75.30**
PageRank	65.56	65.56	65.56	71.26	71.26	71.26
Wordnet Baseline	61.50	61.50	61.50	66.55	66.55	66.55
Corpus Baseline	73.60	58.41	65.13	81.06	63.92	71.48

Table 3: Precision, Recall and F-scores of IWSD, PageRank, Wordnet Baseline and Corpus Baseline

6 Results

We tested our algorithm on tourism and health corpus for English. The corpus was manually sense tagged by lexicographers using Princeton Wordnet 2.1 as the sense repository. We report our results on polysemous words only, *i.e.,* words which have at least one sense listed in the Wordnet. As mentioned earlier, monosemous words are used as the seed input for the algorithm but they are not considered while calculating the precision and recall values. The number of polysemous tokens and the average degree of polysemy in each domain is as mentioned in Table 1.

Domain	# of polysemous tokens	Average degree of polysemy
Tourism	32715	5.62
Health	14508	3.74

Table 1: Corpus size for each domain

We present the following results:

(i) effectiveness of the proposed scoring function *(section 6.1)*
(ii) comparison of IWSD with PageRank and corpus baseline for two domains *(Health and Tourism) (section 6.2)*
(iii) comparison of greedy IWSD with exhaustive graph search method *(section 6.3)*

6.1 Effectiveness of the scoring function: does it represent the training data?

An oft-repeated question in machine learning is: *does the hypothesis learnt at least represent the training data?* Since the scoring function in Equation (2) was arrived at rather intuitively, taking clues from Hopfield network, we wanted to see if it actually represents the training data faithfully. For this, we removed the existing sense labels of the training data and relabeled them using our scoring function by running IWSD described in section 5. Table 2 compares the performance of IWSD and corpus baseline on the training data.

Domain	Algorithm	P %	R %	F %
Tourism	IWSD	84.10	84.10	**84.10**
	Corpus Baseline	81.83	72.93	77.12
Health	IWSD	89.02	89.02	**89.02**
	Corpus Baseline	87.12	78.43	82.54

Table 2: Results on Training Data

F-scores of 84% and 89% on the two domains show that the proposed scoring function not only fits the training data well but also performs better than the corpus baseline.

6.2 Performance on test data

A 4-fold cross validation was done in both the domains. The results of Iterative WSD were compared with PageRank, wordnet baseline (*i.e.,* selecting the first sense from wordnet) as well as corpus baseline (*i.e.,* selecting the most frequent sense from the corpus). The results for are summarized in Table 3. We report both precision and recall values.

We observe that:

1. *IWSD performs better than wordnet baseline:* this is expected since the wordnet sense order does not represent the domain specific corpus sense distribution. Note that here recall is different from coverage. For example, for the Wordnet baseline the coverage would be 100% as every test word has a sense listed in the Wordnet and hence the engine can output the first sense for every test word. However, the recall will be low (61.5%) as recall measures the percentage of test words that were labeled correctly. Hence, in the case of Wordnet baseline, recall is the same as precision.

2. *IWSD performs better than corpus baseline:* IWSD beats the corpus baseline by 4.54% (F-score) in the Tourism domain and around

3.82% (F-score) in the Health domain. This once again establishes the soundness of the proposed scoring function as it shows that combining the self energy and the interaction energy indeed boosts the performance. We also note that in both the domains the precision of most frequent corpus sense is higher than IWSD but the recall is lower than IWSD. This reiterates the fact that domain-specific sense distributions *when available* are pretty accurate (high value of precision), but they may not be available for all words in the test corpus (low value of recall). For such cases where the domain-specific sense distribution is not available the only hope of disambiguation is through the *interaction energy* with neighboring senses.

3. *IWSD performs better than PageRank:* Both IWSD and PageRank make use of the self energy of the node as well as the context dependent energy arising from interactions with the neighboring senses. However, whereas IWSD does better than the corpus baseline in both the domains, PageRank performs only slightly better than the corpus baseline (+0.43%) in the Tourism domain and performs poorly as compared to corpus baseline in the Health domain (-0.22%). The better performance of IWSD over PageRank ($\approx$ 4% in both the domains) shows that the scoring function based on Hopfield network is a better way of combining energies than the iterative formula of PageRank.

6.3 Greedy v/s Exhaustive

Since the exhaustive sense graph search method is exponential in nature we could run it only on a small fraction (1%) of the test data in each fold. The results were compared with greedy IWSD and are summarized in Table 4:

We observe that the exhaustive method performs better than the greedy method in both the domains (F-scores: +1.3% for Tourism and +7.14% for Health). However, the exponential nature of the exhaustive graph search algorithm renders it useless for practical purposes (*e.g.*, even to run on only 1% of the test data the exhaustive search method takes 2 hours whereas IWSD takes only 1 minute). IWSD thus emerges as a practical alternative. But a question which is still left unanswered and which we intend to explore in our future work is whether we can use other graph search algorithms like Beam Search to close the performance gap (around 7.14%) between IWSD

and exhaustive graph search method with some increase in the computational complexity.

Domain	Algorithm	P %	R %	F %
Tourism	IWSD	85.34	84.93	85.13
	Exhaustive graph search method	86.42	86.42	**86.42**
Health	IWSD	82.00	62.26	70.78
	Exhaustive graph search method	77.82	77.82	**77.82**

Table 4: Precision, Recall and F-scores of IWSD and exhaustive graph search method on a small fraction (1%) of the data for both the domains.

7 A qualitative comparison of the three algorithms presented

After the above exposition, we would first like to give an intuitive and qualitative comparison of the three algorithms we have seen. Corpus baseline and Wordnet baseline lie at one end of the spectrum as they rely only on the self energy of the node (in terms of ranking in corpus and ranking in wordnet respectively) and completely ignore the interaction with other senses in the context. PageRank and exhaustive graph search method lie at the other end of the spectrum as they combine the self energy with the interaction energy derived from the interaction with ALL words in the context. However, both these algorithms fail to strike a balance between performance and implementation feasibility. PageRank has implementation feasibility but lacks performance whereas the exhaustive graph search method gives better performance but lacks implementation feasibility. IWSD lies somewhere at the middle of the spectrum as it combines the self energy of a node with its interaction energy based on interaction with only FEW (previously disambiguated) words in the context. By doing so it is able to strike a balance between performance and implementation feasibility.

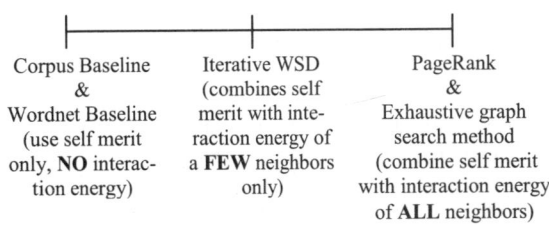

Figure 3: A spectrum showing the position of different WSD algorithms.

8 Conclusion and Future Work:

Based on our study for 2 domains, we conclude the following:

(i) domain-specific sense distributions - if obtainable - can be exploited to advantage.

(ii) combining self energy with interaction energy gives better results than using only self energy.

(iii) making greedy local decisions and restricting more polysemous words from influencing the decision for less polysemous words works sufficiently well for domain-specific WSD.

(iv) IWSD is able to strike a perfect balance between performance and implementation feasibility. None of the other algorithms are able to achieve this balance.

It would be interesting to test our algorithm on other domains and other languages to conclusively establish the significance of the proposed scoring function for WSD. It would also be interesting to check the domain-dependence of our algorithm by testing it on the SENSEVAL-3 dataset which contains general data not specific to any domain.

The exhaustive graph search method gives improvement in performance over IWSD but is computationally infeasible. It would be worth exploring other graph search methods like beam search which are computationally feasible and might perform somewhere in between IWSD and exhaustive graph search.

References

Adam Kilgarriff. 2004. *How dominant is the commonest sense of a word?* In Proceedings of Text, Speech, Dialogue, Brno, Czech Republic.

Agirre Eneko & German Rigau. 1996. *Word sense disambiguation using conceptual density.* In Proceedings of the 16th International Conference on Computational Linguistics (COLING), Copenhagen, Denmark.

Agirre, E. and Lopez de Lacalle, O. On Robustness and Domain Adaptation using SVD for Word Sense Disambiguation. COLING-08

Agirre, E. and Lopez de Lacalle, O. Supervised Domain Adaption for WSD. EACL-09

Agirre, E., Lopez de Lacalle, O. and Soroa, A. Knowledge-based WSD on Specific Domains: Performing better than Generic Supervised WSD. IJCAI-09

Benjamin Snyder and Martha Palmer. 2004. *The English all-words task.* In Proceedings of SENSEVAL-3, pages 41–43, Barcelona, Spain.

Bernardo Magnini, Carlo Strapparava, Giovanni Pezzulo, and Alfio Gliozzo. 2002. *The role of domain information in word sense disambiguation.* Natural Language Engineering, 8(4):359–373.tx

Dipak Narayan, Debasri Chakrabarti, Prabhakar Pande and P. Bhattacharyya. 2002. *An Experience in Building the Indo WordNet - a WordNet for Hindi.* First International Conference on Global WordNet, Mysore, India.

Fellbaum, C. 1998. *WordNet: An Electronic Lexical Database.* The MIT Press.

English Wordnet. http://wordnet.princeton.edu/perl/webwn?s=word-you-want

J. J. Hopfield. April 1982. "Neural networks and physical systems with emergent collective computational abilities", Proceedings of the National Academy of Sciences of the USA, vol. 79 no. 8 pp. 2554-2558.

Lee Yoong K., Hwee T. Ng & Tee K. Chia. 2004. *Supervised word sense disambiguation with support vector machines and multiple knowledge sources.* Proceedings of Senseval-3: Third International Workshop on the Evaluation of Systems for the Semantic Analysis of Text, Barcelona, Spain, 137-140.

Lin Dekang. 1997. *Using syntactic dependency as local context to resolve word sense ambiguity.* In Proceedings of the 35th Annual Meeting of the Association for Computational Linguistics (ACL), Madrid, 64-71.

Michael Lesk. 1986. *Automatic sense disambiguation using machine readable dictionaries: how to tell a pine cone from an ice cream cone.* In Proceedings of the 5th annual international conference on Systems documentation, Toronto, Ontario, Canada.

Mihalcea Rada. 2005. *Large vocabulary unsupervised word sense disambiguation with graph-based algorithms for sequence data labeling.* In Proceedings of the Joint Human Language Technology and Empirical Methods in Natural Language Processing Conference (HLT/EMNLP), Vancouver, Canada, 411-418.

Ng Hwee T. & Hian B. Lee. 1996. *Integrating multiple knowledge sources to disambiguate word senses: An exemplar-based approach.* In Proceedings of the 34th Annual Meeting of the Association for Computational Linguistics (ACL), Santa Cruz, U.S.A., 40-47.

Rajat Mohanty, Pushpak Bhattacharyya, Prabhakar Pande, Shraddha Kalele, Mitesh Khapra and Aditya Sharma. 2008. *Synset Based Multilingual*

Dictionary: Insights, Applications and Challenges. Global Wordnet Conference, Szeged, Hungary, January 22-25.

Resnik Philip. 1997. *Selectional preference and sense disambiguation*. In Proceedings of ACL Workshop on Tagging Text with Lexical Semantics, Why, What and How? Washington, U.S.A., 52-57.

Rob Koeling, Diana McCarthy, John Carroll. 2005. *Domain-specific sense distributions and predominant sense acquisition*, Proceedings of the conference on Human Language Technology and Empirical Methods in Natural Language Processing, p.419-426, Vancouver, British Columbia, Canada.

Roberto Navigli, Paolo Velardi. 2005. *Structural Semantic Interconnections: A Knowledge-Based Approach to Word Sense Disambiguation*. IEEE Transactions On Pattern Analysis and Machine Intelligence.

Véronis Jean. 2004. *HyperLex: Lexical cartography for information retrieval*. Computer Speech & Language, 18(3):223-252.

Walker D. and Amsler R. 1986. *The Use of Machine Readable Dictionaries in Sublanguage Analysis*. In Analyzing Language in Restricted Domains, Grishman and Kittredge (eds), LEA Press, pp. 69-83.

Yarowsky David. 1994. *Decision lists for lexical ambiguity resolution: Application to accent restoration in Spanish and French*. In Proceedings of the 32nd Annual Meeting of the association for Computational Linguistics (ACL), Las Cruces, U.S.A., 88-95.

Yarowsky David. 1995. *Unsupervised word sense disambiguation rivaling supervised methods*. In Proceedings of the 33rd Annual Meeting of the Association for Computational Linguistics (ACL), Cambridge, MA, 189-196.

Finding Humour in the Blogosphere:
The Role of WordNet Resources

Antonio Reyes, Paolo Rosso and Davide Buscaldi
Natural Language Engineering Lab - ELiRF
Departamento de Sistemas Informáticos y Computación
Universidad Politécnica de Valencia, Spain
`{areyes,prosso,dbuscaldi}@dsic.upv.es`

Abstract

Humour is an amazing and challenging topic. Despite the several analyses and researches for understanding its complex mechanisms, it is not completely defined. The studies performed from the Natural Language Processing perspective have demonstrated that, taking into account linguistic resources, statistical methods, machine learning and corpus-based techniques, humour may be handled by means of computational systems in order to automatically generate and recognise it. In this paper we focused on studying humour in the blogosphere. The aim is to evaluate the importance of lexical resources linked to WordNet for recognising blogs with greater probability to contain humour. All the experiments were performed over a corpus integrated by 19,200 blogs. Moreover, a corpus of 16,000 humorous one-liners was used in order to evaluate our results. The findings are encouraging.

1 Introduction

The role of humour is very important in our lives. It impacts on physical, cognitive and social aspects causing, often, different positive effects: from a simple smile up to alleviating stress or improving our interpersonal relationships (Mihalcea, 2007). Also, besides producing well-being sensations, humour is a kind of catalyst which impacts on a broad spectrum of properties linked to cognitive and social information, realising our emotions and feelings, and providing knowledge about the human behaviour. For instance, Ruch (2001) has studied how humour appreciation is associated to personality and how, depending on this property, the kind of necessary stimuli to produce a response changes. However, despite its benefits on human health, humour is a very complex phenomenon whose multifactorial mechanisms can hardly be delimited, generalised and modeled.

The approaches performed in areas such as linguistics (Attardo, 1994), psychology (Ruch, 2001), sociology (Hertzler, 1970), etc., have provided valuable knowledge for explaining humour. Natural Language Processing has also contributed to supply a bit of information in this task through two perspectives: generation (Binsted and Ritchie, 2001) and recognition (Mihalcea and Strapparava, 2006). This paper regards to the second perspective: on the basis of applying different elements reported in the literature as humour features, we focus on studying the importance of lexical resources linked to WordNet for recognising humour in the blogosphere. The task was performed employing a corpus integrated by 19,200 documents divided in 8 sets (7 retrieved from LiveJournal and 1 retrieved from Wikipedia). The underlying aim is to assess the relevance of resources such as WordNet Domains (Bentivogli et al., 2004), WordNet-Affect (Strapparava and Valitutti, 2004) and SentiWordNet (Esuli and Sebastiani, 2006), as well as WordNet (Miller, 1995), for differentiating the sets with greater probability to contain humour. The results are evaluated taking as gold standard the corpus of one-liners (Mihalcea and Strapparava, 2006a) used in the main researches on automatic humour recognition.

The paper outline is organised as follows. Section 2 depicts the related work and establishes our objective. Section 3 describes the corpus and the experiments. Section 4 presents the evaluation. Finally, Section 5 concludes with some final remarks and addresses the future work.

2 Related Work

The interest for humour from a computational viewpoint comes from the last century. In the 90s, the researches in (Binsted, 1996; Binsted and Ritchie, 1997) showed the importance of linguistic patterns, especially phonetic and syntactic ones, for automatically generating humorous punning riddles. In this century, the findings reported in (Stock and Strapparava, 2005) demonstrated how incongruity and opposite concepts are important elements for producing funny senses. Recently, the researches described in (Mihalcea and Strapparava, 2006; Mihalcea and Pulman, 2007; Sjöbergh and Araki, 2007; Reyes et al., 2009a), have provided evidence for automatically recognising elements to characterise humour. Some of the elements reported as humour features are alliteration, antonymy or adult slang (Mihalcea and Strapparava, 2006), likewise similarity, style or idiomatic expressions (Sjöbergh and Araki, 2007). Also, in (Reyes et al., 2009a) it is argued that linguistic ambiguity is an important trigger of humour. All these studies have covered several layers of linguistic analysis: from lexical up to semantics. However, considering the advances achieved from both perspectives, it is clear that the results do not generate/recognise a natural and spontaneous joke. One of the reasons could be the kind of humour analysed: punning riddles and one-liners. The first ones are more related to children and, accordingly, humour tends to be not so funny for adults, whereas one-liners, given their own characteristics by one hand, and the similarity with proverbs by the other one, they often do not provoke a big laugh. Let us consider the following sentences for exemplifying these assertions.

1. What do you call a cold aunt? Aunty-freeze (Binsted, 1996).

2. Ah, nostalgia ain't what it used to be...[1]

Despite their simplicity, both kinds of structures have allowed researchers to make a computational humour treatment with success. On the basis of these achievements, we aim at assessing, given 8 different data sets, the role of WordNet resources for distinguishing the ones with greater probability to contain humour. This objective implies the following tasks:

i. to collect and to validate a corpus related to humour;

ii. to select, given the available resources, a set of features to represent humour;

iii. to measure the humour representativeness, if exists, in the corpus;

iv. to determine a gold standard in order to assess the results.

[1]One-liner taken from the examples given by Wikipedia.

The first task was accomplished by means of retrieving a corpus from one of the most important communities related to blogging: LiveJournal, besides a small set retrieved from Wikipedia. The corpus was evaluated using the measures proposed in (Pinto et al., 2009) for studying corpus features such as domain broadness, stylometry or structure.

The selection of features was performed considering the findings described in the literature: *stylistic* features, (Mihalcea and Strapparava, 2006); *negative orientation*, (Mihalcea and Pulman, 2007); *affectiveness*, (Reyes et al., 2009b). According to each feature, we used WordNet Domains, SentiWordNet and WordNet-Affect, respectively.

The humour representativeness was measured estimating the amount of features per document, plus their semantic ambiguity.

Finally, the fourth task was achieved by means of using the most representative elements from the one-liners corpus, obtained through a clustering process, as gold standard.

3 Experiments on Features Extraction

3.1 Data Sets

The corpus was automatically collected from LiveJournal and Wikipedia. It contains 19,200 documents divided in 8 sets: *angry, happy, humour, sad, scared, others, general* and *Wikipedia*. Every set contains 2,400 documents. The first 6 sets were retrieved taking advantage of the predefined mood tags[2] as well as the users tags[3]. The last two sets were considered as control sets, that is why we did not take into account any mood tag or any seed related to humour for collecting them. The *general* one was also retrieved from LiveJournal considering just blogs related to topics such as news, politics, fashion, religion, technology, weather, computer and cars. For the *Wikipedia* one, we just considered the articles related to technology. This corpus is available at: http://users.dsic.upv.es/grupos/nle/?file=kop4.php.

3.2 Corpus Evaluation

In order to promote the presence of humour in the corpus, except for the control sets, the documents

[2]LiveJournal provides 132 items organised in 15 categories. The sets used in the study correspond to the main categories: *angry, happy, sad, scared*. The set *others* represents the rest of categories.

[3]We just considered the blogs labelled with tags such as humour and joke, which integrate the set *humour*.

	Angry	Happy	Humour	Sad	Scared	Others	General	Wikipedia
Terms	1,314.55	1,114.41	1,577.16	1,193.92	1,342.98	1,027.32	843.44	1,934.07
CVS	132.83	161.33	219.25	119.90	145.42	122.56	107.00	162.30
DL	604.39	542.56	720.50	567.73	625.81	483.44	410.44	937.96
VL	411.10	382.99	503.27	384.47	418.42	341.92	301.68	516.18
VDR	0.94	0.94	0.95	0.94	0.94	0.94	0.95	0.91
UVB	6.91	9.27	9.29	6.78	7.48	7.75	7.80	6.90
SEM	0.39	0.40	0.37	0.38	0.37	0.40	0.46	0.40

Table 1: Assessment corpus features per data set. Measures: corpus vocabulary size (CVS); document and vocabulary length (DL and VL, respectively); vocabulary and document length ratio (VDR); unsupervised vocabulary based measure (UVB); stylometric evaluation measure (SEM).

were retrieved if and only if, they contained keywords such as punch line, humour, funny, laughter, laugh line, gag, joke, and so on. The corpus was evaluated in terms of *shortness*, *broadness* and *stylometry* (Pinto et al., 2009), The results obtained are shown in Table 1.

According to these values, the *shortness* of the data sets is low, both in terms of documents and vocabulary. The vocabulary and document ratio (VDR) measure indicates that, in terms of frequency, all the sets imply high complexity. Regarding to the *broadness*, the unsupervised vocabulary based (UVB) measure indicates that, broadly, all the sets tend to restrict their topics to specific contents, especially, the happy and humour ones. With respect to the *stylometry*, the stylometric evaluation measure (SEM) indicates interesting information related to a common expression style among some sets. Considering these results, we can point out that all the data sets are distinguishable collections with sufficient information for assessing our hypothesis.

3.3 Humour Average

The features for measuring the humour average in the data sets were selected accordingly to the available WordNet resources and, especially, to the results reported in the literature. These ones were: *stylistic* elements, *negative orientation* and *affectiveness*.

The first one, according to (Mihalcea and Strapparava, 2006), represents one of the most relevant features for discriminating humour. The information which better describes the feature is the sexual one. We used WordNet Domains for obtaining the elements related to sexual information. All the words labelled with the tag "sexuality" were retrieved from WordNet Domains.

In (Mihalcea and Pulman, 2007), the authors reported how *negative orientation* may help for discriminating humorous from non humorous data. We used SentiWordNet, for labelling the data sets. We focused on identifying the negative elements, centering on the morphosyntactic categories: nouns, adjectives and verbs, if and only if, they passed an empirically founded threshold ≥ 375 in their negative scores.

Affective information is also considered a focus for identifying humour (Reyes et al., 2009b). We computed, according to WordNet-Affect, the amount of affective elements in every set. It is important to note that we did not considered all the WordNet-Affect categories but only the most informative ones. They were obtained by means of applying an information gain filter (Witten and Frank, 2005). The most informative categories, according to this measure, were: attitude (att), behaviour (beh), cognitive state (cog), emotion (emo) and trait (tra)[4].

A numerical value, plus an ID depending on the feature they belong, were assigned to every element. Then, each document within the set was represented through a feature vector. We just considered the documents, whose sum of features was ≥ 15, i.e., at least 5 elements per feature. The amount of documents which matched this criterion is the following: angry (2,091), happy (1,966), humour (2,074), sad (1,997), scared (2,052), others (2,019), general (1,955), and Wikipedia (1,955). The humour average was obtained summing all the elements per document and dividing the result by the number of documents per set. In order to avoid any tendency in the further experiments, we just considered the 1,000 documents with greater humour average. In Figure 1 we depicted the humour average per set according to these 1,000 documents.

---

[4]All the information about the concepts symbolised by these categories appears in (Strapparava and Valitutti, 2004).

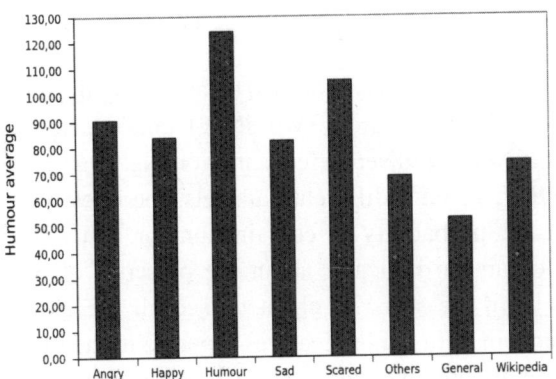
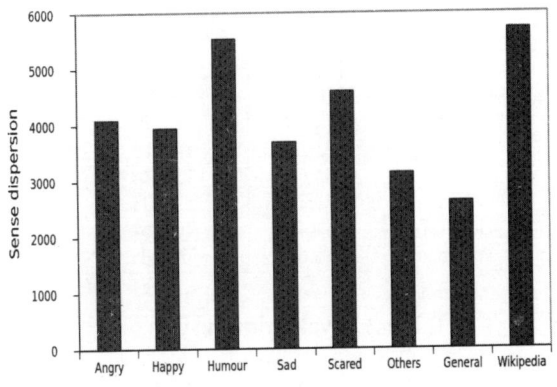

Figure 1: Humour average per set using WordNet Resources.

Figure 2: Semantic ambiguity per set according to the sense dispersion measure.

The results corroborate the *a priori* hypothesis, i.e., the sets which took advantage of the mood and users tags are the ones with greater humour average, whereas the control sets are just comparable with the most heterogeneous set: others.

3.4 Semantic Ambiguity

Ambiguity is one of the characteristics whose impact on humour is very important (Attardo, 1994; Mihalcea and Strapparava, 2006; Sjöbergh and Araki, 2007). From a phonetic level up to a pragmatic one. We decided to estimate this characteristic from a semantic viewpoint. The *sense dispersion* formula in (1), described in (Reyes et al., 2009a), was applied for measuring the semantic ambiguity in the data sets.

This formula is based on the hypernym distance among synsets. Its underlying aim is to quantify the semantic ambiguity through measuring the differences among the senses of a word. The hypothesis is that a word with senses that differ significantly is more likely to be used to create humour than a word with senses that differ slightly.

$$\delta(w_s) = \frac{1}{P(|S|, 2)} \sum_{s_i, s_j \in S} d(s_i, s_j) \quad (1)$$

where S is the set of synsets $(s_1, \ldots, s_n)$ for the word w; $P(n, k)$ is the number of permutations of n objects in k slots; and $d(s_i, s_j)$ is the length of the hypernym path between synsets (s_i, s_j).

We estimated the sense dispersion for the 1,000 documents with greater humour average from all the sets according to the formula in (2):

$$\delta_{TOT} = \sum_{w_s \in W} \delta(w_s) \quad (2)$$

where W is the set of nouns in the collection N. The results are depicted in Figure 2.

According to the results showed in this figure, the fact of considering the semantic ambiguity corroborates the results described in the previous section. It seems that semantic ambiguity would improve a humour recognition task over these data sets, although the improvement is not so significant. On the other hand, we noted that the behaviour of the Wikipedia set is quite different from what expected. Being a control set in which humour does not appear, we would have expected another result. We think that this behaviour is due to the kinds of discourses considered and, especially, to the lexicon employed in the blogs and in the articles. It supposes that the last ones contain less words out of vocabulary and consequently, they have more nouns to estimate their dispersion (since this measure takes only into account nouns), whereas the blogs often contain more misspellings, neologisms, etc., therefore, the amount of elements to be measured decreases.

4 Evaluation

In order to verify the relevance of the results obtained, we decided to evaluate them by means of estimating the similarity between every set (only the 1,000 documents with greater humour average) and a gold standard, in such a way to avoid a subjective and personal assessment[5]. The corpus of one-liners (Mihalcea and Strapparava, 2006a) was employed as gold standard. This corpus has been the main source for the most important research works related to humour recognition. It

---

[5] Let us remember the fuzzy nature of humour: what is humorous for some people could even be offensive for other persons.

	Descriptive	Discriminating
Angry	199.21	113.11
Happy	170.70	106.81
Humour	174.19	117.72
Sad	173.26	143.16
Scared	184.66	128.70
Others	171.28	130.03
General	164.42	101.14
Wikipedia	151.63	79.61

Table 2: Evaluation results.

contains 16,000 humorous one-liners automatically retrieved from the web. The processes performed for evaluating consisted in two phases:

i. we divided every set, including the gold standard, in 10 clusters in order to extract the 20 most descriptive and discriminating items from each one[6]. The 40 items per set were obtained using Cluto (Karypis, 2003);

ii. we applied the Resnik measure implemented in WordNet::Similarity (Pedersen et al., 2004) in order to compare every set of descriptive and discriminating items and to determine how much similarity existed among our sets and the gold standard.

In Table 2 is displayed, based on the most descriptive and discriminating items, the similarity between every single set and the gold standard.

According to the evaluation, the sets whose discourse is more similar to the discourse profiled in the gold standard is the angry (descriptive items) and the sad ones (discriminating items). This means that humour tends to appear often in the sets which denote negative moods (do we laugh for not suffering?). On the other hand, the results corroborate, in some manner, the characterisation performed with the WordNet resources, which indicates a greater probability to find humour in some sets. For instance, both with the descriptive and the discriminating items, the control sets (general and Wikipedia) obtained the worst similarity scores. With respect to the humour set, we would have expected a better similarity score, given the results achieved in the experiments reported in Section 3. However, the results are quite different. Perhaps we have to consider more descriptive and discriminating items in order to verify whether the results change or not.

---

[6]For instance, items such as bed, friend, fun (descriptive), or class, college, summer (discriminating) are examples about the clusters generated in the humour set.

5 Conclusions and Future Work

In this paper we have focused on analysing the role of WordNet resources (WordNet Domains, SentiWordNet, WordNet-Affect and WordNet) for identifying, given 8 different data sets, the ones with greater probability to contain humour. In order to obtain an indicator about the presence of humour in the sets, we characterised all the documents in terms of the features reported in the literature as fundamental in the manner of expressing verbal humour: *stylistic* elements (WordNet Domains), *negative orientation* (SentiWordNet), and *affectiveness* (WordNet-Affect). Moreover, we tried to measure the semantic ambiguity using WordNet (sense dispersion) in order to provide more elements related to humour and to enhance the probability of finding signs of humour in our data sets.

An evaluation over the 1,000 documents with greater humour average was performed in order to verify the similarity between every single set and the gold standard. The results corroborate some of the findings achieved using the WordNet resources, besides indicating that, on the basis of the most descriptive and discriminating items, the angry and sad sets are the ones whose discourses are more similar to the one profiled in the gold standard.

Finally, we plan in the future to verify the results applying more features, assigning weights to every feature depending on their relevance, and assessing other similarity measures.

Acknowledgments

The TEXT-ENTERPRISE 2.0 (TIN2009-13391-C04-03) research project has partially funded this work. The National Council for Science and Technology (CONACyT - Mexico) has funded the research work of Antonio Reyes.

References

S. Attardo. 1994. *Linguistic Theories of Humor*. Mouton de Gruyter.

L. Bentivogli, P. Forner, B. Magnini, and E. Pianta. 2004. Revising the wordnet domains hierarchy: semantics, coverage and balancing. In Gilles Sérasset, editor, *COLING 2004 Multilingual Linguistic Resources*, pages 94–101. COLING.

K. Binsted and G. Ritchie. 1997. Computational rules for punning riddles. *Humour*, 10:25–75.

K. Binsted and G. Ritchie. 2001. Towards a model of story puns. *Humour*, 14:275–292.

K. Binsted. 1996. *Machine humour: An implemented model of puns*. Ph.D. thesis, University of Edinburgh, Edinburgh, Scotland.

A. Esuli and F. Sebastiani. 2006. Sentiwordnet: A publicly available lexical resource for opinion mining. In *Proceedings of the 5th Conference on Language Resources and Evaluation (LREC 2006)*, pages 417–422.

J. Hertzler. 1970. *Laughter: A social scientific analysis*. Exposition Press.

G. Karypis. 2003. Cluto. a clustering toolkit. technical report 02-017. Technical report, University of Minnesota, Department of Computer Science.

R. Mihalcea and S. Pulman. 2007. Characterizing humour: An exploration of features in humorous texts. In *8th International Conference on Computational Linguistics and Intelligent Text Processing, CICLing 2007*, volume 4394, pages 337–347.

R. Mihalcea and C. Strapparava. 2006. Learning to Laugh (Automatically): Computational Models for Humor Recognition. *Journal of Computational Intelligence*, 22(2):126–142.

R. Mihalcea and C. Strapparava. 2006a. Technologies that make you smile: Adding humour to text-based applications. *IEEE Intelligent Systems*, 21(5):33–39.

R. Mihalcea. 2007. Multidisciplinary facets of research on humour. In *3rd Workshop on Cross Language Information Processing, CLIP-2007, Int. Conf. WILF-2007*, volume 4578, pages 412–421.

G. Miller. 1995. Wordnet: A lexical database for english. *Communications of the ACM*, 38(11):39–41.

T. Pedersen, S. Patwardhan, and J. Michelizzi. 2004. Wordnet::similarity - measuring the relatedness of concepts. In *Proceeding of the 9th National Conference on Artificial Intelligence (AAAI-04)*, pages 1024–1025.

D. Pinto, P. Rosso, and H. Jimnez. 2009. On the assessment of text corpora. In *Proceedings of the 14th International Conference on Applications of Natural Language to Information Systems (NLDB) 2009*.

A. Reyes, D. Buscaldi, and P. Rosso. 2009a. The impact of semantic and morphosyntactic ambiguity on automatic humour recognition. In *Proceedings of the 14th International Conference on Applications of Natural Language to Information Systems (NLDB) 2009*.

A. Reyes, P. Rosso, and D. Buscaldi. 2009b. Affect-based features for humour recognition. In *Proceedings of the 7th International Conference on Natural Language Processing ICON-09, (to be published)*.

W. Ruch. 2001. The perception of humor. In World Scientific, editor, *Emotions, Qualia, and Consciousness. Proceedings of the International School of Biocybernetics*, pages 410–425.

J. Sjöbergh and K. Araki. 2007. Recognizing humor without recognizing meaning. In *3rd Workshop on Cross Language Information Processing, CLIP-2007, Int. Conf. WILF-2007*, volume 4578, pages 469–476.

O. Stock and C. Strapparava. 2005. Hahacronym: A computational humor system. In *Proceedings of the 43rd Annual Meeting on Association for Computational Linguistics*, pages 113–116.

C. Strapparava and A. Valitutti. 2004. Wordnet-affect: an affective extension of wordnet. In *Proceedings of the 4th International Conference on Language Resources and Evaluation (LREC 2004)*, volume 4, pages 1083–1086.

I. Witten and E. Frank. 2005. *Data Mining. Practical Machine Learning Tools and Techniques*. Morgan Kaufmann Publishers. Elsevier.

Exploring Hindi WordNet as a Lexical Interface and Subject Headings Tool in Library OPAC

B.A. Sharada
Librarian
Central Institute of Indian Languages
Manasagangotri, Mysore-570 006, INDIA
sharada@ciil.stpmy.soft.net; sharadaba50@gmail.com

Abstract

The most important technical work of the library is cataloging. Previously, for books in Indian languages, the entries were made in Roman transliteration. The software revolution has enabled the preparation of catalog of books in Indian languages in the script of the original language itself. The library management software should be UNICODE compliant for this. Though the cataloging is done in Indian languages, the information retrieval component, 'Subject heading', has to be rendered in English owing to lack of information retrieval tools such as Classification Schedule, Subject Heading (SH) list, etc. in Indian languages. In order to support information retrieval, WordNet was used for English books in the library OPAC as a lexical interface. Similarly, for Indian languages, the Indo WordNet came handy but was available only for Hindi and Marathi. This paper presents a study of how best SH in Indian language can be derived using Hindi WordNet for the books in Hindi, in addition to tools such as subject dictionaries, glossaries, thesaurus etc. if the terms are not included in the WordNet.

1 Introduction

Information processing and retrieval in Indian languages in the digital environment have faced many challenges. The advent of powerful library management software with Unicode support for Indian languages has helped, to a certain extent, in organizing and retrieving the metadata in the original language except Subject Heading (SH). The major drawback is the non-availability of indexing tools in Indian languages for providing Subject Headings. SH is sharp and equal to summarized text. Among the Indian languages, the present study has selected Hindi as the target language. Though the Hindi thesaurus is available, it is in Roget's thesaurus (Kumar & Kumar 2007) pattern that differs from information retrieval thesaurus which can play a complementary role in information retrieval too. Hence, in order to provide the SH and also use Hindi WordNet (HWN) as a lexical interface in the library OPAC, an exploratory study was done in which the Hindi WordNet (HWN) could be used to enhance information search and retrieval in Hindi. This will aid the lay-user to understand better the terminology and the concepts used in the database. Though some studies have been done on the application of wordNet in information retrieval, only few are available in Indo-wordNet applications.

1.1 Controlled Vocabulary

As any natural language, indexing language (IL) too has vocabulary. The IL is an artificial language used in the tools for information retrieval. Since SH list is a part of IL, this also follows 'Controlled Vocabulary'. Owing to the flexibility of natural languages, since many terms representing the same meaning in the IL environment, one standard term or a descriptor to represent a concept will be used. The same pattern is adopted in preparing the thesaurus as well. The main components of the thesaurus Broader Term (BT) and Narrower Term (NT) will be in controlled vocabulary and the Related Term (RT) will be in a normal mode. For example:

Term : Family
BT   : Social Institutions
NT   : Birth Order, Parents, Children

RT : Domestic Relations; <u>Households</u>;
Kinship; Marriage; Matriarchy;
Patriarchy; Adult Children; etc.

In the absence of information retrieval tools in Indian languages such as classification schemes, SH list and information retrieval thesaurus, words used in rendering the title play a vital role in providing the SH. This has to be used without violating the IL rules.

2 Sample for the study

As per the government of India O.M.No.11/20015/21/94-OL (K-2) dated 06.01.1995, it is mandatory to spend 50 % of the amount spent on purchase of Hindi books, excluding the expenditure incurred on journals and standard reference books from the total allocated library grant in any library attached to central government institutions in India. Being the representative of all the languages, the Central Institute of Indian Languages (CIIL) library has more than 60% of its collection in Indian languages and 20% Hindi books. For the present study, two hundred titles in Hindi dealing with disciplines such as Sociology, History, Administration, Linguistics, Folklore, etc., were taken for the analysis. While selecting the titles, due care was taken to select titles dealing with subjects other than Literature that come under the literary forms such as Poetry, Drama, Novel, Short Stories etc. since, in these cases, while rendering the SH, meaning of the title is not considered. In rendering the SH for these titles, same descriptors were followed. For example, the unique SHs for all these titles were 'Hindi Literature', 'Poetry', 'Drama', etc. In case of Collection of Essays, the topics may differ since one book consisting of a collection of essays may deal with a whole range of subjects. Though unique classification number H824.08 was given for Essays, in rendering the SH, the contents of the book could have been highlighted. One advantage in the digital library OPAC is that every component of the MARC tag is a search field. OPAC and MARC are explained in the following section.

3 OPAC

OPAC stands for '<u>O</u>nline <u>P</u>ublic <u>A</u>ccess <u>C</u>atalog'. It is a computerized online catalogue of the materials held in a library. The library staff and the public can usually access it at several computer terminals within the library, or from outside via the Internet. Since the mid-1980s, it has replaced the card catalogue in most libraries. Since the mid-1990s dedicated terminal-based OPACs have been gradually replaced by web-based OPACs.

In an OPAC search screen, one can type in the required title, author, subject or keyword in the text box provided and select the icon that fits the search from the dropdown menu. Usually, for research oriented studies, both subject and keyword searches are frequently used. The result is the list of documents available in the library, arranged randomly. If it is a book, a small icon of a book appears. Similarly, different icons appear corresponding to different document forms such as CD's, maps, microfilms, videos, and newspapers. All searches can be stored in a 'cart' in order to help the readers choose multiple results. The cart contains all the bibliographic information including the call number. From the random search list, after a particular result is selected and clicked, three types of catalogues are normally encountered.

- Full
- Items
- Marc

In 'Full' window, the search term is highlighted with full bibliographic information about a document or book. 'Items' window provides the bibliographic information with specific guidelines to enumerative data. In the Marc window, MARC tags related to bibliographic fields along with the data rendered are depicted.

3.1 MARC

The MARC (MAchine Readable Cataloging) format is the international standard for creating computerized bibliographic records. It encodes various descriptive elements of a resource - title, author, physical elements, subjects, etc. into specified fields, each with numerical 3-digit indicators known as tags, that the program recognizes and translates into the data seen onscreen. Most fields are comprised of at least one subfield, which further details the contents of a field (\a); they are represented alphabetically, with each letter having a different meaning with each field. A sample MARC worksheet is given below.

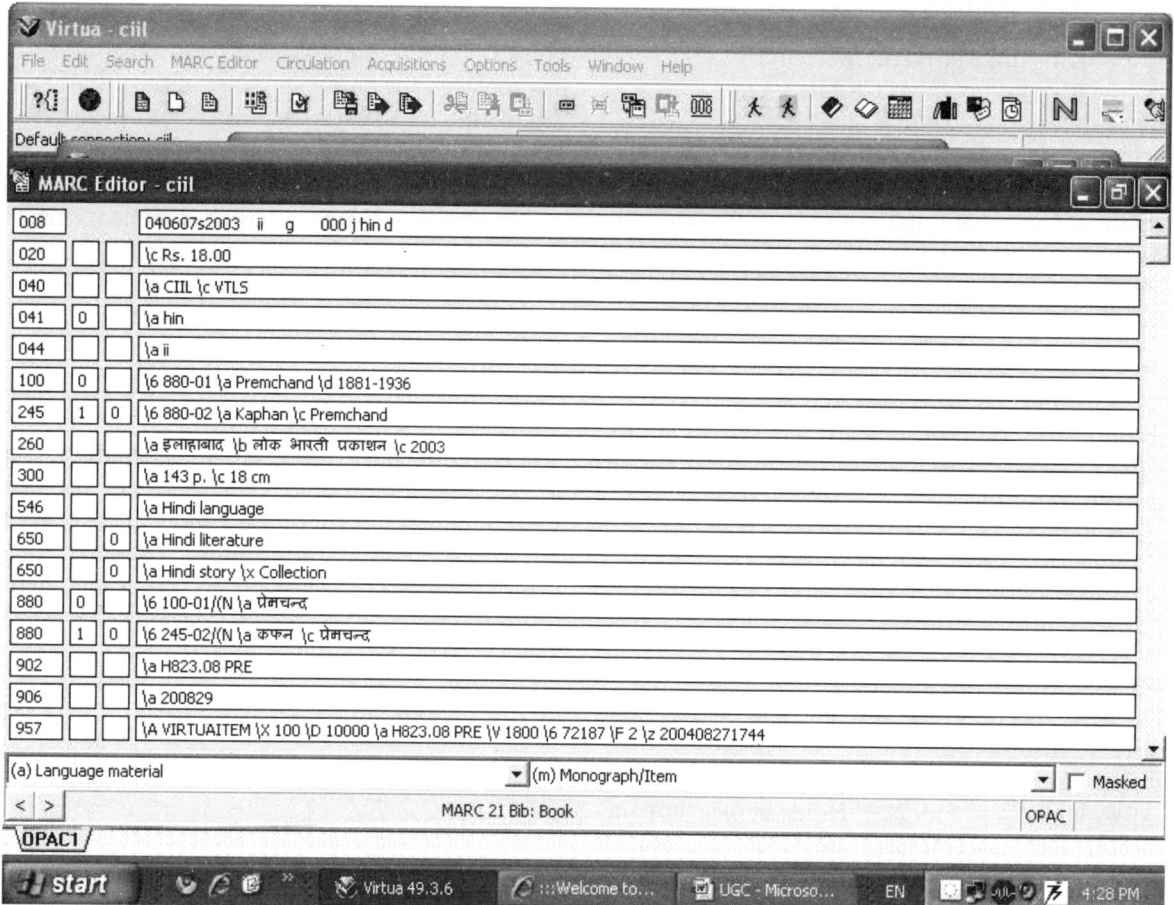

While cataloging, the language code has to be selected from the 008 tag subfield along with other delimiters for entering the data. For instance, Language code in the above example is 'hin' for Hindi. The 008 tag provides coded information about the record as a whole and a special bibliographic aspect of the item being catalogued. These coded data elements are potentially useful for retrieval and data management systems. In a multilingual context, the bibliographic worksheet, should be designed bilingual - Roman transliteration and original language, and though both the entries have the same data in different language scripts, they are entered in different tags. This helps in data extraction in the required form. Normally, in any of the MARC based library software, English is default and MARC tag is 008, which is a controlled field that enables data retrieval. The centralized database is created in English, which is accessible to the rest of the world. In the above example, in tag 245, the title is rendered in Roman script. The same in Devanagari script is rendered in tag '880'. But the tag '650' meant for rendering subject headings (repeatable field) is in Roman script because of the non-availability of indexing tools in Indian languages.

3.2 Providing SH in Cataloguing

Subject access is crucial to the successful utilization of library catalogs. Subject Headings(SH) are very important in cataloging and very helpful in searches. They are excellent ways to narrow or broaden the search and find all the books on the selected topic. While cataloging books for providing the SH, the first approach corresponds to the SH list such as *Sears List of Subject Headings* or *Library of Congress Subject Headings*(LCSH). The next choice is one of subject dictionaries/glossaries, subject thesaurus etc. WordNet was introduced in 2001; since then it has been used both for rendering SH and as a lexical interface for information retrieval for English books.

With reference to books in non-English language, it is necessary to add headings or subdivisions that are necessary for particular interest to the specific geographic area or the needs of the patrons of a given library. Libraries often have local collections of historical nature, or covering a particular regional interest including the language factor. Materials that fit these collections may need some additional or modified subject headings to meet the needs of the collection. Here, one feels the need of SH in different languages. Since the approach for books in Indian languages is in the original language and not in English, rendering the SH in English for these books is compromised. Moreover, it is cumbersome both to translate the subject into English, as well as provide the SH depending on the availability of the term in the SH list.

3.3 WordNet and Subject Heading

Providing thoughtful, carefully done subject analysis of materials added to the library collection is an important step in good library service. Different types of SH are discussed in my earlier study (Sharada 2002) including the advantages drawn from wordNet in deriving the SH. Also it was stated that WordNet can be used in conjunction with SH list and domain specific thesauri to improve information retrieval. Because different domains contain similar concepts described with different terminology. Formerly in a card catalogue there existed the limitation of space, where as in the digital environment, one could choose any number of relevant subject headings in a more user friendly natural language using WordNet in conjunction with subject heading lists and thesauri. Among Indian languages the WordNet is available for Hindi(HWN) and Marathi languages only. In the CIIL Library OPAC these two have been included as a lexical interface for information retrieval. In the present study a trial was made how best HWN could be used to render the SH for books in Hindi, so that SH field also could be in Hindi in the OPAC.

4 Analysis

4.1 Word Frequency Count

Using the 'Corpora Tools' in the 'Indian languages Corpora' prepared by the CIIL (http://www.ciilcorpora.net/frequency.asp) word frequency count was done. Here, the two hundred (200) Hindi titles selected as sample for the study were run in the Word frequency count program. A sorted list of words with their frequency was obtained. The most frequent words are reported in Table 1

Sl.No	Descriptors in Hindi			Frequency	Rank
1	भारत	bhArata	India	32	1
2	हिन्दी	hindI	Hindi	19	2
3	विज्ञान	vijnj'Ana	Science	17	3
4	भाषा	bhASA	Language	13	4
5	संस्कृति	saMskriti	Culture	11	5
6	इतिहास	itihAsa	History	10	6
7	विकास	vikAsa	Development	9	7
8	शिक्षा	shikSA	Education	9	8
9	लोक	lOka	Folk	8	9
10	जीवन	jIvana	Life	6	10
11	सिद्धान्त	siddhAnta	Theory	6	11
12	साहित्य	sAhitya	Literature	5	12
13	कला	kalA	Art	5	13
14	समस्या	samasyA	Problem	5	14

Table 1- Word Frequency Count

In rendering two hundred titles in Hindi, the authors have used 886 words. In order to check the most frequently used words, the close category form words such as 'ka', 'ke', 'aur', 'se', etc. have not been taken into consideration. The content words give an interesting result as depicted in Table-1. This table is prepared limiting the word frequency to 5 times each. Other than the words mentioned in the above table, 24 words have been used 4 times, 16 words 3 times, 57 words 2 times and 339 words single time. This helped in noting down the meanings from different sources.

4.2 Expressive Title

The title of the document is expected to reflect the complete content. It may be rendered in a single word or a phrase. While naming a document, the author focuses more on semantics rather than the syntactic factors, since proper concepts have to be selected to represent the complete content of the document irrespective of any language. Brooks, BC (1968) stated that, ranking of terms/group of terms offers an inefficient, precarious basis for indexing and retrieval system. But in Hindi, it is very much direct in concept representation compared to that in English. An important observation while analyzing the Hindi document titles was, they were too expressive. The advantage of expressive title is, it is enough if the content words/concepts or the subject expressive words are indexed. In the Indian language situation, wherein IL tools are not available, if the titles are expressive, these expressions could be used as they are. Since the IL uses controlled vocabulary, these terms have to be used in such a way that vocabulary of IL is not disturbed.

Example: देवनागरी लिपी तथा हिन्दी वर्तनी का माननीकरण *dEvanAgarI lipI tathA hindI vartanI kA mAnanIkaraNa* - Standerdization of Devanagari script and Hindi spelling

SH would be: *bhASA shAstr* (linguistics), *dEvanAgarI lipI* (Devanagari Script), *hindI* (Hindi), *vartanI* (Spelling), *mAnanIkaraN* (Standerdization).

Usually the concepts will be a single word representation. But in many cases the semantic representation cannot be understood if the related words are not there, for example, आर्थिक विकास *Arthika vikAsa* 'Economic development'.

5 Hindi WordNet (HWN) as SH tool and Lexical interface

Before any new thing is being adopted to the conventional system, one has to check its appropriateness. So is the case in adopting HWN into the OPAC.

5.1 Discussion

In order to use the HWN as an auxiliary tool to search appropriate SH in Hindi for each title, all the terms present in the title were checked in HWN. For illustration, analysis of five titles is presented in Table - 2.

	a. Title of the Document	b. SH suggested by Hindi expert and Thesaurus	c. SH in the LCSH	d. SH found in HWN
1	आर्थिक विकास का केन्द्रीय सिद्धांत Central theory for economic development	*Arthika vikAsa*, (Economic development) *Arthika siddhAMta* (Economic theory) केन्द्रीय सिद्धांत *kEndrIya siddhAMta* (Central theory)	Economic development Economic Policy Economics Industrialization Central theory - Not available (NA)	आर्थिक (economic) वित्तीय (financial) रुपये-पैसे (Rupees-Paise currency) विकास उन्नति, (development) उत्थान तरक्की प्रगति (development) सिद्धान्त (theory) नियम (Rules)
2	भारत की आदिवासी महिलाएं Tribal women of India	भारत *bhArata* (India), आदिवासी *AdivAsI* (Tribal), आदिवासी-महिलाएं	India Tribes Women Tribal women (NA)	भारत, हिंदुस्तान, इंडिया (India) आदिवासी, मूल-निवासी (Tribal)

		AdivAsI mahilAEM (Tribal women)		महिला, स्त्री, औरत, नारी (women)
3	कार्यालय कार्य बोध (work guide to government offices)	कार्यालय *kAryAlaya* (office), कार्य बोध *kArya bOdha* (teaching of work), कार्यालय कार्य *kAryAlaya kArya* (Office work)	NA	कार्यालय, **दफ़्तर** (Office) कार्य, **काम**, **कर्म**, **ड्यूटी** (Official duties) बोध, **संज्ञान**, **ज्ञान** (Teaching)
4	भारत का राजनीतिक संकट (political crisis of India)	भारत *bhArata* (India), राजनीति *rAjanIti* (Politics), राजनीतिक *rAjanItika* (political) संकट *saMkaTa* (crisis)	India political	भारत, **हिंदुस्तान**, **इंडिया** (India) राजनीतिक ((political), राजनीति **विषयक** (Subject of politics) संकट, **आफ़त**, **मुसीबत**, **विपत्ति**, (crisis)
5	नाभिकीय भौतिकी (Nuclear Physics)	नाभिकीय, *nAbhikIya* **न्युक्लियर** *nyukliyar* (Nuclear) नाभिकीय भौतिकी *nAbhikIya bhautikI* (Nuclear Physics)	Physics Nuclear Physics	भौतिकी, भौतिकशास्त्र (Physics), **पदार्थ विज्ञान** (Material Science)

Table - 2 SH in Hindi

The terms that are in bold in column b are taken from the Penguin English-Hindi /Hindi-English Thesaurus (Kumar, Arvind, and Kusum Kumar. 2007). It may be observed in the first title, the concept 'Economic Development'. Column 'b' provides appropriate SH, where as in HWN, the concept has to be split as 'Economic' for which we get three meanings and the word 'Development' gets five meanings. Though we get a clear idea about a particular word in HWN it fails in providing the meaning to the total concept which is a very important factor in providing SH. Also one has to be choosy in selecting the appropriate meaning before selecting the same as SH. For example while checking the term 'Army', four meanings are listed in which दल (*dala*), and फौज (*phauja*) are correct. But the same यूथ (*yUtha*) and संरक्षण (*saMrakSaNa*) are not suitable. This aspect related to compound words in English has been discussed in an earlier study (Sharada 2004). Also for the terms available only in Indian context, for example 'पंचायती राज्य' *paMcAyatI rAjya*, English equivalent is not available in LCSH. Though the term *paMcAyat* is available in HWN, the compound word *paMcAyatI rAjya* is not available.

However out of the two hundred titles selected for the study, approximately 70% terms were available in the HWN as a single term representation. From the above table 2, it is observed that, it is not possible to provide the SH based on either LCSH or HWN. Dependence on experts in Hindi as well as subjects and reference tools in Hindi such as glossary, dictionary and thesaurus are very much essential. For example term नाभिकीय *nAbhikIya* 'nuclear' is not available in HWN but present in LCSH. The same for Sl.No.3 in the above Table 2, the SH are available in HWN but not in LCSH. The exact translation from Hindi to English is too crucial in order to get the exact SH in LCSH.

Even if cataloging is purchased or copied from other sources, subject headings should already be listed in the cataloging record. Often, these cataloging records are copied from MARC records provided by the Library of Congress. This usually ensures that the subject headings are accurately done and usable as they are. Cataloging staff, however, should not assume that all subject headings can just be copied without checking them. For example *Adhunika Hindi kaviyoṃ ke śabda-prayoga* (The usage of words by modern Hindi poets). The SH for this title which will be found in English only are: Hindi language/usage, Hindi poetry, History & Criticism. Problem with this type of cataloging is, the entry is not found in the original language and the English translation is not there. For example: a. *Hindi bhasha aura Devanagari lipi*, b. *Bhasha vijnana aura Hindi bhasha*, c. *Hindi Bhasha aura Sampreshana Prakriya*. The transliteration have different schemes and in some transliteration, capital letters have different value and will not be uniform. Hence it is not possible to adopt this type of cataloging.

5.2 Advantages of HWN

No need to depend upon Roman script for SH

Each synsets chosen for SH will have the link files.

Link files will be with the HWN

In case of doubts with meaning of the words users will have direct access.

5.3 Disadvantage

In HWN single term representation is present.

In many cases of document titles, one has to take the compound word to consideration.

HWN has still to be comprehensive in its coverage. For example, 'खड़ी बोली विकास के आरम्भिक चरण *khaD'I bOlI vikAsa kE Arambhika caraNa* (The beginning of the development of Khadi-boli dialect). Meaning in thesaurus बोली- उपभाषा(dialect), स्थानीय भाषा(Regional language) and खड़ी बोली- कुरु भाषा, तथा हरियाणा की बोली (Khadi-boli: a dialect in the area of Hariyana). But in the HWN five meanings for 'development' - विकास (vikaas), उत्थान (utthaan), तरक्की (tarakki), प्रगति (pragathi), अभ्युदय (abhyuday) are available and the important dialect is missing.

6 Conclusion

Based on the results, it is better to use the HWN and provide the SH in Hindi instead of rendering in English. It will be nearer to the user's approach. Preliminary work has to be done at the database creation level. Each word from the title has to be entered in the online HWN. If these words are available in HWN, those terms could be rendered as SH in the database with the link files. In seeking the appropriate meaning such link files for each word will be useful to the library staff as well as the readers. The user can have access to terms occurring in different context and domains with the result they can search across domain boundaries imposed by the classification. However before providing the link, appropriate words have to be selected. In the library OPAC, since it is included as lexical interface, information retrieval will be easy and even the user will have direct access. This will clarify their idea, meanings of the term and address other vocabulary issues. Also this will help to develop a pre-search modal for user assistance.

If the HWN is made more comprehensive, and includes compound words also, in the absence of information tools in Indian languages, one can completely depend upon it both for rendering the SHs and as a lexical data base to information retrieval. Now the dependency for SH are LCSH, thesaurus, many subject dictionaries in Hindi listed in the reference (Items 2,5,6,7).

It will also save the time for the professionals and at the same time help the readers in getting the pinpointed information in the original language of the document.

References

Brooks, B.C.1988 Stability of keywords in text of radiological report.

De Costa, Joseph, and Ramshankar Shukla, comps. 1988. *Authentic English-Hindi Dictionary.* Publications India, New Delhi

Finkelstein, Lev, et al. Placing search context. *ACM Transactions on Information Systems.* Vol. 20(1); 2002.

http://www.cfilt.iitb.ac.in/WordNet/webhwn/wn.php

Kumar, Arvind, and Kusum Kumar. 2007. *The Penguin English-Hindi /Hindi-English Thesaurus and Dictionary.* Penguin Books, New Delhi.

Kumar, Arvind, and Kusum Kumar.1996. *samaantar kosh, anukram khand.* National Book Trust, New Delhi

Library of Congress Subject Headings. 17th Edition. Library of Congress, 1993

Sharada,B.A. 2002. *Subject heading in Cataloguing and WordNet.* In proceedings of the National Seminar on Cataloguing Digital Resources. Paper G 1-14.

Sharada,B.A. and Girish,P.M.2004. *WordNet has no 'Recycle Bin'.* Proceedings of the Second International WordNet Conference, GWC 2004, Brno, Czech Republic, page no.311-319, 2004.

Tiwari, Bholanath. *Bhasha Vijnaan Kosh.* Jnaanmandal LTD, Varanasi.

Voorhees, Ellen M. *Using WordNet for text retrieval.* In "WordNet" Ed by Christiane Fellbaum. London: MIT Press, 1999, p285-303.

Verbs of Emotion in French and English

Yvette Yannick Mathieu
Laboratoire de Linguistique Formelle
CNRS - Université Paris 7
`ymathieu@linguist.jussieu.fr`

Christiane Fellbaum
Computer Science Department
Princeton University
`fellbaum@princeton.edu`

Abstract

We undertook a detailed investigation of French and English verbs of emotion. Based on a prior classification of French emotion verbs (Mathieu, 2000, 2005), the corresponding English verbs were manually identified. An independent classification for each language yielded 27 shared classes and one class specific to English only. We matched the verbs and the classes crosslinguistically for both semantic and syntactic properties and considered some properties that cut across our classes. Lexically, emotion verbs exhibit the same phenomena familiar from other areas of the lexicon, such as systematic metaphoricity and different kinds of polysemy. We consider possible new ways of representing the emotion verb lexicon in WordNet.

1 Introduction

The lexicon of emotions presents significant challenges for systematic investigation and lexical encoding. Psychologists have identified a small number of basic emotions that are maximally distinct from one another and arguably have universal status; some have physical reflexes (e.g., Johnson-Laird and Oatley, 1989). But languages lexicalize a far greater number of emotion verbs that cannot be easily accommodated within such fairly straightforward schemes; moreover, there is significant crosslinguistic variation, some of which may be culturally conditioned (e.g., Benedict, 1946).

Emotion verbs have been been classified semantically and syntactically for a number of languages Voorst (Belletti and Rizzi, 1988, Levin 1993, Ruwet, 1995, van Voorst, 1995, Mathieu, ibid, *inter alia*). The semantic field of emotion verbs is not clearly delimited. Thus, a number of verbs denote a physical reaction or behavior that may express an emotion:

(1)   It pains/hurts Mary to see John so lonely

Similarly, verbs like *paralyze* may denote both a psychological and a physical change of state.

Verbs like *disillusion, suprise* and *boggle* straddle the border between cognition and emotion. In the work reported here, we took a fairly broad approach and included all verbs that have at least one of their readings in the emotion domain.

Belletti and Rizzi (ibid.) contributed an important distinction to the study of emotion verbs, based on the semantic-syntactic distribution of the arguments and the associated Semantic Roles. One class of verbs projects the Experiencer of the emotion as their structural subject and the Theme or Stimulus (the object of the emotion) as their structural object; the other class realizes the Theme/Stimulus as the subject and the Experiencer as the object. Corresponding examples for English and French are given in (2) and (3):

(2)   Mary loves Paul
        Mary aime Paul

(3)   Paul frightens Mary
        Paul effraye Mary

In this paper we focus exclusively on verbs of the second category, represented by Engl. *frighten* (Fr. *effrayer*).

2 Semantic classification of emotion verbs Credits

Taking a prior classification of French verbs (Mathieu, 2000, 2005) as our point of departure, we manually aligned the English emotion verb lexicon to the French verbs. We consulted standard mono- and bilingual lexicographic resources, such as the *Trésor de la Langue Française Informatisé* and *WordReference.com*.

Our alignment and semantic classification resulted in 27 classes common to English and French and one class that is lexicalized in English only (*shame*). The classes are listed in Table 1 (French classes are in italics). They are labeled with a verb that we judged to be prototypical and most representative for all members of the class. For instance, the class *Frighten* includes all verbs referring to the causation of fear, such as *frighten, scare, panic* and *terrify*. We were surprised that the emotion lexicons of the two languages aligned so well, a result that we had not expected a priori.

Amuse	Annoy	Astonish
amuser	*déranger*	*étonner*
Awe	Bore	Calm
effarer	*lasser*	*calmer*
Comfort	Confuse	Dazzle
rassurer	*déconcerter*	*épater*
Disappoint	Discourage	Disgust
désappointer	*décourager*	*dégoûter*
Distress	Excite	Flatter
meurtrir	*passionner*	*flatter*
Frighten	Frustrate	Interest
effrayer	*frustrer*	*intéresser*
Intimidate	Irritate	Move
intimider	*irriter*	*émouvoir*
Obsess	Offend	Sadden
obséder	*offenser*	*attrister*
Satisfy	Shame	Thrill
satisfaire		*subjuguer*
Worry		
tracasser		

Table 1. Semantic classes of emotion verbs

2.1 French and English verbs of emotion

In French, about 100 verbs belong to the *love* type verb category and 500 to the *frighten* type verb. Contrary to English, there is no verbs expressing a shame feeling, but *frighten* type constructions like "faire honte" (put to shame) or *love* type constructions like "avoir honte" (be ashamed) exist.

For English, our analysis included 370 verbs. These were drawn from WordNet and Levin (1993); additional verbs were translated from the French list.

2.2 Metaphoricity

While many of the verbs we included have a psychological meaning only (*tempt/tenter, amuse/amuser, astonish/étonner,* etc.), the large number of polysemous verbs is striking. In particular, many verbs have two distinct but related meanings, a primary or "basic" one as in (4), and a metaphoric, psychological one (5):

(4)   The sun irritates Mary (her skin)
       Le soleil irrite Mary (sa peau)

(5)   Paul irritates Mary (by his behavior)
       Paul irrite Mary (par son comportement)

An extended emotion reading is particularly common among verbs with a primary physical/contact reading (*strike, touch*) and verbs expressing physical injury (*hurt, wound*).

2.3 Polarity and strength of emotions

Our study highlights three categories of verbs:

a) Negative polarity verbs which express a rather unpleasant feeling, such as fear or disappointment,

b) Positive polarity verbs which express a rather pleasant feeling, such as amusement or fascination, and

c) Neutral polarity verbs which express a neither pleasant nor unpleasant feeling, like astonishment. The polarity of this verbs depends on the context.

This distinction between verbs regarding their polarity corroborate many works in sentiment analysis (Pang *et al.*, 2002, Turney, 2002) which have attempted to classify emotions (in particular those expressing attitudes or reactions) in terms of intuitively positive vs. negative emotions.

A second axis along which the semantics of emtion verbs can be measured is the strength, or intensity, of the emotion. Within each class, members express different degrees of intensity of the core emotion (Mathieu, ibid.). Thus, the *amaze* class includes, in approximately increasing order of intensity, *astonish, surprise, startle, flabbergast, dumbfound, jar, floor, stagger, stun*. Some feelings, such as *anger* or *dislike*, are particularly richly lexicalized and the verbs express strengths of emotions on many points of the scale.

2.4 Intentional vs. unintentional subject stimuli

All the psychological verbs accept non-agentive and hence non-intentional stimuli or causes as subjects. In the examples (6-7), the non-agentive causes are events or states:

(6) The song moved Marie
La chanson a ému Marie

(7) The increasing costs worries John
Les frais croissants tracassent Jean

Another distinction can be drawn stimuli with human referents. Verbs like *frighten* or *amuse* accept both non-intentional and intentional, agentive stimuli (Grimshaw, 1990). Thus, a sentence like *Luc frightens Marie* has two possible meanings: that Luc frightens Marie intentionally (perhaps by jumping at her from behind), or he frightens her unintentionally, as by his behavior or his appearance. In second case, the subject is non agentive. The same two readings can apply to *move*: one can be moved by watching a sleeping child (non-intentional) or by listening to a pianist playing a sad piece (intentional).

3 Syntax

We investigate the behavior of emotion verbs with respect to the exogenic/endogenic properties of the emotions they evoke by considering the middle and the unaccusative constructions. These constructions are linked to the implicit presence of an Agent (middle) and the absence of an Agent (unaccusative). Since any event that evokes an emotion involves an Experiencer who by experiencing an emotion is contributing to the evocation and persistence of a feeling (rather than a Theme, as in the case of verbs like *hit* and *break*), these constructions seem relevant.

3.1 Emotion verbs in middle and unaccusative constructions

The middle construction (Keyser and Roeper, 1984, Fellbaum, 1985, Fellbaum and Zribi-Hertz, 1989, Condoravdi, 1989, *inter alia*) is said to be generic and stative and refer to a property of the syntactic subject. Thus in (8), the car has (had) the property of being easily sellable and the hood of the car has properties that make it not easy to open

(8) This hybrid car sold out fast
The hood doesn't open easily

The English middle construction is roughly paraphrasable with *tough*-movement; thus (8) means approximately the same as (9):

(9) This hybrid car is easy to sell
The hood is not easy to open

The subject of a middle is never an Agent; in most cases, as in (8), it is the Theme. A subclass of psych verbs from the *amuse*-group, which have Experiencer objects, can form middles where the Experiencer appears in the subject position:

(10) John frightens/confuses/discourages easily

(10) expresses that John has properties such as it is easy for someone or something to frighten/confuse/discourage him, or that he is easily frightened/confused/discouraged, independent of any particular Agent of Stimulus[1].

The unaccusative construction, exemplified in (11), superficially resembles the middle:

(11) John saddens easily
Mary enrages quickly

The difference between middles and unaccusatives is that the latter do not imply an Agent, though they may imply a Cause (Fellbaum and Zribi-Hertz, 1989). Thus, only middles accept « agent-oriented adverbs » like « without difficulty », and only middles are paraphrasable with *tough*-movement structures. Moreover, while adverbs in middles always follow the verb, they can either precede or follow the verb in unaccusatives (Fellbaum, 1985) :

(12)a. Mary worries easily/quickly (middle or unaccus.)
b. Mary easily/quickly worries (unaccusative)

---

[1] Verbs with a primary physical sense (*hit, strike, touch*) that cannot form middles cannot do so under a psych reading, either.

This test shows that some psych verbs cannot occur in the unaccusative and require an exernal Agent or Stimulus:

(13)a. Joe embarrasses/disappoints/annoys quickly (middle)
    b. ?Joe quickly embarrasses/ disappoints /annoys (unaccusative)

Many psych verbs, like *worry* and *exhilarate*, can occur in both constructions, showing that the emotion can be evoked by causes both external and internal to the Experiencer.

A priori, one would expect all *amuse*-type verbs can be input to middle formation. However, some verbs do not appear to be felicitous in this construction and we could not find attested examples:

(14) ?John aggrieves/pains/chagrins easily

We suggest that the verbs' compatibility with the middle construction points to a more-fine-grained sub-classification of *amuse*-type verbs, namely *exogenic* and *endogenic* psych verbs. Exogenic verbs denote the experience of emotions caused by an external Agent or Stimulus; endogenic verbs denote the experience of emotions that arise from "inside" the Experiencer and do not merely express a reaction to an external stimulus. The classes *sadden, awe, interest, move, obsess* all include endogenic verbs (Anscombre, 1996) ; others include *rejoice*.

Unlike English, French does not have clear tests for distinguishing unaccusatives from middles, as the two are morphosyntactically identical. However, we can tease out the ability of a verb to receive a middle reading by means of three criteria. First, a middle interpretation is possible in constructions of the form (a) *X se V Adverb* construction, exemplified by

(15) *Marie s'énerve facilement/* Mary enrages easily

As in English, such sentences have an alternative unaccusative reading ("it happens easily/often that Mary enrages") in addition to the middle one ("it is easy for someone/something to enrage Mary"). When the verb is reflexive (*s'énerver*), a manual classification of the results of a corpus search shows that the semantics of this construction is most often unaccusative (in-choative). Zribi-Hertz (2008) points out that when a reflexive sentence can be read either as an unaccusative or as middle, the unaccusative interpretation predominates.

Second, the middle interpretation can be paraphrased as in (16)

(16) One/people in general enrage Mary easily
    It is easy to enrage Mary

Third, the construction allows for an implicit agentive stimuli, as in (16).

Most of the verbs we studied accept this construction (22/23 of the classes in Table 1) while a small number of verbs is not compatible with it (5/6 classes in Table 1): *sadden, move, awe, interest, obsess*. While English and French converge with respect to allowing a middle interpretation (or not), the class *tracasser* (*worry*) allows middles in English but not in French.

Another class of verbs, which includes *annoy* and *depress* cannot occur in unaccusative readings. Thus, sentences like

(17) Mary annoys/depresses easily

can only have middle/causative readings meaning "it is easy to annoy/depress Mary" and not "Mary falls easily into a state of annoyance/depression." These verbs are strongly exogenic.

4 Representing emotion verbs in WordNet

How can our classification of the emotion verb lexicon be accommodated in WordNet? Currently, all verbs are hierarchically arranged by means of a "manner of" relation (troponymy), which distinguishes general from increasingly semantically specified verbs. Like most verb hierarches, the emotion verb "tree" is fairly shallow. The root synset for causative (*amuse*-type) verbs is{arouse, kindle, elicit, evoke, fire, raise, provoke}, which refers to the arousing of an emotion. To make a distinction among the verbs of the 28 classes we identified, a different representation is called for. One possibility would be a cluster of verbs related to the central member. Thus, a group of verbs like *placate, pacify, relax, humor* and appease would be radially arranged around the core verb *calm* that best exemplifies this group. Possibly, the strength of the emotion could be graded and expressed with numerical values (cf. section 2.3).

4.1 Creating a network of verbs

The current WordNet database provides for the clustering of verbs into synsets and the encoding of links from emotion verbs to the corresponding nouns (*please-pleasure*), although currently only homophonic pairs of this kind are in fact encoded (Fellbaum, Osherson and Clark, 2009). In addition, verbs and adjectives (denoting the emotional state) can be paired and linked (*sadden-sad*). Finally, causation links must be added for all relevant pairs (*frighten-fear*, etc.), allowing the user to identify verbs with both causative/middle and unaccusative reading as well as verbs that allow only one of these argument structures (*annoy* vs. *pain*).

4.2 Polysemy and Autotroponomy

The almost regular polysemy found between emotion and communication and cognition readings, as well as between emotion and physical contact readings can be encoded in WordNet and distinguished from less regular and metaphoric polysemy.

Fellbaum (2002) studied a particular kind of polysemy, dubbed autotroponymy, where a single word form has both a more general and a more specific meaning. Among the psych verbs we examined, we found autotroponyms like *concern* and *preoccupy*, which have both a general, neutral reading and a more specific, negative reading, as in (18):

(18) This letter concerns only me (not you)
 This letter really concerns me (I'm concerned aout this letter)

(18') Her job preoccupies her (no time for anything else)
 Her job preoccupies her (she's worried)

5 Conclusion

We undertook a comparative study of the French and English emotion verb lexicon. We found that we could match the verbs semantically and group them into 27 crosslinguistic classes. English has one additional class not lexicalize in French, *shame*. The verbs' participation in the middle and unaccusative constructions may refine the distinction between exogenic and endogenic emotions. Representing the verbs in WordNet in a way that reflects their semantic classification would require a radial, cluster arrangement rather than the present hierarchical one. We are currently restructuring the WordNet database in a way that would allow for a representation of emotion verbs (as well as related nouns and adjectives) along the lines sketched here.

References

Jean-Claude Anscombre. 1996. Noms de sentiment, noms d'attitude et noms abstraits. In *Les noms abstraits*. Villeneuve d'Ascq Presses universitaires du Septentrion, 257 :273.

Adriana Belletti and Luigi Rizzi. 1988. « Psych-Verbs and θ–theory », *Natural Language and Linguistic Theory* 6 : 291-352.

Ruth Benedict. 1946. *The Chrysanthemum and the Sword*. Boston, MA: Houghton Mifflin.

Cleo Condoravdi. 1989. The middle: where semantics and morphology meet, in P. Branigan, J. Gaulding, M. Kubo, and K. Murasugi, eds., *Proceedings of the Student Conference in Linguistics, MIT Working Papers in Linguistics 11, MITWPL*, Cambridge, MA, 16–30.

Christiane Fellbaum. 1985. Adverbs in agentless actives and passives. In; Eiflort, W. et al. (eds.) *Proceedings of the 21st Meeting of the Chicago Linguistic Society*. Chicago, IL: University of Chicago. 21-31.

Christiane Fellbaum. 1998 (ed.) WordNet. *An Electronic Lexical Database*. Cambridge, MA: MIT Press.

Christiane Fellbaum. 2002. The Semantics of Troponymy. In: Green, Rebecca, Myang, Sung Hyon, and Bean, Carol, (Eds), *Relations*, 23-34. Dordrecht: Kluwer.

Christiane Fellbaum, Anne Osherson and Peter E. Clark. 2009. Putting Semantics into WordNet's ``Morphosemantic" Links. In: *Responding to Information Society Challenges: New Advances in Human Language Technologies,* eds. Z. Vetulani and H. Uszkoreit. Springer Lecture Notes in Informatics vol. 5603:350-358.

Christiane Fellbaum and Anne Zribi-Hertz. 1989. La construction moyenne en francais et an anglais: etude des syntaxe et de semantique comparees. *Recherches Linguistiques a Vincennes* 18:19-57.

Jane Grimshaw. 1990. *Argument Structure*. Cambridge, MA: MIT Press.

Philip N. Johnson-Laird and Keith J. Oatley. 1989 The language of emotions: an analysis of a semantic field. *Cognition and Emotion*, 3:81-123.

Le Trésor de la Langue Française informatisé, TLFi. http://atilf.atilf.fr/tlf.htm.

Beth Levin. 1993. *English Verb Classes and Alternations: A Preliminary Investigation*, Chicago, IL, University of Chicago Press.

Yvette Yannick Mathieu. 2000. *Les verbes de sentiments. De l'analyse linguistique au traitement automatique*, Paris, CNRS Editions.

Yvette Yannick Mathieu. 2005. *A Computational Semantic Lexicon of French Verbs of Emotion*, Shanahan, G., Qu, Y., Wiebe, J. (eds.): *Computing Attitude and Affect in Text,* Dordrecht, Springer:109-123.

Bo Pang, Lillian Lee and Shivakumar Vaithyanathan. 2002. Thumbs up? Sentiment Classification using Machine Learning Techniques, In *Proceedings of EMNLP 2002*.

Nicolas Ruwet. 1995. « Les verbes de sentiment peuvent-ils être agentifs? », *Langue française* 105:28-39.

Peter Turney. 2002 Thumbs Up or Thumbs Down? Semantic Orientation Applied to Unsupervised Classification of Reviews », In *Proceedings of 2006 International Conference on Intelligent User Interfaces (IUI06)*.

Jan van Voorst. 1995. Le contrôle de l'espace psycholinguistique. *Langue française* 105 :17-27.

Anne Zribi-Hertz. 2008. Le médiopassif à accord riche en français : pour une approche multifactorielle. Congrès Mondial de Linguistique Française - CMLF'08, Paris : 2645-2662.

Classification of Verbs – Towards Developing a Bengali Verb Subcategorization Lexicon

Somnath Banerjee **Dipankar Das** **Sivaji Bandyopadhyay**
Department of Computer Science and Engineering
Jadavpur University, Kolkata-700032, India
`s.banerjee1980@gmail.com, dipankar.dipnil2005@gmail.com,`
`sivaji_cse_ju@yahoo.com`

Abstract

The acquisition of subcategorization frames for verbs for any language is generally carried out either manually or automatically. The subcategorization lexicon is an important resource for any language and more so for languages such as Bengali that is morphologically rich, free phrase order and above all has no existing full-fledged parser. This paper presents the classification of Bengali verbs and their synonyms with different subcategorization frames according to their sense-based similarities. Syntax plays the main role in the acquisition of Bengali verb subcategorization frames. The main hypothesis on which the work is based is that the subcategorization frames for a Bengali verb are generally same with the subcategorization frames for its equivalent English verb with an identical sense tag. This hypothesis is reexamined to acquire the newly found subcategorization frames for the synonymous Bengali verbs to create verb classes. The classification of Bengali verbs according to their senses is carried out in a recursive way to create as many possible classes covered by the synonymous verbs that share the same types of subcategorization frames. The verb subcategorization frame acquisition system has demonstrated precision, recall and F-measure values of 74.11%, 70.83% and 72.44% respectively on a test set of 120 sentences.

1 Introduction

Several large, manually developed subcategorization lexicons are available for English, e.g. the COMLEX (Macleod *et al.*, 1994), ACQUILEX (Copestake, 1992) and the ANLT (Briscoe *et al.*, 1987) dictionaries. VerbNet (VN) (Kipper-Schuler, 2005) is the largest online verb lexicon with explicitly stated syntactic and semantic information based on Levin's verb classification (Levin, 1993). On the other hand, the lexicographic research project FrameNet (Baker *et al.*, 1998) and PropBank (Kingsbury and Palmer, 2002) have also generated important resources. But, there is no existing subcategorization lexicon available for the less privileged and less computerized Indian languages, e.g., Bengali.

The diverse characteristics of different Indian languages make the subcategorization frame acquisition task more challenging. Apart from other parts of speeches, the subcategorization information of verbs is an essential issue in parsing for the free phrase order languages such as Bengali. As there is no such existing parser available in Bengali, the acquisition as well as the evaluation of the acquired subcategorization frames is a difficult task. The main difference between English and Bengali sentences is the variation regarding the order of phrases.

(Das *et al.*, 2009) identified the subcategorization frames for the Bengali verb *dekha* (see) and (Banerjee *et al.*, 2009) dealt on the subcategorization frame acquisition task for ten different compound verbs that contain *kara* (do) as a component. The pivotal hypothesis in these two works is that the subcategorization frames obtained for a Bengali verb are generally same with the subcategorization frames that may be acquired for its equivalent verb with an identical sense tag in English. In this present task, these above-mentioned eleven Bengali verbs have been considered as the basic set of key verbs to construct different hierarchical sense based classes. The additional hypothesis in this work is that the synonyms of these key verbs containing the same sense share the same subcategorization frames and are classified into the same class with their key verb but the verbs containing multiple senses occupy multiple classes.

The number of different sense based English equivalent synonymous verb groups of a Bengali key verb is extracted from the Bengali to English bilingual dictionary[1] and are termed as Key Synonymous Verb Sets (KSVS). To accomplish the objectives, each class containing the key verb has been formed primarily based on the KSVSs. For each of the eleven key verbs, the synonyms that have been extracted from the Bengali-to-Bengali synonyms thesaurus (Mukhopadhyay, 2007) are termed as the member verbs for that corresponding key verb. Each Bengali synonym is searched in the Bengali to English bilingual dictionary to extract their English equivalent synonyms and the synonyms belonging to the same sense are termed as Member Synonymous Verb Set (MSVS). We have mapped the elements of each MSVS of a Bengali member verb to the elements of each KSVS of its corresponding key Bengali verb. If there is at least one element that belongs to both MSVS and KSVS, then that concerned member verb is included in the key verb class formed for that corresponding KSVS of the key verb.

Each member verb of a key verb class is passed through the subcategorization frame acquisition process (Das and Bandyopadhyay, 2009) carried out on the Bengali news corpus (Ekbal and Bandyopadhyay, 2008) with the help of English VerbNet. The newly acquired subcategorization frames have been evaluated manually with already existing subcategorization frames for the key verb class. This experiment is carried out to identify any valid subcategorization frames not available in the existing frames in that class. It has been observed that all the verbs in a key verb class share the same subcategorization frames as the members of their English equivalent Synonymous Verb Set (SVS) occupy in English VerbNet class.

As there is no WordNet (Miller, 1990) available in Bengali, the main problem here is to acquire the verb synonyms containing same and different senses to build a verb subcategorization lexicon. But, the synonymous member verbs containing same sense identified during the classification process can contribute to make the synsets for Bengali WordNet.

The rest of the paper is organized as follows. Section 2 gives the description of the related work carried out in this area. The classification strategy for the member verbs corresponding to each key verb is specified in Section 3. Section 4 describes the framework for the acquisition of subcategorization frames for the member verbs. Evaluation results of the system are mentioned in Section 5. Finally Section 6 concludes the paper.

2 Related Work

The early works for identifying verbs that resulted in extremely low yields for subcategorization frame acquisition are described in (Brent, 1991). Automatic acquisition strategies of verb subcategorization frames and their frequencies from large corpora are mentioned in ((Ushioda et al., 1993) and (Manning, 1993)). An open class vocabulary of 35,000 words was analyzed manually in (Briscoe and Carroll, 1997) for subcategorization frames and predicate associations. The result was compared against associations in ANLT and COMLEX. Variations of subcategorization frequencies across corpus type (written vs. spoken) have been studied in (Carroll and Rooth, 1998). A mechanism for resolving verb class ambiguities using subcategorization frames is reported in (Lapata and Brew, 1999). All these works deal with English. Several works on the term classification of verb diathesis roles or the lexical semantics of predicates in natural language have been reported in (Korhonen, 2002).

The work on subcategorization frame acquisition of Japanese verbs using breadth-first algorithm is described in (Muraki et al., 1997). Cross lingual work on learning verb-argument structure for Czech language is described in (Sarkar and Zeman, 2000). (Samantaray, 2007) gives a method of acquiring different subcategorization frames for the purpose of machine aided translation system for Indian languages.

Most of the above works have been done manually. The related cross lingual works have been evaluated with the help of parsers. In this present task, the non-availability of Bengali parser makes the evaluation strategy difficult to design. Though Bengali is a free phrase order language, the chunk level similarity with English phrases helps to construct the basic subcategorization frames for Bengali verbs. The contribution of the present work is that the sense-based classification of Bengali verbs shares same type of subcategorization frames.

---

[1] http://home.uchicago.edu/~cbs2/banglainstruction.html

3 Classification Strategy for Member Verbs

The classification strategy of member verbs sharing the same subcategorization frames as their key verb is the first step to create the verb classes. Equivalent English verbs of a key verb for different senses are identified from the Bengali to English bilingual dictionary. The sense wise separated English synonymous elements for each key verb constitute different Key Synonymous Verb Sets (KSVS).

The synonyms of the Bengali key verbs have been extracted from the Bengali-to-Bengali synonyms thesaurus. The thesaurus entries for the synonyms of the key verbs দেখা (*dekha*) [see], তৈরি করা (*toiri kara*) [make] and ব্যবহার করা (*bybohar kara*) [use / behave] are shown as follows where "(ক)" indicates the component part "করা" (*kara*) [do]. These entries have been retrieved from the thesaurus to create the set of synonymous member verbs for the Bengali key verb.

\# < দেখা > তাকানো , চাওয়া, দর্শণ (ক), দৃষ্টিপাত (ক), লক্ষ্য (ক) ।

\# < তৈরি (ক) > নির্মাণ (ক), গঠন (ক), প্রস্তুত (ক), সৃষ্টি (ক), স্থাপন (ক), উৎপাদন (ক) ।
\# < ব্যবহার (ক)> প্রয়োগ (ক), আচরণ (ক) ।

The frequencies of the member verbs collected from the Bengali news corpus (Ekbal and Bandyopadhyay, 2008) are listed in Table 1. It has been observed that the key verbs like ভুল করা (*bhul kara*) [mistake], বন্ধ করা (*bondho kara*) [stop] and পর্যবেক্ষণ করা (*porjobekkhon kara*) [observe] have no direct entries for verb synonyms present in the thesaurus. Constructions of verb classes for these key verbs have not been attempted in this present task.

Each Bengali synonym is searched in the Bengali to English bilingual dictionary to extract their English equivalent synonyms of same and different senses. The elements of MSVS, the English equivalent synonyms carrying same sense are checked for mapping to the elements of each KSVS of its corresponding key verb. If there is at least one element belonging to MSVS and KSVS, the Bengali member verb is then placed in the same class with its key verb.

The classification process is recursive in nature. Each phase for classifying a member verb Xbm that belongs to Bengali synonyms set Cbs of the key verb Ybk is described below.

<Key Verb>: [<Synonym1 {Freq1}>, <Synonym2 {Freq2}>......]

< দেখা (*dekha*) [see]>: [<তাকানো (*takano*) {2}>, < চাওয়া (*chaoa*) {2}>, < দর্শন করা (*darshan kara*) {9}>, < লক্ষ করা (*lakhya kara*) {1}>, < দৃষ্টিপাত করা (*dristipat kara*) {0}]

< তৈরি করা (*tairi kara*) [make] > : [<নির্মাণ করা (*nirman kara*) {0}>, < প্রস্তুত করা (*prostut kara*){11}> , < সৃষ্টি করা (*sristi kara*) {11}>,< উৎপাদন করা (*utpadon kara*) {0} [produce] >, < স্থাপন করা (*sthapon kara*) {6}>,< গঠন করা (*gathan kara*){10}]

< ব্যবহার করা (*babohar kara*) [use/behave] >: [< প্রয়োগ করা (*proyog kara*){7} [apply]>, < আচরণ করা (*achoron kara*) {2} [behave]>]

< বাস করা (*bas kara*) [live] >: [< বসবাস করা (*basobas kara*) {5}>, < অধিষ্ঠান করা (*adhisthan kara*) {0}>, < অবস্থান করা (*abasthan kara*) {0} >]

< কাজ করা (*kaj kara*) [work] >: [< কর্ম করা (*karma kara*) {0} >, < কাজকর্ম করা (*kajkarma kara*) {0} >, < কার্য করা (*karya kara*) {0}>, < পরিশ্রম করা (*porishrom kara*) {2}>, <কাজকাম করা (*kajkam kara*) {0} >, <কাম করা (*kam kara*) {0} >, < কম্ম করা (*kamma kara*) {0}]

< সংগ্রহ করা (*sangroho kara*) [collect]>: [< যোগাড় করা (*jogar kara*) {5}>, < আদায় করা (*aday kara*) {4} >, < উশুল করা (*ushul kara*) {0}>]

< চিৎকার করা (*chitkar kara*) [shout] >: [< চ্যাঁচামিচি করা (*chanchamechi kara*) {0}>, < চেল্লাচেল্লি করা (*chellachelli kara*) {0}>, < গোলমাল করা (*golmal kara*) {0}>, <গন্ডগোল করা (*gandogol kara*) {0} >, < কোলাহল করা (*kolahal kara*) {0} >, < শোরগোল করা (*Shorgol kara*) {0} >, < হট্টগোল করা (*hattogol kara*) {0}>, < হৈচৈ করা (*haichai kara*) {1}>]

< জিজ্ঞাসা করা (*jigyasa kara*) [ask/enquire] >: [< প্রশ্ন করা (*prosno kara*) {6} [ask]>, < জিজ্ঞাসাবাদ করা {1} (*jigyasabad kara*) >, < জেরা করা (*jera kara*) {0} [enquiry]>, < সওয়াল করা (*sawal kara*) {0} >, < জিজ্ঞেস করা (*jigyes kara*) {4}>, < জিগেস করা (*jiges kara*){0}>, < জিগ্যেস করা (*jigyes kara*) {0}>]

Table 1: Frequencies of the member verbs for eight key verbs acquired from the Bengali news corpus

The class corresponding to Ybk is Cbk. The English equivalent classes ECk for the key verb Ybk and ECm for the member verb Xbm are defined as,

ECk = {KSVS1, KSVS2, ..., KSVSq}
ECm = {MSVS1, MSVS2, ..., MSVSp}

If ∃ *Xbm* | (*Xbm* € *Cbs*) for i = 1 to p, j = 1 to q
(Z_{si} ∩ Z_{dj}) ≠ φ
then *Xbm* € *Cbk*
where Z_{si} € $MSVS_i$ and Z_{dj} € $KSVS_j$.

The possible example entries present in the Bengali to English bilingual dictionary for synonymous member verbs প্রয়োগ করা (*prayog kara*) and আচরণ করা (*achoran kara*) and their corresponding key verb ব্যবহার করা (*byabahar kara*) are given as follows.

Member Verbs:
```
< প্রয়োগ করা v. to employ; to
apply, to use ;>
< আচরণ করা v. to behave; to
deal (with), to act (to-
wards); to practice ;>
```

Key Verb:
```
< ব্যবহার করা v. to apply, to
use; to behave, to treat (a
person), to behave towards;
...>
```

In the dictionary, different synonyms for a verb with the same sense are separated using "," and different senses are separated using ";". The synonyms for the different senses of the verbs have been extracted from the dictionary. This yields a resulting set called Synonymous Verb Set (SVS). For example, the English synonyms (*apply, use*) and synonym with another sense (*behave*) have been retrieved for the Bengali key verb "ব্যবহার করা" (*byabahar kara*) and have been categorized as two different KSVS for the Bengali key verb. Each separate class has been formed for each KSVS of the key verb. On the other hand, the English equivalents *apply, use* of the Bengali member verb প্রয়োগ করা (*payog kara*) and *behave* of the Bengali member verb আচরণ করা (*achoran kara*) are different MSVSs for these two member verbs. These two MSVSs consist of two different senses belong to two key classes formed by their corresponding key verb. The English synonym *employ* constitutes another MSVS of the Bengali member verb প্রয়োগ করা (*payog kara*). But this MSVS does not belong to any existing classes formed by its key verb, as it is not satisfied by the classification criterion. Table 2 shows the statistics of the number of KSVSs of the eight (8) key verbs and number of MSVSs of eighteen (18) different member verbs acquired from the corpus after the first phase of the recursive process.

<Key Verb> : { < Member Verb [Number of MSVSs] >}	Number of Verb Classes/ KSVSs for the Key Verb
<দেখা (*dekha*) [see]>: {<তাকানো (*takano*) [1]>, < চাওয়া (*chaoa*) [1]>, < দর্শন করা (*darshan kara*) [2]>, < লক্ষ্য করা (*lakhya kara*) [2]>}	3
<তৈরি করা (*tairi kara*) [make] > : {< প্রস্তুত করা (*prostut kara*) [1]> , < সৃষ্টি করা (*sristi kara*) [2]>,< স্থাপন করা (*sthapon kara*) [2]>,< গঠন করা (*gathan kara*) [2]>}	3
<ব্যবহার করা (*babohar kara*) [use/behave] >: {< প্রয়োগ করা (*proyog kara*) [2] >, < আচরণ করা (*achoron kara*) [2]>}	2
<বাস করা (*bas kara*) [live] >: {< বসবাস করা (*basobas kara*) [1]>}	1
<কাজ করা (*kaj kara*) [work] >: {< পরিশ্রম করা (*porishrom kara*) [1]>}	1
<সংগ্রহ করা (*sangroho kara*) [collect]>: {< যোগাড় করা (*jogar kara*) [1]>, <আদায় করা (*aday kara*) [2] >}	2
<চিৎকার করা (*chitkar kara*) [shout] >: {< হৈচৈ করা (*haichai kara*) [1]>}	1
<জিজ্ঞাসা করা (*jigyasa kara*) [ask/enquire] >: {< প্রশ্ন করা (*prosno kara*) [1] >, < জিজ্ঞাসাবাদ করা (*jigyasabad kara* [2]) >, < জিজ্ঞেস করা (*jigyes kara*) [1]>}	2

Table 2: Number of KSVSs and MSVSs of the member verbs after first phase of the recursive process.

If any MSVS of a member verb remains unclassified, then that member verb is passed through the present classification process considering it as a key verb. But, the process will not be repeated for the synonym entry present in the Bengali synonyms thesaurus if that synonym entry has already been attempted in the classification process as a key verb. The recursive process terminates when no MSVS of a member verb is left unclassified. It has been observed that the preliminary separation of the Bengali member verbs into different verb classes follows the same classification as their English equivalent verbs present in English VerbNet.

4 Subcategorization Frames Acquisition FrameWork

The subcategorization frames acquisition task for the ten key verbs has been reported in the previous work (Banerjee et al., 2009). The subcategorization frames acquisition task is conducted separately for each member verb of a class except the key verb as the acquisition has already been done for the key verbs. This task has been carried out for two reasons. The first reason is to extract any frame that may exist in the corpus and verify the membership of this frame to its corresponding class. The second motive is to classify the newly acquired subcategorization frames into the existing key classes according to the closeness related to their frame sharing properties.

We have developed several modules for the acquisition of verb subcategorization frames for the member verbs from the Bengali newspaper corpus. The modules consist of POS tagging and chunking, identification and selection of verbs, English verb determination, frame acquisition from VerbNet and mapping of the acquired Bengali verb subcategorization frames to their English equivalent VerbNet frames.

We have used a Bengali news corpus (Ekbal and Bandyopadhyay, 2008) developed from the web-archives of a widely read Bengali newspaper. A portion of the Bengali news corpus containing 14000 sentences have been POS tagged using a Maximum Entropy based POS tagger (Ekbal et al., 2008). The POS tagger is developed with a tagset of 26 POS tags[2], defined for the Indian languages. The POS tagger demonstrated an accuracy of 88.2%. We have developed a rule-based chunker to chunk the POS tagged data with an overall accuracy of 89.4%.

To identify the member verbs from the tagged and chunked corpus, the data are analyzed to identify the words that are tagged as main verb (VM) and belong to the verb group chunk (VG) in the corpus. For the compound member verbs containing "করা" (kara) with pattern such as {[XXX] (NN) [kara] (VM)} have been identified and retrieved from the Bengali POS tagged and chunked corpus (e.g. [(prayog(NN) kara(VM))(apply)], [(byabahar (NN) kara(VM))(behave)] etc.).

The verb subcategorization frames for the equivalent English verbs (sharing the same sense) of a Bengali verb are the initial set of verb subcategorization frames that have been considered as valid for that Bengali verb. The different inflected forms in which the member verbs appear in the Bengali corpus have been identified accordingly. Different suffixes may be attached to a verb depending on the various features such as Tense, Aspect, and Person. A Bengali stemmer with an accuracy of 97.09% that uses a suffix list to identify the stem form of the member verbs has been developed. Another table stores the stem form and the corresponding root form.

The determination of equivalent English verbs has been carried out using a Bengali to English bilingual dictionary. The Bengali to English dictionary entry as mentioned in Section 3 for each verb has been analyzed to identify its synonyms and meanings to construct the SVS of that verb.

VerbNet associates the semantics of a verb with its syntactic frames and combines traditional lexical semantic information such as *thematic roles* and *semantic predicates*, with syntactic frames and *selectional restrictions*. Verb entries in the same VerbNet class share common syntactic frames, and thus they are believed to have the same syntactic behavior. The VerbNet files containing the verbs with their possible subcategorization frames and membership information are stored in XML file format. The XML files of VerbNet have been preprocessed to build up a general list that contains all verbs, their classes and possible subcategorization frames (primary as well as secondary). This preprocessed list is searched to acquire the subcategorization frames for each SVS of the Bengali verb.

The acquired VerbNet frames have been mapped to the Bengali verb subcategorization frames by considering the position of the verb as well as its general co-existing nature with other phrases in Bengali sentences (Das et al., 2009).

```
ম্যাক্স       যার          থেকে
(Max)NN (jar) PRP (theke) PSP
হাতপাখা
(NP(Hatpakha) NN )
প্রস্তুত         করেছিলেন
(prostut)NN (korechilen) VM
```

For example, the syntax of "NP-PP" frame for a Bengali sentence has been acquired by identifying the target member verb followed by a NP chunk and a PSP chunk. The above sentence containing prepositional frame "PP" does not appear in the Bengali corpus, as there is no concept of preposition in Bengali. But, when we

---

[2]http://shiva.iiit.ac.in/SPSAL2007/iiit_tagset_guidelines.pdf

compare these types of sentences containing postpositional markers, i.e. PSP (postpositions) as a probable argument of the verb, the system gives the desired output.

There are some frames that did not have any instance in our corpus. A close linguistic analysis shows that these frames can also be acquired from the Bengali sentence. It has been observed that sense wise separated SVS members consist of English equivalent synonyms of a Bengali verb occupy the membership of same class or subclass in VerbNet. The example Bengali verb class for the key verb "দেখা" (dekha) [see] is as follows,

```
<?xml version="1.0" encoding="UTF-8"?>
<VNCLASS ID= দেখা.xml
<MEMBERS>
<MEMBER name="দেখা">
<MEMBER name="লক্ষ্যকরা "
<MEMBER name="দর্শণকরা "
<MEMBER name="চাওয়া"
<MEMBER name="তাকানো "
</MEMBERS>
<FRAMES>
<FRAME name=Basic-Transitive</FRAME>
<SYN>NP-NP-V</SYN>
<Example>আমি কাকাতুয়া দেখি</Example>
<FRAME name=S</FRAME>
<SYN>NP-V-যে-(NP-NP-V) </SYN>
<Example>আমি দেখলাম যে রাম ঐ কাজটি করছে</Example>
</FRAMES>......
```

5 Evaluation Results

The set of acquired subcategorization frames or the frame lexicon can be evaluated against a gold standard corpus obtained either through manual analysis or from subcategorization frame entries in a large dictionary or from the output of the parser made for that language.

As there is no parser available for the Bengali and no existing dictionary for Bengali containing subcategorization frames, manual analysis of the system output with the gold standard corpus data is the only method for evaluation. The gold standard data has been prepared manually from the chunked sentences that contain the member verbs. The verb subcategorization frames acquisition process is evaluated using type precision (*tp*) (the percentage of subcategorization frame types that the system proposes are correct according to the gold standard), type recall (*tr*) (the percentage of subcategorization frame types in the gold standard that the system proposes) and F-measure as

$[2*(tp)*(tr)]/ [(tp) + (tr)]$.

The classification of acquired subcategorization frames for the eighteen member verbs have been carried out accordingly. But, our main objective is to explore the newly found subcategorization frames identified for the member verbs and their classification into the respective classes. Identification of such valid frames in case of Bengali and their presence in the appropriate classes have been conducted to improve the recall and precision values as well. The system has been evaluated with 120 gold standard test sentences containing the eighteen member verbs and the evaluation results are shown in Table 3.

Measures	Results
Recall	70.83%
Precision	74.11%
F-Measure	72.44%

Table 3. The Precision, Recall and F-Measure values of the system for the acquired eighteen (18) member verbs

A detailed statistics of the verbs is presented in Table 4. During the Bengali verb subcategorization frame acquisition process, it has been observed that simple sentences generally contain most of the frames as their corresponding English verb form usually takes in VerbNet. Analysis of a simple Bengali sentence to identify the verb subcategorization frames is easier in the absence of a parser than analyzing complex and compound sentences.

It has been noticed that the absence of other frames in the Bengali corpus is due to the free phrase ordering characteristics of Bengali Language. The proper alignment of the phrases is needed to cope up with this language specific problem. It can help to accelerate the task of disambiguating the arguments from the adjuncts with sufficient accuracy. The number of different frames acquired for these ten verbs is shown in Table 5. Two types of newly found valid frames have been extracted for the two Bengali verb classes. The '*' in Table 5 indicates the new valid frame type as identified by the member verb. These frames have been included in their corresponding key classes and the verification is done manually.

Information	Freq.
Number of sentences in the corpus	14000
Number of key verbs considered in the present task	11
Number of key verb entries available in the Bengali synonyms thesaurus to construct main classes	8
Number of member verbs identified from the Bengali synonyms thesaurus entries	41
Number of member verbs appeared in the corpus with frequency >0	18
Number of sentences containing member verbs in the corpus	120
Number of KSVSs or Verb Classes of the key verbs after first phase of recursive classification task	15
Number of KSVSs or Verb Classes of the key verbs at the end the recursive classification task	22
Number of subcategorization frames acquired from the chunked gold standard 120 sentences	85
Number of subcategorization frames identified correctly from the acquired 85 sentences	63
Number of newly found subcategorization frames only for Bengali	2

Table 4. The frequency information of the verbs acquired from the corpus

Bengali <Key Verb Class>		
(Member Verb)	Type of Subcategory Frames	No. of Frames
< দেখা (dekha)>[see]		
(তাকানো)	Basic Transitive	(1)
(দর্শণ করা)	Basic Transitive	(2)
(লক্ষ করা)	S (Sentential Complement)	(1)
<তৈরি করা (toiri kara) >[make]		
(প্রস্তুত করা)	NP-PP	(2)
	NP-NP	(7)
	Basic Transitive*	(1)
(সৃষ্টি করা)	NP-PP	(9)
(স্হাপন করা)	NP-PP	(2)
	NP-NP	(1)
	Basic Transitive*	(1)
(গঠন করা)	NP-PP	(4)
	NP-NP	(5)
<ব্যবহার করা (babohar kara)>[use/behave]		
(প্রয়োগ করা)	NP-PP	(1)
	NP-NP	(5)
(আচরণ করা)	NP-PP	(2)
<বাস করা (bas kara)>[live]		
(বসবাস করা)	Basic Transitive	(2)
	ADVP-PRED	(1)
	For-PP*	(1)
<কাজ করা (kaj kara)>[work]		
(পরিশম করা)	NP-PP	(1)
< সংগ্রহ করা (sangroho kara)>[collect]		
(যোগাড় করা)	Transitive (Material object)	(1)
(আদায় করা)	PP	(2)
< চিৎকার করা (chitkar kara) >[shout]		
(হৈচে করা)	S (Sentential Complement)	(1)
<জিজ্ঞাসা করা (jigyasa kara)> [ask/enquire]		
(প্রশ্ন করা)	That-S	(3)
(জিজ্ঞাসাবাদ করা)	Basic Transitive	(1)
(জিজ্ঞেস করা)	S-SUBJUNCT	(4)
	Basic Transitive	(1)
	That-S	(3)

Table 5. The frequencies of different frames acquired from corpus

5 Conclusion

The acquisition of subcategorization frames for Bengali verbs and their clustering has helped to build a small verb lexicon for Bengali language. The language specific new frames have been identified in this present task. The sense-based separation of verbs according to syntactical resemblance requires an emphasis on the semantic roles for further exploring the classes towards generalization. For the free-phrase-order languages like Bengali, the error caused in improper argument-adjunct distinction can be reduced and successively the overall performance can be increased with the help of machine learning approaches. Verb morphological information, synonymous sets and their possible subcategorization frames are all important information to develop a full-fledged parser for Bengali. The system can be used for solving alignment problems in Machine Translation for Bengali as well as to identify possible argument selection for Question and Answering systems.

References

Anna Korhonen. 2002. Semantically motivated subcategorization acquisition. *ACL Workshop on Unsupervised Lexical Acquisition*. Philadelphia.

Anoop Sarkar and Daniel Zeman. 2000. Automatic extraction of subcategorization frames for czech. *COLING-2000*.

A. Ekbal and S. Bandyopadhyay. 2008. A Web-based Bengali News Corpus for Named Entity Recognition. *LRE Journal*. Springer.

A.Ekbal, R. Haque and S. Bandyopadhyay. 2008. Maximum Entropy Based Bengali Part of Speech Tagging. *RCS Journal*, (33): 67-78.

Akira Ushioda, David A. Evans, Ted Gibson, Alex Waibel. 1993. The Automatic Acquisition of Frequencies of Verb Subcategorization Frames from Tagged Corpora. *Workshop on Acquisition of Lexical Knowledge from Text*, 95-106.

Ashoke Mukhopadhyay. 2007 ed. Samsad Samarthasabda Kosh. ISBN 81-85626-09-X

B. K. Boguraev and E. J. Briscoe.1987. Large lexicons for natural language processing utilising the grammar coding system of the Longman Dictionary of Contemporary English. *Computational Linguistics*, 13(4): 219-240.

Christopher D. Manning. 1993. Automatic Acquisition of a Large Subcategorization Dictionary from Corpora. *31st Meeting of the ACL*, 235-242. Columbus, Ohio.

Collin F. Baker, Charles J. Fillmore, and John B. Lowe.1998. The Berkeley FrameNet project. *COLING/ACL-98*, 86-90. Montreal.

Copestake A.1992. The ACQUILEX LKB: Representation Issues in the Semi-automatic Acquisition of Large Lexicons. *ANLP*. Trento, Italy.

D.Das, A.Ekbal, and S.Bandyopadhyay. 2009. Acquiring Verb Subcategorization Frames in Bengali from Corpora. *ICCPOL-09*, LNAI-5459, 386-393.Hong Kong.

Grishman, R., Macleod, C., and Meyers, A. 1994. Comlex syntax : building a computational lexicon. *COLING-94*, 268-272. Kyoto, Japan.

George A. Miller. 1990. WordNet: An on-line lexical database. *International Journal of Lexicography*, 3(4):235-312.

Glenn Carroll, Mats Rooth. 1998. Valence induction with a head-lexicalized PCFG. *EMNLP*. Granada.

Karin Kipper-Schuler.2005. VerbNet: *A broad-coverage, comprehensive verb lexicon*. Ph.D. thesis, Computer and Information Science Dept., University of Pennsylvania, Philadelphia, PA.

Kazunori Muraki, Shin'ichiro Kamei, Shinichi Doi.1997. *A Left-to-right Breadth-first Algorithm for. Subcategorization Frame Selection of Japanese Verbs*. TMI.

Levin, B. 1993. English Verb Classes and Alternation: A Preliminary Investigation. The University of Chicago Press.

Michael Brent.1991. Automatic acquisition of subcategorization frames from untagged text. *29th Meeting of the ACL*, 209-214. California.

Maria Lapata, Chris Brew.1999. Using subcategorization to resolve verb class ambiguity. *WVLC/EMNLP*, 266-274.

Paul Kingsbury and Martha Palmer. 2002. From Treebank to PropBank. In *Proceedings of the 3rd InternationalConference on Language Resources and Evaluation*, Las Palmas, Canary Islands, Spain.

S.Banerjee, D.Das and S.Bandyopadhyay. 2009. Bengali Verb Subcategorization Frame Acquisition - A Baseline Model. *(ACL-IJCNLP-2009), ALR-7 Workshop*, 76-83, Suntec, Singapore.

S.D. Samantaray.2007. A Data mining approach for resolving cases of Multiple Parsing in Machine Aided Translation of Indian Languages. *ITNG'07* © IEEE.

Ted Briscoe, John Carroll.1997. Automatic Extraction of Subcategorization from Corpora. *AFNLP-ACL*.

Representing Compound Verbs in Indo WordNet

Soma Paul
International Institute of Information Technology
Hyderabad, India
soma@iiit.ac.in

Abstract

This paper proposes design for representing Indo-Aryan compound verbs in Indo WordNet. Storing these multiword expressions as a whole has been considered not a good idea because generalization will be missed and also some amount of redundancies will creep in the database. In stead we propose to set up a *lexical link* between a light verb and main verbs it combines with. The motivation of the design is triggered by the following observations: a) Light verbs are polysemous to their corresponding full verbs; however they are semantically bleached. b) CVs are lexical variants of their V1 component. By postulating a semantic relation of *Compound verbs* for V1s, we can establish the relation between CV and its V1 associate. By carefully examining the semantic nuances that light verbs add to the meaning of the main verb, the present paper also attempts to present ontology of aspect.

1 Introduction

Development of multilingual Indo WordNet is presently an ongoing endeavour in India (Ramanand et al., 2008, Sinha, 2006) which strives to construct WordNet for several Indian languages using the Hindi WordNet[1](http://www.cfilt.iitb.ac.in/wordnet/webhwn/) as the base. At this opportune moment it is needed that we examine various kinds of complex predicates[2] and determine a suitable representation for them in WordNet like online database.

Compound verb (CV) is a kind of complex predicate that frequently occurs in Indo-Aryan languages. They are composed of two verbs, the first member – main verb (V1) – is either a participial form as in Bangla, Odiya and Assamese[3] (see 1a) or a root (as in Hindi[4], see in (1b)) and the second member – light verb (V2) – is "semantically bleached" and it bears the inflection. For example,

Bangla
    1a. *meeTa heS-e   uTh-lo*
        girl-cl laugh-pf rise – 3 pt
        'The girl burst into laughter'

Hindi
    b. *ləRkI həs   pəR-I*
       girl   laugh fall – 3 pt
       'The girl burst into laughter'

The examination of compound verbs in the context of constructing multilingual Indo WordNet is significant; the motivation being the following:

a. The repertoire of light verbs varies from language to language[5]. For example, Bangla has

---

[1] Among others, Marathi wordnet is now available online (http://www.cfilt.iitb.ac.in/wordnet/webhwn/)
[2] Indo-Aryan languages are replete with various kinds of complex predicates. For example, there exist noun+verb, adjective+verb and verb+verb constructions. Complex predicates represent one single event and are syntactically monoclausal unit (Butt (2003)).
[3] Bangla, Odiya and Assamese are languages spoken in eastern and north eastern zone of India. Bangla is also the official language in Bangladesh. A detailed study of compound verbs in these languages can be obtained from Dasgupta (1977), Mohanty(1992), Paul(2004).
[4] Hindi is a widely spoken language in Northern and central India. The compound verbs of Hindi have been studied by Hook (1974), Abbi(1991), Butt(1995) to name a few.
[5] The attestation of the compound verb is most frequent in Hindi-Urdu (Hook 1974), while it is very rare in Kashmiri (Kaul 1985). Bangla occupies the third position in the scale of frequency. Hook has conducted a contrastive typological study between the *compound-verb-rich* languages such as Hindi-Urdu and *compound-verb-poor* languages such as Marathi and concludes that the occurrence of CV sequences in *compound-verb-rich* languages have acquired a grammatical significance. In languages like Marathi the absence of the V2 has no conventional interpretation on which the hearer can rely on. In Hindi-Urdu, on the other hand, the presence of the V2, even where it is redundant, has

V2 occurrence of the verb *bERano* 'roam' as in *bole bERano, kine bERano* that implies the actor is doing the action of "talking" and "buying" *randomly*, without any discretion. Hindi language shows a lexical gap for such CV. Such gaps require proper treatment during the development of multilingual Indo WordNet.

b. Even when the same light verb occurs in two Indo-Aryan languages, their selection by main verbs might differ in those languages. For example, *pəRna* 'fall' occurs as a V2 both in Bangla and Hindi. However, the following CV is allowed in Hindi and not in Bangla: H[6]. *ro pəRa* – B. **keMde pORa* (B) 'cry+fall'. In Bangla the legitimate CV is *keMde oTha* 'burst in crying', which is not there in Hindi even though *uThna* occurs as a V2 in that language.

WordNet presently deals with complex predicates and does include lexicalized synsets which may contain either single words or MWEs, or sometimes, both together as illustrated below from English and Hindi WordNets:

English WN {*girlfriend, girl, lady_friend*}
 Hindi WN {*uThana, calana, cheRna, arambh_karna, Suru_karna*} "start a discussion"

The present paper argues in favor of lexical status of Compound Verbs and maintains that storing compositional compound verbs as a whole in the lexicon is not a good idea because of the following reasons (Calzolari 2002):

- We lose generalizations;
- We lose the possibility to produce a proper interpretation of these constructions;
- We run into problems when operating in a multilingual environment, when something that is a MWE in a certain language has to be expressed in the target language in terms of a normal syntactic pattern.

We propose in this paper a novel design of representing compositional CVs (which can be extended for other kinds of complex predicate as

well) in WordNet like lexical database. In this kind of representation, there will be no increase in the number of entries that are already present in WordNet. This will be achieved in terms of setting up a *linking* between the two components of CVs. A similar approach has been discussed in Bentvogli et al. (2004) as an alternative to *phraseset* for representing 'recurrent free phrases' in Italian WordNet. Hindi WordNet uses similar strategy for linking synsets across different part of speech, for example, noun – adjective. The idea of adopting the strategy of *linking* for the present task is motivated by the following observations about CVs and their component verbs:

a. V2s are semantically related to their full verb counterpart, they are polysemous. Enlisting V2s under its full verb counterpart captures the polysemy factor.
b. Semantic nuances contributed by a V2 to the overall meaning of CVs remains same for all cases. Those semantic features are attributed to V2 in the lexicon.
c. CVs are lexical variants of their V1 component. By postulating a semantic relation of *Compound verbs* for V1s, we can establish the relation between CV and its V1 associate.

Identification of CV in a language is an issue because there are homotactic sequences that are not to be taken as compound. The next section discusses some criteria for determining a verb sequence to be CV. Section 3 examines semantic contribution of V2s. Section 4 presents the architecture of representing CV in WordNet. The issues are illustrated with Bangla data in this paper with some reference to Hindi.

2 Compound Verbs and their features

CVs are composed of more than one verb. They retain the meaning of the main verb (V1) and the V2 which is semantically bleached adds semantic nuances to the meaning of CVs. Therefore CVs are considered as lexical variant of their V1 component. On the surface, the constituent verbs enjoy a considerable amount of freedom of movement. Other syntactic elements like adverb can intervene between the constituents (The constituents are freer in Bangla compared to Hindi (see Paul 2004, Butt 1995). However, they

---

become an obligatory marker of perfectivity. Its absence has come correspondingly closer to having a conventional interpretation of imperfectivity.
[6] H. = Hindi, B. = Bangla

represent one predicate, a functional semantic unit. Adverbs and negation scope over the whole construction and cannot modify one of the components. Identifying them as representative of one predicate is the main criterion for considering them lexicalized compound and not syntactically compositional construct. The other argument in favor of the lexical status of CVs is the following: Even though CVs are lexical variants of their V1 counterparts, the argument structure[7] of CVs is not always a copy of that of their V1 component. Nor they are licensed by their V2 constituent (for illustration see Paul 2004). On the contrary, the argument structure is licensed by the semantics of the lexicalized CV; an idiosyncratic property of the resultant construct.

In the context of designing architecture of representing compound verb repertoire in WordNet like lexicon, the discussion of "V2 semantics" becomes very significant. The semantic contribution of V2s to the meaning of the V1s creates new semantics for the CVs which can also change the syntactic behavior of the CVs. The next section will illustrate this with examples.

3 Semantics of V2s

In Bangla, we have identified 15 V2s. They are the following:

deoa 'give', *neoa* 'take', *phEla* 'drop', *tola* 'lift', *rakha* 'keep', *oTha* 'rise', *pORa* 'fall', *bERano* 'roam', *bOSa* 'sit', *aSa* 'come', *jaoa* 'go', *cOla* 'move', *ana* 'bring', *mOra* 'die', *paThano* 'send'.

All V2s have full verb counterparts in the language with which they share the core meaning[8]. As light verbs, they undergo semantic loss. Hook (1974) has taken an extreme position and states that V2s becomes lexically empty[9]. Others have conferred a semi-lexical status to V2s[10]. Butt (1995) assumes that the light verb use of a verbal item and its use as a full verb should be identified as a case of lexical polysemy and not as grammaticalization. I will adopt Butt's position and examine the semantic contribution of V2s in this section.

We maintain that semantics of V2 determines how the event structure of the main verb is profiled[11] or focused as it unifies with a V2. The profiled segment constitutes the meaning of the CV. The profiling is accomplished at two levels:

a. By highlighting the *manner of involvement* of the participant(s) engaged in the base-event; and
b. By imposing *temporal* and *aspectual* focus on the event denoted by the resultant CV predicate

I will describe the two levels in the following sub-sections.

3.1 Manner of Involvement of the participants

Some V2s profile manner of involvement of participants engaged in action denoted by V1 component and the profiled information constitutes the semantics of CV. We will examine the issue with respect to the two V2s: *deoa* 'give' and *neoa* 'neoa'. The V2 *deoa* 'give' specifies that the effect of the action denoted by the main verb is directed towards a participant other than the actor; while the V2 *neoa* 'take' entails that the result is directed to the actor himself/herself. This amounts to understanding how participants are affected by the result of the action. I call this *semantics of affectedness*. The semantics of many verbs are inherently marked for *semantics of affectedness*. For example, the meaning of the following verbs *gOchano* 'foist something on somebody', *oSkano*

---

[7] Argument structure is an ordered list associated to lexical representation of a verbal predicate that contains arguments licensed by that predicate.
[8] Paul [2004] has studied the concept of core meaning in detail and how core meaning is shared by the V2s and their corresponding full verb.
[9] Hook describes the phenomenon as *gammaticalization* (Hook 1974:94-97). Sarkar (1975) elucidates Porizka's perception of grammaticalization – a stripping off of the main dictionary meaning from the vector verb in order to reduce them to the role of 'aspective'.

[10] There is a great deal of discussion available in the literature regarding the semantics of V2. Following are some references related to the works on Indo-Aryan Compound verb structure: Hook (1974), Sarkar (1975), Dasgupta(1989), Abbi(1991,1992), Bashir(1992), Mohanty (1992), Butt(1995), Paul(2004).
[11] The theory of *profiling* gives an account of constituting meaning of compound verb is proposed in detail in Paul (2005).

'instigate', *dabano* 'suppress', *goMtano* 'thrust', *bigRono* 'spoil', *mara* 'kill' entails that the result of the action is directed towards an affected entity who is not the doer. These verbs can therefore select the V2 *deoa* 'give' and they are incompatible with V2 *neoa* 'take'. On the other hand, verbs such as *bhaba* 'think', *khaoa* 'eat', *Sekha* 'learn', *paoa* 'get', *bojha* 'comprehend', *dEkha* 'see', *Sona* 'hear' entail that the doer himself is the affected entity – the recipient of the result of the action. They select V2 *neoa* 'take'. There exist verbs which are not inherently marked for *semantics of affectedness*. They are accomplishment verbs such as *banano* 'build', *kena* 'buy', *khoMja* 'search' *raMdha* 'cook', *bhaja* 'fry', *Taŋano* 'hang up', *kaTa* 'cut (vegetables)', *aMka* 'draw', *ana* 'bring', *kOra* 'do' and so on that denotes a situation in which an actor performs some action and the action has a natural outcome. There exists a culmination which borne a result of the action. The semantics of these verbs, however, does not specifically indicate to whom the result of action is directed. For example, in case of the verb *banano* 'build' the builder can build a house for himself (as demonstrated in (3a)) or he can build a house for the benefit of a receiver or beneficiary as shown in (3b):

3. *binu nije-r jonne/ ritu-r jonne*
 Binu self-gen for Ritu-gen for
 baRi-Ta **bana-len**
 house-cl build-3 hon pt
 a. 'Binu has built the house for himself'
 b. 'Binu built the house for Ritu'

For such verbs the V2s *deoa* 'give' and *neoa* 'take' remove this vagueness by categorically focusing on the *manner* in which participants are involved in a situation. The CV *banie neoa* "build-cp take" profiles the self-directedness (or self-beneficiary) reading inherent in the semantics of the verb *banano* 'build'. The CV *banie deoa* "build-cp give", on the other hand, specifies that the effect of the action directed towards an entity other than the doer. Ritu is the beneficiary in the following sentence:

4. *binu ritu-ke Ek-Ta baRi* **bani-e**
 Binu Ritu-obj one-cl house build-cp
 di-lo /***ni-lo**
 give-3pt/ take-3pt
 'Binu built a house for Ritu'

The following table presents the above discussion:

V1	CV with V2 *deoa* 'give'	Semantic overtone	CV with V2 *neoa* 'take'	Semantic Overtone
Banano 'build'	**banie deoa** 'build a thing (for someone)'	Effect of the action directed towards a participant other than the actor	**banie neoa** 'build a thing (and the benefit goes to the doer)'	Effect of the action directed towards the actor himself (self-beneficiary)
Bhaba	**bhebe deoa*		**bhebe neoa** 'think within oneself'	Effect of the action directed towards the actor himself (self-beneficiary)
gOchano	**gochie deoa**	Effect of the action directed towards a participant other than the actor	**gochie neoa*	

Table 1: Manner of Involvement of participants in action denoted by CVs

The above data illustrates how the semantics of V2 profiles the participant role involved in the base structure of the main verb component. The next sub-section substantiates the claim that V2s adds temporal and aspectual focus to the CVs which are lexicalized.

3.2 Telicity and Duration as Inherent Property of CV's Semantics

Scholars in recent years (Vendler 1967, Smith 1991 among others) no longer perceive aspectual notions such as *duration* and *telicity* as an entirely grammaticized concept. Vendler's (1967) classification of verbs into accomplishment, achievement, activity and stative effectively includes *duration* and *endpoints of events* as an integrated part of the semantics of verbs. Carlota Smith has used the concept of aspect in a broader sense and identifies various lexical spans for verbs event structure. For example, "The verb constellation 'arrive in Boston' spans a moment near the end of a chain of events while 'go to Boston' covers a much larger part of chain" (Smith 1991, p 34). We maintain that verbs represent an event structure. The straight line in the following figure indicates the event line. The broken line on left and right sides of the straight line indicates the period prior to the starting of the event and the resultant state respectively. We have attempted to present how V2s profiles lexical span of V1 in the following diagram. The profiled segment determines the aspect of the resultant CV:

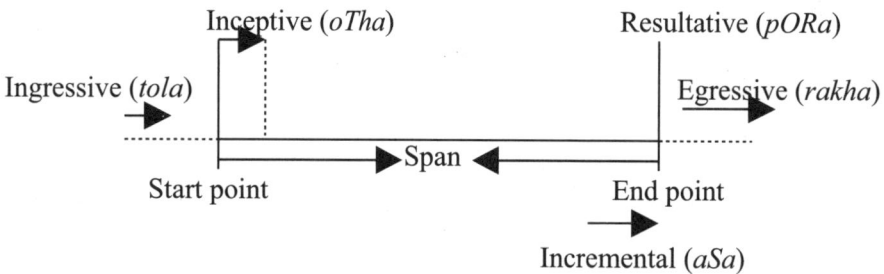

Figure 1: Lexical span profiled by V2s

<u>Inceptive</u>: focus on the entry into an event and thus spans the early portion of the causal chain (Measured by the broken vertical line)
<u>Ingressive</u>: time elapsed before the beginning of the situation[12]
<u>Egressive</u>: focus on the exit from an event and spans the later portion
<u>Resultative</u>: focus on the end of the causal chain
<u>Incremental</u>: focus on the developmental span as the event progress towards its final outcome
<u>Imminent</u>: Approaching towards a goal (not necessarily a developmental span)

Along with the aspects presented in Figure 1, we have more well-known aspectual viewpoints: imperfective and perfective. These aspects have two basic lexical semantic features: *telicity* and *duration*. This section attempts to make evident that these features are inherent of CVs and they are contributed by V2s to the overall meaning of CVs. For example, the main verb *kaMda* 'cry' is an activity which entails duration. When this verb combines with the V2 *phEla* 'drop', the resultant CV becomes non-durative in nature. However, the durative nature prevails when the verb selects V2s such as *cOla* 'move', *bERano* 'roam'. The adverb *EknagaRe* 'at a stretch' conveys duration. As shown in the following examples, this adverb is compatible with *kaMda* 'cry', *keMde cOla* 'continue to cry' and not with *keMde phEla* 'cry unpremeditatedly':

5a. *ritu <u>EknagaRe</u> kaMd-che / keMd-e col-eche*
Ritu at a stretch cry-3 pr ct cry-cp move-3 pr ct
'The girl is laughing continuously'

5b. * *mee-Ta <u>EknagaRe</u> keMd-e phelche*

kaMda 'cry' is an atelic verb because it does not include an endpoint. However, when this verb occurs with *oTha* 'rise', the resultant CV becomes telic in nature and become compatible with completive adverbials as illustrated below:

---
[12] Smith illustrates that the completive adverbial phrase 'in an hour' in the sentence 'He left the house in an hour' refers to the time interval at the end of which the event of 'leaving the house' takes place.

6. *ritu* <u>*muhurt-er moddhe*</u> ***keMd-e uTh-lo***
   Ritu second-gen in   cry   rise-e pt
   'Ritu burst into crying within a moment'

Maraffa (2003) has proposed a solution to represent lexical telicity in WordNets-like computational lexica for PortugUese telic complex predicate. Besides aspectual features, the other lexical property that the CVs inherently reflect is modal information. The following table presents the overall semantic contribution that V2s add to build the semantics of CVs:

	V2	Aspect	Mood	Telicity	Duration	Participant
1	*deoa* 'give'	Perfective		+	-	Non-self
2	*neoa* 'take'	Perfective		+	-	Self
3	*phEla* 'drop'	Perfective	Unpremeditated	+	-	Volitional
4	*tola* 'lift'	Ingressive		+	+	
5	*rakha* 'keep'	Egressive		+	-	
6	*oTha* 'rise'	Inceptive	Suddenness	+	-	Upward
7	*pORa* 'fall'	Resultative	Immediateness	+	-	Downward
8	*bERano* 'roam'	Imperfective		-	+	
9	*bOSa* 'sit'	Resultative	Unwarranted	+	-	
10	*aSa* 'come'	Incremental		-	+	
11	*jaoa* 'go'	Imperfective		-	+	
12	*cOla* 'move'	Imperfective		-	+	
13	*ana* 'bring'	Imminent		-	+	
14	*mOra* 'die'	Imperfective	Futility	-	+	
15	*paThano* 'send'	Perfective		+	-	

Table 2: Semantics of V2s

The following section attempts to present ontology of aspect. All situation types can be represented in this ontology and this will be applicable for all verbs, simple or compound.

3.3 Ontology of aspect

The most abstract ontological category in the following ontology is called *Situation Type*. For the V2s, we postulate the following situation types which subsume various aspects.

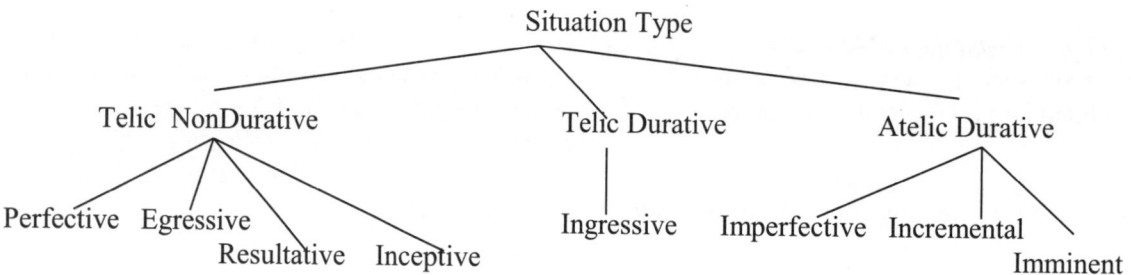

4 Representation of CVs in WordNet

Unlike English WordNet (1998), where phrasal verbs are listed under the main verb, we propose to organize V2s as a synset to their full verb counterpart. Compound verb is specified as a link between V1 and V2. The strategy is very similar to the one that Hindi WordNet is already using for cross part of speech linkage. Hindi WordNet has adopted a device of cross parts of speech linkage by which relations between the synsets of different part of speech is established. For example, the nominal and verbal concepts are linked by *ability link*, *capability link* and *function link*. The following example illustrates *function link* that describes the 'function' or *karma* of the noun referred to by *adhyaapak*.

अध्यापक,शिक्षक,आचार्य,गुरु,मास्टर   (adhyaapak, shikshak, aacaarya, guru, master; *teacher*)

==> पढ़ाना,शिक्षा देना   (paRhaanaa, shikshaa denaa; *teach*)

For compound verbs, linking is established between the main verb and V2 synsets. The link will indicate the meaning of the resultant CV. For every main verb, there will be a link "Compound Verb" which will specify all V2s that the main verb can combine with. Let us illustrate the proposal with an example. The verb *ghumono* 'sleep' can occur with the following V2s (see column 2):

V1	V2	CV	Meaning
ghumono	pORA	ghumie pORA	Fall asleep
ghumono	neoa	ghumie neoa	Take a nap

The information related to the entry *ghumono* will be the following:

Verb
(R)*ghumono* – *nidrar Oboshthay thaka* 'to be in a state of sleep'
  A. Ontology Node
  B. Hypernymy
  C. Compound Verb
  …

Once the link for 'Compound Verb' is expanded the V2s and their semantics will be displayed as illustrated below:

Verb
(R)*ghumono* – *nidrar Oboshthay thaka* 'to be in a state of sleep'
  A. Ontology Node
  B. Hypernymy
  C. Compound Verb

*(R) *neoa* –Result of the action is directed to the actor
  A. Ontological Node

  * Perfective
    * Telic Non-Durative
      * Situation Type

*(R) *pORa* – Action done with an immediateness effect
  A. Ontological Node

  * Resultative
    * Telic Non-Durative
      * Situation Type

The advantage of this kind of representation is linguistically very significant. First, we can assert through the design that V2s and their full verb counterparts are polysemous. They are semantically related. Second, the relation "Compound Verb" on main verb signifies that compound verbs are lexical variant of their main verb counterpart. We will also be able to present all CVs at one place which are lexical variants of a main verb. Third, the design helps us to state that a V2 adds same semantic nuance whenever it unifies a main verb.

5 Conclusion

Compound verbs are viewed as lexicalized items in this work. This paper presents a design of representing compound verbs in Indo WordNet. The proposal is to set up *lexical link* between main verb and the V2s that it selects. The V2s with their gloss is listed as polysemy to their corresponding full verb entry. Ontology of aspect is built to represent the semantic import of the V2s. The present study is done with respect to Bangla data. The task that remains is to handle compound verbs in multilingual scenario with a view of organizing them in Indo WordNet like database.

References

Anvita Abbi. 1991. "Semantics of Explicator Compound Verbs." In *South Asian Languages, Language Sciences,* volume 13:2, 161-180.

Carlota Smith. 1991. *The Parameter of Aspect.* Kluwer Academic Publishers, The Netherlands.

C. Fellbaum et al. 1998. *Wordnet: An Electronic Lexical Database.* MA: The MIT Press.

D. Chakrabarti, D. Narayan, P. Pandey and P. Bhattacharyya. 2002. Experiences in Building the Indo WordNet – A WordNet for Hindi. In *Proceedings of the First International Conference on Global WordNet (GWC02), Mysore, India.*

G. Mohanty. 1992. *The Compound Verbs in Oriya.* Ph. D. dissertation, Deccan College Post-Graduate and Research Institute, Pune.

J. Ramanand, A Ukey, B.K.Singh, P. Bhattacharyya. 2008. *Mapping and Structural Analysis of Multi-Lingual WordNets.* Bulletin of the IEEE Computer Society Technical Committee on Data Engineering

L. Bentivogli and E Pianta. 2004. Extending WordNet with syntagmatic Information. In *Proceedings of Second Global WordNet Conference.*

M. Sinha, M. Reddy, P. Bhattacharyya. 2006 *An Approach Towards Construction and Application of MultilingualIndo-WordNet.* Proceedings of the 3rd Global WordNet Conference (GWC 05), Jeju Island, Korea.

Miriam Butt. 1995. *The Structure of Complex Predicates in Urdu.* Doctoral Dissertation, Stanford University.

N. Calzolari, Fillmore C., Grishman R., Ide N., Lenci A., MacLeod C., Zampolli A. 2002 Towards Best Practice for Multiword Expressions in Computational Lexicons. In *Proceedings of the 3rd International Conference on Language Resources and Evaluation (LREC 2002)*, (1934-1940).

Palmira Marrafa. 2005. The Representation of Complex Telic Predicates in WordNets. In J. Cardenosa et al. *Universal Network Language: Advance in Theory and Application.*

Peter Hook. 1974. *The Compound Verbs in Hindi.* The Michigan Series in South and South-east Asian Language and Linguistics. The University of Michigan.

Probal Dasgupta. 1977. The internal grammar of compound verbs in Bangla. *Indian Linguistics,* 38(3):68-85.

S. Paul. 2004. An HPSG Account of Bangla Compound Verbs with LKB Implementation. Ph.D dissertation, University of Hyderabad, Hyderabad.

S. Paul. 2005. The semantics of Bangla Compound Verbs. *Yearbook of South Asian Languages and Linguistics.* 101-112.

Vijay K. Kaul. 1985. *The Compound Verb in Kashmiri.* Unpublished Ph.D. dissertation. Kurukshetra University.

Unification of Universal Word Dictionaries using WordNet Ontology and Similarity Measures

Sangharsh Boudhh
Center for Indian Language
Technology (CFILT)
IIT Bombay
sboudhh@gmail.com

Pushpak Bhattacharyya
Center for Indian Language
Technology (CFILT)
IIT Bombay
pb@cse.iitb.ac.in

Abstract

We report an exercise that resembles ontology merging. Disambiguated words called *universal words (UW)* from two different sources are attempted to be unified through similarity computation. Using an Ontology based and Extended Gloss Overlap based algorithm, reasonable accuracy is obtained for nouns, followed by decreasing accuracy for adjectives, adverbs and verbs. The context is the Universal Networking Language (UNL) project which is an international endeavor for multilingual information access on the web.

Keywords: UNL, Universal Word, U++ UW dictionary, Hindi-UW dictionary, Extended Gloss Overlap, Lesk's algorithm, WordNet Ontology

1 Introduction

Interlingua-based machine translation systems require disambiguated pivot entries of concepts along with their Parts of Speech, definition and usage instances. For example, the lexeme *spring* is ambiguous and has at least two meanings: *a season* and *a tool*. Possible unique meaning representations of these two senses are

spring(a-kind-of>season)
spring(a-kind-of>tool)

In absence of standardization, the same concepts can be expressed as

spring(a-kind-of>part-of-year)
spring(a-kind-of>instrument)

Humans typically do not have much problem dealing with such variations because of the large amount of world knowledge at their disposal (*season* is indeed a *part-of-year*; *tool* and *instrument* are synonyms). But automatic processes cannot operate correctly with such situations. To give an example, suppose it is required to translate between French and Hindi. To translate a sentence in French, meaning *Spring is a season of festivity* both the French analysis system and the Hindi generator system must agree that the *season* meaning of *spring* is involved. That is, both *French→Pivot* and *Pivot→Hindi* dictionaries should have uniform representation for this sense of *spring*.

The above discussion is in the context of an international project called the *Universal Networking Language (UNL)*[1] which was started in 1996 as an attempt to cross the language barrier on the web. 15 language groups from different parts of the world were involved in this endeavor. The idea was to encode (called *enconversion* in the *UNL* parlance) the sentences of a language L_1 into the UNL form and then generate (*deconversion* in the *UNL* parlance) the sentences of L_2 from the UNL form. It should be evident that both the languages must use the same pivot dictionary.

1.1 Universal Networking Language (UNL): the Framework

UNL is an electronic language for computers to express and exchange information (Uchida *et. al.* 2000). UNL expressions are generated sentence wise and consist of a set of directed binary relations, each between two concepts in the sentence. Tools called *EnConverter* and *DeConverter* which are language independent engines have been conventionally used for converting sentences from the source language to UNL and from UNL to the target language. The constituents of the UNL system are described now.

Universal Words

Universal words are the character-strings which represent simple or compound concepts. They form the vocabulary of UNL and represent the concepts in a sentence without any ambiguity. Universal Words may be simple or compound.

---
[1] http://www.undl.org

Simple unit concepts are called *simple UWs*. For example, *farmer(icl>person)* is a simple UW. Compound structures of binary relations grouped together are called Compound UWs. The syntax of a UW is given below.

<UW> ::= <Head Word> [<Constraint List>]
         [<":"<UW-ID>] [".""<Attribute List>]

where
(i) Head Word: is an English word interpreted as a label for a set of all the concepts that correspond to that word in English.
(ii) Constraint List: is the list of constraints that restricts the scope of the UW to a specific concept included within the Basic UW (explained next).
(iii) UW-ID: is an identifier used to indicate some referential information.

Attributes

Attributes of Universal Words describe the subjectivity of the sentence. They provide information about how a concept is used in a given sentence. The attributes enrich the information content of the UNL by providing information like logicality of UW, time with respect to the speaker, speaker's view on aspects of the event, speaker's view of reference to the concept, speaker's view on emphasis, focus and topic, speaker's attitudes, and speaker's feelings and judgments. The UNL group has provided a very rich set of attributes which makes it possible to capture many real world situations in the UNL form. Currently, there are 87 attribute labels. Some of the attributes are: @past, @present, @future, @imperative, @interrogative, @passive, @topic, @intention, *etc*.

UNL Relations

Binary relations of the UNL expressions represent directed binary relations between the concepts of a sentence. There are a total of 46 relation labels defined in the UNL specifications.

We classify the semantic relations (with overlapping) as the following:
a. Relations between two entities <e_1, e_2>, where e_1 is a verbal concept (29 relations)
b. Relations between two entities <e_1, e_2>, where e_1 is a non-verbal concept

	Arguments <e_2>	Adjuncts <e_2>
DO <e_1>	agt bas ben cag cob con coo dur gol ins obj opl ptn pur rsn scn seq src	man met plc plf plt via tim tmf tmt
Occur <e_1>	ben cob con coo gol obj opl rsn scn seq src	dur man plc plf plt via tim tmf tmt
BE <e_1>	aoj bas ben cao cob con coo dur gol obj plc rsn scn src	plf plt tim tmf tmt man

Table 1: Relations for Verbal Concept

UNL Graph

The UNL representation of a sentence is expressed in the form of a semantic graph, called *UNL graph*. Consider the sentence (1).

(1) *John eats rice with a spoon.*

The UNL expression for (1) is given in (2) and the the UNL graph is illustrated in Figure 1.

(2) [UNL:1]
agt(eat(icl>do).@entry.@present, John(iof>person))
obj(eat(icl>do).@entry.@present, rice(icl>food))
ins(eat(icl>do).@entry.@present, spoon(icl>artifact))
[\UNL]

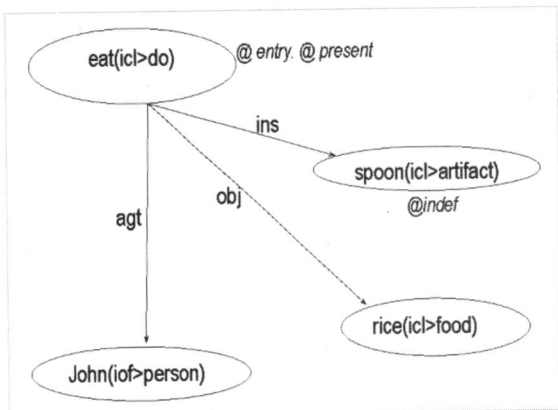

Figure 1: UNL graph of *John eats rice with a spoon*

In figure 1, the arcs are labeled with *agt* (agent), *obj* (object) and *ins* (instrument), and these are the semantic relations in UNL. The nodes *eat(icl>do)*, *John(iof >person)*, *rice (icl>food)* and *spoon (icl>artifact)* are the *Universal Words* (*UW*). These are language words with *restrictions* in parentheses for the purpose of denoting unique sense. *icl* stands for *inclusion* and *iof* stands for *instance of*. UWs can be annotated with attributes like *number*, *tense etc.*, which provide further information about how the concept is being used in the specific sentence. Any of the three restriction labels- *icl, iof* and *equ* (*used for abbreviations*)- can be attached to an UW for restricting its sense.

UNL Hypergraph

UNL has a way of representing coherent sentence parts (like clauses and phrases). It uses the notation :0<n> where <n> is an integer. Compound UW (also called a scope node) is like a graph within a graph and has its own entry node. Compound UWs are powerful constructs in UNL. Scope is a mechanism used in the UNL format to express compound concepts in a sentence as well as coordinating concepts. Clauses can be considered as compound concepts and these are usually marked with a scope. For example, the UNL expression, omitting the UNL restriction information, for the sentence (3) is given in (4).

(3) Mary claimed that she had composed a poem.
(4) [UNL:3]
agt(claim.@entry.@past, Mary)
   obj(claim.@entry. past, :01)
agt:01(compose.@past.@entry.@complete, she)
obj:01(compose.@past.@entry.@complete,poem.@indef)
[\UNL]

The segment *she had composed a poem* is considered as being within a scope, with the predicate *compose* being the entry node. The entire scope is connected to the matrix verb *claim* through the *obj* relation. The scope is represented in the UNL expression by the compound UW ID :01. Any compound concept can be represented using a scope and the scope technique allows us to capture deeply nested constructs in the language.

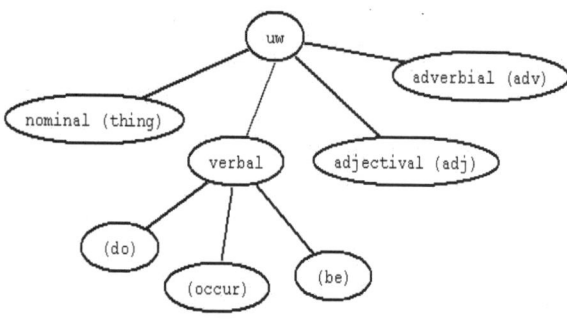

Figure 2: Universal word categorization

Categorization of UWs

UWs are hierarchically categorized (figure 2 above). The most general concept is called *uw*, which is on top of the hierarchy. Then there are four categories, *viz.*, nominal, verbal, adjectival, adverbial concepts represented by *thing, {do, occur, be}, adj, adv* respectively.

2 Problem Definition

Different language groups at different places of the world have been following somewhat different guidelines for UW formation, resulting in non-standard representation for UWs. We have studied two biggest UW dictionaries currently existing in the UNL community. The first is the dictionary developed at Madrid by the U++ consortium[2]: we will call this the **U++ dictionary**[3]. The second is the Hindi-UW dictionary[4] developed for the purpose of enconversion from and deconversion into Hindi at the Center for Indian Language Technology (CFILT [5]), Computer Science and Engineering department, Indian Institute of Technology Bombay (IIT Bombay[6]). We will call this the **H-UW dictionary**.

U++ UW dictionary	Hindi – UW dictionary
dog(icl>canine>thing)	Dog(icl>animal)
dog(unpleasant_woman>thing, equ>frump)	Dog(icl>constellation)
dog(icl>chap>thing)	Dog(icl>mammal)
dog(icl>villain>thing, equ>cad)	Dog(icl>female)

Table 2: UW entries for same word from different dictionaries

We can see a few entries from both the *U++* and *Hindi-UW dictionary* for the headword *dog* (Table 2). The U++ UW *dog(icl>canine>thing)* and the H-UW *dog(icl>animal)* represent the same concept but have been written differently.

The similarity between these two is very evident to human. However it is non-trivial for a

---

[2] U++ Consortium is an open and free association of researchers, business entities and people with a common interest in the development of useful applications to society based in the UNL language. Its main interest focuses on the creation of applications to support multilinguality, in order to overcome linguistic barriers on the Internet.
http://www.unl.fi.upm.es/consorcio/index.php

[3] U++ UW dictionary (web interface)
http://www.unl.fi.upm.es:8099/unlweb

[4] http://www.cfilt.iitb.ac.in/~hdict/webinterface_user/index.php

[5] http://www.cfilt.iitb.ac.in

[6] http://www.iitb.ac.in

machine to be able to pick up this similarity with very high accuracy.

Our goal in this work is to unify the two dictionaries mentioned above, *i.e.*, create mappings between UW entries from the U++ dictionary and the H-UW dictionary.

3 UW construction procedure

The guideline for formation of any new UW for some concept, as proposed in *U++ Consortium* meeting, July 2007 at Grenoble is described briefly [Boguslavsky 2007]:

1. Headword Selection: Choose a word (HW) from English or some language (but using Roman Alphabet), which completely covers the word *W* we are trying to describe
2. Ontological constraints:
   - Noun: *(iof>X)*, if *W* is instance of X and *(icl>Y>thing)*, where *Y* is closest hypernym of *W*, e.g., *dog(icl>mammal>thing)*
   - Verb: *(icl>do)* for action verbs, *(icl>occur)* for process-describing verbs and *(icl>be)* for state-denoting verbs.
   - Adjective: *(icl>adj)*
   - Adverb: *(icl>how)*
3. Semantic constraints: If the HW is broader in scope than *W*, restrict it using UNL relations *(rel>X)* and make equivalent to W.
   - *(icl>Z>Y)* for a narrower hypernym *Z* than *Y*. e.g. *dog(icl>canine>mammal)*
   - *(equ>S)* for synonym *S*. e.g.
   - *(ant>A)* for antonym *A*. e.g.
   - *(pof>A)*, if *W* is part of *A*. e.g. *room(pof>building)*
   - *(icl<V)*, for a hyponym *V*
4. Argument constraints: If W has some obligatory participants, which are usually present in sentence with *W*. e.g. agent or object; *give(agt>thing, obj>thing)*

4 The two UW dictionaries

The structures of two types of UW dictionaries i.e. U++ UW dictionary and L-UW dictionary have been explained in this section. L-UW dictionary is explained with an example of H-UW dictionary which has language L as Hindi which is also more relevant for our context.

4.1 U++ UW dictionary

U++ UW dictionary contains UW, part of speech information, definition and examples. The latest *U++ UW dictionary* has been derived from English WordNet[7] [Fellbaum 1998] version 3.0 (EWN) and entries in it can be traced to corresponding WordNet synsets using the sense key field. This is accepted as the standard dictionary by *U++ Consortium* members. It is maintained by the Spanish language center.

The format of *U++ UW dictionary* is:

UW; sense_key; pos_synset; freq_count

where the first field *UW*, is the Universal Word, *sense_key* is the sense key of the corresponding entry in EWN 3.0, *pos_synset* is the position of headword in the corresponding WordNet synset and *freq_count* is usage frequency for the corresponding synset. Using the sense key, we can link the UW to a unique synset in EWN 3.0. A typical entry from U++ UW dictionary looks like:

dog(icl>canine>thing);dog%1:05:00::;0;42

4.2 H-UW dictionary

The H-UW dictionary[8] is made at the Center for Indian Language Technology[9], IIT Bombay (India) under the supervision of Dr. Pushpak Bhattacharyya.

The format of Hindi-UW dictionary is :

uniq_id; transliteration; hindi_stem; hindi_word; UW_headword; UW_restrictions; attributes; src_lang; priority; frequency; definition; example

A typical entry from the H-UW dictionary looks like:

saMkRipwa; संक्षिप्; संक्षिप् करना; *abbreviate*; *icl>reduce(agt>person,obj>thing)* ; *V,CJNCT,AJ-V,link,VOA,VOAACT, VLTN,TMP,obj-ko,Va; H; 0; 0; Abbreviate 'New York' and write 'NY'.; to shorten*

1. Transliteration of Hindi stem - saMkRipwa
2. Hindi stem - संक्षिप्
3. Hindi word - संक्षिप् करना
4. Headword of the UW- abbreviate
5. UW restrictions icl>reduce(agt>person,obj>thing)

---

[7] http://wordnet.princeton.edu/

[8] Hindi-UW dictionary: http://www.cfilt.iitb.ac.in/~hdict/webinterface_user/index.php

[9] CFILT: http://www.cfilt.iitb.ac.in/

6. Attributes- V,CJNCT,AJ-V,link,VOA,VOA-ACT,VLTN,TMP,obj-ko, Va
7. Source language (H for Hindi)- H
8. Frequency of usage - 0
9. Priority of the word - 0
10. Example - Abbreviate 'New York' and write 'NY'.
11. Explanatory meaning - to shorten

5 Some observations on the U++ and Hindi-UW dictionaries

Statistical data gathered from U++ and H-UW dictionaries and inferences derived from them have been explained in following sub-sections.

5.1 Polysemy distribution

Distribution of number of entries per sense reflects the complexity of problem we would be facing. Tables 3 and 4 show the polysemy distribution in U++ and H-UW dictionaries respectively.

	Unisense	2 Senses	More than 2
Total	130203	15790	9268
Nouns	102041	9733	5321
Verbs	6359	2486	2579
Adjectives	17740	3136	1265
Adverbs	4063	435	103

Table 1: Distribution of senses in each PoS in U++ dictionary

	Unisense	2 Senses	More than 2
Total	166463	38332	20906
Nouns	5553	20629	9938
Verbs	6774	4690	4536
Adjectives	2793	9777	5576
Adverbs	1343	3236	853

Table 2: Distribution of senses in each PoS in H-UW dictionary

5.2 Frequency of relations

We found that out of the 46 semantic relations in UNL only a few appear in the UWs. Here is the percentage of UW in which specific relations appear:

	Total	Nouns	Verbs	Adjs	Advs
icl	92.4%	89.3%	100%	100%	100%
equ	44.3%	44.2%	46.1%	24.3%	38.9%
obj	10.1%	0	85%	0	0
agt	9.21%	0	77.5%	0	0
iof	7.6%	10.7%	0	0	0

Table 3: Frequency of occurrence of relations in different categories in U++ UW dictionary

	Total	Nouns	Verbs	Adjs	Advs
icl	47%	50.2%	53.7%	27.2%	45%
equ	3.4%	2.9%	4.5%	3.4%	2.6%
obj	6.1%	0	22.32%	0	0
agt	3.7%	0	13.4%	0	0
aoj	3.4%	0	0	16%	0

Table 4: Frequency of occurrence of relations in different categories in Hindi-UW dictionary

As is evident from tables 5 and 6, *icl* (meaning *a-kind-of*) is the most frequently used relation while defining UW. Other important relations are *agt* (agent), *obj* (object), *equ* (synonym), *iof* (instance-of), *aoj* (attribute-of-object).

6 Unification algorithm

We developed an algorithm which is a combination of Ontology based and Extended Gloss Overlap based [Banerjee and Perdersen 2003; Perdersen *et. al.* 2004] algorithms:

Basic Pseudo Code

foreach UW *U* in L-UW dictionary {
 upp_uws[] = All U++ UWs with sameHeadWord and Part of Speech as *U*;

 pairs[] = U and elements of *upp_uws* one by one;

 foreach element in *pairs[]* {
  TotalScore = SimpleMatch() + RestrictionScore() + GlossScore() + ExampleScore();
 }

 best_pair = Element from *pairs[]* with maximum *TotalScore*;

 if(*best_pair.TotalScore* >= THRESHOLD_SCORE){
  Finalize and store that pair;
 }
}

Simple Match

This score is based on simple string matching for same relation terms, e.g. *icl-icl, iof-iof,* of *H-UW* and *U++ UW* and *icl-equ, equ-icl* terms, matching of gloss pair, example pair after removing non-word characters and stop words. *icl-icl* means matching of the term with *icl* relation in *U++ UW* with the term with *icl* relation in *H-UW UW*.

Restriction Score

For calculating restriction score, an inverted hypernymy tree is created keeping the *U++ UW* synset at the root and "*icl*", "*equ*" terms of H-UW UW are searched in breadth first manner in the hypernymy tree. The score assigned is inversely proportional to the depth at which match is found.

Gloss and Example Score

All possible pairs of H-UW and U++ glosses and H-UW and U++ examples are considered. Firstly, non-word characters and stop words are removed. Then, maximal string overlap is calculated. Direct hypernym and hyponym glosses are also considered, inspired by Extended Gloss Overlap algorithm.

String Overlap Function

The string overlap function[10] breaks up the string into words and then further into letter pairs. For example, *like god* will be broken into "li", "ik", "ke", "go", "od". Then two times the number of common letter pairs is divided by the total number of pairs.

For example, the score between "doing better" and "better do it" will be:

$$\frac{2 \times |(do, be, et, tt, te, er)|}{|(do, oi, in, ng, be, et, tt, te, er)| + |(be, et, tt, te, er, do, it)|}$$

$$= \frac{2 \times 6}{9 + 7} = 75\%$$

7 Results

Out of the 121696 noun-adjective-verb-adverb *UWs* in H-UW dictionary, our algorithm could score 87287 entries.

Status of H-UW UW	Count	Percentage
No. of candidates	16488	13%
Not aligned	17921	15%
Score >= 50	53144	44%
Score < 50	34143	28%

Table 5: Distribution of alignment of H-UW UWs

Table 7 shows the distribution of UWs with *no sense found*, *not aligned* UW, UW aligned with total *score greater than or equal to 50* as well as those with *score less than 50*.

Recall and Precision

The alignments, with score greater than 50, are considered for recall and precision calculations.

PoS	Total number	(Score >=50)	Recall	Precision
Noun	57147	28662	46.14%	92%
Verb	33433	11361	30.33%	89.25%
Adjective	25302	10239	38.24%	94.5%
Adverb	5814	2882	47.84%	96.5%
Total	121696	53144	40.24%	92.13%

Table 6: Recall and Precision for all Parts of Speech for a threshold score of 50.

8 Results and Discussions

40.24% of UWs were aligned with a precision of 92.13%. Verbs were the toughest to align due to their highly polysemous behaviour and minute difference between senses. Out of the total *87287* aligned UWs, gloss functions gave score for *49246* entries, example functions for *44695* entries and restriction for *11937* entries. Although restriction is a very accurate way to establish alignment, its coverage is small.

UWs in H-UW dictionary which matched no sense in the U++ dictionary mostly have multi-word HeadWords.

9 Conclusion and future work

The exercise of aligning the H-UW UW with U++ UW has various advantages. First of all, now it would be possible to deconvert UNL graphs created using standard U++ UWs at any place into Hindi with better quality output. And EnConverter of Hindi (when it comes) will also

---
[10]

http://www.catalysoft.com/articles/StrikeAMatch.html

be able to create UNL graphs of globally accepted standard.

Although the algorithm has been created with the H-UW dictionary in mind, it can be easily extended to other L-UW dictionaries with similar scenario. As soon as all the countries adjust their systems for U++ dictionary, the exchange of resources becomes easier and quicker. To the best of our knowledge, this is the first attempt at unification of a Language-UW dictionary with the U++ UW dictionary.

Related pieces of work are by Ponzetto and Navigli (2009) and Ehrig and Sure (2004). The latter proposes to use category theory to provide a scheme independent ontology mapping, while the former concentrates on WordNet and Wikipedia mapping.

On the way of achieving this alignment, Java API for H-UW dictionary and U++ dictionary were created as by-products. Moreover, the interface created for manual alignment which shows scores from the algorithm also assists manual alignment to a great extent providing a graphical user interface and highlighting the more likely entries.

Future work is directed at improving the recall of the alignment.

References

Christiane Fellbaum (*ed.*). 1998. *WordNet: An Electronic Lexical Database*, The MIT Press.

Hiroshi Uchida, M. Zhu, and T. Della. Senta. 1999. *UNL: A Gift for a Millennium.* The United Nations University, Tokyo.

Igor Boguslavsky. 2007. *UW construction procedure*, notes of U++ Consortium meeting, Grenoble.

M. Ehrig and Y. Sure. 2004. *Ontology mapping – an integrated approach.* In Bussler C., Davis J., Fensel D. and Studer, R., eds., Proceedings of the First European Semantic Web Symposium, volume 3053 of Lecture Notes in Computer Science. Heraklion, Greece.

Satanjeev Banerjee and Ted Pedersen. 2003. *Extended gloss overlaps as a measure of semantic relatedness.* In Proceedings of the Eighteenth International Joint Conference on Artificial Intelligence (IJCAI).

Simone Paolo Ponzetto, Roberto Navigli. 2009. *Large-Scale Taxonomy Mapping for Restructuring and Integrating Wikipedia.* International Joint Conference on AI (IJCAI).

Ted Pedersen, Siddharth Patwardhan, and Jason Michelizzi. 2004. *Wordnet::Similarity - Measuring the Relatedness of Concepts.* In Daniel Marcu Susan Dumais and Salim Roukos, editors, HLT-NAACL 2004: Demonstration Papers, pages 38--41, Boston, Massachusetts, USA, May 2 - May 7. Association for Computational Linguistics.

Semantic Services in FreeLing 2.1: WordNet and UKB

Lluís Padró
Software Department
TALP Research Center
Universitat Politècnica
de Catalunya
padro@lsi.upc.edu

Samuel Reese
ISAE - Supaero
Université Paul Sabatier
samuel.reese@supaero.org

Eneko Agirre, Aitor Soroa
IXA NLP Group
University of the Basque Country
{e.agirre,a.soroa}@ehu.es

Abstract

FreeLing is an open-source open-source multilingual language processing library providing a wide range of language analyzers for several languages. It offers text processing and language annotation facilities to natural language processing application developers, simplifying the task of building those applications. FreeLing is customizable and extensible. Developers can use the default linguistic resources (dictionaries, lexicons, grammars, etc.) directly, or extend them, adapt them to specific domains, or even develop new ones for specific languages.

This paper presents the semantic services included in FreeLing, which are based on WordNet and EuroWordNet databases. The recent release of the UKB program under a GPL license made it possible to integrate a long awaited word sense disambiguation module into FreeLing. UKB provides state of the art all-words sense disambiguation for any language with an available WordNet.

1 Introduction

Basic language processing tasks such as tokenizing, morphological analysis, lemmatizing, part-of-speech tagging, word sense disambiguation (WSD), dependency parsing, etc. are needed for most natural language processing (NLP) applications such as Machine Translation, Summarization, Dialogue systems, Text mining, etc.

This makes language analyzers a very valuable resources for researchers and developers in NLP. Also, the lack of out-of-the-box state-of-the-art systems is a severe bottleneck for faster progress in the area, both in research and development.

Additionally, a large part of the effort required to develop NLP systems is devoted to the adaptation of existing software resources to the platform, I/O format, or API of the final application.

FreeLing was undertaken with the belief that steps should be taken towards general availability of basic NLP tools and resources, which may be used without restrictions. Thus, to enable faster advances and more portable systems in our area, an open–source model was chosen.

After five years (first version was released on 2004), over 10,000 downloads, and a growing user community which has extended the initial three languages (English, Spanish and Catalan) to seven (adding Galician, Italian, Welsh, Portuguese, and Asturian) prove that the collaborative open model is a productive approach to the development of NLP tools and resources.

In this paper, we focus on the FreeLing services related to semantic processing, namely wordnet access and word sense disambiguation. The next section presents the internal structure of the library. Sections 3 and 4 present the wordnet access and WSD services. Section 5 depicts some examples, and Section 6 outlines some conclusions.

2 Data structure and language analysis services

FreeLing is conceived as a library on top of which powerful NLP applications can be developed, and oriented to ease the integration of language analysis services into higher level applications.

Its architecture consists of a simple two-layer client-server approach: A basic linguistic service layer which provides analysis services (morphological analysis, tagging, parsing, ...), and an application layer which, acting as a client, requests the desired services from the analyzers.

The library is written in C++, since speed is a must for real-world oriented applications. Additionaly, APIs are provided to call the library services from Java, perl, and pyhton.

The internal architecture of the system is based on two kinds of objects: linguistic data objects and processing objects.

2.1 Linguistic Data Classes

The basic classes in the library are used to contain linguistic data (such as a word, a PoS tag, a sentence, a document...). Any client application must be aware of those classes in order to be able to provide to each processing module the right data, and to correctly interpret the module results.

The linguistic classes supported by the current version are:

- `analysis`: A tuple <lemma, PoS tag, probability, sense list>.
- `word`: A word form with a list of possible `analysis` objects.
- `sentence`: A list of `word` known to be a complete sentence, it may include also a parse tree and/or a dependency tree.
- `paragraph`: A list of `sentence` known to be an independent paragraph.
- `document`: A list of `paragraph` that form a complete document. It may contain also coreference information about the entity mentions in the document.

Figure 1 presents a UML diagram with the linguistic data classes.

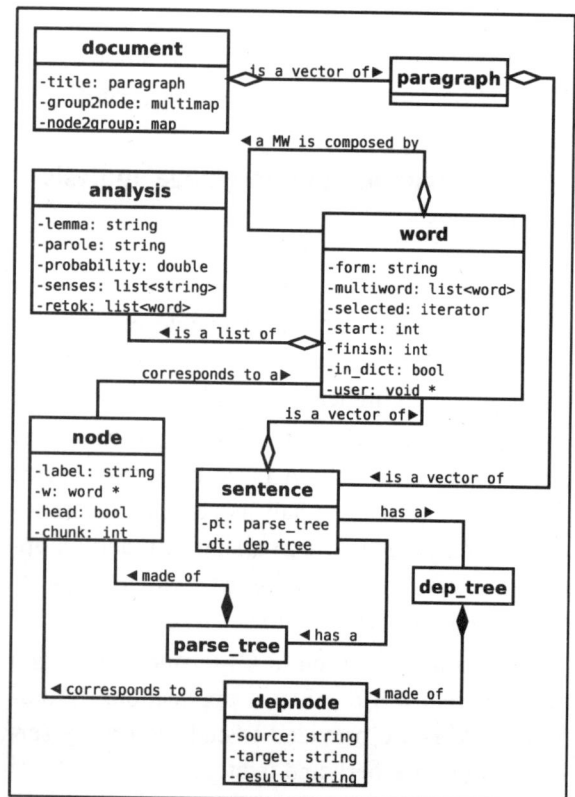

Figure 1: FreeLing-2.1 Linguistic Data Classes.

2.2 Processing Classes

Apart from classes containing linguistic data, the library provides classes able to transform them. See Figure 2 below for a UML diagram.

- `tokenizer`: Receives plain text and returns a list of `word` objects.
- `splitter`: Receives a list of `word` objects and returns a list of `sentence` objects.
- `morfo`: Receives a list of `sentence` and morphologically annotates each `word` of each sentence in the list. In fact, this class applies a cascade of specialized processors (number detection, date/time detection, multi-word detection, dictionary search, etc.) each of which is in turn a processing class:
  - `locutions`: Multi-word recognizer.
  - `dictionary`: Dictionary lookup and suffix handling.
  - `numbers`: Numerical expressions recognizer.
  - `dates`: Date/time expressions recognizer.
  - `quantities`: Ratio and percentage expressions and monetary amount recognizer.
  - `punts`: Punctuation symbol annotator.
  - `probabilities`: Lexical probabilities annotator and unknown word handler.
  - `np`: Proper noun recognizer.
- `tagger`: Receives a list of `sentence` and disambiguates the PoS of each `word` in the given sentences. If the selected analysis carries retokenization information, the word may be split in two or more new words.
- `NE classifier`: Receives a list of `sentence` and classifies all `word` tagged as proper nouns in the given sentences.
- `Sense annotator`: Receives a list of `sentence` and adds synset information to the selected `analysis` for each `word`.
- `Word sense disambiguator`: Receives a list of `sentence` and ranks the possible senses for each `word` selected `analysis`.
- `chunk parser`: Receives a list of `sentence` and enriches each of them with a `parse_tree`.
- `dependency parser`: Receives a list of parsed `sentence` and enriches each of them with a `dependency_tree`.
- `coreference solver`: Receives a document formed by parsed `sentence` and enriches the document with coreference information.

3 Semantic services: WordNet access

There are two basic semantic services: First, a basic database access module that enables the client application to consult a WordNet (Miller et al., 1991) structure (e.g. to find out which synsets a lemma belongs to, which words are contained in one synset, or which are the hypernyms of certain synset). Second, a knowledge-based word sense disambiguator, which has been recently integrated thanks to the release of UKB disambiguator under a GPL license (Agirre and Soroa, 2009).

3.1 SemanticDB module

This module handles WordNet-like structures, which are indexed in a local database. The database sources are provided with FreeLing, and can be adapted –or completely changed– to match the application needs.

The source database consists of two files:

- The WN structure file contains a list of synset codes, with information about its PoS, its hypernyms, its WN semantic file, and its features in EuroWordNet TCO (Álvez et al., 2008). For instance, the entry in this file for WN1.6 noun synset {01630731 cat,true_cat} is:

```
01630731:N 01630126 05 Animal:Object
```

This file is indexed and used to find out synset properties or their hypernyms.

- The language lexical file contains direct and inverse links between lemmas and synset codes. For instance, the first line in the example below establishes a link from the noun lemma *cat* to all the synsets it belongs to. If they are provided sorted by frequency, the first one can be used to perform most-frequent-sense disambiguation. The two last lines define which words are contained in the given synsets:

```
W:cat:N 01630731 07306044 07143161
S:01630731:N cat true_cat
S:07306044:N cat guy hombre
```

Note that this module does not (yet) offer as advanced functionalities as the standard WordNet search library, but it has the following advantages:

- Source files are plain text and easy to build. Indexing programs are provided with FreeLing to enable anyone to create his/her own semantic database.

- Language and WN structure files are separated, making it possible to use the structure file as an ILI and map all languages to the same structure if necessary.

- The synset codes serve as mere concept identifiers, so they can be replaced by any other semantic code (e.g. later WN versions synset codes, or even ad-hoc concept codes).

- Being open-source, the capabilities of the module can be easily extended (e.g. to include more semantic tags or more relations in the structure file), or customized to one specific needs.

Currently, FreeLing includes only semantic data for English, Spanish, and Catalan, that are the only languages that offer a version in the Global Word-Net Grid under an open-source license.

3.1.1 Use of semantic information by FreeLing modules

The Semantic DB module can be used directly by the client application, but it is also used by other modules in FreeLing:

- The sense annotator: Accesses the database and enriches the text with all possible synsets for each form.

- The relaxation–labelling tagger (Padró, 1998): Deals with constraint-grammar-like rules dealing with PoS tag, form, lemma, or sense to guide the selection of the right analysis.

- The dependency parser (Atserias et al., 2005; Carrera et al., 2008): Uses heuristic rules dealing with PoS, syntax, senses, and TCO information to combine into a complete dependency tree the chunks produced by the shallow parser.

- The coreference solver –based on (Soon et al., 2001): Uses TCO and hypernym relations between two mentions as features used by a machine learning classifier to determine whether they corefer.

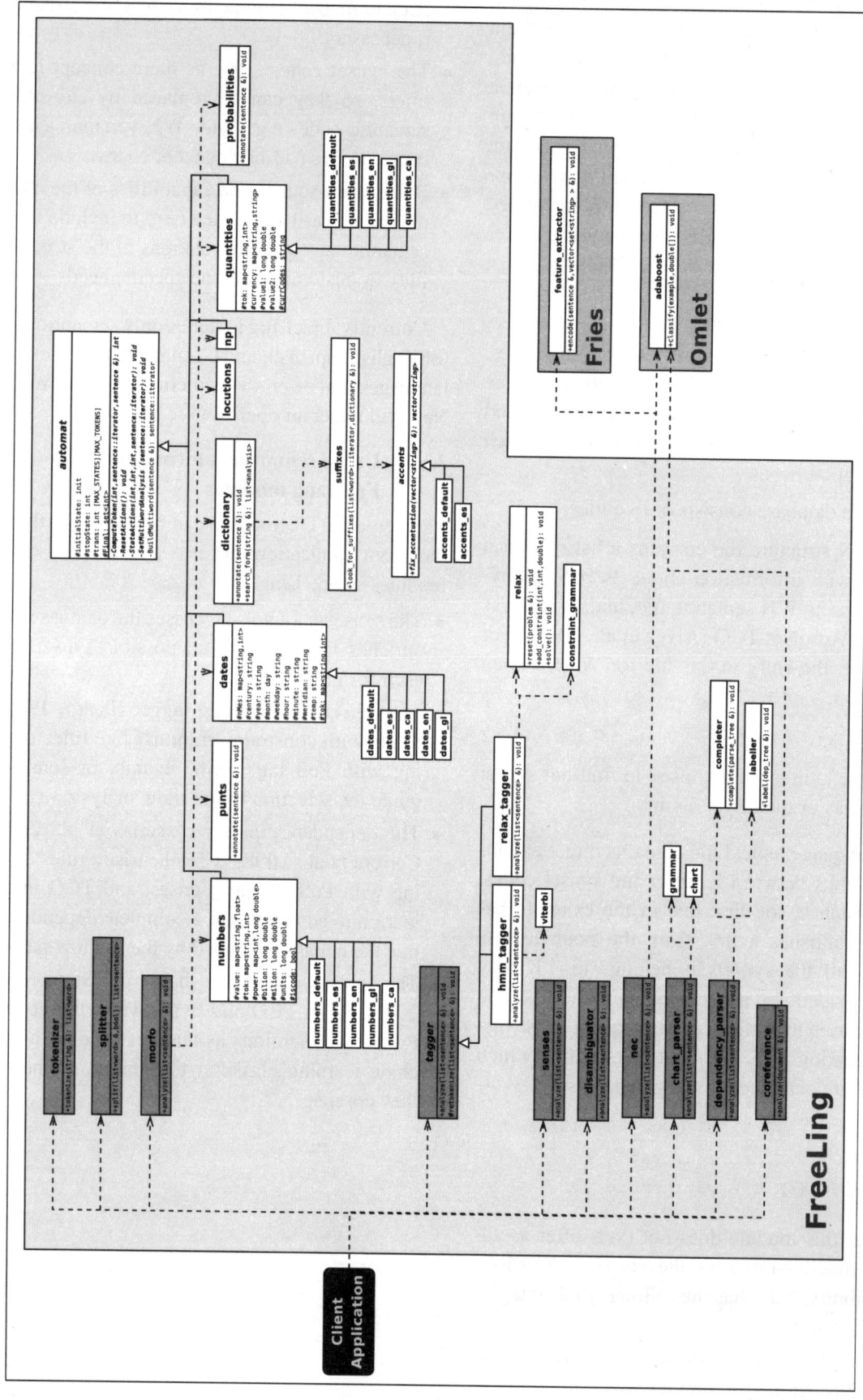

Figure 2: FreeLing-2.1 Main Processing Classes.

4 Semantic services: UKB word sense disambiguation

The PageRank-based word sense disambiguation algorithm UKB (Agirre and Soroa, 2009), and the availability of its code under GPL has recently made it possible to include a long-awaited feature in FreeLing: A language-independent state-of-the-art all-words WSD module. UKB uses the structure of local wordnets in order to perform WSD, and it can be easily applied to any language, with the only requirement of having a wordnet.

The original code has been integrated *as is*, and a simple wrapper has been developed that loads the sentences being analyzed by FreeLing into the appropriate UKB data structure (after the lemmatizer and the tagger have chosen the right PoS and lemma for each word), calls the disambiguator, and loads its results back to the FreeLing data structure. In this way, the UKB module enriches the analysis of a set of sentences with the ranked list of synsets for each word.

Knowledge files handled by this module are:

- The dictionary file, which contains the association between words and synset codes. The same file described above used by the semantic DB module is used. It is converted to the format needed by UKB at installation time. Conversion programs are provided with FreeLing to enable the user to handle his/her own dictionaries.

- The relation graph, containing all relations between synsets to be used by the PageRank algorithm. Since this file contains relations other than hyper/hyponymy, it is currently provided separately, in text format, and indexed at installation time (indexing programs are also provided). Ideally, in the near future this file and the WN structure file used by the SemanticDB should be unified.

Note that, again, the UKB algorithm is a generic graph-based disambiguation tool, which can be fed with any sense dictionary and any relation graph for those senses. Currently, synset codes and relations from wordnets are used, but this module can be used to disambiguate on any sense repository just changing the used knowledge files.

Since this approach of keeping knowledge/data components as separated as possible from processing/code components is also followed by FreeLing, they match easily and both together form a very flexible and sound platform to develop syntax and semantic analyzers for any language.

5 Examples

In this section we will show some simple examples of the semantic capabilities of FreeLing and its UKB component. An online demo of the whole system can be found at http://www.lsi.upc.edu/~nlp/freeling.

5.1 Basic sense annotation

The basic semantic functionality is mere sense annotation, enriching a PoS-tagged sentence with a list of possible senses for each word. An example is shown in Figure 3.

The	cat	ate	my	dinner	sandwich	.
the	cat	eat	my	dinner	sandwich	
DT	NN	VBD	PRP$	NN	NN	Fp
1	1	1	0.998322	1	0.904762	1
	01630731	00794578		05629070	05737298	
	07306044	00793267	my	06128171		
	07143161	00802008	PRP		sandwich	
	02406193	00787073	0.00167785		VB	
	02404497	01205301			0.047619	
	01636523	00187431				
					sandwich	
					VBP	
					0.047619	

Figure 3: Sense annotation of a PoS-tagged sentence.

If this annotation takes place before PoS tagging, the tagger may use the semantic information to help the disambiguation (e.g. a Constraint Grammar based tagger). If that is not the case, the annotation can take place either before or after the tagging, depending on the user's needs.

If the synset codes provided in the sense dictionary are sorted by frequency, the user application only needs to pick the first one to have a basic MFS disambiguator.

5.2 Semantics used by other FreeLing modules

The module in FreeLing that –currently– takes the larger advantage from the availability of semantic information is the dependency parser. The parser is based on a set of heuristic rules that combine chunks and label their dependencies. See (Atserias et al., 2005; Carrera et al., 2008) for details.

Those heuristic rules may refer to certain properties of the chunks (e.g. head PoS tag, head lemma, position relative to other chunks) including semantic features (TCO properties, WN semantic file, hypernyms).

For instance, consider the Spanish sentences *Juan vió a su amigo* (Juan saw his friend) and *Juan escribió a su amigo* (Juan wrote to his friend). In

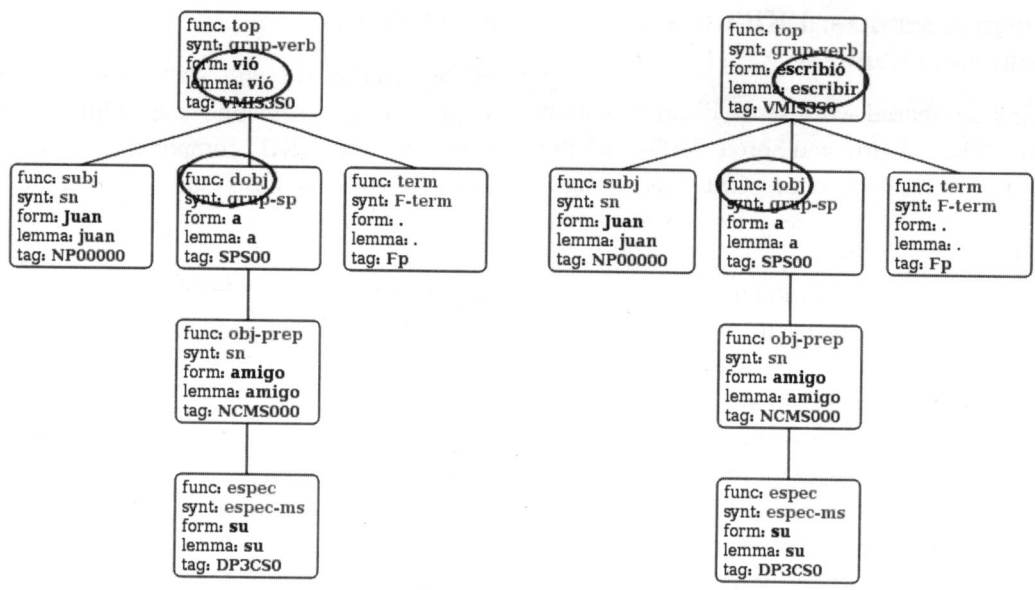

Figure 4: Analysis requiring semantics in dependency parsing

the former, *his friend* is the direct object of the verb *to see*, and in the later, it is the indirect object of *to write*.

The reason is that transitive Spanish verbs such as *to see* that do not have indirect object require the use of the preposition *a* when the direct object is a person. On the other hand, for ditransitive verbs such as *to write* the preposition *a* marks the indirect object.

So, to properly parse these sentences, rules have to be able to check about the `Human` condition of the candidate objects. This is achieved thanks to the TCO access provided by the SemanticDB module, as illustrated in Figure 4.

Another module that benefits from the semantic knowledge included in FreeLing is the machine-learning based coreference solver. The solver considers pairs of nominal mentions (noun phrases and pronouns) and uses a classifier based on (Soon et al., 2001) to determine whether they corefer.

The features used by the classifier include morphosyntax features such as the distance between the mentions, their relative positions, whether they are definite noun phrases, personal pronouns, their gender, number, etc.

They also include semantic information on the kind of entity they may be referring to: If the noun phrase head is a proper noun, a NE classifier is used to determine if it is a person, an organization, or a geographical name. If the noun phrase head is a common noun, its TCO properties are checked to find out whether it is `Human`, `Group` or `Place`.

Then, this information is provided as features to the classifier.

5.3 Word Sense Disambiguation

The frequency-ordered semantic dictionaries enable the user to perform a straightforward most-frequent-sense disambiguation just picking the first sense in the list.

The integration of the UKB module (Agirre and Soroa, 2009) offers a more informed disambiguation mechanism. The sense list is ordered according to the PageRank assigned by the algorithm. The user application can simply select the first one, or use the rank information to perform any desired action.

The example sentences in Figure 5 illustrate how UKB is able to distinguish the two main senses for the word *bank* in different contexts, instead of choosing always the same, as a MFS disambiguator would.

Note that this doesn't mean that UKB has a higher accuracy than MFS at WSD. As reported by (Agirre and Soroa, 2009), the results of UKB at the performed experiments on English and Spanish are quite near of MFS results, and clearly improve those of other unsupervised WSD systems.

6 Conclusions

We presented the semantic services included in the FreeLing 2.1 library, which includes access to wordnets and graph-based all-word sense disambiguation on those wordnet, using the state-

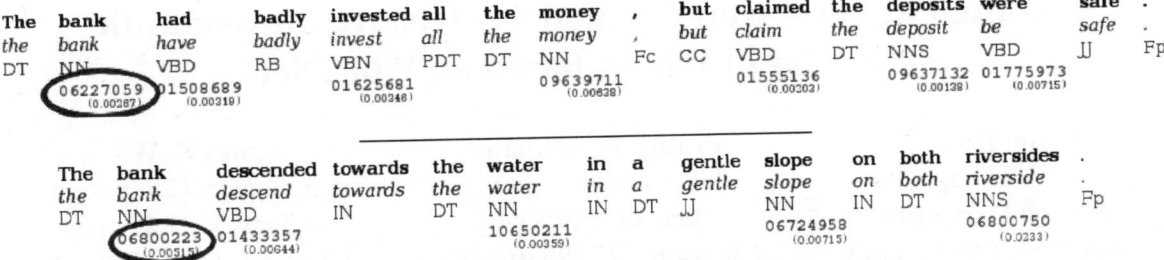

Figure 5: UKB disambiguation of *bank* in different contexts.

of-the-art UKB system (Agirre and Soroa, 2009). The open source licence of these software tools and their architecture, which completely separates code from linguistic data, makes it possible to easily adapt them to any domain or application needs, and provides a platform for affordable development of analyzers for new languages.

Acknowledgements

This work has been partially funded by the Spanish Science and Innovation Ministry, via the KNOW project (TIN2006-15049-C3-03). For further details visit http://ixa.si.ehu.es/know.

References

Eneko Agirre and Aitor Soroa. 2009. Personalizing pagerank for word sense disambiguation. In *Proceedings of the 12th conference of the European chapter of the Association for Computational Linguistics (EACL-2009)*, Athens, Greece.

Jordi Atserias, Elisabet Comelles, and Aingeru Mayor. 2005. Txala un analizador libre de dependencias para el castellano. *Procesamiento del Lenguaje Natural*, (35):455–456, September.

Jordi Carrera, Irene Castellón, Marina Lloberes, Lluís Padró, and Nevena Tinkova. 2008. Dependency grammars in freeling. *Procesamiento del Lenguaje Natural*, (41):21–28, September.

G. A. Miller, R. Beckwith, Christiane Fellbaum, D. Gross, K. Miller, and R. Tengi. 1991. Five papers on wordnet. *Special Issue of the International Journal of Lexicography*, 3(4):235–312.

Lluís Padró. 1998. *A Hybrid Environment for Syntax–Semantic Tagging*. Ph.D. thesis, Dep. Llenguatges i Sistemes Informàtics. Universitat Politècnica de Catalunya, February. http://www.lsi.upc.es/˜padro.

W.M. Soon, H. T. Ng, and D.C.Y. Lim. 2001. A machine learning approach to coreference resolution of noun phrases. *Computational Linguistics*, 27(4):521–544.

Javier Álvez, Jordi Atserias, Jordi Carrera, Salvador Climent, Egoitz Laparra, Antoni Oliver, and German Rigau. 2008. Complete and consistent annotation of wordnet using the top concept ontology. In *Proceedings of the the 6th Conference on Language Resources and Evaluation (LREC 2008)*, Marrakech (Morocco), May.

Weighted Edge: A New Method to Measure the Semantic Similarity of Words based on WordNet[1]

Liang Dong
School of Computing
Clemson University
Clemson, SC 29630, USA
+1-864-650-7580
ldong@cs.clemson.edu

Pradip K. Srimani[1]
School of Computing
Clemson University
Clemson, SC 29630, USA
+1-864-656-5886
srimani@cs.clemson.edu

James Z. Wang
School of Computing
Clemson University
Clemson, SC 29630, USA
+1-864-656-7678
jzwang@cs.clemson.edu

Abstract

Recent study shows that humans are more sensitive to the semantic difference due to categorization than that due to the generalization/specification. We propose a new method to measure the semantic similarity of word pairs based on this discovery. Our method assigns an exponential decreasing weight on each edge along the WordNet hierarchy to measure weighted graph distance between two concepts; it then computes the semantic similarity by employing a set of non-linear transfer functions. Experiments show that this method produces results superior to existing distance-based methods using only hypernym relationship.

1 Introduction

Computing semantic similarity between words has always been a challenge in many areas such as artificial intelligence, natural language processing and information retrieval. It is difficult to model the human perspective on the semantic similarity of words due to two reasons: (1) polysemy and synonymy phenomena widely exist in natural language; (2) psychologists have demonstrated that the human perception of the similarity between words is subject to the context.

Previous studies can be broadly divided into three categories: (1) *distance-based* methods (Rada et al., 1989; Morris and Hirst, 1991; Wu and Palmer, 1994; Yang and Powers, 2005; Alvarez and Lim, 2007) – these are based on the shortest graph distance of words within knowledge resources (dictionaries, thesauri or encyclopedias); (2) *gloss-based* methods (Banerjee and Pedersen, 2003; Patwardhan and Pedersen, 2006; Hughes and Ramage, 2007) – these are

---

[1]Srimani's work supported by NSF grant # CCF-0832582

based on the number of shared words ping with each other's gloss/definition; (3) *distribution-based* methods (Resnik, 1995; Jiang and Conrath, 1997; Lin, 1998; Resnik, 1999; Li et al., 2003; Sevilla et al., 2005) -- they measure the semantic similarity based on information content which is the frequency of occurrence in a corpus (Cilibrasi and Vitanyi, 2007; Gabrilovich and Markovitch, 2007; Wu et al., 2008; Agirre et al., 2009); they take advantage of concurrence statistics discovered from search engine.

We propose a simple yet effective distance-based method solely via hypernym relationship from WordNet (Fellbaum, 1998) without the need of gloss and corpus statistics. The method is based on an observation on the difference of human perception between *categorizing relation* and *inheriting relation* of word pairs. Our recent study shows that humans are more sensitive to the semantic difference due to the categorization than that due to the inheritance/specification. To capture this observation, we improve previous distance-based methods, by assigning non-linear weight on each edge by its depth in WordNet. Further, we introduce hyperbolic functions to transform weighted distances into similarity values. The proposed method has two advantages: (1) it distinguishes the difference between *categorizing relation* and *inheriting relation* of word pairs; (2) it solely relies on hypernym relationship within the WordNet, thus computationally more effective than those requiring extra computations of gloss or corpus statistics. Experimental studies show that our proposed method outperforms existing methods in distance-based category.

2 Weighted Edge Approach

2.1 Inheritance vs. Categorization

When two word-pairs have the same graph distance and their common ancestor are at the same specification level/depth, should any semantic difference exist between them? What is the human perception of it? None of the existing studies has investigated these issues.

To answer these questions, and to further study how human beings judge the semantic similarity of words, we group together two word-pairs that share the same *Least Common Ancestor* (*LCA*) and have the same graph distance between the words in each pair respectively. In one word-pair, the words are both descendents of their *LCA*. We call it *categorization pair* since both words are separated by *LCA* in different categories. In another word pair, one word is descendant of another word. We call it *inheritance pair*.

Inheritance Pair			*Categorization Pair*	
baked-goods :: cookie	30	⇔	bread :: cake	19
beef :: food	48	⇔	meat :: chocolate	2
brownie :: cake	44	⇔	cookie :: fruit-cake	5
ground beef :: meat	24	⇔	pork :: mutton	25
apple pie :: pastry	42	⇔	pie :: puff	8
stove :: device	41	⇔	comb :: fan	8
engine :: machine	18	⇔	computer :: calculator	33
hunting dog :: canine	27	⇔	wolf :: fox	22
minicab :: car	29	⇔	jeep :: sedan	21
gold :: metal	37	⇔	aluminum :: zinc	14
Total	**340**			**157**

Table 1. 2-distant pairs with same *LCA*

Inheritance Pair			*Categorization Pair*	
apple pie :: food	44	⇔	cake :: beef	3
clementine :: fruit	36	⇔	apple :: almond	15
chicken :: food	47	⇔	octopus :: pastry	0
dynamo :: machine	45	⇔	engine :: abacus	4
abbey :: building	26	⇔	hostel :: mansion	23
tabloid :: medium	8	⇔	broadcasting :: journalism	43
laptop :: computer	51	⇔	workstation :: chatroom	0
American football :: athletic game	36	⇔	golf :: basketball	14
cliff diving :: sports	44	⇔	hunting :: swimming	6
collegiate dictionary :: book	41	⇔	atlas :: bestseller	7
Total	**378**			**115**

Table 2. 4-distant pairs with same *LCA*

We collect 20 groups of such word-pairs. The graph distance of the word-pair in the first 10 groups is 2, as shown in Table 1. The graph distance of the second 10 groups, shown in Table 2, is 4. Then we randomly stop people in Clemson University campus and ask them to judge which pair in each group is more similar semantically. 51 individuals finished the questionnaire anonymously. In Table 1 and Table 2, each row contains a group of word-pairs. The left pair is the inheritance pair and the right pair is the categorization pair. The number in the second column represents the number of people who think the inheritance pair is more similar semantically. The number in the last column represents the number of people who feel the categorization pair is more similar. For those who feel both pairs are semantically equal or who cannot tell which pair is more similar, no number is added to any column. The survey results in Table 1 show that in 68.41% of cases, people think the inheritance pairs are more similar, and in only 31.59% of cases, people think the categorization pairs are more similar. The results in Table 2 demonstrate that in 76.67% of cases, people think that the inheritance pairs are more similar, and in only 23.33% of cases, people feel the categorization pairs are more similar.

Our survey results have revealed an important factor in determining the semantic similarity of words. That is, in general, people are more sensitive to the semantic difference caused by categorization than caused by inheritance. This is more obvious when the graph distance of the words gets larger. This important factor has never been considered in any previous studies.

2.2 Weighted Distance Model

In this paper, the similarity of a word pair is measured by their maximum similarity of their synset/concept pairs (Yang and Powers, 2005). Previous studies by Rada (1989) and Resnik (1999) select the concept pair by choosing the shortest graph distance among all concept pairs of a word pair. In our method, we select the concept pair with the highest specification level/depth of *common ancestor* first. This adjustment is based on the observation that the *depth* of *common ancestor* is the most dominant factor in semantic similarity (Li et al., 2003).

We define *Graph Distance* ($Dist_g$) of a concept pair be the number of edges on the shortest path connecting them; and we define *Specification Level (SpecLev)* of a concept as its depth in the WordNet. If a concept is closer to the root, it has a lower *SpecLev* in the WordNet and represents a more general meaning. Vice Versa, higher *SpecLev* represent more specific meanings. We further define *LCA* of a pair be the concept of that pair's least common ancestor along its path.

To reflect the true human perception in measuring the semantic similarity, we use *Specification Level Difference (SLD)* of concept-pair (c_1, c_2) to model the difference between categorization and inheritance:

$$SLD(c_1, c_2) = |SpecLev(c_1) - SpecLev(c_2)| \quad (1)$$

A small *SLD* means categorization factor is dominant, thus a relatively lower similarity value; and vice versa. Given a concept pair (c_1, c_2), with its *LCA* concept c_{lca}, the graph tance $Dist_g(c_i, c_j)$ is:

$$Dist_g(c_i, c_j) = SLD(c_i, c_{lca}) + SLD(c_j, c_{lca}) \quad (2)$$

From Equations (1) and (2), the three *SpecLev* of c_i, c_j, c_{lca} can represent both graph distance and *Specification Level Difference*. We then propose a non-linear weighted edge method to combine these three *SpecLev*s into a single *Weighted Edge Distance ($Dist_w$)*. We assign each hypernym edge in WordNet hierarchy a weighted value, which is a non-linear exponential decreasing value associated to its *SpecLev*, shown in Figure 1. A coefficient $\alpha \in (0,1]$ is set to represent the *weight decreasing rate* along the edge of WordNet hierarchy. The edge connecting two concepts at *SpecLev* k and $k+1$ has a weighted value α^k.

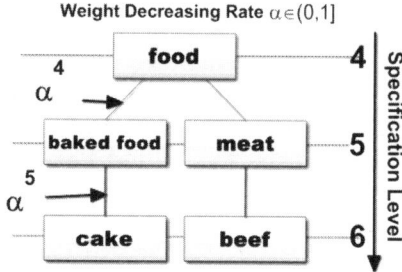

Figure 1. Non-linear Weight on the Edge

Using our weighted edge model, the *Weighted Edge Distance* is the sum of all the edge weight along its shortest path.

$$Dist_w(c_i, c_j) = \sum_{m=SpecLev(c_{lca})}^{SpecLev(c_i)-1} \alpha^m + \sum_{n=SpecLev(c_{lca})}^{SpecLev(c_j)-1} \alpha^n \quad (3)$$

Our weighted edge distance generalizes the traditional graph distance at $\alpha = 1$. When $\alpha \in (0,1)$, the edge value exponentially decreases with the increase of *SpecLev* in the hierarchy.

As illustrated in Figure 2, given two concept-pairs (c_1, c_2) and (c_3, c_4), which have the same *graph distance* and share the same *LCA*, but $SLD(c_1, c_2) = 0$ and $SLD(c_3, c_4) = 2$. We have:

$$\begin{aligned} Dist_w(c_1, c_2) - Dist_w(c_3, c_4) &= \alpha^k - \alpha^{k+1} \\ &= \alpha^k(1-\alpha) \geq 0, \alpha \in (0,1] \end{aligned} \quad (4)$$

Concept pair (c_1, c_2) has a larger weighted edge distance than that of pair (c_3, c_4). This result conforms to our discovery that humans are more sensitive to the semantic difference caused by categorization than that caused by inheritance.

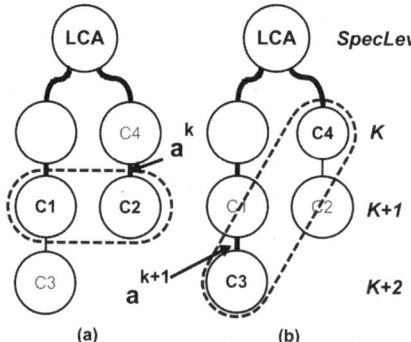

Figure 2. Weighted edge distance depicts difference between categorization and inheritance

2.3 New Transfer Function ϕ

New transfer functions are employed to calculate weighted edge distance to similarity value. We define the semantic similarity of word pair (w_i, w_j) be a function ϕ of its weighted edge distance $Dist_w$ of its max similar concept pair:

$$sim(w_i, w_j) = \phi(Dist_w(c_i, c_j)) \quad (5)$$

Two hyperbolic functions *Hyperbolic Secant* and *Hyperbolic Tangent Cardinal* are used as our transfer functions. Both hyperbolic functions are monotonically decreasing functions with range from 0 to 1.

3 Experimental Studies

3.1 The Benchmark Dataset

Checking the computed similarity against human judgments is a common practice in evaluating the similarity measurement techniques. Many previous studies (Jiang and Conrath, 1997; Lin, 1998; Resnik, 1999; Yang and Powers, 2005; Alvarez and Lim, 2007; Agirre et al., 2009) used either Rubenstein and Goodenough (1965) (RG set) or Miller-Charles (1991) (MC set) as the comparison baseline. In this paper, we conduct similar experiments using our proposed method on three different strategies and calculate the correlation between our computed similarities and the human judgments. Similar to Li's method (2003), we train the optimal parameter (Weighted Decreasing Rate) using the training set D_1 (37 word pairs in RG set but not in MC set), run on the testing set D_0 to get the correlation with human judgments.

3.2 Experiments on Different Strategies

To ensure the computed similarities obtained by transfer function matches the human judgments as closely as possible; we need to find an optimal Weighted Decreasing Rate α. We propose three different strategies. For each strategy, we use the training set D_1 to obtain the optimal α value. We vary α from 0.05 to 1 with an increment of 0.05, and calculate the correlation between the computed similarities and human judgments on training set D_1. The α value that yields the highest correlation between computed similarities and human judgments is selected as the optimal parameter. Previous studies (Li et al., 2003; Yang and Powers, 2005) need to tune multiple parameters to achieve high performance. In our method, the Weighted Decreasing Rate is the only parameter to tune. The optimal parameter obtained by training set D_1 will be used to calculate the semantic similarity values for word-pairs in testing set D_0. In the end, we calculate the correlations between the computed similarity values and MC human judgments on these word-pairs.

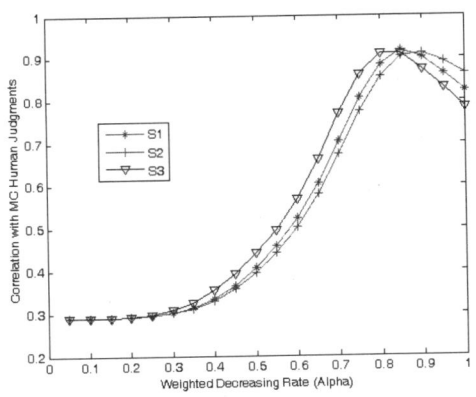

Figure 3. Correlations with human judgments with Weighted Decreasing Rate (α)

Strategy 1: This strategy uses *hyperbolic secant (Sech)* as transfer function:

$$\phi_1 = \operatorname{sech}(x) = \frac{2}{e^x + e^{-x}}$$

$$sim_1(w_i, w_j) = \phi_1(Dist_w(c_i, c_j))$$

As shown S1 in Figure 3, the computed similarities arrive the highest correlation with human judgments on training set D_1 when $\alpha = 0.85$.

Using this parameter to calculate the similarities of word-pairs in testing set D_0 we found their correlation with human judgments to be 0.8111.

Strategy 2: In this strategy, we employ the *Hyperbolic Tangent Cardinal (Tanhc)* function:

$$\phi_2 = \tanh c(x) = \begin{cases} \dfrac{e^x - e^{-x}}{(e^x + e^{-x}) \cdot x}, & x \neq 0 \\ 1, & x = 0 \end{cases}$$

$$sim_2(w_i, w_j) = \phi_2(Dist_w(c_i, c_j))$$

As shown S2 in Figure 3, when α = 0.9, the computed similarities have the highest correlations with human judgments on training set D_1. Using this parameter to calculate the semantic similarities of word pairs in testing set D_0, we found their correlation with human judgments to be 0.8247. This confirms that a better non-linear function can improve the semantic similarity measure.

Strategy 3: The final strategy combines Strategy 1 and Strategy 2 by multiplying the non-linear functions used by these two strategies. The similarity is calculated as:

$$sim_3(w_i, w_j) = \phi_1(Dist_w(c_i, c_j)) \cdot \phi_2(Dist_w(c_i, c_j))$$

As shown S3 in Figure 3, when α = 0.85, the computed similarities have the highest correlation with the human judgments on training set D_1. Using α = 0.85, we calculate the similarities of word pairs in testing set D_0 and found their correlation with human judgments is 0.8350, which is the highest among all strategies tested. The correlations between the computed similarity values and the human judgments on testing set D_0 using four different strategies are summarized in Table 3.

Strategy	Sim_1 $\alpha = 0.85$	Sim_2 $\alpha = 0.9$	Sim_3 $\alpha = 0.85$
Correlation	0.8111	0.8247	0.8350

Table 3. Correlations between computed similarity values and human judgments on testing set D_0 using different strategies

4 Conclusion and Future work

We present a simple yet effective Weighted Edge method to measure the semantic similarity of word pairs solely using pure hypernym relationship in WordNet. This method is based on an observation that human perception are more sensitive to the semantic difference caused by categorization than specification. The experimental results outperform previous studies only employing hypernym relationship. Our future work will take extra meronym (part-of) relationship and gloss factors into consideration. Besides, we will conduct future experiments on Similarity353 dataset.

References

Agirre, E., E. Alfonseca, et al. 2009. A study on similarity and relatedness using distributional and WordNet-based approaches. Proceedings of Human Language Technologies: The 2009 Annual Conference of the North American Chapter of the Association for Computational Linguistics. Boulder, Colorado, Association for Computational Linguistics.

Alvarez, M., A. and S. Lim. 2007. A Graph Modeling of Semantic Similarity between Words. Proceedings of the International Conference on Semantic Computing, IEEE Computer Society.

Banerjee, S. and T. Pedersen. 2003. Extended gloss overlaps as a measure of semantic relatedness. *the Eighteenth International Joint Conference on Artificial Intelligence*, Acapulco, Mexico.

Cilibrasi, R. L. and P. M. B. Vitanyi. 2007. "The Google similarity distance." *Ieee Transactions on Knowledge and Data Engineering* 19(3): 370-383.

Fellbaum, C. 1998. WordNet: An Electronic Lexical Database and Some of its Applications. Cambridge, Mass, MIT Press.

Gabrilovich, E. and S. Markovitch. 2007. Computing Semantic Relatedness using Wikipedia-based Explicit Semantic Analysis *Proceedings of The Twentieth International Joint Conference for Artificial Intelligence*.

Hughes, T. and D. Ramage. 2007. Lexical Semantic Relatedness with Random Graph Walks. *the 2007 Joint Conference on Empirical Methods in Natural Language Processing and Computational Natural Language Learning*, Prague.

Jiang, J. J. and D. W. Conrath. 1997. Semantic Similarity Based on Corpus Statistics and Lexical Taxonomy *Proc. ROCLING X*.

Li, Y. H., Z. A. Bandar, et al. 2003. "An approach for measuring semantic similarity between words using multiple information sources." *Ieee Transactions on Knowledge and Data Engineering* 15(4): 871-882.

Lin, D. 1998. An Information-Theoretic Definition of Similarity. *In Proceedings of the 15th International Conference on Machine Learning*, Morgan Kaufmann.

Miller, G. A. and W. G. Charles. 1991. "Contextual Correlates of Semantic Similarity." *Language and Cognitive Processes* 6(1): 1-28.

Morris, J. and G. Hirst. 1991. "Lexical Cohesion Computed by Thesaural Relations as an Indicator of the Structure of Text." *Computational Linguistics* 17(1): 21-48.

Patwardhan, S. and T. Pedersen. 2006. Using WordNet-based Context Vectors to Estimate the Semantic Relatedness of Concepts. *EACL 2006 Workshop Making Sense of Sense---Bringing Computational Linguistics and Psycholinguistics Together*, Trento, Italy.

Rada, R., H. Mili, et al. 1989. "Development and Application of a Metric on Semantic Nets." *Ieee Transactions on Systems Man and Cybernetics* 19(1): 17-30.

Resnik, P. 1995. Using Information Content to Evaluate Semantic Similarity in a Taxonomy. *In Proceedings of the 14th International Joint Conference on Artificial Intelligence*.

Resnik, P. 1999. "Semantic similarity in a taxonomy: An information-based measure and its application to problems of ambiguity in natural language." *Journal of Artificial Intelligence Research* 11: 95-130.

Rubenste.H and Goodenou.Jb. 1965. "Contextual Correlates of Synonymy." *Communications of the Acm* 8(10): 627-&.

Sevilla, J. L., V. Segura, et al. 2005. "Correlation between gene expression and GO semantic similarity." *Ieee-Acm Transactions on Computational Biology and Bioinformatiocs* 2(4): 330-338.

Wu, L., S. H. Hua, et al. 2008. Flickr distance. *Proceeding of the 16th ACM international conference on Multimedia*, Vancouver, British Columbia, Canada

Wu, Z. and M. Palmer. 1994. Verbs semantics and lexical selection. Proceedings of the 32nd annual meeting on Association for Computational Linguistics. Las Cruces, New Mexico, Association for Computational Linguistics.

Yang, D. and D. Powers, M. W. 2005. Measuring semantic similarity in the taxonomy of WordNet. Proceedings of the Twenty-eighth Australasian conference on Computer Science - Volume 38. Newcastle, Australia, Australian Computer Society, Inc.

LOOK4: Enhancement of Web Search Results with Universal Words and WordNet

Aram Avetisyan
Institute of Informatics and
Automation Problems of NAS RA
/ Yerevan, Armenia
a.avetisyan@undlfoundation.org

Vahan Avetisyan
Technical Manager
UNDL Foundation
/ Geneva, Switzerland
v.avetisyan@undlfoundation.org

Abstract

In this paper we present some results gained from an ongoing experimental project called Look4 that is aimed to enhance the results that we get from popular web search engines by means of a network of concepts, derived from the ontology of WordNet 2.1. We also present some sample statistics and achievements in the fields of multilingual search (Karande Jalindar Baban, 2007) and word sense disambiguation. The key approach for the construction of the concept network is the use of a network from Universal Words (UW) of Universal Networking Language (UNL) (Uchida H. and Zhu M, 2005).

1 Introduction

Today the use of web search engines is an essential part of the ordinary life. It is hard to underestimate the tremendous role they have for internet users. Nevertheless, the merit of these search engines still bypasses essential groups of people lacking the knowledge of the languages that most information is represented in. These limitations affect not only multilingualism of the web but also illustrate the problem of Word Sense Disambiguation (WSD) (Agirre Eneko and David Martinez, 2000) at its best.

In our attempt to find a solution we have used some existing resources such as online services provided by major search engines, semantic ontology of WordNet (Christiane Fellbaum. 1998) and flexibility of UNL for representation of semantic relations among concepts.

Currently many major search providers such as Google or Yahoo have opened their services for the community of developers worldwide. This gives us countless possibilities for research and statistical analysis. In our project we have used these services as a basis for the improvements to come. On the other hand, we have the data from the WordNet which gives us a good chance to get our hands on a structured representation of concepts. Although the WordNet 2.1 is based on the concepts of English, it is still one of the most essential ontological resources available for public use nowadays, and it might be a good basis for something more generic in the future. In any case, in this paper we will not address the questions concerning WordNet or search engines and will try to show their use the way they are.

Thus, if we project these resources on human mind, we'll get the *memory* (keyword search engine) and the *perception of the concept ontology* (WordNet). Now let's *associate* them. In other words let's try to connect what we *understand* with what we *remember*. To do this we will use UNL syntax which serves for representing the relations among concepts. Let's call this the Association Structure.

2 Resources

To build a so called Association Structure we have considered two major resources.

I) The extraction of concepts and relations among them from WordNet 2.1 into a so called Concept Network or UNL WordNet (4). During this extraction all original information is considered. The words are taken as concepts and the relations among the words are marked by means of corresponding UNL relations. The Concept Network data is stored into several SQL tables connected with many-to-many relations.

The concepts with their ontological references form UWs. For example, the concept of *apple fruit* has the following ontology:

```
(Example: 1)
apple > edible fruit;
edible fruit > fruit;
fruit > reproductive structure;
reproductive    structure   >   plant
organ;
plant organ > plant part;
plant part > natural object;
...
```

So the UW for apple can be
`apple(icl>edible fruit)`
or
`apple(icl>edible fruit>fruit)`
or
`apple(icl>edible fruit>fruit>...)`
depending on the ambiguity of the referenced concepts.

Another solution for the ambiguity of the concept names can be the usage of unique numeric IDs with or instead of the strings in English (6).

The many-to-many table structure gives us the flexibility to manage the generation of UWs depending on our needs in the future.

Thus, with this transformation we have a Concept Network which can be searched and navigated by the relations among the Concepts (UWs). Image 1 illustrates the relation browser which is used for navigating over the hyperbolic tree representing the surroundings of the focused concept node.

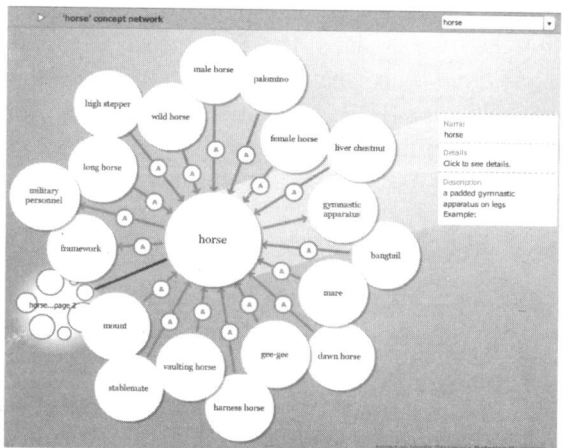

Image 1. Relation browser

II) Another important resource required for the multilingual search is the data on alignment of the UWs with words from the natural language dictionaries. This may be the most expensive task in terms of resources involved, so we have worked on a limited set of dictionaries and natural languages so far.

The dictionary entries are stored in the SQL tables with reference IDs of corresponding UWs.

3 Search Implementation

Now, after the resources are provided the system implements the search in three steps:

I) It tries to "understand" what user is looking for. This is done by an interaction with the user. The system illustrates all possible meanings (UWs) of the searched keyword (image 2). Besides the meaning there is also a possibility to choose a target language (image 3). The realization of the search query is being done by use of attached natural language dictionaries. All entries described in these dictionaries are referencing the synset ids from WordNet representing UWs.

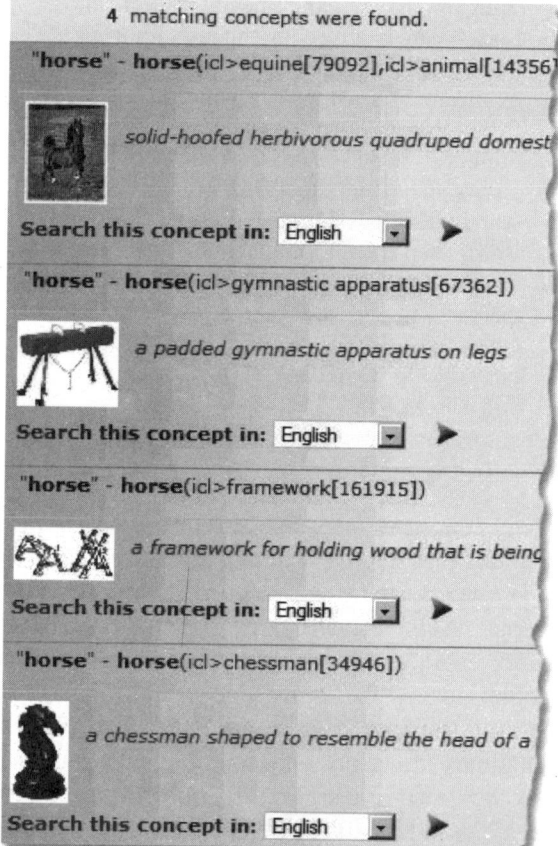

Image 2. Search keywords disambiguation

User can select the meaning he's interested in and the language in which he'd like to see the results (image 3). For example, if the keyword "*horse*" was searched the user will be prompt with several possible meanings for it (such as *animal, gymnastic apparatus, chess piece* etc).

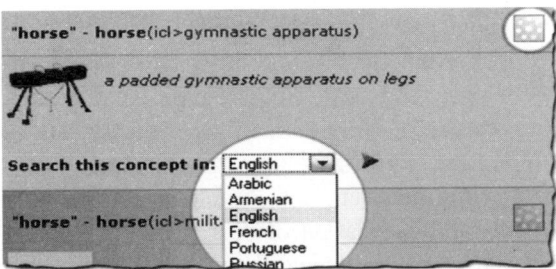

Image 3. Suggested concept

Now, if he is looking for a *gymnastic apparatus* called *"horse"*, he will have to select that exact meaning.

II) After the indications by the user the system generates a more detailed query. In this query the referenced concepts are also included. The new sets of keywords are being translated into target language with corresponding instructions for the search engine, restricting the natural language domain and the priorities of the keywords. For translation the attached NL dictionaries are being used. This operation is dependent on the targeted search engine query specifications.

III) After the new query is generated it is being sent to the search web service and the results in the selected language are being illustrated (Image 4).

Image 4. Multilingual text search results.

4 Results

To evaluate the results we have used the list of most common ambiguous English words from WordNet, which can be found at: http://muse.dillfrog.com/ambiguous_words.php. Here we have selected first 50 words and have done some search in 3 major search engines (Google, Yahoo and Bing). After getting the results for each ambiguous word we have manually analyzed first 50 links to see what are the semantics of the words within the page contexts. Then we have searched the same meanings for the selected words using look4. The

Table 1 illustrates the results for 10 words from the ambiguous word list. The average accuracy level percentage directly from search engines is brought in the "SE avg.". The results gained using Look4 are shown in the "Look4"column.

"root" as	Look4	SE avg.
plant organ	94%	25%
the beginning	40%	30%
root number	94%	4%
other	-	41%
"break" as	Look4	SE avg.
separation	78%	17%
pause	95%	37%
escape	93%	13%
other	-	41%
"cut" as	Look4	SE avg.
decrease	72%	8%
wound	91%	10%
editing	94%	46%
other	-	36%
"charge" as	Look4	SE avg.
cost	92%	17%
electrical phenomenon	100%	20%
attack	89%	13%
other	-	60%
"check" as	Look4	SE avg.
inspection	93%	56%
mark	85%	8%
chess move	68%	4%
other	-	32%
"right"	Look4	SE avg.
position	75%	28%
correctness	31%	16%
law	66%	46%
other	-	10%
"ground" as	Look4	SE avg.
coat of paint	82%	1%
connection	94%	2%
material	72%	53%
other	-	34%
"table" as	Look4	SE avg.
furniture	85%	18%
array	99%	75%
fare	62%	6%
other	-	1%
"scratch" as	Look4	SE avg.
blemish	97%	25%
money	38%	2%
handwriting	83	3%
other	-	70%
"horse" as	Look4	SE avg.
animal	95%	95%
gymnastic apparatus	75%	0%
framework	10%	0%
knight	85%	0%
other	-	5%
AVARAGE	**80.6%**	**21.7%**

Table 1. The comparison of average accuracy

from search engines versus Look4.

Thus, by getting approximately 60% increased precision level it is clear that the experiment was successful. Of course it is obvious that a similar or even higher level of precision can be achieved when providing additional keywords to the search engines manually, but, again, let's remember about the linguistic barrier that exists for an essential part of today's internet users. Also it is important to mention that the results are brought for English only. As for the other languages, tests show that they're highly language dependant. The main factor is the amount of available resources on the web. Some meanings of the words might be never met in any web pages of particular language. Another issue of course is the completeness of attached NL dictionaries.

5   Competitors

Nowadays there are several search engines on the web that provide semantic search. We have studied the most popular ones to compare the result. So what is the main advantage of Look4 over engines like Hakia, Powerset, SenseBot and DeepDive. The generic issue with these engines is that the categorization of the semantic meanings in these engines are done on the statistical bases and cover mainly the most common cases. This approach decreases the coverage of possible meanings. The WordNet is providing a broader coverage for meanings than any of these engines. Another advantage of the Look4 is that it is based on independent and open resources like WordNet and existing open search engines. Which means the advancement of the results in parallel with these resources.

6   The Perspective

To indicate the perspective for the future development of the Look4 system we'll indicate the limitations that exist in its current implementation.

- Considering that the WordNet 2.1 is mainly based on English. It is obvious that the results are reflecting the perception of an English speaker. Of course this issue is not new, and has been addressed in a number of publications. WordNets have been created for several languages reflecting different semantic structures derived from different natural languages. And it is of course a matter of great interest to use them in the Look4 and to compare the results (especially for multilingual search). Thus, it is obvious that the Look4 system itself is somewhat language dependant as far as it uses The English WordNet ontology. On the other hand, again, if we compare the Look4's functionality to a human interpretation, any human translator also has a stamp of the culture and language it belongs to.

- In the current implementation the analysis and translation of search input is being done keyword-by-keyword which limits the possibilities for searching multiword expressions. As a solution in the next stage of this project we plan to integrate UNL modules for analysis (IAN) and generation (EUGENE) (Ronaldo Martins. Vahan Avetisyan. 2009) of natural language texts, which are being developed in a parallel project. These modules will provide some basic translation of the search expressions based on the results of their semantic analysis.

- As UNL provides possibility of storing semantic contents of texts, it is quite interesting to search available corpuses of UNL data based not just on keyword matching, but also on the semantic relations among the concepts in texts and in search expressions. The major issues in this field are is the time and human resources that will be needed to analyze and create essential corpuses to be searched and the expensiveness of graph matching algorithms (the semantic representation of the sentences are graphs). Currently, the research works are being done to resolve these issues.

References

Agirre Eneko and David Martinez. 2000. *Exploring automatic word sense disambiguation with decision lists and the Web In: Proceedings of the Semantic Annotation And Intelligent Annotation workshop.* COLING, Luxembourg.

Christiane Fellbaum. 1998. *WordNet. An Electronic Lexical Database.* MIT.

Karande Jalindar Baban. 2007. *Multilingual search engine: implementation using UNL* http://drtc.isibang.ac.in:8080/xmlui/handle/1849/393.

Ronaldo Martins. 2008. *UNL Wordnet* Mackenzie University – São Paulo – Brazil. http://www.ronaldomartins.pro.br/unlwordnet/UNLWordNet.pdf .

Ronaldo Martins. Vahan Avetisyan. 2009. *Generative and Enumerative Lexicons in the UNL Framework* CSIT 2009, Yerevan Armenia.

Ronaldo Martins. 2008. *Knowledge Vertices in XUNL*. Conference on Information and Knowledge Management, Proceeding of the 2008 ACM workshop on Research advances in large digital book repositories. Napa Valley, California, USA,

Uchida H. and Zhu M. 2005 *The Universal Networking Language (UNL) specifications*. version 7. UNDL Foundation.

Similarity, Comparability and Analogy in WordNet: Squaring the Analogical Circle with *Mondrian*

Tony Veale
School of Computer Science and Informatics
University College Dublin, Ireland.
Tony.Veale@UCD.ie

Mourad el Moueddeb
School of Computer Science and Informatics
University College Dublin, Ireland.
meddebmourad@gmail.com

Abstract

Similarity and comparability are complementary notions that are easy to confuse and difficult to tease apart. Semantic similarity makes comparison meaningful, while comparison is often the pragmatic means through which similarity is perceived and constructed. To date, WordNet has found wide application as a basis for modeling and measuring semantic similarity, but is lacking as a basis for well-formed comparability judgments. In this paper we describe a corpus-based approach to learning a model of sensible comparability, and show how this pragmatic model can be integrated with a WordNet-based notion of semantic similarity. We go on to show how this model of comparability, called *Mondrian*, provides a convenient and efficient means of supporting simple relational analogies between WordNet terms, and how analogies of this kind can be used for the automatic acquisition of enriching relational knowledge in WordNet.

1 Introduction

WordNet is much more than a large list of words, though it is often conveniently used as such in computational contexts. Indeed, it is also much more than an electronic dictionary, since it attempts to place an ontological order onto its inventory of word senses (Fellbaum, 1998). This organization, which is best realized in the taxonomic ordering of noun-senses as a relatively deep IS-A hierarchy, allows WordNet to be used as a lightweight knowledge representation in natural-language processing (NLP) and Artificial Intelligence (AI) systems (e.g., Veale, 2004). Despite any misgivings one might have about viewing WordNet as an ontological model of the world, this taxonomic organization allows WordNet to be used as a robust and efficient basis for semantic similarity judgments that are broadly consistent with human intuition (Miller and Charles, 1991).

The biggest advantage of this approach to similarity – and the reason it has been so widely embraced in NLP/AI applications – is that WordNet can be used to provide a numeric similarity judgment for any two terms that one cares to provide, no matter how dissimilar or oddly-paired they may seem (see Budanitsky and Hirst, 2006). Thus, whether one is comparing prawns and protons or galaxies and footballs, WordNet can be used to provide a reasonably sensible measure of their semantic similarity. These measures are relative, of course, so that one can know that protons are much more similar to electrons than they are to crustaceans. If used sensibly, with meaningful thresholds and cut-offs, WordNet-based similarity measures can play a vital role in many different NLP contexts.

The biggest *disadvantage* to this approach is also its biggest advantage: WordNet can be used to provide a numeric similarity judgment for any two terms at all, no matter how silly the comparison may seem. The space of meaningful comparisons is much smaller than the space of possible comparisons for which WordNet can provide a non-zero similarity judgment. This is fine in some contexts, in which we can trust the client application to only seek similarity measures for term pairs it has good reason to compare. In others, however, a strong semantic similarity score may be used to imply the comparability of terms that no human would ever sensibly compare.

Comparisons between ideas with a high semantic similarity are often fatuous, while comparisons between ideas with low semantic similarity can be highly insightful if used as the basis for a revealing metaphor or analogy (e.g., as when we compare the densely packed protons in an atom's nucleus to the plums in a fruit pudding). From the perspective of analogy *interpretation*, WordNet-based similarity offers limited insights into why two relational structures are comparable (see Veale, 2004, 2006; Turney, 2005), though a numeric measure of semantic similarity does go some way toward quantifying the creative tension exhibited by an analogy (e.g., the low score for plums and protons indicates a considerable analogical leap). In contrast, WordNet-based similarity offers nothing at all to the process of analogy *generation*, since a measure that assigns non-zero similarity to so many term-pairs can hardly be used to pick out a selective few for analogical consideration. A robust measure that is not selective in what it is willing to compare cannot then be selective in the suggestions it makes to a sensitive comparison mechanism like creative analogy generation.

1.1 Goals and Structure of this Paper

In this paper we seek to temper the broadness of WordNet-based semantic similarity to produce a more selective and pragmatically-guided measure of semantic *comparability*. In section 2 we review related work and ideas in re-making similarity as a pragmatic, corpus-based measure, before describing our own approach in this vein in section 3. Section 4 presents the *Mondrian* system, which uses comparability to support analogical reasoning, and in turn uses analogical reasoning (as supported by comparability) to support further knowledge-acquisition. In section 5 we then show how this measure can be used in a process of targeted knowledge-acquisition for enriching WordNet and other lexical ontologies with relational content. We conclude with a summary and some closing remarks in section 6.

2 Related Work and Ideas

Since WordNet organizes its noun-senses according to a hierarchical system of categories, this permits measures of semantic similarity to be operationalized in terms of the categories that are shared by two given terms. Measures differ in how these shared categories are exploited (see Budanitsky and Hirst for a menu of different possibilities): one might consider the minimum link-distance that must be traversed to find the most specific common category of two senses, or the size and generality of the shared categorization (where specific categories imply greater similarity than more general ones), or the *information content* of the categories concerned (e.g., it is more informative to say that two terms denote *mammals* than it is to say that they both denote *animals*). Resnick (1995) looks outside WordNet, to representative text corpora, to determine the extrinsic information content of a term like *animal* or *mammal*, while Seco, Veale and Hayes (2004) use WordNet itself as an intrinsic basis for determining information content, with comparable (but more convenient) results.

But one does not need a curated knowledge-source like WordNet to make sensible similarity judgments. The distributional hypothesis suggests that two words are similar to the extent that they are used in similar contexts (and co-texts) and with the same, or similar, lexical associations (see Weeds and Weir, 2005). Distributional similarity can cut across pre-defined taxonomic structures, to better reflect the dynamics of how words and concepts are actually used in context. For instance, the words "knife", "stove", "tent" and "backpack" are all used in camping contexts, and collectively represent the ad-hoc category *things one takes on a camping trip* (see Barsalou, 1983). An approach based on WordNet alone would be quite inadequate to the task of providing "more words like these" (such as "fishing-pole", "poncho" and "boots") because the context shared by these words, and which makes these words contextually similar, is not shared by WordNet.

The distributional approach can also be ratcheted up to the higher level of relational similarity required for analogical reasoning, in which one compares not terms but term pairs, each pair (such as *jury:verdict* or *courier:package*) representing an implicit relation (such as *delivers*) that must be matched. WordNet-based semantic similarity can only get one so far with these SAT-style analogical problems; Veale (2004) reports results in the 38-44% range using WordNet on a collection of 374 test analogies provided by Peter Turney and Michael Littman, while Turney himself (2005) uses a distributional approach to achieve higher scores approaching human levels of competence on the same test data. Turney uses an approach dubbed *Latent Relational Analysis* (LRA) in which a vector space of distributional features is derived from corpora or web text, and then smoothed using singular value decomposition (SVD).

Though convincing on SAT analogies and other interpretative/evaluative tasks, LRA is not a generative mechanism that can be used to suggest comparable relationships for given term pairs. That is, while it can provide strong results when evaluating comparisons posed by others, it is not (yet) a mechanism that can pose its own comparisons or suggest its own metaphors and analogies. In the sections to follow, we present a simpler corpus-based model of comparison that acquires knowledge of what terms can meaningfully be compared from textual evidence.

3   Learning to Compare from Corpora

WordNet-based similarity measures are decidedly semantic and objective, uninfluenced as they are by more subjective, pragmatic considerations. Any given measurement will implicate just a small number of static category structures, such as *mammal* when comparing *cats* and *dogs*, or *vehicle* when comparing *cars* and *buses*. In contrast, distributed corpus-based approaches implicitly capture the myriad contexts in which we experience two terms/ideas in similar ways. For instance, *pirates, astronauts* and *cowboys* are all semantically similar by virtue of being *human beings*, but are pragmatically similar for a variety of tacit cultural reasons, not least because they represent dashing heroic types that make for "cool" central characters in movies and books, while also making for "cool" costumes on Halloween. The distributed approach is successful because we cannot hope to articulate all the reasons why two terms are pragmatically comparable, much less express these reasons as static category structures in a system like WordNet.

Yet, we desire a representation of similarity that explicitly links terms that are considered comparable within the representation. Recall that the space of pragmatically comparable terms is not the same as the space of semantically similar terms. Since humans only meaningfully compare a tiny subset of the terms that are semantically similar (i.e., that have a non-zero similarity score), we can represent this comparability space as a sparse matrix. This will allow the evaluation of inter-term similarity to be modelled as an efficient look-up of a given cell in the matrix, while the generation of similar terms can likewise be modeled as a look up of the entire (albeit sparse) row corresponding to a given comparison target.

Figure 1 presents a snapshot of such a sparse comparability matrix. Every row corresponds to a different term, as does every column, while the numeric value in each cell (0 … 1) corresponds to the semantic similarity of the corresponding row/column terms. The similarity of a term to itself is 1.0, while the semantic similarity of all other terms is pre-computed using any one of the WordNet measures (at the developer's discretion) described in Budanitsky and Hirst (2006). As such, the numeric values in Figure 1 are all *semantic* similarity scores. But while semantics, not pragmatics, determines these numeric values, the choice of cells to fill is entirely determined by pragmatic factors. Of the 64 cells shown in Figure 1, 42 (or 65%) contain zeros, not because the corresponding term pairs have no semantic similarity, but because they are not deemed to be comparable. The matrix is large, but very sparse.

	A	B	C	D	E	F	G	H	...
A	1.0	0	0	0	0	0	0	0	...
B	0	1.0	0.7	0	0	0.2	0.3	0	...
C	0	0.7	1.0	0	0.4	0	0	0.15	...
D	0	0	0	1.0	0	0	0	0.2	...
E	0	0	0.4	0	1.0	0	0	0	...
F	0	0.2	0	0	0	1.0	0	0.65	...
G	0	0.3	0	0	0	0	1.0	0	...
H	0	0	0.15	0.2	0	0.65	0	1.0	...
...	...	...	...	...	...	...	...	...	

Figure 1. A sparse comparability matrix. Cells contain WordNet-based similarity scores, and are filled on the basis of explicit linguistic evidence.

A given cell holds a non-zero value if the corresponding terms have a non-zero similarity score *and* there is linguistic evidence that the terms are comparable. A myriad subtle factors influence whether one term is comparable to another: are they defined at the same level of specification? Are they inter-changeable in some respect? Do they denote cultural counterparts of one another? We short-circuit this complexity by noting that if any of these (or similar) criteria hold, then we should observe that the terms will tend to be used in the same linguistic contexts by speakers. More specifically, we should observe that the terms will be clustered into the same ad-hoc sets. For instance, we can observe coordinations such as "*scientists and artists*", "*robots and clones*", "*imams and priests*", "*mosques and synagogues*" and "*pirates and cowboys*". Sets like these indicate that a speaker believes the given elements to belong to the same semantic/pragmatic category, even if, in a resource like WordNet, the elements do not share a direct hypernym.

Set-building linguistic constructs such as coordination provide evidence of fine-grained pragmatically-motivated categorizations that a resource like WordNet cannot. Such constructions provide the basis for *Google Sets*, an online tool that allows Google to perform on-demand set completion (see Tong and Dean, 2008). Given a sampling of terms, such as "hamburger" and "pizza", *Google Sets* can infer the implicit category and flesh out the set with additional members such as "taco" and "hotdog". Google also uses this set completion functionality in its online spreadsheet (part of *Google Docs*), allowing a user to specify some values in a column before asking Google to automatically fill it with other values from the same implicit category.

We use the coordination construction to find evidence that two terms can reside in the same ad-hoc set, and thus the same pragmatic category. Google's database of web n-grams (see Brants and Franz, 2006) provides a very large corpus from which to harvest these coordinations. In effect, we harvest all plural coordinations of the form "*Xs and Ys*" (where X and Y are common nouns, as in "*cats and dogs*" or "*zoos and circuses*") and all singular proper coordinations of the form "*X and Y*" (where X and Y are capitalized proper nouns, as in "*Paris and London*" or "*Zeus and Jupiter*"). For each pairing X and Y, we calculate a WordNet-based similarity score and populate the comparability matrix accordingly. In all, the n-grams yield coordinations involving 35,019 different terms, producing a matrix with 35,019 rows and 35,019 columns.

In practice, the matrix is sparse and only a small fraction of these cells are populated. In fact, just 1,363,184 cells have non-zero values, giving the matrix a density of just 0.1%. This matrix is thus compact enough to store in memory, yet contains all of the most plausible comparisons a system is ever likely to consider.

4 Analogical Comparisons in Mondrian

Broadly speaking, coordination patterns provide two different kinds of associations that can be useful for making and understanding comparisons: *substitutive* associations and *contiguous* associations. Substitutive associations are those that suggest that one term might be used as a substitution for another in a simile, metaphor or analogy. For instance, the coordinations "*priests and scientists*", "*scientists and artists*", "*artists and anarchists*", "*churches and mosques*", "*angels and demons*", "*spires and minarets*" and "*rituals and experiments*" all seem to suggest cross-domain equivalences while suggesting alternate ways of looking at a given term / concept. In some contexts then. it might be meaningful (if only figuratively) to view scientists as priests, or experiments as rituals, or artists as anarchists. While substitutive associations often cross domain boundaries, *contiguous* associations relate a term to another term in the same domain. For instance, the coordinations "*mosques and minarets*", "*imams and mosques*", "*artists and studios*", "*priests and sacrifices*" and "*scientists and laboratories*" each express a kind of semantic relatedness rather than strict semantic similarity. Mosques are not similar to imams (at least not in the way that imams are similar to priests), but they are highly related to imams. As such, contiguous associations are better suited to the generation of metonymies than they are to similes, metaphors or analogies.

The comparability matrix contains both kinds of association in abundance; since both arise from the same coordination construction, the matrix does not (and cannot) distinguish the substitutive from the contiguous variety. However, as a rough heuristic, substitutive associations will exhibit high semantic similarity scores (e.g., > .6), while contiguous associations will exhibit much lower similarity scores (e.g., < .25). Figure 2 highlights elements of the Figure 1 matrix that exhibit substitutability because of high similarity (shown with bold lines) and contiguity because of low similarity (shown with dashed lines).

	A	B	C	D	E	F	G	H	...
A	1.0	0	0	0	0	0	0	0	...
B	0	1.0	0.7	0	0	0.2	0.3	0	...
C	0	0.7	1.0	0	0.4	0	0	0.15	...
D	0	0	0	1.0	0	0	0	0.2	...
E	0	0	0.4	0	1.0	0	0	0	...
F	0	0.2	0	0	0	1.0	0	0.65	...
G	0	0.3	0	0	0	0	1.0	0	...
H	0	0	0.15	0.2	0	0.65	0	1.0	...
...	...	...	...	...	...	...	...	...	...

Figure 2. Analogical connections in a comparability matrix. B is highly similar to C, just as H is to F, while B is related to F and C to H.

In Figure 2 we see that B and C have strong similarity (= 0.7), and are seen as comparable because of the linguistic evidence "*Bs and Cs*". F and H are likewise strongly similar (= 0.65). In turn, B and F are weakly similar (= 0.2), as are C and H (= 0.15), while the patterns *"Bs and Fs"* and *"Cs and Hs"* suggests that B and F, as well as C and H, are contiguous in the same domains. In other words, a squaring relationship holds between B, C, F and H: B is contiguous to F, which is strongly similar to H, which is contiguous to C, which is strongly similar to B. This associative square pattern is visible in Figure 2.

As shown by Veale and Keane (1997), this squaring pattern is capable of efficiently leveraging local relationships into global analogical structures. Moreover, the squaring approach, captured here in a model we name *Mondrian*, explicitly views analogical mapping as a data-mining process, in which small regularities of structure are identified in large masses of knowledge that are largely irrelevant to the given analogy. In other words, Mondrian views analogical reasoning as a problem of data-mining in the comparability matrix. Given a starting point B, say, Mondrian can seek out terms that complete the square C, F and H; likewise, given a contiguous relation B:F, Mondrian can find the corresponding relation C:H by examining all comparable terms B and F that also happen to be contiguous. In the most restricted, and efficient, cases, Mondrian can complete the analogical square B:F::C:?, as in the following examples:

```
priest : church  :: imam      : ?   (A: mosque)
mosque : minaret :: church    : ?   (A: spire)
  chef : recipe  :: scientist : ?   (A: formula)
school : bus     :: hospital  : ?   (A: ambulance)
```

Analogical completion is not a deterministic process, and even the most constrained examples above can yield several competing answers (e.g., perhaps a tower or a steeple is a church's answer to a minaret). So it is necessary to rank potential analogies according to their overall similarity. For instance, we might estimate the quality of an analogy based on the quality of the substitutions it involves, as in the following measure:

$$subst\_sim(B:F::C:H) = sim(B, C) \times sim(F, H)$$

However, this *subst_sim* measure does not take into account the actual nature of the contiguous relations between B and F or C and H. For example, the *mosque:minaret::church:spire* analogy implicitly hinges on the fact that minarets are tall, slender parts of a mosque, while spires are likewise tall slender parts of a church. The *part_of* relation is not explicitly coded here, but the pragmatic comparability of minarets and spires means that they are largely interchangeable in many contexts. Nonetheless, without knowledge of the specific relationships between B and F or C and H, we cannot be sure that the analogy is sound. But whatever this relation happens to be, we can expect that if it imposes specific selectional preferences, then the relative similarity of B to F will be comparable to that of C to H. So while mosques relate to minarets in different ways than they relate to imams or mullahs, we can exploit the fact that they are also more similar to minarets than to imams or mullahs. An analogy can thus hinge on a higher-level equivalence of lower-level similarities, suggesting a measure of *balance* such as the following:

$$balance(B:F::C:H) = \frac{min(sim(B, F), sim(C, H))}{max(sim(B, F), sim(C, H))}$$

In other words, if B relates to F in the same way that C relates to H (and we don't know the actual relation), and if this relation imposes specific semantic restrictions on its arguments, then we should expect F to be as similar to B as H is to C, and the balance factor above will be close to 1. An unbalanced analogy, in which B and F have a different relationship than C and H, will have a score closer to 0. Combining both measures, we can now judge the quality of analogy as follows:

$$quality(B:F::C:H) = subst\_sim(B:F::C:H) \\ \times balance(B:F::C:H)$$

This *quality* measure uses only the contents of the comparability matrix as the basis for its judgments. This is a heuristic that often works, since in many cases, semantic relations can be differentiated by their similarity profiles. Nonetheless, to be sure that a proposed analogy is indeed sound, one needs to know the specific semantic relations involved, rather than just the similarity distributions of the terms they are used to relate.

In this regard, we have two options. In the first, we use the *quality* measure above to identify strong candidates for analogical squaring in the comparability matrix, and then use LRA or a similar technique to more rigorously evaluate these candidates from a relational standpoint. In other words, we can use *Mondrian* as a generative precursor to an evaluative technology like LRA, so that the combined system can both generate and evaluate its own relational analogies. In the second option, we attempt to acquire specific semantic relations for the unspecified contiguous pairings we find in the comparability matrix. As we shall see in the next section, we acquire these relations to support analogical reasoning, but analogical reasoning can itself be used to hasten and direct the acquisition of these relations.

5 Layered Knowledge Acquisition

The notion of a contiguous association is highly underspecified. Though the Google n-grams allow us to determine that *scientist* is contiguous with *laboratory, theory, experiment, research* and *grant*, and WordNet allows us to associate a specific similarity score with each pairing, a different semantic relationship holds in each case. It is necessary to do more than heuristically separate comparable terms into substitutive and contiguous groups, and to know the actual relationships (there may be many) that hold in each case.

Interestingly, though contiguous associations lack a specific semantics, they do at least tell us which associations are worthy of semantic description. That is, of all the term pairings one can imagine, contiguous associations indicate those that are most deserving of further elaboration. Contiguous associations can thus drive the process of knowledge acquisition, either in directing a human user's attention to associations that are likely to be important, or in directing the efforts of an automated approach to knowledge acquisition. A middle-ground approach is also tenable here, in which the system hypothesizes a set of candidate relationships for each contiguous association, before asking a human user to choose amongst this set of potential relations. This approach can also work well in a web-based setting, where anonymous contributors volunteer their time and knowledge in updating the system. In such a setting, users are not asked to suggest their own relationships (a request that can elicit an anarchic response) but to vet relationships that the system already considers plausible.

In this semi-automatic approach, knowledge can be acquired in successive layers. Given the contiguous association X:Y (gleaned from the 3-gram "*Xs and Ys*"), the system can look for 3-grams of the form "Xs preposition Ys". For instance, "*imams and mosques*" prompts one to find "*imams in mosques*", which yields the relation "in" as a linkage for *imam:mosque*. Likewise we find, "*priests in churches*", "*artists in studios*", "*scientists in laboratories*" and "*chefs in kitchens*", all comparable (and analogous) uses of the relation "in".

But prepositions like "in" are pseudo-relations at best: they are vague and highly polysemous, and we really desire an additional verb to lock down their relational meaning. Looking to the 3-grams again, this time focusing on patterns of the form "*verb preposition Xs*", we can identify more specific relations that apply to a given object, such as "*work in laboratories*", "*preach in mosques*" and "*cook in kitchens*". These *verb+preposition* combinations can then be presented to a human user as a menu of candidate relations to elaborate a pseudo-relation like "*imams in mosques*".

To summarize, unspecified contiguous associations can be automatically elaborated into preposition-based pseudo-relations by again mining the Google 3-grams. With the computer-guided input of human volunteers, these pseudo-relations can then be further elaborated into specific relations like *work_in* or *preach_in*. At this point, the system can use analogical reasoning to drive the acquisition of further relationships. So, once a system acquires *imam:work_in:mosque* and *imam:preach_in:mosque*, it can reason via the analogy *imam:mosque::priest:church* that the comparable relationships *priest:work_in:church* and *priest:preach_in:church* may also hold true. Conversely, if the system knows the relationship *priest:minister_in:church*, it can use the same analogy to suggest *imam:minister_in:mosque*. If a human user validates the analogical hypothesis *priest:work_in:church*, a system can use another analogy to suggest *teacher:work_in:school* (and conversely, *priest:teach_in:church*), and so on.

The key point here is that a lightweight approach to analogical reasoning, based only on pragmatic comparability and semantic similarity (outlined in section 4 as the *Mondrian* system), can support meaningful analogies even before a specific relational semantics is acquired. Analogy is both the chicken and the egg in this circular situation: lightweight analogies (the egg) drive the acquisition of specific knowledge (the chicken) that in turn supports acquisition of further knowledge in a virtuous cycle of analogy-driven hypothesis generation and validation.

6 Conclusions

WordNet offers a variety of different semantic relations to weave its word-senses together, though the weft is decidedly patchy in parts. Consequently, WordNet's richest resource by far is its structured hierarchy of noun-senses. This hierarchy underpins numeric judgments of semantic similarity that are robust and efficient, and which accord well with human intuitions. In this paper we have teased apart the related notions of similarity and comparability, and provided a convenient, corpus-based approach to determining which term-pairs can be sensibly grouped together and compared. The result is a comparability matrix whose structure is determined by lexical distribution patterns in corpora, and whose numeric content is determined by WordNet-based semantic similarity scores.

Analogy is a knowledge-hungry process, but one that plays a vital educational role in knowledge transfer among humans. As such, analogy can be used to extend the knowledge already possessed by a system (e.g., see Speer, Havasi and Lieberman, 2008), and if properly harnessed, analogy can drive a virtuous cycle of knowledge-acquisition and hypothesis generation. We have shown here how a comparability matrix populated with WordNet-based similarity judgments can provide a lightweight foundation for analogical reasoning, in the absence of a rich relational semantics. Furthermore, we have shown how this lightweight approach can drive a knowledge-acquisition process in a highly targeted fashion, so that an agent acquires precisely the kind of cross-domain knowledge that results in sound, well-structured analogies. By incorporating analogy into the acquisition process at so early a stage, we can ensure that the resulting knowledge-base is not just analogy-rich, but consistent and well-balanced.

The system described here, named *Mondrian* after its penchant for squaring patterns, is available as an on-line demo at *http://Afflatus.UCD.ie* under *Current Projects*. The full comparability matrix, as derived from Google n-grams, is available for browsing here, as are the many analogies that have been mined from this matrix. Ongoing and future research concerns the development of an editor, named *EdMond*, in which *Mondrian*'s contiguous associations can be elaborated through interactions with web-users in the structured fashion outlined in section 5.

References

Lawrence W. Barsalou. 1983. Ad hoc categories. Memory and Cognition, 11:211–227.

Thorsten Brants and Alex Franz. 2006. *Web 1T 5-gram Version 1*. Linguistic Data Consortium, Philadelphia.

Alexander Budanitsky and Graeme Hirst. 2006. Evaluating WordNet-based Measures of Lexical Semantic Relatedness. *Computational Linguistics*, 32(1):13-47.

Christiane Fellbaum (ed.). 1998. *WordNet: An Electronic Lexical Database*. The MIT Press, Cambridge, MA.

George A. Miller and Walter. G. Charles. 1991. Contextual correlates of semantic similarity. *Language and Cognitive Processes* **6**(1):1-28.

Resnick, Philip. 1995. Using Information Content to Evaluate Semantic Similarity in a Taxonomy. *Proceedings of the 14th International Joint Conference on Artificial Intelligence.*

Nuno Seco, Tony Veale and Jer Hayes, 2004. An Intrinsic Information Content Metric for Semantic Similarity in WordNet. Proceedings of ECAI'04, *the European Conference on Artificial Intelligence.*

Robert Speer, Catherine Havasi, and Henry Lieberman. 2008. AnalogySpace: Reducing the Dimensionality of Common Sense Knowledge. *Proceedings of AAAI 2008, the 23rd AAAI conference on Artificial Intelligence.*

Simon Tong and Jeff Dean. 2008. System and methods for automatically creating lists. *US Patent 7,350,187* (assigned to Google; granted March 25, 2008).

Peter Turney. 2005. Measuring semantic similarity by latent relational analysis. *Proceedings of the 19th International Joint Conference on Artificial Intelligence*, 1136-1141.

Tony Veale and Mark T. Keane. 1997. The Competence of Sub-Optimal Structure Mapping on 'Hard' Analogies. *Proceedings of the 15th International Joint Conference on Artificial Intelligence.*

Tony Veale. 2004. WordNet sits the SAT: A knowledge-based approach to lexical analogy. *Proceedings of ECAI'04, the European Conference on Artificial Intelligence*, 606-612.

Tony Veale. 2006. Re-Representation and Creative Analogy: A Lexico-Semantic Perspective. *New Generation Computing* 24:223-240.

Julie Weeds and David Weir. 2005. Co-occurrence retrieval: A flexible framework for lexical distributional similarity. *Computational Linguistics*, 31(4):433–475.

Challenges in Multilingual Domain–Specific Sense-marking

Jaya Saraswati, Rajita Shukla, Sonal Pathade, Tina Solanki
and Pushpak Bhattacharyya
Department of Computer Science and Engineering
Indian Institute of Technology, Bombay
Powai, Mumbai – 400076
Maharashtra, India
{jayas, rajita, sonal, thsolanki, pb}@cse.iitb.ac.in

Abstract

Annotation plays a key role in today's NLP scenario and this paper discusses challenges involved in one of the toughest annotation tasks - sense marking. In an effort to train the machine to understand the written language and thus to ensure speedy and high-quality translation, a huge amount of data needs to be sense-marked accurately by humans using an authentic and standard lexicon. In the work reported here, the corpus is taken from tourism domain and the Princeton wordnet (Version 2.1) is used as the sense inventory for English text while the Hindi and Marathi wordnets have been used for Hindi and Marathi texts respectively. A word may have a number of senses and in identifying which particular sense has been used in the given context, word sense disambiguation becomes a critical necessity. The corpus was independently tagged by different sense-markers and it was found that the inter annotator agreement on word sense disambiguation was about 80 % across the three languages, *i.e.*, English, Hindi and Marathi. Though the sense distinctions in the wordnets are quite fine-grained, there have been cases when the senses provided there have been inadequate and the human sense-markers have faced problems. The study records such challenges and their handling.

Keywords: sense-marking, wordnet, tourism, word sense disambiguation, culture-specific, challenge, inter annotator agreement.

1 Introduction

The famous Princeton University English wordnet[1], an electronic lexical database, has paved the way for other wordnets in different languages across the world. It set the design for having the nouns, verbs, adjectives and adverbs of a language grouped under sets of synonyms, or synsets[2]. Apart from functioning as a dictionary and thesaurus combined into one, it is used greatly in automatic text analysis and artificial intelligence applications.

Hindi[3] and Marathi[4] wordnets have been developed by researchers at the Center for Indian Language Technology, Computer Science and Engineering Department, IIT Bombay. Similar in design to the Princeton wordnet for English, Hindi wordnet incorporates additional features to capture the complexities of Hindi. Since Marathi wordnet is based on the Hindi wordnet, it directly inherits the IDs and semantic relations of words from there.

While working towards building a Machine Translation system from English to any Indian language, word sense ambiguity has been a prominent issue[5]. In a given text, the occurrence of a particular word will correspond to only one sense and nearby words provide strong and consistent clues to the sense of a target word.

The roadmap of the paper is as follows: Section 2 describes the methodology for sense-marking, the sense-marker tool, a description of how it works, and also the screenshot of this tool. Section 3 and all its subsections describe the options for sense-marking that have been considered along with examples to illustrate the point.

---

[1] http://wordnetweb.princeton.edu/perl/webwn/
[2] Fellbaum, C. 1998. *Wordnet: An Electronic Lexical Database*. The MIT Press
[3] http://www.cfilt.iitb.ac.in/wordnet/webhwn/
[4] http://www.cfilt.iitb.ac.in/wordnet/webmwn/
[5] Mitesh Khapra, Sapan Shah, Piyush Kedia and Pushpak Bhattacharyya, *Projecting Parameters for Multilingual Word Sense Disambiguation*, Empirical Methods in Natural Language Processing (EMNLP09), Singapore, August, 2009

Section 4 presents some other challenges faced by the sense-markers. Section 5 presents such cases where inadequacies of the English, Hindi and Marathi wordnets were encountered. The 6th section shows a comparative study of sense marking and the other annotation tasks. The 7th and the final section winds up the discussion by presenting the conclusions and future work on the issues.

2 Methodology followed in Sense Marking

In the process of training the machine to disambiguate a word sense for proper translation in the Tourism domain we use a sense-marking tool[6].
It is a software tool developed to provide the lexicographers with an easy and efficient way of sense tagging the words. A Graphical User Interface based tool using Java facilitates the task of manual sense marking.

The SenseMarker Interface is shown in figure 1 below.

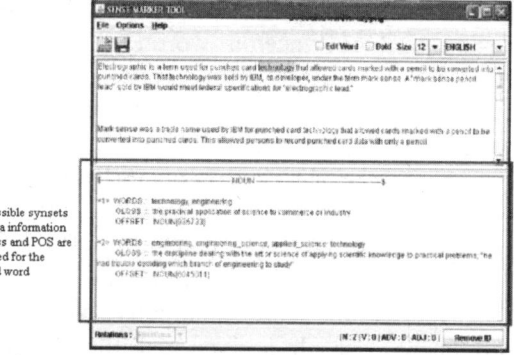

Figure 1: Screenshot of the SenseMarker tool

The tool supports nine languages including English[7], Hindi[8], Marathi[9], Tamil[10], Telugu[11], Kannada[12], Malayalam[13], Bengali[14] and Punjabi[15]. It displays the different senses of a word (as available in the wordnet) along with some other useful information like the gloss and entries of each Synset to which the word belongs. It allows the user to select the correct sense of the word from amongst all the senses. The word can be tagged by just a single click on the correct Synset.

The Steps to Sense-mark a document:

1. The sense-marker sets the Language for which Sense Tagging is to be done.
2. Open the file by clicking on the Open MenuItem of the File Menu or the Tool Bar Open Icon or by pressing CTRL+ O on the key board.
3. A File Chooser menu gets opened. The user has to select the file for tagging and press the open button of the same or double click on the file.

---

[6] Prof. Pushpak Bhattacharyya, Shashank Chauhan, Soumya Nair: Sense Marker Tool : Guide To Sense Marker Tool (B.Tech project report, 2008)

[7] English is the second official language in India. At the time the constitution entered into force, English was used for most official purposes both at the federal level and in the various states The constitution envisaged the gradual phasing in of local languages, principally Hindi, to replace English over a fifteen-year period, but gave Parliament the power to, by law, provide for the continued use of English even thereafter. Accordingly, English continues to be used today, in combination with Hindi (at the central level and in some states) and other languages (at the state level).

[8] Hindi/Khadi boli belongs to the Indo-Aryan language subgroup of Indo-European language family.It is a dialect continuum of the Indic language family in the northern plains of India. 2001 census of India noted 422,048,642 speakers of this language. It is spoken in the Indian states and union territories of Bihar,Chhattisgarh, Delhi, Haryana, Himachal Pradesh, Jharkhand, Madhya Pradesh, Rajasthan, Uttar Pradesh and Uttarakhand.

[9] Marathi is an Indo-Aryan language spoken by the Marathi people of south western India and is the official language of the state of Maharashtra. 2001 census of India noted 71,936,894 speakers of this language.

[10] Tamil is the only surviving Classical language in the world and is a Dravidian language. According to the 2001 census of India there are 60,793,814 speakers of this particular language.

[11] Telugu is a Dravidian language mostly spoken in the Indian state of Andhra Pradesh. According to the 2001 census of India there are 74,002,856 speakers of this particular language.

[12] Kannada is one of the major Dravidian languages of India, spoken predominantly in the state of Karnataka. 2001 census of India recorded 37,924,011 speakers of this language.

[13] Malayalam is one of the four major Dravidian languages of South India. According to the 2001 census of India there are 33,066,392speakers of this particular language.

[14] Bengali or Bangla is an Indo-Aryan language of the eastern Indian subcontinent, evolved from the Magadhi Prakrit and Sanskrit languages. Bengali is native to the region of eastern South Asia known as Bengal, which comprises present day Bangladesh, the Indian state of West Bengal, southern Assam - also known as Barak Valley, and part of Tripura. With nearly 230 million total speakers, Bengali is one of the most spoken languages (ranking fifth or sixth) in the world.

[15] Punjabi is spoken as native language by 44.15% of Pakistanis and 2.85% of Indians is an Indo-Aryan language spoken by inhabitants of the historical Punjab region (in Pakistan and India).According to the Census of India 2001; there are 29,102,477 Punjabi speakers in India.

4. The file/document gets opened in the Tagging Window with added new lines at the end of each statement to demarcate the sentences properly and readability is increased.
5. The word, to be sense tagged, should be single clicked and for a compound word the user is required to drag to select.
6. The synsets for the selected word are displayed in the Synset Window.
7. To assign sense (POS + Offset) to the word the user has to click on the respective synset which makes the right sense and the offset and the pos gets assigned to the word.

However, there have been occasions when this task of sense marking was not a simple one. It was found that either the sense was not present in the wordnets or the existing sense was not sufficient or the components of the compound expressions could not be separately disambiguated to provide the correct sense. We now proceed to discuss these issues.

3 Options for Sense-marking

In light of the things mentioned above, the sense markers had the following options:
      a. Marking the word with the exact sense
      b. Marking with a subsuming sense
      c. Marking with the closest sense
      d. Marking with the exact sense even if the sense does not mention the particular word as a synset member
      e. Creating a new sense

3.1 Marking the word with the exact sense

This is the ideal and most desirable situation. It is the task of the sense-marker to assign senses to as many words as possible. When the word is available in the sense repository with its complete and correct set of senses, the sense marker essentially has to apply her/his knowledge of language and the sense of context to assign the sense accurately.

3.2 Marking with a subsuming sense (using hypernymy)

When the exact sense was not found, sometimes a subsuming sense was tagged as it contained the essence of the original word. For example, the equivalent of various words in Hindi which denote a *container* or a *cooking pot* are not there in English, but they could be tagged to vessel or pan respectively.

3.3 Using a close sense

The basic observation was that in the absence of an exact match of the sense for a given word, it was decided that a close or nearby sense should be tagged. The word *festival*, for example, shows two senses in the wordnet, (a) a day or period of time set aside for feasting and celebration, and, (b) an organized series of acts and performances (usually in one place); "a drama festival". In the Indian context, a sense like *An occasion for feasting or celebration, especially a day or time of religious significance that recurs at regular intervals*[16] looked more appropriate, but since the wordnet sense (a) did not look too out of place, it was tagged.

3.4 Marking with the exact sense even though the sense does not mention the particular word as a synset member

If the exact sense was found in some other existing synset of the wordnet, then the word was made a part of that synset. It was decided that such words should be enclosed with a hash mark followed by the ID of that synset. Quite a few words fell in this category. For example:

a. *Ganga*: This word was tagged to the concept (an Asian river; rises in the Himalayas and flows east into the Bay of Bengal; a sacred river of the Hindus) where the existing synset was Ganges, Ganges River. The ID of this synset was given to the word Ganga as, by right, it should have been a member of this synset. The tagging looked like this - #Ganga#_9153625.

b. *Pulao*: The concept was same as that of pilaf, pilaff, pilau, pilaw (rice cooked in well-seasoned broth with onions or celery and usually poultry or game or shellfish and sometimes tomatoes), and so it was tagged with this ID.

Another instance was when the concept was present in the wordnet but there was a different word for it in Indian English. For example, the word *raw* as in *raw mangoes* where it conveyed the sense of being *green, unripe, unripened, immature*, (the gloss being – *not fully developed or mature; not ripe*) could be directly traced to this concept. A similar case was with the concept of

---
[16] www.thefreedictionary.com

salad leaves, the way the word *lettuce* is used in Indian English.

3.5 Creating a new sense

This option was adopted on occasions where a word appears in the document, the sense of which is either present in the wordnet but is not appropriate in the context or is completely absent from the wordnet. This is clearly obvious in cases of culture-specific word entities. It was decided that a new sense should be created for them and stored in the local copy of the wordnet. All such words were enclosed between an opening # and a closing # symbol. A script to parse the words between these symbols would be written and new synsets for these words would be created. The synset IDs will start from 200000. The categories for these are:

Culture-specific words
Specific words from all cultures cannot be stored in any lexicon. There are certain terms which express a concept which is not universal in nature. They are embedded in the culture of that particular land where they originated. Such words are not sufficiently present in the wordnets. These concepts pertain more specifically to places which were European Colonies at some point of time. However, since English is the most important language of communication all over the world, the sense inventories are expected to contain most of them. In the Indian context, the Princeton wordnet at times does come up to this expectation and has captured little-known concepts as well. An interesting instance is that of the word *Raita* which has the gloss *an Indian side dish of yogurt and chopped cucumbers and spices* in the English wordnet. This is a common North Indian dish which is not very familiar elsewhere in India itself and yet it has found its way in an English lexicon. Other English dictionaries have also incorporated many Indian words like *guru, Brahmin, chapatti, gherao, etc*. Yet the fact remains that many of the culture-specific words are not there. For the purpose of marking such words with a proper sense, it is of utmost importance that senses be created for them. The examples for this are:

    i. Temple car – The concept here is that of chariots that are used to carry the idols of Hindu gods. The chariot or car is usually used on festival days, when many people pull it.

    ii. Auto rickshaws; autos – a motorized version of the traditional rickshaws, has a tin/iron body resting on three small wheels (one in front, two on the rear), a small cabin for the driver (called an auto-wallah in some areas) in the front and seating for three in the rear[17].

The Hindi and Marathi sense markers did not have to resort to hash marking the words from the Tourism text that were not found in the wordnets. Since the two sense inventories are being made indigenously, the lexicographers could inform the wordnet creators about their needs and get the words/senses inserted in the wordnets. The Hindi/Marathi sense markers usually did not find culture-specific words in the sense inventories while sense-marking the tourism text. For example, in Marathi, the word मंगळागौर *(mangalaagaur)* which has the sense

(1) लग्नानंतरच्या श्रावणात मंगळवारी माहेरी व सासरी केलेली पार्वतीची पूजा व समारंभ
- After-marriage Tuesday of ShraavaNa month fathers house or at the house of inlaws performed Parvatis worship
-lagnaantarchyaa shraavaNaat mangala-vaarii maaherii va saasarii keleli Parvatichi poojaa va samaarambha
- a religious ceremony to worship Goddess Parvati performed on any Tuesday of the month of Shravan, (fifth month of the Hindu calendar) by a married woman either at her fathers house or at the house of her in-laws.

The word मंगळागौर also has the sense of *the name of a goddess* which has not been created so far[18].

Species names:
Though some common flora and fauna names are present in the wordnet, it is lacking in *species names* which commonly occur in the text related to Tourism domain. Names like *elephant grass, Himalayan griffin, blue sheep, snow trout, black-necked grebe, hog deer, Impeyan pheasant, blood pheasant, Bengal florican, etc.* needed to have senses created for them. For example, *snow trout* refers to a particular species of fish which is a cold water riverine and short migratory fish belonging to the family *Cyprinidae* and sub-family *Schizothoracinae*. These are widely distributed in the Himalayan and sub- Himalayan region. This sense would not be captured if the

---

[17] www.wikipedia.org
[18] http://en.wikipedia.org/wiki/Marathi

components of the name *snow trout* are separated as *snow+ trout*.

In the Hindi wordnet too, for example, the senses of species such as दलदली घड़ियाल (marsh crocodile), or विशाल धनेश (Great Hornbill), and in the Marathi wordnet, the sense of पल्लवपुच्छ कोतवाल (Racket-tailed Drongo) are missing.

Words with affixes

Affixed words have been stored separately in the wordnets. The ones that are not there are such words as *trans*-border, *sub*-alpine, *post*-independence, *eco*-friendly, *multi*-cuisine, *bio*-diverse, stress-*free*, sugar*less*, *etc.*, which appear quite frequently in the documents. It was felt that they, along with their affixes, should be treated as a single word entity and a new sense should be created for them. This was decided keeping in view the fact that an affix may have more than a single sense. For example, the prefix *sub* may have any of the three following senses: (a) under, beneath (as in subterranean, submarine); (b) subsidiary, secondary (as in subplot); and (c) almost, nearly (as in subhuman)[19]. The same would apply to words with suffixes, such as motorable, jeepable, modernish, etc. The suffix *–ish* may mean any of the following, depending on the context in which it is used: (a) Typical or similar to (when appended to many kinds of nouns), as in, *Her face had a girlish charm*; (b) about, approximately (when appended to numbers, especially times and ages), as in, *We arrived at tennish* or *We arrived tennish*; (c) of a nationality, or the language associated with a nationality (when appended to roots denoting names of nations or regions), as in, *Danish, Spanish, etc.*; and (d) somewhat (when appended to adjectives), as in, *His face had a greenish tinge*.

In Hindi too, one comes across a suffix like वाला (*wala*) which gives different meanings to the words it is attached to. For example, when it occurs with words like दूध (*doodh* - milk) or मिठाई) mithai - sweets), it conveys the sense of seller of these things. With words like गाड़ी (gaadii – vehicle) or बँगला (bangalaa – bungalow/cottage), it refers to the owner of these. A word like पुलिसवाला (pulisawala - policeman) would mean a person in the police force. When the word is, say, दिल्लीवाला, then this suffix denotes a person belonging to Delhi. Meaning of about to is apparent when the word is आने वाला (aanewala – about to come) or जाने वाला (jaanewala – about to go). An expression like मूँछवाला (moustached – having moustache) gives altogether different meaning because of this suffix *wala*. A different kind of case was encountered in Marathi; for example, the word आपलेपणा (aapalepaNaa - intimacy, closeness) has the suffix पणा (paNaa) which denotes a state, and the whole word conveys the sense of being familiar or close to someone. However, both these words are not found in the respective wordnets for the reason that all the words with the affixes have not been incorporated. The list of such words would be extremely exhaustive and hence a decision has been taken to include them in the later stages of wordnet development.

Multi-words in the corpus

Tourism corpus contains descriptions of places and landscapes, and hence one comes across many rather unexpected multi-words as translation candidates which are not found in the wordnet. Given the frequency of the appearance of compound-word and multi-word expressions, the coverage in the wordnets is insufficient. In the framework of WSD, this becomes an important concern.

There are two kinds of multiword expressions (MWE): one which can have compositional interpretation and the other conveying the non-compositional. Machine cannot infer non compositional multiword expressions, so they have to be stored in the sense repositories. For example, the English expression *green card* conveys the sense of *a card that identifies the bearer as an alien with permanent resident status in the United State*. This could not have come from the meanings of the individual components of this MWE and so we find it stored in the dictionaries, including the wordnet. An example of this in Hindi is चूल्हा चौका (cuulhaa-caukaa). In the sentence

(3) इन्हें आगे चलकर चूल्हा चौका ही तो संभालना है
  - They in future the work of the kitchen take care of -aux
  - inheM aage cala kara cuulhaa-caukaa hii to samhaalanaa hai

---

[19] http://en.wiktionary.org/wiki/Wiktionary

- They have to take care of only the work of the kitchen in the future,

the multi-word has the sense of रसोई से संबंधित काम (rasoi se sambandhit kaam - *the work related to the kitchen*). Here, the sense of the components चूल्हा (cuulhaa), meaning

(4) मिट्टी, ईंट या लोहे का बना आग का पात्र जिस पर भोजन पकाते हैं

- clay, bricks, or iron made artifact on which food cooked is
- mittii, iiMta yaa lohe kaa banaa aag kaa paatra jis para bhojan pakaate hain
- an artifact made of clay, bricks or iron used for cooking food),

and चौका (caukaa) meaning भोजन बनाने का कमरा या स्थान (bhojan banaane kaa kamaraa yaa sthaan - *a room or place for cooking food*) would not convey the sense of रसोई से संबंधित काम (rasoi se sambandhit kaam) or the work related to the kitchen.

The MWEs conveying compositional interpretation pose a challenge to the sense markers as they can have multiple senses where some of them are compositional and some are not. The Hindi example of such a case is the expression धूप-छाँव (*sunshine and shade*). On the literal level, this is a compositional expression, if used in a sentence like the following:

(6) नैनीताल में धूप-छाँव के बीच तालों की सैर का अपना ही मज़ा है।

- Nainital in sunshine and shade amidst lakes' visit own enjoyment-aux
- Nainital mein dhuup-chhanv ke beech taaloM kii sair kaa apnaa hii mazaa hai
- Visiting the lakes in Nainital amidst sun shine and shade has its own enjoyment.

On a metaphorical level, this refers to the ups and downs in one's life; as in जीवन की धूप-छाँव, (jeevan kii dhuup-chaanv) which is non-compositional. So is its third usage, as in the expression धूप-छाँव साड़ी (dhuup-chhanv saree), where it conveys the sense of a colour which is composed of two intermingling hues.

Furthermore, there is no consistency in the way the compositional expressions appear in the text – they may be written with a hyphen, or without a hyphen with just a blank space in between the components, or they could appear as one unit. Expressions such as *sun-washed* (beaches), *snow-laden* (mountains), *low-impact* (camping) were not present in the wordnet. As a solution it was decided to remove the hyphen and tag the words separately. Thus in the expression *sun-washed* the word *sun* was given the sense – *a typical star that is the source of light and heat for the planets in the solar system*; and *washed* was sense-marked as - *wet as from washing*. In this manner the sense of the entire multiword was tagged. In Hindi and Marathi, the expression नारी-निकेतन (naarii-niketan) was dealt with in the same way.

Adjectival Phrases

In the Tourism domain, the sense markers came across a number of adjectival phrases which acted like pre-modifiers of nouns and, at times, behaved like predicatives too. The expressions such as *melt-in-the-mouth* chocolates, a *never-before* adventure, *get-away-from-it-all* appeal, the frenetic *cigarette-and-coffee* pace, etc. have been decided to be lexicalised. Similar is the case with phrases like *sit-out* (as in *to rest in the sit-out*), *a must check-out* (as in *A must check-out is the restaurant at the hotel*).

Figurative language

The sense-markers working in English language came across quite a few idioms and figurative expressions in the tourism corpus as there is a proclivity to use such language in this particular domain. However, this tendency was not found so much in the Hindi and the Marathi corpuses as they comprise of translated matter from English where such examples tend to acquire their literal senses on translation. For English sense-marking, it was decided that these should be lexicalized and thus were enclosed within # marks. For example, in a sentence like *The ambience is good but the food is not much to write home about*, the idiom *not much to write home about* would be lexicalized as *something being mediocre; not as good as you expected or to not be especially good or exciting*. In another sentence, *The palace situated in the lake is a gem of a place for the tourists,* the word *gem* is used metaphorically, conveying the sense of *something that is valued for its beauty or perfection*.

4 Other Challenges

There were some other language issues in the tourism corpus which the sense-markers encountered. Decisions regarding each category of such words and phrases were taken keeping in mind the general principles of English grammar as well as the requirements of machine translation.

4.1 The participle issue

In words such as *glowing diamonds, shaking towers* or *fluttering butterflies*, the words *glowing, shaking* and *fluttering* did not have a sense given under the adjective category as here the verb participle is acting as an adjective. Therefore, it was decided to pick up the sense from the verb category. So, for the word *glowing*, the verb sense conveying *emit a steady even light without flames* was picked up.

4.2 Named Entity issue

In the domain of Tourism, it is but natural to come across a large number of named entities as names of destinations and places of interest, such as Coffin Bay or Port Lincoln. It was decided that here the proper Noun part of the name would not to be tagged, but the common noun part would be tagged. So in the above example, the word Coffin was not tagged, whereas the word Bay was given the sense as *an indentation of a shoreline larger than a cove but smaller than a gulf*. Similarly in Hindi, names such as त्रिपोलिया बाजार (Tripoliya Bazaar) and in Marathi टेंमडील तलाव (Tomdil talaava), which are not available in the Hindi and the Marathi wordnets respectively, had only their common noun parts tagged. Thus बाजार (bazaar), which has the sense of

वह स्थान जहाँ तरह-तरह की चीज़ें बिकती हों

(that place where variety of things are sold)

and तलाव (talaava) which has the sense of मोठे तळे (big lake) were tagged to the respective senses.

5 Inadequacies of the English, Hindi and Marathi wordnets as encountered by sense-markers

Besides the above-mentioned challenges, various inadequacies of the wordnets were also encountered. For instance, the adjective senses of many common nouns are absent from the English wordnet; as in the expression *a vegetarian diet*, the word *vegetarian* requires an adjective sense which should mean *consisting primarily or wholly of vegetables and vegetable products*; or the word *budget* as used in the expression *a budget hotel* where the sense of budget should consists of *being as appropriate for a restricted budget or inexpensive*.

Proper nouns such as *Moghul, Rajput,* or *Khmer,* which appear in the wordnets, do not have their adjective senses, as in *the Khmer culture*, or *the Moghul architecture*.

The adverb sense of many words needs to be included in the wordnet. For example: *chillingly* - as in *the worlds most chillingly famous horror attraction*; *fleetingly* - as in *visitors do not merely wanting to experience the attractions fleetingly*; *on-line* - as in *to book accommodation on-line*; *archaeologically* – as in *the cave being archaeologically significant, etc.*

Some verbs appear in the wordnet only in the intransitive sense. For example, the verb *dilate* has the sense *become wider* in the sentence "*His pupils were dilated*"; but its transitive sense, that of *make wider* which should correspond to sentence like *It dilates the blood vessels* has not been given in the English wordnet.

The sense-markers also came across concepts in the Princeton wordnet which, they felt, should have had a broader sense but they appeared in a restricted form. For example, the word *Lord* in the wordnet is defined as *a term referring to the Judeo-Christian God*. When the concept of *Lord* is found in other religions, for example, *Lord Rama* or *Lord Buddha*, it becomes difficult to tag it to the sense quoted above. It would have been much better to have the gloss like *a term referring to God* as given in the English wordnet, instead of restricting it to the Judeo-Christian religion. The words like *Creator, demon, gateway, etc.* posed the same kind of challenge.

6 Comparison with Other Annotation Tasks

Other annotation efforts include Part-of-speech tagging, Chunking and Named Entity Recognition.

	Sense Marking	POS Tagging	NER	Chunking
Options	Typically large	2-3	2-3	Very little
Training Corpus	Very large	30-60K	30K	20K
Complexity of Algorithm	Highly Complex	Medium	Medium	Simple
Language Proficiency	High	Medium	Little	High
Time Taken	Typically much	Not much	Little	Much
Inter Annotator Agreement	Low	Medium	High	High
Language Divergence	Not Affected	Affected	Not Affected	Affected

Table 1: Comparison of Annotation Tasks

Table 1 above shows a comparative study of all the annotation tasks.

Part-of-speech tagging, also called grammatical tagging or word-category disambiguation, is the process of marking up the words in a text (corpus) as corresponding to a particular part of speech, based on both its definition, as well as its context - *i.e.*, relationship with adjacent and related words in a phrase, sentence, or paragraph. Chunking, in computational linguistics, is a method for parsing natural language sentences into partial syntactic structures (noun groups, verbs, verb groups, etc.). Named Entity annotation task seeks to locate and classify atomic elements in text into predefined categories such as the names of persons, organizations, locations, expressions of times, quantities, monetary values, percentages, etc.[20]

7 Conclusion

In this paper we have discussed problems faced in annotating tourism domain corpora in three languages using the sense repositories of English, Hindi and Marathi wordnets. English, as used across the world, varies from country to country and state to state. It is, therefore, a challenge to accurately mark words with their senses. Culture specific words like *curry/gravy* from India, *wanton* from China and *Doro Wat* from African cuisine are such cases in point. Similar is the case with Hindi which has wide variations inside and outside India. Besides culture specific words, different region-specific usages of existing words (meaning expansion), absence of words and absence of senses of existing words are other challenges facing a sense annotator. Of course, the wordnet built for a particular language cannot always accommodate borrowed words, borrowed senses, and meaning contractions and expansions influenced by other languages. But in an increasingly globalized world where code mixing and all other phenomena as listed above are becoming a norm, lexical resources have to evolve strategies of staying useful while maintaining purity and faithfulness to the languages and cultures they represent.

In conclusion, we would like to say we found problems in assigning senses to

1. Culture-specific words
2. Words particular to Indian English
3. Words denoting fractional quantities
4. Species names
5. Words with affixes
6. Multiword expressions
7. Adjectival phrases
8. Figurative language

Partitioning the wordnet into id-regions dedicated to native words and senses, expanded senses and borrowed senses is a concrete suggestion our paper makes to wordnet creators of all languages.

Plans are underway to see that the wordnets link with DBpedia[21], Wikipedia[22] and Yago[23].

References:

Collins Essential English Dictionary 2nd Edition 2006 © HarperCollins Publishers 2004, 2006

Collins Essential Thesaurus 2nd Edition 2006 © HarperCollins Publishers 2005, 2006

Date, Yashwant Rao and Karve, Chintamana Ganesha, 1995. *Maharashtra Shabdakosh*. Varada Books, Pune, Maharashtra

Dhongde, Ramesh, 2009. *Oxford English-Marathi Dictionary*. Oxford University Press, New Delhi

Kernerman English Learners Dictionary © 1986-2008 K Dictionaries Ltd and partners

The American Heritage® Dictionary of the English Language, Fourth Edition copyright ©2000 by Houghton

www.khandbahale.com/englishmarathi

---

[20] http://en.wikipedia.org/wiki

[21] http://en.wikipedia.org/wiki/DBpedia
[22] http://en.wikipedia.org/wiki
[23] http://www.mpi-inf.mpg.de/yago-naga/yago

Hindi Semantic Category Labeling using Semantic Relatedness Measures

Siva Reddy
LTRC
IIIT Hyderabad, India
gvsreddy@students.iiit.ac.in

Abhilash Inumella
LTRC
IIIT Hyderabad, India
abhilashi@students.iiit.ac.in

Navjyoti Singh
Center for Exact Humanities
IIIT Hyderabad, India
navjyoti@iiit.ac.in

Rajeev Sangal
LTRC
IIIT Hyderabad, India
sangal@iiit.ac.in

Abstract

In this paper, we evaluate and compare six semantic relatedness measures used for Hindi semantic category labeling. Our experiments show that the measure "adapted lesk" performed better than other measures. However, a simple baseline system achieved better accuracy than all the measures.

1 Introduction

The task of semantic category labeling has been introduced in (Reddy et al., 2009). Given a word, its admissible semantic categories and its context, the task of semantic category labeling is to assign the most appropriate semantic category to the word. Our language of interest is Hindi [1]. An example is shown in *Table 1*. We used Hindi WordNet Ontological categories (Narayan et al., 2002) as semantic category inventories rather than WordNet synsets which are conventionally used in word sense disambiguation.

1.1 Ontological Categories

Hindi WordNet Ontological Categories are coarse grained distinctions of word senses. These categories are organized in a hierarchical fashion based on 'is-a' relation. A separate ontological hierarchy exists for each syntactic category (noun, verb, adjective adverb). Total number of categories in noun, verb, adjective and adverb hierarchy are 101, 31, 25 and 11 respectively and the maximum depth of the hierarchy is 5. There are 28,663 synsets in Hindi WordNet. Every synset is mapped to a category in the ontological hierarchy. Figure 1 depicts ontological hierarchy of the word *billA*.

2 Related Work

Inspired by the original Lesk algorithm (Lesk, 1986), a number of WordNet based disambiguation algorithms were proposed. Lesk algorithm disambiguates a target word by assigning the sense whose gloss (definition) maximally overlaps with the neighbouring words gloss. Banerjee and Pedersen (2002) used hierarchical relationships in WordNet to include the glosses of words that are related to the target word and its neighbours. Patwardhan et al. (2003) takes the view that gloss overlaps are just another measure of semantic relatedness. They evaluated a number of semantic relatedness measures for English word sense disambiguation.

Our work builds on the earlier work of (Patwardhan et al., 2003). We evaluated a number of semantic relatedness measures in the light of Hindi Semantic Category Labeling.

3 Experimental Setting

In this section, we describe our method of labeling and various semantic relatedness mesures used.

3.1 Labeling Algorithm

We used a variation of simplified Lesk algorithm to label the semantic category for a given target word in a given context. Unlike simplified lesk algorithm which uses gloss overlap of target word's category and sentential context as a relatedness measure, our algorithm generalizes by using other semantic relatedness measures. It chooses the semantic category of the target word which is maximally related with its context. We used the immediate neighbours of the target word W_T, word to the left W_L and word to the right W_R, as context of the target word. The semantic category 'C' which maximizes the following equation is chosen to be the label of the target word.

$$\max_{C \in cat(W_T)} (\mathit{leftRelatedness}(C) + \mathit{rightRelatedness}(C))$$

where

cat(w) are the categories of the word 'w'

$$\mathit{leftRelatedness}(C) = \max_{L \in cat(W_L)} Rel(C, L)$$

---
[1] Hindi is the official language of India. Urdu is a close cousin to Hindi. Hindi and Urdu are spoken by approximately 500 million people in the world.

1. kuwwe/Dog ko xeKawe/seeing hI billA/cat pedZa/tree para/on caDZa/climbed gayA
   Mammal   *NaturalEvent*   *Mammal* *NaturalObject*   *VerbOfAction*

2. saBA/Meeting meM/in Aye/came saBI/all svayaMsevaka/volunteers billA/badge
   Event   *VerbOfAction*   *Group*   *Artifact*
   lagAye/wear hue We
   VerbOfState

Table 1: Examples showing the task of semantic category labeling. *wx-notation* is used here to write Hindi.

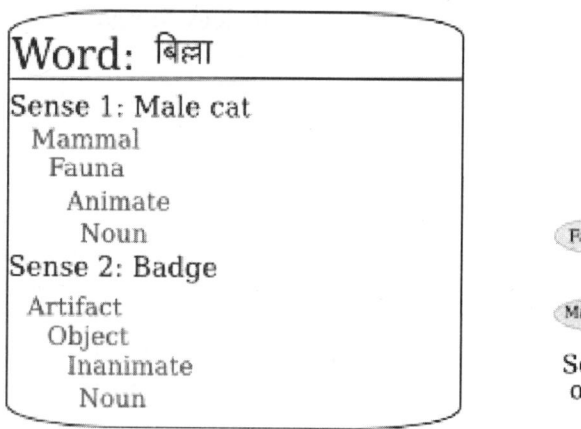
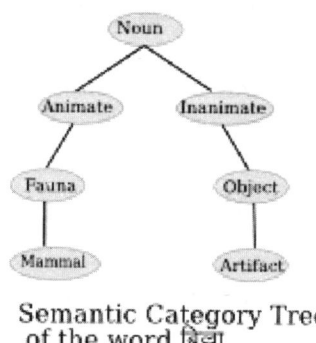

Figure 1: Hindi WordNet entry of the word *billA*. The word has two senses meaning male cat and badge. Ontological category mappings of the two senses are shown on the left side of the figure. On the right, the semantic category tree(SCT) of the word is shown.

$$rightRelatedness(C) = \max_{R \in cat(W_R)} Rel(C, R)$$

and *Rel()* gives the semantic relatedness value between two categories measured using semantic relatedness measure

The next section describes the semantic relatedness measures used by us.

3.2 Semantic Relatedness Measures

Semantic Relatedness Measure gives a metric to measure the relatedness of two concepts. A concept can either refer to a semantic category or a synset. We conducted our evaluation using the following Semantic relatedness metrics: Lesk (lesk), adapted Lesk (adpLesk), Leacock & Chodorow (lch), Wu & Palmer (wup), Lin (lin), and Jiang & Conrath (jcn). We provide below a short description for each of these six metrics.

We view gloss overlaps as just another measure of semantic relatedness. Simplified and adapted lesk relatedness measures are based on this assumption.

The Lesk Measure

Lesk relatedness between two concepts is the number of gloss overlaps of the two concepts. Hindi WordNet Ontological categories does not contain adequate gloss (and examples). To provide more gloss for an ontological category, we used the gloss of the synsets which correspond to this ontological category.

$$Rel_{lesk} = Overlap\ (\ gloss_{concept1},\ gloss_{concept2}\ )$$

The Adapted Lesk Measure

Adapted lesk relatedness between two concepts is defined as

$$Rel_{adpLesk} = Overlap\ (\ extendedGloss_{concept1},\ extendedGloss_{concept2}\ )$$

where extendedGloss of a concept is the total gloss of all the concepts in the hierarchy of the given concept (including itself).

The Leacock-Chodorow Measure

The (Leacock and Chodorow, 1998) relatedness between two concepts is determined as:

$$Rel_{lch} = -log\frac{length}{2D}$$

where length is the length of the shortest path between two concepts using node-counting, and D is the maximum depth of the hierarchy.

The Wu-Palmer Measure

The Wu and Palmer (Wu and Palmer, 1994) relatedness metric measures the depth of two given concepts in the WordNet taxonomy, and the depth of the least common subsumer (LCS), and combines these figures into a relatedness score:

$$Rel_{wup} = \frac{2 * depth(LCS)}{depth(concept_1) + depth(concept_2)}$$

The Lin Measure

The (Lin, 1998) relatedness between two concepts is defined as

$$Rel_{lin} = \frac{2 * IC(LCS)}{IC(concept_1) + IC(concept_2)}$$

where IC is defined as:

$$IC(c) = -logP(c)$$

and P (c) is the probability of encountering an instance of concept c in a large corpus. As we don't have a large sense tagged corpora, we calculated this probability by making the assumption done in (Patwardhan et al., 2003): each category of a word is equally likely. We used a Hindi web corpora of size 324 MB to collect these statistics.

The Jiang-Conrath Measure

The Jiang and Conrath (1997) Measure used by us is similar to the one used in (Patwardhan et al., 2003)

$$Rel_{jcn} = \frac{1}{IC(concept_1) + IC(concept_2) - 2 * IC(LCS)}$$

4 Evaluation

In our experiments, we labeled only nouns. We evaluated our experiments on manually annotated sense (semantic category and synset) tagged data developed by Indian language machine translation consortium(ILMT). It comprises of articles from news and tourism domain. In all, there are 7200 manual annotated sentences covering 133 semantic categories. The average semantic category ambiguity of a word is 2.18 i.e. on an average each word can have 2.18 semantic categories whereas synset ambiguity of a word is 2.57.

4.1 Results

The results of the experiment are shown in tables 2 and 3. In table 2, the accuracies for the task of semantic category labeling are shown and in table 3, the results for word sense disambiguation using synsets are shown. As we can see from the results the semantic categories are coarse grained and hence it turns out to be an easier task compared to synset assignment. This is expected because in a number of cases multiple synsets correspond to same semantic category in Hindi WordNet.

Also, the accuracies of baseline system, which assigns the first sense is considerably higher than others. WordNet senses are listed in the order of its frequency from which the sense inventory is created. Our testing corpus might have fallen along these lines of WordNet creation. This might be the reason of having higher accuracies for baseline. On a different corpus(domain), the first sense in WordNet might not be the frequent sense in the domain of interest. This effects the accuracy of the baseline system. This is not the case with the algorithms based on relatedness measures.

4.2 Observations

It is interesting to observe that adapted Lesk performs well on semantic category labeling than on synset labeling whereas Lesk performs well on synset labeling. This gives an insight that gloss information of Hindi WordNet ontological category is not sufficient for semantic category labeling and has to depend on the ontological heirarchy. In the case of synsets, the gloss information is adequate and the addition of hierarchial information may create noise.

Results show that lesk and adapted lesk are performing well (recall) compared to other semantic relatedness measures. This might be due to the reason that lesk and adapted lesk can relate two words across the syntactic categories (part-of-speech tags) which is not the case with other relatedness measures used in this paper.

Model	Precision	Recall
Baseline	84.76	84.76
lesk	74.75	72.73
adpLesk	76.05	74.09
lch	74.87	61.30
wup	75.33	61.68
lin	74.11	60.17
jcn	71.93	51.43

Table 2: Semantic Category Labeling Evaluation of Nouns

Model	Precision	Recall
Baseline	78.23	78.23
lesk	65.27	63.51
adpLesk	63.36	61.73
lch	67.14	54.98
wup	67.45	55.23
lin	65.05	52.81
jcn	62.52	44.70

Table 3: Synset Assignment Evaluation of Nouns

5 Conclusion

In this paper, we evaluated a number of semantic relatedness measures in the light of semantic category labeling. We hope these statistics will be helpful in providing insights for any work which aim to use semantic relatedness measures. For the task of semantic category labeling, the measure **adapted Lesk** performs better than all other measures.

Acknowledgements

We would like to thank Prof. Ted Pedersen for his valuable suggestions on semantic relatedness measures.

References

S. Banerjee and T. Pedersen. 2002. An adapted Lesk algorithm for word sense disambiguation using WordNet. *Computational Linguistics and Intelligent Text Processing*, pp. 117-171.

J.J. Jiang and D.W. Conrath. 1997. Semantic similarity based on corpus statistics and lexical taxonomy. *International Conference Research on Computational Linguistics (ROCLING X) (September 1997)*

C. Leacock and M. Chodorow. 1998. Combining local context and WordNet similarity for word sense identification. *WordNet: An electronic lexical database*, 49(2):265–283.

M. Lesk. 1986. Automatic sense disambiguation using machine readable dictionaries: How to tell a pine cone from an ice cream cone. In *Proceedings of the 5th annual international conference on Systems documentation*, pages 24–26. ACM New York, NY, USA.

D. Lin. 1998. An information-theoretic definition of similarity. In *Proceedings of the 15th International Conference on Machine Learning*, pages 296–304.

D. Narayan, D. Chakrabarty, P. Pande, and P. Bhattacharyya. 2002. An experience in building the Indo WordNet-a WordNet for Hindi. In *International Conference on Global WordNet*.

S. Patwardhan, S. Banerjee, and T. Pedersen. 2003. Using measures of semantic relatedness for word sense disambiguation. *In Proceedings of the Fourth International Conference on Intelligent Text Processing and Computational Linguistics (CICLING-03) (2003)*

S. Reddy, A. Inumella, R. Sangal, and S. Paul. 2009. All Words Unsupervised Semantic Category Labeling for Hindi. In *Proceedings of Recent Advances in Natural Language Processing*.

Z. Wu and M. Palmer. 1994. Verbs semantics and lexical selection. In *Proceedings of the 32nd annual meeting on Association for Computational Linguistics*, pages 133–138. Association for Computational Linguistics Morristown, NJ, USA.

An Intelligent Framework for Reasoning on Story Plots using WordNet

A. Jaya
Research scholar
Dept. of Computer Science Engineering
Anna University
jaya_venky@yahoo.com

G.V. Uma
Assistant professor
Dept. of Computer Science Engineering
Anna University
gvuma@annauniv.edu

Abstract

Reasoning refers to mental process that generates conclusion, based on the activities of the mind such as analyzing, comparing, inferring, and predicting. It helps in taking decision based on the facts. Reasoning is a casual process for the human beings whereas making the system to reason with the available facts to take decision is a tedious process. But in the Artificial intelligence era, reasoning helps the system to take decision with available facts and also makes the system as an intelligent one. People are interested in reading the various kinds of stories like romantic, comedy, thriller and etc. They are having the capability to analyze the story by means of characters involved, settings, location, situation and etc. An intelligent framework is developed using WordNet to benefit the system in order to reason the facts in the story and to arrive at conclusion. The Wordnet ontology helps the system by providing the concepts from many domains. This can be extended to other languages apart from English.

(Keywords – Framework, Reasoning, story, word net)

1 Introduction

Reason is a type of thinking process and the ability of reasoning shows the intelligence of a person deriving conclusion based on the facts and figures. It helps for the system to take decision. Reasoning is the process of using a rational, systematic series of steps based on sound mathematical procedures to arrive at a conclusion; the drawing of conclusions from given facts and mathematical principles; often used as a problem solving strategy. The automatic story generation system aims to generate the stories based on the user's wish. The efficiency of the Purdom's algorithm is used for language generation and using this language generator, sentences are constructed to represent the story. Since the sentences are generated by the system, it needs to undergo the semantic validation. Mainly, the validation can be performed by two ways. They are:

1. Syntactic oriented validation
2. Semantic oriented validation.

Syntactic oriented validation concentrates on the language structure and the grammar adhered for the sentence generation. For example, 'Lion was come to den'. The above sentence has the problem with sentence formation structure. System has to reason the sentence based on the sentence grammar and detects the problem in the language structure. It suggests the corrected sentence as 'Lion came to den or Lion was coming to Den.' which helps to correct the sentence in the story by selecting any one of the above.

Semantic oriented validation focuses on the real world meaning of the generated sentences. Reasoning helps in validating the sentences semantically to produce the meaningful stories. For example, one of the generated sentences for the lion story is 'Rat killed the Lion. '. Even though the sentence is syntactically correct, based on the reality, rat cannot kill the lion. Because, rat is a domestic animal and Lion is a wild animal. Human beings can understand the reality easily. Similarly, the system has to detect the semantic problem and should change into meaningful sentence. Utilization of WordNet lexical database helps in reasoning process that system has to understand as human being that rat cannot kill the Lion. The validator suggests the sentence as 'Lion killed the rat or Rat killed by the Lion'

WordNet is efficiently utilized for these kinds of sentence validation in both ways which include syntactic and semantic ways .WordNet is a large lexical database of any language. Nouns, verbs, adjectives and adverbs are grouped into sets of cognitive synonyms (synsets), each expressing a distinct concept. Synsets are interlinked by means of conceptual-semantic and lexical relations. The resulting network of meaningfully related words and concepts can be navigated with the browser. WordNet's structure makes it a useful tool for computational linguistics and natural language processing.

Section 2 discusses the related work and Section 3 gives the reasons for reasoning the stories. Section 4 discusses about the intelligent frame work for reasoning the stories. Section 5 focuses on the role of Wordnet in reasoning. Section 6 discusses the conclusion and future works.

2 Related works

There are different types of story generators available for the purpose of automatic story generation and their evolution is described below.

Propp (1968) discussed the story generation as; a tale is a whole that may be composed of thirty one moves. A move is a type of development proceeding from villainy or a lack, through intermediary functions to marriage, or to other functions employed as a denouement (ending). One tale may be composed of several moves that are related between them. One move may directly follow another, but they may also interweave; a development, which has begun pauses and a new move, is inserted.

Bailey (1999) described an approach to automatic story generation based on the twin assumptions that it is possible for the generation of a story to be driven by modeling of the responses to the story of an imagined target reader, and that doing so allows the essence of what makes a story work (its 'storiness') to be encapsulated in a simple and general way.

Charles, F et al (2001), presented results from a first version of a fully implemented storytelling prototype, which illustrates the generation of variants of a generic storyline. These variants result from the interaction of autonomous characters with one another, with environment resources or from user intervention.

Dimitrios N. Konstantinou et al (2002) discussed about the story generation model HOMER. It receives natural language input in the form of a sentence or an icon corresponding to a scene from a story and it generates a text-only narrative apart from a story line and it includes a plot, characters, settings, the user's stylistic preferences and also their point-of-view.

Riedl et al (2004) had provided planning algorithm for story generation. The story planners are limited by the fact that they can only operate on the story world provided, which impacts the ability of the planner to find a solution story plan and the quality and structure of the story plan if one is found, but which lacks semantics.

George miller (1998) provided a wonderful environment to have the collection of words and their synonyms and they are put together to form a lexical database. It helps to retrieve the meaning for any kinds of words in any language.

Feinerer (2009) discussed about WordNet package and it provides Java interface to the WordNet1 lexical database of English which is commonly used in linguistics and text mining.

Reasoner framework helps to overcome the semantic lacking of story which can be resolved by reasoning the stories in a systematic and efficient way using the advantages of WordNet.

3 Reasons for reasoning the story

As described earlier part of the paper, many story generation model generates different kinds of story. Jaya et al (2007) stated the development of automatic story generation with ontology. Generated story may lack in meanings which pull down the interest of the readers. In order to afford meaningful stories, they need to undergo the reasoning process. It provides the semantically validated stories in neat and efficient way. The main reasons for reasoning the stories are given below:

- To check the syntactical structure of the story
- To provide the semantics to the sentence by means of
    - characters and their attributes
    - Events in stories which helps to generate new ones.
- To avoid ambiguity over the sentences
- To assist in validation of any kinds of stories
- To strengthen the stories, by acquiring knowledge from the WordNet.

Framework for reasoning the stories

The framework for reasoning the stories are shown in Figure – 1 and it helps in story analysis to perform the validation. Mainly, this framework has been designed for the story which is automatically generated by the system. This framework mainly divides into two phases such as parser and reasoner.

4.1 Parser

Parser contains the two phases namely separator and analyzer. Separator helps to separate the story into story segments called sentences. The separation of sentences helps to check the sentences by its form of sentence structure and the meaning of the story. Analyzer used to identify the noun, verb, settings, location and etc from the story which helps in semantic validation.

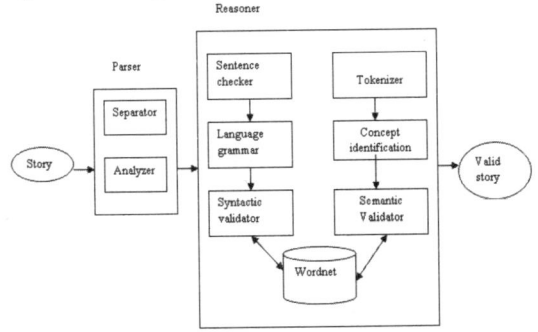

Figure – 1 Framework for reasoning the story

For example, location: forest, character: noun, if one of the sentences in the story is, "Lion was walking in to mall", and then validator needs to correct the sentence as "Lion was walking in to den". As a human beings, know that forest based stories will not have a location called mall and the city based the stories will have the mall. This kind of simple reasoning helps to provide the semantic validation to the story.

4.2 Reasoner

Reasoner divides its path into two such as syntactic validation framework and semantic validation framework. Syntactic validation framework helps to check the sentence structure of the sentences. If the generated sentence is "Lion was sleep den" in the 'Lion and mouse 'story then, it needs to undergo the syntactic validation and the generated sentence should be either as "Lion was sleeping in the den" or "Lion slept". The Figure - 2 shows the syntactic validation of sentence using WordNet. Since WordNet provides the clear view of noun, verb and their tense, helps to change the tense too. It is a large lexical database of any language. Figure -3 provides the extraction of the word "Lion" from the word net. It gives four dimension of lion such as animal, social animal, astrology, zodiac sixth sign. Based on the context, the word lion has been identified and the suitable phrase can be utilized for the validation.

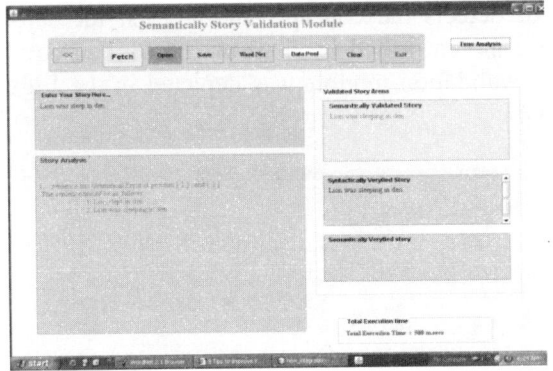

Figure – 2 syntactic validation of story using Wordnet

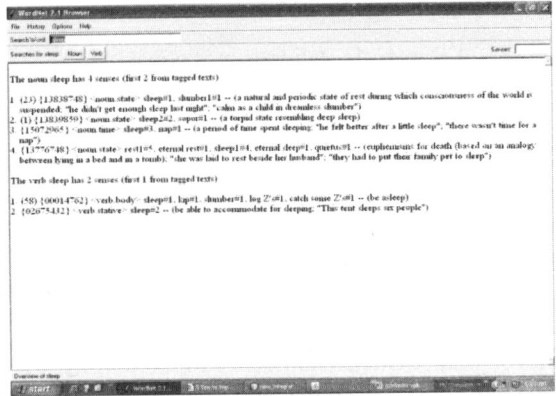

Figure – 3 Extraction of word from Wordnet

For the semantic validation, machine generated stories definitely needs to undertake the validation criteria. The generated sentences may be meaningless for the real world aspects; it needs to come across the semantic validation. For example, Automatic Story Generator generates the following sentence, "cat killed lion". In the reasoner module, the sentence has been tokenized in the tokenizer module. The noun and verb has been extracted from the sentence, each token parsed to the Wordnet and their characteristics has been extracted from the WordNet which helps in semantic validation. As discussed earlier, the lion has four dimensions in Wordnet.

Since 'cat' is already in the sentence, animal dimension for lion in the Wordnet has been identified, extracted and validated.

In the next level of validation, Even though cat and lion are animals, but the difference here is, the cat belongs to domestic animal family, lion belongs to wild animal family. In the concept identification module, domestic has lower value than the wild. Therefore, the conclusion here is,' the cat cannot kill the lion'. So the semantic validator detects the concepts and suggest the sentence as 'cat killed by lion' or 'lion killed cat'. This validation module was depicted in the Figure 4

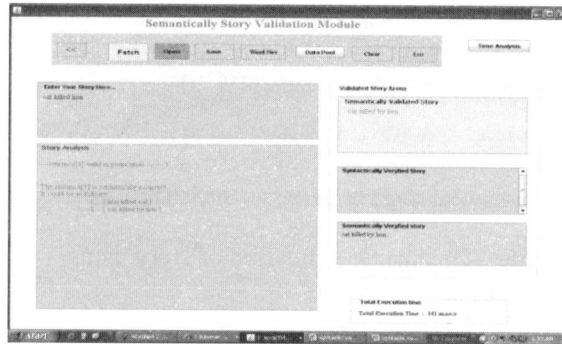

Figure – 4 Semantic validation of story using Wordnet

Similarly, consider one more sample sentence as;" donkey was crossing the bank in forest". The noun bank refers to different dimensions. Since donkey and forest exists in the Sentence, ambiguity of the word 'bank' has been resolved, and the correct dimension of the bank is river bank which has been extracted from the WordNet. Otherwise, the bank which is the place for transaction of money can also brings the ambiguity of the word. The Figure 5 shows the multi dimensional view of the word 'Bank'. All the sentences in the story should be validated in both ways which includes syntactic and semantic. The semantic Validation elevates the interest of the reader on the story.

5 Role of Wordnet in reasoning

WordNet acts as brain of the system to provide artificial intelligence to the system for reasoning the stories. WordNet is independent of domains and it provides knowledge for any word given to the system. Wordnet helps the system for reasoning in the following ways

- Provides common understanding for the multi disciplinary group of people.
- Provides all possible meaning for the particular word.
- Easy integration with automatic story generation system.

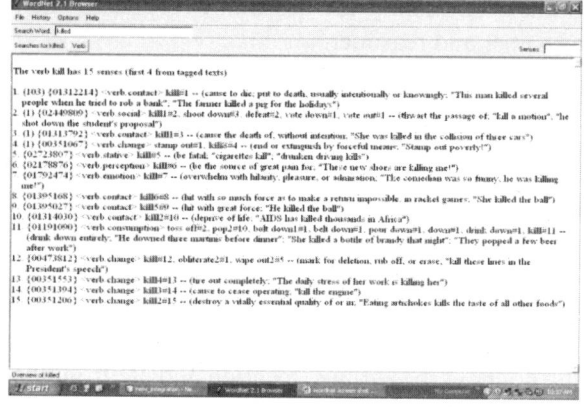

Figure – 5 Multidimensional view of a word in WordNet

WordNet is organized by the concept of synonym sets (synsets), groups of words that are roughly synonymous in a given context. Nouns, verbs, adjectives and adverbs are grouped into sets of cognitive synonyms (synsets), each expressing a distinct concept. Synsets are interlinked by means of conceptual-semantic and lexical relations. A Synsets represents a concept, and contains a set of Words, each of which has a sense that names that concept. The Wordnet is a system for bringing together different lexical and semantic relations between the words.

6 Implementation and Results

The above framework has been implemented in Java and uses the Java JDBC to connect to MySQL server and retrieve the relevant values. GUI is developed using Java Swing. For retrieving the single word, the frame work utilizes the lexical database and it helps to retrieve the different senses of the word with their identification number of synsets. The synset_id for each sense are identified by the extractor and by using the look up operation relative synsets information are retrieved. The retrieved results are used for the semantic checking.

The framework has been built and tested for various stories. The system parses the sentence to the framework for the reasoning purpose. Charles (2002) proposed a set of factors that are considered to check the quality of the story. These factors are utilized to check the quality of reasoned stories. Based on the above factors, the generated stories are given to a group of people to give their opinions about the generated stories with following scaling factors and with above said features. Excellent – 5; V. Good – 4; Good - 3; Fair – 2; needs improvement – 1;

S.no	Factor	describes
1	Overall	How is the story as an archetypal fairy tale?
2	Style	Did the author use an appropriate writing style?
3	Grammaticality	How would you rate the syntactic quality?
4	Flow	Did the sentences flow from one to the next?
5	Diction	How appropriate were the author's word choices?
6	Readability	How hard was it to read the prose?
7	Logicality	Did the story seem out of order?
8	Believability	Did the story's characters behave as you would expect?

Figure 6: Factors for Assessment of Story

S.no	Parameters	Before reasoning (max = 5)	After reasoning (max = 5)	Improvement
1.	Overall	4.3	4.7	1.09
2.	Style	4.0	4.5	1.13
3.	Grammaticality	4.1	4.8	1.17
4.	Flow	4.2	4.5	1.07
5.	Diction	2.8	3.4	1.21
6.	Readability	3.7	4.0	1.08
7.	Logicality	3.6	4.1	1.14
8.	Believability	4.4	4.7	1.07

Table1: Results of Story Assessment

The Table 1 depicts the calculated values for the stories before reasoning and after reasoning. The Figure – 7 shows the assessment value of story. After reasoning, the quality of the story is improved on an average of 1.12 times better than the before reasoning. The believability factor and overall content have very good feedback among other factors. The other factors like style of the story, grammar content in the story, flow of the story are the good factors in the next level and also the other good factors in the next level are diction, readability, and legibility.

7 Conclusion

Since the WordNet is not domain specific, the framework can be applied for all kinds of sentences in the story.

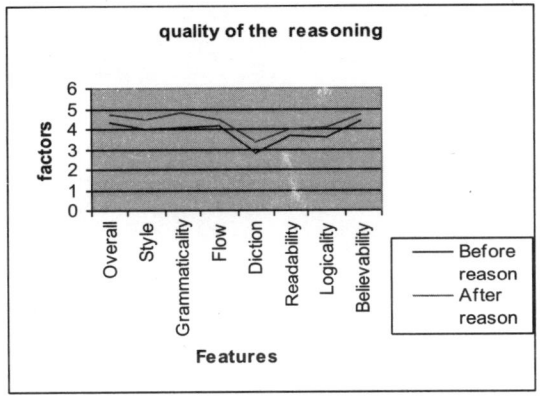

Figure 7: Assessment of the story

The framework can be improved by reasoning the sentences in the story as means of cause and effect. The sentences in the system generated story should be related with each other. If not so, the system has to reason the story and identify the relative order of sentences in the story. This will helps to make the Automatic Story Generation as effective one. The concept of automatic story generation helps the entertainment world in various aspects like automatic script writing, plot generation, screenplay writing etc.

References

Charles, F.; Mead, S.J.; Cavazza, M. "Character-driven story generation in interactive storytelling" Virtual Systems and Multimedia. Proceedings. Seventh International Conference on Virtual Systems and Multimedia. 25-27 pp no: 609 – 615, Oct. 2001

Dimitrios N. Konstantinou, Paul Mc Kevitt," HOMER: An Intelligent Multi-modal Story Generation System" Research plan. Faculty of Informatics, University of Ulster, Magee, Londonderry, 2002

George Miller, "WordNet. An electronic lexical database". Edited by Christiane Fellbaum, with a preface by. Cambridge, MA: MIT Press; 1998. 422 p

Ingo Feinerer, "Introduction to the wordnet Package" may 2008

Jaya A., J. Sathishkumar, G.V. Uma ,"A Novel Semantic Validation Mechanism For Automatic Story Generation Using Ontology" The 2007 International Conference on Artificial Intelligence (ICAI'07: June 25-28, 2007), Los Vegas, USA

Paul Bailey, "Searching for storiness: Story generation from a Reader's perspective" Symposium on Narrative Intelligence, AAAI Press, 1999

Propp. V "Morphology of the Folktale", University of Texas Press, 1968.

Riedl, M. and Young, RM, "Open-World Planning for Story Generation" Proceedings of the 19th International Joint Conference on Artificial Intelligence. California USA 2004.

Exploring the Integration of WordNet and FrameNet

Egoitz Laparra
IXA group, UPV/EHU
Donostia, Spain
egoitz.laparra@ehu.com

German Rigau
IXA group, UPV/EHU
Donostia, Spain
german.rigau@ehu.com

Montse Cuadros
TALP Research Center, UPC
Barcelona, Spain
cuadros@lsi.upc.edu

Abstract

This paper presents a novel automatic approach to partially integrate FrameNet and WordNet. In that way we expect to extend FrameNet coverage, to enrich WordNet with frame semantic information and possibly to extend FrameNet to languages other than English. The method uses a knowledge-based Word Sense Disambiguation algorithm for matching the FrameNet lexical units to WordNet synsets. Specifically, we exploit a graph-based Word Sense Disambiguation algorithm that uses a large-scale knowledge-base derived from existing resources. We have developed and tested additional versions of this algorithm showing substantial improvements over state-of-the-art results. Finally, we show some examples and figures of the resulting semantic resource.

1 Introduction

Predicate models such as FrameNet (Baker et al., 1998), VerbNet (Kipper, 2005) or PropBank (Palmer et al., 2005) are core resources in most advanced NLP tasks, such as Question Answering, Textual Entailment or Information Extraction. Most of the systems with Natural Language Understanding capabilities require a large and precise amount of semantic knowledge at the predicate-argument level. This type of knowledge allows to identify the underlying typical participants of a particular event independently of its realization in the text. Thus, using these models, different linguistic phenomena expressing the same event, such as active/passive transformations, verb alternations and nominalizations can be harmonized into a common semantic representation. In fact, lately, several systems have been developed for shallow semantic parsing and semantic role labeling using these resources (Erk and Pado, 2004), (Shi and Mihalcea, 2005), (Giuglea and Moschitti, 2006).

However, building large and rich enough predicate models for broad–coverage semantic processing takes a great deal of expensive manual effort involving large research groups during long periods of development. Thus, the coverage of currently available predicate-argument resources is still unsatisfactory. For example, (Burchardt et al., 2005) or (Shen and Lapata, 2007) indicate the limited coverage of FrameNet as one of the main problems of this resource. In fact, FrameNet1.3 covers around 10,000 lexical-units while for instance, WordNet3.0 contains more than 150,000 words. Furthermore, the same effort should be invested for each different language (Subirats and Petruck, 2003). Following the line of previous works (Shi and Mihalcea, 2005), (Burchardt et al., 2005), (Johansson and Nugues, 2007), (Pennacchiotti et al., 2008), (Cao et al., 2008), (Tonelli and Pianta, 2009), we empirically study a novel approach to partially integrate FrameNet (Baker et al., 1998) and WordNet (Fellbaum, 1998). The method relies on the use of a knowledge-based Word Sense Disambiguation (WSD) algorithm that uses a large-scale graph of concepts derived from WordNet (Fellbaum, 1998) and eXtented WordNet (Mihalcea and Moldovan, 2001). The WSD algorithm is applied to coherent groupings of words belonging to the same frame. In that way we expect to extend the coverage of FrameNet (by including from WordNet closely related concepts), to enrich WordNet with frame semantic information (by porting frame information to Wordnet) and possibly to extend FrameNet to languages other than English (by exploiting local wordnets aligned to the English WordNet).

WordNet [1] (Fellbaum, 1998) is by far the most widely-used knowledge base. In fact, WordNet is being used world-wide for anchoring different types of semantic knowledge including word-

---
[1] http://wordnet.princeton.edu/

nets for languages other than English (Atserias et al., 2004), domain knowledge (Magnini and Cavaglià, 2000) or ontologies like SUMO (Niles and Pease, 2001) or the EuroWordNet Top Concept Ontology (Álvez et al., 2008). It contains manually coded information about English nouns, verbs, adjectives and adverbs and is organized around the notion of a *synset*. A synset is a set of words with the same part-of-speech that can be interchanged in a certain context. For example, <*student, pupil, educatee*> form a synset because they can be used to refer to the same concept. A synset is often further described by a gloss, in this case: "a learner who is enrolled in an educational institution" and by explicit semantic relations to other synsets. Each synset represents a concept that are related with an large number of semantic relations, including hypernymy/hyponymy, meronymy/holonymy, antonymy, entailment, etc.

FrameNet [2] (Baker et al., 1998) is a very rich semantic resource that contains descriptions and corpus annotations of English words following the paradigm of Frame Semantics (Fillmore, 1976). In frame semantics, a Frame corresponds to a scenario that involves the interaction of a set of typical participants, playing a particular role in the scenario. FrameNet groups words or lexical units (LUs hereinafter) into coherent semantic classes or frames, and each frame is further characterized by a list of participants or lexical elements (LEs hereinafter). Different senses for a word are represented in FrameNet by assigning different frames.

Currently, FrameNet represents more than 10,000 LUs and 825 frames. More than 6,100 of these LUs also provide linguistically annotated corpus examples. However, only 722 frames have associated a LU. From those, only 9,360 LUs[3] where recognized by WordNet (out of 92%) corresponding to only 708 frames.

LUs of a frame can be nouns, verbs, adjectives and adverbs representing a coherent and closely related set of meanings that can be viewed as a small semantic field. For example, the frame EDUCATION_TEACHING contains LUs referring to the teaching activity and their participants. It is evoked by LUs like *student.n*, *teacher.n*, *learn.v*, *instruct.v*, *study.v*, etc. The frame also defines core semantic roles (or FEs) such as STUDENT, SUBJECT or TEACHER that are semantic participants of the frame and their corresponding LUs (see example below).

[Bernard Lansky]$_{STUDENT}$ studied [the piano]$_{SUBJECT}$ [with Peter Wallfisch]$_{TEACHER}$.

The paper is organized as follows. After this short introduction, in section 2 we present the graph-based Word Sense Disambiguation algorithm and the additional versions studied in this work. The evaluation framework and the results obtained by the different algorithms are presented and analyzed in section 3. Section 4 shows some examples and figures of the resulting semantic resource, and finally, in section 5, we draw some final conclusions and outline future work.

2 SSI algorithms

We have used a version of the Structural Semantic Interconnections algorithm (SSI) called SSI-Dijkstra(Cuadros and Rigau, 2008)(Laparra and Rigau, 2009). SSI is a knowledge-based iterative approach to Word Sense Disambiguation (Navigli and Velardi, 2005). The original SSI algorithm is very simple and consists of an initialization step and a set of iterative steps.

Given W, an ordered list of words to be disambiguated, the SSI algorithm performs as follows. During the initialization step, all monosemous words are included into the set I of already interpreted words, and the polysemous words are included in P (all of them pending to be disambiguated). At each step, the set I is used to disambiguate one word of P, selecting the word sense which is closer to the set I of already disambiguated words. Once a sense is disambiguated, the word sense is removed from P and included into I. The algorithm finishes when no more pending words remain in P.

In order to measure the proximity of one synset (of the word to be disambiguated at each step) to a set of synsets (those word senses already interpreted in I), the original SSI uses an in-house knowledge base derived semi-automatically which integrates a variety of online resources (Navigli, 2005). This very rich knowledge-base is used to calculate graph distances between synsets. In order to avoid the exponential explosion of possibilities, not all paths are considered. They used a context-free grammar of relations trained on Sem-

---

[2] http://framenet.icsi.berkeley.edu/
[3] Word-frame pairs

Cor to filter-out inappropriate paths and to provide weights to the appropriate paths.

Instead, SSI-Dijkstra uses the Dijkstra algorithm to obtain the shortest path distance between a node and some nodes of the whole graph. The Dijkstra algorithm is a greedy algorithm that computes the shortest path distance between one node an the rest of nodes of a graph. BoostGraph[4] library can be used to compute very efficiently the shortest distance between any two given nodes on very large graphs. As (Cuadros and Rigau, 2008), we also use already available knowledge resources to build a very large connected graph with 99,635 nodes (synsets) and 636,077 edges (the set of direct relations between synsets gathered from WordNet[5] (Fellbaum, 1998) and eXtended WordNet[6] (Mihalcea and Moldovan, 2001). For building this graph we used WordNet version 1.6 and the semantic relations appearing between synsets and disambiguated glosses of WordNet 1.7. To map the relations appearing in eXtended WordNet to WordNet version 1.6 we used the automatic WordNet Mappings[7] (Daudé et al., 2003). On that graph, SSI-Dijkstra computes several times the Dijkstra algorithm.

Previously, the SSI-Dijkstra algorithm have been used for constructing KnowNets (Cuadros and Rigau, 2008).

Initially, the list I of interpreted words should include the senses of the monosemous words in W, or a fixed set of word senses. Note that when disambiguating a Topic Signature associated to a particular synset, the list I always includes since the beginning at least the sense of the Topic Signature (in our example *pupil#n#1*) and the rest of monosemous words of W. However, many frames only group polysemous LUs. In fact, a total of 190 frames (out of 26%) only have polysemous LUs. Thus, SSI-Dijkstra provides no results when there are no monosemous terms in W. In this case, before applying SSI, the set of the LUs corresponding to a frame (the words included in W) have been ordered by polysemy degree. That is, the less polysemous words in W are processed first.

Obviously, if no monosemous words are found, we can adapt the SSI algorithm to make an initial guess based on the most probable sense of the less ambiguous word of W. For this reason we implemented two different versions of the basic SSI-Dijkstra algorithm: **SSI-Dijkstra-FirstSenses-I** (hereinafter FSI) and **SSI-Dijkstra-AllSenses-I** (hereinafter ASI). Thus, these two versions perform as SSI-Dijkstra when W contains monosemous terms, but differently when W contains only polysemous words. In fact, FSI and ASI always provide an interpretation of W.

While FSI includes in I the sense having minimal cumulated distance to the first senses of the rest of words in W, ASI includes in I the sense having minimal cumulated distance to the all the senses of the rest of words in W. The rationale behind the FSI algorithm is that the most frequent sense for a word, according to the WN sense ranking is very competitive in WSD tasks, and it is extremely hard to improve upon even slightly (McCarthy et al., 2004). Thus, this algorithm expects that the first sense in WordNet will be correct for most of the words in W. Regarding ASI, this algorithm expects that the words in W (corresponding to a very close semantic field) will establish many close path connections between different synsets of the same word (because of the fine-grained sense distinction of WordNet).

At each step, both the original SSI and also the SSI-Dijkstra algorithms only consider the set I of already interpreted words to disambiguate the next word of P. That is, the remaining words of P are not used in the disambiguation process. In fact, the words in P are still not disambiguated and can introduce noise in the process. However, the knowledge remaining in P can also help the process. In order to test the contribution of the remaining words in P in the disambiguation process, we also developed two more versions of the basic SSI-Dijkstra algorithm. **SSI-Dijkstra-FirstSenses-P** (hereinafter FSP) and **SSI-Dijkstra-AllSenses-P** (hereinafter ASP). When a word is being disambiguated, these two versions consider the set I of already interpreted words of W and also the rest of words remaining in P. That is, at each step, the algorithm selects the word sense which is closer to the set I of already disambiguated words and the remaining words of P all together. While FSP selects the sense having minimal cumulated distance to I and the first senses of the words in P, ASP selects the sense having minimal cumulated distance to I and all the senses of the words in P.

---

[4] http://www.boost.org/doc/libs/1_35_0/libs/graph/doc/index.html
[5] http://wordnet.princeton.edu
[6] http://xwn.hlt.utdallas.edu
[7] http://www.lsi.upc.es/~nlp/tools/mapping.html

	FN	GS	10	VM
#Frames	708	372	195	299
Nouns	5.87	7.90	13.58	4.18
Verbs	5.77	6.49	9.70	11.32
Adjectives	2.49	3.24	5.36	1.27
Other	0.11	0.14	0.24	0.05
Not in WN	1.07	1.30	2.13	1.02
Monosemous	4.40	5.79	9.87	4.50
Polysemous	8.77	10.68	16.88	11.30
#senses	3.64	3.45	3.63	4.31
Total	14.24	17.77	28.88	16.82

Table 1: Number of frames and average distribution of words per frame of the different datasets

3 Experiments

We have evaluated the performance of the different versions of the SSI algorithm using the same data set used by (Tonelli and Pianta, 2009). This data set consists of a total of 372 LUs corresponding to 372 different frames from FrameNet1.3 (one LU per frame). Each LUs have been manually annotated with the corresponding WordNet 1.6 synset. This Gold Standard includes 9 frames (5 verbs and 4 nouns) with only one LU (the one that has been sense annotated). Obviously, for these cases, our approach will produce no results since no context words can be used to help the disambiguation process[8]. Table 1 presents the main characteristics of the datasets we used in this work. In this table, *FN* stands for FrameNet[9], *GS* for the Gold-Standard, *10* for those Gold-Standard frames having at least 10 LUs and *VM* for the FrameNet–WordNet verb sense mapping[10] from (Shi and Mihalcea, 2005). Note that *VM* refers here to the characteristics of the frames appearing in the resource, not the mapping itself. The table shows for each dataset, the number of frames and the average distribution per frame of each POS, the words not represented in WordNet, the number of monosemous and polysemous words, the polysemy degree and the total words. The number of words per frame in this Gold Standard seems to be higher than the average in FrameNet.

Table 2 presents detailed results per Part-of-Speech (POS) of the performance of the different SSI algorithms on the Gold Standard in terms of Precision (P), Recall (R) and F1 measure (harmonic mean of recall and precision). In bold appear the best results for precision, recall and F1 measures. As baseline, we also include the performance measured on this data set of the most frequent sense according to the WordNet sense ranking (*wn-mfs*). Remember that this baseline is very competitive in WSD tasks, and it is extremely hard to beat.

We also included in the empirical evaluation the WordNet–FrameNet Verbal Mapping (**VM**) from (Shi and Mihalcea, 2005). As they work focused on verbal predicates for Semantic Parsing, *VM* does not provide provides results for nouns and adjectives. The annotation process between FrameNet 1.2 verb LUs and WordNet 2.0 verbal senses was performed manually. Since WordNet sense distinctions are very fine-grained, many verbal LUs in FrameNet were associated to multiple WordNet senses. We transport WordNet 2.0 sensekeys to version 1.6 by using the sense mappings from WordNet. Obviously, both FrameNet versions, that is 1.2 and 1.3, also presents differences in coverage of frames, LUs and correspondences between them. The final mapping covers a total of 299 frames and 2,967 verbal LUs.

As expected, the manual annotation provided by *VM* obtains the best results for verbs. However, possibly because of the different coverage of the FrameNet and WordNet versions, the recall is not as high as expected. In fact, the best recall for verbs is obtained by FSP.

All the different versions of the SSI-Dijkstra algorithm outperform the baseline. Only SSI-Dijkstra obtains lower recall for verbs because of its lower coverage. In fact, SSI-Dijkstra only provide answers for those frames having monosemous LUs, the SSI-Dijkstra variants provide answers for frames having at least two LUs (monosemous or polysemous) and the baseline always provides an answer.

As expected, the SSI algorithms present different performances according to the different POS. Also as expected, verbs seem to be more difficult than nouns and adjectives as reflected by both the results of the baseline and the SSI-Dijkstra algorithms. For nouns and adjectives, the best results are achieved by both FSI and ASI variants. Remember that these versions perform as SSI-Dijkstra on frames having monosemous LUs but performing an initial guess on frames having only polysemous LUs. While FSI makes an ini-

---

[8] In fact, FrameNet has 33 frames with only one LU, and 63 with only two.

[9] We removed frames without assigned LUs or not represented in WordNet

[10] Available at http://www.cse.unt.edu/~rada/downloads.html

	nouns			verbs			adjectives			all		
	P	R	F	P	R	F	P	R	F	P	R	F
VM	0.00	0.00	0.00	0.93	0.66	0.77	0.00	0.00	0.00	0.93	0.34	0.50
wn-mfs	0.75	0.75	0.75	0.64	0.64	0.64	0.80	0.80	0.80	0.69	0.69	0.69
SSI-Dijkstra	**0.84**	0.65	0.73	0.70	0.56	0.62	**0.90**	0.82	0.86	**0.78**	0.63	0.69
FSI	0.80	**0.77**	**0.79**	0.66	0.65	0.65	0.89	**0.89**	**0.89**	0.74	0.73	0.73
ASI	0,80	**0,77**	**0,79**	0,67	0,65	0,66	0,89	**0,89**	**0,89**	0,75	0,73	0,74
FSP	0.75	0.73	0.74	**0.71**	**0.69**	**0.70**	0.79	0.79	0.79	0.73	0.72	0.72
ASP	0.72	0.69	0.70	0.68	0.66	0.67	0.75	0.75	0.75	0.70	0.69	0.69
SSI-Dijkstra+	0.79	0.77	0.78	0.70	0.68	0.69	0.89	**0.89**	**0.89**	0.76	**0.74**	**0.75**

Table 2: Results of the different SSI algorithms on the *GS* dataset

tial guess including in I the sense of the less polysemous word having minimal cumulated distance to the *first senses* of the rest of words in W, ASI makes an initial guess including in I the sense of the less polysemous word having minimal cumulated distance to *all* the senses of the rest of words in W. In fact, FSI and ASI behave differently than SSI-Dijsktra in 73 frames having only polysemous LUs in the data set. Interestingly, the best results for verbs are achieved by FSP, not only on terms of F1 but also on precision. Remember that FSP always uses I and the first senses of the rest of words in P as context for the disambiguation. It seems that for verbs it is useful to consider not only the disambiguated words but also the most frequent senses of the rest of words being disambiguated. However, for nouns and adjectives the best precision is achieved by the original SSI-Dijkstra. This fact suggests the importance of having monosemous or correctly disambiguated words in I at the beginning of the incremental disambiguation process, at least for nouns and adjectives.

To our knowledge, on the same dataset, the best results so far are the ones presented by (Tonelli and Pianta, 2009) reporting a Precision of 0.71, a Recall of 0.62 and an F measure of 0.66[11]. Although they present a system which considers the most frequent sense, the most frequent domain and overlappings between the WordNet glosses and the FrameNet definitions of the LUs, in fact these results are below the most-frequent sense according to the WordNet sense ranking.

As a result of this empirical study, we developed **SSI-Dijkstra+** a new version of SSI-Dijkstra using ASI for nouns and adjectives, and FSP for verbs. SSI-Dijkstra+ clearly outperforms the baseline. Interestingly, the performance of this new algorithm improves overall, but obtains lower results for nouns than FSI and ASI and lower results for verbs than FSP.

	P	R	F
mfs-wn	0.67	0.67	0.67
SSI-Dijkstra	**0.79**	0.74	0.76
FSI	0.78	0.78	0.78
ASI	0.78	0.77	0.78
FSP	0.72	0.71	0.71
ASP	0.70	0.70	0.70
SSI-Dijkstra+	**0.79**	**0.79**	**0.79**

Table 3: Results using FrameNet–WordNet Verbal mapping from (Shi and Mihalcea, 2005) as gold standard

Table 3 shows presents detailed results of the performance of the different SSI algorithms on the FrameNet–WordNet Verbal mapping (*VM*) produced by (Shi and Mihalcea, 2005) in terms of Precision (P), Recall (R) and F1 measure. In bold appear the best results for precision, recall and F1 measures. Again, we also include on the most frequent sense according to the WordNet sense ranking (*wn-mfs*).

On this dataset, the overall results are much higher because this dataset provides several correct verbal senses per LU. Again, the knowledga-based WSD algorithms perform over the most frequent sense baseline.

In fact, we expect much better results performing the disambiguation process including in I, when available, the manually assigned FrameNet–WordNet Verbal mappings. Possibly, using this approach very high accuracies for nouns, adjectives and the remaining verbs could be obtained.

4 WordFrameNet

The contribution of this new resource we call WordFrameNet is threefold[12]. First, we extend

---

[11] In fact, both evaluations are slightly different since they divided the dataset into a development set of 100 LUs and a testset with the rest of LUs, while we provide results for the whole dataset.

[12] Available at http://anonymous-web-page

the coverage of FrameNet. That is, by establishing synset mappings to the FrameNet LUs, we can also add their corresponding synonyms to the frame. For instance, the frame EDUCATION_TEACHING only considers *instruct.v* and *instruction.n*, but not *instructor.n* which is a synonym in WordNet of the LU *teacher.n*. Thus, while the original FrameNet have 9,328 LUs corresponding to 6,565 synsets, WordFrameNet have 20,587 LUs. That is, more than the double. Tables 5 and 6 show respectively, the original and new LUs for the EDUCATION_TEACHING frame. In this case, 24 of the original LUs have been associated to WN synsets, thus producing 18 new LUs for this frame.

Second, we can extend the coverage of semantic relations in WordNet. That is, by establishing new semantic relations among all the LUs of a particular frame. For instance, in WordNet there is no a semantic relation connecting <*student, pupil, educatee*> and <*teacher, instructor*> directly. In that way, we obtain 124,718 new semantic relations between the original 6,565 synsets. 121,813 of these relations that connect synsets of the same frame do not appear in WordNet. In table 4 we show the number of existing WordNet relations between synsets of the same frame.

Hypernymy	2028
Antonymy	408
Similar-to	328
Also-see	178
Part	97
Attribute	82
Entailment	44
Verb-group	22
Derived-from	18
Cause	14
Member	8
Substance	4
Participle-of-verb	1

Table 4: WordNet relations in FrameNet

Third, we can also automatically extend FrameNet to languages other than English by exploiting local wordnets aligned to the English WordNet. For instance, the Spanish synset aligned to <*student, pupil, educatee*> is <*alumno, estudiante*> and the Italian one is <*allievo, alunno, studente*>. In Spanish, we obtain a WordFrameNet with 14,106 LUs. In fact, the current version of the Spanish FrameNet consists of 308 frames with 1,047 LUs[13] (Subirats and Petruck, 2003). Table 7 presents the Spanish version of WordFrameNet for the EDUCATION_TEACHING frame. In this case, 30 Spanish LUs have been associated to this particular frame, while the current version of the Spanish FrameNet only have 2 LUs (*aprender.v* and *enseñar.v*).

Furthermore, we can also transport to the disambiguated LUs the knowledge currently available from other semantic resources associated to WordNet such as SUMO (Niles and Pease, 2001), WordNet Domains (Magnini and Cavaglià, 2000), etc. For instance, now the LU corresponding to *student.n* can also have associated the SUMO label *SocialRole* and its corresponding logical axioms, and the WordNet Domains *school* and *university*.

5 Conclusions and future work

In this work, we have presented an ongoing work aiming to integrate FrameNet and WordNet. The method uses a knowledge based Word Sense Disambiguation (WSD) algorithm called SSI-Dijkstra for assigning the appropriate synset of WordNet to the semantically related Lexical Units of a given frame from FrameNet. This algorithm relies on the use of a large knowledge base derived from WordNet and eXtended WordNet. Since the original SSI-Dijkstra requires a set of monosemous or already interpreted words, we have devised, developed and empirically tested different versions of this algorithm to deal with sets having only polysemous words. The resulting new algorithms obtain improved results over state-of-the-art.

Finally, using the same automatic approach, we also plan to disambiguate the Lexical Elements of a given frame. Thus, the resulting resource will also integrate the core semantic roles of FrameNet. For example, for the frame EDUCATION_TEACHING we will associate the appropriate WordNet synsets to the Lexical elements STUDENT, SUBJECT or TEACHER.

---

[13] http://gemini.uab.es:9080/SFNsite/sfn-data/current-project-status

train.v	00407541-v	prepare for a future task or career
instruct.v	00562446-v	impart skills or knowledge to
educational.a	02716766-a	relating to the process of education
tutee.n	07654181-n	learns from a tutor
schoolteacher.n	07551404-n	a teacher in a school below the college level
educate.v	00407541-v	prepare for a future task or career
study.v	00405251-v	be a student of a certain subject
instruction.n	00567704-n	activities that impart knowledge
teacher.n	07632177-n	a person whose occupation is teaching
student.n	07617015-n	a learner who is enrolled in an educational institution
schoolmistress.n	07550942-n	a woman schoolteacher
tutor.v	00562981-v	be a tutor to someone; give individual instruction
lecturer.n	07367816-n	someone who lectures professionally
training.n	00574678-n	activity leading to skilled behavior
pupil.n	07617015-n	a learner who is enrolled in an educational institution
schoolmaster.n	07551048-n	any person (or institution) who acts as an educator
school.v	01626656-v	educate in or as if in a school
master.v	00403563-v	be or become completely proficient or skilled in
tutor.n	07162304-n	a person who gives private instruction (as in singing or acting)
professor.n	07504465-n	someone who is a member of the faculty at a college or university
learn.v	00562446-v	impart skills or knowledge to
teach.v	00562446-v	impart skills or knowledge to
coach.v	00565367-v	teach and supervise, as in sports or acting
education.n	00567704-n	activities that impart knowledge

Table 5: LUs corresponding to EDUCATION_TEACHING frame

develop.v	00407541-v
prepare.v	00407541-v
educate.v	00407541-v
instruct.v	00562446-v
school_teacher.n	07551404-n
read.v	00405251-v
take.v	00405251-v
teaching.n	00567704-n
pedagogy.n	00567704-n
educational_activity.n	00567704-n
instructor.n	07632177-n
educatee.n	07617015-n
schoolmarm.n	07550942-n
mistress.n	07550942-n
preparation.n	00574678-n
grooming.n	00574678-n
get_the_hang.v	00403563-v
private_instructor.n	07162304-n

Table 6: New LUs associated to EDUCATION_TEACHING frame

adiestrar.v	00407541-v
amaestrar.v	00407541-v
enseñar.v	00562446-v
instruir.v	00562446-v
educacional.a	02716766-a
maestra.n	07551404-n
maestro.n	07551404-n
profesor.n	07551404-n
profesora.n	07551404-n
aprender.v	00405251-v
educación.n	00567704-n
enseñanza.n	00567704-n
instructor.n	07632177-n
monitor.n	07632177-n
profesor.n	07632177-n
alumna.n	07617015-n
alumno.n	07617015-n
estudiante.n	07617015-n
maestra.n	07550942-n
profesora.n	07550942-n
tutelar.v	00562981-v
conferenciante.n	07367816-n
formación.n	00574678-n
preparación.n	00574678-n
instructor.n	07162304-n
preceptor.n	07162304-n
profesor_particular.n	07162304-n
tutor.n	07162304-n
profesor.n	07504465-n
entrenar.v	00565367-v

Table 7: Spanish LUs inferred for EDUCATION_TEACHING frame

References

J. Álvez, J. Atserias, J. Carrera, S. Climent, A. Oliver, and G. Rigau. 2008. Consistent annotation of eurowordnet with the top concept ontology. In *Proceedings of Fourth International WordNet Conference (GWC'08)*.

J. Atserias, L. Villarejo, G. Rigau, E. Agirre, J. Carroll, B. Magnini, and Piek Vossen. 2004. The meaning multilingual central repository. In *Proceedings of GWC*, Brno, Czech Republic.

C. Baker, C. Fillmore, and J. Lowe. 1998. The berkeley framenet project. In *COLING/ACL'98*, Montreal, Canada.

Aljoscha Burchardt, Katrin Erk, and Anette Frank. 2005. A WordNet Detour to FrameNet. In *Proceedings of the GLDV 2005 GermaNet II Workshop*, pages 408–421, Bonn, Germany.

Diego De Cao, Danilo Croce, Marco Pennacchiotti, and Roberto Basili. 2008. Combining word sense and usage for modeling frame semantics. In *Proceedings of The Symposium on Semantics in Systems for Text Processing (STEP 2008)*, Venice, Italy.

M. Cuadros and G. Rigau. 2008. Knownet: Building a large net of knowledge from the web. In *22nd International Conference on Computational Linguistics (COLING'08)*, Manchester, UK.

J. Daudé, L. Padró, and G. Rigau. 2003. Validation and Tuning of Wordnet Mapping Techniques. In *Proceedings of RANLP*, Borovets, Bulgaria.

Katrin Erk and Sebastian Pado. 2004. A powerful and versatile xml format for representing role-semantic annotation. In *Proceedings of LREC-2004*, Lisbon.

C. Fellbaum, editor. 1998. *WordNet. An Electronic Lexical Database*. The MIT Press.

Charles J. Fillmore. 1976. Frame semantics and the nature of language. In *Annals of the New York Academy of Sciences: Conference on the Origin and Development of Language and Speech*, volume 280, pages 20–32, New York.

Ana-Maria Giuglea and Alessandro Moschitti. 2006. Semantic role labeling via framenet, verbnet and propbank. In *Proceedings of COLING-ACL 2006*, pages 929–936, Morristown, NJ, USA. ACL.

Richard Johansson and Pierre Nugues. 2007. Using WordNet to extend FrameNet coverage. In *Proceedings of the Workshop on Building Frame-semantic Resources for Scandinavian and Baltic Languages*, at *NODALIDA*, Tartu, Estonia, May 24.

Karen Kipper. 2005. *VerbNet: A broad-coverage, comprehensive verb lexicon*. Ph.D. thesis, University of Pennsylvania.

Egoitz Laparra and German Rigau. 2009. Integrating wordnet and framenet using a knowledge-based word sense disambiguation algorithm. In *Proceedings of RANLP*, Borovets, Bulgaria.

B. Magnini and G. Cavaglià. 2000. Integrating subject field codes into wordnet. In *Proceedings of LREC*, Athens. Greece.

D. McCarthy, R. Koeling, J. Weeds, and J. Carroll. 2004. Finding predominant senses in untagged text. In *Proceedings of ACL*, pages 280–297.

R. Mihalcea and D. Moldovan. 2001. extended wordnet: Progress report. In *Proceedings of NAACL Workshop on WordNet and Other Lexical Resources*, Pittsburgh, PA.

R. Navigli and P. Velardi. 2005. Structural semantic interconnections: a knowledge-based approach to word sense disambiguation. *IEEE Transactions on Pattern Analysis and Machine Intelligence (PAMI)*, 27(7):1063–1074.

R. Navigli. 2005. Semi-automatic extension of large-scale linguistic knowledge bases. In *Proc. of 18th FLAIRS International Conference (FLAIRS)*, Clearwater Beach, Florida.

I. Niles and A. Pease. 2001. Towards a standard upper ontology. In *Proceedings of the 2nd International Conference on Formal Ontology in Information Systems (FOIS-2001)*, pages 17–19. Chris Welty and Barry Smith, eds.

Martha Palmer, Daniel Gildea, and Paul Kingsbury. 2005. The proposition bank: An annotated corpus of semantic roles. *Computational Linguistics*, 31(1):71–106, March.

Marco Pennacchiotti, Diego De Cao, Roberto Basili, Danilo Croce, and Michael Roth. 2008. Automatic induction of FrameNet lexical units. In *Proceedings of Empirical Methods in Natural Language Processing (EMNLP)*, Honolulu, Hawaii, USA.

Dan Shen and Mirella Lapata. 2007. Using semantic roles to improve question answering. In *Proceedings of the Joint Conference on (EMNLP-CoNLL)*, pages 12–21.

Lei Shi and Rada Mihalcea. 2005. Putting pieces together: Combining framenet, verbnet and wordnet for robust semantic parsing. In *Proceedings of CICLing*, Mexico.

Carlos Subirats and Miriam R.L. Petruck. 2003. Surprise: Spanish framenet! In *Proceedings of the International Congress of Linguists*, Praga.

Sara Tonelli and Emanuele Pianta. 2009. A novel approach to mapping framenet lexical units to wordnet synsets. In *Proceedings of IWCS-8*, Tilburg, The Netherlands.

Towards Universal Multilingual Knowledge Bases

Gerard de Melo
Max Planck Institute for Informatics
Saarbrücken, Germany
`demelo@mpi-inf.mpg.de`

Gerhard Weikum
Max Planck Institute for Informatics
Saarbrücken, Germany
`weikum@mpi-inf.mpg.de`

Abstract

Lexical, ontological, as well as encyclopedic knowledge is increasingly being encoded in machine-readable form. This paper deals with knowledge representation in multilingual settings. It begins by proposing a generic graph-based knowledge base framework, and then, in three case studies, explains how pre-existing knowledge can be cast into this framework. The first case study involves enriching WordNet with information about human languages and their relationships. The second study shows how machine learning techniques can be used to bootstrap a large-scale multilingual version of WordNet where semantic relationships between terms in many languages are captured. The final study examines how information can be extracted from Wiktionary to produce a lexical network of etymological and derivational relationships between words.

1 Introduction

Knowledge of various sorts, including lexical, ontological, and encyclopedic knowledge, is increasingly being captured in machine-readable form. When multiple human languages are involved, additional challenges need to be addressed. For instance, it is not evident how one best represents languages and their relationships, or how related words from different languages may be connected. This paper proposes a generic framework for representing multilingual knowledge in terms of semantic entity-relationship graphs in the spirit of WordNet (Fellbaum, 1998), a well-known monolingual lexical database. It presents three multilingual lexical knowledge bases that exemplify how one can accommodate pre-existing knowledge within the framework using automatic or semi-automatic techniques and simultaneously addresses the following three questions:

1. How can relationships between languages be captured?
2. How can semantic relationships between words in different languages be captured?
3. How can superficial (etymological, derivational) relationships between words in different languages be captured?

The rest of this paper is organized as follows. Section 2 defines the basic framework and discusses approaches to model terms (words and expressions), word senses, and languages. Section 3 introduces the first case study where WordNet is enriched with domain-specific knowledge about human languages and their relationships, addressing the first question. Section 4 describes a large-scale extension of WordNet to cover not just English words but over 800,000 terms from many different languages, which aims at the second question. Section 5 presents a lexical network that encodes etymological and derivational relationships between words, answering the third question. Finally, Section 6 provides concluding remarks.

2 Data Organization Framework

We begin with a few basic assumptions that define the general framework.

2.1 Preliminaries

Definition 2.1. A *statement* is an item from $\mathcal{U} \times \mathcal{R} \times \mathcal{U} \times [0,1] \times \Sigma$, where the universe $\mathcal{U}$ is a set of entities, $\mathcal{R}$ is a set of relations, and Σ is a labelling alphabet. A statement (x, r, y, c, a) expresses that two entities x, y stand in relation r to each other with degree of confidence c and additional attributes given by $a \in \Sigma$.

For example, one can specify that the English word "*snow*" stands in an `etymology` relation to the reconstructed Proto-Germanic form *"*snaiwaz*" with confidence $c < 1$, and an attribute a denoting the source of this claim. The universe $\mathcal{U}$ may include both real world entities as well as abstractions and conceptualizations. We use entity identifier strings to refer to them. In Semantic Web knowledge bases, the entities can be arbitrary real-world entities or Web resources. Relations like `dc:creator` express that one entity is the creator of another entity. In WordNet, the entities one deals with are mainly words and word senses, i.e. meanings of words. Relations include word-to-sense relations that connect words to their meanings and vice versa. Additionally, there are sense-to-sense relations like the hyponymy/hypernymy relation, which connects a word or word sense to a more general word or word sense, e.g. "*school*" is a hyponym of "*educational institution*". The statement attributes can for instance be used to capture data provenance, or to specify that a relation between two words applies with respect to specific senses of those words.

Definition 2.2. A *knowledge base* is a set of statements that are asserted to be true (to the extent given by their respective degrees of confidence).

A knowledge base of this form can also be seen as a graph or network, and statements can be viewed as edges or links in the network. Note that statements not in the knowledge base are not assumed to be false, i.e. there is no formal commitment to the Closed World Assumption. Hence one can freely extend a knowledge base with whatever information is available or required for a specific task, without implicitly asserting that other statements are false. For example, in Section 3, we extend WordNet with extensive information about a specific domain, and in Section 4 we add new terms to WordNet without being able to guarantee that all senses of those terms are covered. A knowledge base may also be created collaboratively by multiple stakeholders with different foci.

Up to this point, the definitions are generally compatible with the W3C RDF standard (Hayes, 2004). The following principle goes beyond the common practices on the Semantic Web.

Principle 2.3. $x = y$ should hold for any two entities $x, y \in U$ considered semantically identical.

This means that, within a single knowledge base, ideally only a single, shared set of entities should be used, without semantic duplicates. For example, when linking word senses to specific categories such as law, sports, etc., some knowledge bases rely on a separate vocabulary of domain labels, e.g. Bentivogli et al. (2004). We instead advocate following WordNet in using identifiers already present in the knowledge base instead of a separate vocabulary. In WordNet, the sense for "*plaintiff*" is connected to the primary sense of "*law*". This has the advantage of extensive information about the domains being readily available, e.g. the hypernym hierarchy can be used to relate domains to each other.

2.2 Representation Choices for Entities

In what follows, we elaborate on how specific real-world entities can be represented.

2.2.1 Terms

When considering entities for words, expressions, or more generally 'terms', different levels of abstraction can be considered. For the term entities, we choose to consider two homonyms, e.g. the animal noun "*bear*" and the verb "*bear*", as the same term, because, typically, one wishes to look up terms in the lexical knowledge base without already knowing what senses exist. This distinction is instead made at the level of sense entities instead of for term entities. In contrast, we do consider the Spanish term "*con*", which means "*with*", distinct from the French term "*con*", which means "*idiot*". This level of abstraction allows us to model relationships between words in different languages using statements like (`eng:"digital"`,`etymology`,`lat:"digitus"`,$1,\emptyset$) to express that the English word "*digital*" stems from the Latin word "*digitus*" (finger or toe). If one instead used pure string literals without language information, it would be necessary to specify the two respective languages as additional attributes of the statement.

We consider different word forms distinct terms. There are a few minor subtleties of term identity regarding string encoding. For multilingual applications, the ISO 10646 / Unicode standards offer an appropriate set of characters for encoding strings. Since Unicode allows encoding a character such as "à" in either a composed or in a decomposed form, NFC normalization (Davis and Dürst, 2008) is applied to avoid duplicate entities.

2.2.2 Senses

Lexical knowledge bases are generally based on the assumption that the meanings of a word can be enumerated as a list of word senses. In the EuroWordNet approach (Vossen, 1998), also adopted for BalkaNet and other related projects (Tufiş et al., 2004; Atserias et al., 2004), each individual wordnet has its own inventory of senses, and a separate interlingual index (ILI) is intended to serve as a language-neutral repository of senses. Whenever possible, senses in the individual wordnets are linked to the ILI by means of synonymy, near-synonymy, hyponymy, or other relations.

Such a representation can be transformed into one that is in accordance with Principle 2.3, where sense identifiers are directly shared whenever these can be thought of as existing in multiple languages. Such sharing is in fact one major difference between WordNet and traditional dictionaries: In WordNet, synonymous terms are tied to a single shared sense identifier, while in conventional dictionaries the respective senses have distinct, unconnected entries. What WordNet does for synonymous terms within a language can be generalized to terms across languages by allowing a sense entity to apply to words in more than one language. The general idea is that the set of terms associated with a sense should be either near-synonymous or translational equivalents (with respect to specific contexts).

Note that this principle does not imply that language-specific subtleties be neglected, since distinct entities may co-exist whenever semantic differences persist. For example, if in one language the word for "*tree*" has a meaning that includes shrubs, then that meaning should not be conflated with the meaning of the English word "*tree*", which generally does not include shrubs. In a similar vein, if in one language birds and insects are considered animals and in another they are not, then there are actually distinct concepts that need to be demarcated. This is similar to how the vernacular English concept of "*nuts*" should be distinguished from the corresponding botanical concept, which excludes peanuts and almonds.

2.2.3 Languages and Language Collections

Sense entities for individual human languages are of particular interest in a multilingual knowledge base. The English word "*language*" can be viewed from either a countable or an uncountable perspective. One might think of Spanish, Hindi, and so on, as individual *instances* of languages. Alternatively, language can be conceived as a phenomenon, and words like "*Spanish*" as referring to certain varieties of that phenomenon. In this latter conception, "*Spanish*", "*Hindi*", etc. can be regarded as hyponyms of "*language*", as in WordNet. This allows us to easily model a hierarchy that keeps making finer distinctions as one follows hyponymy links. For instance, from language families like the Semitic or Sinitic languages one may move down to macrolanguages like Arabic or Chinese, and then to more specific forms like Moroccan Arabic or Mandarin Chinese, dialect groups like Ji-Lu Mandarin, or even dialects of particular cities. Similar distinctions can be made with respect to temporal classifications, or writing systems and orthographies. Subjective or controversial distinctions between language families and macrolanguages, or between languages and dialects or sociolects can be avoided.

3 Extension of WordNet with Language-related Information

Our first case study deals with modelling relationships between human languages. More specifically, it involves enriching WordNet with domain-specific information about languages and their relationships, as elaborated earlier in Section 2.2.3. WordNet already contains certain languages and language families as hyponyms of "*language*". We extend WordNet's language hierarchy to cover a significantly larger range of languages, with additional background information. This allows multilingual applications to use language identifiers specified within the knowledge base in accordance with Principle 2.3, while simultaneously also facilitating interoperability with international standards. An application can look up information about a language, e.g. where it is spoken.

3.1 Knowledge Extraction

We draw on the following sources to extract relevant information:

- the ISO 639-3 specification[1], which defines codes for around 7,000 languages and lists relationships between macrolanguages and individual languages
- the ISO 639-5 specification[2], which describes a limited number of language families (e.g. Tai languages) and other collections (e.g. sign languages)
- the ISO 15924 specification[3], which lists a number of writing systems, e.g. Cyrillic, Devanagari, and Hangul
- the Ethnologue language codes database (Lewis, 2009), which provides additional language names, geographical regions, etc.

---

[1] http://www.sil.org/iso639-3/
[2] http://www.loc.gov/standards/iso639-5/
[3] http://unicode.org/iso15924/

- the Linguist List[4], which contributes information on extinct languages as well as constructed languages
- the Unicode Common Locale Data Repository[5] (CLDR), which connects languages to their geographical regions and writing systems, and delivers names in many languages
- the English Wikipedia[6], from which we can extract multilingual names, glosses, and language family information for several hundred languages

In order to abide to Principle 2.3, we attempt to merge duplicates.

1. Those resources that rely on codes defined by ISO 639 Part 1, 2, or 3 are consolidated simply by means of those codes, possibly relying on the ISO 639-3 mapping tables.
2. Wikipedia's languages are merged with languages from ISO 639-3 by extracting the codes from the respective Wikipedia articles.
3. Wikipedia's language families are merged with corresponding families from ISO 639-5 where possible, by extracting links from Wikipedia's "*List of ISO 639-5 codes*" article, which also provides equivalences between ISO 639-5 and ISO 639-3.
4. Finally, we attempt to map each sense entity x derived from the resources to existing WordNet senses y, using scores computed as

$$m(x,y) = \sum_{t \in \Gamma(x)} \frac{\mathbf{1}_{\Gamma(t) \cap \Delta(x)}(y)}{|\Gamma(t) \cap \Delta(x)|}.$$

Here, $\Delta(x)$ returns the set of all WordNet senses in the same WordNet branch where x will be placed. These branches are defined as hyponyms of the "*language*" or "*script*" senses, or as meronyms of the hemisphere senses for geographical areas (parts of one of the hemispheres). The function Γ yields the set of terms for a sense x, or the set of senses of a term t (i.e. the out-neighbourhood in the graph of all term-sense links). For a given set S, $\mathbf{1}_S$ is the corresponding set membership indicator function.

Those languages and writing systems (scripts) that could not be mapped to WordNet are connected to

[4]http://linguistlist.org/
[5]http://cldr.unicode.org/
[6]http://en.wikipedia.org/

the WordNet hypernym hierarchy as new senses in accordance with Section 2.2.3. The language senses are made hyponyms of the respective language family sense if such information is available, or simply added as direct hyponyms of "*language*" or similar words (e.g. "*artificial language*") if no explicit language family information is available.

Similarly, the writing systems defined by ISO 15924, e.g. Cyrillic and Devanagari, are made new instances of the sense for "*script*", and geographical regions are made new instances of "*geographical area*". These, too, are merged with existing entries already in WordNet when possible.

3.2 Results

Even for scores with a low threshold $m(x,y) > 0$, an accuracy rate of $94.3\% \pm 4.1\%$ is obtained for 100 random WordNet language mappings. Ambiguous and low-score mappings were corrected manually by an annotator to ensure the quality of the resulting extension. The process also adds over 7,000 new languages to the roughly 600 existing ones in WordNet, as well as smaller numbers of language families and scripts. Languages often have their name provided not only in English but in many different languages, sometimes over 100.

When new terms are added, these may not satisfy the lexicographic inclusion criteria that other entries are subjected to, e.g. certain language names may not be sufficiently lexicalized within a language to warrant an inclusion in WordNet. This problem is addressed by flagging the newly added term-sense statements appropriately.

The languages are integrated into WordNet's hypernym hierarchy, using macrolanguages and language families as intermediate hypernyms when possible. In addition to the hypernymy links, the language senses are also equipped with other statements that provide further background information, for instance geographical regions, identification codes, writing systems (links to writing system entities), etc. Table 1 shows an example for the African Bemba language (ChiBemba). Geographical regions are provided by the CLDR and Ethnologue based on ISO 3166 / UN M.49, and the respective entities are merged with the corresponding WordNet senses using the mapping procedure described above.

In the future, we would like to address automatically mapping ISO 639-6 identifiers to WordNet

Relation	Values*
has_gloss	"The Bemba language, Chibemba, also known as Cibemba, Ichibemba, Icibemba and Chiwemba, is a Bantu language that is spoken primarily in Zambia by the Bemba people and about 18 related ethnic groups. [...]" (eng)
lexicalization	eng:"Bemba", ukr:"бемба", cmn:"姆巴文", many more
hypernym	Central_Bantu_languages
iso_639_2B_code	"bem"
iso_639_3_code	"bem"
region	Zambia, etc.
described_by	http://en.wikipedia.org/wiki/Bemba_language
described_by	http://www.ethnologue.com/show_language.asp?code=bem
script	Latin_script
...	...

* The entity identifiers are presented here in a slightly more human-readable form than actually stored in the KB.

Table 1: Example Language Entity: Bemba language (ChiBemba)

to cover dialects and additional variations, once the respective data has been made publically available.

4 Multilingual WordNet Translation

The next case study addresses how semantic relationships between terms in different languages can be captured. As explained earlier in Section 2.2.2, the principles that WordNet is based on can be extended to the multilingual case by treating semantic relationships between terms in different languages in the same way as semantic relationships between terms of a single language: Terms with the same meaning are linked to the same sense node, and terms with related meanings are connected indirectly via connected sense nodes. In order to accomplish this at a large scale, we automatically link terms in different languages to the word senses already defined in WordNet. This transforms WordNet into a multilingual lexical knowledge base that covers not only English terms but hundreds of thousands of terms from many different languages (de Melo and Weikum, 2009).

4.1 Knowledge Extraction

Following Principle 2.3 and Section 2.2.2, we share sense identifiers between languages where appropriate. In the past, several authors have assumed a similar stance and proposed using translation dictionaries to attach non-English terms to sense identifiers from the English WordNet, e.g. Atserias et al. (1997), Isahara et al. (2008). Such techniques fall within what has been called the 'expand' paradigm for building wordnets (Vossen, 1998). Unfortunately, a straightforward translation runs into major difficulties because of synonyms and homonyms. For example, a word such as "*bat*" has 10 senses in the English WordNet, but a German translation like "*Fledermaus*" (the animal) only applies to a small subset of those senses. This challenge can be approached by harnessing machine learning techniques.

An initial input knowledge base graph G_0 is constructed by extracting information from existing wordnets, translation dictionaries including Wiktionary[7], and the FreeDict project dictionaries[8], multilingual thesauri and ontologies like the GEMET thesaurus[9], and parallel corpora like the OpenSubtitles corpus (Tiedemann, 2004). Additional heuristics are applied to increase the density of the graph and merge similar statements.

A sequence of knowledge graphs G_i are iteratively derived by evaluating paths from a new term x to an existing WordNet sense z via some English translation y covered by WordNet. For instance, the German word "*Fledermaus*" has the English word "*bat*" as a translation and hence initially is tentatively linked to all senses of "*bat*" with a confidence of 0. In each iteration the confidence values are then updated to reflect how likely it seems that those links are correct. The confidences are predicted using RBF-kernel SVM models that are learnt from a training set of labelled links between

---
[7] http://www.wiktionary.org
[8] http://www.freedict.org
[9] http://www.eionet.europa.eu/gemet/

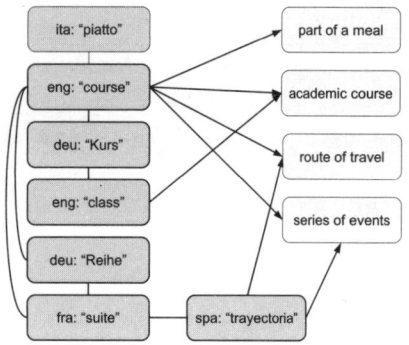 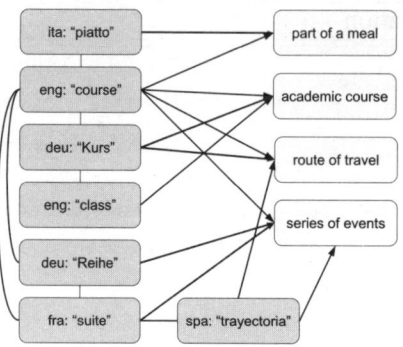

Figure 1: Connections in the input graph G_0 (left) and the desired output graph G_i (right). Lines with arrows represent links from terms to senses, while lines without an arrow represent `translation` links.

words and senses. The feature space is constructed using a series of graph-based statistical scores that represent properties of the previous graph G_{i-1} and additionally make use of measures of semantic relatedness and corpus frequencies. The most significant features $x_i(x,z)$ are computed as:

$$\sum_{y \in \Gamma(x, G_{i-1})} \phi(x,y) \operatorname{sim}_x^*(y,z) \qquad (1)$$

$$\sum_{y \in \Gamma(x, G_{i-1})} \frac{\phi(x,y) \operatorname{sim}_x^*(y,z)}{\operatorname{sim}_x^*(y,z) + \operatorname{dissim}_x(y,z)} \qquad (2)$$

The formulas consider the out-neighbourhood $y \in \Gamma(x, G_{i-1})$ of x, i.e. its translations, and then observe how strongly each y is tied to z. The function sim* computes the maximal similarity between any sense of y and the current sense z. The dissim function computes the sum of dissimilarities between senses of y and z, essentially quantifying how many alternatives there are to z. Additional weighting functions ϕ, γ are used to bias scores towards senses that have an acceptable part-of-speech and senses that are more frequent in the SemCor corpus.

Relying on multiple iterations allows us to draw on multilingual evidence for greater precision and recall, due to mutual reinforcement and propagation effects. For instance, in the first iteration, one might determine that the German word "*Fledermaus*" is linked to the animal sense of "*bat*" with high probability, and then in the next iteration this can aid in inferring that the Turkish translation "*yarasa*" has the same meaning. For further details of this approach, please refer to de Melo and Weikum (2009).

	Term-Sense Links	Distinct Terms
Nouns	1,048,003	589,536
Verbs	221,916	88,189
Adjectives	289,328	147,257
Adverbs	36,095	26,254
Overall	1,595,763	822,212

Table 2: Coverage of multilingual wordnet graph

4.2 Results

We have successfully applied these techniques to automatically create UWN, a large-scale multilingual wordnet. Evaluating random samples of term-sense links, we find that for French the precision is 89.2% ± 3.4% (311 samples), for German 85.9% ± 3.8% (321 samples), and for Mandarin Chinese 90.5% ± 3.3% (300 samples). The overall number of new term-sense links is 1,595,763, for 822,212 terms, as shown in Table 2. The three most well-represented languages are currently German, French, and Esperanto, which is largely due to the choice of input dictionaries. These figures can easily grow even further as the input is extended by tapping on additional sources.

The structure of the extended wordnet is reasonably rich, including hyponymy/hypernymy and several other generic relations for which it is fair to assume that they apply to the new terms as well. The next step would involve manual revision and extension, since our approach does not necessarily generate complete sense listings and the set of senses associated with a word may not always result in sense distinctions that would seem perfectly adequate to a lexicographer compiling a monolingual dictionary. Additional experiments however have shown that the wordnet is already beneficial in several application tasks even in this raw form. Examples studied include cross-lingual text classification and semantic relatedness estimation, where high-quality manually created resources are outperformed (de Melo and Weikum, 2009).

5 An Etymological Word Network

As a final case study, we investigate capturing relationships between multilingual word forms, i.e. etymological and derivational information. Traditionally, lexical knowledge bases have focussed on synchronic relationships. We produce an etymological word network that additionally captures diachronic information by representing how words originated from other previously existing words. By navigating this network, one can easily see that the English "*doubtless*" is derived from "*doubt*", which in turn comes from Old French "*douter*", which evolved from the Latin word "*dubitare*". Starting from these latter entities, cognate forms are also discoverable.

5.1 Knowledge Extraction

The knowledge base is mined from the English version of Wiktionary using custom pattern matching techniques. We process the XML dump of Wiktionary, and segment articles by language, since a single article can cover unrelated words in different languages. The "Etymology" sections in the articles may contain arbitrary text describing the roots of a word. Fortunately, certain patterns are very frequent, as one can observe in Figure 2. We thus recursively parse the section using a set of regular expressions that cover many of the etymological relationships described in Wiktionary. Regular expressions extract the language (if mentioned), the original term, and the rest, i.e. the next element in an etymological chain. In addition, the English glosses of words are also parsed, as these often hold links to root forms for derivations, or links to standard forms when there are orthographic variations or other alternative forms. For instance, the English word "*booking*" is attached to the verb "*to book*". Many articles also have separate sections listing derived forms and alternative spellings, which we harvest as well.

Etymological print dictionaries often do not cite their sources due to space constraints. In our case, the Wiktionary page that provided the etymological link can be referenced. Frequently, this is not the article page for the word itself, but rather some other page that references that word while tracing a longer etymological history. For example, the etymological link from Anglo-Norman "*estorie*" back to the Latin "*historia*" is found on the page for the English word "*story*".

Another issue arising in etymology is that some words are known only as reconstructed forms. We represent this at the statement level, adding attributes that specify that the links as well as the unattested forms are hypothetical.

5.2 Results

We obtain a lexical network with over 1,000,000 terms, 200,000 etymological links between terms, and 1,700,000 derivational links between terms. Note however that the distinction between derivational and etymological relations is not always completely clear. For example, many words developed due to quite regular processes of affixation or compound formation, e.g. "*sexism*", "*microwave*", and "*website*". In this regard, our knowledge base follows the conventions adopted in Wiktionary.

Existing standards like TEI P5 (Burnard and Bauman, 2009) define a semi-structured representation of etymological data, rather than a genuinely structural one that exposes relationships between words using a network-like graph model. Graph representations expose the connections between words much more explicitly. Due to affixes such as "*non-*", "*-ize*", etc., it turns out that much of the graph actually constitutes a single connected component that can be navigated by following links. In addition, graph representations are machine-readable and more language-neutral, which makes them reusable in different contexts. Information that they cannot directly capture faithfully can still be retained in textual form, e.g. using additional statement attributes. Fortunately, most forms of etymological information, including e.g. when a word's use was first attested, historic examples of a word's use, or even the presence of multiple conflicting etymological hypotheses could easily be couched in a machine-readable graph representation without resorting to textual comments.

Etymological relationships are essentially links between words in different language, which can naturally be modelled as relations between terms as defined in Section 2.2.1. Of course, statement

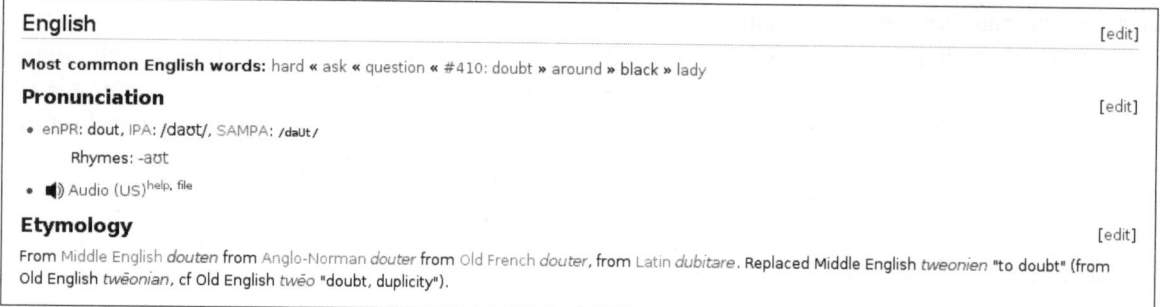

Figure 2: Excerpt from Wiktionary article on "*doubt*", which explains the etymological roots going back to the Latin "*dubitare*"

attributes could be added to specify that an etymological relationship only applies to specific senses of a term. Indeed, one could also specify relationships of regular polysemy between senses, which would enable a clearer distinction between genuine homonyms and polysemy in the narrow sense than is currently possible in WordNet. Such issues are possible directions for future work.

6 Conclusion

We have analysed principles for representing multilingual knowledge and proposed a general framework as well as techniques to organize existing knowledge within this framework. The first case study involved enriching WordNet with additional information about the vast number of languages in the world, and their relationships. The second demonstrated the use of machine learning to bootstrap a preliminary version of a generic multilingual wordnet describing relationships between terms in different languages. Our final study examined how derivational information between terms in different languages can be extracted from Wiktionary to produce a lexical network of etymological relationships. Together, they demonstrate not only how knowledge bases can universally capture multiple languages simultaneously, but also the additional level of interlinking that this enables.

References

Jordi Atserias, Salvador Climent, Xavier Farreres, German Rigau, and Horacio Rodríguez. 1997. Combining multiple methods for the automatic construction of multilingual WordNets. In *Proc. International Conference on Recent Advances in NLP (RANLP)*, pages 143–149.

Jordi Atserias, Luís Villarejo, German Rigau, Eneko Agirre, John Carroll, Bernardo Magnini, and Piek Vossen. 2004. The MEANING Multilingual Central Repository. In *Proc. 2nd Global WordNet Conference (GWC)*, pages 80–210.

Luisa Bentivogli, Pamela Forner, Bernardo Magnini, and Emanuele Pianta. 2004. Revising the Wordnet Domains hierarchy: semantics, coverage and balancing. In *Proc. COLING 2004 Workshop on Multilingual Linguistic Resources*, pages 94–101, Geneva, Switzerland.

Lou Burnard and Syd Bauman, 2009. *TEI P5: Guidelines for Electronic Text Encoding and Interchange, Version 1.4.1*. TEI Consortium, July.

Mark Davis and Martin Dürst. 2008. Unicode normalization forms, rev. 29. Technical report, Unicode.

Gerard de Melo and Gerhard Weikum. 2009. Towards a universal wordnet by learning from combined evidence. In *Proc. 18th ACM Conference on Information and Knowledge Management (CIKM 2009)*. ACM.

Christiane Fellbaum, editor. 1998. *WordNet: An Electronic Lexical Database (Language, Speech, and Communication)*. The MIT Press.

Patrick Hayes. 2004. RDF semantics. W3C recommendation, World Wide Web Consortium, February.

Hitoshi Isahara, Francis Bond, Kiyotaka Uchimoto, Masao Utiyama, and Kyoko Kanzaki. 2008. Development of the Japanese WordNet. In *Proc. LREC 2008*, Marrakech, Morocco.

M. Paul Lewis. 2009. Ethnologue: Languages of the world, sixteenth edition (online version).

Jörg Tiedemann. 2004. The OPUS corpus - parallel & free. In *Proc. LREC 2004*.

Dan Tufiş, Dan Cristea, and Sofia Stamou. 2004. BalkaNet: Aims, Methods, Results and Perspectives. A General Overview. *Romanian J. Information Science and Technology*, 7(1–2):9–34, 4.

Piek Vossen, editor. 1998. *EuroWordNet: A Multilingual Database with Lexical Semantic Networks*. Springer.

Division of Semantic Labor in the Global WordNet Grid

Piek Vossen
De Boelelaan 1105,
1081HV Amsterdam
VU University Amsterdam
p.vossen@let.vu.nl

German Rigau
Donostia, Basque Country, Spain
IXA Group,
University of the Basque Country
g.rigau@ehu.es

Abstract

In this paper, we describe an implementation of the Global WordNet Grid in the KYOTO project that distinguishes 3 layers of knowledge: domain vocabularies, wordnets and a central ontology. The layers are distinguished according to the principle of the division of linguistic labor, as defined by Putnam (1975). Such a division is required to handle and structure the large quantities of domain vocabulary and its linguistic diversity. We define the relations between the layers and explain how they can be used for reasoning and inferencing.

1 Introduction

Since the introduction of the English WordNet (Fellbaum 1998), wordnets have been developed in many languages, more or less along the same basic principles. In the EuroWordNet project (Vossen 1998), wordnets in different languages have also been connected to each other, which since then has been followed in many other projects all over the world. The English WordNet has always been the connecting medium as the Inter-Lingual-Index or ILI. Through the years also other semantic frameworks have been used as language neutral representations of meanings that can be shared across wordnets, such as the EuroWordNet top-ontology (Vossen 1998), WordNet domains (Magnini 2002), etc. Most notably is SUMO (Niles and Pease 2002), which was mapped to the English WordNet but also to other wordnets such as Arabic, Chinese, Dutch, Spanish, Catalan or Basque. In most cases, the mapping to SUMO was carried over from English to the other languages, using the ILI.

A large ontology as a language independent representation of meaning holds many promises for future research and usage provided that it is tightly connected to these wordnets. Universalia and idiosyncracies of lexicalizations in language can be expressed in a systematic way, allowing language-independent reasoning over linguistically expressed knowledge. This has led to the idea of the Global Wordnet Grid (GWG), in which all wordnets are anchored to a shared ontology (Fellbaum and Vossen 2007, Pease, Fellbaum, Vossen 2008, Vossen and Fellbaum 2008).

The KYOTO project[1] can be seen as a first attempt to implement the GWG on a practical scale for specific domains. The goal is to develop a knowledge sharing and transition platform that can be used by communities in the world. The KYOTO platform operates as a Wiki for establishing semantic interoperability across languages for a specific domain by creating domain wordnets that get interlinked through a shared ontology. The resulting semantic knowledge base is further used to apply automatic fact mining on document collections. The platform allows for continuous updating and modeling of the vocabulary by the people in the community, while their domain wordnets remain anchored to a generic wordnet. If successful, the GWG can be built by the massive labor force of the Internet community and the results become available to the global community.

When applying the principle of GWG to a specific domain, one is confronted with numerous practical and fundamental problems to handle the domain data. First of all, existing background knowledge should be re-used to build the domain wordnet. Secondly, other new terms are automatically learned from the documents and web sites used in the community. Both background knowledge and domain terminology need to be aligned with existing generic wordnets to make

---

[1] KYOTO is an Asian-European project funded under project number 211423 in the 7th Frame Work in the area of Digital Libraries: FP7-ICT-2007-1, Objective ICT-2007.4.2: Intelligent Content and Semantics.

the domain wordnet interoperable with general concepts. The third aspect, is that any domain wordnet needs to be mapped to a shared domain ontology, which in itself is anchored to a common top and mid-level ontology.

In previous projects, plugin relations have been proposed to relate domain wordnets to generic wordnets. Similar relations can be defined for background vocabularies and wordnets. In addition, we need to define the semantics for the relations between the synsets and the ontology to separate the language specific properties from the language neutral properties. For instance, basic mapping relations have been defined to map SUMO to WordNet (Niles and Pease 2002, Vossen et al 2008) but none of these proposals provide an explicit semantic model for these relations. In fact, semantic information is duplicated in both wordnets and ontologies and it is not clear what knowledge should be expressed where and how this knowledge can be used.

In addition to the complex relations between the different knowledge repositories, we also have to deal with volume. Our experience is that vocabularies in domains are very large, covering millions of concepts. Representing and maintaining these vocabularies in domain wordnets and in the central ontology raises various problems in terms of maintenance and the kind of reasoning and inferencing that one might want to apply. In the case of the ontology, representing those amounts of concepts and applying reasoning is currently completely unfeasible.

A final issue is that background vocabularies are often maintained outside the wordnet community, without connecting their resources to the wordnet infrastructure.

To handle these practical and fundamental issues in the KYOTO project, we defined a three-layered model of semantic resources that are interconnected. Firstly, the **vocabulary layer** including background vocabulary and mined text terminology. Secondly, the **wordnet layer** integrating generic and domain wordnets. Finally, the **ontology layer** containing generic and domain ontologies. We also provide first definitions for the semantics of the mappings between these layers. Furthermore, we explain how different types of inferencing can be applied to each layer for different practical applications such as fact mining from textual repositories. For modeling the semantics, we use the division of labor principle from Putnam (1975), which we apply to the knowledge bases and computer systems that interact with human knowledge and language.

The structure of this paper is as follows. We first give some background information on the KYOTO project. Next, we describe the problems handling the knowledge resources in the domain of the environment. In section 4, we explain our three-layered model and, in section 5, we explain the different types of relations between the layers. Finally in section 6, we discuss how inferencing can be applied to each layer and how factual data can be extracted from text as an instantiation of the model.

2 The KYOTO project

The KYOTO project allows communities to model terms and concepts in their domain and to use this knowledge to apply text mining on documents. The knowledge cycle in the KYOTO system starts with a set of source *documents* produced by the community, such as PDFs and websites. Linguistic processors apply tokenization, segmentation, morpho-syntactic analysis and some semantic processing to the text in different languages. The semantic processing involves detection of named-entities (persons, organizations, places, time-expressions) and determining the meaning of words in the text using a given wordnet in a language.

The output of this linguistic analysis is stored in an XML annotation format that is the same for all the languages, called the KYOTO Annotation Format (KAF, Bosma et al 2009). This format incorporates standardized proposals for the linguistic annotation of text but represents them in an easy to use layered structure. In this structure, words, terms, constituents and syntactic dependencies are stored in separate layers with references across the structures. This makes it easier to harmonize the output of different linguistic processors for different languages and to add new semantic layers to the basic output, when needed (Bosma et al 2009). All modules in KYOTO draw their input from these structures. In fact, the word-sense-disambiguation process is carried out to the same KAF annotation in different languages and is therefore the same for all the languages (Agirre, Lopez de Lacalle & Soroa 2009). In the current system, there are processors for English, Dutch, Italian, Spanish, Basque, Chinese and Japanese.

The KYOTO system proceeds in 2 cycles (see Figure 1). In the 1st cycle, the **Tybot** (Term Yielding Robot) extracts the most relevant terms from the documents. The Tybot is another generic program that can do this for all the different languages in much the same way. The terms are organized as a structured hierarchy and, wherever possible, related to generic semantic databases, i.e. wordnets for each language. In Figure 1, italic terms occur in the text, and underlined terms are not found in wordnet. Straight terms are hyperonyms in wordnet that do not necessarily occur in the text but are linked to ontological classes. The domain experts can view the terms in the term database and edit them, i.e. adding or deleting terms, changing their meaning, adding definitions, changing relations, etc.

The result is a domain wordnet in a specific language. Each new term can be seen as a possible proposal to also extend the ontology. Through the ontology, the domain experts can establish the similarities and differences across the languages and hence cultures.

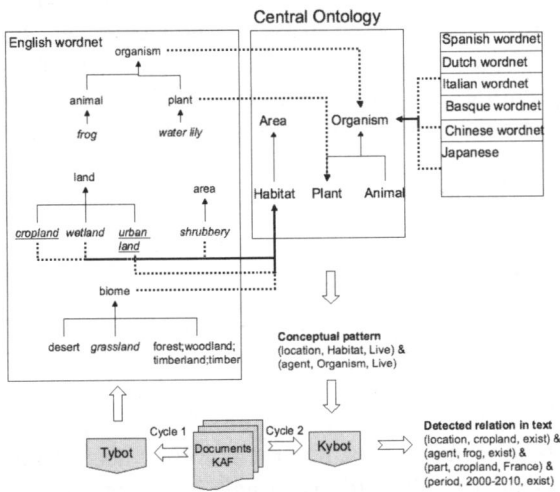

Figure 1: Two Cycles of processing in KYOTO

The 2nd cycle of the system involves the actual extraction of factual knowledge from the annotated documents by the **Kybots** (Knowledge Yielding Robots). Kybots use a collection of profiles that represent patterns of information of interest. In the profile, conceptual relations are expressed and their realization in a language is achieved through the domain wordnets and so-called expression rules. Since the semantics is defined through the ontology, it is possible to detect similar data across documents in different languages, even if expressed differently. In Figure 1, we give an example of a conceptual pattern that relates organisms that live in habitats. The Kybot can combine this pattern with words from the wordnet and morpho-syntactic structures. When a match is detected, the instantiation of the pattern is saved in a formal representation, either in KAF or in RDF. Since the wordnets in different languages are mapped to the same ontology and the text in these languages is represented in the same KAF, similar patterns can easily be applied to multiple languages.

3 Knowledge integration

The multilingual knowledge base plays an important role in the KYOTO project. It is designed as an implementation of the Global Wordnet Grid. The wordnets for seven languages have been represented in the Wordnet-LMF format (Soria, Monachini and Vossen 2009) and stored in a DebVisDic server (Horak et al. 2005). The DebVisDic server also contains the SUMO ontology and a first version of the KYOTO ontology in OWL-DL. The SUMO ontology is fully mapped to WordNet3.0. The KYOTO ontology (version 1) consists of 786 classes divided over three layers. The top layer is based on DOLCE (DOLCE-Lite-Plus version 3.9.7, Masolo et al 2003) and OntoWordNet. This layer of the ontology has been modified for our purposes (Herold et. al 2009). The second layer consists of concepts coming from the so-called Base Concepts in various wordnets (Vossen 1998, Izquierdo et al 2007). Examples of base concepts are: *building, vehicle, animal, plant, change, move, size, weight*. The Base Concepts (BCs) are those synsets in WordNet3.0 that have the most relations with other synsets in the wordnet hierarchies and are selected in a way that ensures complete coverage of the nominal and verbal part of WordNet. This has been completed for the nouns (about 500 synsets) and is currently being carried out for verbs and adjectives in WordNet 3.0. Through the BCs, we will ensure that any synset in the wordnets is mapped to some concept in the ontology either directly or indirectly[2]. The most specific layer of the ontology contains concepts representing species and regions relevant to the KYOTO domain. These concepts were provided by the end users, and in certain cases, concepts have been added to link the domain specific terms to the ontology.

The wordnets and the ontology play an important role for mining facts from text. They form the basis for the conceptual patterns of the Kybots. For resolving the constraints in these patterns, Kybots need to apply some kind of inferencing over the available knowledge.

---

[2]This set of BCs is more minimal than the BCs defined in EuroWordNet and BalkaNet. The original BC set contained too much redundancy and arbitrariness for our purposes.

During the project, new terms and concepts will be added to the knowledge repository. Partly, these terms and concepts are learned from the domain corpus and partly they will be derived from existing background knowledge basis. Combining these resources and defining the semantics of the mappings across these resources presents a major knowledge integration task.

Concept mining systems for specific domains usually assume that the domain corpus provides the basis for building the vocabulary and, eventually, learning the associated domain ontology. However, modeling of the domain vocabulary requires to consider that:

- Every domain text contains general vocabulary in addition to domain terms;
- Every domain text contains references to named entities in the world;
- Every domain has large quantities of background concepts and terms, which are not all mentioned in the texts;

The KYOTO knowledge model assumes that the terminology from the domain text corpus is merged with a generic wordnet in a language so that the domain terms are anchored to more general terms and concepts. This requires that the term hierarchy for the domain is somehow disambiguated to match specific word meaning from the generic wordnet. Once the term hierarchy is aligned with a generic wordnet, existing mappings from wordnet to ontologies can be used to apply the ontological distinctions to the domain terms. Named entities are more likely to be found in other resources such as Wikipedia, DBPedia and GeoNames. This requires another alignment operation, where the concepts in the external sources need to be matched to wordnet as well and through wordnet to the ontology. The situation becomes more complex when existing domain thesauri and taxonomies are added to the knowledge base. Modeling the vocabulary and concepts in a domain is a complex knowledge integration problem.

The following knowledge repositories are relevant or the environment domain in KYOTO:

- Generic wordnets in each language ranging from 50,000 to 120,000 synsets.
- A term databases with about 500,000 terms extracted from about 1,000 documents in each language.
- Existing ontologies such as the EuroWordNet top-ontology (Vossen 1998), SUMO (Niles and Pease 2002) and DOLCE (Masolo et al 2003).
- Wikipedia: over 3 million articles in English and large volumes in other languages, by September 2009[3].
- DBPedia: 2.6 million things and 274 million pieces of information (RDF triples), by September 2009[4].
- GeoNames: 8 million geographical names and 6.5 million unique features whereof 2.2 million populated places and 1.8 million alternate names, by September 2009[5].
- The Species 2000 database with 2.1 million species, having taxonomic relations and labels in many different languages[6].

We will describe our approach to the problem of integrating these in a useful knowledge repository. We propose a solution with 3 layers of repositories with different types of links between them that support different types of inferencing.

4 Division of knowledge over different layers

The amount and complexity of the knowledge repository is enormous. The Global Wordnet Grid architecture suggests that the wordnets extended with the domain vocabulary are anchored through the domain extension of the ontology. In practice this means, that the ontology needs to be extended with millions of new concepts. For example, the KYOTO ontology needs to make a distinction between taxonomic groups and individual organisms. Instances of species are *members* of a taxonomic group and *instances* of an organism. Likewise, we can predict that if an instance of a *frog* ceases to exist, it is not implied that the taxonomic group *Anura* ceases to exist but only an instance of the organism *Anura*. The former is only the case when all members of *Anura* cease to exist. As a consequence, the ontology that represents all species in this domain should include all 2.1 million species twice (!), once as group and once as a type of organism.

Such a model leads to various practical problems. First of all, ontologies of that size cannot be loaded in any existing inferencing system. Inferences as the above can thus not be made be-

---

[3] http://www.wikipedia.org/
[4] http://dbpedia.org/About
[5] http://www.geonames.org/about.html
[6] http://www.sp2000.org/

cause of the size of such an ontology. Another problem is that the vocabularies are linguistically too complex and diverse. Whereas the species can be considered as rigid concepts, as defined by Welty and Guarino (2002), this is not the case for most of the terms that are learned from the document collection. In the environment domain, the documents typically include terms for roles of species rather than the species as such, e.g. *invasive species*, *migration species*, *threatened species*. For mining facts from documents, these non-rigid role terms have more information value than the defining properties of the species.

For a knowledge sharing system as modeled by the Global Wordnet Grid, it is thus more important to precisely define what the roles and processes are in which species participate than to provide the defining properties of the species as such. Likewise, we propose a model of division of knowledge along the lines of the division of linguistic labor defined by Putnam (1975). Putnam argues that linguistic communities rely on the fact that experts know the defining properties of natural kind terms such as *gold* and can thus determine which instances of matter are gold and which are not. Most natural language users therefore have a shallow definition of what gold is and can still use this definition to communicate valuable information on gold, such as for trading gold or buying jewelry.

Along the same lines, we propose a digital version of this principle, where we state that a computer does not need to know the defining properties of each rigid concept but can rely on the capacity of the domain expert to determine what the instances are of, for example, a particular species. Vast amounts of words for rigid concepts can likewise remain in the vocabularies as long as we indicate their status as rigid concepts.

More useful is to properly represent the roles and processes in which the rigid concepts participate. These need to be represented both in the vocabularies and in the ontology to be able to process information in a proper way and to carry out the necessary inferencing.

In addition, terms from the term database are mapped to the most specific synset as well. In the example shown in Figure-2, we see typical role concepts as terms. For these role concepts, we infer that they do not represent rigid subtypes but can be used to refer to instances of concepts that play a specific role. The role relation to the process needs to be defined more specifically through a mapping relation with the ontology. To properly define the semantics of this model, we need to define the precise relations between the concepts represented in the different repositories. This will be discussed in the next section.

5 Relations between the different layers

We thus have three different types of repositories: vocabularies, wordnets and ontologies. Each repository has internal relations and also there are relations from vocabularies to wordnets and from wordnets to the ontology. Thus, wordnet can be seen as conceptual bridge between the vocabulary and the ontology.

Following the DOLCE model, the KYOTO ontology has major hierarchies for **endurants** (e.g. things such as 'plant', 'highway'), **perdurants** (processes such as 'migration', 'obstruction'), and **qualities** (e.g. properties such as 'endemic', 'poisonus'). Endurants include both types and roles such as 'frog' or 'EndangeredRole'. Events, processes and states are classified under Perdurants. Properties are classified under Quality. The following relations are used within the ontology:

- subClassOf, equivalentTo, generic-constituent relations between Endurant:Endurant, Perdurant:Perdurant, Quality:Quality.
- playedBy relation between Role:Endurant.
- hasRole[7] relation between Perdurant:Role.

For example, the Endurant concepts 'plant' and 'animal' have a subClassOf relation to 'organism' and the Endurant 'highway' is a subClassOf 'physical-object', Perdurant 'AnimalMigrationProcess' is a subClassOf 'MigrationProcess'. Endurants 'MigrationRole' and 'BreedingRole' both have a subClassOf relation to 'AnimalRole' and 'AnimalRole' has a playedBy relation to the Endurant 'Animal'. Finally, a 'MigrationRole' playedBy 'Animal' is part of the Perdurant 'MigrationProcess' through the hasRole relation.

The ontology is used to model the shared and language-neutral concepts and relations in the domain. Instances are excluded from the ontology. Instances will be detected in the documents and will be mapped to the ontology through instance to ontology relations (see below). There are two relations that we need for this: instanceOf from instances to Endurant, Perdurant, or Quality and instancePlay from instances to Role. Specific entities in discourse, such as an

---

[7] The hasRole relation is compliant to the participant relation in DOLCE. Whereas participant is between Perdurant and Endurant, hasRole is more specific: between Perdurant and Role.

animal identified as *Duck1*, are then instances of a class in the type hierarchy of objects, e.g. Duck1 *instanceOf* Duck and can play roles, e.g. Duck1 *instancePlay* BreedingRole. The latter states that Duck1 could cease being a breeder while the former states that he cannot cease being a duck. Likewise, we will get a clear separation between the ontological model and the instantiation of the model as described in the text.

In addition to the ontology, we will have a wordnet for each language in the domain. In addition to the regular synset to synset relations in the wordnet, we will have a specific set of relations for mapping the synsets to the ontology, which are all prefixed with *sc_* standing for synset-to-concept. For rigid synsets, we have an *sc_equivalenceOf* or *sc_subclassOf* relation to Endurant, Perdurant or Quality. For non-rigid synsets, we have an *sc_domainOf* between synsets and Endurants, and an *sc_playRole* relation between synset and Roles. For each of these relations, the logical implications are defined as follows:

- **sc_equivalenceOf**: the synset is fully equivalent to the ontology Type & inherits all properties; the synset is *Rigid*
- **sc_ subclassOf**: the synset is a proper subclass of the ontology Type & inherits all properties; the synset is *Rigid*
- **sc_domainOf**: the synset is not a proper subclass of the ontology Type & is not disjoint (therefore orthogonal) with other synsets that are mapped to the same Type either through *sc_subclassOf* or *sc_domainOf*; the synset is *non-Rigid* but still inherits all properties of the target ontology Type; the synset is also related to a Role with a *sc_playRole* relation
- **sc_playRole**: the synset denotes instances for which the context of the Role applies for some period of time but this is not essential for the existence of the instances, i.e. if the context ceases to exist then the instances may still exist (Mizoguchi et al. 2007).

Only the *sc_equivalenceOf* and *sc_subclassOf* relations are used in the SUMO to Wordnet mapping, represented by the symbols '=' and '+' respectively. The SUMO-Wordnet mapping likewise does not systematically distinguish rigid from non-rigid concepts. In our model, we separate the linguistically and culturally specific vocabularies from the shared ontology while using the ontology as a point of interface for the concepts used by the various communities.

The lexicalization of the concepts can differ considerably across languages. Consider the following examples of different lexicalizations that can now be elegantly modeled:

{meat}Noun, English
-> sc_domainOf *Cow, Sheep, Pig*
-> sc_playRole *EatenRole*
{名 肉, 食物, 餐 }Noun, Chinese
-> sc_domainOf *Cow, Sheep, Pig, Rat, Dog*
-> sc_playRole *EatenRole*
{غذاء, لحم, طعام}Noun, Arabic
-> sc_domainOf *Cow, Sheep*
-> sc_playRole *EatenRole*

In these examples, we see that words for *meat* in English, Chinese and Arabic are defined by the same role relation but have different ranges of domains, indicating what animals are considered as food. Similar cultural differences can be represented in this way.

6 Inferencing over the different layers

In text mining, there is a tight connection between the computational model for representing knowledge and the inferencing capabilities supported by the model. However, current logic based reasoning systems do not scale to the amount of information and the setting that is required for KYOTO to match text with the semantic model. For instance, state of the art machinery like formal reasoners such as Pellet or Fact++ are unable to deal with large and complex ontologies as the ones the KYOTO project is currently envisaging. Thus, a knowledge representation and reasoning infrastructure must be designed and built that can scale and can be flexibly adapted to the varying capabilities required by the different modules of the whole KYOTO System.

New approaches to the problem follow a rather loose definition of inference, mainly relying on the use of large amounts of automatically acquired informal and inaccurate knowledge and approximate inferences (Agirre and Soroa 2009). For KYOTO, we can combine such loose approaches with more strict reasoning, each being applied to the different layers. Large amounts of named entities like those appearing in YAGO (Suchanek et al 2008) or DBpedia (Auer et al 2007) or Species2000, etc. are stored in advanced XML databases such as Virtuoso. Wordnets are stored in relational or XML databases (DebVisDic, Horak et al 2005), but for inferencing a more complex graph representation is required (Agirre and Soroa 2009; Laparra and Rigau 2009). Finally, formal ontologies are stored in standard OWL-DL.

Each type of knowledge repository allows different inferencing capabilities with its own benefits and drawbacks. For instance, Virtuoso allows to store millions of instances but only have a minimal inferencing ability when querying on SPARQL, while OWL-DL allows to perform complex logical operations on the stored data (like consistency, etc.) but it scales poorly. However, the three knowledge repositories are connected by different relationships, which allows computer programs to use different representational layers and different inferencing capabilities. SPARQL queries on Virtuoso provide in simple lookup and relation tracking facility until a match with a wordnet synset is found. Within the wordnet knowledge base more complex operations can be applied such as measuring distances and similarities in a graph-structure. The ontological structures applied to the wordnet can be used to perform formal inferencing over a limited set of fundamental implications (Álvez et al. 2008).

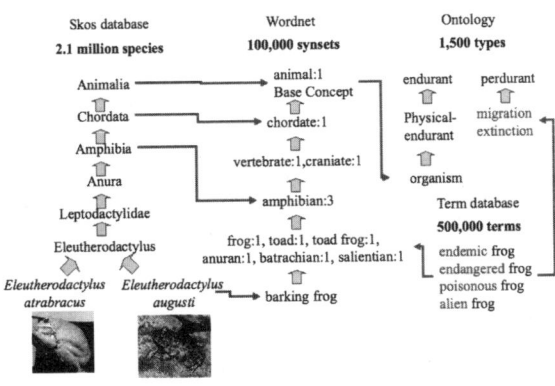

Figure 2: Division of knowledge over 3 layers

In Figure 2, we show an example of the three layers of the KYOTO model. We include in the vocabulary vast quantities of species represented as a SKOS hierarchy in Virtuoso database[8]. The species hierarchy is partially linked to a generic wordnet. SPARQL queries can be used to extract the hierarchical relations to find the most specific matching wordnet synset. The wordnet synset hierarchy can be traversed to find the most specific Base Concept that is matched to the ontology. In this way, we can infer for all species in the vocabulary that they are both *members* of a taxonomic group and *rigid subtypes* of organism.

[8] http://virtuoso.openlinksw.com/

For instance, expressions such as "migration of Hirundo rustica" can be semantically processed to obtain an appropriate interpretation. Querying the vocabulary database for "Hirundo rustica", we obtain a Species2000 entry corresponding to the WordNet3.0 synset 01594787 <barn_swallow, chimney_swallow, Hirundo_rustica>. Although this synset has not a direct connection to the KYOTO ontology, following the hypernym hierarchy, we find <bird> which is connected to the Endurant type Bird in the KYOTO ontology, which in turn is a subClassOf Animal. Our graph-based Word Sense Disambiguation algorithm can also assign the synset 07312616 to "migration". This synset is directly connected to AnimalMigrationProcess in the ontology, which is a subclassOf the Perdurant MigrationProcess type. MigrationProcess hasRole MigrationRole, which is playedBy the type Animal. Thus, different inferencing mechanisms can be applied to each knowledge repository in order to obtain the most appropriate interpretation for "migration of Hirundo rustica".

7 Conclusions

We described a three-layered model for representing vast and diverse amounts of knowledge in the Global Wordnet Grid. We defined the relations between these layers and the ways of inferencing on each layer. This model gives a more precise definition of linguistic and ontological knowledge and a more realistic implementation. The KYOTO model allows more flexibility to divide the burden of semantics to different layers and different communities. The KYOTO model can be used to represent wordnet families both in ILI style and in GWG style. It also allows a gradual transition from ILI to GWG representation of data.

8 Acknowledgements

The KYOTO project is co-funded by EU - FP7 ICT Work Programme 2007 under Challenge 4 - Digital libraries and Content, Objective ICT-2007.4.2 (ICT-2007.4.4): Intelligent Content and Semantics (challenge 4.2). The Asian partners from Tapei and Kyoto are funded from national funds.

References

Agirre, E., & Soroa, A. (2009) Personalizing PageRank for Word Sense Disambiguation. Proceedings of the 12th conference of the European chapter of the Association for Computational Linguistics (EACL-2009). Athens, Greece.

Agirre, E., Lopez de Lacalle, O., & Soroa, A. (2009) Knowledge-based WSD and specific domains: performing over supervised WSD. Proceedings of IJCAI. Pasadena, USA. http://ixa.si.ehu.es/ukb

Álvez J., Atserias J., Carrera J., Climent S., Laparra E., Oliver A. and Rigau G. (2008) Complete and Consistent Annotation of WordNet using the Top Concept Ontology. Proceedings of LREC'08, Marrakesh, Morroco. 2008.

Auer A., C. Bizer, G. Kobilarov, J. Lehmann, R. Cyganiak and Z. Ives. DBpedia: A Nucleus for a Web of Open Data. In Proceedings of the International Semantic Web Conference (ISWC), volume 4825 of Lecture Notes in Computer Science, pages 722-735. 2007.

Black, W., Elkateb. S., Rodriguez, H., Alkhalifa, M., Vossen, P.,Pease, A., Bertran, M., & Fellbaum, C. (2006). The Arabic WordNet Project. In: Proceedings of the Conference on Lexical Resources in the European Community. Genoa, Italy.

Bosma, W., Vossen, P., Soroa, A. , Rigau, G., Tesconi, M., Marchetti, A., Monachini, M., & Apiprandi, C. (2009) KAF: a generic semantic annotation format. In Proceedings of the 5th International Conference on Generative Approaches to the Lexicon Sept 17-19, 2009, Pisa, Italy.

Fellbaum C., & Vossen, P. (2007) Connecting the Universal to the Specific: Towards the Global Grid,In: Proceedings of The First International Workshop on Intercultural Collaboration (IWIC 2007), KYOTO, Japan, January 25-26, 2007, also in LNCS Vol.4568, Springer-Verlag, 2007.

Fellbaum, C. (Ed.) (1998) WordNet: An Electronic Lexical Database. Cambridge, MA: MIT Press.

Freitag, D. (1998) Information extraction from html: Application of a general machine learning approach. In Proceedings of the Fifteenth National Conference on Artificial Intelligence, 1998.

Gangemi A., Guarino N., Masolo C., Oltramari A., Schneider L. (2002) Sweetening Ontologies with DOLCE. Proceedings of EKAW. 2002

Herold, A., & Hicks, A., (2009). Evaluating Ontologies with Rudify Knowledge. Proceedings of the International Conference on Knowledge Engineering and Ontology Development, Madeira, Portugal, October, 2009.

Herold, A., Hicks, A., Rigau, G., & Laparra, E. (2009) KYOTO Deliverable D6.2: Central Ontology Version – 1 www.kyoto-project.eu.

Horak, Ales - Pala, Karel - Rambousek, Adam - Povolny, Martin. (2005) *DEBVisDic - First Version of New Client-Server Wordnet Browsing and Editing Tool*. In Proceedings of the Third International WordNet Conference - GWC 2006. Brno, Czech Republic: Masaryk University, 2005. pp. 325-328. ISBN 80-210-3915-9.

Izquierdo R., Suárez A. & Rigau G. Exploring the Automatic Selection of Basic Level Concepts. Proceedings of RANLP'07, Borovetz, Bulgaria. September, 2007.

Laparra E. and Rigau G. Integrating WordNet and FrameNet using a knowledge-based Word Sense Disambiguation algorithm. Proceedings of RANLP'09. Borovets, Bulgaria, September, 2009.

Magnini B. & Cavaglia, G. (2000) Integrating Subject Field Codes into WordNet. In Gavrilidou M., Crayannis G., Markantonatu S., Piperidis S. & Stainhaouer G. (Eds.) Proceedings of LREC-2000. Athens, Greece, 31 May- 2 June 2000

Masolo, C., Borgo, S., Gangemi, A., Guarino, N. & Oltramari, A. (2003) WonderWeb Deliverable D18: Ontology Library, ISTC-CNR, Trento, Italy.

Mizoguchi R., Sunagawa E., Kozaki K. & Kitamura Y. (2007 A Model of Roles within an Ontology Development Tool: Hozo. Journal of Applied Ontology, Vol.2, No.2, 159-179.

Niles, I. & Pease, A. (2001) Formal Ontology in Information Systems. Proceedings of the international Conference on Formal Ontology in Information Systems – Vol. 2001 Ogunquit, Maine, USA

Pease A., C. Fellbaum, P. Vossen, (2008) Building the Global WordNet Grid. In Proceedings of the 18th International Congress of Linguists (CIL18), Seoul, Republic of Korea, July 21-26, 2008.

Putnam, H., (1975) The Meaning of "Meaning". In Philosophical papers: Volume 2. Mind, language and reality, Cambridge University Press, 215-271.

Soria C., M. Monachini, P. Vossen: "Wordnet-LMf: fleshing out a standardized format for wordnet interoperability", in: Proceedings of IWIC2009, Stanford, USA, February 20-21, 2009.

Suchanek F., G. Kasneci and G. Weikum. YAGO - A Large Ontology from Wikipedia and WordNet. Journal of Web Semantics 6(39). 2008

Vossen, P. (Ed.) (1998) EuroWordNet: a multilingual database with lexical semantic networks for European Languages. Kluwer, Dordrecht.

Using DEB Services for Knowledge Representation within the KYOTO Project

Aleš Horák and Adam Rambousek
Faculty of Informatics, Masaryk University
Botanická 68a, 602 00 Brno, Czech Republic
{hales,xrambous}@fi.muni.cz

Abstract

Within the EuroWordNet projects the national wordnets were interlinked with a interlingual index, ILI. In the subsequent Balkanet project, mostly pragmatic decisions stood as the reason for choosing the English as the pivot language instead of ILI. The Global WordNet Grid, as an approach, and the KYOTO project, as an instantiation of this approach are shifting the idea of the pivot from lexical meanings to real semantics - the languages will be interlinked through the shared ontology.

In this paper, we describe the design and implementation of the KYOTO database, which is based on the Dictionary Editor and Browser (DEB) platform. The main ideas and assets of the platform are presented and the necessary additions and adaptation for the needs of the KYOTO project are depicted.

1 Introduction

The wordnet semantic networks, regarding the Princeton WordNet (Fellbaum, 1998) as well as its national derivatives in more than fifty languages,[1] have been already used in many projects of intelligent text processing. The main benefits of wordnets are the hypero-hyponymic hierarchy and its translatability, i.e. the fact that most of the national wordnets are linked to the English one as a pivot. Further on, we will show the insides of the database part of a project that moves this pivot to the semantic part, i.e. tries to "replace" the English pivot with a shared ontology.

In the following text, we describe the KYOTO project (Vossen, 2008), which aims at a favourable application of the WordNet like ontologies in the multilingual form (denoted as the *Global WordNet Grid*) and a shared common ontology corresponding to the level of the *Suggested Upper Merged Ontology* (SUMO) as the central knowledge backbone. The ontology here serves as a meaning description tool for all the terms and facts that are extracted, compared and stored within the KYOTO system.

2 The KYOTO Project – WordNets, Ontologies and Text

WordNet semantic networks allow to express basic language relations[2] in a multigraph structure directly processable by computer systems.[3] However, description of more complicated structured knowledge, e.g. relations with more than one participants, cannot be encoded in a WordNet-standard way that could be further analysed and used by computers.

In the KYOTO system, this (potential) drawback of WordNet is solved by the idea of extending the WordNet into a *Global WordNet Grid* of multiple languages with a shared ontology in the center. Interlinking of national wordnets is not a new idea, it was introduced e.g. in the EuroWordNet (Vossen, 1998) and Balkanet (Christodoulakis, 2004) projects. In these projects the "pivot," i.e. the *interlingual index*, was represented directly by the English WordNet. This solution had several advantages and several disadvantages. From the point of view of the knowledge analysis, the biggest disadvantage was that the lexical knowledge structure was "hidden" in the English lexicon without the possibility to really extract it for the purpose of further computer processing. The shared ontology provides a way of adding structural semantics to the interlingual links.

The KYOTO project will incorporate and expand the Global WordNet Grid and will be the first system that exploits the benefits of storing the definitions of terms and facts in a computer processable logical system using the Grid's shared ontology.

---

[1]see http://www.globalwordnet.org/ for information about particular national wordnets

[2]hyperonymy/hyponymy, synonymy/antonymy, holonymy/meronymy, etc.

[3]deriving sets of similar objects, classes of more general objects or objects with opposite meaning

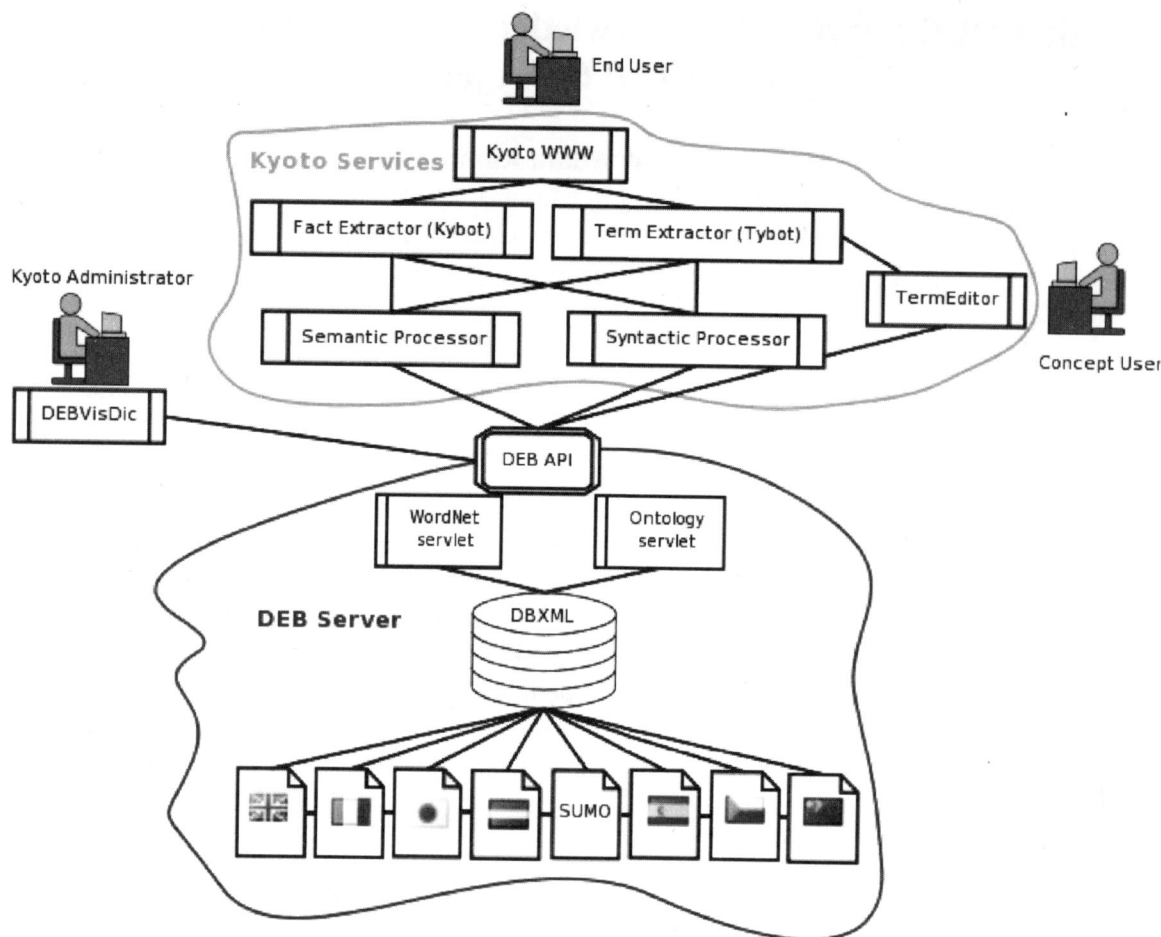

Figure 1: The schema of the KYOTO database within the KYOTO system.

3 The KYOTO Databases

The KYOTO database is built over the DEBVis-Dic application with the DEB server either set up at one central locality or it can be set up by several KYOTO partners. The DEB platform provides important backgrounds for the KYOTO project universal features (see Figure 1).

3.1 The DEB Architecture

The Dictionary Editor and Browser (DEB) platform (Horák et al., 2006; Horák and Rambousek, 2007; Horák et al., 2008) has been developed as a general framework for fast development of wide range of dictionary writing applications. The DEB platform provides several very important foundations that are common to most of the intended dictionary systems.

These foundational features include:

- strict client-server architecture with communication based on standard HTTP(s) protocol including authentication.

- the communication between the server and the client is based on predefined Application Programming Interface (API) and works with data in the XML form. The actual storage system (denoted as "storage backend") is hidden for the user. Thus it is possible to replace the backend and add new backend as the request arises. For instance, in the following text we describe adopting the OpenLink Virtuoso database as a new DEB backend for its SPARQL data query language abilities.

- the standard DEB clients (DEBDict, DEB-VisDic, DEBTerm, PRALED, ...) for the data presentation and manipulation use the Mozilla Extensions (Oeschger and others, 2002), which allow a separation of the graphical interface from the application logic.

- data checking and presentation are provided by means of XML standards such as XML Schema or XSLT.

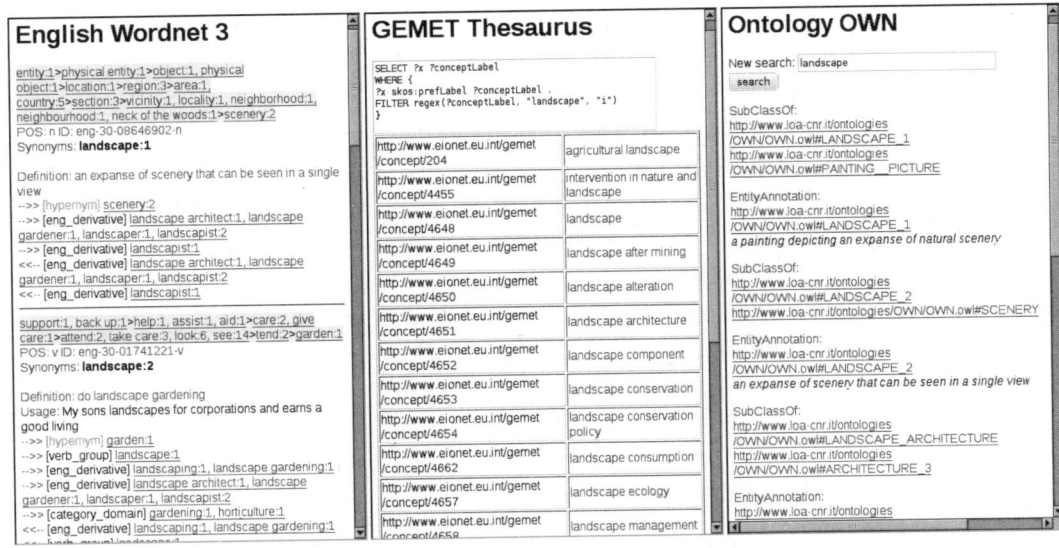

Figure 2: Linking wordnets, thesauri and ontologies within KYOTO database.

Query: `https://server_name/wneng30?action=runQuery&outtype=editor&displayonly=POS&query=eng-30-02084071-n`
Result: `{"SYNSET":{"ID":{"$":"eng-30-02084071-n"},"POS":{"$":"n"}}}`

Query: `https://server_name/wneng30?action=save&id=eng-30-02084071-n&data=New definition&saveonly=DEF`
Result: *Synset definition is changed.*

Table 1: API call for obtaining the Part-of-Speech and changing the synset definition instead of full synset information, useful in lightweight clients.

4 New DEB Features within the KYOTO Project

4.1 Synset API Calls Granularity

Standard DEBVisDic API supports loading and saving synsets including the complete synset data. However, modern AJAX-like[4] lightweight applications frequently need to change just specific parts of the whole synset structure. Supporting this requirement, the client applications that access the wordnet data by means of the DEB application programming interface (API) do not need to get or save all the data at once and can parse less data faster. For these reasons, the API was extended with arguments to read or write specific parts of the synset. Example of such "micro" read and write calls are presented in Table 1.

4.2 Translate Synsets

One of the main advantages of wordnets is their multilinguality, i.e. the design of interlingual index used as a pivot between several national wordnets. Currently, the most commonly used pivot is the English wordnet due to its size, completeness and good maintenance. The link to the pivot is encoded either by assigning the English wordnet synset ID directly to the national synset, or by means of *external relations* (ELR) as specific "pointers" to other synsets outside the actual dictionary.

A common operation in multilingual projects is thus "translating" a word (in all synsets) to another language by means of the selected pivot. Since the mapping from national wordnets to English wordnet is not always unambiguous, each synset can point to one or more synsets in common wordnet. The DEB API call thus provides all possible synsets in the target language.

For instance, when we take the word *bosque* (forest) in Spanish, we can find this word in two synsets *bosque:1* and *bosque:2* that are linked to *forest:1, wood:2, woods:1* and *forest:2, woodland:1, timberland:1, timber:4* in the English

---
[4]*Asynchronous JavaScript and XML*, see (Rosenfeld and Morville, 1998)

Query: `https://server_name/wnspa?action=translate&query=bosque&target=wnjpn`
Result: { "translated": [{
  "elr": ["eng-30-09284015-n"],
  "value": "jpn-09-09284015-n",
  "label": "[n] 森林地:, 森:, 樹林:, 森林地帯:, ラフォーレ:, 林:, 森林:, 林地:"
},{
  "elr": ["eng-30-08438533-n"],
  "value": "jpn-09-08438533-n",
  "label": "[n] 森:, 樹林:, 林:, 森林:, 林地:"
}]}

Table 2: Translating API call – translate *bosque* (forest) from Spanish to Japanese

Query: `https://server_name/wnen30_d?action=nextSense&literal=Dusky+gopher+frog&callback=jsonp1253866807430`

Result without the 'callback' parameter:
  `{"literal":"Dusky gopher frog","recommended_sense":3}`

JSONP compatible response:
  `jsonp1253866807430({"literal":"Dusky gopher frog", "recommended_sense":3});`

Table 3: Variant of API calls supporting the JSONP protocol with callbacks.

wordnet. Through the obtained English IDs, we can enlist direct equivalents e.g. in the Japanese wordnet – see the example in Table 2.

4.3 Links between Wordnets and Ontologies

All wordnets in the KYOTO database are interlinked using the common central ontology. The solution is not limited to one ontology only, and different domain ontologies can extend the information for some synsets. Apart from the KYOTO Central Ontology, four different thesauri are used:

- GEMET (GEneral Multilingual Environmental Thesaurus)[5]
- SPECIES 2000[6]
- WWF Ecoregions database
- EUNIS[7]

All the ontologies are converted to the standard RDF/SKOS (Miles and Bechhofer, 2009) format and stored in the OpenLink Virtuoso Database backend (Wilensky and Idehen, 2009) (see Figure 2 for an example of interlinking these resources).

---

[5] http://isegserv.itd.rl.ac.uk/skos/gemet/
[6] http://www.sp2000.org
[7] http://eunis.eea.europa.eu

The main reason for using the Virtuoso database as a new DEB storage backend is the built-in support for the RDF SPARQL query language (Prud'hommeaux and Seaborne, 2009), which is designed for complex queries over ontological relations encoded in RDF triplets. Also the open-source license of Virtuoso is a necessary prerequisite for inclusion into DEB. Thanks to DEB platform architecture, the Virtuoso service is seamlessly integrated to all DEB interfaces. A user enters a SPARQL query (or a client application prepares one as a result from graphical user formulation) in the DEBVisDic interface and the results are retrieved by the server using Virtuoso AJAX API and presented to the user in the same format as other wordnets.

4.4 Importing Full Subtree

During the work on adding new items to the wordnet ontology, users often consults different ontological resources, such as the above mentioned GEMET or EUNIS. Including specific parts of these ontologies into WordNet often works with the same hierarchy as it is defined in the source ontology.

For such cases, the new DEB API provides a

Query: `https://server_name/wnen30_d?action=saveTree`
```
[ { "SYNSET": {
    "INTERNAL_ID": "1",
    "SYNONYM": { "LITERAL": { "$":"frog", "@sense":"2" } },
    "DEF": { "$":"Def frog" },
    "POS": { "$":"n" },
    "ELR": [ { "$":"term_frog_id","@type":"equivalent","@system":"KYOTOterminology" },
             { "$":"eng-30-01639765-n","@type":"equivalent","@system":"enwn30" } ]
  },{ "SYNSET":
    "INTERNAL_ID": "2",
    "ILR": [ { "$":"1","@type":"hypernym" } ],
    "SYNONYM": { "LITERAL": { "$":"robber frog", "@sense":"2" } },
    "DEF": { "$":"Def robber frog" },
    "POS": { "$":"n" },
    "ELR": [ { "$":"term_robber_frog_id","@type":"equivalent","@system":"KYOTOterminology" } ]
  },{ "SYNSET":
    "INTERNAL_ID": "3",
    "ILR": [ { "$":"1","@type":"hypernym" } ],
    "SYNONYM": { "LITERAL": { "$":"poison frog", "@sense":"3" } },
    "DEF": { "$":"Def poison frog" },
    "POS": { "$":"n" },
    "ELR": [ { "$":"term_poison_frog_id","@type":"equivalent","@system":"KYOTOterminology" } ]
  },{ "SYNSET":
    "INTERNAL_ID": "4",
    "ILR": [ { "$":"3","@type":"hypernym" } ],
    "SYNONYM": { "LITERAL": { "$":"endemic poison frog", "@sense":"4" } },
    "DEF": { "$":"Def endemic poison frog" },
    "POS": { "$":"n" },
    "ELR": [ { "$":"term_endemic_poison_frog_id","@type":"equivalent","@system":"KYOTOterminology" } ]
  },{ "SYNSET":
    "INTERNAL_ID": "5",
    "ILR": [ { "$":"1","@type":"hypernym" } ],
    "SYNONYM": { "LITERAL": { "$":"golden frog", "@sense":"5_sense_number" } },
    "DEF": { "$":"Def golden frog" },
    "POS": { "$":"n" },
    "ELR":[ { "$":"term_golden_frog","@type":"equivalent","@system":"KYOTOterminology" } ]
  } } ]
```
Result: *All synset from the tree are added with correct link IDs.*

Table 4: API call for merging a full sub-tree from a selected source to a wordnet.

---

technique for efficient saving of several synsets and their hierarchical structure in one step. With this API call, DEBVisDic can store several synsets at once, while keeping their defined structure. Of course, before saving the synsets, the user does not know the unique synset database IDs regarding the new synsets. To be able to define the synset hierarchy, the user uses temporary identifiers in the request and the DEBVisDic server replaces them with real IDs.

For example, we want to enrich the WordNet with the following hierarchy of ontological concepts:

- frog
  - robber frog
  - poison frog
    * endemic poison frog
  - golden frog

The user will copy the hierarchy to the WordNet editor and add more synset data, like definition, other synonyms or more relations. When the editing is done, all the data are processed by the DEB server part and stored in the database. An example of the corresponding request and result is displayed in Table 4. In this example, the INTERNAL_ID elements are temporary identifiers that will be replaced with the actual IDs during the save process. This new extension to the DEBVisDic API offers a very effective way of building new WordNets.

4.5 JSONP Support

For security reasons, JavaScript client applications may send requests only to server on the same domain as the application. However, when working with several services hosted on different servers, the application needs to overcome this limitation. This kind of API requests is supported by so-called JSONP (JSON with padding) protocol. JSONP is a jQuery extension that passes the obtained server response to a specified JavaScript function. To be able to provide the results of all API calls in the form of the JSONP protocol, all the DEBVisDic API calls accept a new parameter 'callback'. With this parameter, the response is encapsulated in the requested JavaScript function. An example of the JSONP support in the DEB API calls is showed in Table 3.

4.6 External WordNet Relations

In a complex system like Global WordNet Grid or KYOTO database, where the different wordnets are connected together, usually through one pivot wordnet, sometimes with several center wordnets.

There are several types of external relations used in inter-wordnets links. The most common relations are:

- EQ_Synonym,
- EQ_Near_Synonym,
- EQ_Has_Hyperonym, and
- EQ_Has_Hyponym.

New API function allows to quickly find all the synsets from several wordnets that are related with the pivot synset. This is very useful for a multi-language projects.

5 Conclusions

We have presented the exploitation of the DEB platform as the main part of the database system within the KYOTO project. The DEB architecture shows here the benefits of its versatility and adaptability to news requirements, which allow to add new storage backend of OpenLink Virtuoso database or add the JSONP support to all previous API calls.

Even though the KYOTO project is just in the middle, we believe that the project will be a valuable step forward in defining future standards for semantic network architectures.

Acknowledgements

This work has been partly supported by the Ministry of Education of CR within the Center of basic research LC536 and in the National Research Programme II project 2C06009 and by the Czech Science Foundation under the project 102/09/1842.

References

C. Fellbaum, editor. 1998. *WordNet: An Electronic Lexical Database*. MIT Press.

Aleš Horák and Adam Rambousek. 2007. Dictionary Management System for the DEB Development Platform. In *Proceedings of the 4th International Workshop on Natural Language Processing and Cognitive Science (NLPCS, aka NLUCS)*, pages 129–138, Funchal, Portugal. INSTICC PRESS.

Aleš Horák, Karel Pala, Adam Rambousek, and Pavel Rychlý. 2006. New clients for dictionary writing on the DEB platform. In *DWS 2006: Proceedings of the Fourth International Workshop on Dictionary Writings Systems*, pages 17–23, Italy. Lexical Computing Ltd., U.K.

Aleš Horák, Karel Pala, and Adam Rambousek. 2008. The Global WordNet Grid Software Design. In *Proceedings of the Fourth Global WordNet Conference*, Szegéd, Hungary. University of Szegéd.

D. Christodoulakis. 2004. *Balkanet Final Report*. University of Patras, DBLAB. No. IST-2000-29388.

Alistair Miles and Sean Bechhofer. 2009. SKOS Simple Knowledge Organization System, http://www.w3.org/2004/02/skos/.

Ian Oeschger et al. 2002. *Creating Applications with Mozilla*. O'Reilly and Associates, Inc., Sebastopol, California.

Eric Prud'hommeaux and Andy Seaborne. 2009. SPARQL Query Language for RDF, http://www.w3.org/TR/rdf-sparql-query/.

Louis Rosenfeld and Peter Morville. 1998. *Information Architecture for the World Wide Web*. O'Reilly and Associates, Inc., Sebastopol, California.

P. Vossen, editor. 1998. *EuroWordNet: a multilingual database with lexical semantic networks for European Languages*. Kluwer.

Piek Vossen. 2008. KYOTO Project (ICT-211423), Knowledge Yielding Ontologies for Transition-based Organization. http://www.kyoto-project.eu/.

Alan Wilensky and Kingsley Idehen. 2009. OpenLink Virtuoso Database, http://virtuoso.openlinksw.com/.

Developing the Persian WordNet of Verbs: Issues of Compound Verbs and Building the Editor

Masoud Rouhizadeh
NLP Research Laboratory
Shahid Beheshti University
Tehran, Iran
mrouhizadeh@gmail.com

Mahsa A. Yarmohammadi
NLP Research Laboratory
Shahid Beheshti University
Tehran, Iran
yarmohamadi@gmail.com

Mehrnoush Shamsfard
NLP Research Laboratory
Shahid Beheshti University
Tehran, Iran
m-shams@sbu.ac.ir

Abstract

In this paper we mostly focus on the behavior of Persian compound verbs and the way we propose to deal with them. Most of the Persian verbs are compound verbs and they are formed by two major patterns of combination and incorporation. In many cases the compound verbs are semantically transparent. This behavior of the verbs has some important consequences in the Persian semantic lexicon hence; we design an editor to fully support it. The system architecture is three-tier model and in analysis, design and implementation of this editor we used prototyping methodology. The database consists of 11 tables which are related to each other by definite relations and store Persian verbs, nouns, adjectives, adverbs, prepositions and synsets. The results are compatible to other WordNets and the information is exportable to XML.

1 Introduction

Persian is the official language of three countries and it is also spoken in more than six other countries. There is no doubt in the necessity of constructing basic language processing resources and tools for it, like many other less-studied languages. On the other hand, one of the most urgent problems in language technology is the lexical semantics bottleneck, the unavailability of domain-independent lexica with rich semantic information on lexical items. Such lexica could greatly improve the quality of current applications.

There have been some attempts for reaching this goal (Famian & Aghajaney 2006; Keyvan et al., 2006; Mansoori & Bijankhan, 2008); however, most of them are only considering design of the structure and, in practice, limited sets of words or lexemes are entered in the lexicon.

This paper is a report of an ongoing project of developing the Persian WordNet of verbs, persuading our previous work (Rouhizadeh et. al. 2007 and 2008). It is a part of a larger project of building a semantic lexicon for Persian called FarsNet (Shamsfard, 2008).

Here we mostly focus on the behavior of Persian compound verbs and the way we propose to deal with them. Then we will review the editor of the WordNet of Persian verbs which is designed to handle the compound verbs phenomena in Persian.

This paper is divided into two parts; first, we give some theoretical considerations about Persian compound verbs and then we briefly review the editor of the Persian WordNet of verbs.

2 Compound verbs in Persian WordNet

Persian verbs can be divided into two major morphological categories: simple and compound verbs. Compound verb formation is highly productive in Persian. The number of simple verbs in Persian today, is less than 200 verbs while the number of compound verbs is more than 4000. compound verb formation is highly productive in Persian today. Persian compound verbs show interesting semantic behavior and a good semantic lexicon of Persian should deal with such particular characteristics. In the following subsections we briefly review different types of compound verb formation in Persian and their semantic properties, then, we review the consequences of these properties in Persian WordNet.

2.1 Persian compound verbs and their semantics

According to Dabirmoghaddam (1997) there are two major types of compound-verb formation in Persian which are *Combination* and *Incorpora-*

tion. These two types of verb formation are described below.

2.1.1 Combination

In this type of compound-verb formation the non-verbal and the verbal constituent are combined in the following patterns. The Persian examples are shown in front of each item.

Adjective + Auxiliary: *delxor-shodan* 'to become annoyed' 'annoyed-become'

Noun + Verb: *bâzi-kardan* *'to play'* *'play-do'*

Prepositional Phrase + Verb: *be donya âmadan* 'to be born' 'to-world-come'

Adverb + Verb: dar yâftan *'to perceive'* *'in-find'*

Past Participle + Passive Auxiliary: *sâxte šodan* 'to be built' 'built-become'.

2.1.2 Incorporation

In Persian, the direct objects (losing its grammatical endings) can incorporate with the verb, to create a compound verb, which is a conceptual whole as shown in the following example:

1-a. mâ qazâ-y-e-m-ân- râ   xor-d-im
     we food-our-pl.-DO   eat-past-we
     'We ate our food'

1-b. mâ qazâ- xor-d-im
     'We did food eating'

In direct object incorporation the argument structure of verb changes and the transitive verb changes to intransitive, as a result of incorporation.

Also, some prepositional phrases can incorporate with verbs. Here, the proposition disappears after incorporation:

2-a. ân-hâ be zamin   xor-d-and
     that-pl. to ground   eat-past-they
     'They fell to the ground.'

2-b. ân-hâ zamin xor-d-and
     'They fell down.'

2.1.3 Compound verbs semantics

As far as the semantic behavior of the different types of compound verbs are concerned, statistical findings show that the verbal constituent has *transparent* meaning in "Direct Object Incorporation" and "Adjective + Auxiliary" combination. In other word, in these types of compound verb, the meaning of the compound unit is the summations of the meanings of its verbal and its non-verbal constituents. In the other processes, however, there is a metaphorical extension and/or semantic bleaching of the verbal constituent of the compound, that is, the meaning of the whole compound *cannot* be considered as the summation of its units. Interestingly, in "Noun + Verb" compounding the verbal constituent is lexicalized to serve as an aktionsart marker and it shows how the action of the whole verb is performed. A detailed study of this behavior in Persian WordNet can be found in Mansoori and Bijankhan (2008).

2.2 New relations for Persian compound verbs

According to the properties mentioned above, we define the two new relations for Persian compound verbs. The first one is TRANSPARENT_COMPOUND relation which exists between the verbal and non-verbal constituent of the compound verbs which are combination of adjective or past participle and the auxiliary. Here the meaning of the compound verbs is transparent and it is the summation of the adjective or past participle and the following auxiliary.

We also define the TRANSAPRENT_INCORPORATION relation between the verbal and non-verbal constituents of the compound verbs which are formed by *direct object incorporation*. The meaning of these verbs is also transparent.

We defined also collocation relation between verbal and non-verbal constituents of all compound verbs regardless of their compounding process. This is not a semantic relation but it is very effective relation for detection of the verbs in syntactic/semantic processing.

2.3 Compound verbs and the structure of Persian WordNet

This classification of Persian verbs has five consequences in the structure of Persian WordNet of verbs.

The first consequence is the possibility of defining Hyponymy/Hyperonymy relation between the verbal constituent and the whole compound verb in all transparent compounds. In other words the compound verb is the Hyponym of its verbal constituent.

The second consequence shows itself in the relations between different parts of speech. The transparent compound verbs have direct semantic relations to their non-verbal constituents. Every relation and characteristic of these non-verbal constituents can be transferred to their compound verbs.

The third consequence is about the compound verbs which are formed by combination of adjective and auxiliaries budan (to be), šodan (to become) and kardan (to do). Once we have entered their semantic information in our database, we can predict systematically, the meaning of their compound verbs – a function of an adjective and an auxiliary.

The fourth consequence is about the verbs formed by direct object incorporation. Their non-verbal consequent was in fact the direct object of the simple verb. Thus, their hyperonyms, hyponyms and co-hyponyms are very good candidates for the direct object (without 'râ', the direct object marker in Persian) of that simple verb.

The fifth consequent is about the verbs formed by the combination of noun + verb. In this kind of verbs the simple verb is lexicalized to serve as an aktionsart marker. The real or metaphoric viewpoints are stored in Persian our database and in the case of their combination to nouns this information is transferred into the whole compound verb.

These kinds of relationship are special characteristics of the Persian verbs lexicon. All these special features of Persian verbs are completely supported in our editor. In the following section we briefly review the editor and its technical aspects.

3 The editor for Persian WordNet of verbs

Considering the above-mentioned properties of the Persian compound verbs we required an editor to fully support those special characteristics and semantic behavior.

We were using VisDic, the BalkaNet multilingual editor (Tufis et. al. 2004) for a while but it was not supporting compound verbs special characteristics and semantic behavior. It was also not appropriate for Persian scripts in the sense that since it could not support the right-to-left direction and some encodings of Persian scripts. On the other hand, the information in our verb lexicon is not limited to WordNet relations and we are going to put some more information like semantic restriction, verbs frames and so on.

On the base of these facts, we started to design the editor from scratch to fulfill our needs. We focus on the WordNet information of verbs since the FarsNet project concerns this at the first phase. However, the editor and its database are extendible to support many other kinds of relations and information such as those in FrameNet and VerbNet.

What will be discussed in the rest of this sections is the first[1] editor that we developed for WordNet of verbs. The editor is designed based on relational database model and the results can be exported to standard XML format. This feature makes our results compatible to the WordNets of the other languages. In this section we discuss about the design methodology of the editor, its graphical user interface and different parts of it and the editor's database model. Finally there is a note of compatibility of the editor's output with the other WordNets.

3.1 Methodology

In the analysis, design and implementation of this editor we used prototyping methodology. The programming language is Visual Basic 6. The software architecture is based on three-tier model, which are: 1) Data Access layer, 2) Business Logic layer and 3) Presentation layer. We use an adaptor between the first and the third layers to keep the adaptability to other prospective DBMSs. Each of these three layers has a dedicated and special responsibility. As a result, experts can make different changes in any layer with no interference to the other layers. To produce the web version of the editor, we simply used the first and the second layers of the desktop version. Then we design only the third layer.

3.2 The Graphical User Interface (GUI)

The graphical user interface of this editor is designed to make the manual lexicography task easy and straight-forward. It has two forms to edit verb entries and synsets separately. This provides the facility for the lexicographer to edit individual verb or the verbs within the synsets independently. When launching the editor, the main menu appears and one can select to go for "Verbs" or "Synsets". This directs the lexicographer to the "List of Verbs" or the "List of synsets" forms which are described below in details.

---

[1] We have ported and expanded this editor to the second one in Java working on XML data to be able to work platform free. We have also developed a web based version of the editor to enable collaborative lexicography over the internet. The theoretical foundations and design criteria of the first editor is inherited to its successors too.

3.2.1 Verbs entries

The first window of the verb editor is a "List of Verbs". Here one can view all the existing verbs of the database, edit a verb by double clicking on it, delete a verb and add a new verb. If the lexicographer chooses to add a new verb he/she will be redirected to another window of "Add New Verb". This window is quite similar to "Verb Properties" window which will be appeared if he/she selects a verb to edit (Figure 1).

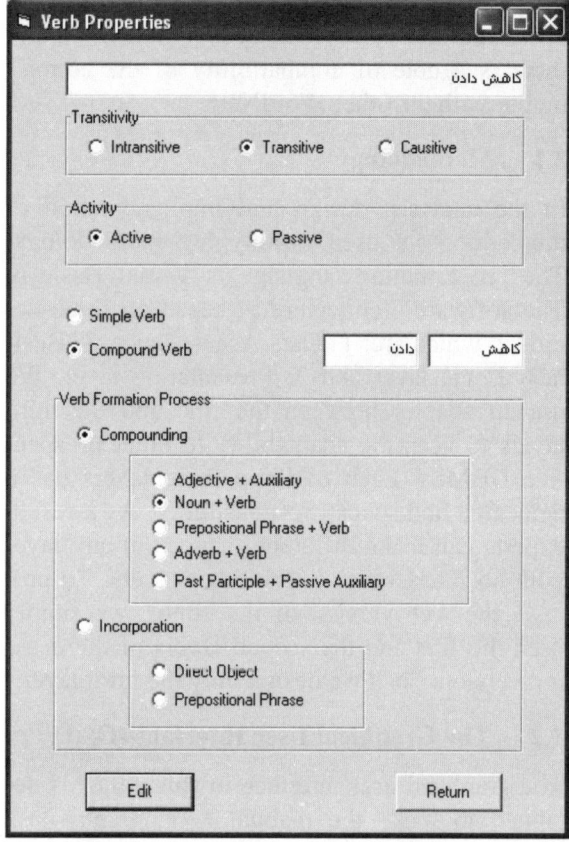

Figure 1: The window of "Verb Properties"

In this window all the necessary information should be presented for a single verb entry. At first the lexicographer selects the transitivity of a verb that is weather the verb is "Intransitive", "Transitive" or "Causative". In the next part he/she selects if the verb is "Active" or "Passive". The most important part is defining the morphological structure of the verb. He/she can select if the verb is "Simple" or "Compound". If he/she selects the verb as a compound verb, the two verbal and non-verbal constituents are automatically separated. No information will be saved in the database about the constituent structure of the verb until he/she selects the type of "Verb Formation Process". If he/she chooses the "Compounding Process", then it is necessary to select whether the verb is composed of "Adjective + Auxiliary", "Noun + Verb", "Prepositional Phrase + Verb", "Adverb + Verb" or "Past Participle + Passive Auxiliary". If he/she chooses the "Incorporation" process then it is necessary to choose whether the verb is formed through "Direct Object" or "Prepositional Phrase" incorporation.

As the verb formation process is selected, all the non-verbal constituents are saved separately in their related tables i.e. the tables of Nouns, Adjectives, Prepositions, etc.

As mentioned before, verbal constituent has transparent meaning in "Direct Object Incorporation" and "Adjective + Auxiliary" verb formation processes. The meaning of the resulting compound verb in these cases is the function of the meaning of its verbal and non-verbal constituents. So following information will be saved about such kind of entries: a) the compound verb, b) the non-verbal constituent, c) the verbal constituent (if this constituent is not entered previously, a new window will appear to add it) and d) a direct link between verbal and non-verbal constituent to show transparency of the meaning of the compound verb. The TRANSPARENT_COMPOUND and TRANSAPRENT_INCORPORATION relations are defined automatically as we select one of these types of compounding process. A collocation relation between the verbal and non-verbal constituent is also saved here.

The abovementioned two types of verbs inherit also the relationships which belong to their non-verbal counterparts. This is the way in which we connect lexicon of Persian verbs to the lexicon of Persian adjectives (in compounding process of Adj.+ V.) and the lexicon of Persian nouns (the direct objects incorporation process).

We also mentioned that in the other compound verb formation processes there is a metaphorical extension and/or semantic bleaching of the verbal constituents and this constituent does not have a transparent meaning. As a result we would save the following information: a) the compound verb, b) the non-verbal constituent and c) the verbal constituent (if not exists, a new window will appear to add this verb) but *no* direct link between the two constituents. Instead, we save the type of verbal constituent in Noun + Verb compounds. This constituent serves as the aktionsart marker. A collocation relation is saved for these kinds of verbs too.

Once the lexicographer entered the information of each verb in this form, the verb will be ready to be a part of a synset (group of synsets). To define the synsets there are separate forms in the editor which will be described in the next subsection.

3.2.2 Synsets

The editor goes to list of the whole synsets if you select the "Synsets" option from the main menu. Is the lexicographer selects to bottom of "Synsets" he/she can view all the existing synsets of the database, edit a synset by double clicking it, delete a synset and or a new synset. If he/she chooses to add a new synset he/she will be redirected to another window of "Add New Synset" (Figure 2). This window is quite similar to "Synset Properties" window which will be appeared if he/she selects a synset to edit.

For each synset it is possible to enter the following information:

Synset ID: This ID can be defied automatically or manually. Our lexicon could be connected to other existing WordNets via the links of Persian synsets IDs to their equivalent synset IDs in Princeton WordNet 3.0.

Definition: A definition of a synset is given in this field which is very similar to existing definitions in mono-lingual dictionaries.

Usage: An instance of the synset (or particular word(s) of it) usage is given in this filed.

Synonym words: Here the lexicographer should enter all the synonym words which form a synset. He/she can add every verb by typing it in the blank input box. If the verb was not defied before, the editors opens "Add New Verb" window and the new verb is added after definition process. In addition he/she can select the synonym verbs from the list of existing verbs. The list of verbs appears as he/she presses this bottom and it is possible to select one or more verbs from the list. Finally, he/she can delete any verbs of the synonym sets, or edit it by double clicking on it.

Relations: it is possible to establish a relation among the current synset and the other synsets via different kinds of relations. These relations, which are mainly derived from EuroWordNet, include:
HAS_HYPERONYM
HAS_HYPONYM
ANTONYM
NEAR_ANTONYM
CAUSES
IS_CAUSED_BY
HAS_SUBEVENT
IS_SUBEVENT_OF

These relation exist among *verb* synsets, however, there are some other relations which exist among verbs and other parts of speech:
XPOS_NEAR_SYNONYM
HAS_XPOS_HYPERONYM
HAS_XPOS_HYPONYM which exists between a verb and a noun and:
XPOS_NEAR_ANTONYM between a verb and an adjective and:
IN_MANNER and
MANNER_OF which exist between a verb and adverb and vice versa.

It is possible to select the above relations among the verb synsets and the synsets of other parts of speech.

3.3 The database model

The relational database of Persian WordNet of verbs consists of 11 related tables. The tables contain data for Persian Verbs, Nouns, Adjectives, Adverbs, Prepositions and Synsets. Table of VERB for instance stores verbs and their properties such as the verb's transitivity, verb's morphological structure and verb's compounding process. There are also three tables for storing the information of Persian synsets and their different relations. Figure 3 shows the database architecture of Persian WordNet of verbs.

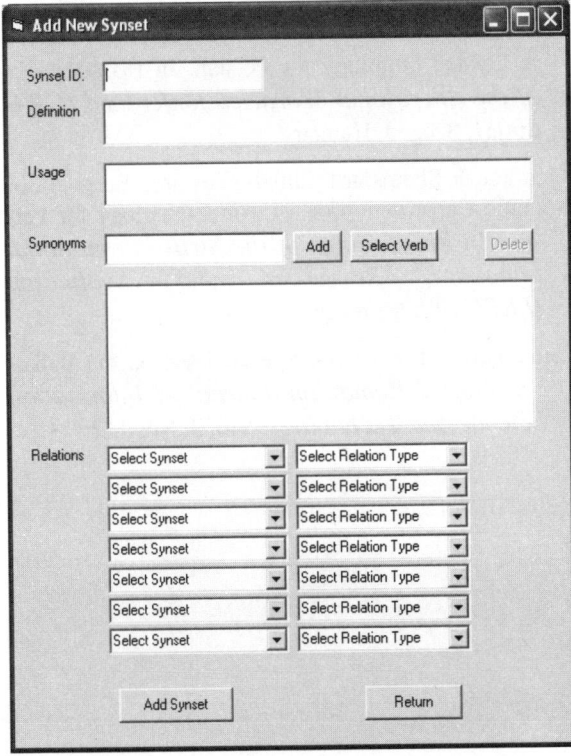

Figure 2: The "Add New Synset" form

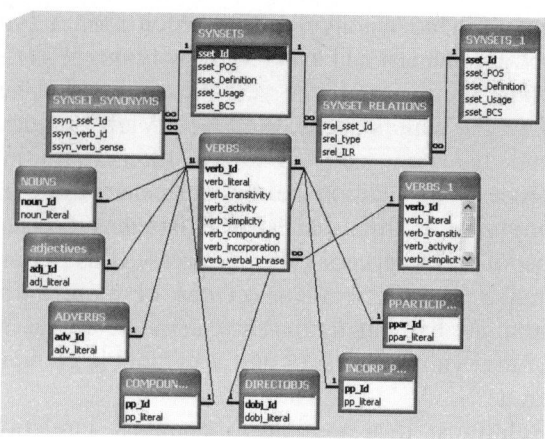

Figure 3: The database architecture of Persian WordNet of verbs

3.4 Compatibility

Our verb lexicon is structurally compatible to the other existing WordNets. All the information in the database is exportable to XML format. The data in SYNSETS table and its related tables i.e. SYNSET_SYNONYMS and SYNSET_RELATIONS could be exported to standard XML of WordNets. In this format each synset is defined within a <SYNSET></SYNSET> including some other inner tags such as <ID>, <POS>, <DEF>, <USAGE> and <SYNONYM>.

4 Conclusion and further work

In this paper we have discussed some linguistic issues of Persian compound verbs and their effects on developing the Persian WordNet of verbs. We also showed the features of the first editor which is specially designed for Persian verbs and their characteristics. Defining a web service for our verb lexicon to retrieve and publish data in XML format for other NLP softwares or websites is among our further works.

Once we have a larger lexicon, the editor may be set for deeper semantic processing. We can provide hierarchical definition of the verbal constituents to predict the meaning of the whole compound verbs. This feature reduces redundancy in the database to a great extent.

Adding the argument structures of verbs and their semantic restrictions are also in our future planning of this project.

Acknowledgments

This work has been funded in part by Iran Telecommunication Research Center (ITRC) under contract no. T/500/19231.

References

Mohammad Dabir-Moghaddam. 1997. Compound Verbs in Persian. *Studies in the Linguistic Science*, 27(2), 25–59.

Ali Famian, Darioush Aghajaney. 2006. Towards Building a WordNet for Persian Adjectives. In *Proceedings of the 3rd Global WordNet conference*, pp. 307–308. South Korea.

Christiane Fellbaum (ed.), *Wordnet: an Electronic Lexical Database*, MIT Press, 1998.

Farhad Keyvan, (et. al.). 2006. Developing PersiaNet: The Persian Wordnet. In *Proceedings of the 3rd Global WordNet conference*, pp. 315-318. South Korea

Niloufar Mansoory, Mahmood Bijankhan .2008. The Possible Effects of Persian Light Verb Constructions on Persian WordNet. In *Proceedings of the 4th Global WordNet conference (GWC 2008)*, Szeged, Hungary.

Masoud Rouhizadeh, Mostafa Assi, Mahsa A.Yarmohamadi. 2007. Designing Persian Verbs WordNet. In *Proceedings of the 7th Iranian Conference on Linguistics*, Tehran, Iran.

Masoud Rouhizadeh, Mehrnoush Shamsfard, Mahsa A.Yarmohamadi. 2008. Building a WordNet for Persian Verbs. In *Proceedings of the 4th Global WordNet conference (GWC 2008)*, Szeged, Hungary.

Mehrnoush Shamsfard. 2008a. Developing FarsNet: A Lexical Ontology for Persian. In *Proceedings of the 4th Global WordNet conference (GWC 2008)*, Szeged, Hungary.

Mehrnoush Shamsfard. 2008b. Towards Semi Automatic Construction of a Lexical Ontology for Persian. In *Proceedings of the Sixth International Language Resources and Evaluation (LREC'08)*, Morocco.

Dand Tufis, et. al. 2004. Special Issue on the BalkaNet Project. *Romanian Journal of Information Science and Technology*, Vol. 7, Nos 1–2.

slo WNet: Construction and Corpus Annotation

Darja Fišer
Department of Translation, Faculty of Arts
University of Ljubljana, Slovenia
`darja.fiser@guest.arnes.si`

Tomaž Erjavec
Department of Knowledge Technologies
Jožef Stefan Institute
`tomaz.erjavec@ijs.si`

Abstract

This paper presents a wordnet for Slovene which was created semi-automatically with a combination of approaches and multilingual resources, in particular a bilingual dictionary, a parallel corpus and Wikipedia. Analysis of the results shows that the dictionary approach yields a good core wordnet but requires substantial manual editing due to a lack of automatic word-sense disambiguation. This was successfully improved with the corpus approach which, however, was limited to single-word literals. The last approach, based on Wikipedia, was only used for domain-specific monosemous terms, and can deal with multi-word literals and therefore usefully complements the previous two approaches. The created sloWNet was then used to semantically annotate a corpus for Slovene: one hundred high frequency nouns were annotated in a corpus of 100,000 words. The paper reports on the method and results of this manual annotation. Both the Slovene wordnet and annotated corpus are to be publicly available.

1 Introduction

sloWNet is a lexico-semantic resource for Slovene, in which words that describe the same concept and therefore have the same meaning (literals) are organized into sets of synonyms (synsets). Synsets are linked into a semantic network with various lexical and semantic relations. Slovene wordnet is based on Princeton WordNet (Fellbaum 1998) and was built automatically following the expand model (Vossen 1998) according to which PWN concepts are rendered in the target language but the relations that hold among those concepts are preserved. Three different approaches and several bi- and multilingual resources were used to generate sloWNet which currently contains about 20,000 synsets and 24,000 literals, 17,000 of which are monosemous. It is aligned to all wordnets for other languages that use PWN synset ids.

The topic of this paper is a project in which frequent nouns from a corpus of Slovene were manually annotated with wordnet senses. The result of the annotation process is a list of concordances in which each nucleus word has an assigned sense called semantic concordances. Semantic concordances are a useful resource for a wide range of applications, such as automatic word sense disambiguation, or for corpus-based studies of sense frequency, distribution and co-occurrence. They are also invaluable as an aid for translation as well as for vocabulary acquisition in a foreign language.

The paper is organized as follows: Section 2 presents the approaches used to construct sloWNet and analyses the results, Section 3 presents manual annotation of a corpus with sloWNet synsets and Section 4 concludes the paper with a discussion and suggestions for future work.

2 Slovene wordnet

For the construction of Slovene wordnet we have leveraged the resources at our disposal, namely a bilingual dictionary, a multilingual parallel corpus and encyclopaedic resources from the Wikipedia family. Based on the assumption that the translation relation is a plausible source of semantics (Dyvik 1998) and that it will reveal words which can have more than one meaning on the one hand and different expressions that share the same meaning on the other, we have used these resources in combination with BalkaNet wordnets (Tufis et al. 2000) to extract semantically relevant information in three different approaches we describe below.

First, we used a bilingual dictionary to translate basic concepts into Slovene. At this stage of the project, our aim was to obtain a core wordnet, which is why we only included synsets from Base Concept Sets (see Tufis et al. 2000). The translations were checked and corrected by hand (see Erjavec and Fišer 2006).

With the second approach we wished to extend the core wordnet as well as to improve automatic disambiguation of polysemous words in order to avoid subsequent extensive manual editing of the generated synsets. A parallel corpus for five languages was word-aligned and the extracted multilingual lexicon was disambiguated with the existing wordnets for these languages from the BalkaNet family (see Fišer 2009). If there was an overlap between all possible synset ids for lexicon entries, the same id was assigned to their Slovene equivalent in the lexicon. All Slovene entries in the lexicon with the same assigned id were treated as synonymous and therefore added to the same synset (e.g. *armada* and *vojska* for *army*). On the other hand, if the same Slovene expression appeared in several lexicon entries and was assigned different synset ids in each case, it was treated as polysemous and therefore added to different synsets (e.g. *stranka1* for *political party* and *stranka2* for *client*).

In the last approach, our goal was to overcome a limitation of the corpus-based approach, which used a 1:1 word-alignment algorithm and could therefore only deal with single-word literals, and to enlarge sloWNet with domain-specific terminology. We used open-source resources, such as Wikipedia and Eurovoc from which we extracted Slovene equivalents for monosemous PWN literals.

We also used Wikipedia articles to extract additional synonyms and definitions for synsets that were left in English in the previous approaches (see Fišer and Sagot 2008).

Synsets obtained from all three approaches were merged and filtered according to the reliability of the sources of translations. The structure of PWN synsets for which no translation could be found with any of the approaches was adopted from PWN based on the hierarchy preservation principle (Tufis 2000), only the literals were left empty. These synsets will be translated in the future. The entre network of synsets was then formatted in XML and loaded to the DEBVisDic editor for viewing and editing (Horak 2005).

An example of a Slovene synset with its corresponding English equivalent can be seen in Figure 1. The synset is marked with a Part-of-Speech label, a unique id and a Base-Concept-Set category. The Synonyms field, the most important one in the synset, contains all the literals that are used to describe the concept. They share a common definition which is in most cases still in English at this point of the project. What follows is domain information, mapping to the SUMO/MILO ontology and lexical and semantic relations, such as hypernymy, meronymy and hyponymy. The Stamp field contains information about when the synset was validated and who validated it.

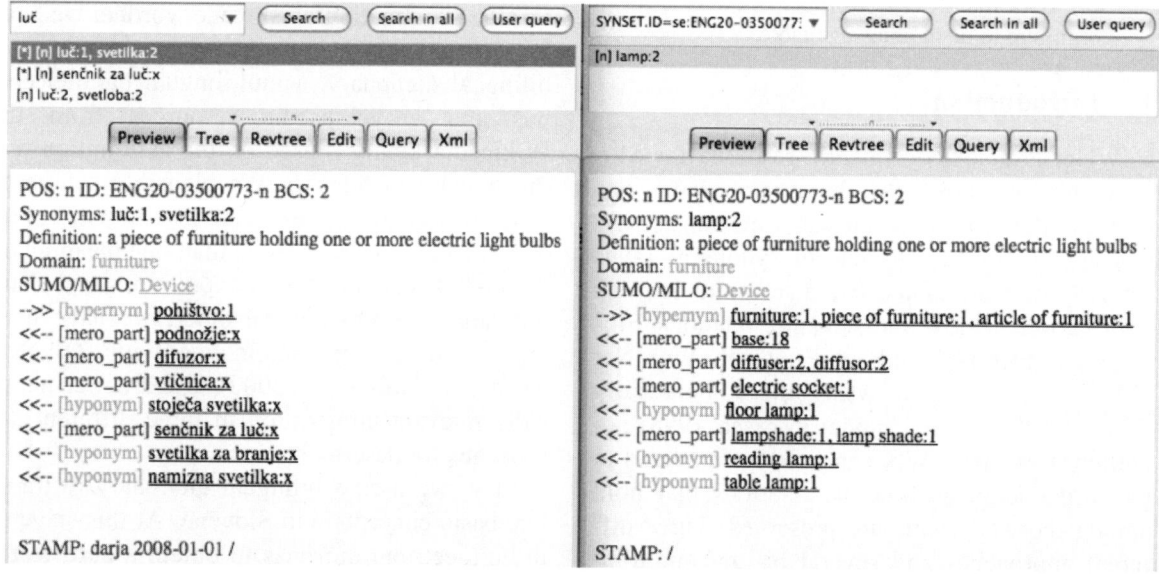

Figure 1. Slovene synset *{luč:1, svetilka:2}* with its English equivalent *{lamp:2}* in DEBVisDic.

2.1 Analysis of sloWNet

The latest version of sloWNet (2.1, 30/09/2009) contains about 24,000 literals, which are organized into almost 20,000 synsets, covering about 15% of PWN 2.1. 17,000 or about 71% of the literals in sloWNet are unique, i.e. appear in only one synset.

Base Concept Sets 1 & 2 are fully covered but there are also many specific synsets. The most frequent domain in sloWNet is Factotum (25%) which was mostly obtained from the dictionary and a parallel corpus while the following three are Zoology (17%), Botany (13%) and Biology (7%) and come from Wikipedia.

sloWNet mostly contains nominal synsets (91%), although there are some verbal and adjectival synsets as well. We have not been able to obtain adverbial synsets with the approaches described above. Apart from single word literals, there are also plenty of multi-word expressions (43%). These too mostly come from Wikipedia. Synsets in sloWNet are relatively short as 66% of them contain only one literal, average synset length being 1.16. The longest synset contains 16 literals (for verb *goljufati*, Eng. *to cheat*).

The most common relation in sloWNet is hypernymy, which represents almost half of all relations in wordnet (46%). Hypernymy is by far the most prevalent relation for nouns (91%). Nominal hypernymy chains tend to be quite long, the longest ones contain as much as 16 synsets. Since sloWNet does not cover the entire inventory of PWN concepts, there are some gaps (empty synsets) in the network. An investigation of nominal hierarchies revealed that all of the nine top nodes exist in Slovene and that almost half (46%) of the chains do not contain a single gap. What is more, only 2% of chains contain five or more gaps. These gaps will have to be filled in the future in order to obtain a denser hierarchy of nodes.

A comparison of nominal synsets from sloWNet and the jos100k corpus showed that sloWNet nouns cover 30% of the common nouns present in jos100k. Most frequent nouns in the corpus (freq. ≥ 30) have 91% coverage in sloWNet, medium-frequency nouns (freq. 4-29) have 65% coverage while infrequent nouns (freq. ≤ 3) only have 28% coverage in sloWNet (Fišer and Erjavec 2008). While coverage of the most frequent words is good, we will try to improve overall coverage of sloWNet in the future in order to make the resource more useful.

3 Semantic annotation with sloWNet

The main goal of our annotation process was to obtain the first semantically annotated corpus for Slovene which can be used in corpus-based linguistic research as well as a resource for HLT applications requiring training data. However, because sloWNet had been created automatically and had been based on a foreign-language resource, our secondary goal was to check coverage of the senses it contains compared to the senses represented in the corpus and thereby evaluate and improve the developed lexicon in a practical semantic task.

As opposed to sequential annotation, in which all the words in the corpus are annotated, we followed the targeted semantic annotation principle (Miller, et al. 1994) which aims at determining senses only for a selection of polysemous corpus words. Targeted annotation is preferred by many researchers (see Kilgarriff 1998) because this way the semantic characteristics of each word are taken into consideration only once, and the whole corpus achieves greater consistency.

In addition, we followed the joint approach of coordinated wordnet validation and corpus annotation as proposed by Agirre et al. (2006) because it ensures that word senses in the lexicon reflect real usage and guarantees a better fit between sense distinctions in the lexicon and the corpus.

3.1 The jos100k corpus

The corpus used for semantic annotation was jos100k, which is part of the JOS project that is developing annotated corpora and associated resources meant to facilitate developments in human language technologies for the Slovene language. At present, the JOS resources comprise morpho-syntactic specifications, two word-level annotated corpora, and two web services. The developed resources are available under the Creative Commons licenses.

The jos100k corpus (Erjavec and Krek 2008) is a 100,000 word Slovene corpus which contains sampled paragraphs from the Slovene reference corpus FidaPLUS. The corpus is annotated with manually validated morphosyntactic descriptions and lemmas. The corpus has been carefully composed and checked and is intended to serve as a gold-standard reference corpus. In the scope of the JOS project we are currently annotating it for syntactic structures, and for lexico-semantic information, which is the topic of this paper.

3.2 Annotation of the corpus

In the first attempt of semantically annotating Slovene, we limited the task to nouns only because sense assignment for nouns is the easiest and because their coverage in sloWNet is currently by far the best. We extracted 100 most frequent common nouns from the jos100k corpus which also exist in sloWNet. Multi-word expressions that already exist in sloWNet were not included in the annotation as multi-word expressions are typically monosemous and therefore do not require manual sense assignment; it is also harder to automatically identify them in the corpus.

The annotation procedure consisted of several stages: the annotators started from sloWNet in which they checked all the senses of the target word and corrected any errors they found. In the second step, the annotators turned their attention to the concordances and tried to assign a wordnet sense to each occurrence of the given word in the corpus. If they came across a meaning of a word or a phrase they could not find in sloWNet, they added it to wordnet. In the final stage, the annotations were tested for errors and consolidated.

Because no tailor-made annotation software was available, the annotation was performed in MS Excel. Annotators received xls files with the concordances containing the target word that were extracted from the jos100k corpus. After studying an occurrence of the target word in context they determined which synset was the most appropriate for it and annotated it with the corresponding synsed id from wordnet to column C. Any comments that were required for this target word were added to column D. An example of the annotation process can be seen in Figure 2 where a multi-word expression *zemljiška knjiga/cadaster* was identified and the appropriate synset id and comment were added for this line in columns C and D.

The goal of the annotation process was to assign a sense to all occurrences of the target words. If more than one sense seemed appropriate despite best efforts to disambiguate them, the annotators were instructed to choose the most basic sense.

If an occurrence of the target word belonged to a multi-word expression (MWE), it was annotated with that sense and marked as a MWE. In case the target word was (part of) a proper name that does not exist in wordnet, the word was flagged as (part of a) proper name. If the appropriate sense could not be found in either sloWNet or PWN, the word was left unannotated and flagged as an out-of-vocabulary item. Most of these senses are language-specific and should therefore be added as such to sloWNet at a later stage of wordnet development.

3.3 Analysis of the annotations

While the annotation is still undergoing some minor revision, we report here on the current state of the semantic concordances over jos100k. Table 1 gives the basic statistics over the annotation set. Each of the 100 nouns has, on average, 54 occurrences in the corpus, which range between 30 (e.g. *oče/father*) and almost 350 (*leto/year*) with the next most frequent being *dan/day* (150). The annotators assigned over 500 different synsets to this set, i.e. over 5 senses per noun. Five of the nouns were monosemous (e.g. *muzej/museum*), while the most polysemous noun annotated was *čas/time* for which a total of 15 senses were used. Finally, almost 50 tokens were proper names, or parts of proper names not present in PWN, and for a further 25 tokens (0.5%) no appropriate synset could be found, e.g. for *voda/water* in *voda na [nekogaršnji] mlin / water for [somebody's] mill*, a Slovene idiom.

tokens	5,384
literals	100
avg tokens/literal	53.8
min tokens/literal	30
max tokens/literal	346
synsets	502
avg synsets/literal	5.4
min synsets/literal	1
max synsets/literal	15
proper names	46
no synset	25

Table 1. Annotation statistics

A	C	D	E	F	G
n	pomen	Opomba	levi kontekst	beseda	desni kontekst
5			aje lenari in prebira	knjige	, predvsem tiste za osebno:
6			prebral prvo takšno	knjigo	, za njo so se zvrstile druge
7	ENG20-06100818-n	*zemljiške knjige	natizacija zemljiške	knjige	
8			ilelfu , da je napisal	knjigo	zgodb , ki so jih opisali kot "

Figure 2. Annotation of the target word *knjiga* (*book*) in MS Excel.

Although MWEs were not explicitly selected for annotation, a surprisingly large number of focus nouns turned out to be part of MWEs which had, or could sensibly have their own literals in the wordnet. Table 2 gives the number of instances tagged as MWEs, almost 10% of the overall tokens, of which almost half had to be annotated with an approximate synset. Altogether, MWEs were tagged with 170 synsets, a third of the overall total.

MWE tokens	471
MWE tokens with approx. synset	223
MWE tokens with approp. synset	248
MWE synsets	170

Table 2. Multi-word expressions

As expected, the complexity of sense assignment to the target nouns correspond to their level of polysemy in sloWNet. On the other hand, it turned out that the lexicon was still missing some senses for nouns which are frequent in the corpus but have very few senses or are even monosemouns in the initial version of sloWNet, which is why these nouns had to be carefully examined as well (e.g. *člen*, freq. 57 appeared in sloWNet only in the sense of *link* but not in the sense of *article in a legal document* or the *grammatical article*).

There were quite many synsets containing the target nouns that were not used by the annotators. There is a good reason for not using some of these synsets because the target nouns appeared in them only due to insufficient disambiguation during wordnet generation and were deleted by the annotators during wordnet revision. An example is the word *sodišče/court* which appears in some synsets because the English word court was wrongly translated into Slovene in three synsets:

(1) *a yard wholly or partly surrounded by walls or buildings* – the correct translation is *dvorišče*,
(2) *the sovereign and his advisers who are the governing power of a state* – the correct translation is *dvor* and
(3) *the family and retinue of a sovereign or prince* – the correct translation is *dvor*.

Other senses were not used because they did not appear in the corpus. However, they should not automatically be treated as irrelevant for Slovene because the 100.000 word corpus that was used is far too small for making such conclusions and it would do more harm than good if such senses were deleted from sloWNet at this stage. One such example is the noun *stran* (*page*) which has seven senses in sloWNet, four of which do not appear in the corpus not because they are not used in Slovene at all but because they simply did not appear in our corpus:

(1) *an extended outer surface of an object,*
(2) *a distinct feature or element in a problem,*
(3) *a sheet of any written or printed material (especially in a manuscript or book)* and
(4) *one side of one leaf (of a book or magazine or newspaper or letter etc.) or the written or pictorial matter it contains.*

A comparison of annotations for the same target word that were submitted by two different annotators shows that their annotations vary to a great extent: they chose the same synset id for only 60% of the annotated tokens. It has also been observed that target words differ substantially in the level of agreement between the annotators, which means that some words were much easier to annotate than others. Perfect agreement was reached only with the words that were assigned only one sense (e.g. *odstotek/percentage*). Words with a low number of assigned senses (3 or 4, such as *člen/article* or *oče/father*) have an agreement exceeding 90%. The level of agreement decreases with the increase of target word frequency in the corpus. This suggests that highly frequent and polysemous words were harder to annotate.

As the inter-annotator agreement was rather low, we checked whether annotators agreed on the most frequent sense for a given word. The most predominant sense is very useful for many HLT applications because it has been found that the predominant sense baseline is quite hard to beat by word sense disambiguation algorithms. It turns out that the distribution of senses of the annotated words are in favour of the predominant sense, and that non-predominant senses chosen are in the minority. Also, annotators agreed on the most frequent sense almost in all the cases.

One of the words in which the annotators disagreed even on the most frequent sense is *predstavnik/representative* for which the share of the most frequent sense is similar (56.7% and 46.7%) with both annotators but the synsets they used to annotate the most occurrences of this noun in the corpus are different. One annotator most frequently chose the synset *agent: a representative who acts on behalf of other persons or organizations* while the other one preferred the synset *representative: a person who represents others*. When we study both synsets in detail, we find that they are both very similar and it is indeed hard to distinguish between them. This shows that sense distinctions in wordnet are not clear-cut and are very fine-grained, which is a common criticism of the resource as a sense repository for practical applications.

4 Conclusions

The paper presented sloWNet, in particular the method of its construction and the annotation of selected high-frequency nouns with wordnet senses in the jos100k corpus.

The main findings are that automatic methods can lead to reasonably high-quality wordnet construction. The validation of sloWNet with corpus annotations has shown that most senses that were required to annotate the corpus had already been present in sloWNet whereas the same is not true for non-core senses and especially for multi-word expressions which had to be added by the annotators in many cases. Multi-word expressions were especially difficult, as in almost half of the cases no exactly appropriate sense could be found in wordnet. This suggests that sloWNet will have to be further extended in order to ensure a thorough coverage of the sense inventory relevant for Slovene.

Semantic annotation of a corpus, be it manual or automatic, is still one of the challenging annotation tasks. It is very different from e.g. morpho-syntactic annotation in which all the units are annotated with the same set of categories, whereas in determining the meaning of a word, different categories have to be used for each unit we wish to annotate. This is why inter-annotator agreement is typically lower for semantic annotation than other annotation tasks.

In our annotation, we encountered significant problems in determining the best sense for each token, often involving lengthily discussions, and inconclusive decisions.

One way of simplifying and improving the annotation process in the future is collapsing fine-grained hard-to-distinguish senses into more general categories, called supersenses. This had already been done manually by Palmer, Dand and Fellbaum (2007) and automatically by Bruce and Wiebe (1998) who achieved a 10% improvement on the results.

Notwithstanding the difficulties of the annotation, the result is the first Slovene corpus that is annotated at the semantic level. The corpus will be freely available for linguistic analysis or as a training set for applications in human language technologies on the project website: http://nl.ijs.si/jos/index-en.html, while sloWNet is already publicly available via the Creative Commons license: http://nl.ijs.si/slownet.

Acknowledgments

The work was supported in part by the Slovenian Research Agency grant J2-9180 "Linguistic annotation of Slovene language: methods and resources" and by the EU 6FP-033917 project SMART "Statistical Multilingual Analysis for Retrieval and Translation".

References

Agirre, E., Aldezabal, I., Etxeberria, J., Izagirre, E., Mendizabal, K. & Quintian, M. (2006). A methodology for the joint development of the Basque WordNet and SemCor. Proceedings of LREC'06. Genoa.

Bruce, R., & Wiebe, J. M. (1998). Word sense distinguishability and inter-coder agreement. Proceedings of the Third Conference on Empirical Methods in Natural Language Processing (pp. 53–60). Granada.

Dyvik, H. (1998): Translations as semantic mirrors. In: Proceedings of Workshop W13: Multilinguality in the lexicon II of the 13th biennial European Conference on Artyificial Intelligence, ECAI 1998, pp. 24-44, Brighton, Gret Britain.

Erjavec, T., & Krek, S. (2008). The JOS Morphosyntactically Tagged Corpus of Slovene. Proceedings of LREC'08. Marrakech.

Erjavec, T. & Fišer, D. (2006): Building Slovene WordNet, In: Proceedings of the 5th International Conference on Language Resources and Evaluation, LREC 2006. Genova, Italy, 24.-26. May 2006.

Fellbaum, C. (Ed.). (1998). WordNet: An Electronic Lexical Database. Cambridge, London: MIT.

Fišer, D., & Erjavec, T. (2008). Predstavitev in analiza slovenskega wordneta. Proceedings of IS-LTC'08 (pp. 37–42). Ljubljana.

Fišer, D., & Sagot, B. (2008). Combining Multiple Resources to Build Reliable Wordnets. Proceedings of TSD'08. Brno.

Fišer, D. (2009). Laveraging parallel corpora and existing wordnets for automatic construction of the Slovene wordnet. In: Human language technology: challenges of the information society, (LNCS 5603). Berlin; Heidelberg: Springer, pp. 359-368.

Horak, A., Pala, K., Rambousek, A., & Povolny, M. (2005). DEBVisDic - First Version of New Client-Server Wordnet Browsing and Editing Tool. Proceedings of the GWA'05 (pp. 325–328). Brno.

Kilgarriff, A. (1998). Gold Standard Datasets for Evaluating Word Sense Disambiguation Programs. Computer Speech and Language. Special Use on Evaluation, 12 (4), 453–472.

Mihalcea, R., Chklovski, T., & Kilgarriff, A. (2004). The Senseval-3 English lexical sample task. Proceedings of ACL/SIGLEX Senseval-3.

Miller, G. A., Chodorow, M., Landes, S., Leacock, C., & Thomas, R. G. (1994). Using a semantic concordance for sense identification. Proceedings of the workshop on Human Language Technology. Plainsboro, NJ.

Palmer, M., Dand, H. T., & Fellbaum, C. (2007). Making fine-grained and coarse-grained sense distinctions, both manually and automatically. Natural Language Engineering (13), 137–163.

Tufis, Dan; Dan Cristea in Sofia Stamou (2000): BalkaNet: Aims, Methods, Results and Perspectives. A General Overview. V: Dascalu, Dan (ur.): Romanian Journal of Information Science and Technology Special Issue. 7/1-2, 9-43.

Veronis, J. (1998). A study of polysemy judgements and inter-annotator agreement. Programme and advanced papers of the Senseval workshop. Herstmonceux Castle.

Semi Automatic Development of FarsNet: The Persian WordNet

Mehrnoush Shamsfard
Computer Engineering Dept., Shahid Beheshti University, Tehran, Iran
m-shams@sbu.ac.ir

Akbar Hesabi
Linguistic Dept., Allameh Tabatabaiee University, Tehran, Iran
a.hesabi11@yahoo.com

Hakimeh Fadaei
Computer Engineering. Dept., Shahid Beheshti University, Tehran, Iran
Shafagh4@yahoo.com

Niloofar Mansoory
Payam Noor University Iran
nmansoory@gmail.com

Ali Famian
Payam Noor University Iran
famianali@yahoo.com

Somayeh Bagherbeigi
Allameh Tabatabaiee University, Tehran, Iran
sb_4715@yahoo.com

Elham Fekri
Shahid Beheshti University, Tehran, Iran
elham.fekri@gmail.com

Maliheh Monshizadeh
Shahid Beheshti University Tehran, Iran
monshizadeh@ce.sharif.edu

S. Mostafa Assi
Institute for Humanities and Cultural Studies, Tehran, Iran.
s_m_assi@ihcs.ac.ir

Abstract

This paper describes the development process of FarsNet; a lexical ontology for the Persian language. FarsNet is designed to contain a Persian WordNet with about 10000 synsets in its first phase and grow to cover verbs' argument structures and their selectional restrictions in its second phase. In this paper we discuss the semi-automatic approach to create the first phase: the Persian WordNet.

1 Introduction

WordNet (Miller 1995, Fellbaum 1998) is an electronic lexical database originally designed for English and replicated in several other languages. WordNet organizes words into sets of cognitively synonymous sets, called synonym sets or synsets. A synset is a set of words with the same part-of-speech that can be interchanged in a certain context. Actually, each synset represents a distinct concept, which can be expressed by its members in a range of different contexts. Synsets are interrelated by means of lexical (word-to-word) and conceptual-semantic (synset-to-synset) relations. The relations may relate words within a POS category (such as Synonymy, Antonymy, Hyponymy, Meronymy) or between different categories (such as Attributes and Derivationally related form,).
WordNet presently contains approximately 155287 different word forms organized into some 82115 word meanings synsets.

Nowadays WordNet is developed for more than 40 languages around the world. EuroWordNet, BalkaNet, AsiaNet and WordNets for Dutch, Italian, Spanish, German, French, Czech and Estonian are among them. Unfortunately some languages such as Persian (Farsi) lack such a semantic resource for use in NLP works.
There have been some efforts to create a wordnet for the Persian language too (Keyvan, et al, 2007; Mansoory & Bijankhan, 2008; Famian & Aghajani, 2007) but no available product have been announced yet. The only available lexical resources for Persian are some lexicons containing phonological and syntactic knowledge of words (such as Eslami, et al. 2004). This paper describes the semi automatic construction of FarsNet 1.0; the first WordNet for the Persian Language (Shamsfard, 2008). In this paper after an introduction to Persian Wordnet and its features and general construction methodology and resources, we will describe the language specific issues and our semi-automatic methods for building the WordNet.

2 Persian WordNet

FarsNet is designed to contain a Persian WordNet with about 10000 synsets in its first phase and grow to cover verbs' argument structures and their selectional restrictions in its second phase. FarsNet has also inter-lingual relations connecting Persian synsets to English ones (in Princeton WordNet 3.0). Persian WordNet goes closely in the lines and principles of Princeton WordNet,

EuroWordNet and BalkaNet to maximize its compatibility to these WordNets and to be connected to the other WordNets in the world to enable cross lingual tasks such as MT, multilingual IR and developing multilingual dictionaries and thesauri.

In this section after a brief description of Persian Language, we talk about the general methodology and lexical resources we used for FarsNet 1.0.

2.1 The Persian Language

The Persian language, also known as Farsi, is a member of the Iranian group of the Indo-Iranian sub-family of the Indo-European languages. It is the official language of Iran, Afghanistan and Tajikistan with more than 100 millions speakers. As far as the lexicon is concerned, Persian has borrowed many loanwords mostly from Arabic, English, French, and the Turkish languages. The Arabic influence has been great in both number of borrowed words and their frequency in use. Syntactically, Persian is primarily an SOV language with many ordering exceptions which makes it almost a free word order language. We will mention some specific features of Persian language for different parts of speech in the following sections.

2.2 Features and Coverage

FarsNet 1.0 is going to include the lexical, syntactic and semantic knowledge about more than 15000 Persian words and phrases organized in about 10000 synsets of nouns, adjectives and verbs. The size of this WordNet is more than some small scaled wordnets such as Hebrew and less than large scaled ones such as Princeton or EuroWordNet. According to size, it falls in the same category as medium scaled WordNets like the Arabic one.

- *Concepts*

The base concepts covered in FarsNet are classified into two groups: (a) Language independent base concepts which are those counted as base or important in many languages (b) Persian base concepts which are the most frequent words or common or important concepts among Persian speakers.

From the first group, FarsNet covers most of the base concepts BCS1 and BCS2 of BalkaNet to achieve compatibility with other WordNets. The base concepts of European languages which do not have equivalent or are not common in Persian are eliminated from this set.

The second group is extracted from the most frequent words of two Persian corpora: Peykareh (Bijankhan, 2004) and PLDB (Assi, 1997) to preserve the Persian specific structures. Many of the members of this group are present in the first group as well.

- *Relations*

There are two main types of relations defined in FarsNet: inner language and inter-language relations. As FarsNet is mapped to WordNet 3.0 there are two inter-language relations; equal-to and near-equal-to between FarsNet and WordNet synsets. Inner language relations which are held between different senses and synsets of FarsNet are the same as the relations in WordNet 2.1. They include synonymy, hypernymy and hyponymy, different types of meronymy, Antonymy and cause. FarsNet 1.0 does not cover inter-POS relations. So the domain and range of all relations are from the same POS currently.

2.3 General Methodology

The fact that already there are no taxonomies or ontologies that provide a formalized description of concepts of Persian language and also the lack of machine readable Persian (mono- or bi-lingual) dictionaries led us to choose and adopt the expand strategy in constructing the Persian synsets and hierarchy. Following the methods applied for creating EuroWordNet (Vossen, 1998), at the first step we manually develop the core WordNet of Persian concepts and then we will semi-automatically expand it by adopting a top-down process.

In other words, our general methodology consists of three major steps: (1) Construction of a Core-Wordnet for a set of common base concepts (2) enrichment of this set providing relational links and incorporating their direct semantic contexts and (3) top-down extension of this core-WordNet by new concepts and relations. To construct the core concepts of FarsNet we have translated the BalkaNet concepts sets BCS1 and BCS2 (Tufis, 2004). Also the most frequent and language specific concepts will be added in the next phases using electronic Persian corpora. Adding hyperonyms and the first level hyponyms to these Base Concepts will result to the core WordNet of Persian. This core WordNet has to be expanded (semi) automatically using specifically available resources, e.g. monolingual and bilingual dictionaries, lexicons, ontologies, thesauri, corpora, etc.

This approach maximizes compatibility across WordNets and at the same time preserves the language specific structures of Persian.

2.4. Lexical Resources

There are some lexical resources we use to construct the Persian WordNet. Some of them are paper copies which are used in manual creation of the lexicon and some others are electronic resources which are used in employed automatic methods as well. Our main lexical resources are as follows.

- monolingual Dictionaries
  - Sokhan dictionary (Anvari, 2004) is our main reference for lexical definitions, examples, and other lexical information. This monolingual dictionary in eight volumes (available in paper format only) is widely acknowledged as the most complete, reliable Persian dictionary.
  - Sadri Afshar Dictionary (Sadri Afshar, et al. 2008) with 50000 entries is another resource to ensure the satisfying coverage.
- Corpora
  - Persian Linguistic Database (PLDB)[1], (Assi, 1997) is an on-line database for the contemporary (Modern) Persian. The database contains more than 50 million words of all varieties of the Modern Persian language in the form of running texts. Some of the texts are annotated with grammatical, pronunciation and lemmatization tags. PLDB has been our main resource for determining words' frequency.
  - Peykareh (Bijankhan, 2004): is a collection gathered form Ettela'at and Hamshahri newspapers of the years 1999 and 2000, dissertations, books, magazines and weblogs. Written and spoken texts ware collected randomly from 68 different subjects in order to cover varieties of lexical and grammatical structures. The version of Peykareh (also known as Bijankhan corpus) which we use contains about 10 millions manually tagged words with a tag set that contains 109 Persian POS tags. A subset of this collection tagged with smaller tag set is also prepared and distributed by DBRG at Tehran University.
- Bilingual Dictionaries
  - English-Persian Farhange Mo'aser Dictionary (Bateni,1992)
  - English-Persian Millennume Dictionary (Haghshenas, 2007)
  - Aryanpour (2008) English-Persian electronic Dictionary containing more than 200000 entries.

- Others
  - Khodaparasti (1997) is a dictionary of Persian synonyms and antonyms (in paper format).
  - Persian Thesaurus (Fararooy 2008) is an electronic thesaurus used for automatic mapping between Persian and English synsets.

3 Nouns

To make the noun part we move from two sides as well; translating English synsets and choosing Persian concepts. For the first side, we manually translate the PWN Synsets of selected base concepts, using our linguistic knowledge of English and Persian and English-Persian Farhange Mo'aser Dictionary (Bateni, 1992) and then enter the Persian equivalences in our WordNet editor. Then we refer to Anvari (2004), to check out the consistency and correctness of our equivalences. For the second side, we use the most frequent nouns from Persian Linguistic Database (PLDB) and Bijankhan corpus, and add the nouns which are missed in the first side to the lexicon. In the next step, the suggestions are defined, some glosses and examples are added and some relations are held between synsets.

To complete the relations between nouns or their synsets and also doing the mapping between Persian and English synsets (especially for the cases in which we move from Persian side) we use semi-automatic methods to suggest new relations and mappings.

3.1 Automatic Mapping Suggestion Between English and Persian Words and Synsets

Our goal is finding the most appropriate mapping between Persian words (or synsets) and English synsets. We used the adaptation of farreres' approach [Farreres, 2005] for Persian [Dehkharghani & Shamsfard, 2009] which needs bilingual Persian-English and English-Persian dictionaries, monolingual Persian-Persian dictionary, Persian thesaurus and English WordNet as resources. The results show 72% precision in mapping Persian words to English synsets and 69% precision in mapping Persian synsets to English synsets

3.2 Semi-automatic Extraction of Conceptual Relations

Conceptual relations are classified in two categories: Taxonomic and Non-taxonomic relations, both of which could be learned by our relation learning system. These relations are extracted from either raw or tagged texts of two sources:

---

[1] http://www.pldb.ihcs.ac.ir

Bijankhan corpus and Wikipedia articles using the following approaches.

3.2.1. Pattern based approach

We exploit pattern based approaches to extract both taxonomic and non-taxonomic relations from Persian texts.

To extract taxonomic relations we define a set of 24 patterns containing the adaptation of Hearst patterns [Hearst, 1992] for Persian and some other new patterns. We have also extracted some patterns for some well known non-taxonomic relations such as "Part of", "Has part", "Member of" and "synonymy". The translations of some of these patterns are shown in table 1 (TW stands for target word).

Table1: Some patterns for extracting relations

	Pattern	Relation
1	TW is (a) X.	Hypernymy
2	TW is considered as X	Hypernymy
3	TW is known as X	Hypernymy
4	TW is called X	Hypernymy
5	TW is named as X	Hypernymy
6	TW is a part of X	Part of
7	TW includes X	Has part
8	TW means X	Definition
9	TW is defined as X	Definition
10	TW1 or TW2 or … are	Synonymy
11	TW has X	Has

Pattern-based approaches in extracting relations are usually of high precision but low recall in a corpus. Searching Wikipedia articles thus is mush simpler as Wikipedia articles are high informative and in the first section of these articles we can usually find some occurrences of our patterns. To start the pattern matching phase we extracted the 1000 most frequent Persian Nouns and extracted the Wikipedia articles related to these words. For each word the related article is searched for the phrases matching any of the patterns. The translations of some of the extracted relations by this method are mentioned in table2.

It should be mentioned that searching the patterns need some text processing tools (e.g. chunker) to find the constituents of sentences. While there is no efficient chunker for Persian, we did some post-processing to eliminate incorrectly extracted relations. This phase includes eliminating the stop words, applying some heuristics such as matching the head of the first noun phrase in the sentence with the head of the extracted TW in copular sentences, eliminating prepositional phrases for taxonomic relations, replacing long phrases with their heads and so on.

Table2: Some extracted relations

1	Isa (blood, liquid)
2	Isa (newspaper, publication)
3	Isa (prison, location)
4	Isa (heart, organ)
5	Isa (pen, tool)
6	Isa (representative, person)
7	Isa (organization, collection)
8	Has part (Tehran, Tajrish)
9	Has (Greece, history)
10	Synonym (thought, idea)

3.2.2. Structure based approach

In Wikipedia pages Structures such as tables, bullets and hyperlinks are informative pieces of text. For example in many Wikipedia documents we can find some information given via bullets. This information usually shows some taxonomic relations. In these cases the title of the section which only contains bulleted text is considered as the domain of the relation and each bullet forms the range of the relation.

Hyperlinks are other sources of information. In the whole document each important word which has an article in Wikipedia is linked to its related article. These linked words especially the ones locating in the first section of the text are usually related to the title of the document. We use this fact to extract some taxonomic and non-taxonomic relations. That means for a given word we search the first section of its related article in Wikipedia and extract the linked words. These linked words are usually related to the original word but to reduce the error rate, for each linked word in this section we search its related article to see if we can find a link to the article of original word or not. If such a link exists it means that these two documents are interrelated and there is a high probability that the two words are related.

This method is used over the articles of 1000 most frequent nouns. The types of the extracted relations are not known in this method but they can be mostly found by using some extra searches on the web. Some learned relations from this approach are shown in table 3.

Table 3: Extracted relations from Wikipedia structures

	First word	Related word
1	fire	flame
2	water	earth
3	professor	university
4	marriage	wife
5	face	human
6	path	street
7	tree	wood
8	North sea	sea
9	heart attack	disease
10	Brighton	city in England

3.2.3. Statistical approach

Statistical methods are widely used in extracting relations in many systems. In this system we use this approach to extract co-occurrence relations. To extract these relations, for each pair of words within the 500 most frequent nouns of Persian we searched a 100,000 word subset of Bijankhan corpus to find in how many sentences these two words co-occur. If this number is above a certain threshold, these two words are considered as co-occurrent. Experimental investigations show that 19 would be a proper threshold in this method. Some of these relations and their frequencies are shown in table4.

Table 4: Statistically extracted related words

	First word	Second word	Freq.
1	interest	sale	19
2	price	merchandise	23
3	market	Price	29
4	manufacture	product	36
5	manufacture	merchandise	70
6	stock	merchandise	142

4 Adjectives

In Persian, adjectives are either simple or are formed through adding a number of affixes to other lexical categories, especially nouns. These affixes range from highly productive [-i:irani (Iranian)], to fairly productive [-mand: servatmand (rich)], and nonproductive [-nâk: dardnâk (painful)].

In building the adjective part of FarsNet, we use three Persian dictionaries (Sokhan, Sadri Afshar and Khodaparasti) and the PLDB database as our main lexical resources.

Following a modified version of GermaNet adjective classification[2], we have organized Persian adjectives in 12 main semantic categories and 57 sub-classes. At this stage, just the following 12 general categories have been implemented. For each category some examples are provided.

1- Conceptual: torS (sour); rošan (light); narm (smooth)
2- Temporal: dir (late); râyej (popular)
3- Spatial: nazdik (near); čap (left); xâli (empty)
4- Movement moteharrek: (moving); sâken(fixed); sâbet (stable)
5- Material: felezi (metal); sangin (heavy); garm (warm)
6- Body: gorosne (hungry); bimâr (ill); mozakkar (male)
7- Emotion: xošhâl (happy); qamgin (sad); afsorde (depressed)
8- Intelligence: bâhuš (intelligent); ahmaq (dull); âgâh (aware)
9- Behavior: (tanbal: lazy), dust (friendly); mâher (skilled)
10- Social: (melli: national); servatmand (rich); xosusi (private)
11- Quantity: do(two); kam (few,little); arzân (cheap)
12- Relational (saxt:difficult); sâlem (safe); mohem (important)

About 1500 Persian adjective synsets have been put to the system to date. This covers about 1800 adjective word forms.

4.1 Semi-automatic extraction of adjectives and their features

In semi-automatic development of adjective part we extract the antonymy relations by applying morphological rules and testing on a corpus.
On the other hand we automatically cluster adjectives. The goal is to put adjectives that are defining different degrees of the same attribute in one cluster. For example words {hot, warm, cool, cold, chilly} describe temperature attribute with different intensity, and so they must be put into the same class. To cluster adjectives we compute dissimilarity between them. Our system employs known linguistic and statistical methods for adjective clustering. In linguistic side we use a pattern based approach and search for co-occurring adjectives in noun phrases. If two adjectives are co-occuring in an Ezafe-construction, they may not be in a cluster while if they occur in a positive or negative conjunction they probably belong to a cluster. For example, adjectives "سرد" [sard, cold] and "گرم" [garm, hot] which belong to one cluster, usually cannot be used in one

---
[2] http://www.sfs.uni-tuebingen.de/lsd/

Ezafe-construction ("آب سرد گرم" [äb - e sard -e garm: cold hot water]) because one thing cannot be hot and cold at the same time. While they can occur in a conjuction such as ("نه سرد و نه گرم" [na sard va na garm: neither cold nor hot]).

On statistical side we assume that similar adjectives appear with common set of nouns. Suppose that frequency of occurrence of adjective i with noun j is Fij. For each two adjective, A and B and nouns X and Y If Fax<Fay and Fbx<Fby, or, Fax>Fay and Fbx>Fby the two adjectives are concordant and otherwise they are discordant.
Similarity is define as: Similarity= Pc - Pd , where Pc is the probability of being concordant, and Pd is the probability of discordance, so it's range is between -1(dissimilar) and 1(similar).
Then we cluster adjectives according to their dissimilarity value by minimizing the following objective function by hill climbing approach.

$$\varphi(p) = \sum_{i=1}^{R} [1/|Ci| \sum_{\substack{x,y \in Ci \\ x \neq y}} d(x,y)]$$

In which R shows the number of classes, Ci shows the ith class, |Ci| is the total number of elements in ith class. d(x, y) is dissimilarity parameter calculated for adjectives x and y.
The best results of evaluation for some groups of test data show %54.50 precision, %74 recall and 60.50% F-measure.

5 Verbs

The construction of the verb hierarchy in FarsNet also follows a top-down strategy on a expand methodology to achieve a high level of overlapping between English and Persian, at least in the highest levels of the hierarchy.
In our current project we are linking our verbal synsets with basic relations such as synonymy, hypo/ hypernymy, antonymy and the cause relation As the hypo/ hypernyms are constructed along with the structure of PWN and its verbal hierarchy, it is clear that in most of the cases there is a one-to-one correspondence between the two languages. But regarding the antonymy and cause relations there are some language specific features which affect the structure of Persian WordNet of verbs.
Beside the manual process, we have used some semi-automatic techniques for extraction of verbal synsets. In the following two sub-sections first we will discuss some specific Persian verbal features and their effects on determining the semantic relations among verbs and then will explain the semi-automatic method used in synset extraction.

5.1. Particularities of Persian verbal system

One of the significant characteristic of the Persian verbal system is its small number of simple verbs. Actually most of the verbal concepts are expressed by compound verbs in this Language. The syntactic and semantic features of Persian compound verbs have been the subject of interest for many linguists and some authors (Mansoory & Bijankhan 2008; Rouhizade, et al. 2008) have discussed the issue in WordNet framework or actually from relational semantic perspective .

Each compound verb in Persian is the combination of a nonverbal element and a light verb. The non-verbal elements which come before the light verb and in this sense are called the preverbal elements range over a number of lexical and phrasal categories such as noun, adjective, adverb and prepositional phrase.
For the construction of WordNet, this morphological information can help the lexicographer to determine some semantic relations among the compound verbs and also to predict the relations that may connect two verbal synsets.
In determining the antonymy relations among the verbal synsets we found that in most of the cases when the verbs are compound and their preverbal elements are adjectives and nouns, the existence of the antonymy between the two adjectives or nouns will lead us to connect the two verbs with the same lexical relations (e.g. dorugh goftæn (to lie) vs. rast goftæn (to tell the truth)).
The other interesting issue about the Persian compound verbs is the cause relation among them. Like English, Persian has lexicalized causative pairs but in contrast with English, the number of Persian causative pairs is very high. This fact results from a morpho-semantic pattern among the Persian simple and Compound verbs. Regarding the simple verbs, Persian has the suffix "–andæn" which can be replaced with the infinitive maker suffix "–idæn" and change a intransitive, anticausative verb to a simple transitive, causative one. The pair *lærzidæn/ lærzandæn* (shake/ shake) is of these kinds. Referring to PWN you will find no cause relation between the two senses of the first verb (shake). Actually these two meanings are fused in one synset and the definition "*move or cause to move back and forth*" shows that both causative and anticausative meanings are referred to the same

lexical element and same synset respectively. But regarding the corresponding Persian concepts, because we have two different lexical items we must construct two different synsets and relate the causative one to the other by means of the cause relation.

The other productive pattern in making the causative/anticausative pairs in Persian is the replacement of one light verb with the other in Persian compound verbs. The replacement of *kærdæn* with *shodæn* in *?ævæz kærdæn* (change: cause to change) / *?ævæz shodæn* (change: undergo a change) and also the replacement of *dædæn* with *kærdæn* in *ta?ghir dædæn* (change: cause to change) / *ta?ghir kærdæn* (change: undergo a change) are of these kinds.

One interesting point which causes a clear difference between English verbal synsets and Persian one with respect to cause relation is that because in most of the cases in English there is no morphological realization for causation, this semantic relation is ignored and both causal and non-causal meaning are presented with one verb or synset. For example {close1} is defined as "*cease to operate or cause to cease operating*" in WordNet 2.0 So in construction of their equivalent synsets in FarsNet because there are two different lexical entries for both causative and noncausative meanings, we have made two different synsets and linked one to the other by means of the cause relation.

5.2. Semi automatic extraction of compound verb's synsets and relations

According to wide usage of compound verbs in Persian, we present a new methodology to semi-automatic enriching of Persian verbs WordNet by using Persian WordNet of nouns and adjectives.

Generally the semi-automatic extraction of compound verb synsets involves using synsets of their preverbal elements. To achieve this goal first the most important (36) Persian light verbs were selected. Then, the process of constructing verbs was done in two phases: first using noun synsets and second using adjective synsets. As these two categories are the most common preverbal elements, it was proposed that adding the common light verbs to members of each nominal or adjectival synset will result in well constructed verbal synsets.

Some resources containing monolingual and bilingual dictionaries along with a Persian corpus were used to evaluate the validity of the constructed compound verbs.

To test the idea we first add the light verbs to each noun or adjective and count the frequency of occurrence of the created compound verbs in the corpus to find the valid common compound verbs. Then we selected three types of structures to form a synset: (1) same preverbals plus synonym light verbs (2) synonym preverbals plus same light verbs (3) synonym preverbals plus synonym light verbs. The created synsets are evaluated both manually by a lexicographer and automatically by looking at the English –Persian dictionary. If there is an entry for which all elements of this synset are within the translation then the synset is accepted. for example combining synonym light verbs 'kardan', 'nemudan' and 'sakhtan' with the same preverb 'Ashkar' can form a valid verbal synset while the same light verbs combing with 'laneh' do not make a synset. Using this method and adding 6467 nouns (organized in 3625 nominal synsets) to 36 light verbs we have constructed 232812 compound verbs from which 4270 were accepted. These verbs were involved in the synset construction method and 3271 verbal synsets were built and accepted by compounding synonym nouns and same LVs and 2822 synsets from same or synonym nouns plus synonym LVs. The same process was performed on one hundred adjectives which resulted in 180 accepted verbal synsets.

6 The Developed Tools

We have developed two sets of tools for FarsNet. The first set consists of a browser (for users) and an Editor (for lexicographers) to view and edit the content manually. They are developed as both local and web-based applications. The second set contains some tools for automatic extraction of lexical and semantic knowledge from resources and proposing them to lexicographers for confirmation before inserting to the lexicon.

FarsNet is both stored in XML files and in a database. In both formats, for each word, its POS category, its different forms of writing (orthography) and its phonetic, syntactic and morphological information are stored. Also different senses of the word with the synsets they occur in, along with their gloss and examples are represented. For each sense and also each synset the relations are stored as well. For each synset, there is also a link to its equivalent or near equivalent synset in WordNet 3.0.

7 Results and Conclusion

In this article we had a review of the on-going project on building a Persian WordNet. The current statistics of FarsNet is shown in table 5. The numbers show the number of items entered to the editor and passed to evaluation phase.

Table 5-Statistics of FarsNet at current position

Category	Words	Synsets	Relations
Noun	8868	4081	8437
Adjectives	1691	1502	231
Verbs	2596	3683	391
Total	13155	9266	9059

To evaluate this WordNet: first, we have to compare the results with 3 reliable bilingual dictionaries; second, some human experts check and evaluate the synsets, third, when completed, we have to use the WordNet in some applications and evaluate the results.

Adding more entries to this lexicon, adding the argument structures and selectional restrictions of Persian verbs, adding inter-POS relations and mapping FarsNet to other general upper ontologies like SUMO are among our further works to complete the project. We are also working on enhancement of our automatic knowledge acquisition methods to enable faster and more reliable ontology construction.

Acknowledgements

This work has been funded in part by Iran Telecommunication Research center (ITRC) under contract no. T/500/19231.

References

Hassan Anvari. 2004. *Sokhan Comprehensive Dictionary*. Sokhan Publishing Co.

S. Mostafa Assi. 1997. *Farsi Linguistic Database (FLDB)*. International journal of Lexicography, V10, Euralex Newsletter.

Mohammad R. Bateni. 1997. *Moasers's - English-Persian Dictionary*. Mazda Pub.

Mahmood Bijankhan. 2004. *Role of language corpora in writing grammar: introducing a computer software*. Iranian Journal of Linguistics, No. 38.

Rahim Dehkharghani., Mehrnoush Shamsfard.,2009. Automatic Mapping of a Thesaurus to WordNet, NLPCS workshop, Italy.

Moharam Eslami, M. Sharifi Atashgah, L. S. Alizadeh, T. Zandi. 2004. *Persian Generative Lexicon*. The first workshop on Persian language and computer. Tehran, Iran.

Ali Famian, D. Aghajani. 2007. Towards Building a WordNet for Persian Adjectives. proceedings of the 3rd Global WordNet conference.

Jamshid Fararooy. 2008. *Thesaurus of Persian Words and Phrases*. Ibex Publishers Inc.

Javier Farreres. 2005. *Automatic Construction of Wide-Coverage Domain-Independent Lexico-Conceptual Ontologies*. PhD Thesis, Polytechnic University of Catalonia, Barcelona

Christian Fellbaum. 1998. *WordNet: An Electronic Lexical Database*. MIT Press.

Ali M. Haghshenas, H. Samei, N. Entekhabi. 2004. *Farhang-e- moaser English Persian Millennium Dictionary* (2Vol.), Sokhan Publishers, Tehran.

Marti A. Hearst. 1992. *Automatic Acquisition of Hyponyms from Large Text Corpora*, Proceedings of the Fourteenth International Conference on Computational Linguistics, Nantes, France.

Farhad Keyvan, H. Borjan, M. Kasheff, C. Fellbaum. 2007. *Developing PersiaNet: the Persian WordNet*. proceedings of the 3rd Global WordNet conference.

Farajollah Khodaparasti. 1997. *A Comprehensive Dictionary of Persian Synonyms and Antonyms*, Fars Encyclopedia.

Niloofar Mansoory, Mahmoud Bijankhan. 2008. *The possible effects of Persian Light verb construction on Persian WordNet*. proceedings of the 4th global WordNet conference.

George A. Miller. 1995. *WordNet: a lexical database for English*. Communications of the ACM archive. Volume 38, Issue 11. Pages: 39 – 41.

Masoud Rouhizadeh, Mehrnoush Shamsfard, Mahsa A. Yarmohammadi. 2008. *Building a WordNet for Persian Verbs*. In: proceedings of the 4th global WordNet conf.

Golam H. Sadri Afshar, N. Hakami, N. Hakami. 2008. *Farhang-e Moaser, Contemporary Persian Dictionary*.

Mehrnoush Shamsfard. 2008. *Developing FarsNet: A Lexical Ontology for Persian*, In proceedings of the 4th global WordNet conference.

Dan Tufis. 2004. *Balkanet: Aims, Methods, Results and perspectives*. Romanian journal of Information Science and Technology. V7, pp.9-43.

Peik Vossen , (ed). 1998. *EuroWordNet: A Multilingual Database with lexical Semantic Networks*. Kluwer academic Publishers.

Experiences in Building the Nepali WordNet - Insights and Challenges

Alok Chakrabarty
Department of Computer Science
Assam University Silchar
mcscalok@gmail.com

Bipul Syam Purkayastha
Department of Computer Science
Assam University Silchar
bipul_sh@hotmail.com

Arindam Roy
Department of Computer Science
Assam University Silchar
arindam_roy74@rediffmail.com

Abstract

Machine translation in Nepali language is in an infant stage in comparison to other scheduled languages of India like Hindi, Sanskrit, Tamil, etc. One of the major reasons behind this is the non-availability of rich lexical resources in Nepali. The Nepali WordNet is thus an endeavour to prepare a rich lexical resource for the Nepali Language for effective machine translation and to facilitate the development of Information and Communication Technologies in Nepali. The endeavour is inspired by the famous English WordNet and the Hindi Word-Net. In the present paper we discuss some of the preliminaries involved in this attempt like the expansion approach of WordNet creation, the linguistic challenges involved, WordNet creation tool interface and the synsets' storage structure. We also discuss some of the special characteristics of the Nepali language.

1 Introduction

According to Miller, et al. (1993), "WordNet is an online lexical reference system whose design is inspired by current psycholinguistic theories of human lexical memory." In a WordNet, nouns, verbs, adjectives and adverbs are grouped into sets of cognitive synonyms (synsets), each expressing a distinct lexical concept or sense. These synsets are interlinked by means of conceptual-semantic and lexical relations. With each synset, WordNet provides a short and general definition for that sense. As it stores the lexical information in terms of word meanings whose organization conforms to the current psycholinguistic theories of human lexical memory it can be termed as a lexicon based on psycholinguistic principles.

The Nepali WordNet is an attempt to prepare such a lexical reference system for the Nepali language along the lines of the famous English WordNet (Fellbaum, 1998; Miller, 1995) and the Hindi WordNet (Chakrabarti et al., 2002) so that it can be used as a tool for enhancing the performance of Machine Translation and cross lingual information retrieval systems involving Nepali and to facilitate the development of various Information and Communication Technologies in Nepali.

The roadmap for the rest of the paper is as follows:

Section 2 is on some of the special characteristics of the Nepali language. Section 3 is on the expansion approach of WordNet creation, the *relation borrowing* concept and the challenges faced therein. Section 4 presents a discussion on the WordNet creation tool interface and the synsets' storage structure, and finally Section 5 concludes the paper.

2 Special Characteristics of Nepali

Nepali (नेपाली) is a language in the Indo-Aryan branch of the Indo-European language family with approximately 40 million speakers in Nepal, Bhutan, Myanmar and parts of India. It is the lingua-franca of Nepal and is one of 23 official languages of India, incorporated in the Indian constitution. It has official language status in the Indian states of Sikkim and in West Bengal's Darjeeling district. Further it is widely spoken in the Indian states of Uttaranchal and Assam (Nepali language, 2009).

Unlike English, Nepali, like Hindi and its ancestor Sanskrit is a *Subject Object Verb* (SOV) language, i.e., in Nepali, the subject, object, and verb of a sentence usually appear in that order. For example:

Sentence:	उसले	मेरो	केरा	खायो।
Transliteration:	*usle*	*mero*	*keraa*	*khaayo.*
Gloss:	he	my	banana	ate.
Parts:	Subject		Object	Verb
Translation:	He ate my banana.			

Nepali is written left to right in the Devanagari script. It is written phonetically, that is, the sounds correspond almost exactly to the written letters. Nepali has many loanwords from Arabic and Persian languages, as well as some Hindi and English borrowings.

A deviating feature of Nepali among the Indo-Aryan languages is in terms of grammatical gender. Nepali possesses an "*attenuated gender*" system in which the gender accord is typically restricted to non-human female animates (Masica, 1991). For example:

[Human: Male, female]

Sentences:	केटो आयो,	केटी आई
Transliterations:	*keTo aayo,*	*keTi aaee*
Translations:	Boy came,	Girl came

[Non-human: Male, female]

Sentences:	गोरु आयो,	गाइ आयो
Transliterations:	*goru aayo,*	*gaai aayo*
Translations:	Bull came,	Cow came

The above issue raises problem in deciding some Nepali synsets as discussed in the next section. The old English (Anglo-Saxon) had such kind of distinction in grammatical gender but modern English is normally described as lacking grammatical gender.

As per verb morphology, Nepali has only two genders *masculine* and *feminine* for nouns. Gender in Nepali is a syntactic property. For both the genders a common pluralizing suffix 'हरु', '*haru*' can be used for nouns in Nepali, like केटाहरु, '*keTaaharu*' (boys), केटीहरु, '*keTeeharu*' (girls). Unlike English its usage is not mandatory and may be left unused if plurality is already indicated in some other way like by explicit numbering, or agreement (Cardona and Jain, 2003).

3 The Expansion Approach of WordNet creation

The Expansion Approach of WordNet creation is an effective method for creation of a new WordNet for a language from a well-established one. It was first proposed within the EuroWordNet project (Vossen, 2002). Thereafter it has been used by a number of WordNet development teams for the creation of new WordNets. Examples include the WordNets for Spanish, French (Vossen, 2002), Hungarian language (Alexin et al., 2006), Hindi, Marathi (Sinha et al., 2006), etc.

In the Expansion Approach, synsets of a pre-existing WordNet are understood by the lexicographer and the corresponding target language synsets expressing the same sense are created.

The Nepali WordNet also is under construction using this Expansion Approach as a consortium project with IIT Bombay. The WordNet is presently at an infant stage.

Because of the high degree of similarity between the two languages Hindi and Nepali, the Hindi WordNet has been used as the pivot WordNet in this approach. In the software tool in use for this purpose, almost all Hindi synsets are linked with the corresponding synsets of the English WordNet. The English WordNet is thus in use presently for the resolution of ambiguity of senses for the synsets in the Hindi WordNet (in a linked fashion with the Hindi WordNet). Once done with the Hindi synsets the process may further be extended to include additional synsets in Nepali WordNet from the English WordNet using English as pivot language.

Henceforth we will refer to the Nepali WordNet, Hindi WordNet and English WordNet as NWN, HWN and EWN respectively.

The main idea behind the Expansion Approach is the concept of *relation borrowing*. It refers to the relation establishment for one WordNet using the relations of another WordNet. The technique is automatic for semantic relations which link concepts or senses, but semi-automatic for lexical relations which link individual words. Different cases of relation borrowing from HWN to NWN are as follows:

a. *A sense is present in both Nepali and Hindi*:
Since Hindi and Nepali belong to the same linguistic family (Indo-Aryan) and exist in almost identical cultural setting, this is the commonest case. In this case relations are established in NWN for that sense.

b. *A sense is present in Hindi but not in Nepali*:

In this case the relations will not get established for this sense. For example, {आठवारा [aaThwaaraa, a period of eight days, like Monday to Monday]} is a sense in Hindi for which there is no corresponding sense in Nepali. Such a sense may be termed as a Hindi specific sense. In such case a lexicographer should adopt the following methods:

1. Transliteration
2. Use of multiword expression (short phrases)
3. Coining of new words

The steps should be used in the mentioned order of priority.

c. *A sense is present in Nepali but not in Hindi*:

Such a sense may be termed as a Nepali specific sense. The relations for such a sense in Nepali have to be established manually. For example, {पेवा [pewaa, a portion of the property of family owned by a female member]} is a sense in Nepali which does not have any correspondence in Hindi.

Similar cases of relation borrowing also exist from EWN to NWN.

WordNets deal with the content words, or open class category of words. Thus, the NWN also contains the open category of words viz. Noun, Verb, Adjective and Adverb. As per HWN, in the NWN also there are various semantic and lexical relations. In total there are 16 such relations (Hindi WordNet Documentation, 2009). They are:

1. General relations between synsets: *Hypernymy, Hyponymy, Meronymy, Holonymy*

2. General lexical relations: *Antonymy, Gradation*

3. Verb specific lexical relations: *Entailment, Troponymy, Causation*

4. Cross parts of speech linkage

a) Linkages between nominal and verbal concepts (Semantic relations): *Ability Link, Capability Link, Function Link*
b) Linkage between nominal and adjectival concepts: *Attribute (semantic relation), Modifies Noun*

c) Linkage between adverbial and verbal concepts: *Modifies Verb, Derived From*

3.1 Challenges faced in the Expansion Approach

We now discuss about the challenges that are faced in using the Expansion Approach. For each case of relation borrowing discussed above, following challenges were encountered:

Case a: Even if this is the commonest case and for most of the synsets it is easier to do so, a specific challenge arises for this case also:

1. When a sense in Hindi, expressed through a single word expression cannot be expressed so in Nepali and requires a multi-word synthetic expression. For example the sense of लड़ना, 'laRna', (quarrel), a verb in Hindi, is expressed in Nepali by the synset {झगडा गर्नु [jhagRa garnu], भनाभन गर्नु [bhanaabhan garnu], कलह गर्नु [kalah garnu], कुटाकुट गर्नु [kuTaakuT garnu], कुटामारी गर्नु [kuTaamaari garnu]} all synonyms requiring two-word noun + verb expression [गर्नु, 'garnu', is the verb]. In such cases the way-out is to put the multiword expressions in the synset of the target WordNet (here NWN) joined by underscores as under:

{झगडा_गर्नु, भनाभन_गर्नु, कलह_गर्नु, कुटाकुट_गर्नु, कुटामारी_गर्नु}

However problems may arise if the multiword expression becomes too long.

Case b: Out of the three solutions proposed above, transliteration is comparatively easy and straightforward. In many languages adoption of new words by transliteration has been done. Examples include the adoption of words like 'mobile', 'typewriter', 'cycle', 'station', 'coffee', 'machine', 'driver', 'pilot', 'table', 'chair', etc. from English to Hindi and Nepali and words like 'cheetah', 'brahmin', etc. from Hindi to English. For many of the words mentioned above, for one language there existed no corresponding word with exact sense in the other language, like 'mobile', 'typewriter', 'cycle', 'station', 'coffee', 'driver', 'pilot' of English had no counterparts in Hindi and Nepali. However because of the difference in pronunciation due to regional factor, many of these words got slightly changed or deformed. For example:

'doctor' = डाक्टर, 'daaktar' (Nepali)
'cycle' = साइकल, 'saaikal' (Nepali)

However due to literal issues as well as cultural acceptance issues many lexicographers do not favour transliteration. In such case they may coin new multiword expressions like:

'binary' = द्वि_आधारी_अंक 'dwi_aadhaari_ank' or 'binder' = बाँध्नका_लागि_प्रयोग_गरिने_वस्तु 'baandhnaka_laagi_prayog_garine_wastu'

as well as new words like:

'pilot' = विमानचालक, 'vimaanchaalak',
'cycle'= द्विचक्रयान 'dwichakrayaan',
'rickshaw' = त्रिचक्रयान 'trichakrayaan'

as a solution to this case.

But in many cases such new words or multiword expressions may not be user friendly and thus will be limited in use in literary works and official works only. Common people more often will use the transliterated forms (in exact or deformed). For example a rickshaw puller or a passenger will prefer to use 'rickshaw' instead of त्रिचक्रयान.

Multiword expressions may get very long. For example: {मठरी, [maTharee, an eatable made of wheat flour prepared during the Hindu festival of छट पूजा 'chhaT poojaa']} is a culture-specific sense in Hindi with no counterpart in Nepali. Transliteration will give मठरी as it is in Nepali. However a possible multiword expression in Nepali can be, 'गहुँको_पीठोले_बनाएको_खाने_कुरा', 'gehũko_piThole_banaaeko_khaane_kuraa' but it will be quite long, still lacking information about the festival name.

Coining of new word in the target language is also a challenge because this needs synchronization among lexicographers.

In such a case, if the sense will never be required in Nepali context then the creation of the corresponding synset in Nepali may be avoided.

Case c: This is the reverse of Case b. In this case after the manual creation of synset and relation establishment in NWN if we wish to introduce the sense in HWN then we will have to face the same challenges as mentioned for Case b above. Further deciding upon a sense as Nepali-specific needs synchronization among lexicographers of Nepali which is again a challenge.

There are other linguistic challenges also that are faced in the development process like:

1) The attenuated gender system in Nepali raises a peculiar problem. The same word have to be used to mean both genders of non-human animates, like, 'peacock' and 'peahen' both are referred to as 'मुजुर', 'mujur' in Nepali. Sometimes the difference is established using a prefix 'पोथी', 'pothi' forming a multiword expression in Nepali for the non-human female animates, like 'पोथी_बाघ', 'pothi_baagh' for 'tigress. Though for some commonly referred non-human female animates like 'cow' etc. feminine terms like गाइ, 'gaai' exist, but in general it is not so.

2) When a lexicographer conceptualizes the synset creation process at word level then it may so happen that the lexicographer may find a word in Hindi that has more number of senses in Nepali than in Hindi. In that case a Nepali lexicographer may get tempted to add the additional senses also in the NWN. Then for those uncommon Nepali-specific senses the lexicographer will have to face the problems for Case c.

3) Nepali contains fewer synonyms in comparison to the Hindi synsets for most of the senses.

4 The WordNet creation tool

The development of the NWN is being carried out presently using the Expansion Approach with the help of a browsable-searchable software tool for the WordNets. The software tool provides an interface for each field (discussed later) of the synsets of the HWN and NWN as shown in figure 1. The tool does not allow the fields of HWN to be modified as it is the pivot. It also contains a link (read-only) to refer the English WordNet for reference. The tool has been developed at CFILT, IIT Bombay (http://www.cfilt.iitb.ac.in/). The front-end of the tool has been implemented in Java. The Java interface is connected at the backend with text files of synsets, called "syns" files, for Hindi and English. As the lexicographer inserts corresponding synsets in Nepali against the Hindi ones (sometimes referring the corresponding English ones) the output syns file for the synsets of Nepali is created. The choice of textual database is for simplicity and to extend support for multiple platforms without the need of installation of any DBMS server like MySQL etc. by the end user. Each synset entry in a "syns" file has five fields:

ID: The synset identifier.
CAT: The syntactic category of the sense.
CONCEPT: It explains the concept represented by the synset. For example, "यस्तो कुरा वा काम जसले कसैको मान वा प्रतिष्ठा कम गराउँछ" (*yasto kuraa waa kaam jasle kasaiko maan waa pratishTha kam garaaūcha*) explains the concept of insult as some saying or deed which diminishes somebody's reputation.
EXAMPLE: It gives the usage of the words of the synsets in the sentence. In general, the words in a synset are replaceable in the sentence. For example: "हामीले कसैलाई पनि अपमान गर्नुहुँदैन" (*haameele kasailaaee pani apmaan garnuhūdain*) gives the usage for the words in the synset of 'अपमान', '*apmaan*' representing insult as something that should not be done to anybody.
SYNSET-(LANGUAGE): It keeps the set of synonyms for the sense in the LANGUAGE designated. In the output syns file for NWN this field has the name SYNSET-NEPALI.

It is important to mention that the synset identifier 'ID' is the key to connect two WordNets. Also for a given polysemous word, for each of the sense of the word, there will be a separate ID.

The tool depicted in figure 1 has an intuitive interface and contains several features ideal for the expansion approach. Features such as searching a synset by ID or by a word, listing all complete, incomplete or all synsets of target language Nepali and font increasing/decreasing for better readability are also there. Provision is also there for adding extra comment, if necessary, with a synset in NWN.

The NWN presently has around 3000 synsets consisting of nouns, verbs, adjectives and adverbs. Since it is currently under development so at different stages in its development phase different numbers of new synsets will get introduced in NWN as such the "syns" text file format for synsets' storage and exchange seems quite ideal. A text file is easy to exchange for purposes like verification and rectification, however such plain text file are always vulnerable to error due to mishandling. Once all the synsets of Hindi gets linked with their Nepali counterparts the set of all error-free 'syns' files can then be coalesced together and stored in a DBMS server like MySQL with proper security implementations for online browsing (Online Hindi WordNet, 2009) or in DBMS like JavaDB (JavaDB, 2009) for embedded systems.

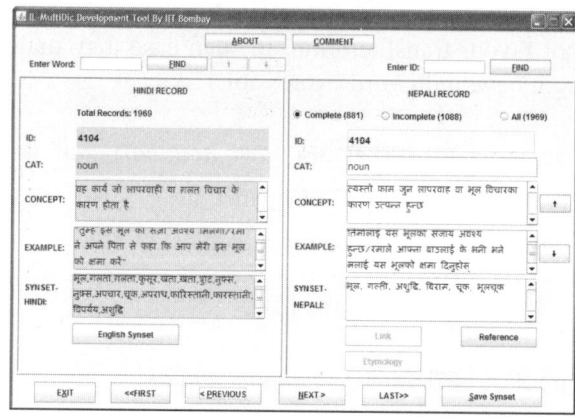

Figure 1: The WordNet creation tool from CFILT, IIT Bombay

5 Conclusion

In this paper we have discussed some characteristic features of Nepali, the expansion approach of Nepali WordNet creation using relation borrowing, linguistic challenges involved, software tool that is in use for the development of Nepali WordNet and the storage structure for WordNet entries.

The expansion approach is very useful considering the time and effort needed in creating WordNets. It avoids duplication of effort. The linguistic challenges discussed in context of Nepali mainly imply the challenge of obtaining a one-to-one correspondence for senses in the Hindi WordNet in to Nepali WordNet.

One of the aims of developing the Nepali WordNet is to overcome the problem of language barrier for the common Nepali speaking peoples who solely use Nepali. When completely implemented, the Nepali WordNet will turn out to be a milestone for the Nepali language. As a future work the authors are interested in implementation of Lesk algorithm and the like for Nepali Word Sense Disambiguation.

Acknowledgements

This research and development was supported by a grant from the Department of Information Technology, Ministry of Communication and Information Technology, Govt. of India. We also acknowledge the WordNet Group at IIT Bombay for their support and specially Prof. Pushpak

Bhattacharyya, Consortium Leader, NE WordNet project for his constant encouragement and support. Further we acknowledge the efforts of Dr. Khagen Sharma, Linguist, Nepali WordNet group and Mr. Tek Narayan Upadhaya, Lexicographer, Nepali WordNet group, in the preparation of this paper. Finally we convey our thanks to Assam University Silchar for the help and support offered.

References

Colin P. Masica. 1991. *The Indo-Aryan Languages.* Cambridge University Press, Cambridge, UK. http://books.google.com/books?id=J3RSHWePhXwC&pg=PA221

Debasri Chakrabarti, Dipak Kumar Narayan, Prabhakar Pandey, and Pushpak Bhattacharyya. 2002. Experiences in building the Indo WordNet - A WordNet for Hindi. 1st Global Wordnet Conference (GWC 02), Mysore, India, January, 2002.

Fellbaum, C. (ed.) 1998. *WordNet: An Electronic Lexical Database*. MIT Press.

George A. Miller, Richard Beckwith, Christiane Fellbaum, Derek Gross, and Katherine J. Miller. 1993. Five Papers on WordNet. MIT press. http://www.mit.edu/~6.863/spring2009/readings/5papers.pdf

George A. Miller. 1995. English WordNet - A Lexical Database for English. *Communications of the association for Computing Machinery*, 38(11):39-41.

George Cardona and Dhanesh Jain (eds.) 2003. *The Indo-Aryan languages*, volume 2. Routledge Language Family Series, London and New York. http://books.google.com/books?id=jPR2OlbTbdkC&pg=PA554

Hindi WordNet Documentation. 2009. http://www.cfilt.iitb.ac.in/wordnet/webhwn/other/hwn_docs_2.doc.

JavaDB. 2009. http://developers.sun.com/javadb

Manish Sinha, Mahesh Reddy, Pushpak Bhattacharyya. 2006. An Approach towards Construction and Application of Multilingual Indo-WordNet. 3rd Global Wordnet Conference (GWC 06), Jeju Island, Korea, January, 2006

Nepali language. 2009. http://en.wikipedia.org/wiki/Nepali_language.

Online Hindi WordNet. 2009. http://www.cfilt.iitb.ac.in/wordnet/webhwn/wn.php

Piek Vossen. 2002. EuroWordNet General Document. EuroWordNet Project LE2-4003 & LE4-8328 report, University of Amsterdam.

Zoltán Alexin, János Csirik, András Kocsor, and Márton Miháltz. 2006. Construction of the Hungarian EuroWordNet Ontology and its Application to Information Extraction. 3rd Global Wordnet Conference (GWC 06), Jeju Island, Korea, January, 2006.

Growth and Revision of Estonian WordNet

Kadri Kerner
University of Tartu
Institute of Estonian and
General Linguistics
Liivi 2–308, Tartu, Estonia
kadri.kerner@ut.ee

Heili Orav
University of Tartu
Institute of Estonian and
General Linguistics
Liivi 2–308, Tartu, Estonia
heili.orav@ut.ee

Sirli Parm
University of Tartu
Institute of Estonian and
General Linguistics
Liivi 2–308, Tartu, Estonia
sirli.parm@ut.ee

Abstract

Up to the present day, the main goal has been the increasing process of Estonian WordNet (EstWN) and currently it consists of more than 27 000 concepts (November 2009). Now we have started also the revision process of existing data in EstWN, since we have educated personnel and also the knowledge of the deficiency and needs of the thesaurus. Firstly an overview of current data in EstWN is given. Then we will address the different problems of automatically transferred synsets, also this paper describes the mini-test made to check the adverb's sense distinctions and definitions in EstWN. One of the problems is the revising the hierarchies and one study has been carried out – the checking of the taxonomy of human being in EstWN. Finally we address the representation of systematic polysemy in EstWN. The paper concludes with some of the future plans and connections with other projects.

1 Introduction

There are two thesauri available for Estonian. First thesaurus (Saareste, 1979) has an historic value (compiled by Andrus Saareste as war refugee in Uppsala in 1979) and second, the modern one is the *wordnet*-type thesaurus of Estonian. Estonian WordNet's basic idea is the creation of theoretically systematic and applicably proper network of meanings because it is useful for some natural language applications. WordNet as a valuable resource can be used for example in Semantic Web, ontology, word sense disambiguation systems, machine translation etc.

The Estonian team joined the wordnet community (EuroWordNet-2[1]) from the beginning of January 1998. In the framework of the project of Estonian Language Technology the Estonian WordNet has been created during the years 1997–2000. After some discontinuation this project was awaken again. In 2006 started the project for increasing EstWN and is supported by Estonian National Programme on Human Language Technology. Thanks to governmental program our thesaurus has enlarged a lot. The EstWN at the present stage includes about 19600 noun synsets, 1700 adjective synsets, 4000 verb and 1700 adverb synsets.

Our chosen approach so far for enlarging has been manual and domain-specific, i.e we have added concepts from semantic fields like architecture, transportation, personality traits and so on. There are 45 different types of semantic relations present. The most frequent relation among nouns and verbs is hyperonymy/hyponymy. Near_synonymy and near_antonymy are more frequent among adverbs and adjectives. Since one person is dealing with one domain at the time, then it makes the relations between different concepts (in one domain) easier to determine. For example from the domain of architecture the concept *antiiktempel* ('antique tempel') has 1 hyperonym, 11 hyponyms, 1 has_holo_part and 8 has_mero_part relations.

Besides adding new concepts to EstWN we have started the checking of existing language material.

2 Revising automatically transferred synsets in EstWN

New synsets to EstWN have been and are mostly added manually, but during the increasing process of EstWN around 3000 noun synsets were automatically transferred from the Estonian Synonym Dictionary (Õim, 1991). The Synonym

---

[1] http://www.illc.uva.nl/EuroWordNet/

Dictionary represents synonyms both in written and spoken language, also there are present some old words and dialect words. This dictionary includes different word senses and in some cases diminutive forms (especially for adjectives). The synonym line in this dictionary does not indicate only to absolute synonyms, since that was not the goal. The goal according to the author was to provide guidance of how to express something with different words. This dictionary is meant for a sensible user, who can choose wisely between all the proposed synonyms.

The Synonym Dictionary does not include any semantic relations (except synonymy), so it was possible to import only synonym lines. The definitions, examples, semantic relations and ILI-links were planned to add manually. Also, the manual check-over of these synsets was required, because many of synsets needed to be revised and corrected in order to include them to EstWN. During the manual work different kinds of problems about the imported synsets aroused.

Firstly, there were cases of old and dialect words that are not present in nowadays general language. For the most part old and dialect words are not includes to EstWN. So, some of the old word synsets and dialect word synsets were completely removed (for example the synset *kupulasja, kuppar, kupumoor*; in English it is a kind of a healer who uses special kind of glass-shaped instruments for healing cough). Some of the imported synsets had one or two old/dialect words and the inappropriate words were removed from the synset. For example the synset *seelik, undruk, kört* ('skirt'), where Estonian word *kört* is rarely used dialect word and which carries slightly different meaning than the other two words in this synsets. (Villem, 2009:65)

Secondly, there were synsets, which needed to been joined together, because there were no difference between the senses, even the words in the synset were mostly the same. Another reason for uniting similar word senses is to avoid the over-grained sense distinctions. For example, *põlgus1, põlgamine1, põlg1, põlastus1, halvakspanu1, jälestus1* ('contempt', insolence') and *põlgamine2, põlgus2, põlg2, põlastus2, halvakspanu2, halvustus1* ('derogative', 'contempt', 'insolence'). Also, if these synsets stood separate, then it could not be possible to connect both with eq_synonym relation to ILI, instead each synset would have got near_synonym link. (Villem, 2009:68)

One of the most frequent problems was that both hyperonyms and hyponyms were included in one synset. Also, if hyponyms as more specific senses are in the same synset with their hyperonyms, there is a problem of choosing the appropriate ILI-linkFor example *teller, klienditeenindaja* ('teller, customer service representative'), where teller is a customer service worker in a bank. In a wordnet it is nessecary to keep specific meanings from the general ones. Another example is *vahuvein* ('sparkling wine'), *šampanja* ('Champagne, more a spoken language variant'), *šampus* ('Champagne'), where both sparkling wine and Champagne are hyponyms of wine. (Villem, 2009:78)

Many of the synsets transferred contained also plural forms. Some synsets contained only plural forms; some consisted of both plural and singular word forms. It was necessary to determine, which of these plural forms actually carry a different meaning than its singular form. In some cases nothing needed to be corrected, for example, *kedrid, säärised* ('spat, spats, gaiter'), because these are plural words consisting of two same objects. Also, some synsets containing both plural and singular word forms held the same meaning left unchanged. For example, *kard* (singular form), *inglijuuksed* (plural form), ('tinsel'), because the singular form of the word *inglijuuksed* ('tinsel') does not hold the same sense than the plural form. But there were quite many cases where the words were groundlessly in plural. Although in real texts these words are usually used in plural, there is no difference of meanings between plural and singular forms. For example *memoriaal, mälestusvõistlused* ('memorial, memorials'), where m*älestusvõistlused* ('memorials') should be in singular form. (Villem, 2009:90)

The next problem deals with singular and plural forms. In lexicography it is advised to mark the use of singular and plural more explicitly. So-called complect-words describe things, which are in a sense the same, they are tied with the same action, they are meant to perform together, for example, *bikini* and *parents*. Also, a group representing an individual is described with plural for example *boys*. (Langemets, 2004: 745)

Finally we faced the genus issues. Often one synset contained neutral, feminine and masculine gender. In some cases it was possible to organize the words in these synsets into hyperonyms and hyponyms, and then it was also possible to connect synsets with appropriate links to ILI. For example, *klassikaaslane, klassiõde, klassivend* ('classmate', "class-sister", "class-brother"), where classmate could be the hyperonym for class-sister and class-brother. Another example, *lesk, leskmees, lesknaine* ('widow, widowman (widower), widow (widowwoman)'), where both genders are present in one synset, but it would be clearer if they were separated. (Villem, 2009:92)

3 Revising adverbs in EstWN

Another line of work has been with adverbs. We started to add adverbs into EstWN only few years ago and mostly we added adverbs of time, degree and also adverbs of manner and place. Estonian frequent adverbs of time have also multiple senses, for example adverb *veel* ('more, still, yet') has altogether 5 senses in EstWN. Previous work with nouns (Kerner, 2004) showed that human annotators cannot perceive too fine-grained sense distinctions in EstWN, so it was interesting to get some feedback from human judges about adverbs. So we carried out a questionnaire type of mini-test to check granularity of senses, definitions, and explanations of adverbs. Although we asked about three adverbs, it provided us with the information of how to improve the process of adding new adverbs in the future.

We selected three adverbs from the EstWN which are: *täna* ('today'), *veel* ('still/yet'; 'more'), *nimelt* ('namely'). The questionnaire was represented electronically on the Internet. We selected 10 sentences from the corpus of Estonian Written Language[2] for every adverb and asked people to choose an appropriate sense according to EstWN for each adverb. In addition, they were able to tag senses as 'not able to disambiguate' or 'correct sense missing'.

We received approximately 25 answers per each adverb, which gave us some information about these senses (usually manual disambiguation is performed by two people only).

The first adverb *täna* ('today') had two possible senses to choose from and we presented these sentences first, so the answerer could get the idea, and didn't feel too overwhelmed with too many senses.

> '**täna1**' – *today, at this moment, on this day* (*I can't meet with you today.*);
> '**täna2**' – *today, at this time, at the present time, at present, nowadays, now, presently* (*They now live in California*)

Based on human judges these two senses didn't combine with each other that often, so we could assume, that the sense distinctions in the EstWN are similar to the ones in real texts and also in human annotators mind.

The second adverb *veel* ('yet, still, more') had altogether 5 senses.

> '**veel1**' – *still* (*It's still warm outside.*)
> '**veel2**' – *yet* (*Mary is not yet at school; I have yet to see the results.*)
> '**veel3**' – *in an additional manner or place or at an additional time: more, in addition, else, further, other* (*There's nothing more we can do.*)
> '**veel4**' – *more, to a greater extent* (as in "*more interesting*")
> '**veel5**' – a modal adverb with so called 'empty meaning'

For the adverb *veel* we assumed, that people do not distinguish between two time-related senses, sense number one and sense number two. The time senses 1 and 2 did not combine explicitly, but after a closer look, we discovered, that if people didn't know whether to choose one or the other time sense, they rather prefer the sense with empty meaning (the sense number 5). So we could assume, that these time senses one and two are still similar enough, so that human annotators cannot precisely disambiguate between them. Another conclusion is that the empty meaning of adverb *veel* is currently somewhat vaguely defined. The assumed result of clearly distinguishing between the time senses and in-addition sense also appeared.

The third adverb *nimelt* (eng namely, specifically etc) had three senses to choose from.

> '**nimelt1**' – *precisely, exactly, on the dot, just* ("*Precisely, my lord,*" *he said*);
> '**nimelt2**' – *namely, viz., that is to say, videlicet* (*That's how he is basically/namely*);
> '**nimelt3**' – *spitefully, with spite, despitefully* (*He answered his accusers spitefully*).

We assumed that some of the senses of adverb *nimelt* will combine with each other, and results show that indeed senses 1 and 2 tend to combine often and senses 1 and 3 also combine in some cases. Considering the problem of wordnets being too over-grained for some applications, we will consider probably joining these senses into

---

[2] http://www.cl.ut.ee/korpused/baaskorpus/

one. Also, it is useful to add antonymy relation to sense number three (for example: *accidentally* and *unwittingly, unintentionally* etc), in order to facilitate the distinction.

Considering this questionnaire it was draw some conclusions for future work: it is important to make the definitions of senses more clear and specific and to add more example sentences. The sense distinctions are not too fine-grained, they are quite in accordance with real texts.

4 Revising the Taxonomies in EstWN

In this year one BA student defended her thesis which topic was taxonomy of human being in EstWN. In EstWN word *inimene* ('person') is the word with most hyponyms –more than 800 all together (Kirt, 2009). This study presented solutions of how to decrease the amount of the '*person's*' hyponyms. For example the division of human beings was proposed accordingly to their professions (*professor, doctor*), place of living (*Estonian, Jew, American*), activity (*organizer, agitator*), relationships (*friend, mother, lover*), (emotional) state (*schlimazel, failure, beggar, waif*) and personality (*cheat, adventurer, hippie, hermit, yokel*). Every here described group has some sub-group also. All these were looked through and focus was concentrated on *hyponymy – hyperonymy* relation (Kirt, 2009). It became clear that it is necessary to review the current hierarchies, because it helps to correct the existing organization and creates a good foundation for the new accompanying synsets. Similar research has been done for Danish Wordnet (see Pedersen and Braasch, 2009) which shows that others compilers of wordnet-type thesauri have became to opinion how important is checking process parallel with composing.

5 Revising the Systematic Polysemy in EstWN

In this summer a PhD thesis about the systematic polysemy of nouns in Estonian was completed (Langemets, 2009) and EstWN can also profit from this thesis. This thesis provides the systematic patterns of Estonian noun polysemy. Systematic polysemy is defined as a situation where several senses of at least two words regularly imply a similar semantic relation (Langemets, 2009:28). Systematic polysemy is one type of metonymy (Peters and Peters, 2000), for example, the pattern BUILDING-INSTITUTION ('school, theatre'). In Estonian WordNet the systematic polysemy is not marked explicitly, also it has been marked quite arbitrarily, for example 'school' has both BUILDING-INTITUTION senses, 'theatre' is only in a INSTITUTION sense, 'university' in only in a INSTITUTION sense etc. In this thesis around 80 different types of systematic polysemy patterns are presented, so it is possible to add the missing senses and to make the representation of systematic polysemy more persistent. Another issue is how to represent systematic polysemy, one way is to add it as a complementary sense; the representation should be clear to human users as well as useful to some applications (for example in word sense disambiguation so-called underspecified senses, where an option of further specification exists (Buitelaar, 2000)).

6 Conclusion

The main line of work is the revising the present data and at the same time extending Estonian WordNet with new concepts. Since 2006 we have added around 12 000 new concepts, EstWN contains of more than 27 000 concepts at present. There are more than 55 000 semantic relations currently present from which approx. 25 000 are added during last 3 years.

From the 3000 automatically transferred synsets around 60% needed to be corrected and revised. Also we had to insert semantic relations manually and the correction-work took up more time than we originally expected.

More semantic relations for the adverbs are needed to determine the appropriate senses, for example the derivational relation. The list of semantic relations for adverbs in EstWN is actually currently in creation.

Also, we plan to include labels from WordNet Domains (Magnini and Cavaglià, 2000) to EstWN. From the project of manually disambiguated word sense corpora it is possible to get feedback to current sense divisions; also information about missing concepts and words.

References

Bentivogli, Luisa; Forner, Pamela; Magnini, Bernardo; Pianta, Emanuela. 2004. *Revising WordNet Domains Hierarchy: Semantics, Coverage, and Balancing.* In COLING 2004 Workshop on "Multilingual Linguistic Resources", Geneva, Switzerland, August 28, pp. 101–108.

Buitelaar, Paul. 2000. *Reducing Lexical Semantic Complexity with Systematic Polysemous Classes and Underspecification.* In: Proceedings of the

ANLP2000 Workshop on Syntactic and Semantic Complexity in Natural Language Processing Systems , Seattle, USA.

Kerner, Kadri. 2004. *Sõnatähendused tekstides ja tesauruses ühestajate erimeelsuste põhjal*. BA thesis. University of Tartu.

Kirt, Riin. 2009. *Inimesega seotud hierarhiapuu eesti wordnetis*. BA thesis. University of Tartu.

Langemets, Margit. 2004. *Mõnda nimisõnade semantikast*. - Keel ja Kirjandus nr.10.

Langemets, Margit. 2009. *Systematic Plysemy of Nouns in Estonian and its Lexicographic treatment in Estonian Language*. Phd Thesis. University of Tallinn.

Pedersen, Braasch. 2009. *What do we need to know about humans? A view into the DanNet database*. Proceedings of the 17th Nordic Conference of Computational Linguistics NODALIDA 2009. Editors: Kristiina Jokinen and Eckhard Bick, pp 158–166.

Peters, Wim; Peters, Ivonne. 2000. *Lexicalised Systematic Polysemy in WordNet*. In: Proceedings of the Second International Conference on Language Resources and Evaluation, Athens, Greece.

Saareste, Andrus. 1958—1968. *Eesti keele mõisteline sõnaraamat I-IV. Dictionnaire analogique de la Estonienne I—IV*. Kirjastus Vaba Eesti, Stockholm.

Villem, Olga-Annikki. 2009. *ILI-kirjete lisamine Eesti wordnetti ja selle käigus ilmnenud automaatselt genereeritud sünohulkade probleemkohad.* BA thesis. University of Tartu.

Õim, Asta. 1991. *Sünonüümisõnastik*, Tallinn.

French WordNet progress and Structured Concepts Embodiment Inside WordNet

Dominique Dutoit
MEMODATA
LITIS (Univ. of Rouen)
CRISCO (Uni. of Caen)
do.dutoit@gmail.com

Patrick de Torcy
MEMODATA
17 rue Dumont d'Urville
14000 CAEN
p.detorcy@memodata.com

Yann Picand
MEMODATA
17 rue Dumont d'Urville
14000 CAEN
y.picand@memodata.com

Abstract

In this paper, first, we will give some global measures of the French WordNet progress and, second, we suggest the introduction of new relations inside WordNet which are part-whole relations. In that part, we study the benefits of these relations in morphology, syntax and semantics, including some intensional semantics.

1 Introduction

This paper deals with the embodiment of structured concepts, such as part of grammar or meaning inferences, inside the wordnet structure.

As many researches, this particular research is based on the substrate outputs of the past works. Working since 1989 in the field of lexical semantics, of course this substrate contains different layers which apparently could use specific algorithms to be accessed and played. One goal of this embodiment is to unify all these algorithms in a single one, allowing us to converse between distinct steps of the analyses. Focusing on the structured concepts introduction techniques inside wordnet, we will not deal about its necessity. Nevertheless, we will have to remember the main algorithm and some particularisms of our ongoing concepts and relations. The given work is based on *The Integral Dictionary* (TID, [Dutoit 1992]), a French semantic net, which is today fully merged in Princeton' WordNet. The older infrastructure of TID is based on the structuralistical point of view called *componential semantics*.

Then, the paper plan is:
- Data input : sample concepts
  - The French Wordnet inside TID
  - Other models
  - Algorithm
- New : structured concepts
  - Formalism
  - Some use cases

This proposal about the introduction of structured concepts inside a graph was announced and argued in a long academic document (in French) [Dutoit 2009] which is a "Habilitation à Diriger des Recherches" (Habilitationschrift).

2 French data input : sample concepts

We were a partner for the French in EuroWordnet [Vossen 1999], and in Balkanet [Stamou 2002]. In this section, we summarize the current state of the French WordNet with quantitative measures, we give details about Wordnet and TID integration, we give details about specific TID formalism and we give a short view of the algorithm used in text analysis

2.1 Current state of the French WordNet

Table 1 shows the main figures:

Princeton synset with a French Literal	79.562
Princeton synset with a French gloss	38.252
Princeton synset with a French label that is not a literal (an entry for the French dictionary) but only an explanation or a suggested translation	2.357

Table 1: the French regular Wordnet

2.2 WordNet and TID integration

Originally (before 2000), TID had not the benefits of the synset object. Then, once introduced this structure, TID was able to share its data with WordNet. Having the synset compounds, the notion of gloss was also reachable. Fortunately, we had an explanatory dictionary for French not linked. Then, we use some heuristics (see below the main one: semantic distance), to fill semi-automatically the French Synsets derived from Princeton. This approach yields to the statistics given in Table 1 relating to the French glosses.

Today, TID is fully compatible with Wordnet. But, as TID contained some other layers, of course, we maintained these data. The other layers was derived from the Meaning-Text Theory (MTT) (Melcuk, 1996) which is influenced by a generative point of views and from the componential theories (for instance Pottier, 1992) that are pure structuralism.

2.3 The MTT model inside TID

Here, we will not explain the whole model but only some features related to the aim of this paper.

The MTT model manages some formal RELATION between word-meanings. A word meanings is a kind of word, but not a kind of synset. In TID, we decided to allow MTT relations between: word-meaning and word meaning, word meaning and synset, and synset to synset, due to some needs in terms of redundancy and accurateness.

All the MTT relations are more precise than the wordnet relations between synsets. For instance, where Wordnet defines a bidirectional relation between one *improvement synset* and one *improve synset*, the MTT model defines a directional relation between them (in this example, the nominalization case with a formal label meaning *action of* or *result of*).

Most of the MTT relation are not included into the wordnet model or TID, and reify some complex relationship between terms, hiding inside a partially composite formal label a kind of structured complex concept which is one aim of this paper. Then, the MTT relations are formally only binary relations, and can not define directly structured forms.

Table 2 shows the main figures concerning the implementation of MTT in TID (and by inheritance in the French WordNet):

Number of different MTT types of relations	45
Number of MMT relations between synset or word meanings	112540

Table 2: the French Wordnet implementing MTT

Of course, when the French synsets are merged to the Princeton synsets, Princeton synsets inherit of the improvements given by MTT.

2.4 Componential models inside TID

All the componential models create a formal distinction between words or forms and meanings or formal concepts. Then, TID which is an empiric work originally induced by this saussurian distinction, contains some objects that are not words but only "concepts". This paper has not the goal of dealing with advantages or disadvantages of this dualism. Sometimes the formalism seems heavy, sometimes it is clear that it allows the description of some particular features, for instance when "natural" hypernyms are not available in the lexicon of a given language.

Then, with that distinction, we have to accept that could exist:
- a word meaning "horse-equine",
- a synset "horse-equine",
- a class of "horse-equine",
- a kind of topic "horse-equine"
- and some other things like this.

Figure 1 gives some details about this:

Relation	Node
-	cheval-horse (synset) [1]
generic [2]	horse (class) [2]
spec, encyclop. [2]	animal breeding (class) [2]
spec, encyclop. [2]	mount (class) [2]
spec, encyclop. [2]	beast of burden (class) [2]
spec, taxonomic. [2]	equid (familly of) (class) [2]
To topic [2]	Horse (theme) [2]
holo_member [3]	type genus of the Equidae… (synset) [1]
hypernym [4]	hoofed mammals … (synset) [1]
derivative [3]	provide with a horse … [1]

Figure 1: Wordnet, TID and MMT sharing their details

Legend:
 1: WordNet and TID
 2: only TID
 3: only WordNet
 4: WordNet and MMT

Have a look to http://dictionary.sensagent.com/cheval/fr-en/#analogical to get a better view of these details. Let's notice that on this site, most types of relation have been simplified and/or merged.

Table 3 shows the main figures relating to the implementation of a part of componential semantics in TID (and by inheritance in the French WordNet):

Number of different TID concepts	23
Number of TID concepts	40.000
Number of different TID relations	36
Number of TID relations	340.000
Number of WordNet Synsets linked to TID	see table 1
Number of TID synsets for French	220.000

Table 4: Componential semantics in TID

2.5 One Algorithm

The algorithm goal is to reach a subset of concepts (or sometimes synsets) which links two words-meanings. For instance,

samurai & warrior	H a v e		warrior (class)
			warrior (synset)
samurai & saber			war (theme)
	e		fight (theme)
samurai & katana			war (theme)
			fight (theme)
	t		Japan (theme)
samurai & Tokyo	o		Japan (theme)
samurai & to ennoble			nobility (theme)
florist & tulip		s	flower (theme)
florist & to sell		e	trade (theme)
florist & to exchange		l	exchange (theme)
florist & person		e c	person (class)
			person (synset)
florist & shop		t	shop (theme)

Figure 2: Expected concepts extracted from TID and/or WordNet

In figure 2, we can observe that the extracted concepts are not relations between the two terms but a (A) sample abstraction (common compound, componential compound, semantic feature, analogy) which subsumes the two given words(-meaning).

It is important to notice that most of the extraction could not be found in a concrete text inside a local area, such as a phrase or a short sentence. The good unit to discover these terms together is often a large portion of a discourse. For instance, a sentence like "florist sells flowers" is uncommon, except, of course, in a dictionary. Then, (B) a dictionary could not explain easily: "the advocate sells his pen".

In this condition, the integration of structured concepts could have the both A and B roles.

Finally, we have to give an idea about the algorithm itself. We proposed an original way to measure the semantic proximity between two word senses. This measure takes into account the similarity between words (their common features) but also their differences. It was described first in [Dutoit 2000]. Also this article could give some details about some uses in concrete text [Dutoit 2002].

Comparison between two words is based on the structure of the graph: the algorithm calculates a score taking into account the common ancestors but also the different ones. The notion of "nearest common ancestor" is classical in graph theory. We have extended this notion to distinguish between "symmetric nearest common ancestor" (direct common ancestor for both nodes) and "asymmetric nearest common ancestor" (common ancestor, indirect at least for one node).

Definition: Distance between two nodes in a graph

We note d the distance between two nodes A and B in a graph. This distance is equivalent to the number of arcs between two nodes A and B. We have $d(A, B) = d(B,A)$.

Let's say:

$h(f)$ = the set of ancestors of f.

$c(f)$ = the set of arcs between a node f and the graph's root from the point of view of f.

Definition: Nearest common ancestors (NCA)

The nearest common ancestors between two words A and B are the set of nodes that are daughters of $c(A) \cap c(B)$ and that are not ancestors in $c(A) \cap c(B)$.

It is possible to define a measure to calculate the similarity between two words from these sets. We call this measure *activation* (see Dutoit 2002), but as this paper is not focused on this measure we will not give more details. Let's remember that it's possible to use the activation to measure the semantic proximity between two word senses following a particular *point of view*. As this paper is focused to introduce some other points of view on the net (then: other type of concepts, not only shared semantic feature), we work on the hypothesis that *the same algorithm could be used to extract these new concepts in a larger, more heterogeneous set of NCA*.

Another interesting subset of shared concepts could participate to the measure of the smaller differences between meanings.
For instance, the smaller differences between *samurai & Tokyo* have to be:

d(samurai, Tokyo)=f(aristocracy, warrior)
d(Tokyo, samurai)=f(town)

whereas similarity is immediately a function of *Japan*.

This anti-symmetric measure of differences is particularly interesting for several tasks, such as calculation of the saturation of a word or a set of words by another word or another set or words. It used the subset of *Asymmetric nearest common ancestor (ANCA)*. The asymmetric nearest common ancestors from a node A to a node B are contained into the set of ancestors of c(B) ∩ c(A) which have a direct node belonging to h(A) but not to h(B).

2.6 Some uses of the algorithm

The algorithm was used to:
- measure one semantic weight of each word in a text related to the other words of the text
- make a reverse dictionary service computed from the graph (TID, WordNet etc)
- compare sentences, for instance, to merge TID with WordNet

We think that if we introduce in the net some other concepts, which will be structured concepts, then several other services will be reachable.

3 Introducing structured concepts and dynamic concepts

This section defines structured concepts and some rules to reach and saturate them. The most effective use of these structured concepts, when they are validated, is to generate some dynamic concepts which were not directly reachable before their activation. A deep discussion about these concepts, in philosophic, linguistic or computational terms can be found on Dutoit [2009].
To discuss these notions, we will introduce the following simplest examples:
- compound words
- finite expression
- infinite expression

and, more essential for our conference:
- lexical semantics.

3.1 Compound words

The French compound *pomme de terre* is a translation to the simple word *potato*. Of course, it is possible to design a particular compound term processor to localize this expression in a given text. But, this tool can not decide itself, with its privative morphological knowledge if the right interpretation of the compound is the compound itself (the whole) or its parts. For instance, is a *lung neoplasm* a simple term or a compound term? It is related to the point of view. Interpretation of *pomme de terre* is the same. For instance, in term of lexical reduction, you get [*pomme de terre*] in French and can get [*potato*] in English. But in term of grammatical rules you have to consider 3 separate words. Introducing structured concepts in our graph (TID, WordNet) could answer to this instability of these points of view using an instable graph containing several structured concepts.

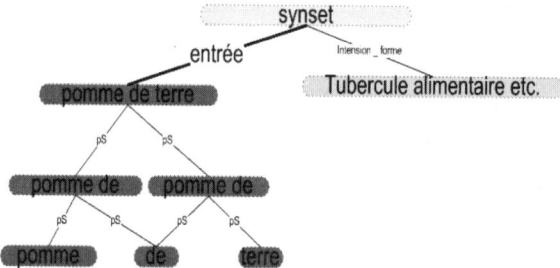

Figure 3: A compound term

This graph defines a partially ordered set which is a lattice. The binary character of the graph is influenced by the algorithm presented above. Using this algorithm, it appears that the entry point to the analyzers becomes the lexicon itself and not the syntax. In that approach, syntactical constraints (such as relative token position, belonging to a given chunk or able to support a particular syntactic relationship) are applied when the (structured) concept is detected by the lexicon, and not before, as a result of these rules. Then, the algorithm stays unchanged, but, in the cases of structured concepts, augmented by a constraint section.
Let's highlight the procedure.

Structured concept

The part of the figure 3 with relations labeled e_i, where e means *element* and *i* is an index.

Dynamic concept

The part of figure 3 with a relation labeled *entrée*, where entrée means that the created whole *pomme de terre* is also an entry of the dictionary.

Formally, we do not use the relation label: *entrée*, but the label λ$_{t\_whole}$, where *t* means "token" and *whole* means that the whole *pomme de terre* could be considered as a simple *token* **in** the point of view found by the structured concept.

Remark: *the area of the structured concept presented above is very close to the popular Google index.*

3.2 Finite expression

Let's take the example of a date.

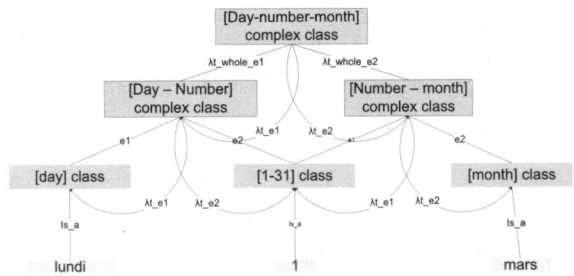

Figure 4: Building a date using the classes of the graph

This graph does not introduce a strong innovation except lambda calculus. The previous one was simpler due to absence of classes. With presence of classes, of course, the built date is not (in the French order) [[*day* [*number*] [*month*]] but, in this example [[*lundi*] [1] [*mars*]] (literally *Monday 1 March*).

Structured concept

In the figure, [day-Number] is a structured concept (it needs one day name and one particular number, with a specific syntactical constraint) to be activated. The figure shows 3 structured concepts like [day-Number].

Dynamic concept

In that figure, when satisfied, [day-Number] emits the order of placing 3 identified tokens:
- λt_e1 : *lundi*, as a token, which means that *lundi* in *lundi 1* is a day. This result is not innocent. For instance, *lundi*, in a phrase like *the noun lundi*, has to be *viewed* as a noun and not as a (for instance : hyponym of a) day.
- λt_e2 : *1*, as a token, which means that *1* in *lundi 1* is a number of day. This result is not innocent. For instance, it should very useful to "understand" a very short dialog like:

Laura: Could you come "lundi 1"?
Elie: No, "le 1", I will be very busy.

In fact, this process creates a local extension of the date concept that is not admissible in a dictionary because *1 may co-refer everything* except when you have spoke about the day *lundi 1 Mars* or the horse number 1, or the boat number 1 etc.

- Λt_whole_e1 : *lundi 1*, as a token, which means that *lundi 1* in *lundi 1 mars* could be considered as a non-dependant thing and could be re-used as is.

3.3 Infinite expression

The case is given by the evaluation of arithmetic expressions which are not aprioristically sizable. Dutoit 2009 shows how to close the expression in the graph before attempting the calculation.

3.4 Several phrases

We are going to deal with the following phrases:
a) the noun samurai a') the noun fortunately
b) a white horse b') a white thing
c) the color of that horse c') the color of that thing

Cases (a) and (a')

Case (a) interest is that it exists somewhere a place where this particular phrase has a meaning. Unfortunately, this place which establishes links between POS and words is not reachable for the NCA: assuredly, the point of view of componential semantics (based on shared part or meaning) is different to the POS point of view. But, this difference does not modify deeply the relations nature. If we say:

samurai has one hypernym *warrior* (generative point of view)
samurai is a kind of the concept [*warrior*] (componential point of view)
samurai is a kind of [*noun*] (POS point of view), we do not say the same thing at all.

But, if we examine the case (a'), it appears that the previous discourse is not sufficient. For instance, the sentence *the noun fortunately does not exist in English* is trivial. Then, what could be the nature of the relationship between *noun* and *samurai* or *fortunately*? To simplify our answer, we can remember a very classical thesis due to Aristotle. For our example, his analysis should be:
- in (a) and (a'), *noun* is an active power and predicated terms are passive powers.
- in all situation, one active power tries to apply its program to its environment, and success of this procedure is in dependence to the aptitude of the passive power to support the active power transformation.

In our example, *samurai* which have an active power in other situation, here, is only a passive power that can support the transformation (point of view, a focus to one part of its whole) *noun*. Of course, *fortunately* does not support this in our current state of knowledge in English.

Then, the mechanism of this structured concept is something like:

noun previous (a_word) → try to consider a_word as a kind of *noun*.

Then, one **v**irtual instance of **a_word** (**va**_word) is created has a kind of *noun*. If both elements a_word & vaword exist together in that area, the related NCA will be returned.

Figure 6 shows this situation:

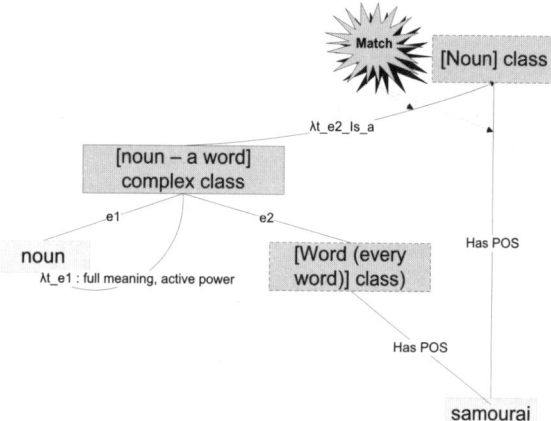

Figure 5: Building the intension of *the noun XXX* using the classes of the graph

Structured concept

In the figure, [noun- a_word] is the single structured concept and it reifies one active power of meaning the word *noun*.

Dynamic concept

Elsewhere, [noun] class is both a static concept (because it returns Noun as POS when accessed by a potential noun token via the dictionary entry *samurai*) and a dynamic concept because it could be filled by a session token which is *samurai: noun* in the phrase the *noun samurai*. It is a first very short example of intensional semantics (not intentional in the Husserl use in phenomenoly). Von Fintel [2002] write in that purpose:

We need to move to a semantics that is intensional in the following sense: it has to contain operators, like former, that "displace" the evaluation of their complements from the actual here and now to other points of reference ...

Case (b)

The most frequent approach that deals with these phrases consists to assume simply world knowledge where a horse has a color property or can be colored. As we have read it, these considerations are not based on lexical semantics (for instance, explanatory dictionary) but on our world experiment. Then, this approach is close to CYC (Lenat, 1999) and far from WordNet. Is there somewhere in WordNet a source that could compute a *linguistic* relation between *color* and *horse,* or *white* and *thing?* We suppose that this source is inside the gloss itself, and could be computed if we improve the formal representation of the glosses.

Reading WordNet gloss, it is visible that *color* is a visual appearance of an object. To simplify the discourse, we consider that this object has a strong opacity, and, then, we suggest the part of an object that gives this visual appearance is its surface part. Then, we can try to define again this meaning of *color.* It could be: *a property of the surface of an object that...*

At this point, it appears that *color,* similarly to the word *noun,* in certain position, has an active behavior that moves a *referent* word, like *horse,* from its places (given by its definition) to another place like a *surface,* or more precisely, like a *thing viewed from its color.*

In figure 6, the structured concept [color of a_noun] emits the fact that the **token** *horse* **could be viewed** as a [thing viewed for its color]. By inheritance, such thing **could** reach, **could** be activated as a [surface], a [volume] ... and finally as a [concrete thing]. In another point of view, a general linguistic knowledge inherits from the fact that an animal could have a body (body is defined in WordNet as *a entire structure of an organism*) that the **original** token *horse* could be viewed as an [equid] ... an [animal] and finally as a [thing having a body] (in the definite meaning). At bottom of figure 6, $\lambda t\_property(e2,e1):Is\_a$ (1), where (1) is a comment, creates a new token *property(horse,color)* with this place.

At top of the figure, you have the expression λt_whole. This expression is a concatenation of the new token *horse* and the older token *horse:color.* It is a kind of identification. Then,

- $\lambda t\_whole:Is\_a$ (2) claims that *horse_ property(horse,color)* is an attested member of [concrete thing]

- $\lambda t\_e2:Is\_a$ (3) claims that *horse_ property(horse,color)* is also an attested member of [thing having a body]

Rem. 1: in our example, a such *horse_ property(horse,color)* selects the different meanings of *horse* that are defined as an animal, but a similar expression will select some other meanings for *horse*, such as *heroin,* in another similar path.

Rem. 2: the stranger expression horse_ *property*(*horse,color*) could be considered as a mean to memorize that these understandings of *horse (concrete thing* and *thing having a body)* have been **simultaneously** checked by two paths, where the first one is the predication (which is not enough) and the second one is a linguistic inference resembling to a world knowledge (which is not enough). Before this simultaneous event, nothing exits (no latent ambiguity), after this simultaneous event a new thing exists with two congruent interpretations available for future calculations.

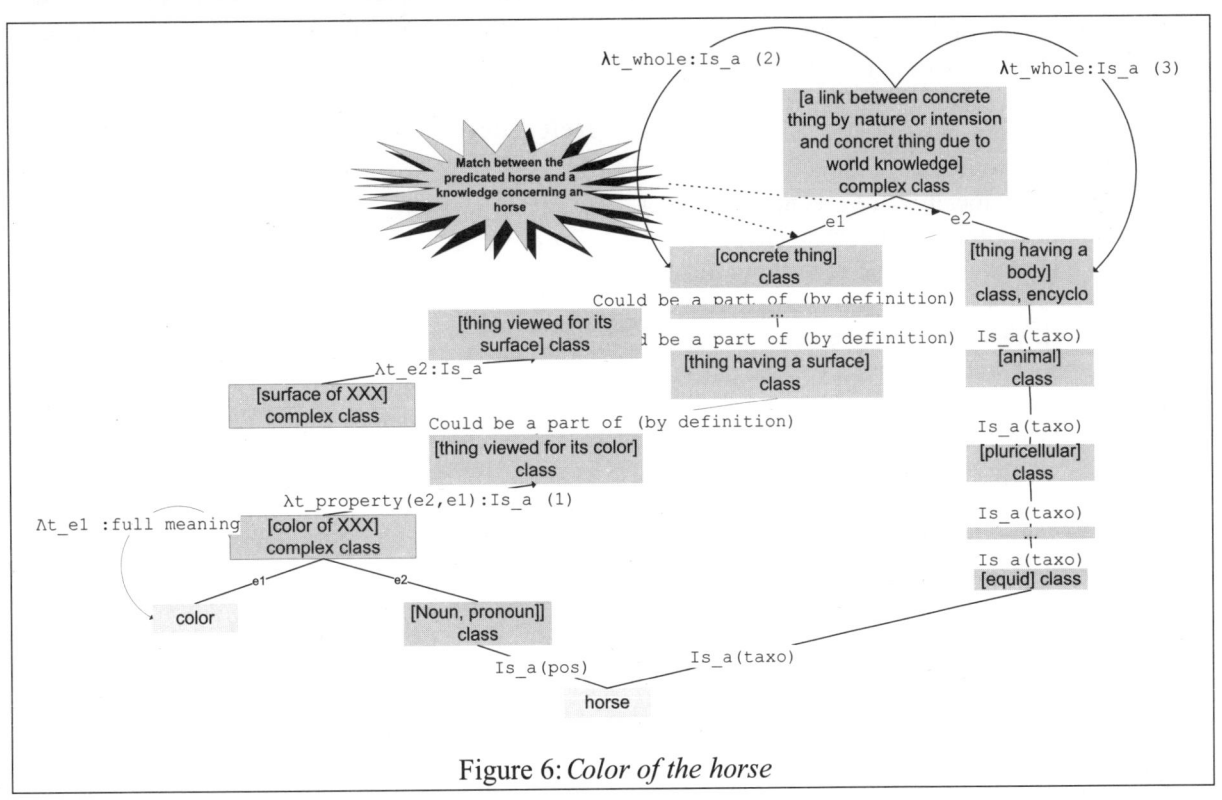

Figure 6: *Color of the horse*

It is not possible to draw in a single figure, the dictionary and its running effects. The built instances will be shown at the end of this section.

Case (c)

Drawing *white horse* is very similar with *horse color* in the direction of concrete thing. Nevertheless, we have a particular task with this phrase. As our goal is to embody a part of the meaning (the glosses) inside the graph itself, we have to implement the fact that *white* invokes itself the concept *color* as top attribute. Bottom of figure 7 shows the relation: *e2, added.* Role of this relation is to allow such invocation.

The view of instances

Lambda operators have the role of moving tokens but also of creating tokens. It could be useful to draw this result. Figure 8 shows this result. As mereotopology [Smith B., 1996] is one source of this work, the resulting figure is not a surprise: the part-whole relations are fully maintained.

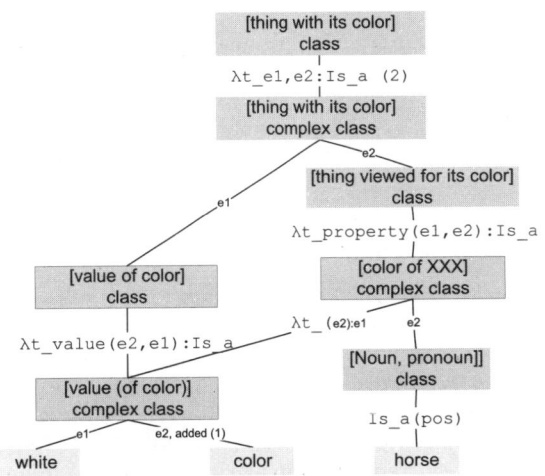

Figure 7: *White horse.*

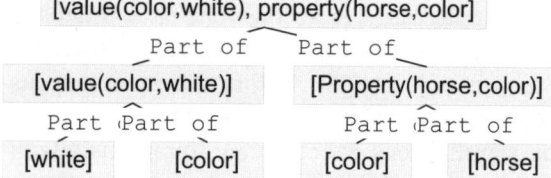

Figure 8: Instance for *white horse*.

Case (b') and (c')

Could a thing support *color* or *white* as predication? If we consider *thing* as *anything*, the answer is *no*, considering that only particular things (such as *concrete thing*) could support the predicate. Therefore, it is why *color of the thing* could not, in our opinion, be directly computed. As we have to localize the [concrete thing] subset, it appears that an old mechanism could help us in this matter: it is the reverse dictionary technique [Dutoit, 200]. Contrarily to the previous work that runs from bottom to top of the graph, the reverse dictionary runs partially from top to bottom in order to induce *concrete thing* subset from the things set.

A funny application of the built graph

Words after words, the graph builds more complex instances linked together by mereotopological relationships, as in *pomme de terre*. We have shown [Dutoit 2009] that playing the graph on a question like "what is the color of a white thing?", after a formal introduction or one meaning of *what*, could finally creates the following tokens:

[
  [value(color,white), property(thing,color)]
  [value(color, ?what), property(thing, color]
]

where *?what* and *white* co-refer a same thing. This result is due to the fact that it does not depend to external knowledge (world knowledge, local knowledge or reverse dictionary), but only to a lexical semantics formalization of the explanatory dictionary glosses.

4 Conclusion

In a first part, we have described the French WordNet current state in various statistic tables. In that part, we have also summarized the environment of the French WordNet, which is strongly linked to other works in lexical semantics, where all these works make together the body of *The Integral Dictionary (integral* means this integration of theoretical point of views*)*. In a second part, we have suggested improvements of WordNet formalism by introducing some new relationships which are part-whole input / output relations. We studied the opportunities of these relations with various lexicon problems, from morphological area to naive world knowledge area. Introduction of these relations was both motivated by improving the static model of the dictionary, including an *intensional* point of view which is then available for a dynamic building of phrases "understanding".

Reference

Christian Fellbaum, 1998. *WordNet: An Electronic Lexical Database*. Cambridge: The MIT press.

Dominique Dutoit, 1992. *A set theoritic approach to lexical semantics,* COLING.

Dominique Dutoit, 2000, *Quelques opérations sens→texte et texte→sens→texte utilisant une sémantique universaliste apriorique,* PhD, Greyc, Univ. of Caen.

Dominique Dutoit, Thierry Poibeau., 2002. *Combining knowledge sources for resource acquisition*. (COLING), Taipei.

Dominique Dutoit, Pierre Nugues, 2002. *The right word*, full paper, LREC, Las Palmas

Dominique Dutoit, 2009. *Intégration structurale des points de vue componentiel et compositionnels*. HDR, Univ. of Rouen : http://www.memodata.com/2004/fr/publications.shtml

von Fintel, 2002. *Lecture Notes on Intensional Semantics,* http://www.phil-fak.uni-duesseldorf.de/summerschool2002/fintel.pdf

Douglas B. Lenat, 1999. *From 2001 to 2001: Common Sense and the Mind of HAL*, http://www.cyc.com/halslegacy.html.

Igor Mel'čuk, I. 1996. *Lexical Functions: A Tool for the Description of Lexical Relations in the Lexicon*. In L. Wanner).

Bernard Pottier, 1992. *Théorie et analyse en linguistique*, Coll. Hachette Supérieur.

James Pustejovsky, 1995. *The generative lexicon*, Cambridge, Mass. MIT press

Barry Smith, 1996. *Meretopolopy: a theory of parts and bundaries,* http://ontology.buffalo.edu/smith/articles/Mereotopology1.pdf

Piek Vossen, 1999, *Final report*, EuroWordNet, LE2-4003, LE4-8328.

Domain Specific WordNet on Customs Law

Zoltán Alexin
Department of Software Engineering
University of Szeged
Árpád tér 2., Szeged, Hungary
alexin@inf.u-szeged.hu

János Csirik
Research Group on Artificial Intelligence
Hungarian Academy of Sciences and
University of Szeged
Aradi vértanúk tere 1. Szeged
csirik@inf.u-szeged.hu

Attila Almási
Department of Informatics
University of Szeged
Árpád tér 2., Szeged, Hungary
vizipal@gmail.com

Veronika Vincze
Department of Informatics
University of Szeged
Árpád tér 2., Szeged, Hungary
vinczev@inf.u-szeged.hu

Abstract

The NLP research group at the University of Szeged took part in the development of the Hungarian WordNet between 2005 and 2007. In 2008, they developed a smaller, domain specific WordNet on customs law. This knowledge base contains about 650 concepts cautiously selected by legal experts from the relevant Hungarian statutory legal texts, above all, from two acts and from other laws and decrees. The resulted hierarchic net of concepts is used in an information retrieval system for quick access to documents that have been previously indexed according to the concepts. In addition to this, the WordNet can be used in the daily routine work or in the training of customs officers as it contains detailed definitions of concepts and precise references to legal places where the given concept is defined. Although the WordNet is not a general legal ontology, it shares common concepts with the LOIS multilingual legal WordNet.

1 Introduction

Hungary became full member of the Schengen Treaty in December of 2007.[1] At the same time, Hungary became the Eastern gate of the European Union. The security of the whole Schengen Zone demands empowering the border guard and tightening passenger control. This includes the improvement of the existing information systems.

A consortium led by the Montana Knowledge Management Ltd.[2] won the support of the National Office for Research and Technology[3] in 2008. During the project named TUDORKA7, the *InfoVadász* document repository and retrieval system developed by the Montana Ltd. was to be tailored to the requirements of the project. The purpose of the planned system was to give the necessary help in the fight against crimes such as drug trafficking, smuggling, excise duty crimes etc. by providing simple and fast access to a large number of documents, legal resources, warrants, protocols, and reports – sometimes written in English, German, or French.

A multilingual knowledge base within this international environment should be a central part of the information system. A knowledge base that contains the most important customs law concepts in several languages in parallel would make search in the document sources easier. In EuroWordNet technology, Inter-Lingual Indices (ILI) connect concepts in different languages and provides an excellent representation method for such a knowledge base (Alonge et al., 1998).

The authors of this paper took part in the development of the Hungarian WordNet (Alexin, Csirik et al, 2006; Miháltz, Hatvani, et al. 2008)

---

[1] http://abiweb.obh.hu/abi/pdf/Schengen.pdf
[2] http://www.montana.hu/index.php?lang=en
[3] http://www.nkth.gov.hu/english

containing 40 thousand general synsets. They were also involved in a project that created a domain specific extension to this WordNet from 3000 concepts related to economy.

The planned document repository and retrieval system would store not only the documents themselves but relevant metadata like creation date, author, and the language of the document. After providing translations of concepts to different languages, the querying subsystem would apply translated query expressions i.e. list of translated keywords corresponding to the language of the selected document when it computes the fitness or relevance measure to the query. The advantages of a parallel language knowledge base can be exploited in the above manner.

Researchers were unable to create a complete multilingual knowledge base within the given time frame, therefore, they started looking for a multilingual database to connect to, possibly a WordNet knowledge base that would serve as a basis for a Hungarian ontology. The LOIS (Legal Ontologies for Knowledge Sharing) multilingual legal WordNet was that database.

Legal experts found better reasons to create such a knowledge base. The *gloss/definition* field can contain not only an informal but the official definition of concepts that usually originates from legal rulings like laws, decrees, or commands. In the *note* field the exact legal reference can be provided.

During the creation of the knowledge base, legal experts had an opportunity to scrutinize the legal texts. This way, they explored conflicts or ambiguities between the definitions. Sometimes a concept is defined in two legal places in a different manner, or the Hungarian rule does not correspond exactly to the EU principles. Several deficiencies like this were found during the work.

In the following sections this customs law WordNet is presented. It consists of about 650 concepts related to customs crimes, excise duty crimes and taxation procedure. It contains the relevant official definition of the concepts whenever it exists, as well as the exact legal reference to the place of definition. If there is more than one relevant definition for a concept it is also marked in the knowledge base, which can be considered as a Hungarian part of the LOIS WordNet although its topic is somewhat different. The Hungarian concepts are connected to their LOIS WordNet counterparts by ILI indices. Whenever customs law concepts have hypernyms in the general Hungarian WordNet it is also marked in the semantic relation field.

2 The LOIS Legal WordNet

The LOIS (Legal Ontologies for Knowledge Sharing) multilingual WordNet was created during an EU funded project EDC 22161 between 2003 and 2006 (Dini, Peters, et al. 2005, Peters, Sagri and Tiscordia 2007). The LOIS consortium was led by the Italian Institute of Legal Information Theory and Techniques in Florence. After a short negotiation a research agreement between the Institute of Informatics at Szeged and the LOIS consortium was signed according to which, Hungarian researchers were granted access to the LOIS multilingual legal WordNet.

The LOIS WordNet originally contained 35000 concepts in five European languages (English, German, Portuguese, Czech and Italian), roughly 7000 concepts in each.

```
<WORD_MEANING ID="1429"
 PART_OF_SPEECH="N" STATUS="FINISHED">
 <SOURCEBASE>LEXDB</SOURCEBASE>
 <NOTE/>
 <GLOSS>a person who has not reached full legal age</GLOSS>
 <CONCEPTS/>
 <VARIANTS>
   <LITERAL LEMMA="minor" SENSE="1">
    <EXAMPLES>not of legal age; &quot;minor children&quot;</EXAMPLES>
   </LITERAL>
   <LITERAL LEMMA="minor" SENSE="1">
    <EXAMPLES>a person who has not reached full legal age; a child or juvenile</EXAMPLES>
   </LITERAL>
   <LITERAL LEMMA="juvenile" SENSE="1">
    <EXAMPLES>a person who has not reached the age (usually 18) at which one should be treated as an adult by the criminal justice system</EXAMPLES>
   </LITERAL>
 </VARIANTS>
</WORD_MEANING>
```

Fig. 1. The concept of *juvenile* as defined in the LOIS WordNet

The LOIS WordNet uses its own Inter-Lingual Indices to identify the concepts (synsets). The IDs of the semantically identical synsets are the same in each of the five languages. Synsets, mostly nouns, are taken from the general legal science and there are few verbs, adjectives and adverbs. Generally, each synset has a definition which sometimes comes from Celex[4], the legal

---
[4] http://eur-lex.europa.eu/en/index.htm

document repository of the EU or from legal handbooks. In Figure 1 an example of a LOIS synset is shown.

3 The customs law WordNet

In the framework of the customs law WordNet project, the researchers from Szeged first began to collect a term vocabulary from Hungarian legal texts by automatic methods. The consortium finally decided that two acts should be processed: Act on taxation procedure[5] and Act on excise duty[6]. Legal experts from the Department of Constitutional Law were invited to the project. They manually checked the terminology and advised to augment them with other important terms e.g. from the Penal Code. Unfortunately, they had no other digitized resource to begin with. Later the consortium asked the researchers from Szeged to add further terms from the publicly available commands of the Commissioner. When the list of terms was finalized, legal experts began to collect glosses. The related laws, decrees and legal handbooks were systematically thumbed over. If more than one gloss was found for a term, then all explanations – having made a record of their source – were included in the knowledge base.

```
<SYNSET>
  <ID>HuWN-911671085</ID>
  <SYNONYM>
  <LITERAL>fiatalkorú
      <SENSE>0</SENSE>
  </LITERAL>
  </SYNONYM>
    <DEF>Fiatalkorú az, aki a bűncselek-
mény elkövetésekor tizennegyedik élet
évét betöltötte, de a tizennyolcadikat
még nem.</DEF>
    <SNOTE>1978. évi IV. tv. Btk. 107.§.
(1)</SNOTE>
    <SNOTE>LOIS ID="1429"; a magyar jog-
rendben kis- és fiatalkorú megkülön-
böztetés létezik</SNOTE>
    <SNOTE>jog</SNOTE>
    <POS>n</POS>
    <ILR>HuWN-148541600
       <TYPE>hypernym</TYPE>
    </ILR>
</SYNSET>
```

Fig. 2. The concept of *fiatalkorú* (*juvenile*) as defined in the customs law WordNet

When the term vocabulary was finished, computational linguists together with legal experts ordered the terms in a hierarchy. The originally paper-based notes and Microsoft Excel spreadsheets were compiled into a WordNet by linguists using the VisDic editor program (Horák and Smrž, 2004). Principally, the hypernymy relation was implemented but also holonymy occurred several times.

The <DEF> node (gloss) contains the definition of the synset, which legal experts usually took from an act being in force or from legal handbooks. The part-of-speech of the synset is marked in the <POS> node. Synonyms of a term were collected from legal handbooks. In several cases, synonyms were multiword expressions due to the characteristics of the legal terminology. Linguistic relations like hypernymy or holonymy were coded in <ILR> nodes. The <ID> nodes contain the ILI indices of the synsets.

In Figure 2 an example of a synset from the Hungarian customs law WordNet is shown. It can be seen, that the Hungarian counterpart of the LOIS synset "juvenile" has a Hungarian WordNet <ID> due to the fact that the customs law WordNet was made as an extension to the Hungarian WordNet.

In the first <SNOTE>, one can find the exact reference to the legal place where the gloss is taken from, namely Penal Code (Law IV. of 1978.), section 107. In the second <SNOTE>, the LOIS ILI index and an explanation in Hungarian are included.

3.1 Conflicts between linguistic and legal requirements

When building the WordNet it was often found that the requirements of linguistics and law were contradictory so researchers had to make priorities. It was decided that, first, they meet the requirements of law and, then, take linguistics into consideration where possible.

As a consequence, the customary linguistic rule applied in WordNets that the definition of a synset must contain a hypernym of the concept or its synonym (Miller et al., 1990) has been modified for, in most cases, definitions are mere lists of words.

In the Hungarian WordNet (Alexin et al., 2006; Miháltz et al., 2008), within synsets, notes are units that make short, supplementary comments possible. However, in the customs law WordNet notes have been given a new function. They are used to include information that cannot be entered as a part of the definition but provide substantial, indispensable data e.g. exact place of the definition in the legal texts, numerical data

---

[5] Hungarian Act no. XCII. of 2003.
[6] Hungarian Act no. CXXVII. of 2003.

(e.g. alcohol concentration, quantity of importable goods, etc.)

When creating the hierarchy, the *bottom-up* method was followed because concepts derived from legal sources proved to be rather specific and they were usually used to create base-level synsets only. This, however, made the work simpler because hypernyms could be selected relying on the hierarchy of Hungarian WordNet.

In the customs law WordNet there are nine *unique beginner* synsets. Due to the decision mentioned above, it may happen that an element identified as an object on the base-level gets linked to a non-object hypernym synset or occurs in the tree of the *unique beginners* e.g. *abstraction* or *state*. This linguistically indefensible state was impossible to eliminate. Due to the phraseology of law these apparent "inconsistencies" have remained.

4 Connections between the Hungarian customs law WordNet and the LOIS Legal WordNet

The last step of the work was to establish connections between the two WordNets. Legal experts examined the English version of the LOIS WordNet and produced a list of synsets that may have connections to the customs law WordNet. A linguist and a legal expert then – taking the definitions into consideration – checked manually the list item by item to figure out whether the relation between the two concepts is valid, It was also checked whether the LOIS synset was more general than the synset in the customs law WordNet. In several cases the LOIS WordNet did not contain glosses for the synsets therefore the decision on identicality could not be made.

When the two synsets proved to be undoubtedly identical, the connection has been marked in the *note* field of the synset in the customs law WordNet as follows: LOIS ID="nnnn", where nnnn is the ILI index of the corresponding synset in the LOIS WordNet. A short explanation was also added. See Figure 2.

	Connected to LOIS	Cannot be connected to LOIS	All
General legal synset	81	116	197
Excise duty synset	113	337	450
Total	194	453	647

Table 1. The number of connections between the customs law WordNet and the LOIS WordNet

In Table 1, statistics on the customs law WordNet is presented. 194 out of the 647 (30%) synsets from the customs law WordNet have a counterpart in the LOIS WordNet. Among them 113 synsets are closely connected to the excise duty terminology (declaration, payment, definitions, crimes etc.), while 81 synsets are general legal terms.

In the whole customs law WordNet, 450 out of the 647 synsets were taken from the excise duty terminology. Their definitions come from legal rulings (laws, decrees, orders, etc.) being in force, e.g. tax warehouse, licensee of the tax warehouse, the onset of tax paying obligation. The remaining 197 synsets are general legal terms with definitions taken from handbooks, e.g. interest, loss, official, representation.

The number of adjectives, nouns and verbs in the two WordNets are shown in Table 2.

	LOIS WordNet (English)	Customs Law WordNet
adjectives	0	0
nouns	6720	647
verbs	51	0

Table 2. The distribution of the adjectives, nouns, and verbs among the synsets of the two WordNets

5 Conclusion

The presented Hungarian customs law WordNet was made with a view of a multilingual information retrieval and query system which would be capable of returning the relevant documents written in any of the supported languages by answering a query expression entered in Hungarian. This task can be accomplished in a narrow semantic domain like customs law. A multilingual knowledge base, a WordNet can provide the semantically correct translations of the most frequent terms.

A multilingual legal knowledge base is essential in international administration, business, insurance, jurisdiction or counseling. This knowledge base should be the kernel of later information systems, and can be used for other purposes as well. For example, it may help to understand the differences between jurisdictions of countries i.e. it may be used as a legal definition (reference) database.

The presented Hungarian customs law WordNet was an experiment on this approach. The developed WordNet has fulfilled our expectations towards such a knowledge base.

Finally, it has a well-founded connection to the LOIS multilingual legal WordNet and to its synsets in several languages. At the same time, it has evoked new questions whether to translate all of the LOIS synsets to Hungarian, or to broaden the current customs law WordNet. Both are possible objectives of forthcoming R&D projects.

Acknowledgments

The authors wish to thank Márton Sulyok, Judit Tóth and other members of the Department of Constitutional Law at the Faculty of Law of the University of Szeged for their contribution to the project.

The research presented in this paper was supported by the TUDORKA7 and MASZEKER projects of the Jedlik Ányos 2007 and 2008 Programs of the National Office for Research and Technology (NKTH, http://www.nkth.gov.hu/) of the Hungarian government.

References

Alexin, Z., Csirik, J., Kocsor, A., Miháltz, M., Szarvas, Gy. 2006. Construction of the Hungarian EuroWordNet Ontology and its Application to Information Extraction, Project report, In: *Proceedings of the Third International WordNet Conference GWC 2006*, South Jeju Island, Korea, 2006, pp. 291–292.

Antonietta Alonge, Laura Bloksma, Nicoletta Calzolari, Irene Castellon, Maria Antonia Marti, Wim Peters, Piek Vossen. 1998. The Linguistic Design of the EuroWordNet Database. *Computers and the Humanities*, 32(2–3):91–115.

Dini, L., Peters, W., Liebwald, D., Schweighofer, E., Mommers, L., and Voermans, W. 2005. Cross-lingual legal information retrieval using a WordNet architecture. In *Proceedings of the 10th international Conference on Artificial intelligence and Law* (Bologna, Italy, June 06–11, 2005). ICAIL '05. ACM, New York, NY, 163–167.

Horák, A., Smrz, P. 2004. VisDic — Wordnet Browsing and Editing Tool, In: *Proceedings of the Second International WordNet Conference GWC 2004*, pp. 136-141.

Miháltz, M., Hatvani, Cs., Kuti, J., Szarvas, Gy., Csirik, J., Prószéky, G., Váradi, T. 2008. Methods and Results of the Hungarian WordNet Project, In: *Proceedings of the Fourth Global WordNet Conference. GWC 2008*, University of Szeged, Department of Informatics, 2008, pp. 311–320.

Miller, G. A., Beckwith, R., Fellbaum, C., Gross, D., Miller, K. 1990. Introduction to WordNet: an Online Lexical Database. *International Journal of Lexicography*, 3(4):235–244.

Peters, W., Sagri, M. and Tiscornia D. 2007. The structuring of legal knowledge in LOIS, *Artificial Intelligence and Law,* Volume 15, Issue 2 (June 2007), pp. 117–135. Springer Verlag, ISSN: 0924-8463.

Hierarchy of Perceptional Adjectives in RussNet

Irina Azarova
St-Petersburg State University /
Universitetskaya nab. 11, 199034
St-Petersburg, Russia
`ivazarova@gmail.com`

Maria Yavorskaya
St-Petersburg State University /
Universitetskaya nab. 11, 199034
St-Petersburg, Russia
`Yav.mas@gmail.com`

Abstract

The group of perceptional adjectives in RussNet is presented. The structuring of adjectival synsets follows different patterns: bipolar clustering, hyponymy, and troponymy. Several complex problems of hyponymy linking are discussed.

1 Introduction

Adjectives is a class of ambivalent words, which may share features with nouns or verbs forming noun-verb continuum (Wetzer, 1996), that is, some are closer to nouns, others — to verbs. The difference is expressed in grammatical behaviour: attributive-only, predicative-only or attributive-and-predicative (Quirk et al, 1985) syntactic usage and derivational productivity — forming degrees of quality or intensifications/ diminutives, - that is considered in Russian grammatical tradition to be the evidence of their descriptive origin.

The semantic approach to adjectives is based on prototypical semantic classes (Dimension, Age, Value and Colour) (Dixon, 2004) and other miner classes denoting difficulty, similarity, quantification, position, etc. The attribute expressed by an adjective refers to a wide or narrow class of objects, so it may more or less definitely combine the concept of quality with that of an object features. For example, Russian adjective *rusyj* (*fair*) clearly specifies the object class — hair (or a human with such hair), and its definition 'light brown' in the explanatory dictionary looks incorrect (the gloss for *fair* in WordNet is more adequate: 'pale yellowish to yellowish brown'). This quality of descriptive adjectives affords them to substitute a noun phrase, and they are considered to be conceived on a class of objects as its domain.

A sequence of adjectives may specify the intersection of classes as in *big brown shoes* (intersection of a class of big shoes with that of brown shoes). In relation to logical behaviour of adjectives, they are differentiated as intensional and extensional (intersective vs subsective) (Peters & Peters, 2000). The construction of a noun with several adjectives is normally represented by a positional pattern as in an example above, confer *brown big shoes*.

The usual structuring of descriptive adjectives word meanings is considered to be "bipolar clusters" (Miller, 1998), that is, pairs of focal adjectives form the centres of opposite poles for attribute values, a number of descriptive adjectives being associated to centres by semantic similarity. This pattern is very typical for different wordnets, however, in (Azarova and Sinopalnikova, 2004) it was shown that in some groups of adjectival meanings the proper hierarchy may be set up. In some cases it looks like noun hyponymy, e.g. *bolshoj1 (big)* 'having great or greater than average spatial extension' has hyponyms *dlinnyj1 (long)* 'having great or greater spatial extension between two extreme points in *horizontal* direction' and *vysokij2 (high)* — 'having great or greater spatial extension between two extreme points in *vertical* direction', etc. The meaning of a hypernym is specified in a particular manner (an exact direction) in hyponyms.

In this paper we deal with adjectives from the semantic field of Perception. We suppose that this group represents the core elements of our cognitive space and a hypothetical hierarchy may be outlined in this domain. The most frequent Russian adjectives from (Sharoff, 2001) with reference to different spheres of perception: visual, auditory, tactile, gustatory, and olfactory.

The RussNet technique (Azarova et al., 2005) of data processing involves marking up the random samples of 150-300 contexts from the balanced corpus of contemporary texts in order to extrapolate the frequency distribution of word meanings to the general aggregate of adjective occurrences in the corpus. This procedure allows us to order word meanings according their frequencies in the format *bolshoj1, bolshoj2, etc.* (in contrast with traditional dictionary enumeration of meanings, which is rather subjective and sometimes arbitrary). We'll use an abbreviation WM for this specified pair word-meaning, and measure a WM frequency of co-occurrences in *ipm* (instances per million words in the corpus). Experiments with distributions of word meanings in the corpus showed that WMs with ipm-index more than 60 are concepts from the top ontology, and less than 0.1 are potential, because a list of these rare WMs tends to be unlimited. The ipm-index is very helpful as an evidence in hypernym-hyponym relation. The sum of all processed WMs in the adjectival perception group is about 3,500 ipm, that covers 73,500 corpus contexts.

We use also the following dictionaries: the Dictionary of Russian in 4 volumes (Evgenjeva, 1981–1984) for preliminary word meaning definitions, the Russian Associative Dictionary (Karaulov et al., 2002) for checking semantic links by means of an associative rank (the number of similar responses to the word stimulus).

We suppose that WMs of frequent adjectives outline the general structure of perceptional domains. In order to prove its comprehensibility we process a number of rare WMs. We'll demonstrate that there are several modes of group structuring, the special attention being focused to the types of hypernym-hyponym relation.

2 Hyponymy link

The hyponymy linking between a pair of WMs is based on 3 evidences.

The first one is dictionary definition, for example, *rozovyj1* (rose-coloured, pink) 'pale red' (Evgenjeva, 1981–1984), the colour is defined as a tint of red, that is, a variant or a hyponym.

The second is the corpus evidence: the hypernym and the hyponym are to have similar collocations, though the hypernym has wider usage, and, consequently, higher ipm-index. *Krasnyj1* (red) ipm is 120.59, and *rozovyj1* (rose-coloured, pink) — 17.31, which conforms to requirements of ipm-indices correlation between the hypernym and hyponym. The value of ipm for *krasnyj1* indicates that this concept is from top ontology (as well as *belyj1* 'white' – 152.44, *chernyj1* 'black' – 138, and *zelenyj1* 'green' – 82.7).

The third evidence is used in doubtful cases, it is the association rank in (Karaulov et al., 2002), usually there is a response with highest rank or one the upper part of the article. *Rozovyj1* (rose-coloured, pink) has a response *krasnyj1* (red) with a rank 3. Association response is usually oriented from a hyponym to the hypernym. This association rank is not the highest, which is 17 for a noun *tsvet* (colour).

The 3 sources may disagree: the first and the second are in favour of hyponymy linking of *rozovyj1* and *krasnyj1*, but the third one hardly supports this relation.

It may be easily seen that the hyponymy in this pair is of a troponymy type (as in a verb pairs *walk–strike*), it is peripheral realisation of an action or a quality (in the case of adjective WMs).

The different instance is a relation between *bol'shoj1* (big) and *ogromnyj1* (huge) 'very big', the latter being the realisation of a lexical function MAGN (Zholkovskij & Mel'chuk, 1965) — intensification of an attribute, confer other functions: ANTIMAGN, BON and ANTIBON. In this pair all evidences are in favour of hyponymy linking. An association response for *ogromnyj* is *bol'shoj* with rank 40. The realisation of a lexical function MAGN is stylistically marked, this link is typical for attachments of expressive designations in bipolar clusters, which is a traditional wordnet relation in attributive structuring. The difference is in direction of relations: similarity presupposes symmetry, which is not proved by RussNet data.

The third type of hyponymy in attributive structures is logically similar to true hyponymy. For example, *vysokij2* (high) and *vysokij6* (tall), the latter in relation to the former is subsective in a SIMPLE sense (Peters & Peters, 2000), that is, *vysokij6* refers to the subclass of that for *vysokij2*.

2.1 The controversial points of hyponymy

Normally the hyponymy relation presupposes that synsets are from one POS, the meaning of a hyponym incorporates the meaning of the hypernym and its specification.

The first disputable point of adjectival hyponymy is that the top-level concept for some parameter specification may be represented by a noun WM. This is manifested by the highest association rank of a noun WM *tsvet* (colour) in an example above.

We can use the unilateral implication test for verification of the semantic relation: let B be a hyponym for A, then

A={*vkus (taste)*}, B={*kislyj2 (acid)*} =>
C=*The fruit is _____*.

T*he fruit is acid* implies that *the fruit has (certain) taste* (true). But *the fruit has taste* doesn't imply that *the fruit is acid* (false).

The second point concerns the uniqueness of the hypernym. For example, the adjective WM *seryj1* (grey) according to (Evgenjeva, 1981–1984) denotes 'of a colour resulted from blending black and white, as of ashes', thus WM *seryj1* (grey) has 2 different hypernyms *chernyj1* (black) and *belyj1* (white). This is an intersection in a monochromic designation, but similar connections are very common in a structure of coloured attributes. For example, *ognennyj2* (flame-coloured) is defined as "orange-red", where the main colour is red (it is a standard superordinate notion of the troponymy type described above), but the second one (*orange*) is a troponym of *red*. So two hypernyms (or co-hypernyms) may be from the same level of hierarchy (intersective) or from hypernym-hyponym levels of hierarchy

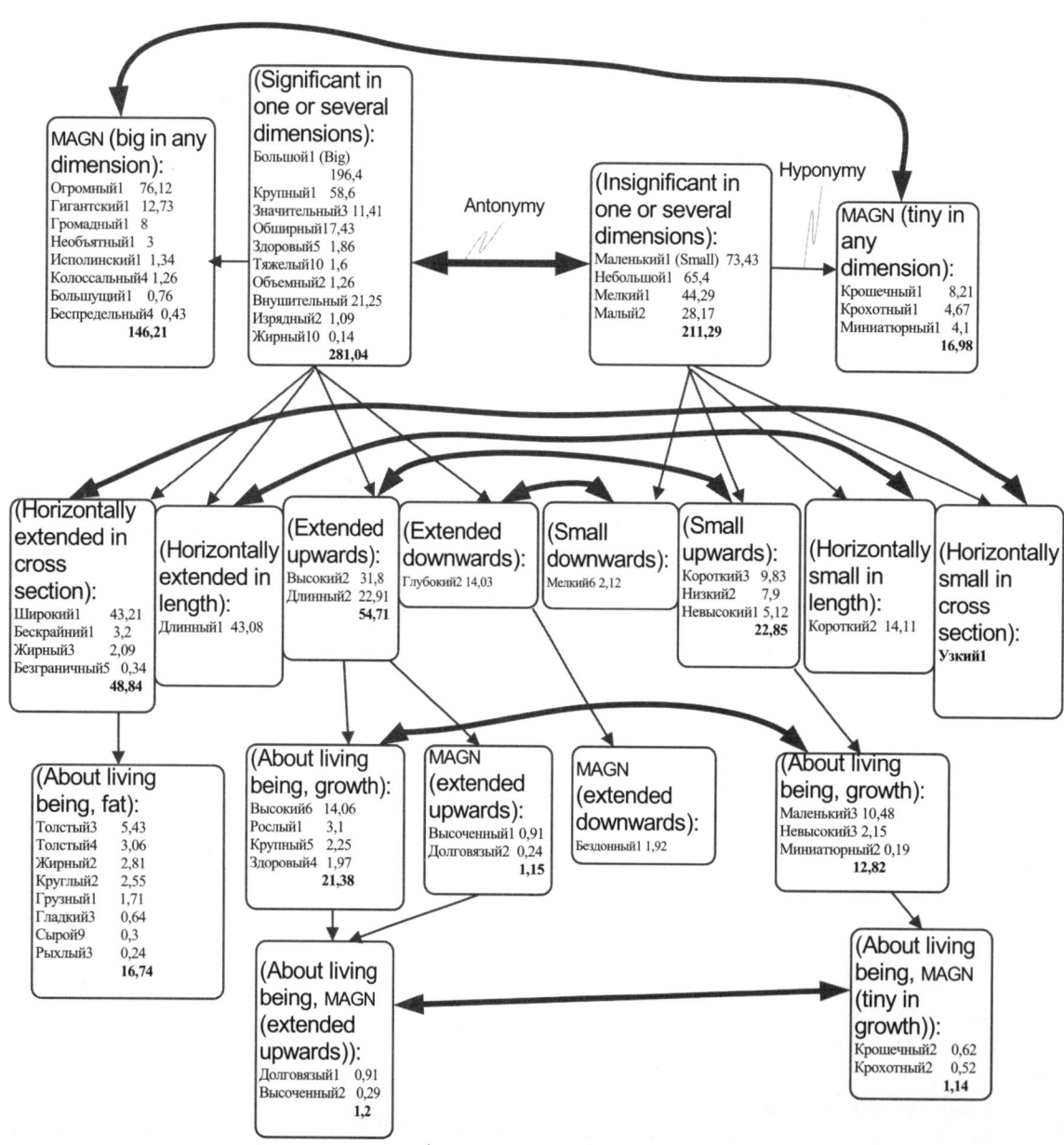

Figure 1. Adjectives of size.

(subsective). We propose to make weaker the connection with the subordinate concept *orange* inserting a prefix into the relation type — LIGHT-HYPONYMY.

The third point is connected with a prototypical pattern for an attribute, as is the case with a description of *seryj1* (grey) '...as of ashes'. It may be useful for text interpretation procedures to gain information of this type. In a way this link is similar to INVOLVED or ROLE relations.

Thus, this *seryj1* (grey) is connected to noun WM *pepel* (ash) with a link ATTRIBUTE.

3 Adjectives of visual perception

This group includes such parameters as size, colour, shape, surface property etc., the characteristics perceived by eyesight. It is the most elaborate structure of different perceptional spheres.

3.1 Adjectives of size

Size is a prototypical concept field for attributive meanings. Fig.1 represents semantic relations in this group. Squares configure synsets, its members — WMs — are ordered according to their ipm indices. The number of line shows the place of a WM in the synset, the bold total at the bottom of a square shows the ipm index of a synset. Arrows indicate semantic relations between two synsets. One-side links mark the link from the hypernym to hyponyms, two-sides links are used for symmetrical relations — antonyms.

The top synset *bolshoj1 (big)* has antonymic synset *malenkij1 (small)* and is adjoined by several types of hyponyms.

MAGN synsets *ogromnyj1 (very big, huge)* and *kroshechnyj1 (very small, tiny)* are linked with *bol'shoj1 (big)* and *malen'kij1 (small)* as traditional adjectival clusters.

Another type of hyponymy is represented by 8 synsets (*shirokij1 (wide)* — *dlinnyj1 (long)* — *vysokij2 (high)* — *glubokij2 (deep)* and their antonyms: *uzkij1 (narrow)* – *korotkij2 (short)* – *korotkij3 (low)* – *melkij6 (shallow)*) and specifies size according to one of the dimensions, so their co-occurrence is narrower than that of the hypernym (**deep column*) anyway all of them are visible objects. The relation between superordinate and subordinate synsets is of the noun hyponymy type, they are subsective.

The third type of hyponyms is represented by very specific co-occurrence with nouns. For example, some synsets have attributes defined only over the class of living beings (*dolgovyazyj1 (lanky)* or *kroshechnyj2 (tiny – about creatures)*). This type resembles both

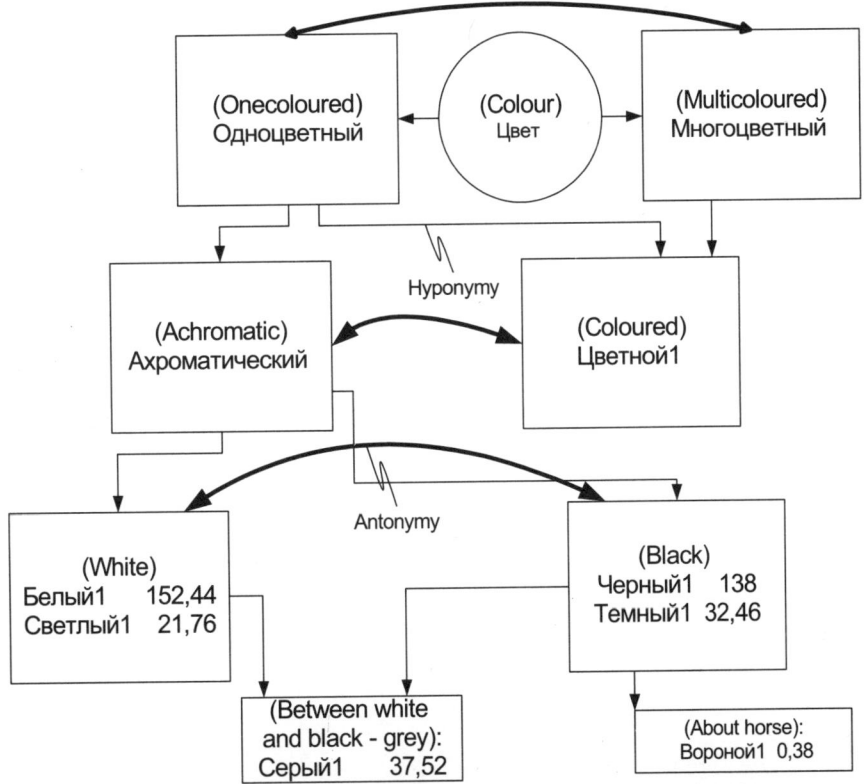

Figure 2. Adjectives of colour. Top of the hierarchy.

hyponymy of nouns and troponymy of verbs.

3.2 Adjectives of colour

Colour is another prototypical field of adjectival meanings. Fig.2 represents the top levels of the Colour structure. In this structure there are two substructures: black and white structure (achromatic) and coloured attributes (chromatic). The root of the structure is represented by the noun WM (colour). Antonymy exists only in monochromic substructure.

Synsets *achromaticheskij (achromatic)* or *mnogotsvetnyj (multicoloured)* are low frequent and inserted to conform with scientific picture of the world, they may be considered virtual, because there is no true lexicalised expression for them. They are inserted to support the hierarchy, meanwhile they make more convenient representation of mixed colours or merge of colour with a black and white palette: *cherno-belyj, cherno-krasnyj (black-and-white, black-and-red)* etc.

Fig.3 represents a part of the "coloured" hierarchy with brown tints. This structure includes troponymy-like hyponyms (*red + yellow + brown +...=coloured*) and hyponyms defined over specified semantic classes (*hair, horse, meal* etc.)

In this structure there are examples of LIGHT HYPONYMY: a synset belongs to one co-hypernym MORE than to the other. Ex.: *rumyanyj2* is defined as "glittering gold-and-brown, about roasted meal". The main hypernym is obviously *brown* but we can't ignore *glittering gold*, although *rumyanyj2* doesn't belong to the yellow tints. The new type of hyponymy is marked by dashed and dotted arrows on the Fig.3 (LIGHT_HYPONYMY).

In this structure WM for adjectives of colours are connected with noun synsets as a prototypical representatives by means of a link of a new type ATTRIBUTE: *belyj1 (white)* is defined as "of a colour of milk, snow, chalk" or *fistashkovyj2 (pistachio)* has a definition "of a colour of pistachio nut nucleus".

In some projects our colleagues prefer to regard relations between nouns, denoting these objects, and adjectives of colour as regular polysemy (Barque et al. 2008). We can't agree with them. First of all, polysemy is a relation between members of the same POS, so adjectival synset *{cerise1, cherry4}* just can't be polysemic to the noun *{cherry}*. The real reason for this may be the inflectional character of Russian, in which adjectives differ from nouns in form (cf. *vishnevyj3 (cerise)* and *vishnya (cherry)*). Obviously, such objects are prototypical for the

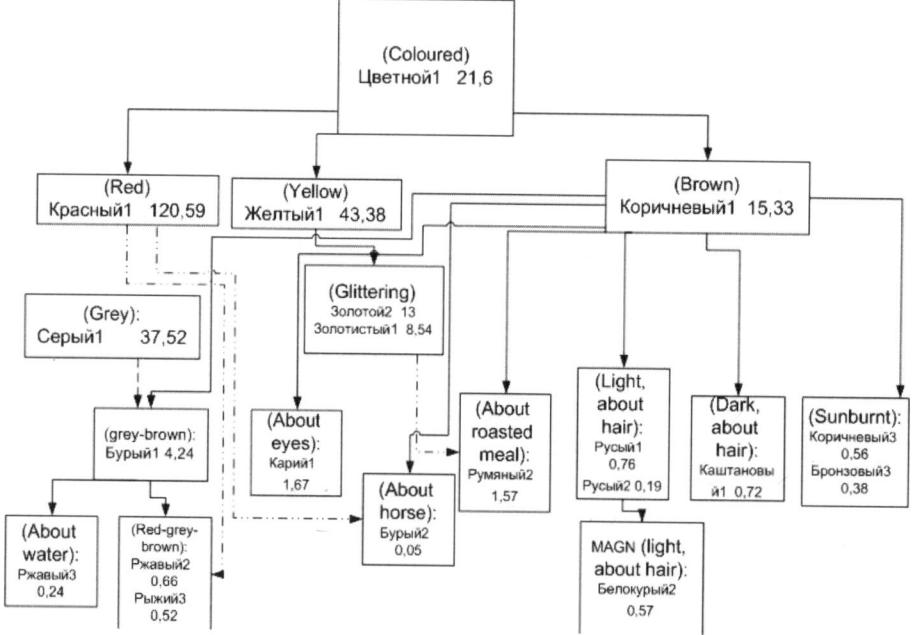

Figure 3. Adjectives of colour. Brown tints.

colours and there has to be a relationship between them. The primary colours are not motivated from the contemporary point of view, and the existed relation XPOS_NEAR_SYNONYMY is not applicable, so ATTRIBUTE link would be useful.

4 Adjectives of auditory perception

It is common knowledge that Sound can be estimated in terms of its volume, pitch (diapason), time-value, purity and site of generation. It's curious that according to frequency the main dichotomy here is not the pair *gromkij1-tikhij1 (loud-quiet)* but *dlinnyj5-korotkij6 (long-short)*.

It ought to be noted that the whole group is though numerous but rather low frequent. Even the dominant doesn't exceed 17 ipm. Nevertheless, we plan to structure it in the similar way.

5 Adjectives of olfactory perception

This group of adjectives in this group is concise, and low frequent. Its total ipm index doesn't exceed 30 ipm. This fact can be easily explained by a very productive syntactic phrase in Russian "*smell of N*" which may describe practically every odour without adjectival elements. The specific feature of adjectives in his group is a representation of lexical functions BON and ANTIBON (attractive or not), MAGN and ANTIMAGN (strong or weak). Sometimes components are specified.

Fig.4 represents the structured subgroup of smell attractiveness. There are also such individual synsets as "very strong smell", "combined smell" and "smell that leaves certain sensation in the mouth" (*solonovatyj2 – slightly salty smell*).

6 Adjectives of gustatory perception

Fig.5 represents adjectives of taste, where noun-hypernym is crucial to create any structure at all. Such adjectives as *bitter, sweet, salty etc.* have nothing in common but certain sensation they leave on a tongue that means Taste. Core tastes differ from each other by collocation with noun classes. Sometimes, *sladkij* (sweet) and *kislyj* (sour) are considered to be antonyms, though opposition in contexts is sporadic: in combination with a noun *jabloko* (apple).

Moreover, the data of (Karaulov et al., 2002) show no sign of antonymic opposition in association responses.

But the ultimate argument from our point of view is a composite word *kislo-sladkij* (sour and sweet).

The group is to the great extent alike the adjectives of colour:

- there are several main tastes and their shades, some of which can be described by means of co-hypernymy.
- We can't clearly distinguish tastes and in several cases are forced to rely on dictionary definitions.
- Antonymy is rare and disputable. We should decide by ourselves if any pair like "*light*

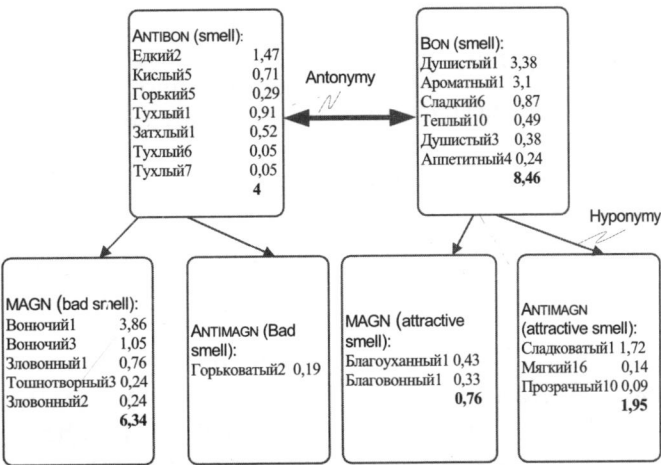

Figure 4. Adjectives of odour. Attractiveness.

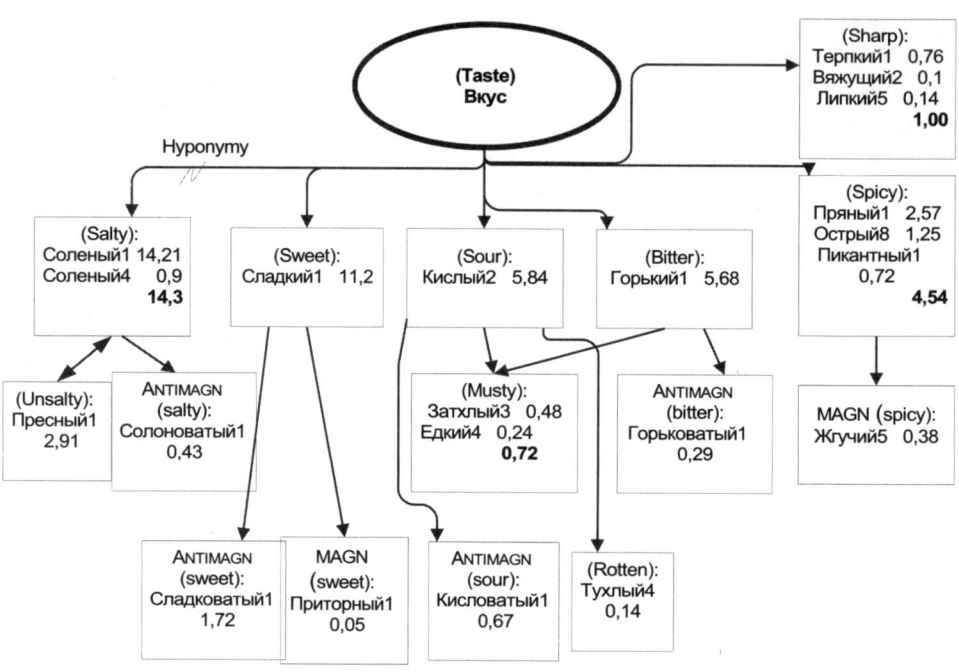

Figure 5. Adjectives of taste.

attribute" – "*strong attribute*" demonstrate antonymy or not. And the decision is pragmatic. For example, we don't regard WM *sladkovatyj1* (slightly sweet) and WM *pritornyj1* (very-very sweet) as antonyms, neither we did in other subgroups: *blagouhannyj1* (very attractive smell) – *sladkovatyj1* (slightly attractive sweet smell).

But due to the fact that taste perception is less verbalised and perhaps the human classification of the taste itself is less elaborated than that of visual images, we don't expect to meet light hyponymy in this group.

7 Adjectives of tactile perception

This group is divided into adjectives of weight, heat, moisture, characteristics of the whole body (*myagkij1, lomkij1 – soft, fragile*) and characteristics of its surface (*skol'zkij1, pushistyj1, lipkij1 – slippery, fluffy, sticky*) – everything we can feel by our skin.

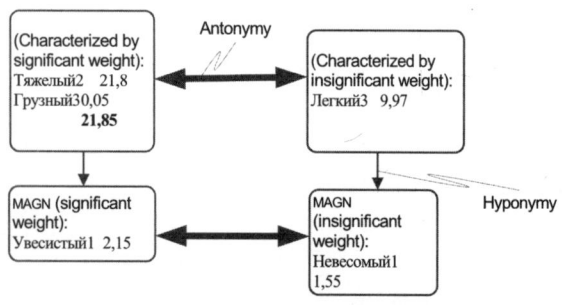

Figure 6. Adjectives of weight.

Some of these subgroups, like adjectives of weight, have rather obvious hierarchy: see Fig.6.

Others, like characteristics of surface, seem to be very flat in structure with variety of troponym-like hyponyms.

8 Conclusions

As we have seen, the groups of perceptional adjectives are not uniform both on the level of their lexicalisation in Russian and on the level of a number of synsets and the depth of hierarchy of subgroup structuring.

Nevertheless, we have shown that in many cases we just can't be content with the conventional point of view, which doesn't foresee any type of the hyponymy in adjectival structures. Moreover, we demonstrated types of hyponymy for adjectives, which combine the hyponymy for typical nouns and the troponymy for verbs with several particularly adjectival features:

- noun-like classical HYPONYMY
- specific mainly for verbs TROPONYMY.
- CO-HYPERNYMY (there exit two hypernyms, for one hyponym)
- LIGHT HYPONYMY (there exit two hypernyms, one of which is the main and the other is the secondary for the hyponym).

We hope that proper structuring of perceptional adjectives will help to represent the whole group of adjectival WMs in RussNet database.

References

Alonge, Antonietta & others. Encoding information on adjectives in a lexical-semantic net for computational applications.
http://www.aclweb.org/anthology-new/A/A00/A00-2006.pdf

Azarova, Irina and Sinopalnikova, Anna (2004) Adjectives in RussNet. *Proc. of the 2nd Global WordNet Conference.* Brno: Masaryk University. Pp. 251–258.

Azarova I.V., Ovchinnikova E.A., Ivanov V., Sinopalnikova A. A.. (2005) RussNet as a Semantic Component of the Text Analyser for Russian. In *Proceedings of the Third International WordNet Conference.* Brno Masaryk University. Pp. 19–28.

Barque, Lucie and Chaumartin, François-Régis. (2008). Regular Polysemy in WordNet.

Dictionary of Russian in 4 volumes (1981–1984) Ed. A.P.Evgenjeva, Moscow.

Dixon R.M.W. (2004) Adjective Classes in Typological Perspective. In R.M.W. Dixon and A.Y. Aikhenvald, Eds. Adjective Classes. A Cross-Linguistics Typology. Oxford: Oxford University Press, pp. 1-49.

Mendes, Sara. (2006). Adjectives in WordNet. *Proc. of the 3nd Global WordNet Conference*: pp.225-230.

Miller, Katherine J. (1998). Modifiers in WordNet. In C/Fellbaum, Ed. *WordNet. An Electronic Lexical Database.* MA, The MIT Press. Pp. 47-67.

Naumann, K. (2000). Adjectives in GermaNet.
http://www.sfs.uni-tuebingen.de/GermaNet/Adj.html

Peters, Ivonne and Peters, Wim. (2000). The Treatment of Adjectives in SIMPLE: Theoretical Observations. *Proc. of the 2nd International Conference on Language Resources & Evaluation.*

Russian Associative Dictionary (2002). Ju.N.Karaulov et al. Moscow.

Sharoff, Serge. (2001). The Frequency Dictionary for Russian.
http://www.artint.ru/projects/frqlist.asp

Soler, Clara. (2004). Extension of the SpanishWordNet. *Proc. of the 2nd Global WordNet Conference.*

Vasilevich A.P. et al. (2008). Colour and colour names in Russian. Moscow: URSS.

Wetzer, Harrie. (1996) The typology of adjectival predication. Berlin: Mouton de Gruyter.

Yavorskaya, Maria and Azarova, Irina (2009) Structuring of attributive word meanings in RussNet (in the group of Russian perceptional adjectives). *Proc. of the 15th International "Dialog" Conference,* Moscow.
http://www.dialog-21.ru/dialog2009/materials/html/87.html

Zholkovskij, A., Mel'chuk, A. (1965). O vozmozhnom metode i instrumentax semanticheskogo sinteza. (*On a Possible Method and Instruments for Semantic Synthesis.*) Nauchno-texnicheskaja informacija.
http://www.neuvel.net/meaningtext.html

Modeling Attitude, Polarity and Subjectivity in WordNet

Isa Maks
Faculteit der Letteren
De Boelelaan 1105,
1081 HV Amsterdam
The Netherlands
e.maks@let.vu.nl

Piek Vossen
Faculteit der Letteren
De Boelelaan 1105,
1081 HV Amsterdam
The Netherlands
p.vossen@let.vu.nl

Abstract

In recent years techniques have been developed to mine wordnets for sentiment-bearing words. They annotate synsets with labels for subjectivity and polarity. These techniques assume that all members of a synset are similar with respect to these annotation labels. In this paper we show that this is often not true, especially not when fine-grained polarity and subjectivity is taken into account. Therefore, we propose an extension to the wordnet model which will be better tailored to the description of fine-grained subjectivity and polarity and yet remains useful for the above mentioned mining techniques.

1 Introduction

In recent years much attention has been paid to the automatic detection of opinions, sentiments, beliefs and emotions (*subjectivity*) in text. Most of the techniques use some kind of word list annotated with polarity and subjectivity features. Initially, simple word lists were compiled and automatically annotated for negative or positive polarity only (Kamps et al. (2004), Hatzivassiloglou (1997)). The word lists were limited in size, often consisting of adjectives only. In these lists *friendly* would be tagged as positive, *sad* as negative and *chemical* as neutral. One of the main problems with these lists is that the annotation is at the word level, ignoring the possibility that a word may have both objective and subjective senses, like the Dutch word *burgerlijk*, meaning *civil* and *narrow-minded,* or may have both positive and negative senses, like the Dutch word *wreed* meaning *cruel* and *fantastic* (cf. examples 2 and 3 below).

Such subjectivity-ambiguous and polarity-ambiguous words may cause major errors in the applications they are used in (Andreevskaia et al. 2006). To overcome this problem, Wiebe (2003, 2006) introduced annotation at the word-<u>sense</u> level. The most recent and comprehensive annotation scheme (Su and Markert (2008)) combines labels for subjectivity and polarity and applies them at the word-sense level.

What most sense-based approaches have in common is that they use wordnet as a lexical resource. Automatic methods are developed to annotate synsets with subjectivity and polarity labels (Esuli et al. (2006), Andreeskva et al. (2006)) For example, the synset below would be labelled as 'objective' and having 'no polarity':

Ex. (1) (Objective: noPolarity)
lion, king_of_beasts, Panthera_leo
[large gregarious predatory feline of Africa and India having a tawny coat with a shaggy mane in the male]

As the annotation refers to the whole synset, only one set of labels for all members of the synset is provided. The methods obviously assume subjectivity-unambiguous and polarity-unambiguous synsets. The question is whether this is correct? Do these different synonyms for *lion* all have the same connotation and polarity? One might argue that the *king_of_beast* has a positive connotation while the other synonyms do not. In that case, subjectivity and polarity labels should be stored for each synonym separately. But should that be done by splitting the synset in two synsets or by further defining the synonyms?

In this paper we further elaborate these questions and describe the consequences of these choices for the architecture of the wordnet structure. In the next section we will briefly describe the concepts, models and resources which will be used and referred to in this paper. Section 3 discusses the nature of synsets and in section 4 this is related to subjective language. Section 5 concludes with answering the core question of this paper: is the synset the appropriate unit for the annotation of subjectivity and polarity and if not, what are the alternatives.

2 Method and Resources

2.1 Attitudinal Language

Various definitions have been given for the notion of subjective language. Within the domain of sentiment analysis and opinion mining the most widely used definition is by Wiebe et al. (2005, 2008). They define subjective language as language that is used to express private states such as emotions, beliefs, opinions, doubts, etc.

A detailed and comprehensive definition of subjective language is given by Martin and White's Appraisal Model (2005). They describe subjective language or appraisal language as part of a more comprehensive language model. It distinguishes the following interacting components: (1) Attitude, for the expression of feelings, including emotions, emotional reactions, evaluations of people, things and places; (2) Engagement, for the ways people express their commitments towards what they evaluate and (3) Graduation, for the amplification or weakening the strength of these evaluations and commitments. Attitude, is considered to be the core of the model and is described in three dimensions: Affect, Judgement and Appreciation. Affect words refer to emotions and emotional reactions (e.g. *sorrow, happy, fear, loath, cry, upset*), to desires (e.g. *want, abhor*), etc. Judgement refers to words used for giving moral evaluations of people and the way they behave (e.g. *deceptive, intelligent, neurotic, unreliable, nag*). Appreciation refers to the value and evaluations of 'things', performances and natural phenomena. It typically includes aesthetic evaluations (e.g. *beautiful, ugly, shapeless*).

Examples (2a)-(3b) illustrate the annotation of polarity and subjectivity in combination with Attitude Labels based upon the Appraisal Model.

Ex. (2a) (Objective: noPolarity) burgerlijk (*civil, civilian*) ex.: burgerlijke recht-*civil law disobedience* [objective - no Attitude]

Ex. (2b) (Subjective: negative) burgerlijk, bekrompen (*narrow-minded*) ex.: zijn buren zijn vreselijk burgerlijk *his neighbours are terribly narrow-minded* [Judgement of character/behaviour]

Ex. (3a) (Subjective: negative) wreed, hardvochtig, etc. (*cruel*) ex.: een wrede despoot *a cruel tyrant* [Judgment (of character/behaviour)]

Ex. (3b) (Subjective: positive) wreed, fantastisch, geweldig, etc. *fantastic, cool* ex.: ze rijden daar in vet wrede auto's rond *They drive around in really cool cars/* [Appreciation]

In the next sections we will focus on the Attitude component of the Appraisal model. Subjective or attitudinal words are considered – within the scope of this paper – as words belonging to one of the Attitudinal categories.

2.2 Lexical Resources

In this paper we will refer to three different lexical resources: the Dutch Wordnet –(part of the Cornetto database); the Dutch Reference Lexicon (also part of the Cornetto database) and the Princeton Wordnet (versions 3.0 or other if mentioned).

The Cornetto database (Vossen et al. 2008a) combines two resources with different semantic organisations: the Dutch Wordnet with its synset organisation and the Dutch Reference Lexicon with its form-meaning composites or lexical units. The description of the lexical units includes definitions, usage constraints, selectional restrictions, syntactic behaviours, illustrative contexts, etc. Within the Cornetto Database, each synonym in a synset is linked to the corresponding lexical unit of the Dutch Reference Lexicon.

3 What makes a synset?

To give an answer to the question whether wordnet synsets are appropriate for sentiment encoding, we must first know in more detail what synsets are. What are the criteria for composing a synset and for words to be members of the same synset? Synsets consist of interchangeable words or synonyms. However, according to Miller (1998) synsets do "not entail interchangeability in *all* contexts; by that criterion natural languages have few synonyms." Therefore, the notion of synonymy in WordNet is less strict: synset synonyms can be interchanged in *some* contexts.

This notion, however, may lead to different criteria for forming synsets, as illustrated by the comparison of the synset of *lion* (cf. example (1)) and the synsets *dog* and *doggie* (cf. examples (5a and b)). There are three variant terms denoting the concept *lion:* a neutral one, a scientific one and an affective one which expresses admiration for the strength and beauty of the animal. All three terms denote the same concept, but one might wonder if there is any context in which *Panthera_Leo* and *King of Beasts* are indeed interchangeable. The notion of synonyms is not only vague with respect to what terms should be included in a synset, it is, of course, equally vague in setting criteria for terms that are *not* synonyms.

Ex. (5a) `dog, domestic dog, Canis familiaris` (a member of the genus Canis..) "*the dog barked all night*"

Ex. (5b) `pooch, doggie, doggy, barker, bow-wow` (informal terms for dogs)

Although the terms of synsets (5a) and (5b) refer to the same animal, this time they are not considered synonyms. Style labels (cf. the definition of (5b) *informal terms for dogs*) cause the distribution of the synonyms over different synsets. Usage constraints can be good criteria for splitting up synsets, but - as can be seen in synset (1) - they are not applied consistently. Furthermore, they seem to contradict the general rule of synonymy. It is probably much easier to find contexts in which *dog* and *doggy* are interchangeable than contexts in which the synonyms of synset (1) are interchangeable.

Other criteria for splitting up synsets are selectional restrictions and syntactic behaviour, which we will not discuss further here.

Thus we see, that the lack of a precise definition of synonyms within the framework of Wordnet gives rise to different sets of criteria ranging from rather loose (example 1) to rather strict ones (example 5). This leads not only to inconsistencies within wordnets but also to differences among wordnets. In the case of EuroWordNet, the number of synonyms per synset, varies from 1.35 to 2.16. In the case of more recent wordnets used in the Kyoto project (Vossen et al. 2008b), the rate varies between 1 for the Chinese wordnet to 1.76 for the English WordNet (cf. Table 1).

Wordnet	Synonyms/synset
Chinese Wordnet 1.6	1.00
Italian Wordnet 2.0	1.36
Japanese Wordnet 3.0	1.39
English WordNet 3.0	1.76
Dutch Wordnet 2.0	1.69
Basque Wordnet 1.6	1.66
Spanish Wordnet 1.6	1.49

Table 1: synonyms per synset in different wordnets

Clearly, the English WordNet has most synonyms per synset, even though it is the largest wordnet in size. As the difference between the English and the Dutch Wordnet is relatively small (1.76 versus 1.69), we assume that their criteria for synset splitting are rather similar.

4 Subjective language in Wordnet

In this section we explore how attitudinal language is described in the English and Dutch Wordnets.

4.1 Large synsets

Subjective words seem to cluster together in large synsets more than other words do. The top 50 of the largest synsets of the Dutch Wordnet – ranging from 62 to 16 members - consists for the major part of Judgement and

Appreciation words: mostly evaluations of persons and of the way they behave.

Ex. (6a) judgement of persons:
`etterbuil, lelijkerd, schoft, smeerlap, pokkenlijder, etc. (skunk, bastard, son-of-a-bitch)`

Ex. (6b) judgement of persons:
`leeghoofd, sufkop, uilskuiken, uilebal, etc. (featherbrain, nitwit, rattlebrain)`

Ex. (6c) judgement of behaviour:
`apekool, geouwehoer, wijvenpraat, leuterpraat, quatsch, lulkoek (drivel, piffle, rubbish, poppycock)`

Some of these synsets could easily be put together in even larger ones. At the same time, they might be split up according to certain criteria, like usage constraints: differences in frequency, differences in style (ranging from informal to vulgar), differences in social group, etc. They have two things in common: firstly, they all have a rather strong connotation and seem to have little denotational meaning. This common feature makes is possible to regard them as synonyms. Secondly, all of them have a clear polarity in most cases, but the intensity of the polarity may differ considerably within a synset. A synset containing *lelijkerd (rascal)* and *etterbuil (son-of-a-bitch)* might be considered 'intensity-ambiguous' as the first synonym is much less negative than the second one. It will be quite difficult to split up synsets using criteria like weak or strong polarity since polarity values are scalar rather than categorical.

4.2 Smaller synsets

Not all attitudinal words are members of large synsets. On the contrary, many of them have more explicit denotational meanings and are not as one-dimensional as the examples given in the previous section. Most Affect words, most Appreciations and many Judgement words as well, refer to specific and complex concepts, which makes them members of different synsets. These synsets, however, are often subject to another type of ambiguity. They are subjectivity–ambiguous as their members all have the same, clear denotation but some of them also have a positive or negative connotation, as in the following example:

Ex. (7)
`Nederlander:1, Hollander:1, kaaskop: 1 (inhabitant of the Netherlands)`

Nederlander and *Hollander* are quite synonymous and interchangeable in many contexts. The third synonym *kaaskop* also refers to a Dutch person. Its literal meaning is 'cheese head' and it has a negative, affective meaning which cannot be inferred from the way it is presented in this synset.

5 Pilot

In the previous section we saw some examples of inconsistent synsets. We carried out a small experiment to manually mark the subjectivity of synset members with the aim to determine (1) how consistent or inconsistent synsets are with respect to attitudinal language and (2) if there are any differences between different categories of attitudinal language.

We selected about 75 words including Affect, Engagement and Appreciation words covering nouns, verbs and adjectives. We manually linked the words to the correct synsets and collected some synonyms of the involved synsets. Synsets with only one synonym were excluded. The synset members (approx. 250) were presented in alphabetical order to avoid synset membership associations. Each synonym was given its own definition taken from the lexical unit in the Cornetto database (cf. section 2.2).

The synonyms were individually annotated by two people and were given labels for subjectivity (subjective, objective and both). 'Subjective' is defined as belonging to one of the three attitudinal categories (Affect, Engagement or Appraisal); 'objective' as not belonging to any of them; and 'both' for lexical units permitting both readings. An example of the category 'both' is *zwaar (heavy)* which can be used in contexts as referring to an objective and precise measure of weight or as merely expressing 'not light' often having a negative connotation.

The annotators disagreed in 45 cases. These were excluded from the analysis. For this evaluation, we are only interested in clear cases. The results (Table 2) consist of 205 lexical units linked to 75 synsets. A synset is considered as ambiguous when at least one synonym has a different annotation than the any of the others.

part-of-speech	number of synsets	subjectivity-ambiguous
Adjective	15	3
Noun	35	10
Verb	25	6
total	75	19

Table 2: subjectivity-ambiguous synsets

We see that 25% of the synsets in total (19) are inconsistent in terms of subjectivity. For nouns this is 28%, for verbs 24% and for adjectives 20%. Even though the total set is small compared to the full wordnet, we can still clearly see a pattern.

The following points are noticeable:
- Most ambiguities involve judgements of behaviors and persons, where words denoting the concept of that particular behaviour or trait are mixed with words which denote the same concept but have also a judgement connotation. Synsets (8) – (9) exemplify some of these cases, which are comparable to the earlier examples of *Dutch man/ kaaskop*:

Ex.(8)
[s:neg]scharrel (*flirt*)
[o:neutral]affaire (*love affair*)

Ex.(9)
[o:neutral] zijn (*be, stay*)
[s:pos] vertoeven (*stay, dwell*)
[s:neg] uithangen (*stay*)

- We found no synsets which refer to emotions and expressions of emotions (Affect) that are ambiguous.

To summarize, we have seen that:
(1) The vague criteria for synset membership lead to inconsistencies in a wordnet, also with regard to Attitudinal Language. (2) Attitudinal language is not homogeneous with respect to polarity- and subjectivity-ambiguity. Both Judgement and Appreciation words fall into different categories: they are either words with a strong connotational and weak denotational meaning or, vice versa, words with a strong denotational and a weak connotational meaning. In the first case, the words cluster in large synsets, which in most cases are ambiguous with respect to the intensity of the polarity. In the latter case, the words with connotation often cluster with their objective counterpart into subjectivity-ambiguous synsets.

6 Discussion: splitting or lumping?

How can we solve these synset internal ambiguities? As explained above (section 3), the vague concept of synset permits a strict and a loose approach to synset forming. These approaches lead to two systematic rules that we can apply:

- "One denotation and one connotation per synset". This rule dictates that ambiguous synsets should be split as they cannot represent different connotations (including positive, negative and neutral). As a consequence, different synsets may have the same denotation (cf. examples 5a and 5b). or
- "One denotation and several connotations per synset". This rule dictates that all words that denote the same concept are stored together in one synset regardless of their connotations (cf. examples (8) and (9)).

A strict application of the first rule results in a wordnet with a large amount of very small synsets and many hypernym relations to links these synsets to higher concepts. Basically this technique is being applied in many cases in the English WordNet as shown in the following examples:

Ex. (11a)   Kraut, Krauthead, Boche, Jerry, Hun (*offensive term for a person of German descent*)

    is a direct hyponym of

Ex. (11b)   German (*a person of German nationality*)

There are however, some major disadvantages to this approach:
- It leads to an 'unintuitive' wordnet structure with hardly any synonyms in the synsets.
- One might ask if the result is correct. *Kraut, Boche, etc.* will then be presented as a direct hyponym of *German* just as *Berliner, Prussian* etc. But *Krautheads* and *Jerries* are not a kind of Germans; they <u>are</u> Germans. The use of these words tells us something about the attitude of the speaker. Splitting synsets will thus lead to ISA-overloading (Guarino 1998), where genuine subtypes of Germans are mixed with synsets that refer to roles or subjective labels. A solution could be to differentiate many different subtypes of hyponymy relations, one for each type of connotation.

An important question is which criteria should apply? Wiebe et al. (2006) propose that "subjectivity labels should provide principled criteria for refining word senses in Wordnet, as well as for clustering similar meanings to create more course-grained sense inventories". If we return to example (1) with the three variant terms for *lion*, this would imply that this synset will be split into two synsets: an objective one for *lion* and *Pantera-leo* and a subjective one with positive polarity for *King-of-beasts*. This raises the question whether these newly formed synsets are interesting and useful for other applications as well? For example, 'an informal vs. formal-language' classifier, or 'a scientific vs. non-scientific language' classifier, would prefer yet another type of categorisation of these synonyms. In the end - when all splitting criteria have been applied - all synsets may have been reduced to one member, eliminating the basis of the wordnet structure. This extreme differentiation of information would reduce a wordnet database to a database with lexical units.

A strict application of the second rule results in a wordnet with extremely large synsets. This approach also has some disadvantages:
- For example, the lumping of the following terms into one synset denoting 'man', connotes all kinds of mostly negative and positive qualities and would lead to highly unconventional structures:

Ex.(12)

```
man, buster, fellow, old boy,
old man, stiff, hunk, rotter,
dirty dog, rat, skunk, stink-
er, stinkpot, bum, puke,
crumb, lowlife, scum bag, so-
and-so, git , hunk, ironside,
studd, machoman  etc., etc.,
etc.
```

- Such synsets permit very low interchangeability of synonyms as their connotational meanings differ too much.
- It leads to low interoperability between Wordnets: on the one hand it is relatively easy to link complete synsets of different languages to each other, but on the other hand precise translation equivalence is impossible.
- There is a major loss of information since all information would be specified at the lexical-unit level and applications need to acces both the synsets and each lexical unit individually.
- Just as with the previous solution, it leads to very 'unintuitive' synsets.

Therefore, we propose a two-layered and hybrid approach. Hybrid because it will be a combination of applying loose and strict criteria for synset forming depending on the explicitness of subjectivity and polarity characteristics. Thus, synsets are formed by basic connotation groups of positive, negative and neutral connotation. The solution is two-layered because subjectivity will be described at both the synset and the lexical unit level. Subjectivity and polarity are often characteristics which depend on context; lexical units are the typical units where illustrative contexts and usages of words (implicitly or explicitly) are given. At the level of the lexical unit this information can be associated with fine-grained subjectivity and polarity.

Figure (1) illustrates the proposed model with regard to nouns. Following Guarino (1998) a distinction is made between *Roles* and disjoint *Types* to avoid ISA-overloading. Regular Roles and Types are considered to be neutral with respect to connotation. Words with connotations are considered as "subjective near-synonyms" of their neutral denotational counterparts. They can be near-synonyms of either Types or Roles. They are themselves always considered to be attitudinal Roles as they are only true in a personal worldview (i.e. that of the speaker or writer or of a participant). In our example (cf. figure 1), *woman* is a neutral Type which may have neutral Roles like *nanny, nursemaid, prostitute,* and *girlfriend*. A *woman* can also 'play the role' of a *cow, bitch, stunner, super woman,* etc., but only according to the subjective opinion of the speaker or writer. The relations are therefore labelled as a subjective negative Roles.

By linking synonyms to their respective lexical units, it will be possible to assign a scalar value for fine-grained polarity to each synonym separately. The subtle, internal ambiguity with regard to the intensity of the polarity can thus be handled without splitting synsets any further. Figure (1) shows these synonym-to-lexicalunit-links of one synset only; they express the differences with regard to polarity between *bag, cow,* and *bitch* ranging from relatively weak to relatively strong.

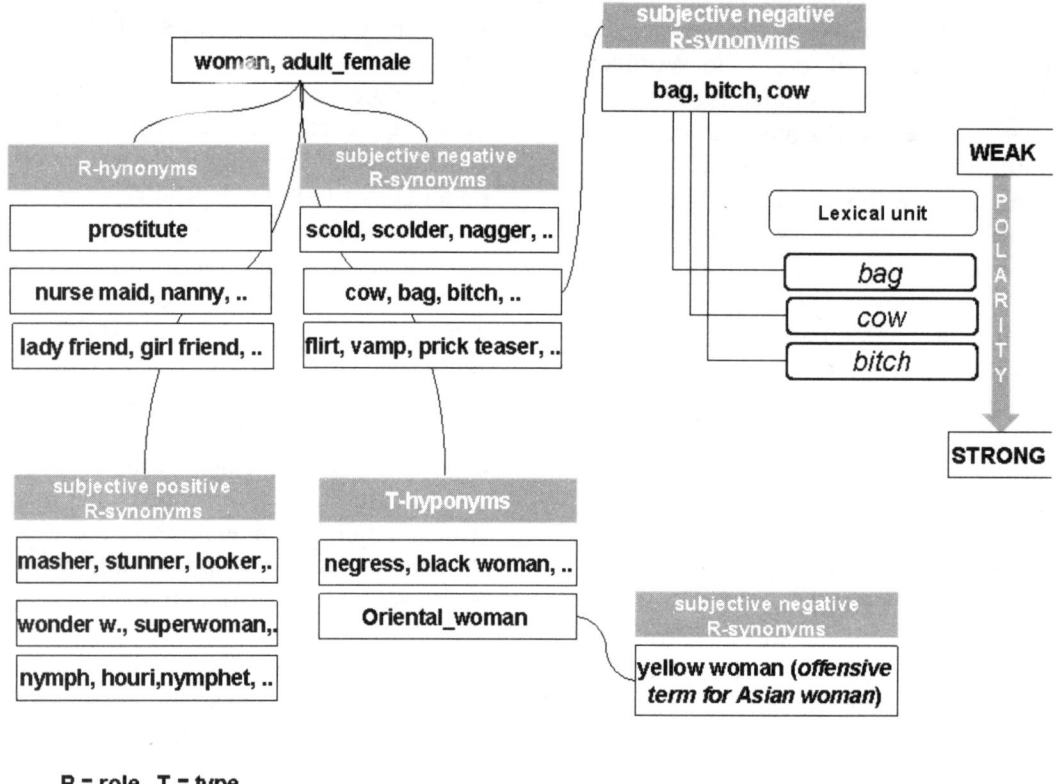

Figure 1: Attitudinal nouns in Wordnet

Likewise, with regard to verbs, the model allows us to make a distinction between words with a connotation and their neutral counterparts. Real troponyms, indicating an action performed in a particular manner or for a particular purpose, are distinguished from 'subjective near-synonyms'. In our example (cf. figure 2), *gorge, stuff, devour, fress* etc. are not considered as manners of eating but they are interpreted as expressing the negative opinion of the speaker or writer about someone's eating behavior.

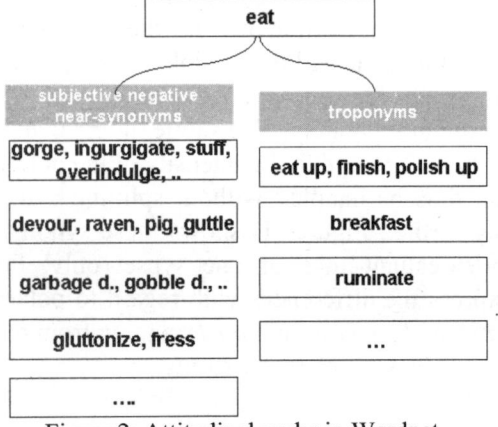

Figure 2: Attitudinal verbs in Wordnet

For adjectives the situation is different: it is not possible to form hierarchical networks of neutral adjectives and relate them to subjective counterparts as almost all adjectives do have some kind of negative or positive connotation. Adjective synsets, however, are often internally ambiguous with regard to polarity and would benefit greatly from the possibility to assign a scalar value for fine-grained polarity to each of its synonyms.

The combination of two resources offers the advantages of both. Applications can directly use the synset structure to determine the coarse-grained affective value of complete synsets. To use more fine-grained connotations they can access the lexical units individually. Moreover, the synset structures remain 'intuitive' with all neutral synonyms grouped together and with negative and positive synonyms grouped in distinct synsets. Furthermore, clearer criteria can be used to define synset-membership and less well-defined or agreed criteria can be used to encode fine-grained distinctions at the lexical unit level. This makes it easier to match synsets across languages and to establish equivalence relations across wordnets. Finally, software for deriving a sentiment wordnet using page-rank and sentiment propagation will benefit from the homogeneous synsets and perform better.

7 Conclusions

We have shown that wordnet is not the appropriate structure for the description of Attitudinal Language. Especially if we want to describe fine-grained subjectivity and polarity, there are serious limitations caused by the possible internal ambiguity of synsets with regard to these features. To overcome these limitations we propose a modification and extension of the current wordnet architecture.

In future we will refine the guidelines for the new categories and perform annotation excercises to test and further improve the model.

8 Acknowledgments

This research has been carried out within the project From Text To Political Positions (http://www2.let.vu.nl/ oz/cltl/t2pp/). It is funded by the VUA Interfaculty Research Institute CAMeRA.

References

Andreevskaia, A. and S. Bergler (2006) Mining WordNet for Fuzzy Sentiment:Sentiment Tag Extraction fromWordNet Glosses. In: EACL-2006, Trento, Italy.

Argamon, S, K. Bloom, A. Esuli, F.o Sebastianiy (2007) *Automatically Determining Attitude Type and Force for Sentiment Analysis.* In: Proceedings of the 3rd Language and Technology Conference, Poznan, Poland.

Esuli, Andrea and Fabrizio Sebastiani. (2006). *SentiWordNet: A Publicly Available Lexical Resource for Opinion Mining.* In: Proceedings of LREC-2006, Genova, Italy.

Guarino, N. (1998) *Some ontological principles for designing upper level lexical resources.* In Proceedings of LREC-1998, Granada, Spain.

Hatzivassiloglou, Vasileios and Kathleen McKeown.1997. *Predicting the Semantic Orientation of Adjectives.*In: Proceedings of ACL'97, Madrid, Spain.

Kamps, J., R. J. Mokken, M. Marx, and M. de Rijke (2004). *Using WordNet to measure semantic orientation of adjectives.* In: Proceedings LREC-2004, Paris.

Martin, J. R. and P. R. R. White. 2005. The Language of Evaluation: Appraisal in English. Palgrave, London, UK. (http://grammatics.com/appraisal/).

Miller, G. (1998) *Introduction.* In: WordNet: An Electronic Lexical Database (C. Felbaun (ed.). The MIT Press, Cambridge, Mass.

Su, F.and K. Markert *Eliciting Subjectivity and Polarity Judgements on Word Senses.* In: Proceedings of Coling-2008, Manchester, UK.

Wiebe, Janyce and Rada Micalcea.(2006) . Word Sense and Subjectivity. Proceedings of ACL'06, Sydney, Australia.

Wiebe J., Theresa Wilson , Rebecca Bruce , Matthew Bell , and Melanie Martin (2004). Learning subjective language. Computational Linguistics 30 (3).

Vossen, P., I.Maks, R. Segers and H. van der Vliet (2008). *Integrating Lexical Units, Synsets, and Ontology in the Cornetto Database.* In Proceedings of LREC-2008, Marrakech, Morocco, 2008

Vossen, P., E. Agirre, N. Calzolari, C. Fellbaum, S. Hsieh, C. Huang, H. Isahara, K. Kanzaki, A. Marchetti, M. Monachini, F. Neri, R. Raffaelli, G. Rigau, M. Tescon, J. van Gent (2008). KYOTO: A System for Mining, Structuring, and Distributing Knowledge Across Languages and Cultures , in: Proceedings of GWC 2008, Szeged, Hungary.

WNMS: Connecting the Distributed WordNet in the Case of Asian WordNet

Kergrit Robkop[1]
Sareewan Thoongsup[1]

Thatsanee Charoenporn[1,2]
Virach Sornlertlamvanich[1,2]
Hitoshi Isahara[3]

[1]Thai Computational Linguistics Lab., NICT Asia Research Center, Thailand
{kergrit, sareewan, thatsanee, virach@tcllab.org}

[2]National Electronics and Computer Technology Center Thailand, Thailand
[3]National Institute of Information and Communication Technology, Japan
isahara@nict.go.jp

Abstract

This paper deals with the development of a platform for Asian WordNet (AWN) construction. Not only for the diversity of the languages using in Asia, we also need a platform that can connect the distributedly developing WordNet to establish a network for the cross language WordNet. Each WordNet is created independently by referring to the original Princeton WordNet (PWN) as the focal representation. The Asian WordNet Management System (WNMS) is proposed as a distributed management system that allows the server for each WordNet interchange requests with each other to perform a cross language WordNet interfacing, including the fundamental web service utilities for editing, visualizing and exporting.

1 Introduction

The Princeton WordNet (PWN) (Fellbuam, 1998) is one of the most semantically rich English lexical banks widely used as a resource in many research and development. Nowadays, there have still been some efforts in developing WordNets of some languages in Asia. Some of them can make a progress on their own Wordnets, for example, Japanese WordNet (Isahara and et al., 2008; Bond and et al., 2009), Chinese WordNet (Huang, 2007), Korean WordNet (KorLex, 2006), and so on. The achievement of these projects will lead to the development of linguistic database and the cooperation among languages in Asia.

However, many languages in Asia are still in the initial stage of the development for their own WordNet. Sharing the language resources among the richer and lesser resource languages can be found in many recent efforts (Virach, 2008). Starting from the seed dictionaries we proposed an efficient way to creating a WordNet from the existing bi-lingual dictionaries (Virach and et al., 2008a). The results are now extended to share among the WordNet of each language.

To facilitate the development of the WordNet for languages in Asia, the AsianWordNet Project (AWN) is initiated based on the collaboration manner in creating an interconnection among the WordNets. The goal of AWN is to provide a communication platform to realize the cross language manipulating between the WordNet of the Asian languages. The AWN is built based on the English PWN. Therefore, the original structural information is inherited to the target WordNet through its sense translation and sense ID. The AWN finally connects each WordNet to build the complete Asian WordNet via the English Princeton WordNet.

In the first stage, we adopted KUI (knowledge Unifying Initiator) for collaborative editing to review and complete the translation (Virach and et al., 2008b). We have found that KUI is suitable for building such a community, however, it fails to show the relation between senses; the translation is for word translation rather than sense translation; and the system is also not fully distributed. As a result, we propose a new system called WNMS (Asian WordNet Management System) to dedicate its features to the Asian WordNet construction and visualization.

The following section gives an overview of the tools provided in WNMS (Asian WordNet

Management System) that are Editor, Web Service API, Visualization and Exporting tool. In Section 3 the progress report of Asian WordNet development is given. Section 4 concludes our work.

2 Asian WordNet Management System (WNMS)

WNMS is a distributed management system that makes the servers interact with each other in order to construct Asian WordNet. In the Princeton WordNet database the word entry is organized by linking of semantic relation to the word meaning. It is therefore possible to provide such semantic relation for better understanding in the translation process.

To achieve the goal of AWN, providing a communication platform for finishing WordNet, WNMS has been developed to facilitate the process of the connection between the members, the database storages, and the English WordNet translation. WNMS is easily, freely and publicly available for download. The installed WNMS server will be connected to the other servers to form the AWN network.

Tools in WNMS are Editor, Web Service, Visualization and Export. These tools are clearly explained in the following subsections.

2.1 Asian WordNet Editor

Asian WordNet Editor is a user-friendly tool that supports users in developing their local WordNet by using the sense translation method. This tool allows an editor or a translator to translate synsets (synonym of word) of PWN with minimal assistant from software developers or programmers.

The important features in AWN Editor are in the followings:

- **By category**: the base types of WordNet synsets has been shown in the By Category window. These base types are based on categories from PWN. An editor or translator can start to translate by searching from the base type and then go down to a synset of its. Figure 1 shows the By Category window with the base types. Base types are categorized as followings: 25 primitive groups for noun, 15 groups for verb, 3 groups for adjective and only one group for adverb.

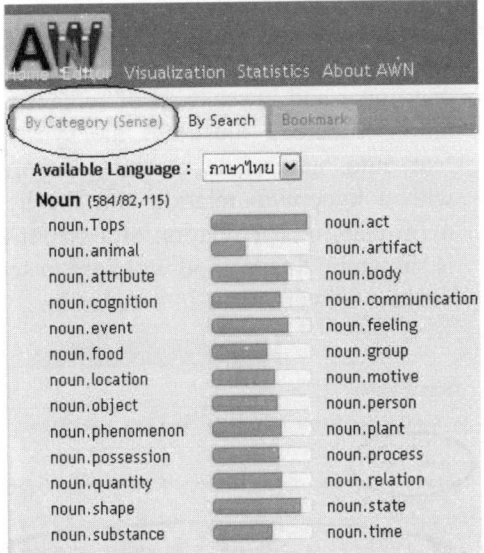

Figure 1. Asian WordNet search by category

- **By Search**: By Search window is another way to start editing or translating in AWN. Figure 2 illustrates search box where an editor or translator can start creating WordNet by searching the target word on the page of WordNet Search Engine.

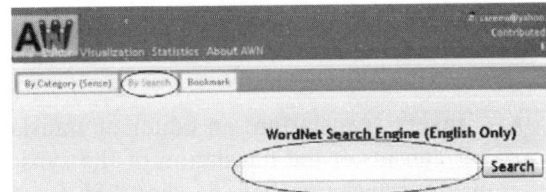

Figure 2. Asian WordNet search box

- **Bookmark**: While working on the translation, the editor or translator can create a bookmark for placing some unclear synsets for further checking. Figure 3 shows the Bookmark page on AWN Editor.

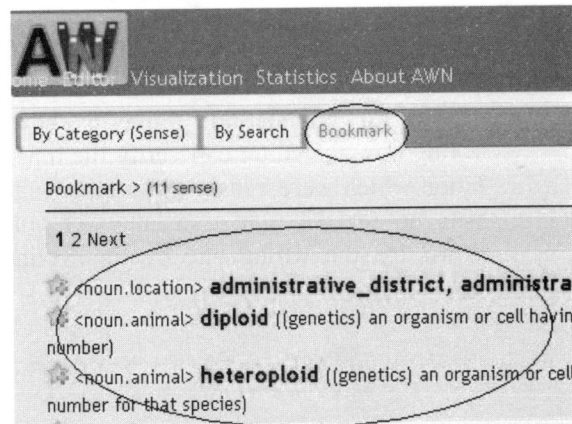

Figure 3. Bookmark page

- **Semantic relation of a synset**: The synsets of English WordNet show the relation one upper and lower level of semantic relation. Figure 4 illustrates the synset of 'car, auto, automobile, machine, motorcar' with a hypernym relation and the hyponym relation. The relation of a synset that is shown by this method will help to scope the idea of word sense in translation.

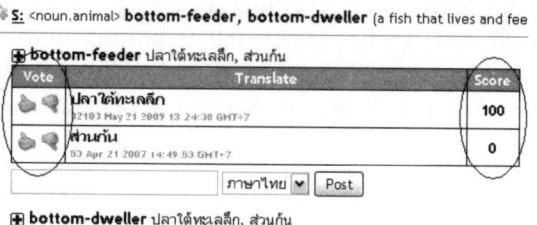

Figure 6. Vote for translation

To reach the objective in working together in AWN construction, AWN Editor has been designed to make the user's translation as simple and efficient as possible.

Next section is about Web Service API that functions as the connector between servers in different languages.

2.2 Web Service API

In WNMS, Web Service is designed to support machine-to-machine interaction over the network of AWN. AWN Web Service is Internet Application Programming Interfaces (API) that can be accessed over the network and executed on a remote system hosting the requested services. When running Web Service, each WordNet in AWN network can be considered autonomous. Each language WordNet in AWN network works independently. Web Service API will function as the connector among membership's servers. By this way, data in AWN network can be exchanged among the membership.

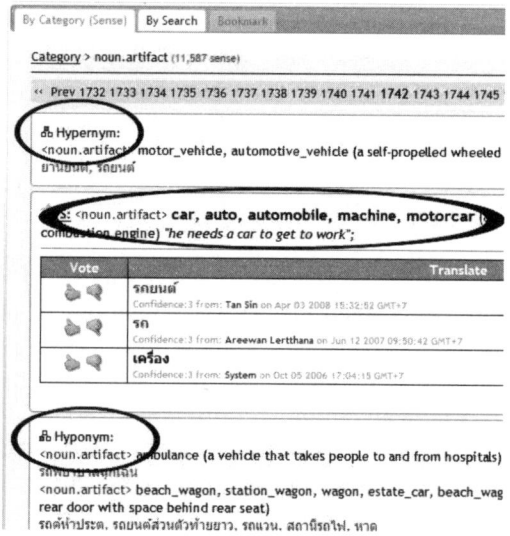

Figure 4. Semantic relation of a synset

- **Insert translation**: an editor or translator can insert the translation of the synset in the translation box, as shown in figure 5.

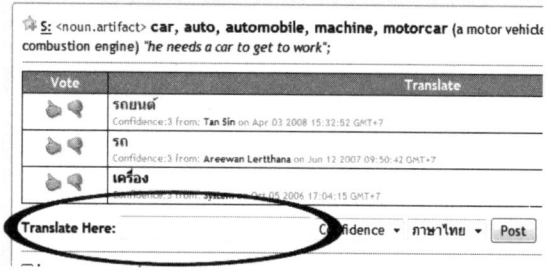

Figure 5. Insert Translation

- **Vote for translation**: figure 6 shows voting box, the editor can verify the translation which were translated by others and vote up for the right translation or vote down for the wrong one by this voting box.

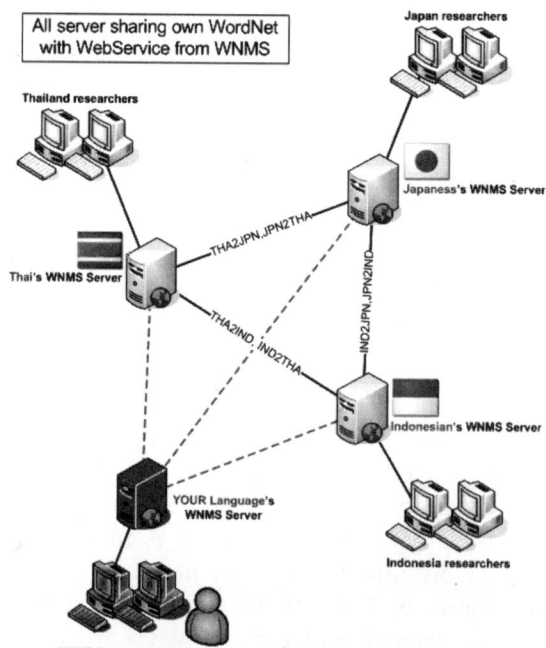

Figure 7. All server sharing own WordNet with WebService from WNMS

Figure 7 shows one-to-one connection among languages in AWN network, for example, THA2JPN is the linking between Thai and Japanese to exchange the data through English WordNet.

The different file format and data index cause some problem for information retrieval. Sometimes, an information file in each WordNet is formatted differently. So the requester needs to know how to access different file formats and to specify which file format that the WordNet local provider should use to access the data source.

words. Finally they will be transferred back to Thai server.

By using Web Service API, an unfamiliar language database does not need to be stored in the server. The data of other languages will be transferred to the target server by Web Service API tool when they are required. Membership countries are therefore only responsible for their own language database.

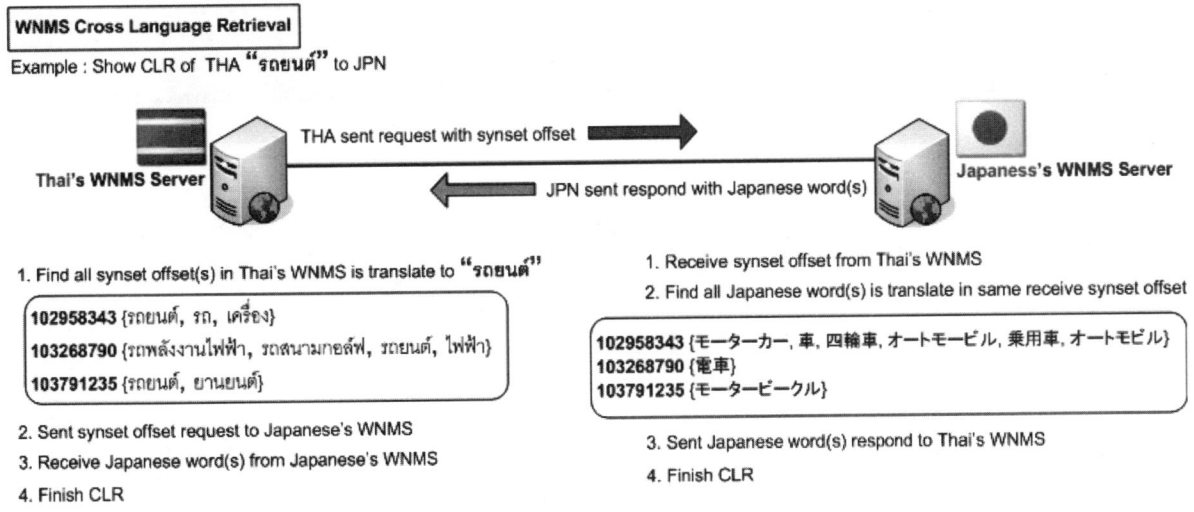

Figure 8. WNMS Cross Language Retrieval

WNMS has been developing to adjust this problem. We attempt to set the standard of WordNet information retrieval by using WNMS in Asian WordNet.

Actually, a language database based on PWN structure is indexed by the WordNet sense index that provides for accessing synsets and word senses in the WordNet database. By using WNMS, a membership of AWN can use the WordNet sense index to retrieve synsets or other information related to a specific sense in WordNet from another.

Figure 8 shows the process of data transferring between Japanese and Thai. A Thai user needs to search Japanese words that relate with รถยนต์ rod4-yon0 'car' in Thai word. This word will be searched for synset_offsets from English WordNet by Web Service API. All of "รถยนต์" synset_offsets will be transferred to Japanese server. Then the synset_offsets of รถยนต์ rod4-yon0 'car' will be searched for the information of Japanese

2.3 Visualization

Visualization tool allows fast interactive viewing of WordNet structures organized in a tree. The Treebolic program (Bernard Bou, 2009) has been used for visualizing the result of WordNet structure received from Web Service API.

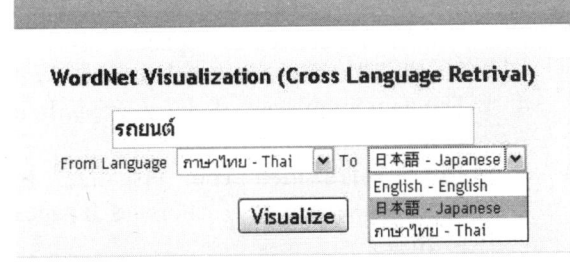

Figure 9. Asian WordNet Visualization

In the AWN Visualization page, a user can visualize the structure of WordNet by typing a word in the box and choose the source and target language, as in figure 9 and figure 10 visualizes the result of transferring data.

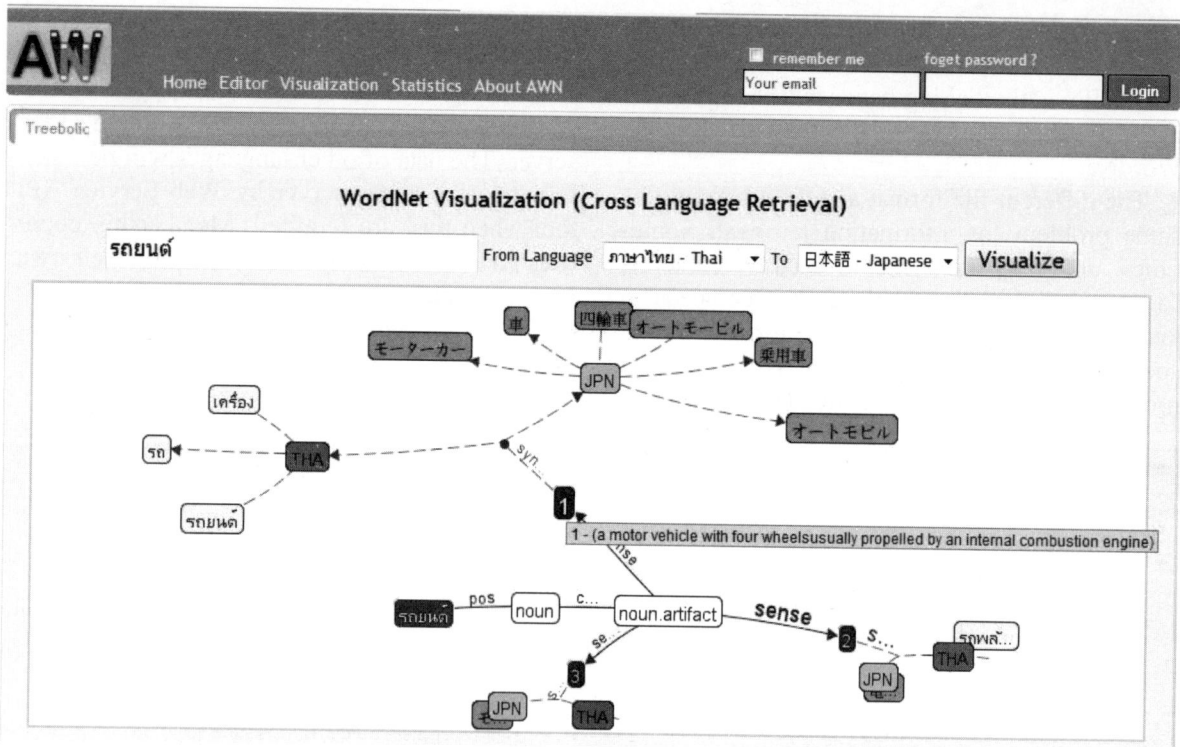

Figure 10. Asian WordNet Visualization

The process of transferring are:
1. When receiving the surface of word, Web Service API will search for the senses of Thai word รถยนต์ rod4-yon0 'car' in Thai WordNet database.
2. The information of Thai word รถยนต์ rod4-yon0 'car' that will be taken from the database is:
   a. Synset of Thai word
   b. Synset_offsets of English WordNet
   c. POS with category of base type and
   d. Synset of English word
3. The synset_offsets of English WordNet will be transferred to Japanese server to search for information of Japanese word.
4. The synonym sets of Japanese will be sent to Thai server.
5. The Visualization Tool visualizes the WordNet structure of Thai and Japanese word.

The following is the example of the information of Thai word รถยนต์ rod4-yon0. There are three concept for Thai word รถยนต์ rod4-yon0.

Sense 1 of Thai word รถยนต์ rod4-yon0
Synset_offset: 102958343
POS.base type: <noun.artifact>
English synset: car 0 auto 0 automobile 0 machine 1 motorcar 0
Gloss: (a motor vehicle with four wheels usually propelled by an internal combustion engine)
Thai synset words: รถยนต์, รถ, เครื่อง
Japanese synset words: モーターカー, 車, 四輪車, オートモービル, 乗用車, オートモビル

Sense 2 of Thai word รถยนต์ rod4-yon0
Synset_offset: 103268790
POS.base type: <noun.artifact>
English synset: electric 0 electric_automobile 0 electric_car 0
Gloss: (a car that is powered by electricity)
Thai synset words: รถพลังงานไฟฟ้า, รถยนต์, รถสนามกอล์ฟ, ไฟฟ้า
Japanese synset words: 電車

Sense 3 of Thai word รถยนต์ rod4-yon0
Synset_offset: 103791235
POS.base type <noun.artifact>
English synset: motor_vehicle 0
automotive_vehicle 0
Gloss: (a self-propelled wheeled vehicle that does not run on rails)
Thai synset words: รถยนต์, ยานยนต์
Japanese synset words: モータービークル

This information will be visualized in a tree by using Visualization in AWN, as in figure 10.

2.4 Export tool

The Export tool in WNMS allows the membership user to export data to the following format: LMF (Lexical Markup Framework) (Takenobu and et. al, 2009), XML (Extensible Markup Language), CSV text file format, and so on, so the user can use WordNet for other related projects, for example, machine translation, word sense disambiguation, and so on.

3 Progress Work on Asian WordNet

Asian WordNet has been being developed to reach the goal of the project. The success of AWN project needs to develop not only some tools for construction but also the cooperation among Asian languages. At present, there are ten Asian languages in AWN, as the following table.

Language	Synsets
Thai	80,098
Lao	72,672
Japanese	66,648
Korean	65,483
Burmese	26,033
Indonesian	21,584
Vietnamese	17,767
Mongolian	2,283
Bengali	1,775
Sinhala; Sinhalese	177

Table 1 The number of synsets in AWN

Each language has a difference in the linguistic resources, so it needs to use several methods to create and share the WordNet among Asian languages. We try to use available resources of each language to build AWN. The several methods for building are:

- Using local WordNet to link with AWN.

By supporting and cooperating from Japanese WordNet by NICT, Thai WordNet can be linked and interchange the data with Japanese WordNet by using WNMS in AWN.

- Mapping local word surface to English WordNet

Bilingual dictionary can be a resource for WordNet construction. The surface words in language have been mapped to English WordNet. However, it needs to recheck by native language. Those languages in AWN are Korean, Burmese, Indonesian, Vietnamese, Mongo, Bengali and Sinhalese.

- Using a phoneme-based transfer method for machine translation.

This method can be used for languages that are very similar in terms of grammar, lexicon, and character encoding scheme. Thai and Lao languages have these characteristics (Virach and et al., 2008).

- Using manual translation

This method has been used for Thai WordNet. We use the Editor interface on AWN to translate the concepts (synset) of English in PWN into Thai synonym sets.

The number of the synsets of English WordNet has been continuously translated into Thai synsets. From 117,659 synsets in PWN, there are:

49,514 synsets translated

40,425 translated synsets have been approved.

57,047 Thai unique lemmas

4 Conclusion

In this paper we have described tools used for Asian WordNet construction. The development of tools is to facilitate the construction and to make a better connection among WordNets of Asian languages. These tools will help extend the network of Asian WordNet. WNMS is easily, freely and publicly available for download. The installed WNMS server will be connected to the other servers in AWN network. WNMS can be downloaded at www.asianwordnet.org.

Acknowledgements

AWN project would not have been possible without our enthusiastic partners and community contributors. We gratefully thank Dr. Hitoshi Isahara and Dr. Francis Bond from NICT, Japan, Professor Chi Mai Luong from Institute of Information Technology, National Center for Science and Technology of Vietnam, Vietnam, Valaxay Dalaloy from Science Technology and Environment Agency, LAOS, Hammam Riza from Agency for the Assessment and Application of Technology, Indonesia, Professor Purev Jaimai from Center for Research on Language Processing, National University of Mongolia, Mongolia, Dr. Myint Myint Than from Myanmar Computer Federation (MCF), Myanmar, StarDict and ADD school supporters.

References

Bernard Bou. 2009. *Treebolic.* Available at http://treebolic.sourceforge.net/

Chu-Ren Huang. 2007. *Chinese WordNet.* Academica Sinica, Available at http://bow.sinica.edu.tw/wn/

Fellbum, C. 1998. *WordNet: An Electronic Lexical Database.* MIT Press, Cambridge, Mass.

Francis Bond, Hitoshi Isahara, Sanae Fujita, Kiyotaka Uchimoto, Takayuki Kuribayashi and Kyoko Kanzaki. 2009. *Enhancing the Japanese WordNet.* in The 7th Workshop on Asian Language Resources, in conjunction with ACL-IJCNLP 2009, Singapore.

Hindi Wordnet, 2007. Available at http://www.cfilt.iitb.ac.in/wordnet/webhwn/

Hitoshi Isahara, Francis Bond, Kiyotaka Uchimoto, Masao Utiyama and Kyoko Kanzaki. 2008. *Development of the Japanese WordNet.* In LREC-2008, Marrakech.

KorLex, 2006. *Korean WordNet*, Korean Language processing Lab, Pusan National University, 2007. Available at http://164.125.65.68/

Takenobu Tokunaga, Dain Kaplan, Nicoletta Calzolari, Monica Monachini, Claudia Soria, Virach Sornlertlamvanich, Thatsanee Charoenporn, Yingju Xia, Chu-Ren Huang, Shu-Kai Hsieh and Kiyoaki Shirai. 2009. *Query Expansion using LMF-Compliant Lexical Resources*, Proceedings of The 7th Workshop on Asian Language Resources (ALR7), Joint conference of the 47th Annual Meeting of the Association for Computational Linguistics (ACL) and the 4th International Joint Conference on Natural Language Processing (IJCNLP), Suntec, Singapore, August 6-7.

Virach Sornlertlamvanich. 2008. *Cross Language Resource Sharing*, Proceedings of Workshop on NLP for Less Privileged Languages, Hyderabad, India, January 11.

Virach Sornlertlamvanich, Chumpol Mokarat, and Hitoshi Isahara. 2008. *Thai-Lao Machine Translation based on Phoneme Transfer*, Proceedings of the 14th NLP2008, University of Tokyo, Komaba Campus, Japan, March 18-20.

Virach Sornlertlamvanich, Thatsanee Charoenporn, Chumpol Mokarat, Hitoshi Isahara, Hammam Riza, and Purev Jaimai. 2008. *Synset Assignment for Bi-lingual Dictionary with Limited Resource*, Proceedings of the Third International Joint Conference on Natural Language Processing (IJCNLP2008), Hyderabad, India, January 7-12.

Virach Sornlertlamvanich, Thatsanee Charoenporn, Kergrit Robkop, and Hitoshi Isahara. 2008. *KUI: Self-organizing Multi-lingual WordNet Construction Tool*, Proceedings of the Fourth Global WordNet Conference (GWC2008), Szeged, Hungary, January 22-25.

Linking CoreNet to WordNet - Some Aspects and Interim Consideration

In-Su Kang
Kyungsung Univ.
608-736 Busan
South Korea
dbaisk@ks.ac.kr

Sin-Jae Kang
Daegu Univ.
712-714 Daegu
South Korea
sjkang@daegu.ac.kr

Se-Jin Nam
KAIST
305-701 Daejeon
South Korea
jordse@gmail.com

Key-Sun Choi
KAIST
305-701 Daejeon
South Korea
kschoi@cs.kaist.ac.kr

Abstract

CoreNet, which is built on 2,937 semantic categories, is a multilingual lexico-semantic network aiming at bridging multiple languages/parts-of-speech for a variety of NLP applications. To foster its more widespread use, we have attempted to link semantic categories of CoreNet to Princeton WordNet. To ameliorate translation problems between CoreNet (mostly written in Korean) and English WordNet and to enhance recall of WordNet equivalents, two are partially indirectly linked through a Korean WordNet which shares most synset IDs with English WordNet. As an interim report, this paper describes a mapping methodology and current considerations.

1 Introduction

CoreNet (Choi and Bae, 2004) is a concept network of word senses, which has been constructed in KAIST for the Korean, Chinese, and Japanese languages since 1994 based on CoreNet concept hierarchy originated from NTT Goi-Taikei (Ikehara *et al.*, 1997) concept hierarchy. For Korean, it encompasses 31,384 general words (Biemann *et al.*, 2004), and a total of 62,632 senses of them are linked to one or more concepts in CoreNet concept hierarchy which is comprised of 2,937 high-level concepts mainly taxonomically organized into 12 depths. Unlike other lexico-semantic networks such as WordNet (Fellbaum, 1998) or Goi-Taikei (Ikehara *et al.*, 1997), CoreNet was designed to function as a single shared resource to bridge the semantics of not only different languages but also several parts-of-speech (POS) in the same language. For this, a single CoreNet concept hierarchy is used to link word senses of different lexical categories such as nouns, verbs, and adjectives for Korean, Chinese, and Japanese.

To start extending CoreNet's multi-lingualism into Indo-European languages and to promote its broader utilization for diverse NLP application, we have attempted to map CoreNet concept hierarchy to Princeton WordNet (PWN). This paper describes such efforts.

The rest of the paper is organized as follows. Section 2 presents a methodology to map between CoreNet and PWN. Section 3 describes current considerations while linking, and Section 4 gives a conclusion. For writing Korean expressions, Yale Romanization is used with a syllable delimiter '-'.

2 Mapping Methodology

2.1 Bottom-up Mapping

There are two strategies in assigning the mapping-order to CoreNet concepts: top-down and bottom-up approaches. A top-down method starts from topmost nodes and determines mappings of higher-level nodes first and then lower-level nodes. A bottom-up one does the contrary.

When the former locates target-hierarchy equivalents of a source-hierarchy concept, it might be intractable to take into account all descendants of the source concept. Due to that, the top-down approach may produce the mapping result where target equivalents of source hyper-concepts do not include those of some source hypo-concepts as progeny. Although the bottom-up approach could avoid such inconsistency, it may yield numerous candidate-equivalents for higher-level source concepts, which would need to be generalized to a manageable number of higher concepts. However, such generalization can be accelerated by an automatic method such as discovering nearest-common-ancestors from known offspring nodes within the target hierarchy.

A top-down scheme could be beneficial for the case where two concept hierarchies are similar. However, CoreNet and PWN are inherently different in languages, sizes, and concept granularities. Moreover, CoreNet concepts are not clearly defined compared to PWN synsets. These may raise problems in a downward mapping approach. Our team thus decided to employ a bottom-up method.

2.2 Indirect Mapping through KorLex

Since CoreNet concepts are described in non-English languages (mostly in Korean), linking CoreNet to PWN requires a language translation process. Translation between different languages in general involves disambiguating word senses, handling the cases that simple word-for-word correspondences do not exist.

To alleviate such difficulties in Korean-to-English (K-E) translation and to increase recall of PWN equivalents, we pursue to indirectly associate CoreNet with PWN through KorLex[1], a Korean WordNet. Although KorLex does not cover all PWN synsets or vice versa, overlapped synsets between KorLex and PWN contribute not only to reduce K-E translation problems but also to recall most synonymous K-E translations.

KorLex-based indirect-linking corresponds only to the case where a KorLex synset is found for a CoreNet concept and there exists a PWN synset of which ID is identical to that of the KorLex synset.

2.3 Mapping of Individual Concepts

To find PWN equivalents for a CoreNet concept, we exploit a CoreNet concept term (in Korean), a list of CoreNet concept words (in Korean), K-E dictionaries, and some utility programs such as PWN/KorLex/CoreNet browsers. First, for a CoreNet concept c and its concept term t_c, an equivalent-generation program produces a worksheet that includes the following.

- [I-1] Information (a concept term, a taxonomic hierarchy, concept words) of c
- [I-2] Information (taxonomic hierarchy, gloss, usage) of KorLex-noun/verb/adjective synsets $Ksyn_c$ such that at least one synonym of $Ksyn_c$ partially matches t_c.
- [I-3] Information (taxonomic hierarchy, gloss, usage) of PWN-noun/verb/adjective synsets $Esyn_c$ such that ID[2] of $Esyn_c$ is the same as that of $Ksyn_c$.
- [I-4] Information (taxonomic hierarchy, gloss, usage) of PWN-verb/noun/adjective synsets $Esyn_c$ such that at least one synonym of $Esyn_c$ partially matches one of English translations of t_c.

Each of [I-2], [I-3], and [I-4] may have multiple records for each POS (part-of-speech) such as noun, verb, and adjective. In [I-4], English translations are automatically obtained from Korean-to-English translation dictionary. The above worksheet is presented to human judges who review its contents to decide some PWN equivalents for c. If a human cannot find any related synsets within the worksheet, he/she looks up K-E dictionaries for relevant translations and browse synsets' information to select PWN equivalents of c by using PWN browsers.

As semantic relations used for linking between a CoreNet concept and a PWN synset, we employ the following seven relation types used in PWN: synonymy, hypernymy, hyponymy, troponymy, proper inclusion, presupposition, cause (Fellbaum, 1998). For instance, when a CoreNet concept corresponds synonymously to PWN synset {department_store,emporium}, its mapping is represented as follows.

{department_store,emporium^noun:03061806 ^synonym[3]}

3 Considerations

While associating CoreNet concepts to PWN synsets, the following considerations and issues have been raised. First, note that CoreNet concepts are designed to be applied to multiple POSs, but PWN concept system is divided into PWN-noun, PWN-verb, PWN-adjective, etc., according to POS. This requires us to link CoreNet to PWN separately for each of three parts-of-speech.

---

[1] KorLex is PWN-referenced Korean WordNet which has been developed since 2004, and it contains about 130,000 synsets and 150,000 word senses for nouns, verbs, adjectives, adverbs, and classifiers (Yoon et al., 2009).

[2] KorLex is constructed by using the synset IDs of PWN 2.0.

[3] {synset^POS:synset_ID^mapping_relation}

Second, some non-terminal concepts of CoreNet are represented in the form of enumerating child concept terms using a delimiter '/' (e.g. '*kyu-chik/pep-lyul/co-ngyak*' (rule/law/treaty), '*ngyun-li/cong-kyo*' (ethics/religion), '*mun-cang/ku/tan-nge*' (sentence/phrase/word), etc.) rather than a single concept term. So, it is non-trivial to find PWN equivalents for this type of concepts (called an enumeration-concept). For example, we have to search a PWN synset which signifies both 'ethics' and 'religion' for a CoreNet concept termed '*ngyun-li/cong-kyo*' (ethics/religion). Enumeration-concepts cover about 429 (14.6%) out of a total of 2,937 CoreNet concepts. To solve this, a set representation is introduced, which assigns an enumeration-concept a set of all PWN equivalents of its child concepts with a hyponymy relation. The mapping result for '*ngyun-li/cong-kyo*' (ethics/religion) is as follows.

{{morality^noun:04614989^hyponymy}, {religion,faith^noun:07591116^hyponymy}}

Third, there are CoreNet concepts termed '*pin-pu*' (rich/poor), '*cu-kayk*' (host/guest), etc. This type of concepts (called an antonyms-concept) exists as a single word in Korean but contains both meanings of antonym words in English. Antonyms-concepts cover about 29 (1%) out of entire CoreNet concepts. For this, we use the set representation again to encompass all PWN equivalents of each antonym. For example, the mapping result for '*cu-kayk*' (host/guest) is as follows.

{{host^noun:09530955^hyponymy}, {guest,invitee^noun:09498008^ hyponymy}}

Forth, there are CoreNet concepts called a complementary-concept. For concept *c*, this refers to the remnant of the scope of *c* that all children concepts of *c* specify. Complementary-concepts cover about 184 (6.3%) among all CoreNet concepts. For example, 'the other workers' concept in Figure 1 is a complementary concept.

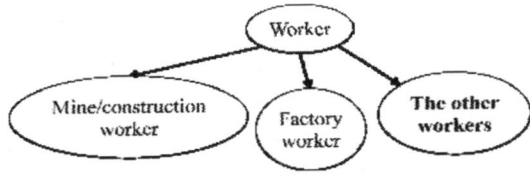

Figure 1. Example of a complementary concept

This type of concepts is mapped to the synset of its parent concept with a hypernymy relation. For example, the mapping result for 'The other workers' in the above is as follows.

{worker^noun:09025575^hypernymy}

Note that 'Worker' in Figure 1 is linked to PWN synset ID 09025575.

Fifth, there are some phrasal-concepts, which are hard to find their PWN equivalents (e.g. '*ka-kyek-ngin-sang*' (price advance), etc). In this case, we first find the headword of a phrasal-concept term, and map the phrasal-concept to synsets corresponding to the headword with a hypernymy relation. For '*ka-kyek-ngin-sang*' (price advance), its headword is '*ngin-sang*' (advance), which is mapped to PWN synset {advance,gain} with synset ID 00152358. Thus, the mapping result for '*ka-kyek-ngin-sang*' (price advance) is as follows.

{advance,gain^verb:00152358^hypernymy}

4 Conclusion

We have almost completed mapping terminal concepts (2,100) and non-terminal concepts (837) in CoreNet, except the cases belonging to the previously mentioned issues. After completing our work, we plan to distribute CoreNet with mappings to PWN in the form of LMF (Lexical Markup Framework)[4], the ISO standard for Natural Language Processing (NLP) lexicons and Machine Readable Dictionaries (MRD).

References

Aesun Yoon, Soonhee Hwang, Eunryoung Lee, and Hyuk-Chul Kwon. (2009). "Construction of Korean Wordnet KorLex 1.5". *Journal of KIISE (Korean Institute of Information Scientists and Engineers): Software and Applications*, 36(1):92-108.

Chris Biemann, Sa-Im Shin, Key-Sun Choi. (2004). "Semiautomatic extension of CoreNet using a bootstrapping mechanism on corpus-based co-occurrences". *Proceedings of the 20th International Conference on Computational Linguistics*, Geneva, Switzerland.

Christiane Fellbaum. (1998). WordNet: An Electronic Lexical Database (Language, Speech, Communication), MIT Press.

---

[4] http://www.lexicalmarkupframework.org/

Key-sun Choi and Hee-sook Bae. (2004). "Procedures and Problems in Korean-Chinese-Japanese Wordnet with Shared Semantic Hierarchy". *Proceedings of Global WordNet Conference*, Brno, Czech Republic, pp.91-96.

Satoru Ikehara, *et al.* (1997). The Semantic System, volume 1 of *Goidaikei: A Japanese Lexicon*, Iwanami Shoten, Tokyo.

A WordNet for Tulu

B.S. Shivakumar
Dept. of Tulu and Translation Studies
Dravidian University, Kuppam 517425, India
shivabharany@yahoo.co.in

Abstract

Tuḷu WordNet is an attempt to build a lexical resource for Tuḷu language using IndoWordNet as a base. The issues and problems in building a WordNet for Tuḷu are discussed in brief with proper examples.

1 Introduction

Tuḷu is a Dravidian language of India with over three million speakers in Karnataka [karnāṭaka], known as Tuḷuvas [tuḷuwaru]. It is one of the oldest languages which sprout from the proto south-Dravidian subgroup. According to linguists Tuḷu is as old as Prākrit. Most Tuḷuvas live in the districts of Dakshina Kannaḍa and Udupi [uḍupi] in the west of the state of Karnataka [karnāṭaka]. It is also spoken in the Kasaragod [kāsaragōḍu] district of Kerala [kēraḷa] state. There are a sizeable number of Tuḷuvas in the gulf as well as in Mumbai and other parts of Maharashtra [mahārāṣṭra]. The originally used script of the Tuḷu language, which was an adapted from of the Grantha Script and from which the present day Malayalam script also evolved, is rarely used today. Since the beginning of the twentieth century, it has, mostly, been written in the modified Kannaḍa script.

1.1 Geographic Distribution

The scholars have divided Tuḷu speaking region into five geographical areas, i.e. northeast (covers Karkala [kārkaḷa] and Belthangadi [beḷtaṅgaḍi] Taluks), northwest (Covers Udupi and Mangalore), South central (Covers Bantwala [baṇtwāḷa] and Puttur [puttūru] area), southeast (covers Sullia [suḷḷya] and subrahmanya) and south west (covers Manjeswara [mañjēśwara] and Kasaragod [kāsaragōḍu] of Kerala [kēraḷa]). There are several caste groups in each area which distinguish primarily the four major divisions: Brahmin (śiwaḷḷi and śaiwa), Common Group castes (including castes such as bunt, billawa, gauḍa, mogawīra), Jaina, and the rest (Harijans and tribals). Accordingly, four sociolects have been recognized. Those are Brahmin Dialect, Common dialect, Jaina Dialect, and Harijan and Dalit Dialect. There is a tendency among speakers of the fourth group to abandon their own caste dialects and adopt the common variety of their area, particularly in the north. Brahmins, at the other end of the social spectrum, generally maintain their distinctive caste dialect, and use Common Tuḷu only for communicating with other, non-Brahmin Tuḷu speakers.

1.2 Script

Tuḷu has been written in two orthographic systems. Old Tuḷu script is an early adaptation of Grantha script used by Tuḷu Brahmins traveling to Kerala to study Sanskrit texts. Inscription in Tuḷu script have been discovered and dated to the fifteenth century. The two epics Sri Bhagawato [bhāgawatō] and Kaweri [kāwēri] both from the seventeenth century were originally set down in this script. To retain these texts and some other writings, old Tuḷu script has been primarily used by handful of Brahmins to transcribe Sanskrit texts, a practice that continues to the present. It is otherwise no longer used for writing or publishing Tuḷu texts. During the early nineteenth century, Christian missionaries introduced Kannaḍa script for Bible translations and other related materials. The practice continues and is followed in Brigel's (1872) Tuḷu grammar, Manner's (1886 & 1888) dictionary of Tuḷu and Paniyadi's (1932) Tuḷu grammar. The renaissance of Tuḷu writing in the twentieth century has further consolidated the practice of using Kannaḍa script for Tuḷu.

Recently, serious attempts were made by Tuḷu traditional scholars to revive the original script. The movement is not successful and the efforts have been failed to the extent that it may not reoccur again. In the light of the fact, the project will go with modified Kannaḍa script.

Existing modern literature in Tuḷu is available only in modified Kannaḍa script and it is the only available hard copy corpus available for the present day Tuḷu.

1.3 Major Linguistic Features

Tuḷu has three morphologically distinct word classes: nouns, verbs and indeclinables. The language has only two types of inflectional suffixes: nominal suffixes and marking number and case, and verbal suffixes marking such categories as causative, reflexive, completive; tense and mood; and person, number and gender. Indeclinables, including what have been called adjectives and adverbs, generally take no inflection when they are used to modify nouns and verbs.

Tuḷu has eight cases, of which the nominative is unmarked. The remaining seven are signaled by case markers suffixed directly to the nominal base in the singular and to the plural marker in the plural. Tuḷu is a tense prominent language in which the verbal inflections fundamentally denote tense distinctions. Distinctions of mood and aspect are conveyed by auxiliary verb construction or by secondary usages of tense markers.

2 Building the Tulu WordNet

Aim of the project is to develop an e-lexical reference resource for the Tuḷu language i.e., Tuḷu WordNet. The project has been inspired by the land marking electronic lexical reference resource developed for English by the team of Cognitive linguists at Princeton University, headed by George A Miller, known globally by the name 'WordNet', unmarked meaning of which is English WordNet.

The design of the project is based on the Indo WordNet, unmarked meaning of which is Hindi WordNet, developed by the Dipak Kumar Narayan and team.
Tuḷu being a non-scheduled language of India does not have many linguists working fulltime on it. And as the consequent result we find nil work on the lexical studies in Tuḷu. The concept of synonymy, antonymy, hypernymy, hyponymy, meronymy, and holonymy are not well exercised in the Tuḷu linguistic studies.

As a result, developing a WordNet for Tuḷu takes lot of exercise of the above mentioned theoretical notions independently throughout the project. To avoid the unusual span of time delay the Tuḷu WordNet is being built on the basis of Hindi WordNet.

The project is not officially initiated, yet, at Dravidian University. However, at personal capacity the project has been initiated before three months and awaiting to be funded. The project is very much at an initial stage. The project was initiated with 1969 synsets provided by the IndoWordNet team.

We are initially concentrating on developing the synsets at the earliest. Till now, without having project personnel, other than the principal investigator and the co-investigator 909 synsets have been completed. Care has been taken to collect native synsets too. Categorical details of the completed synsets are as follows:

Total Synsets ▫ Classified Synsets ▫	Synset – Taken	Synsets – Completed
	1969	0909
nouns	1512	0722
verbs	0225	0057
adjectives	0180	0107
adverbs	0052	0023

The completed synsets have been data entered into the Indian Language Multilingual Sense-Based Dictionary Development Tool (IL-Multidic tool Jan 2007) developed by IIT Bombay (IndoWordNet team).

2.1 Methodology

Effort has been made to give equivalents to the Hindi synset as well as for illustrations. However, while giving equivalents to the Hindi synsets we are referring to the English synsets too. The 1969 synsets provided by the Indo WordNet are already linked with English synsets of Princeton University WordNet. Giving equivalent to the concept in Tuḷu and later finding synonyms for the word in Tuḷu are having its own theoretical problems which are discussed in the forthcoming sections (cf. 2.2.1).

As a part of methodological adequacy we are at a time giving equivalents both in Tuḷu and Kannaḍa. This process overloads the project with double work. But the process allows us to cross check with Kannaḍa, whenever there are problems in recognizing compounds (compound nouns, compound verbs, or compound adjectives), multiword lexical units and phrasal lexemes which are idiomatic by meaning (in all categories). In future we would like to tag up with Kannada WordNet Project. Negotiation in the respect is going on. It will be conclusive when the project is officially initiated.

2.1.1 Resources for Tulu WordNet

Resources from Tuḷu linguistics and lexical studies to develop any computerized data bases for Tuḷu are very less. The project pools up whatever the available resources which are given in the subsections below as part of the methodological process applied in the project. These are the existing resource reference works which are considered and in hand to develop the Tuḷu WordNet. As we have already mentioned that we do have lack of resources and we are working with whatever the minimum resources that we do have. Three resources those we can mention are dictionary resources, corpus resources and reference resources, details of which are given in the following section.

2.1.1.1 Dictionaries

A handful of dictionary resources which were developed in different span of the late second millennium starting form late nineteenth century, are the only resources. A land marking publication in the late twentieth century publication is the major resource. All those works are listed below.

Two dictionaries (Tuḷu-English & English-Tuḷu) compiled by Manner (Manner 1886 & 1888)
Tuḷu lexicon Vol – 1 to 6 (Tuḷu-Kannaḍa-English Upadhyaya (1988, 1992, 1995, 1997a, 1997b, & 1999)
Tuḷu-English dictionary of Madras University (Mariappa Bhat, M & Shankar Kedilaya, A. 1967)
Bernard Kolver's Tuḷu glossary (Kolver 1969)

Shivakumar's common Man's Multilingual dictionary (A Pocket dictionary) (Shivakumar, B S et al. 2008)

Certain Kannaḍa resources are also kept on the side line to the project, which are as follows:

English-Kannada dictionary of Mysore University publication

Mysale's Hindi-Kannada dictionary

2.1.1.2 Corpus

We have two hard copy publications with respect to the corpus resource, which are:

1. Janert, Klaus Ludwig & Narasimhan Poti, N. 1981
2. Kolver, Bernhard. 1969.

Out of the two former one is the corpus of Tuḷu folk songs and poetry with English translation and glossary and later one is the corpus of Tuḷu folk tales with English translation and glossary, which are suppose to be converted into soft copies by direct data entry method. To get the copy-right for the process, we are still waiting for funding.

Other than these the Rashtrakavi Govinda Pai Research Centre, an NGO at Udupi, Karnataka [karnāṭaka] has published certain books in Tuḷu using Kannaḍa script and the soft copies of those books are available in the centre. Still negotiation with the NGO is going on for utilizing their soft copies of the books as corpus. We did not receive the complete statistical details of the word count from them.

In the same way Karnataka [karnāṭaka] Tuḷu Sahithya Academy, the state Government body has published few books in Tuḷu with Kannaḍa script and we are negotiating with them to utilize the soft copies of those books for the Tuḷu corpus. A complete statistical detail of the word count is not available yet.

Dravidian University published eight books in Tuḷu, including the one of the work by the present researcher, soft copies of which is available, so that we can utilize them as raw corpus. Word count is around 70,000. Certain private authors are also publishing Tuḷu books in Kannaḍa script, but how many of them still maintaining the soft copy of those books are still under survey. Until the project gets funded we have to hold up the negotiation on remuneration grounds. However, a rough sketch of the word count may be around 250, 000.

At this stage utilizing the corpus for developing synsets and finding equivalent is not practically applied. We need to pool up the above mentioned resource for the purpose and to develop soft version of it. It will be a byproduct of this project.

2.1.1.3 Reference resources

For the structural aspects of Tuḷu language and word formation rules of Tuḷu Shetty's (2001), Paniyadi's (1932) and Brigel's (1872) grammars are considered as reference grammars. For lexical studies in Tuḷu Acharya 1983, Dey & Shetty 1976, Kekunnaya 1995, Shetty 1986, 1992, 1983, 2003 are considered as basic works on Tuḷu language.

2.1.1.4 Morphological Tools

Till now, to my knowledge, no computational tools like morphologic parsers or generators are developed for Tuḷu. In future the project may attempt to develop certain tools as byproduct of the WordNet project.

2.2 Issues and Problems of building Tuḷu WordNet

2.2.1 Theoretical issues

2.2.1.1 Finding Synonyms - Lexical Category in Tuḷu

Adjectival synsets pose specific problems in providing equivalent from Hindi and English. Moreover, they result into new synsets too. For Example:

Hindi ID 27:
CAT :: adjective
CONCEPT :: jise buddhi na ho yā bahut kam ho
EXAMPLE :: "mūrkh logoṁ se bahas nahīṁ karnī cāhie"

SYNSET-HINDI :: mūrkh, bevakūph, mūḍh, buddhū, ujabak, jaḍ, bhoṁdū, gāvār, nāsamakṣ, nādān, ajñāni, buddhihīn, budhṁgaḍ, mūrakh, bhucc, bhuccaḍ, ahamak, bāwalā, bāwarā, poṁgā, aṁdh, acatur, acet, ajñān, besamakṣ, cūtiyā, ghanacakkar, bhakua, bhakuwā, anasamakṣ, jāhīl, apaṁḍit, caṁḍūl, gāwadī, bilallā, matihīn, mūḍhātmā, mūḍhamati, muhir, abudh, abukṣ, abūkṣ, abodh, cabhok, baklol, ghoṁgha, nirbuddhi, ayānā, cugad, mūsalacaṁd, mūsaracaṁd, śīn, bāṁgaḍū, mugdhamati, pāsar, arbhak, arabhak, alpabuddhi, awicakṣaṇ, avid, avidh, avidvān, mūsar, avibudh

English ID 2655665
CAT :: adjective
CONCEPT :: devoid of intelligence
EXAMPLE :: "the shrieking of the mindless wind"
SYNSET-ENGLISH :: asinine, fatuous, inane, mindless, vacuous

Equivalent synset of Tuḷu will be as follows:
CAT :: adjective
CONCEPT :: buddi dāṁtinaṁcina attiḍa buddi kammi uppunaṁcina
EXAMPLE :: "heḍḍi janakkule sahawāsa āwaṁdī" 'company of asinine folks is no good'
SYNSET-TUḶU:: heḍḍi, eḍḍi, peddu, aṁḍe, bajibaḍḍi, daḍḍi, bōsi, bajiboddu, detti pāḍina, teriyaṁdina, matidāṁtina, matiyijjaṁdina, taredāṁtina, tareyijjaṁdina, ariwudāṁtina, ariwuyijjaṁdina, tiḷuwaḷikedāṁtina, tiḷuwaḷikeyijjaṁdina, buddidāṁtina, buddiyijjaṁdina, prajñedāṁtina, prajñeyijjaṁdina, wiwēkadaṁtina, wiwēkayijjaṁdina, awiwēki, maṁdabuddi, mūrka,

There are 27 lexical items in this synset which are good enough to fill the adjectival slot given in the example sentence. Hindi is having more than 60 synonyms. English is having 5.

However, 5 lexical items given aṁḍe, bajiboddu, detti pāḍina, awiwēki, and maṁdabuddi, are nouns also.

Here the concept homonymy plays role and these lexical items are suppose to be taken into the relevant synset of nouns with the concept 'a human / person who is devoid of intelligence'. Here we get a new synset.

The 15 synonyms of the synset, teriyaṁdina, matidāṁtina, matiyijjaṁdina, taredāṁtina, tareyijjaṁdina, ariwudāṁtina, ariwuyijjaṁdina, tiḷuwaḷikedāṁtina, tiḷuwaḷi-keyijjaṁdina, buddidāṁtina,buddiyijjaṁ-dina, prajñedāṁtina, prajñeyijjaṁdina, wiwēkadaṁtina, and wiwēkayijjaṁdina, are extracted form the noun inflection process through which any given noun in Tuḷu produces adjectival forms. All these forms are negative forms of the nouns which means 'without the [meaning of noun]'. These are the output forms of the regular inflection process that every regular noun in Tuḷu undergo and yield paradigms. Hopefully it is the same case with other Dravidian languages too.

At present we are adding all such type of forms to the synsets, but still we are not sure that it fits the theory and practice of the Global WordNet family. So this paper calls for the suggestions from the WordNet family of linguists to opinionate on this specific issue.

The adjectival lexemes heḍḍi, eḍḍi, peddu, bajibaḍḍi, daḍḍi, and bōsi, produces nouns two per each with masculine and feminine markers which are as follows:

Masculine set: heḍḍe, eḍḍe, pedde, bajibaḍḍe, daḍḍe, and bōse 'a male who is devoid of intelligence'
Feminine set: heḍḍi, eḍḍi, peddi, bajibaḍḍi, daḍḍi, and bōsi 'a female who is devoid of intelligence'

Therefore, here again we are getting another two synsets. However, since our work is based on Hindi synsets which are tagged or linked to English synsets, our search for the synsets with concepts 'a human / person who is devoid of intelligence', 'a male who is devoid of intelligence', and 'a female who is devoid of intelligence' did not yield result. We are preserving these lexical items with a note that these are the synsets sprout out of the Indo WordNet synset ID 27. The ID numbering process for the new synsets awaits the regular methods followed in the Global WordNet family. Rather than keeping them pending to attend at the end, if we can accommodate them immediately it helps to simplify the methodological practice.

2.2.1.2 Recognizing Compound Verbs

As we have already mentioned that lexical studies are not there for Tuḷu we need to recognize many compound verbs which are not listed in the Tuḷu dictionaries. However, we need to develop criteria to recognize the compound verbs which are highly active during actual communication in Tuḷu.

Eg: 1 detti pāḍina 'vacuous' ID 27

In this example the form /detti/ is past participle of the verb /deppu/ 'lift up'. The form /pāḍina/ is the relative participle of the verb /pāḍi/ 'drop'. Historically this must be a syntactic construction; however, now it is a lexical item belonging to the category of adjectives.

Eg: 2 pado paṇu 'sing' ID 236

In this synset regular verb pāḍu 'sing' is also there. pado paṇu 'sing' literally mean that 'say a song' [pado 'song' + paṇu 'sing']. This is semantically a near synonym and to pāḍu 'sing'. However, a speaker may choose a particular item depending upon the context.

The process of recognizing such compounds requires linguistic rules. Till now we are managing with the native speaker's intuition to detect such compound synonyms. We need to get work on the nature of compounding with relevant consultants.

2.2.1.3 Recognizing Phrasal Lexical Items

Phrasal lexical items are also not included in the standard Tuḷu dictionaries. These lexical items are also important in developing an efficient WordNet.

Eg: karakailu pidāyi 'evacuation' literally meaning "threw out the vessels and other utensils"
    bētāḷa lekka untu 'stand like a fool'

2.2.2 Standard Style Related Issues

As already mentioned, since Tuḷu is not a constitutionally scheduled language in India and its usage in written medium is just a century old. We still find the issues of Standard style to be used for the collection of the lexical items for the WordNet. Tuḷu has a minimum of five regional dialects and four recognizable sociolects, which are being used by the Tuḷu speakers all over coastal Karnataka [karnāṭaka].

Therefore we do not decide which regional dialect and which sociolect is suppose to be standard. In spite of it we consider common Tuḷu sociolect of all the four regional dialects as the primary source of Data. This would be more acceptable to the Tuḷu native speakers. Acceptability and usage are the main parameters in providing synsets.

However, Bramhin Tuḷu and Jain Tuḷu of all the regional dialects will be given focus too. As far as Harijan and Dalit sociolect is considered whatever it is available through the written works only those words can be taken. It is also necessary to mention that for a given synset words from all the dialects should not be there; because, some words may be common to all dialects.

For example:
ID: 226   Hindi synset: sukr, sukr grah, sūk, vīnus, ṣoḍaśāṁśu, śvētrath, sit
Tuḷu synset: bolli, sukra, sukre, sukra graho bolli (Common Tuḷu.)
sukra, sukre, sukra graho (Br.Tu & J. Tuḷu).

2.2.3 Technical issues

Tuḷu is not taught as a subject either in schools or in colleges. Moreover, it is not a scheduled language of India. There are attempts of pleading the Indian Government to consider Tuḷu under eighth-schedule. As a consequence the linguists who focused on Tuḷu were either foreign scholars or Tribal linguists (even though the Tuḷu is not a tribal language).

Therefore, for project personnel, it is inevitable to depend on the Tuḷu speakers who are having academic qualifications either in Kannaḍa or Hindi. There is no dictionary for Hindi –Tuḷu and one has to depend on Hindi- Kannaḍa Dictionary to find out lexical items for Tuḷu synsets.

The concept of synonymy, antonymy, hypernymy, hyponymy, meronymy, and holonymy are not well exercised in the Tulu linguistic studies. As a result the developing WordNet for Tulu takes lot of exercise of the above mentioned theoretical notions independently throughout the project. However, to cope with the requirements of the project we need to train the project fellows with the theory of sense relations as practiced in the WordNet project, which may take six weeks of a program for the project personnel. We need to develop samples for each sense-relation with Tuḷu examples and to run the program like an actual six week course in Lexical semantics and sense-relation.

3 Conclusion

I conclude here that developing an electronic lexical resource for Tuḷu based on the theoretical and applied grounds of Princeton University English WordNet is quite promising and novel one for the revival of Tuḷu language. The technical support from IndoWordNet team is promising and helpful. However, developing Tuḷu WordNet definitely poses many challenges than what we initially presumed due to lack of resources and expert hands. This will be overcome when the project funding comes through.

Acknowledgements

I hereby thank the three anonymous reviewers whose suggestions helped me to frame this paper into proper shape. My sincere thanks are due to Dr. Jyoti D. Pawar for her help in finding preliminary resources. My heartfelt thanks are due to Dr. Arulmozi who introduced me to the WordNet family. I express my sincere gratitude to Dr. B.P. Hemananda for his enormous help in giving a good shape to this paper.

References

Acharya, A S. 1983. 'Kinship terms in Tulu' *BDCRI* Vol. 42 pp. 1-4.

Balasubrahmanya, N. 1989. *English-Kannada Dictionary*. Vol. I Mysore: Prasaranga, Mysore University.

Balasubrahmanya, N. 1996. *English-Kannada Dictionary*. Vol. II Mysore: Prasaranga, Mysore University.

Balasubrahmanya, N. 1999. *English-Kannada Dictionary*. Vol. III Mysore: Prasaranga, Mysore University.

Balasubrahmanya, N. 2004. *English-Kannada Dictionary*. Vol. IV Mysore: Prasaranga, Mysore University.

Brigel, Rev. 1872. *A Grammar of the Tulu Language*. Mangalore: Basel Mission Book and Tract Depository.

Dey, Pradip & Shetty, Ramakrishna T. 1976. 'Echo-word construction in Tulu'. *BDCRI* Vol. 35 3-4 pp. 33-39.

Dipak Narayan, Debasri Chakrabarty, Prabhakar Pande and P. Bhattacharyya. 2002. *An Experience in Building the Indo WordNet- a WordNet for Hindi*, in First International Conference on Global WordNet, Mysore, India.

Fellbaum, Christiane (ed.). 1998. *WordNet*. Cambridge, Massachusetts: The MIT Press.

Fellbaum, Christiane. 1998. 'A Semantic network of English Verbs' *In* Fellbaum, Christiane (ed.). *WordNet*. Cambridge, Massachusetts: The MIT Press.

Janert, Klaus Ludwig & Narasimhan Poti, N. 1981. *Yakka Salare Kathe: Tulu texts of Dravidian folk poetry from South India with an English translation and glossary*. Wiesbaden: Franz Steiner Verlag.

Kekunnaya, Padmanabha. 1995. *A Comparative Study of Tulu Dialects*. Rashtrakavi Govida Pai Research Centre, Udupi.

Kolver, Bernhard. 1969. *Tulu texts with Glossary. Dravidian Tales from South India*. Wiesbaden: Franz Steiner Verlag Ljmbk.

Krishnamurti, Bh. 2003. *Dravidian Languages*. Cambridge University Press, Cambridge.

Manner, A. 1886. *Tulu-English Dictionary*. Mangalore: Basel Mission Press.

Manner, A. 1888. *English-Tulu Dictionary*. Mangalore: Basel Mission Press.

Miller, George A. 1998. 'Nouns in word net' *In* Fellbaum, Christiane (ed.). *WordNet*. Cambridge, Massachusetts: The MIT Press.

Miller, Katherine J. 1998. 'Modifiers in word net' *In* Fellbaum, Christiane (ed.). *WordNet*. Cambridge, Massachusetts: The MIT Press.

Mysale, J D. 2004 (1950). Hindi-Kannada Dictionary. Dharawad: Raamaashraya Publication.

Paniyadi, S.U. 1932. *Tulu Wyakarana*. Udupi: Tulu Press.

Shetty, Ramakrishna T. 1983. 'Post-positions in Bunt's Tulu' In *AIUTTA*: collection of papers in the thirteenth conference of Dravidian Linguistics. Annamalai Nagar.

Shetty, Ramakrishna T. 1986. 'Lexical opposites in Tulu: A brief sketch' Aayvukkovai. pp. 325-328.

Shetty, Ramakrishna T. 1992. 'Word meaning analysis in Tulu (with special reference to polysemous words)' Paper presented at the national seminar on *Word-meaning Analysis* held at Rashtrakavi Govinda Pai Research Centre. (Memeo)

Shetty, Ramakrishna T. 2001. *A Comprehensive Grammar of Tulu*. Annamalai Nagar: Annamalai University publication.

Shetty, Ramakrishna T. 2003. 'Word structure of Tulu morphology' In Ramakrishna Reddy, B (ed.) *Word Structure in Dravidian*. Kuppam: Dravidian University Publication. pp. 291-306.

Shivakumar, B S. et al. 2008. *Common Man's Multilingual Dictionary: Tulu-Kannaḍa-Telugu-Tamil-Malayalam-English*. Kuppam: Prasaaraanga, Dravidian University. (A pocket dictionary of around two thousand entries).

Subrahmanyam, P.S. 1968. 'Position of Tulu in Dravidian'. *Indian Linguistics* Vol.29.

Upadhyaya, U. P. (ed.). 1988. *Tulu Lexicon* Vol.1., Udupi: Rashtrakavi Govinda Pai Research Centre.

Upadhyaya, U. P. (ed.). 1992. *Tulu Lexicon* Vol.1., Udupi: Rashtrakavi Govinda Pai Research Centre.

Upadhyaya, U. P. (ed.). 1995. *Tulu Lexicon* Vol.1., Udupi: Rashtrakavi Govinda Pai Research Centre.

Upadhyaya, U. P. (ed.). 1997a. *Tulu Lexicon* Vol.1., Udupi: Rashtrakavi Govinda Pai Research Centre.

Upadhyaya, U. P. (ed.). 1997b. *Tulu Lexicon* Vol.1., Udupi: Rashtrakavi Govinda Pai Research Centre.

Upadhyaya, U. P. (ed.). 1997c. *Tulu Lexicon* Vol.1., Udupi: Rashtrakavi Govinda Pai Research Centre.

Vossen, P. 2001. *EuroWordNet General Document* [Computer file] Available from: http://www.hum.uva.nl/~ewn [2006, November 2]

Building a WordNet for Dravidian Languages

S. Rajendran
Department of Linguistics
Tamil University, Thanjavur
raj_ushush@yahoo.com

G. Shivapratap, V. Dhanlakshmi, KP. Soman
CEN, Amrita Vishwa Vidyapeetham
Coimbatore, India
{g_shivapratap, v_dhanalakshmi, kp_soman}
@ettimadai.amrita.edu

Abstract

This paper attempts to emphasize the need for a standalone and independent Dravidian WordNet. Since the morphology and lexical concepts of Dravidian languages are closer to each other than to a language from a different family, it is proposed to base the Dravidian WordNet on a Dravidian Language. A significant amount of work has already been done in Tamil language to understand the ontological structure and vocabulary. Based on the findings of these studies, it is proposed to build a Tamil WordNet first and then extend it to complete the Dravidian WordNet. A prototype model for the Tamil WordNet is also proposed in this paper.

1 Introduction

The current work in Machine translation from English to Indian languages and between Indian languages demands strong lexical knowledge and resources. WordNet (Fellbaum, 1998) emerges as one of the natural and indispensible tool for this cause. The WordNet by its nature turns to be an ideal lexical accessing system as it links concepts with another concept by multifarious meaning relations. WordNet not only links one concept with another concept through semantic relations, but also captures the contextual meaning variations of a particular word i.e. the polysemy of a word.

Analogous to EuroWordNet, building an Indo WordNet needs individual WordNets for all the major Indian languages. Currently, WordNets are being developed at IIT-Bombay (Hindi and Marathi), Gujarati University, Ahmedabad (Gujarathi), IIT-Kharagpur (Bengali), and Tamil University, Thanjavur in collaboration with Amrita University and Kuppam University (Dravidian languages).

Among Indian languages, Dravidian languages such as Tamil, Telugu, Kannada and Malayalam share a number of lexicalized concepts in terms of morphology and semantics besides others as in typological and culture-specific features. The authors firmly believe that building a common WordNet for Dravidian languages will make it easier in developing an Indo-WordNet.

2 Need for Dravidian Wordnet

Dravidian WordNet is a natural chunk in the Indo-WordNet. It is only ideal that we should have Dravidian WordNet before we develop a larger Indo-WordNet, because the genealogical relationship among the Dravidian languages can be maximally exploited in a more natural way. It allows, for example, a search tool to infer other terms, from the terms provided by the user and coming up with the most optimal search for retrieving information.

Currently, the IndoWordNet is built using the Hindi wordnet as the source language. This approach is simpler and economical considering the interlinking of synsets of different languages. However, using source words from a different language family as a base to create synsets for Dravidian languages will restrict the syntactic envelope of the words in Dravidian languages. Hence, in order to capture the entire semantics, morphology and lexicalized concepts in Dravidian languages, we propose to build an independent WordNet for Dravidian languages.

3 Design of Dravidian WordNet

The design and implementaion of the Dravidian WordNet will be based on EuroWordNet as explained by Pike Vossen (1998). The WordNet database will be built (as much as possible) from available existing resources and databases with semantic information developed in various projects. This will be not only more cost-effective given the limited time and budget of the project, but also will make it possible to combine information from independently created Word-

Nets. Two models (Vossen, 1999) will be involved in the built up.

- **Merge Model**: the selection will be done in a local resource and the synsets and their language-internal relations will be first developed separately, after which the equivalence relations to Tamil WordNet will be generated.
- **Expand Model**: the selection will be done in Tamil WordNet and the Tamil WordNet synsets will be translated (using bilingual dictionaries) into equivalent synsets in the other language. The WordNet relations will be later on adopted across languages.

The Merge Model will result in a WordNet that will be independent of Tamil WordNet, possibly maintaining the language-specific properties. The Expand model will result in a WordNet that is very close to Tamil WordNet but which is also biased by it.

3.1 Dravidian WordNet as Extension of Tamil WordNet

The design of the Dravidian WordNet-database will be first of all based on the ontological structure of Tamil WordNet which in turn is based on a thesaurus for Tamil prepared by Rajendran (2001). Tamil WordNet relies on extensive preliminary investigations of the vocabulary of Tamil (Rajendran, 1976-2003) based on the componential analysis of meaning (Nida, 1975a & 1975b) and structural semantics (Lyons, 1977). Portions of this work have been compiled into a Tamil thesaurus (Rajendran, 2001). The Tamil thesaurus in electronic form represents the Ontological Structure of Tamil (OST) vocabulary giving scope to take care of any kind of semantic/lexical relations that hold between lexical items. The notion of a synset and the main semantic relations will be taken over in Dravidian WordNet. However, some specific changes will be made to the design of the database, which are mainly motivated by the following objectives:

- to create a multilingual database;
- to maintain language-specific relations in the WordNet;
- to achieve maximal compatibility across the different resources;
- to build the WordNets relatively independently (re)-using existing resources;

The most important difference of Dravidian WordNet with respect to a language specific WordNet is its multilinguality, which however also raises some fundamental questions with respect to the status of the monolingual information in the WordNets. In principle, multilinguality will be achieved by adding an equivalence relation for each synset in a language to the closest synset in Tamil WordNet. Synsets linked to the same Tamil WordNet synset will be supposed to be equivalent or close in meaning and can then be compared. However, we have to take into consideration the differences across the WordNets. If 'equivalent' words are related in different ways in the different resources, we have to make a decision about the legitimacy of these differences.

In Dravidian WordNet, we will take the position that it must be possible to reflect such differences in lexical semantic relations. The WordNets are seen as linguistic ontologies rather than ontologies for making inferences only. In an inference-based ontology it may be the case that a particular level or structuring is required to achieve a better control or performance, or a more compact and coherent structure. For this purpose it may be necessary to introduce artificial levels for concepts which are not lexicalized in a language or it may be necessary to neglect levels that are lexicalized but not relevant for the purpose of the ontology. A linguistic ontology, on the other hand, exactly reflects the lexicalization and the relations between the words in a language. It is a "WordNet" in the true sense of the word and therefore captures valuable information about conceptualizations that are lexicalized in a language: what is the available stock of words and expressions in a language. In addition to the theoretical motivation there is also a practical motivation for considering the WordNets as autonomous networks. To be more cost-effective, they will be derived (as far as possible) from existing resources, databases and tools. Each site therefore will have different starting points for building their local

WordNet, making it necessary to allow for a maximum of flexibility in producing the WordNets and structures.

3.2 Prototype Implementation

An initial prototype for Tamil WordNet is proposed which can be extended for Dravidian WordNet. In this approach, we try to define and formalize synsets and their relationships using Set theory and first-order logic. A synset is considered as a unique record which consists of the following attributes:

1. Synonyms: words are interchangeable without modifying the context.
2. POS tag: specifies if the synonyms are nouns, verbs, adjectives or adverbs
3. Description
4. Example

The synsets are basically classified into 4 top level sets, namely Nouns, Verbs, Adjectives and Adverbs. Whenever a synset S_i is read into the database by the WordNet interface, the POS tag attribute is checked and the synset is included into the appropriate top level set. Each synset is given a unique id. In parallel, the list of synonyms in the synset is extracted and compiled into a dictionary. While building the dictionary, it is ensured that each word is mapped to list of all the synsets containing that word.

$$D(w) = \{S_1, S_2, ...S_n\} \quad n >= 0$$

We must now establish semantic relations between synsets in each of the top level set. For the Nouns set, we define hyponymy, hypernymy, meronymy, and holonymy. The synsets in the Verb set are related to each other by hyponymy, hypernymy and similarity. The synsets in the Adjectives and Adverbs set relate to each other using similarity. For each top level set, a relationship matrix R can be maintained that captures the semantic relationship between synsets. The rows of R will correspond to the unique synsets in that top level set and the columns of R correspond to the different semantic relations. Each r_{ij} in R can be considered as the set of all synsets S_k that are related to S_i using the semantic relation j.

Alternatively, using first order logic, we can define the semantic envelope of a word w as:
$SE(w_{noun}) = Hyponym(S_i) \cup Hypernym(S_i) \cup Meronym(S_i) \cup Holonym(S_i)$ where $S_i \in$ Nouns
$SE(w_{verbs}) = Hyponym(S_i) \cup Hypernym(S_i) \cup Similar(S_i) \; S_i \in$ Verbs
$SE(w_{adjectives}) = Similar(S_i) \; S_i \in$ Adjectives
$SE(w_{adverbs}) = Similar(S_i) \; S_i \in$ Adverbs

A simple block diagram of the prototype is shown in Figure 1

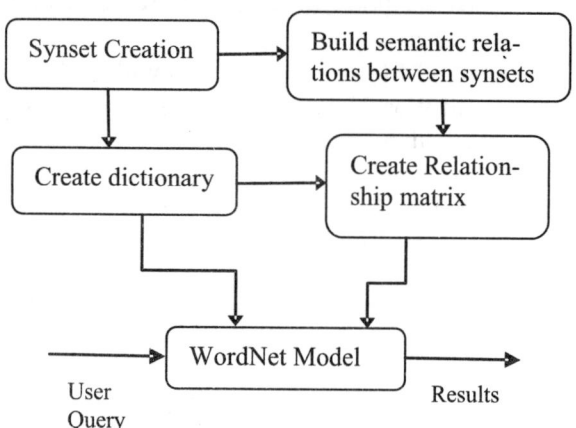

Prototype of Wordnet

4 Utilities and Applications

Dravidian WordNet will provide a multilingual network of words linked by semantic relations. This will allow, for example, a search tool to infer other terms, from terms provided by the user, which should be used in searching for information. The network will also provide support across different languages converting terms from one language into other languages. This is particularly useful for users working in a second language and may not have appropriate knowledge of vocabulary. The network will also be used as a basic resource for supporting other applications. The semantic knowledge embodied in the network makes it suitable as a component in expert systems, language translation aids, language learning systems and automatic summarizers.

For application developers the production of a multilingual set of word nets will allow applications to be developed, which can work with a selected language or over a range of languages. This will allow Dravidian developers to compete effectively in the now predominantly (American) English market, providing solutions which work with the user's own language. In addition, it will be possible to create applications which can access and provide information in languages other than the user's own language.

Users will be provided with more effective and powerful tools that they can use in their own language. Applications such as information retrieval will allow non-expert users to access the information they want without the need for familiarity with indexing schemes and terms. Improved access to information will itself provide benefits for European industry, administration and citizens. The support for different languages will reduce language barriers to information whilst retaining the benefits of diversity in expression and culture that the range of Dravidian languages provides.

The resources produced by DWN will have a wide range of users. The current user group, which provides feedback on intermediate project results, comprises members from libraries, software developers, universities and publishers interested in language learning, language generation, machine aided translation, language understanding, information retrieval, electronic publishing and the production of WordNet in additional languages. The end users of the resources will be all those people who utilize the applications that incorporate DWN resources.

5 Conclusion

This paper has attempted to illustrate the need for an independent Dravidian WordNet. As a first step towards building a Dravidian WordNet, a prototype design for Tamil WordNet has also been proposed. WordNet is a natural answer in machine translation systems. It has the potential to interpret source language words and come up with lexical equivalents in the target language in a more natural way as a bilingual does. Building of WordNet is an immediate requirement in the context of information technology equipped with internet in which the web sites in Dravidian languages are getting added up day by day.

References

Alonge, A., N. Calzolari, P. Vossen, L. Bloksma, I. Castellon, T. Marti, W. Peters. 1998. *The Linguistic Design of the EuroWordNet Database*. In: Nancy Ide, Daniel Greenstein, Piek Vossen (eds). Special Issue on EuroWordNet. Computers and the Humanities, Vol 32, Nos. 2-3, 91-115.

Beckwith, R. and G.A. Miller. 1990. *Implementing a Lexical Network*. International Journal of Lexicography, Vol 3, No.4, 302-312.

Cruse, D.A. 1986. *Lexical Semantics*. Cambridge: Cambridge University Press.

Fellbaum, C. 1990. *English Verbs as a Semantic Net*. International Journal of Lexicography, Vol 3, No.4, 278-301.

Fellbaum, C. 1998. *A Semantic Network of English Verbs*. In: Fellbaum, C. (ed.). WordNet: An Electronic Lexical Database. Cambridge: MIT Press.

Fellbaum, C. (ed.) 1998. *WordNet: An Electronic Lexical Database*. Cambridge, MA: MIT Press.

Gross, D. and K.J. Miller 1990. *Adjectives in Wordnet*. International Journal of Lexicography, Vol 3, No.4, 265-277.

Lyons, J. 1977. *Semantics* (vol.1). Cambridge: Cambridge University Press.

Miller, G.A.1990. *Nouns in WordNet: a lexical inheritance system*. International Journal of Lexicography Vol 3, No. 4, 245-264.

Miller, G.A. 1991. *Science of Words*. New York: Scientific American Library.

Miller, G.A. 1998. *Nouns in WordNet*. In: Fellbaum, C. (ed.). 1998. WordNet: An Electronic Lexical Database. Cambridge: MIT Press

Miller G.A., R. Beckwith, C. Fellbaum, D. Gross, K.J. Miller. 1990. *Introduction to WordNet: An On-line Lexical Database*. International Journal of Lexicography, Vol 3, No.4, 235-244.

Miller, K.J. 1998. *Modifiers in WordNet*. In: Fellbaum, C. (ed.). 1998. WordNet: An Electronic Lexical Database. Cambridge: MIT Press

Nida, E.A. 1975a. *Compositional Analysis of Meaning: An Introduction to Semantic Structure*. The Hague: Mouton

Nida, E.A. 1975.b. *Exploring Semantic Structure*. The Hague: Mouton

Pustejovsky, J. 1995. *The Generative Lexicon*. Cambridge: MIT Press.

Rajendran. S, 1983. *Semantics of Tamil Vocabulary*. (Report of the UGC sponsored Postdoctoral Work in manuscript). Poona: Deccan College Post-Doctoral Research Institute.

Rajendran. S, 1995. *Towards a Compilation of a Thesaurus for Modern Tamil*. South Asian Language Review 5.1:62-99.

Rajendran. S, 2001. *taRkaalat tamizc coRkaLanjciyam* [Thesaurus for Modern Tamil]. Thanjavur: Tamil University.

Rajendran. S, 2002. *Preliminaries to the preparation of a Word Net for Tamil.* Language in India 2:1, www.languageinindia.com

Rajendran. S, 2003. *Pre-requisite for the Preparation of an Electronic Thesaurus for a Text Processor in Indian Languages.* Language in India 3:1, www.languageinindia.com

Rajendran, S., S. Arulmozi, B. Kumara Shanmugam, S. Baskaran, and S. Thiagarajan. 2002. *Tamil WordNet.* Proceedings of the First International Global WordNet Conference. Mysore: CIIL, 271-274.

Tengi, R.I. 1998. *Design and Implementation of the WordNet Lexical Database and Searching Software.* In: Fellbaum, C. (ed.). 1998. WordNet: An Electronic Lexical Database. Cambridge: MIT Press.

Vossen P. (eds.) 1999. *EuroWordNet: a multilingual database with lexical semantic networks for European Languages.* Dordrecht: Kluwer Academic Publishers,.

Vossen P. 1999 fc., *EuroWordNet as a multilingual database.* In: Wolfgang Teubert (ed). Berlin: Mouton Gruyter.

Tamil WordNet

S. Rajendran
Department of Linguistics
Tamil University, Thanjavur 613010
raj_ushush@yahoo.com

Abstract

Wordnets for Indian Languages have been getting built on a massive scale under the stewardship of Pushpak Bhattacharyya, who is the torch bearer of the wordnet development in India. Wordnet preparation for Indian languages is in full swing. Wordnet building for Tamil has been started quite earlier parallel to Hindi wordnet. A Tamil wordnet model has been prepared and put as an open source in a website. Now the Tamil team has joined hands with the Indo-wordnet teams to build Tamil wordnet as one of the components of the bigger Dravidian wordnet. The paper presents the experience of the Tamil wordnet team.

1 Introduction

A wordnet plays an important role both in the development of NLP applications such as a machine translation system and a question-answering system as well as for lexical studies of a language. While wordnets have been already compiled for most of the European languages, these resources are under preparation for Indian languages. This paper presents the lexicographic and computational issues faced in an attempt to build a Tamil wordnet.

2 Characteristics of Tamil

Tamil is a Dravidian language. It is a verb final, relatively free-word order and morphologically rich language. Like other Dravidian languages, Tamil is agglutinative. Computationally, each root word can take a few thousand inflected word-forms, out of which only a few hundred will exist in a typical corpus. Subject-verb agreement is required for the grammaticality of a Tamil sentence. Tamil allows subject and object drop as well as verbless sentences. In addition, the subject of a sentence or a clause can be a possessive Noun Phrase (NP) or an NP in nominative or dative case. As Tamil is an agglutinative language, several suffixes can be added to the root word, thus forming thousands of different word forms.

The verb is the chief constituent of a sentence. Verbs take different argument structures based on their semantic nature. These argument structures define the case markers of noun phrases, which are, for instance, direct and indirect objects to the verb. In addition, the predicate which is in finite form has to agree with the subject in terms of person-number-gender (e.g. *avan vandtaan* 'he came_3PMS'). In Tamil, two noun phrases can constitute a sentence (*avan maaNavan* 'he student' 'He is a student'). As Tamil has relatively free word-order, the constituents of a sentence can be shuffled retaining the same meaning (*avan pazham caappiTTaan* 'he fruit ate_3PMS', *pazham avan caappiTTaan* 'fruit he ate_3PMS' 'He ate a fruit').

Tamil nouns are inflected for case and number (plural). The morphotactics of nominal forms of Tamil is as follows:

Noun + (Plural maker) + Case marker

Consider the morphological decomposition of *kaalkaLai* 'legs_ACC':

kaalkaLai => *kaal* <N> + *kaL* <plural> + *ai* <accusative case>

Verbs are inflected for tense and finite and nonfinite markers. A finite verb shows subject-agreement marker.

Verb + Tense + Subject agreement marker (person-number-gender)

Consider the morphological decomposition of the word *paTittaan* 'he read':
paTittaan => *paTi*<V> + *tt* <past tense> + *aan* <3rd person, singular, masculine>

The agreement marker can simultaneously represent three distinct grammatical features: person, number and gender. For example, the morpheme –*aan* itself indicates the third person, singular number and masculine gender.

3 Challenges of representing lexical knowledge in Tamil

There is often a clash between scientific taxonomy and folk taxonomy, particularly in such areas as those of flora and fauna. As Tamil is aiming to equip itself for scientific use, preference may be felt for a scientific classification over that enshrined in folk taxonomy which reflect culture. Modern scientific taxonomy excludes *iraal* 'shrimp' from its traditional place in the class of fish, and classifies *vauvaal* 'bat' not as a bird but as an animal. We would wish to place *puumi* 'earth' and *cantiran* 'moon' separately from *naTcattirankaL* 'stars' and *cuuriyan* 'sun' along with 'stars', and to eliminate *iraaku* 'a mythical serpent believed to consume the sun and the moon and cause eclipses' and *keetu* 'a mythical celestial dragon believed to cause eclipses' from the class of astronomical phenomena. Preference for astronomy over astrology reflects a contemporary scientific approach to ontology.

Tamil being a Dravidian language holds some unique features which cannot be represented in the "expansion approach" of finding equivalents to Hindi synsets.

Tamil forms pronominalized nouns from verb stems by a productive derivative process:

va-ndt-a-van 'come_PAST_RP_3PMS' 'he who came'
paTi-tt-a-van 'study_PAST_RP_3PMS' 'he who studied/educated male person'

Adjective also forms such pronominalized forms: *nalla-van* 'good_3PMS' 'good male person'

Such derivative forms are not found in Hindi. Similarly syntax of adjective is different form that of Hindi. In Hindi, like English, adjective can occur as a complement to the 'be' verb occupying predicate position. In Tamil adjective cannot occur independently in the predicate position. Only the pronominalized forms of the adjectives can occur in the predicate position. For example, *vah acchaa hai* in Hindi has been translated into Tamil as *avan naalavan* 'he good_3PMS' 'He is good'.

4 Challenges to creating synsets

Creating synset for a concept, though appears simple at the outset, the complexity arises when synsets are created based on Hindi/English glosses. The untrained lexicographers are tempted to find out equivalents for the set of words grouped under a synset. Mostly they get biased by the words listed under each Hindi synset. The co-synonyms given under a synset are mostly misleading; words which are different in meaning are put under the same synset.

The arrangement of co-synonyms given under each synset need to be considered seriously. Though a number of words are given as synonyms, they may vary by style or register. The order of precedence of co-synonyms in a synset can be based on the frequency of occurrence in a corpus. But in the absence of a corpus with the information on frequency of occurrence of words, this is not feasible. One has to depend on ones own intuition. But in Tamil context, this too creates problem. For example, though *cuuriyan* 'sun' and *candtiran* 'moon' are the frequently used words, because of their Sanskrit origin, they are not be given precedence over other items.

There is a unique set of verbal nouns in Tamil formed by the suffixation of *–kai, -tal* and *–al* to verb stems (e.g. *varukai, varutal, varal;* they all mean 'coming'). Though the corresponding three members can be considered as synonyms belonging to a synset, they differ in their syntactic distribution.

5 Challenges to linking with English and Hindi synsets

Linking English and Hindi synsets with their Tamil equivalents throw challenges in a number of cases. The following problems are noted by the lexicographers:

ID 591: *maarnaa* 'beat' is given a wrong gloss 'land'

ID 1392: Hindi synset of the concept *bhaims* which means 'buffalo' is given gloss in English as 'buffalo'. But in ID 1411 for Hindi *bhaimsa* which means 'female buffalo', English gloss is given as 'buffalo' instead of 'female buffalo'.

ID 1427: For the Hindi synset of the concept *duniyaa* which means 'world', the words *mrutyulook* which means 'dead world' and *jiivlook* which means 'living world' are given as co-synonyms.

ID 1492 : For Hindi concept which means 'balcony', the example is given to mean 'shed'.

ID 1683: For the Hindi concept which means 'lion', the synset includes words denoting tiger. In Tamil separate words are used for 'lion' and 'tiger'.

ID 9199: The Hindi word *sambandhini* which means 'lady member of the person related by a marriage alliance', Tamil equivalent is not available. Tamil *campati* means 'person related by a marriage alliance'.

ID 6672: For Hindi word *hiraN* 'male dear', English gloss is given wrongly as "sheet, flat_solid".

ID 4226: For Hindi *daND* 'punishment', English gloss is given wrongly as 'music, medicine'.
ID 120, 121: The synonyms given for the Hindi concepts *preem* 'love' and *sneeh* 'affectionateness' are misleading.

ID 24: For the Hindi *sheerni* which means "female lion", the words denoting tiger are given as co-synonyms. This causes confusion.

ID 172: For the Hindi *aparaadhi* which means 'accused', Tamil has an equivalent only in nominal form. The word which appears at the modifier position of a compound word is given adjective status in Hindi. If all the nouns at the modifier position in compounds are given adjective status, then there will be multiple categorical status for a single lexical item.

The senses relation metonymy sometimes creates problem. For example, the names of trees and fruits which are metonymically related have same forms in Hindi. This creates confusion in Tamil. For example, *aam* in Hindi means both tree as well as fruit, where as in Tamil separate words are available to denote mango tree and mango fruit: *maamaram* 'mango tree' and *maampazham* 'mango fruit'.

6 Computational environment and tasks in linking

The synset correspondences are made for individual words. The working tool goes by synsets. There is always a chance of misinterpreting the meaning even though meanings are provided in Hindi and English with examples. (Some of the examples and descriptions are not free from ambiguity.) If the synsets are given keeping mind the hierarchical relations (or thesaurus-classification), the lexicographers can do the job of finding equivalents in their languages for Hindi concepts efficiently.

7 Interfacing issues

The working tool in which the synsets corresponding to Hindi have to be filled up does not contain information on semantic relations such as hyponymy-hypernymy, meronymy-holonymy, antonymy, troponymy, etc. Such information may help the lexicographers to find correct correspondences.

8 No. of synsets linked, difficult synsets etc.

2000 synsets have been linked. 2851 unique words are found for 1969 synsets. The following table gives the number of synsets in each grammatical category based on the number of co-synonyms found.

	Nouns	Verbs	Adj	Adv
Synsets	2403	223	172	53
1	1938	153	105	30
2	291	47	38	15
3	89	18	20	5
4	28	4	7	3
5	29	1	2	--
6	15	--	--	--
7	7	--	--	--
8	3	--	--	--
9	1	--	--	--
10	1	--	--	--
11	1	--	--	--

As verbs are more polysemous than other categories and their meaning depends on the words associated with them, deciding on the co-synonyms needs to be done with great care.

9 Conclusion

Presently only the concepts, synsets and examples have been dealt with. The semantic relations such like antonymy, hypernymy, hyponymy, meronymy, holonymy, troponymy, entailment etc. are ignored. If the individual wordnets are built based on the underlying ontology (at least on a thesaurus-classification) and semantic relations linking concepts, the lexicographers will find it easy to build their wordnet with their native intuition. But at present we are asked to give equivalents for Hindi concepts. Such approach is unnatural and ad hoc. That makes the job of building wordnet uninteresting and unscientific. This approach leads to committing mistakes. What we are engaged to make is creating a Hindi-Tamil bilingual dictionary, rather than a wordnet.

The expansion approach, though economical, will be biased over Hindi. For a language like Tamil which has rich lexical resources already available in electronic and paper forms, it is advisable to build its own wordnet independently and then link it with Indo-wordnet.

References

English WordNet - A Lexical Database for English, http://wordnet.princeton.edu/, 2009.

George A. Miller, Richard Beckwith, Christiane Fellbaum, Derek Gross, and Katherine Miller. 1993. *Five Papers on WordNet*, MIT press. www.mit.edu/~6.863/spring2009/readings/5papers.pdf

Hindi WordNet - A Lexical Database for Hindi, http://www.cfilt.iitb.ac.in/wordnet/webhwn/, 2009.

Hindi WordNet Documentation, http://www.cfilt.iitb.ac.in/wordnet/webhwn/other/hwn_docs_2.doc, 2009.

Manish Sinha, Mahesh Reddy, Pushpak Bhattacharyya. 2006. *An Approach towards Construction and Application of Multilingual Indo-WordNet*, Third International Conference on Global WordNet, Jeju Island, Korea.

Rajendran, S. 2001. *taRkaalat tamizc coRkaLanjciyam* [Thesaurus for Modern Tamil]. Tamil University, Thanjavur.

Rajendran, S. 2002. '*Preliminaries to the preparation of a Word Net for Tamil.*' Language in India 2:1, www.languageinindia.com

Rajendran, S., S. Arulmozi, B. Kumara Shanmugam, S. Baskaran, and S. Thiagarajan. 2002. "*Tamil WordNet*." Proceedings of the First International Global WordNet Conference. CIIL, Mysore, 271-274.

Vossen P. (eds.) 1998. EuroWordNet: A Multilingual Database with Lexical Semantic Networks. Kluwer Academic Publishers, Dordrecht.

Telugu WordNet

S. Arulmozi
Department of Dravidian and Computational Linguistics
Dravidian University, Kuppam 517425, India
arulmozi@gmail.com

Abstract

This paper describes an attempt to develop Telugu WordNet, particularly construction of synsets in Telugu language along the lines of Hindi synsets using the expansion approach. Based on the Hindi WordNet synsets, we assign Telugu synsets manually using the Offline Tool Interface. We share the challenges faced in the construction of core synsets from Hindi into Telugu language. A brief account on Telugu language and its notable features are also provided.

1 Introduction

WordNet building activities in Dravidian languages started with the work of Tamil WordNet[1] at AU-KBC Research Centre using Rajendran's (2001) ontological classification of Tamil vocabulary. Work on Dravidian WordNet (comprising WordNets in four major Dravidian languages, viz. Kannada, Malayalam, Tamil and Telugu) started during a Workshop[2] held at Chennai in which synsets were built for Construction Domain. Currently Dravidian WordNet[3] activity is being carried out for Kannada at University of Hyderabad, Malayalam at Amrita Vishwa Vidyapeetham, Tamil at Tamil University and Telugu at Dravidian University.

In this paper, we describe the construction of synsets for Telugu language. Based on the Hindi WordNet synsets, we aim to develop synsets in Telugu using the expand model. The paper is organized as follows: Section 2 gives a brief account on the morphological features of Telugu language. This section also provides the language technology activities pertaining to Telugu language. Section 3 details the Telugu synset building activity, challenges/problems faced during the construction of synsets.

Section 4 gives a statistical account on the synsets developed. The last section summarizes the work.

2 The Telugu Language

Telugu belongs to the South Central Dravidian subgroup of the Dravidian family of languages. It has recorded history from 6th Century A.D. and literary history dating back to 11th Century A.D. It has been recently awarded the Classical Status. It is the second most spoken language after Hindi in India. Telugu has been the language of choice for lyrical compositions for its vowel ending words, rightly called the "Italian of the East".

The vocabulary of Telugu is highly Sanskritized in addition to the Persian-Arabic borrowings కబురు/ kaburu/ `story ', జవాబు /javaabu/ `answer '; Urdu తరాజు /taraaju/ `balance'. It does have cognates in other Dravidan languages such as పులి /puli/ `tiger ', ఊరు /uuru/ `village'; తల /tala/ `head'.

Words in Dravidian languages, especially in Telugu are long and complex. i.e. because it also suffixation, words are build up from many affixes that combine with one another. Telugu, like other Dravidian languages is highly rich in morphology and hence agglutinative in nature; it also allows polyagglutination.

Telugu has the state-of-the-art Morphological Analyser [4] and Telugu-Hindi, Hindi-Telugu, Telugu-Tamil, Tamil-Telugu MT systems[5]. In addition to this, the Resource Centre for Indian Language Technology Solutions-Telugu (RCILTS) established by the Ministry of Communications and IT, Govt.of India during 2000-2003 has developed several products,

---

[1] Project partially funded by Tamil Virtual University.
[2] Workshop on WordNet for Dravidian Languages organized from 2-3 June 2003
[3] Project funded by the Ministry of HRD, Govt. of India.

[4] Developed by G.Uma Maheswar Rao at the Centre for ALTS, University of Hyderabad.
[5] Consortia on Indian-Language-Indian Language MT systems established by MCIT, GoI.

services and knowledge bases pertaining to Telugu language. They include Drishti, the first comprehensive OCR system in Telugu, Tel-Spell, Spell checker for Telugu, Telugu Corpus (9.2 m words)[6], etc.

This effort on building a WordNet for Telugu is the first of its kind along the lines of Hindi WordNet.

3 Construction of Telugu WordNet

Various approaches are followed in the construction of WordNets across the languages of the world. For the Indian languages, WordNets are constructed using the expand model.

For the construction of Telugu WordNet, we also follow the expand model. i.e. Hindi WordNet synsets are taken as a starting point of departure. The concepts provided along with the Hindi synsets are first conceived and appropriate concepts in Telugu are manually provided by language experts. The Telugu synsets are then built based on the concepts created keeping in view the three principles, viz. Minimality, Coverage and Replaceability.

For the building of synsets, we use the OfflineTool provided along with Hindi WordNet synsets. This standalone interface allows users to view the Hindi synsets, concepts, example sentence on the one side and simultaneously keying the target language (Telugu in our case) synsets, concepts and example sentence. The tool also has the Princeton WordNet English synsets interlinked. This helps the language experts to cross check with English WordNet synsets.

Below we present the challenges/problems faced in the construction of 2000 core synsets from Hindi into Telugu.

3.1 Expansion from Hindi/English into Telugu

For the construction of Telugu synsets, we use the OfflineTool provided by Hindi WordNet group. We have encountered certain problems with regard to the tool. We have also faced specific problems while rendering corresponding synsets, concepts in Telugu. Below we present few of the computational and lexicographical concerns.

---

[6] Achievements of RCILTS-Telugu, TDIL

3.1.1 Computational Concerns

The interface[7] has the following problems:

1. In the target language box, complete option does not show how many synsets are completed. It was working in the earlier version.

2. By mistake, if the user opens the tool for the second time, there shall be a message displayed stating, that the tool is already open.

3. The tool does not work when logged-in as a Guest user (in Windows Vista). Whenever guest user is logged in and opens the tool, it does not allow to SAVE the data.

4. When X-Link (Synset Linker) is invoked, the popup window does not display any options.

5. Everytime the user has to use the exit button to close the tool, instead the close option X shall be enabled.

3.1.2 Lexicographical Concerns

1. Hindi synsets ID 5499:

Synset IDs are the same in both versions (2.0 and 2.1) of Offline Tool. Subsequently, the concept, example and sysnets are the same.

But in version 2.0 of the OfflineTool, EWN ID is 1214525 and it displays the Concept as: "the social act of assembling"; Example as: "they demanded the right of assembly"; Synset: "assembly, assemblage, gathering" and in version 2.1, PWD ID is 8069519 displaying the Concept as: "a large number of things or people considered together"; Example: "a crowd of insects assembled around the flowers"; Synset: "crowd".

Now, this is a problem when one tries to manually assign synsets in Telugu based on the Hindi/English synsets.

2. Hindi ID Number 7379:

The concept भाई का लड़का /bhai ka ladka/ which means `brother's son' is an interesting problem. The synsets given for this concept in Hindi are

---

[7] Offline Tool Version 2.1

"भतीजा, भ्रातृज, भ्रातापुत्र, भ्रातृपुत्र, भतीज, अवतंस, अवतन्स" /BatIjA, BrAtRuja, BrAtAputra, BrAtRuputra, BatIja, avataMsa, avatansa/ which all means 'brother's son' in Hindi. When it comes to Telugu, providing concept is a challenge. Straightforward, one can assign సోదరుని కుమారుడు /sOdaruni kumAruDu/. But

when assigning synsets, one has to cope up with the ambiguity in the concept. i.e. whose brother;s son.

In any case, we have provided equivalent as అన్న కొడుకు /anna koDuku/.

Similar challenge faced in ID 1804.

3. Hindi synset ID: 7531

Concept:
चालीस सेर की एक तौल

cAlIsa sera kI eka taula

which means 'a measure of 40 kg'.

For this concept, there is no corresponding equivalent in Telugu. But there are different usages in different dialects of Andhra Pradesh. For example, in Kuppam, the measure is equal to 10 kg whereas in Kadapa it is 14 kg.

When it comes to providing equivalent synsets, Hindi and Telugu uses the same, i.e. *manu*.

4. Hindi Synset ID: 1602

Concept:
व्यापार करनेवाला व्यक्ति

vyApAra karanevAlA vyakti

which means 'bookbinder'

The English IDs given for the above mentioned Hindi synset ID is different from Version 2.0 to Version 2.1.

In Version 2.0 of OfflineTool, EWN ID is 10560080 and the concept given is "someone who purchases and maintains an inventory of goods to be sold", and synsets are "trader, bargainer, dealer, monger".

In Version 2.1, under PWN ID 9736400, the concept is "a person engaged in commercial or industrial business (especially an owner or executive) and the synsets are "businessman, man of affairs".

5. Hindi Synset ID: 1680

Concept:
बहुत बड़ा या विशेष ऊँचाई का या जिसका विस्तार ऊपर की ओर अधिक हो
bahuta baDxA yA viSeSha UMcAyI kA yA jisakA vistAra Upara kI ora adhika ho

For the above mentioned Hindi concept, the corresponding English synsets in both the versions are completely different.

In the 2.0 version, for the EWN ID 1250892, the concept given is "the action of establishing on a socialist basis"; example given is "the socialization of medical services" and the synsets are "socialization, socialisation".

In 2.1 version, for the PWN ID 1250892, the concept given is "(literal meaning) being at or having a relatively great or specific elevation or upward extension (sometimes used in combinations like "knee-high"", example is "a high mountain", and so on and the synset is "high".

These kinds of synsets pose a real problem for the language experts because whenever they assign a concept/synset, it creates a confusion. Further, it

We have presented only few challenges and problems faced in the construction of Telugu WordNet using Hindi synsets. The real challenge will come up once we start working horizontally on synsets.

4 Statistics

The status of Telugu WordNet after completion of core (2k) synsets is given below:

No. of Core Synsets: 2000
No. of unique words: 4270

Out of 2000 core synsets in Telugu, 3489 are noun synsets with synsets ranging from 1-11; 521 are verb synsets ranging from 1-6; 498 adjective synsets ranging from 1-8 and 145 adverb synsets ranging from 1-7. The unique words from all the POS categories for the 2000 core synsets is 4270.

	Nouns	Verbs	Adj	Adv
Synsets	3489	521	498	145
1	495	50	34	8
2	454	90	53	15
3	334	58	43	16
4	131	21	31	9
5	53	3	12	2
6	13	3	5	1
7	15	0	1	1
8	8	0	1	0
9	3	0	0	0
10	1	0	0	0
11	1	0	0	0

Table 1: Status of Telugu Synsets

5 Summary

In this paper, we have described the approach that is followed for the construction of Telugu WordNet. A brief note on the characteristics of Telugu language and the language technology activity in Telugu is also provided. The manual synset building activity of 2000 core synsets with specific problems faced is discussed. Work is in progress for completing 10k common synsets and this will be made available during the presentation.

Acknowledgements

The work on Telugu WordNet activity is part of the larger effort on building a Dravidian WordNet and funded by the Ministry of Human Resource Development, Government of India.

References

Brown, C.P. 1857. *A Grammar of the Telugu Language*. Christian Knowledge Society's Press, Madras.

Burrow, T. and Emeneau, M. B. 1984. *Dravidian Etymological Dictionary*. Munshiram Manoharlal Publishers, New Delhi.

Fellbaum, C. (ed.). 1998. *WordNet: An Electronic Lexical Database*. The MIT Press.

Krishnamurti, Bh. 1961. *Telugu Verbal Bases*. University of Chicago Press, Berkeley.

Krishnamurti, Bh. And Gwynn, J.P.L. 1985. *A Grammar of Modern Telugu*. Oxford Univeristy Press, New Delhi.

Krishnamurti, Bh. 2003. *The Dravidian Languages*. Cambridge University Press, Cambridge.

Narayan, D., Chakrabarty D., Pandey P. and Bhattacharyya, P. 2002. `An Experience in Building the Indo WordNet- a WordNet for Hindi', *International Conference on Global WordNet*, Mysore.

Miller, G.A. 1995.` WordNet: A Lexical Database for English', *Communications of the ACM*. Vol.38, No.11.

Rajendran, S. 2001. *taRkaalat tamizhc coRkaLanjciyam* [Modern Tamil Thesaurus]. Tamil University Publication, Thanjavur.

Toward plWordNet 2.0

Maciej Piasecki
Institute of Informatics
Wrocław Univ. of Technology
maciej.piasecki@pwr.wroc.pl

Stanisław Szpakowicz
SITE, University of Ottawa and
ICS, Polish Academy of Sciences
szpak@site.uottawa.ca

Bartosz Broda
Institute of Informatics
Wrocław Univ. of Technology
bartosz.broda@pwr.wroc.pl

Abstract

Three years in development, the first release of a Polish wordnet contains almost 27000 lexical units grouped into some 17700 synsets. We look back at this completed first stage of the project, beginning with its main assumptions. We reconsider the challenges; we show how well they have been met and how many remain for the future. We discuss the benefits of semi-automatic wordnet expansion based only on information extracted from corpora. Next, we outline the plan for another three years, now devoted to growth – in the size of the network and in the variety of the underlying semantic relations.

1 All about plWordNet 1.0

There were no Polish wordnets or other NLP-friendly thesauri as late as in 2006[1]. The plWordNet project has set out three years ago to build such a resource[2] (Derwojedowa et al., 2009; Piasecki et al., 2009). Given very modest funding and the pressing need for a Polish wordnet, we assumed semi-automatic construction with a multi-purpose wordnet-builder's software tool and a significant input from semantic analysis algorithms. Such algorithms, notably to extract linguistic knowledge from large corpora of Polish, had to be designed and implemented first. We then constructed an integrated linguist's workbench – the WordNet Weaver (WNW) (Piasecki et al., 2009, section 4.5.3). It makes it much more efficient for the linguists to work on continual wordnet expansion, and helps increase the appropriateness of new entries. The WNW algorithm suggests additions – instances of wordnet relations – but the wordnet editors make all final decisions.

We wanted to make the first Polish wordnet suitable for a range of applications, not the least for linguistic research. It had to be an accurate description of the system of Polish lexical semantics, including its peculiarities. We followed the general idea of the Merge Model (Vossen, 2002) of wordnet development (Piasecki et al., 2009, Section 1.3.1), but the limited budget forced us to postpone mapping to other wordnets. We took a data-driven approach to the construction process: we based it on automated extraction of liguistic knowledge from large corpora of Polish. Details – see section 2 and (Piasecki et al., 2009).

With a clear focus on potential applications of plWordNet in language studies, we thought it consistent to put its structure on a solid linguistic footing. We started with lexico-semantic relations, zooming in on those usually featured in wordnets. Such relations link *lexical units*[3] (LUs) rather than synsets or other word groupings. This had led to the adoption of the LU as a type of vertex in the graph which underlies plWordNet – the basic building block of plWordNet's structure.

A team of linguists, assisted by the wordnet-builder's tool, manually created the first version of plWordNet with nearly 16500 LUs (Piasecki et al., 2009, Section 2.5). This was semi-automatically expanded to 26990 LUs in 17695 synsets (Piasecki et al., 2009, Section 5.2). The procedure can be summarised in 5 steps.

1. A set of candidate lemmas was collected from dictionaries and supplemented by the most frequent lemmas in a few large corpora of Polish (Piasecki et al., 2009, section 3.4.5).

2. Several data sets describing lexico-semantic relations were automatically extracted from morpho-syntactically tagged corpora. The extraction methods included measuring semantic relatedness and using lexico-syntactic patterns (Piasecki et al., 2009, chapters 2–3).

3. Selected groups of semantically close lemmas identified by a clustering algorithm

---

[1] There are two now; see (Vetulani et al., 2009).
[2] The Polish name is *Słowosieć*, literally word-net.
[3] A lexical unit is a word in a broad sense, possibly an idiom or a collocation, but not a productive syntactic structure. A lexical unit is represented by a lemma (a basic morphological form) and its meaning.

were loaded into WNW. The algorithm of activation-area attachment (Piasecki et al., 2009, section 4.5) suggested places in the plWordNet graph where LUs corresponding to the new lemmas might be added.

4. Linguists browsed suggestions in any order they found advisable, and edited the wordnet structure. (Reruns of the algorithm– triggered at will by editors – take into account the richer, enlarged wordnet structure).

5. A coordinator of the linguistic team reviewed the effects of such expansion, using the same WNW system.

In the remainder of the paper we will discuss how well we could keep the initial assumptions, what was helpful, what we had to change, and what we could recommend. We will also outline our plans for the recently begun next phase of the plWordNet project. We expect that its conclusion in three years will see a much larger plWordNet, with richer structures and built using improved methods of semi-automatic expansion.

2 Lessons learned

We applied the WordNet Weaver on a practical scale in the semi-automatic expansion of plWordNet from a manually-created *core* plWordNet to the present version 1.0. An effort of a mere 3.4 person-months resulted in the addition of 8316 new lemmas, 10537 new LUs, 8729 synsets and 11063 instances of lexico-semantic relations. The work performed encompassed also many improvements to the core plWordNet structure. It is our rough estimate that the expansion process was sped up 5–6 times in comparison to purely manual work. This estimate, however, is based only on observations made during an experiment whose goal was wordnet expansion. A systematic evaluation of the method is still to be performed. With the pressing goal of constructing a Polish wordnet as large as possible in the limited time, we could not afford working with the same lemma list independently in two different ways.

The semi-automatic approach means a process which is essentially data-driven. Extracted senses of lemmas were filtered by two factors: their coverage in the corpora and the ability of the extraction methods to recognize certain lexico-syntactic structures as clues during knowledge extraction.

Even so, the editors always could – and occasionally did – override any suggestions and add missing LUs. The suggestions, however, often drew their attention to senses present in the data but not obvious; see (Piasecki et al., 2008) for a large collection of such cases. Here is an example of a word frequent in general language: *wigilia* 'eve' was also extracted as a sense of *święto* 'holiday'. And an example from domain-specific language: *ocieplenie* 'insulation' was automatically linked to *izolacja* 'insulation', turned down by an editor but reinstated by the coordinator.

The activation-area attachment algorithm heavily relies on wordnet structure. An odd-looking, though consistent, suggestion may sometimes arise in the absence of hypernyms not entered yet into the plWordNet version under editing. The algorithm once suggested that certain types of food be linked to an incomplete, shallow hierarchy of *napój* 'drink'. That happened because *potrawa* 'dish (food)' and its hierarchy were absent in that version of plWordNet. The linking of *potrawa* to *napój* (as a hypernym/hyponym or synonym) was also suggested because the algorithm found it to be the closest match in that unfinished network.

New hyponyms were often associated with several co-hyponyms already present in plWordNet, because a link to a common hypernym was missing. As a result, several separate activation areas were suggested instead of one. For example, *pojazd mechaniczny* 'mechanical vehicle' appeared unconnected to many LUs denoting types of mechanical vehicles. Another example: for *bezpiecznik* 'fuse' the algorithm suggested three senses: *włącznik* 'switch (for turning on)', *przełącznik* '(change-over) switch', *wyłącznik* 'switch (circuit breaker)'. This was caused by the lack of a hypernym such as *element elektroniczny* 'electronic element'. Such discoveries were a sure sign of likely mis-attachments or omissions in the network.

WNW's focus on the hypernymy structure is twofold. First, hypernymy drives most of the search for a suitable location for new LUs,[4] so we lose structural information encoded in the instances of other relations. Second, WNW suggests only hypernymy links, while the generated suggestions relate a new LUs by other types of wordnet relation. We lose potentially valuable proper-

---
[4]One of the extraction algorithms (Piasecki et al., 2009, Chapter 4.5.1) is trained on data which include LU pairs associated by several wordnet relations.

ties if we present the suggestions to linguists only in terms of hypernymy and synonymy.

The hypernymy hierarchy of plWordNet is shallow for gerunds. A manual inspection of the WNW results gave an impression of suggestion accuracy[5] much lower for gerunds than for nouns. Yet, the accuracy is similar: 61.43% for gerunds or lemmas which are ambiguous between gerunds and nouns, 64.12% for lemmas unambiguously recognised as nouns (Piasecki et al., 2009, p. 169). The discrepancy may be due to the much higher number of suggestions generated on average per gerundial lemma than per noun. Most suggestions generated for gerunds rely only on the measure of (distributional) semantic relatedness, but evidence of different types increases the accuracy significantly. An effective description of gerunds requires different lexico-syntactic features. We return to this issue in Section 3.4.

Synonymy is an elusive phenomenon. There are many takes on it in linguistics. A synset is often described as a set of "words" referring to the same lexicalised concept (Fellbaum, 1998a; Vossen, 2002; Koeva, 2008). It is an even more demanding task to identify a concept, its extension and the corresponding set of "words" which lexicalise it. It seems easier to recognise, and consistently assign, lexico-semantic relations to pairs of LUs than to work with concepts. The analysis of LU meaning can be supported by usage examples found in corpora, while the connection between concepts and their uses can seldom be directly observed in language data.

The decision to make the LUs the centrepiece of plWordNet influenced its character a lot. First of all, the synset is no longer a primary element of the structure. A synset is defined via the lexico-semantic relations in which its members participate; it groups those LUs which share a set of lexico-semantic relation targets (Piasecki et al., 2009, section 2.1). A synset thus can be perceived as a *sui generis* "shortcut" for the fact that two or more LUs share the same relations. All structural links originate from the relations well studied in the linguistic tradition and the lexicographic practice. The centrality of LUs also allowed us to introduce substitution tests, similar to those applied in EWN (Vossen, 2002), in support of the linguists' work (Piasecki et al., 2009, Appendix A). The test were also automatically generated and available for every edit decision. Clearly, experienced editors could ignore the tests when making simple decisions, but tests instantiated with the appropriate lemmas were always at hand if needed.

We strive to base our definitions of lexico-semantic relations on facts observable in texts – such as those which substitution tests help uncover – and to avoid relying only on the editors' language competence. To support our decisions, we consulted with a few dictionaries and looked at material retrieved from large corpora. This stance leaves aside a variety of psychological and philosophical considerations around the issues of lexical meaning. We believe that such minimal commitment works to plWordNet's advantage: it is transparent to possible applications. For example, while plWordNet is not meant to be an ontology, it can be mapped to different ontologies if necessary.

Wordnet relations are usually categorised into those which link synsets and those which go between "words" or "literals". Making the LU a basic element of a wordnet makes this dichotomy unnecessary. All relations are defined at the level of LUs and are only inherited at the level of synsets.

The structure of plWordNet resembles – perhaps more closely than usual in wordnets – that of a monolingual dictionary with a dense network of lexico-semantic relations added. What makes plWordNet significantly different from a dictionary meant for human readers is the primary role of lexico-semantic relation; what makes it similar to a typical wordnet is the presence of synsets, even if they are defined in an unorthodox manner.

A consequence of our decisions is that plWordNet's hypernymy structure tends to be deeper (this was found out by manual inspection), while synsets are often smaller and represent a rather strict form of near-synonymy. For example, 79.5% of nominal synsets have only one lexical unit, 12.67% have two. A statistical comparison with Princeton WordNet (PWN) would be misleading so early in our project. WordNet's size and coverage are far above what we have achieved thus far: plWordNet only covers adequately the more general LUs and the upper levels of hypernymy. A selective manual comparison of plWordNet and PWN has revealed significant differences in the top hypernymy levels, but we have found no important differences beyond the discrepancy due to the obvious disparity of coverage and the rather

---

[5]We calculate it as the percentage of new lemmas for which the editors took up at least one suggestion.

predictable differences between the Polish and English lexical system, such as specific senses of some LUs. Our longer-term plans include a mapping between plWordNet and PWN, so we postponed a detailed, methodical comparison to that phase. Because plWordNet is developed bottom-up from extracted data, the top-level hypernymy hierarchy is mostly accumulated as new lemmas arrive and lower levels are linked. Only for some general lemmas in the initial version of plWordNet the upper hypernymy structure was created in advance. It is therefore difficult to draw any conclusions about the nature of divergences between the top levels of hypernymy in plWordNet and PWN.

We also statistically compared plWordNet with wordnets created during the first phase of the EWN project, with a similar duration of this phase. The average number of LUs in a synset is lower in plWordNet than in any other wordnet we analysed, but similar to the version of GermaNet from that period: 1.36 in plWordNet and 1.37 in GermaNet as reported in (Vossen et al., 1999).

3 Phase 2: A Deeper and Broader Wordnet

3.1 Triple the Size

The results of the plWordNet 1.0 project are encouraging, but the wordnet is still small. While it has generated solid interest, it must grow considerably to became a real asset in NLP research and development. The WordNet Weaver, though already quite useful, must be extended in several ways. These are some of the themes of the follow-up project, funded for another three years.

Is there a *best* size of a wordnet? More is better, and in any event a large wordnet should at least match the size of PWN 3.0. That, however, costs time and money. Our *realistic* target for plWordNet 2.0 is 70000-80000 lexical units in 45000-55000 synsets. One of our objectives is to construct a mapping between plWordNet and PWN, as well some other wordnets (possibly in another project), we want to make plWordNet 2.0 comparable in size to contemporary large European wordnets, among them GermaNet[6] (Kunze and Lemnitzer, 2002).

In the plWordNet 1.0 project, we targeted 11 relations (Piasecki et al., 2009, Section 2.2), meant mostly to develop the nominal part of the wordnet. The follow-up project will put more resources into the verbal part and the adjectival part. When selecting new relations for inclusion in plWordNet 2.0, we will consider four main factors: lexico-semantic relations identified in linguistic study (especially for Polish), the requirements of plWordNet's expected applications of in Natural Language Engineering (NLE), the existing language resources for Polish (including those still in development), and relations described so far in wordnets (for compatibility).

In the following sections we describe three main research areas planned in the plWordNet 2.0 project. We focus on the inclusion of new lexical relations; a richer description of verbs in particular seems important for practical applications. On the other hand, we will also turn our attention to derivational relations, because derivational mechanisms are very productive and important in Slavic languages. Last but not least, we want to improve the methods of semi-automatic wordnet expansion for supporting linguists' work: as previously, we have little money and little time.

3.2 Enriching the Verbal and Adjectival Parts of plWordNet

In order to analyse quantitatively the description of LUs in terms of wordnet structural elements which deliver information about LUs, we have introduced the notion of *network density*. It is based on the number of relational instances – links – going from a LU to any other LU in the wordnet. Instances of symmetrical relations (such as antonymy) are treated as consisting of two links going in the opposite directions. In order to register the synset structure in the measure, two LUs occurring in one synset are treated as mutually linked. The network density in the verbal part of plWordNet 1.0 is high when we count synonymy (3.83), but quite low (1.52) if calculated without including synonymy represented by synsets; the density of coverage of nouns is 3.55 (2.48 without synonymy). The density corresponds to how well a LU is described on average by means of a set of different links, which defines the meaning of the LU according to the principles of a wordnet. Obviously the density is only a helpful factor and cannot be interpreted as an absolute measure.

Only several relations in plWordNet 1.0 can link verbal units[7]. For applications, it appears important to have a description of verb selectional

---

[6] www.sfs.uni-tuebingen.de/GermaNet/

[7] Those relations are hypernymy/hyponymy, troponymy, antonymy and conversion. We also considered some forms of derivation.

preferences in relation to verb subcategorisation frames. Such description, however, does not associate roles in verb frames with LUs. Rather, it considers semantic categories which can be defined as regions in the hypernymy structure. There is ongoing independent work on the construction of a Polish semantic valence dictionary (Hajnicz, 2009); role description in this work is based on plWordNet. We will thus focus on adding to plWordNet 2.0 several lexico-semantic relations based on the general notion of verbal entailment and modelled after the particular relations of this type used in PWN (Fellbaum, 1998b) and EuroWordNet (EWN) (Vossen, 2002). For example, we can consider *subevent* or *cause*; *manner* is already covered in plWordNet by troponymy.

For the Portuguese wordnet, WordNet.PT, Amaro (2006) proposed a set of much finer-grained verbal relations, motivated by the Generative Lexicon model (Pustejovsky, 1991). While the rich information expressed in that way could be valuable for NLE, such a set of relations would be very laborious to develop on a large scale and would make hard-to-meet demands on the automatic extraction of wordnet relations from text.

Initially only antonymy and derivational relations described adjectives in plWordNet 1.0. Grouping into synsets was based directly on near-synonymy (the construction of adjectival synsets was supported by the appropriate substitution tests (Piasecki et al., 2009, Apendix A). Adjectival hypernymy was added later in the project. The final network density is a low 2.72 (1.02 without synonymy), but this could be expected given the limited set of relations. Most solutions proposed in the literature for increasing network density would add cross-categorial relations to link adjectival LUs with nominal and verbal LUs; examples include *is a value of / attributes* known from PWN (Fellbaum, 1998c) or relations introduced in WordNet.PT (Marrafa and Mendes, 2006). Many such associations are expressed by derivational relations, so we want first to developed a semantic description of derivational relations, and only later to analyse those subsets of adjectival LUs which will still not be acceptably covered.

3.3 Towards a Rich Derivational Description

Derivational mechanisms, productive in Slavic languages, feature to some extent in all Slavic wordnets. Their builders – for example, Pala and Hlaváčková (2007) and Koeva (2008) – emphasize the importance of derivation. We also take this position (Derwojedowa et al., 2008; Piasecki et al., 2009). In plWordNet 1.0 derivational links appear as one of two relations: relatedness and pertainymy; the former covers more regular derivates. Irregular derivational LU pairs also belong to fuzzynymy. It is not enough, however, just to register the presence of a derivational link; its semantic status should be clarified. The idea is not new. Miller and Fellbaum (2003) introduced "morphosemantic links" into PWN to connect synset members. Fellbaum et al. (2009) proposed a semantic classification of types of associations expressed by the derivational relations.

Among the cross-categorial relations of EWN there are several whose instances in Polish would be associated by derivational links. Let us show example pairs of Polish words for the EWN relations. *Cross-categorial near synonymy*: *poruszyć$_{verb}$* 'move [highly polysemous]' – *poruszenie* 'motion; commotion'. *Role/involved*: *wkręcać* 'screw in' – *wkrętak* '(a type of) screwdriver', *kierować* 'drive (a car)' – *kierowca* '(car) driver', *wypiekać* 'bake (bread, pastry)' – *wypieki$_{plurale\ tantum}$* 'baked bread or pastry products'. *Co-role*: *pianino* '(upright) piano' – *pianista$_{masculine}$* 'pianist', *gra* 'game' – *gracz* 'player', *sąd* 'court (of trial)' – *podsądny$_{masculine}$* 'plaintiff'. *Be in state*: *biedak* 'poor or pitiful person' – *biedny$_{adjective}$* 'poor'.

We want to follow this approach: adopt the classes for derivational relations proposed in (Fellbaum et al., 2009) to Polish and possibly extend the set, especially with NLE applications in mind. We will carefully examine the practice and experience of the EWN project (Vossen, 2002) in encoding cross-categorial relations and in their classification. For example, we will consider adopting for Polish the subtypes of the *role* relation[8]. Another interesting problem is the development of a semantic classification of aspectual pairs of verbs (such as *malować$_{habitual}$* 'paint' – *pomalować$_{perfective}$* 'have painted') in a way compatible with a relatively simple structure of a wordnet and conducive to NLE applications.

Derivational relations create in Polish (and in other Slavic languages) chains of associated LUs. An example: *bomba$_{noun}$*

---
[8]`agent, instrument, patient, location, direction, result, manner, source_direction, target_direction.`

'bomb', *bombardować*$_{verb}$ 'bomb', *bombowiec* 'bomber (plane)', *bombardier* 'bombardier (rank)', *bombowy*$_{adjective}$[9] 'related to bombs'... Another, rather breathtaking, example: *barwa*$_{noun}$ 'colour, hue', *barwić*$_{habitual}$ 'colour', *odbarwić*$_{perfective}$ 'remove colour', *zabarwić*$_{perfective}$ 'colour', *barwiarz*$_{masculine}$ 'dyer (person)', *barwiarka*$_{feminine}$ 'dyer (person)', *barwiarnia* 'dyeing shop', *barwny*$_{adjective}$ 'colourful', *pstrobarwny*$_{adjective}$ '≈ motley'... Jadacka (1995) describes 64 (!) elements in a chain for *barwa*. It is a challenging task to make a semantic classification cover a wide range of indirect derivational association, while keeping the system's complexity in check.

We will introduce in plWordNet 2.0 a two-level model of the description of derivational relations between LUs: each link will be described by a pattern of a formal derivational dependency and a semantic type of the association. Pala and Hlaváčková (2007) constructed a tool for automatic prediction of derivational links between LUs from their word forms, and populated CzechWordNet with thousands of automatically generated derivational links. Since Czech and Polish are fairly close, a similar solution ought to be easily constructed for plWordNet; Rabiega-Wiśniewska (2006), for example, describes the lexical derivation in Polish with special focus on nouns and adjectives. Pala and Hlaváčková (2007) identified 10 productive derivational patterns, for example "action, verb → noun", and the produced links were labelled according to the pattern applied.

Derivational patterns often lead to ambiguous semantic classification of the LU links (Fellbaum et al., 2009; Koeva, 2008). For example, the affix *-ka* encodes different semantic relations in *miara* 'measure' – *miarka*$_{diminutive}$ 'measure' and in *krasnal*$_{masc.}$ 'brownie (dwarf)' – *krasnalka*$_{fem.}$ 'brownie (dwarf)'. LU pairs apparently related by derivation may have no semantic association, for example *mine* (bomb) – *mining* (industry) (Koeva, 2008) or *nakręcić* 'confuse (in a message)' – *nakrętka* '(threaded) nut'. We will deal with this difficulty by combining the pattern-based identification of derivationally linked lemma pairs with automatic extraction of information on the semantic nature of the association between the pair elements. We will rely on the positive experience with the combinations of different types of evidence extracted from corpora and classification methods based on Machine Learning (Piasecki et al., 2009, Section 4.5). WNW will be supplemented by a tool to suggest derivationally motivated links and their semantic classification.

Interestingly, the semantic ambiguity of derivational links is yet another good reason to base the wordnet structure on LUs. Ambiguity tends to disappear when we analyse semantic types of derivational relations at the LU level. For example, the semantic difference between the derivations *forma* 'form' – *foremny* 'shapely' and *forma* 'form' – *formalny* 'formal' is clarified when we know that the lemma *forma* represents two different LUs.

The introduction of new semantic relations via a semantic classification of derivational links creates a small dilemma. We should extend this description to LUs associated semantically in a similar way, but not linked derivationally. For example, *wykładać* 'to lecture' is derivationally related to *wykład* 'lecture'. The link can be seen as the `object` type, but this is also true of the pair *wykładać* – *przedmiot* 'subject matter', where there is no derivational relation. In plWordNet 1.0, pairs of the latter kind appear in the fuzzynymy relation. It is not a clear-cut decision whether to extend the semantic classification beyond derivational pairs and where to put the limits; associations of this kind have different strengths, are influenced by typicality, conventions, frequency of use and so on. For example, the definition of `involved/role` in EWN refers to typicality: "is typically involved" (Vossen, 2002, p. 29). This selection problem is not unlike difficulties with collocation, if one were to construct a dictionary of collocations. We will investigate all these matters for the needs of plWordNet 2.0 structure.

3.4 Deeper Research on Semi-automatic Methods of WordNet Expansion

There are at least two good reason why the plWordNet 2.0 project should expend much effort on the further development of extraction methods and on WNW: the limitations of the present version of WNW mentioned in Section 2 and the need to expand its operation to semantic classification of derivational links. WNW is based on several extraction methods delivering evidence for the final multi-criterial decision. Besides improving the accuracy and recall of the methods, we want to develop a uniform measure of the reliability of infor-

---

[9] ... and an idiomatic meaning: great, fantastic, etc.

mation extracted by particular methods. All methods we used so far extract semantic associations between lemmas in the same part of speech. For the needs of semantic classification of derivational relations we will extend our methods to the description of cross-categorial pairs.

The description of nouns, in particular, is based on the occurrences of lexico-syntactic relations which characterise contexts of noun occurrences. Yet, three of four types of relations (Piasecki et al., 2009, p. 67) focus on those small parts of the sentences structure which include the noun (such as modification by a specific adjective) but not the verb. Only one type, "occurrence of *a specific verb* for which a given noun can be its subject" relates the noun to a verb. This limited view of syntactic relations was caused by the lack of a robust, shallow parser of Polish. A truly wide-coverage parser is yet to emerge. We will therefore continue work on morpho-syntactic constraints (Piasecki et al., 2009, Chapter 3.4.3) in order to collect a set of lexico-syntactic relations which can be recognised by the constraints with sufficient precision and describe lemma co-occurrences of more than one part of speech, for example verbs and nouns. The required changes are located mainly in the area of lexico-syntactic descriptions of occurrence contexts of the analysed lemmas. We will also develop a dedicated way of describing gerunds by adding morpho-syntactic constraints focused on the identification of possible elements of the gerund argument structure, motivated by derivation of gerunds from verbs.

WNW's algorithm of suggestion generation will be extended by taking into account links other than hypernymy. Additional evidence for the algorithm will come from derivational links already encoded in plWordNet and those automatically discovered when processing new lemmas. Cross-categorial information in the processing of verbal and adjectival lemmas could be the most reliable means of improving the performance of the next version of WNW with respect to lemmas in these two parts of speech. In parallel, WNW's User interface will be redesigned to give linguists properly visualisation of the whole wordnet structure. We want to make a flexible and scalable graphical presentation of the plWordNet structure the central element of the user interface, to set it as the default when presenting suggestions and editing the structure. List-based and record-based panels will be preserved to facilitate other kinds of tasks.

We will improve as well the mechanisms which support group cooperation and the management of the linguist team. We will build into the system access to external sources of knowledge, such as lexicons and encyclopaedias.

4 A Few Early Conclusions

We have carried out a long and generally fruitful experiment in semi-automatic wordnet construction. We have made steady progress in developing methods of automated extraction of linguistic knowledge on a scale which makes them practically useful, and we deployed them with a most promising effect for a language significantly different than English. Our work also made good economic sense: a core Polish wordnet of some 16400 lexical units has been almost doubled in size fast and reliably (and that helped us make a convincing case for renewed funding).

We want to make plWordNet transparent with respect to theories of meaning and to applications in Natural Language Engineering. We hope to achieve it by reducing the methodological basis of the project to several linguistic notions such a lexical unit or a lexico-semantic relation. The present size of plWordNet is too low for drawing definite conclusions, but it seems to be developing in a good direction. It also is not as drastically different from other wordnets as we initially suspected it might become.

Methods of automatic extraction of lexical-semantic knowledge appeared to be mature enough for application by linguists in the practice of expanding the wordnet. The extracted data describe well the overall complexity of lexico-semantic relations, so the automatic support should be rather easily extended from hypernymy to many other types of relations.

The development of a wordnet in isolation from wordnets for other languages has several advantages (from our point of view – see Section 2). There is a risk: mapping to other wordnets and knowledge representation structures (perhaps some kind of general ontology) may not be an easy task. The separation of plWordNet construction and future mapping to other wordnets (or a general ontology) will most probably cost more than if both processes ran in parallel, but this choice of ours aimed at providing a faithful description of the Polish system of lexical meanings via plWordNet structures.

Acknowledgments

Work financed by the Polish Ministry of Education and Science, Project N N516 068637.

References

Raquel Amaro. 2006. WordNet as a Base Lexicon Model for the Computation of Verbal Predicates. In Petr Sojka, Key-Sun Choi, Christiane Fellbaum, and Piek Vossen, editors, *Proc. Third Global WordNet Conf.*, pages 9–17.

Magdalena Derwojedowa, Maciej Piasecki, Stanisław Szpakowicz, Magdalena Zawisławska, and Bartosz Broda. 2008. Words, Concepts and Relations in the Construction of Polish WordNet. In A. Tanács, D. Csendes, V. Vincze, Ch. Fellbaum, and P. Vossen, editors, *Proc. Fourth Global WordNet Conf.*, pages 162–177.

Magdalena Derwojedowa, Maria Głąbska, Maciej Piasecki, Joanna Rabiega-Wiśniewska, Stanisław Szpakowicz, and Magdalena Zawisławska. 2009. plWordNet 1.0 — The Polish Wordnet. Visit at www.plwordnet.pwr.wroc.pl, Apr. 09.

Christiane Fellbaum, Anne Osherson, and Peter E. Clark, 2009. *Putting Semantics into WordNet's "Morphosemantic" Links*, pages 350–358. In Vetulani and Uszkoreit (Vetulani and Uszkoreit, 2009).

Christiane Fellbaum. 1998a. A Semantic Network of English: The Mother of All WordNets. *Computers and the Humanities*, 32:209–220.

Christiane Fellbaum, 1998b. *A Semantic Network of English Verbs*, chapter 3, pages 69–104. In (Fellbaum, 1998c).

Christiane Fellbaum, editor. 1998c. *WordNet – An Electronic Lexical Database*. The MIT Press.

Elżbieta Hajnicz. 2009. Problems with Pruning in Automatic Creation of Semantic Valence Dictionary for Polish. In V. Matoušek and P. Mautner, editors, *Proc. 12th International Conf. Text, Speech and Dialogue, Plzeň, Czech Republic, September 2009*, volume 5729 of *LNCS*, pages 131–138. Springer.

Hanna Jadacka. 1995. *Rzeczownik polski jako baza derywacyjna [The Polish noun as a basis for derivation]*. PWN, Warszawa.

Svetla Koeva. 2008. Derivational and Morphosemantic Relations in Bulgarian Wordnet. In Kłopotek et al. (Kłopotek et al., 2008), pages 359–368.

Claudia Kunze and Lothar Lemnitzer. 2002. GermaNet – representation, visualization, application. In *Proc. LREC 2002, main conference*, volume V, pages 1485–1491.

Mieczysław A. Kłopotek, Adam Przepiórkowski, Sławomir T. Wierzchoń, and Krzysztof Trojanowski, editors. 2008. *Intelligent Information Systems XVI. Proc. International IIS'08 Conf., Zakopane, Poland, June 2008*. Advances in Soft Computing. Academic Publishing House EXIT, Warsaw.

Palmira Marrafa and Sara Mendes. 2006. Modeling Adjectives in Computational Relational Lexica. In *Proc. COLING/ACL 2006 Main Conf. Poster Sessions*, pages 555–562, Sydney, Australia.

George A. Miller and Christiane Fellbaum. 2003. Morphosemantic links in WordNet. *Traitement automatique de langue*, 44(2):69–80.

Karel Pala and Dana Hlaváčková. 2007. Derivational Relations in Czech WordNet. In *Proc. Workshop on Balto-Slavonic NLP*, pages 75–81, Prague, Czech Republic.

Maciej Piasecki, Bartosz Broda, and Michał Marcińczuk. 2008. The WordNet Weaver – support for semi-automatic wordnet expansion. Examples of suggestions automatically generated during the expansion of plWordNet, June 2008: plwordnet.pwr.wroc.pl/browser/graphs.jsp.

Maciej Piasecki, Stanisław Szpakowicz, and Bartosz Broda. 2009. *A Wordnet from the Ground Up*. Wrocław University of Technology Press. www.site.uottawa.ca/~szpak/pub/A_Wordnet_from_the_Ground_Up.zip.

James Pustejovsky. 1991. Generative Lexicon. *Computational Linguistics*, 17(4):409–441.

Joanna Rabiega-Wiśniewska. 2006. *A Formal Description of Lexical Derivation in Polish. Nouns and Adjectives* [in Polish[. Ph.D. thesis, Faculty of Polish Studies, Warsaw University.

Zygmunt Vetulani and Hans Uszkoreit, editors. 2009. *Human Language Technology. Challenges of the Information Society, Third Language and Technology Conf., Poznań, October 2007, Revised Selected Papers*. LNCS 5603. Springer.

Zygmunt Vetulani, Justyna Walkowska, Tomasz Obrębski, Jacek Marciniak, Paweł Konieczka, and Przemysław Rzepecki, 2009. *An Algorithm for Building Lexical Semantic Network and Its Application to PolNet - Polish WordNet Project*, pages 369–381. In Vetulani and Uszkoreit (Vetulani and Uszkoreit, 2009).

Piek Vossen, Claudia Kunze, Andreas Wagner, Karel Pala, Pavel Sevecek, Kadri Vider, Leho Paldre, Laurent Catherin, and Dominique Dutoit. 1999. Final WordNets for Czech, Estonian, French, and German. Deliverable 2D014, WP3, Wp4 LE4-8328, The EuroWordNet Project.

Piek Vossen. 2002. EuroWordNet General Document Version 3. Technical report, Univ. of Amsterdam.

Representation of Complex Predicates in WordNet

G. Uma Maheshwar Rao
Centre For ALTS
University of Hyderabad
guraohyd@yahoo.com

K. Rajyarama
Centre For ALTS
University of Hyderabad
krajyarama@gmail.com

Abstract

Indian languages exhibit a large number of complex predicate constructions comprising of a V+V combination or an N+V combination. The present paper focuses on issues related to the representation of complex N+V constructions in wordnet. We have attempted to evolve a mechanism based on the semantic features of the nouns involved in the N+V constructions for predicting the compositionality of a complex N+V construction. Such an analysis it is felt will help in classifying complex predicates into various types and an appropriate mechanism for representing each of these types has been suggested.

Transliteration: a,A,i,I,u,U,e,E,ai,o,O,au,M,H, k,kh,g,gh,ng,c,ch,j,jh,ny,T,Th,D,Dh,N,t,th,d,dh,n, p,ph,b,bh,m,y,r,l,L,v,sh,S,s,h

1 Introduction

Telugu and almost all Indian languages possess a large number of complex word constructions which comprise of (a) verb + verb or (b) non-verb + verb. The non-verb in (b) type of constructions can be a noun, an adjective or an adverb. These constructions are variously referred to as Compound verbs (Hook, 1974), Conjunct verbs (Wallace, 1985), Composite verbs and Complex predicates (Krishnamurti, 1992; Verma, 1993). Depending on the grammatical category of the non-verb constituent they are also referred to as 'NV compounds', 'AV compounds' (cf. Kachru, 1980; Hook, 1993; Verma, 1993). In recent literature the term Complex Predicates has become more or less stabilized to refer to these constructions. Complex predicates of N+V type are discussed in this paper. Even though complex predicates structurally comprise of two words, syntactically and semantically they behave like single constituents. Such structurally complex but semantically unique constructions can raise important issues of processing and representation for lexical storage and retrieval purposes. In this paper we would like to focus on issues of the following sort:

- a. How should complex predicates be processed and represented in wordnets?

- b. What are the principles/assumptions which underlie storage and retrieval of complex predicates in wordnets?

The paper is organized as follows: In section 1 we provide a brief introduction to complex predicates. In section 2 we discuss about wordnets and their organization. Section 3 deals with complex predicates in Telugu. Section 4 discusses issues related to representing complex predicates in Wordnets. Sections 4.1 and 4.2 deal with the proposals for representing complex predicates in wordnets. Section 5 concludes the paper.

2 Introduction to Wordnet

Large scale lexical data bases like wordnets are essential prerequisites for various NLP related tasks like machine translation, information extraction and retrieval. From the theoretical point of view, identification of word senses (including multi-word sequences) their representation and their diambiguation is of great concern for computational studies. In Wordnets, words are represented as related to each other by a set of semantically statable relations. In wordnets nouns, verbs, adjectives and adverbs are grouped into sets of cognitive synonyms or synsets, each expressing a distinct concept. Miller's (1993) paper spells out the objectives and the architecture of wordnet. Miller (1993), Fellbaum et al. (1993) and Fellbaum

(1993) describe the organization of nouns, adjectives and verbs in wordnet respectively.

Wordnets for major grammatical categories viz. nouns, verbs, adverbs and adjectives have been created. Nouns in wordnets are organized on the basis of lexical inheritance system and are related to each other on the basis of relations like hyponymy, hypernymy, synonymy and meronymy (Miller, 1993). The organization of the nouns in the wordnet is based on the intuition that common nouns provide a superordinate term along with their distinguishing features. This generates a lexical inheritance system in which each word inherits the distinguishing features of all its superordinate words.

Fellbaum (1993) proposes a different set of semantic relations for verbs, since verbs differ substantially from other categories like nouns and adjectives in terms of the semantic relations that hold between them. Verbs are divided into different semantic groups based on semantic criteria. Semantic relations like polysemy, synonymy, entailment and troponymy form the basis for the organization of relations among verbs. In wordnet adjectives are divided into two types viz. descriptive and relational. According to Fellbaum et al. (1993), "Descriptive adjectives ascribe to their head nouns values of (typically) bipolar attributes and consequently are organized in terms of binary oppositions (antonymy) and similarity of meaning (synonymy)". Relational adjectives are classified to be stylistic variants of the nouns they modify and so are cross referenced to the noun files. (Fellbaum et al., 1993).

In addition to the single lexemic representations in terms of their grammatical categories, it is also necessary to represent morphological relations expressed by constructions like complex predicates in wordnets.

3 Complex Predicates in Telugu

In this section, we focus on the complex predicates of the N+V type in Telugu. The high frequency and productivity of N+V can be attributed to the fact that Telugu is a verb final language and hence does not require any special efforts to incorporate a noun in the complex predicate. More over this appears to be a very handy mechanism to accommodate into Telugu loan words from the domains of science and technology.

The following dicussion involves verbs, both transitive and intransitive, which occur as constituents of NV constructions.

3.1 Transitive Verbs in Telugu

Rajyarama (1998) identifies an exhaustive list of 22 transitive verbs which occur as heads in N+V constructions. Verbs like *ceyyi* 'to do', *peTTu* 'to keep', *koTTu* 'to beat', *paTTu* 'to hold', *tiyyi* 'to take', *veyyi* 'to throw' are a few examples of this category. Out of these *ceyyi* 'to do', *veyyi* 'to throw' are very frequently used (both transitively and intransitively). A few examples illustrate the use of the verbs mentioned above:

- nidra paTTu 'fall asleep'
  'sleep hold',

- Ita koTTu 'to swim'
  'swimming hit

- guraka peTTu 'to snore'
  'snoring keep'.

Consider a verb like *ceyyi* 'to do' as in 1. *snAnaM ceyyi* 'to bathe' which has a literal meaning 'do/make bath' and in 2. *jalubu ceyyi* 'to catch cold' which literally means 'to do cold' as illustrated below:

- 1. sIwa snAnaM cEsiMdi.
  Sita bath-do -pst-3p-sg-f
  'Sita bathed'

- 2. sIwaki jalubu cEsiMdi
  Sita -dat. cold do-pst-3p-sg-f
  'Sita caught cold'

3.2 Intransitive verbs in Telugu

Nearly around 11 verbs occur as constituents of N+V constructions. Some of them are *avvu* 'to become', *paDu* 'to fall', *kalugu* 'to occur', *puTTu* 'to be born'. Consider the following examples:

- 3. bAdha paDu 'to be pained'
  'pain fall'

- 4. Akali avvu 'to be hungry'
  'hunger become'

- 5. digulu paDu 'to worry'
  'worry fall'

It is important to note that in none of the examples cited above the meaning of the N+V sequences is compositional. The verb loses its lexical meaning in this particular context.

Most of the earlier works on complex predicates (Hook, 1974, 1993; Dasgupta 1977; Verma, 1993; Krishnamurti, 1992; Uma Maheshwara Rao, 1995; Rajyarama, 1998) have applied a number of morphological and syntactic tests in order to test their compositionality. Some of these include tests like scrambling, coordination, modification and interrogation. These tests help in distinguishing between N+V constructions which are combinations of direct object+verb and N+V constructions which are instances of an incorporated noun and the verb. The outcome of these tests is that complex predicates with non-compositional semantics and which do not yield themselves to any of the tests mentioned above should be treated as 'wholes' and not as independent units.

4 Representing Complex Predicates in Word net

Complex predicates comprising of a noun and a verb involve a number of processes which can be morphologically stated and are used basically to represent newer verbal concepts. Although the verbs which are constituents of these constructions are a finite set, the non-head constituent nouns are not. Therefore it is important to evolve a mechanism which can predict the meaning of the complex N+V constructions from the meaning of these non-head constituents in the context of the head.

From a lexicographic point of view these constructions pose problems of representation and storage. In this paper we seek to address and resolve some of the vital problems faced by a lexicographer while handling such constructions.

We propose that complex N+V constructions like *bhaya paDu* 'to fear' can be represented in Wordnet by adopting one of the following approaches:
(a) List based approach
(b) Rule based approach
In the following sections, we discuss the basic assumptions and the consequences of each of these approaches:

4.1 List based approach

Under this approach we assume that it is possible to list all the N+V sequences in the lexicon. Such a listing begins with identifying the verbs that can occur as constituents of the complex predicates. In any language only a finite set of verbs can occur as complex predicate constituents.

Once the verbs are identified, the nouns that can co-occur with each of these verbs will also have to be exhaustively listed.

Following this all possible N+V combinations in a language will be listed. Theoretically such an approach may appear feasible especially taking into consideration the huge memory available with the computer and also the speed and accuracy with which the machines operate. However, this method of merely listing the N+V combinations may be constrained by various limitations like:

- 1. Thousands of forms (N+V combinations) will have to be listed which can be quite cumbersome.

- 2. There is always a possibility of a new N+V combination entering a language.

- 3. There is also the problem of unnecessary redundancy which can be avoided.

In order to overcome the limitations cited above we propose an alternate approach which takes its cues from human language processing mechanisms. We strongly argue for an approach which simulates how humans process, store and retrieve complex predicates.

4.2 Rule based approach

The basic assumption is that it is possible to process and store complex predicates in a way similar to how human beings recognize and store these constructions in their mental repertoire. Human beings do not list and store each and every complex predicate form whenever they come across one. Rather, human behavior seems to be rule governed. It seems that humans formulate rules based on the abstractions derived from the semantic features of the words involved in such constructions.

In this approach we argue for a method which is rule based. The rules are based on the generalizations drawn form the semantic and syntactic features of the words involved in a complex predicate. This approach is based on the assumption that it is possible to predict the nature of a complex N+V construction on the basis of the semantic features of the nouns involved. This is evident from the behavior of some of the most frequently used verbs like *ceyyi* 'to do', *veyyi* 'to throw', *peTTu* 'to keep' and *koTTu* 'to beat/hit' when they function as heads of complex N+V constructions. In the following section we illustrate the semantic behavior of each one of these verbs mentioned above:

Let us consider the verb *ceyyi* 'to do'. The following examples demonstrate the types of nouns that this verb can combine with:

- 6. vaMTa ceyyi 'to do cooking'
  cooking do

- 7. kUra ceyyi 'to cook curry'
  curry do

Therefore it is possible to say that the verb *ceyyi* 'to do' when it combines with any noun which is characterized by the features [+artifact, +edible] the complex verb denotes 'to make'.
ceyyi 'to do' on the other hand when it combines with nouns which are [+artifact, -edible] as in:

- 8. bomma ceyyi 'to make a toy'
  toy do

- 9. kuMDa ceyyi 'to make a pot'
  pot do

the verb *ceyyi* 'to do' functions as a resultative verb bringing about change in the state denoted by the N. Consider the nature and function of the verb *ceyyi* 'to do' when it combines with nouns which denote states both physiological and psychological, as in the examples (10-13):

- 10. jalubu ceyyi 'to catch cold'
  cold do

- 11. jabbu ceyyi 'to fall sick'
  sickness do

- 12. mOsaM ceyyi 'to cheat'
  cheating do

- 13. alavAtu ceyyi 'to create habit'
  habit do

- 14. snAnaM ceyyi 'to bathe'
  bath do

- 15. type ceyyi 'to type'
  type do

- 16. print ceyyi 'to print'
  print do

Here the verb is completely bleached of its lexical content and functions as a verbalizer. Consequently, the verb *ceyyi* 'to do' functions differently in each case depending on the semantic nature of the noun that is incorporated. The same can be represented as follows:

- 6-7. N   ceyyi
  [+af.,+edi.]

- 8-9. N   ceyyi
  [+ af.,-edi.]

- 10-13. N   + ceyyi
  [+ abs.]

Another verb *peTTu* 'to keep' behaves in a similar way. Let us consider the contexts in which *peTTu* 'to keep' occurs:

- 17. guraka peTTu 'to snore'
  snore   keep

- 18. parugu peTTu 'to run'
  pain   keep

- 19. maData peTTu 'to fold'
  fold   keep

- 20. kharcu peTTu 'to spend'
  spend   keep

- 21. lekka peTTu 'to count'
  count   keep

In the examples (17-21) the nouns are characterized by the feature [+action]. In this context the verb functions as only a verbalizing element. Similarly in the following complex predicates (22-25) nouns belong to the category of [+psychological state] and the output of the predicate is 'to cause' the state denoted by the noun.

- 22. bAdha peTTu 'to hurt'
  hurt   keep

- 23. bhaya peTTu 'to scare'
  fear   keep

- 24. sukha peTTu 'to comfort s'one'
  comfort   keep

- 25. kaSTa peTTu   'to cause hardship to s'one'
  hardship   keep

- 26. annaM peTTu 'to serve rice'
  rice   keep

- 27. bhojanaM peTTu 'to serve food'
  food   keep

- 28. kUra peTTu 'to serve curry'
  curry   keep

The complex predicates in examples (26-28) involve nouns which are characterized by the feature [+af.,+edi]. Here also the verb *peTTu* does not retain its lexical meaning of 'to keep something somewhere' but functions as a verbaliser.

Another verb *koTTu* combines with nouns and exhibits similar behavior. Consider the following examples:

- 29. Ita koTTu 'to swim'
  swim   hit

- 30. jebulu koTTu 'to pick pocket'
  pockets   hit

- 31. dArulu koTTu 'to way lay'
  ways   hit

- 32. mamdu koTTu 'to booze'
  liquor   hit

- 33. kampu koTTu 'to stink'
  stink   hit

- 34. vasana koTTu 'to smell'
  smell   hit

The noun in the example(29) is characterized by the feature [+action] as in *Ita* 'swimming' or [+concrete,+count] as in *jEbulu* 'pockets', *dArulu* 'ways', *maMdu* 'medicine' (examples; 30-32) and [+physiological state] as in *vAsana* 'smell' and *kaMpu* 'stink' (examples:33-34).

In the following, yet another verb *veyyi* 'to throw' combines with nouns of different types as in the examples (35-41):

- 35. Akali veyyi 'to be hungry'
  hunger-throw

- 36. bAdha veyyi 'to be pained'
  pain-throw

- 37. bhayam veyyi 'to be afraid'
  fear-throw

- 38. dAham veyyi 'to feel thirsty'
  thirst-throw

- 39. cali veyyi 'to feel cold'
  cold-throw

- 40. siggu veyyi 'to be ashamed'
  shame throw

- 41. ettu veyyi 'to tricks one'
  trick throw

In the above cases, complex predicates involving nouns and the verb *veyyi* 'to throw' denote psychosomatic states and these nouns are characterized by the semantic features [+psychological state] and [+physiological state].

Similarly consider the set of nouns that enter into complex predicate involving *veyyi* 'to throw':

- 42. tALaM veyyi 'to lock'
  lock   throw

- 43. muggu veyyi 'to draw designs'
  designs   throw

- 44. gaDiya veyyi 'to bolt'
  bolt   throw

- 45. ceyyi veyyi 'to lay hand'
  hand   throw

Nouns in examples (42-45) are characterized by the semantic feature [+concrete]. Consider another set of concrete nouns which are either self benefactive or other benefactive with which the verb *veyyi* 'to throw' combines:

- 46. baTTalu vEsuko
  'to wear[self] clothes'

- 47. ceppulu vesuko
  'to wear[self] chappals'

- 48. nagalu vesuko
  'to wear[self] jewellery'

Also Consider another verb *paDu* 'to fall'. This verb is found to be co-occurring with nouns characterized by the semantic feature [+psychological state] and even in this context the verb functions as a verbalizer. Consider the examples (49-53) which illustrate this observation:

- 49. bhaya paDu 'to fear'
  fear   fall

- 50. bAdha paDu 'to suffer'
  suffer   fall

- 51. kaSTAlu paDu 'to face hardships'
  hardships   fall

- 52. siggu paDu 'to be ashamed'
  shame   fall

- 53. niMda paDu 'to be blamed'
  blame   fall

The examples sited in 6 to 59 demonstrate the approach we would like to adopt. As illustrated above specification of a noun for its semantic feature(s) will help in determining the syntactic and semantic behavior of the verb. This may also help us in drawing generalizations like: When a N with a specific semantic feature combines with a given verb then the outcome is either a compositional or a non-compositional complex predicate.

Nouns identified with specific semantic features enable one to predict the meaning of the complex predicate.

5 Conclusion

We may draw the following conclusions based on the dicussion in section 4. We need to adopt a hybrid approach which combines both List-based and Rule-based approaches, while handling complex N+V constructions. In the case of synthetic constructions the semantics of the noun and the verb undergoes a complete change and these constructions become Idioms. For example: *kannu koTTu* 'to wink' which literally means 'eye hit'. Such compounds have to be listed in the lexicon. However these constructions may not be very large in any language.

Complex N+V constructions which are regularly and productively formed like *bhaya paDu* 'to be scared' can be represented in the lexicon using the rule-based approach.

If wordnets have words populated with semantic features it would be redundant to list exhaustively all such complex predicates with their meanings. Hence, the semantic properties of the head (verb) and the non-head (noun) may be listed in the lexicon and the appropriate sense of the complex predicate may be realized automatically from the rules.

References

Beckwith, R., Miller, G. A. 1993. *Design and Implementation of the WordNet Lexical Database and Searching Software.* [ftp.cogsci.princeton.edu/pub/wordnet].

Fellbaum, C., Gross, D., and Miller, K. 1993. *Adjectives in WordNet.* [ftp.cogsci.princeton.edu/pub/wordnet].

Fellbaum, C. 1993. *English Verbs as a Semantic Net.* [ftp.cogsci.princeton.edu/pub/wordnet].

Hook, P.E. 1974. *The Compound Verb in Hindi.* Ann Arbor University of Michigan, USA.

Hook, P.E. 1993. *Aspecto Genesis And The Compound Verb In Indo-Aryan. In Verma.* M.K. (ed.) Complex Predicates In South Asian languages. pp. 97-113.

Krishnamurti, Bh. 1992. *Complex Predicates in Telugu.* In Bulletin of The Deccan College Post Graduate and Research Institute. S.M. Katre felicitation volume. pp. 314-327.

Miller, G. A., Beckwith, R., Fellbaum, C., Gross, D., and Miller, K. 1993. *Introduction to WordNet: An On-line Lexical Database.* [ftp.cogsci.princeton.edu/pub/wordnet].

Miller, G. 1993. *Nouns in WordNet: A Lexical Inheritance System.* [ftp.cogsci.princeton.edu/pub/wordnet].

Rajyarama. 1998. *A Study On Some Aspects Of Derivational Morphology In Telugu With Special Reference To Compounds.* Ph.d. Thesis submitted to University of Hyderabad.

Uma Maheshwar Rao, G. 1994. *On certain Aspects Of Word Formation Processes : A Case Study Of Telugu.* Paper presented in National Seminar on Word Formation in Indian Languages. Osmania University, Hyderabad, February 9-10, 1994.

Verma, M. K. 1993. *(ed.) Complex Predicates in South Asian languages.* Manohar Publishers and Distributors. New Delhi.

The Representation of Idioms in WordNet

Anne Osherson
St. Hilda's College
Oxford University
anne.osherson@gmail.com

Christiane Fellbaum
Computer Science Department
Princeton University
fellbaum@princeton.edu

Abstract

WordNet's very extensive coverage does not systematically include idiomatic expression, multi-word units that are semantically compositional to varying degrees. This gap must be filled if WordNet is to be successfully used in applications requiring Word Sense Disambiguation and language pedagogy. Our focus here is on Verb Phrase and sentential idioms. We propose a classification of idioms based on their semantic compositionality and suggest a specific mechanism for integrating them into WordNet.

1 Introduction

We define idioms as multi-word units with specific, conventionalized meanings. A hallmark of idioms is their semantic non-compositionality, i.e., their meanings typically are not the sums of the meanings of their constituents. Idioms fall along a scale of semantic compositionality, ranging from the completely opaque (*buy the farm, have a chip on one's shoulder*) to fairly transparent (*point a finger at, throw pearls before swine*) expressions. Idioms are frequent in all genres and registers and constitute an integral and large, important part of the lexicon (Jackendoff, 1997). They present a challenge to Natural Language Processing systems, which must recognize the constituents as part of a larger unit and assign the appropriate meaning to the phrase (Fazley et al., 2009; Lin and Sporleder, 2009). A resource like WordNet can help with both tasks. Matching strings in text to WordNet's entries will identify lexically relevant multi-word units, and WordNet's relational structure will provide the level of semantic interpretation that has been shown to be useful in many tasks (see Alonge and Loenneker 2004 and Fellbaum, 1998, 2002 for related work).

2 A Semantic Classification of Idioms

The idioms we have encoded can for the most part be divided between two groups: compositional and non-compositional idioms. In compositional idioms, the meaning of the phrase can be deduced from the sum of its parts, although how literal that meaning is varies greatly (Nunberg et al., 1994; Moon, 1998; Cowie 1998 *inter alia*). This is not the case in non-compositional idioms, and we found that most often, non-compositional idioms take the form of evocative images, which serve to illustrate the idiom's meaning in a more abstract manner. Taken individually, the parts of these idioms may have no connection at all with the idiom's meaning and usage. We examine several classes of idioms for their compositionality and their metaphoric character of their constituents with an eye towards their representation in WordNet.

2.1 Compositional Idioms

Compositional idioms work most often by extending metaphorical significance to real and recognizable events. Their meanings may be culture-specific and thus intuitively accessible to native speakers but not to others.

A subclass of compositional idioms whose idiomatic readings are closely related to their literal ones are those referring to physical behaviors. These can be reactions that accompany an emotional or cognitive response, and the idiomatic reading focuses on this response. Examples are listed in (1).

(1) *raise eyebrows*
   bat an eyelid/eye/eyelash
   cut to the quick
   hit a nerve
   get on your nerves
   turn your nose up
   take your breath away

bite your tongue/lips
bite off more than you can chew

These idioms are derived from the addition of psychological/cognitive meanings to physical events. The phrase preserves a literal meaning but can also be used in an extended sense. Some of the idioms in this category (2) are less plausible in their literal interpretation than those listed above – these have an added element of exaggeration or figurative language, but because the imagery used is almost exclusively sensory, and therefore implicitly understood, these idioms remain as transparent as those in (1). These expressions below may be even more culture-specific than those in (1) and depend on the speaker and audience being familiar with the customs and ideas behind them.

(2) *make your flesh crawl*
make your blood boil
melt your heart

The first kind of idiom is more likely to undergo variations, due to its transparency and plausibility. As well as the tendency to substitute components of these phrases for similar ones (hence the ability to say "bat an eyelid" as well as "bat an eyelash") there also seems to be a greater freedom in using the phrases themselves – contextual words can be easily added into the phrase, and the original components are subject to morphological changes (Ernst, 1981; Langlotz, 2006; Fellbaum, 2006, 2007). Indeed, internet searches reveal usages such as

(3) Schiavo case hit a political nerve
http://findarticles.com/p/articles/mi_qn4188/is_20050410/ai_n13598785/

(4) without the merest bat of a judicial eyelash…
http://visibleprocrastinations.wordpress.com/2006/12/

(5) the fact that no original Shakespeare manuscripts survive raise a few scholarly eyebrows.
http://74.125.93.132/search?q=cache:1BJuwTCAbJUJ:www.ricksteves.com/plan/destinations/britain/strtfrd.htm+raise+scholarly+eyebrow&cd=10&hl=en&ct=clnk&gl=us&client=firefox-a

But variation is also found for idioms of the second kind:

(6) John Saul can make readers' skin crawl
http://www.highbeam.com/doc/1P2-4067887.html

(7) Hundreds point a collective finger at Crew and Board of Ed.
http://connection.ebscohost.com/content/article/1032458628.html;jsessionid=BAA395F60ABB08BD1078EDE8EA451610.ehctc1

Since they are based on cultural constructs, which change, evolve, and are forgotten with time (unlike human physical reactions listed in (1) and (2), which we can assume remain fairly constant) these idioms are much more susceptible to changes in use and meaning. Certain idioms have even become completely opaque to native speakers of the language, who learn and use it as a set phrase with a set meaning, but are now completely unaware of its original meaning or etymology.

A related subclass of "cultural-construct" idioms in current usage are still arguably transparent:

(8) *take your hat off*
blow the whistle
blow s.b./s.th. out of the water
point the finger at
pull the trigger

Even if the speaker has never actually taken his hat off in respect, he may recognize the gesture and the meaning behind it. Most people have probably never fired a gut, but would understand the idiomatic meaning of *pull the trigger* (but see Keysar and Bly, 1995). *Blow the competition out of the water* is still widely used, but the reference to battleship warfare is quickly fading from our cultural memory, as is the metallurgy origin of *strike while the iron is hot* (Dobrovolskij and Piirainen, 2005). The meaning here resides in the entire idiom rather than in that of the constituents. Consequently, the entire idiom must be regarded as a lexical item.

The idioms listed in in (9) encode cultural references that are probably no longer current to most modern speakers:

(9) *cry wolf* (from a morality story)
  rest on your laurels (Ancient Roman laurel crowns)
  wash your hands of… (Biblical: Pontius Pilate)
  look a gifthorse in the mouth (few people today acquire horses)

These idioms are likely learned and stored as set phrases and probably exhibit less variation since speakers do not assign meaning to their components. We found no attested examples like *kick the pail, check a gifthorse's teeth, cry coyote*. Nevertheless, some constituents are referential, e.g., *gifthorse*, and could therefore merit a lexical entry.

2.2 Non-compositional Idioms

The phrases in (10) use imagery to illustrate the idioms' meanings, which do not arise from the constituents' meanings. Rather, the words paint a picture, which, in most cases, conjures up a concrete situation.

(10) *spill the beans*
walk on eggshells
beat/flog a dead horse
add fuel to the fire
bury your head in the sand
see the light
a watched pot never boils

In some of the idioms, the constituents may have metaphoric character.

2.3 Idioms with mixed properties

The classification suggested above is only approximate; a number of idioms, including those in (11), cannot be straightforwardly fit into any one category.

(11) Rise from the ashes
Throw s.b. to the wolves
See red
Tear your hair out

For example, the reference to a mythical phoenix may be lost to speakers, but *rise from the ashes* nevertheless evokes the intended meaning. Similarly, *tear your hair out*, which refers an ancient mourning ritual, is no longer culturally relevant; yet the original meaning remains perhaps on the strength of the image. *Seeing red* does not literally happen when the idiom is invoked, but the meaning relies on the understood significance of the color red, perhaps specific to Western culture.

The change from transparency to opacity and the loss of meaning of the idioms' components to contemporary speakers is of course consonant with the overall tendency of the lexicon (and language) to shift and evolve. Idioms are learned, re-hashed, re-interpreted and used in different contexts, resulting in gradual changes in use and meaning, as with many other aspects of language. Idioms that can be classified in more than one way may simply be in a transitional stage.

3 Representing Idioms in WordNet

Currently, only few idioms are included in WordNet. For example, *kick the bucket* and *buy the farm* are members of the synset that also includes *die* (WordNet synsets do not respect connotational or stylistic differences but are purely based on denotational equivalence). Treating idioms as "long words" in this manner is convenient in the case where the idiom is not composed of constituents that have a meaning, i.e., metaphors. But in many cases, the components of idioms can be said to be lexical items (form-meaning pairs) in themselves. For example, in *spill the beans*, the verb arguably carries the meaning "reveal" and *beans* refers to "secret or confidential information." Speakers assign such meanings to the idiom components, as can be seen by the fact that they modify them or substitute semantically similar items (see papers in Fellbaum 2007). We need to reflect, first, the metaphorical status of such words and, second, the fact that their use is limited to the particular context of an idiom.

An on-line idiom dictionary (http://www.usingenglish.com/reference/idioms) was manually examined and over 200 idioms were paraphrased and analyzed for their compositionality by a native English speaker. For each idiom, we identified those components that have a literal meaning. We then manually determined with WordNet synset expressed that meaning and recorded its sense key. The following are representative examples.

Old flames die hard
    It's very difficult to forget old things, especially the first love.
    flames – **feeling%1:03:00::** the experiencing of affective and emotional states
    die - **fade%2:30:00::** disappear gradually

Rain on your parade
    If someone rains on your parade, they ruin your pleasure or your plans.

rain on - **spoil%2:41:02::** make a mess of, destroy or ruin

parade – **plan%1:09:00::** a series of steps to be carried out or goals to be accomplished

    fun%1:04:00:: activities that are enjoyable or amusing

See the light
When someone sees the light, they realise the truth
see - **realise%2:31:00::** perceive (an idea or situation) mentally
light - **truth%1:26:00::** conformity to reality or actuality

In many cases, some constituents have a literal meaning, as is the case with *keep* in the following example:

Keep at bay
If you keep someone or something at bay, you maintain a safe distance from them.
keep - **keep%2:42:07::**continue a certain state, condition, or activity
bay – **distance%1:07:00::** the property created by the space between two objects or points
    distance%1:12:00:: indifference by personal withdrawal

Given these data, the idioms can be straightforwardly integrated into the WordNet database.

3.1 Idiom-specific Relations in WordNet

Wordnet is currently being converted from its text-based format to a relations (SQL) database. One distinct advantage of the new format over the old one will be that it allows the addition of a large number of relations among synsets and synset members. The integration of idioms into WordNet is therefore unproblematic.

The first step is to create a new synset containing the idiom component. In most cases, the synset will have only a single member, though in some cases, different word form, restricted to different idioms, may express the same concept. For example the members of the synset{cat, beans} both refer to a secret in the context of the idioms *let the cat out of the bag* and *spill the beans*. Next, a link will be established between these synsets and the synsets containing the appropriate word form(s) with literal readings; in this case {secret}, which were manually identified as described above. Finally, the synsets (or synset members if the synset contains more than one) containing the idiom constituents must be interlinked by another kind of pointer, which assures that only those idiom components that co-occur in the context of a specific idiom are related. For example, {beans} and {spill} are linked, as are {cat} and {bag}, but {beans} and {bags} are not, as they do not share the same distribution.

3.2 A Remaining Problem: Prepositions

The proposed approach to integrating idioms into WordNet will help the automatic recognition of idiomatic strings in a text by identifying the meanings of idiom components. However, we are not able at present to handle prepositions that are specific to an idiom. WordNet does not include prepositions among the major parts of speech that are encoded. Part of the reasoning was that prepositions have a status somewhere between content and function words.

Clearly, the choice of a particular preposition in an idiom is not entirely arbitrary. In some phrases, like *sweep something under the rug/carpet,* which conveys the sense of hiding in a way that *sweeping something on the rug/carpet* could not (and carpet/rugs are a kind of *covering*), the choice of preposition is crucial. In other cases, however, the choice of preposition can be much looser without changing much of the meaning of the phrase - it could *rain **on** your parade* or ***over** your parade*, and you *could look **on** the bright side* or ***at** the bright side*, and even *look **for** the bright side*, all of which convey the same meaning. These idiosyncracies make it difficult to treat all prepositions in the same way - they don't all need to be clearly defined, but neither can they simply be left out.

The absence of prepositions in WordNet does not allow us at present to represent their semantic contribution to the idioms. In cases like *take a leaf out of s.o.'s book* (copy s.th. from s.b. to one's advantage), reanalysis was the solution. We analyze *take_out* as a unit (a phrasal verb) and mapped it to an existent sense in WordNet.

4 Conclusions

There are several advantages to representing idioms in this way. Besides closing a serious gap in WordNet's coverage, we distinguish opaque and transparent idioms on the one hand, and partially from fully transparent ones on the other hand. In addition, the proposed representation takes into account the fact that idioms are not fixed strings or "long words." Rather, they show a remarkable range of syntactic and lexical modification, including lexical substitution (Langlotz, 2006; Fellbaum 2006, 2007)). This flexibility stumps applications that rely on lexical databases treating idioms as long strings, making it impossible to recognize syntactically or lexically "deviations" from the standard citation form that sets an often arbitrary norm (Sag et al., 2001). By contrast, our proposal potentially enables automatic systems to recognize and interpret idioms in all their varieties.

Statistical approaches that measure the collocational properties of idiom components can perform well in recognizing idiomatic phrases (Church and Hanks, 1990). For example, they recognize that *cat* and *bag* frequently cooccur, and they can do so independently of syntactic variation or modification. However, they are unlikely to recognize idioms where a lexeme has been substituted, but see Herold (2007) for a solution.

Acknowledgments

This work has been supported by grant CI-ADDO-EN 0855157 from the National Science Foundation under the American Recovery and Reinvestment Act. We thank Jordan Boyd-Graber and Bettina Burgett for helpful discussions.

References

Antonietta Alonge and Birte Lönneker. 2004. The Heart of the Problem: How Shall we Represent Metaphors in Wordnets? Proceedings of the Second International WordNet Conference. Brno, p. 10.

Kenneth W. Church, K. and Patrick Hanks. 1990. Word Association Norms, Mutual Information, and Lexicography. *Computational Linguistics* 16:22-29.

Alan. P. Cowie. 1998. *Phraseology: Theory, Analysis, and Applications.* Oxford: Oxford University Press

Dmitrij Dobrovol'skij and Elizabeth Piirainen. 2005. *Figurative Languge: crosscultural and crosslinguistic perspectives.* Amsterdam: John Benjamins.

Thomas Ernst. 1981. Grist for the linguistic mill: Idioms and "extra" adjectives'. *Journal of Linguistic Research,* 1:51–68.

Afsaneh Fazly, Paul Cook and Suzanne Stevenson. 2009. Unsupervised type and token identification of idiomatic expressions. *Computational Linguistics*, 35(1):61–103.

Christiane Fellbaum. 1998. Towards a representation of idioms inWordNet. In S. Harabagiu (ed), *Proceedings of the Workshop on Usage of WordNet in Natural Language Processing Systems.* Montreal: COLING/ACL 1998, pp. 52–57.

Christiane Fellbaum. 2002. VP idioms in the lexicon: Topics for research using a very large corpus. In S. Busemann (ed), *Proceedings of KONVENS 2002.* Saarbrücken, Germany: DFKI, pp. 7-11.

Christiane Fellbaum. 2006 (ed.) Corpus-based Studies of German Idioms and Light Verbs. *International Journal of Lexicography* 19.4.

Christiane Fellbaum. 2007 (ed.) *Idioms and Collocations*. Birmingham, UK: Continuum Press.

Axel Herold. 2007. *Corpus Queries*. In: Fellbaum (2007, ed.) 54-63.

Ray Jackendoff. 1997. Twistin' the Night away'. *Language,* 73:534–559.

Boaz Keysar and Bridget Bly. 1995. Intuitions of the transparency of idioms. Can one keep a secret by spilling the beans? *Journal of Memory and Language*, 34, 89–109.

George Lakoff and Mark Johnson. 1980. *Metaphors We Live By.* Chicago: University of Chicago Press.

Andreas Langlotz. 2006. *Idiomatic Creativity*. Amsterdam: John Benjamins.

Rosamund Moon. 1998. *Fixed Expressions and Idioms in English. A Corpus-Based Approach*. Oxford Studies in Lexicography and Lexicology. Oxford: Clarendon Press.

Geoffrey Nunberg, Ivan Sag and Thomas Wasow. 1994. Idioms. *Language* 70, 491–538.

Ivan Sag, Timothy Baldwin, Francis Bond, Anne Copestake and Dan Flickinger. 2001. Multiword Expressions: A pain in the neck for NLP. *LinGO Working Papers*, No. 2001-03.

Linlin Li and Caroline Sporleder. 2009. Classifier Combination for Contextual Idiom Detection Without Labelled Data. *EMNLP*.

Enriching the Romanian WordNet using Semi-automatically Identified Hyponymic Patterns

Verginica Barbu Mititelu
Romanian Academy Research Institute for Artificial Intelligence
13, Calea 13 Septembrie, Bucharest 050711, Romania
vergi@racai.ro

Dan Ştefănescu
Romanian Academy Research Institute for Artificial Intelligence
13, Calea 13 Septembrie, Bucharest 050711, Romania
danstef@racai.ro

Alexandru Ceauşu
Romanian Academy Research Institute for Artificial Intelligence
13, Calea 13 Septembrie, Bucharest 050711, Romania
aceausu@racai.ro

Abstract

This paper presents the algorithm used for the semi-automatic identification of Romanian hyponymic patterns, the precision of these patterns, which we further use for identifying on the web and filtering instances or Named Entities to be introduced in the Romanian WordNet.

1 Introduction

The development of the Romanian WordNet (RoWN) started in the BalkaNet project (Tufiş et al., 2004). Since then it has been being enriched so that at the moment of this writing, RoWN contains 55,985 synsets (with 49,439 lemmas) classified according to the DOMAINS3.1 taxonomy (Bentivogli et al., 2004), aligned to the SUMO&MILO ontology concepts (Niles and Pease, 2001), labeled with subjectivity markups (Tufiş, 2009) of the SentiWordNet type (Esuli and Sebastiani 2006). All words in glosses have been lemmatized, tagged and parsed (with dependency links).

RoWN has been used as a lexical resource for most of the system applications developed in our Institute: TREQ-AL (Tufiş et al., 2003), COW-AL (Tufiş et al., 2006a), SynWSD (Ion and Tufiş, 2007), QA systems (Puşcaşu et al., 2006, Ion et al. 2008, Ion et al., 2009). The very good results of these systems in competitions are, in great part, due to the quality of the linguistic resource they use, i.e. the RoWN.

This paper presents the way we enriched the RoWN with instances from the geographical domain using hyponymic patterns. We present the methodology for identifying these patterns for English and Romanian (section 2), alongside with their precision (section 3). We compare the Romanian hyponymic patterns with the English ones. Section 4 describes the methodology for selecting the target concepts from the geography domain for which we identified instances on the Internet (section 5). For refining the results, we process the snippets extracted by Google (section 6). We present the results in section 7, the related work in section 8, and then conclude our paper, envisaging further work.

2 Patterns Identification

In (Barbu Mititelu 2008) we presented the methodology for semi-automatic identification of hyponymic patterns. For English we ran an experiment on over 38 million words from British National Corpus (BNC) from which we automatically extracted those sentences containing nouns in hyponymy relation, which we recognized using Princeton WordNet 2.0[1]. We automatically grouped the extracted sentences according to the similarity of the lexical material (i.e. lemmas) between the hyponym and its co-occurring hypernym, thus resulting groups of examples with identical lexical material between the hyponym and its hypernym. These examples were then manually inspected to extract the hyponymic patterns.

For Romanian we did not have such a large corpus at that moment, so we proceeded to two different methods for identifying the patterns: one was the translation of the English ones found as described above, and the second was the running of the same experiment as for English but on a small Romanian corpus (1 million words) and using the RoWN (a version having more 46,000 synsets) as source of hyponym-hypernym pairs.

---

[1] In version 2.0 of Princeton WordNet the INSTANCE-OF relation does not exist; instances are recorded as hyponyms.

A comparison between the English and Romanian hyponymic patterns shows that different languages have the tendency to "lexicalize" this lexicon-semantic relation in similar ways (the intersection of the sets of patterns in the two languages contains 70% of the English ones and 66.6% of the Romanian ones).

3 Patterns Testing

The English patterns were tested in order to establish their precision on a file (of 7 million words) from BNC. The most representative results are in Table 1:

English Pattern	Precision (%)
NP *other than* NP	100
NP *especially* NP	100
NP *principally* NP	100
NP *usually* NP	100
NP *such as* NP	99.2
NP *in particular* NP	92.3
NP *e(.)g(.)* NP	91.4
NP *become* NP	91
NP *another* NP	87
NP *notably* NP	86.8
NP *particularly* NP	84.6
NP *except* NP	84.6
NP *called* NP	81.5
NP *like* NP	81.3
NP *including* NP	80.6
NP *mainly* NP	75
NP *mostly* NP	70.8

Table 1. Precision of English hyponymic patterns

For the present study we tested the Romanian hyponymic patterns on a sub-corpus of the OPUS corpus[2], namely the EMEA (European Medicines Agency) documents (11,914,802 tokens). However, it abounds in repeated expressions and a specialized vocabulary (Tiedemann, 2009). The results are in Table 2.

Romanian Pattern	Precision (%)
NP *chiar și* NP ("even")	100
NP *de obicei* NP ("usually")	100
NP, *ci (și/doar)* NP ("but also")	100
NP *în special* NP ("especially")	96.88
NP *precum* NP ("such as")	94.83
NP *cum ar fi* NP ("such as")	93.75

[2] http://www.let.rug.nl/~tiedemann/OPUS/

NP *(în) afară de* NP ("except")	92.11
NP *și (orice) alt* NP ("and (any) (an)other")	90.1
NP *fi un* NP ("be a")	87.98
NP *sau alt* NP ("or (an)other")	86.96
NP *mai ales* NP ("especially")	85.71
NP *alt decât* NP ("other than")	85.71
NP *sine numi* NP ("be called")	84
NP *inclusiv* NP ("including")	83.51
NP *de exemplu* NP ("for example")	79.57
NP *fi considerat* NP ("be considered")	79.17
NP *care fi* NP ("that be")	74.12
NP, *adică* NP ("namely")	66.66
NP *cu excepția* NP ("except")	54.55
NP *și (tot) celălalt* NP ("and (all) other")	54.29

Table 2. Precision of Romanian hyponymic patterns

Comparing the precisions of the Romanian and the English patterns, we notice that many of them are quite similar (or even identical). This is a further proof that different languages tend to lexicalize hyponymy in similar ways.

4 Selection of Target Concepts

To proceed to the semi-automatic identification of instances in the geographical domain to include in the RoWN, we needed to select from the RoWN those concepts whose daughters are instances we are interested in identifying. The RoWN was aligned to the XML version of PWN 2.1 (Tufiș et al., 2006b). We extracted from it those synsets that have synsets in INSTANCE-OF relation with them (i.e. parent synsets whose daughters are in INSTANCE-OF relation with them).

From the resulted synsets we selected only those that belong to the geography domain: 38 synsets containing 54 literals.

5 Extracting Snippets with Geographical NEs

We introduced these literals in the position normally occupied by the hypernym in five Romanian hyponymic patterns with high precision (see Table 3), thus obtaining some "seeds". For each seed, we extracted its occurrences on the Internet using a Google Screen Scraper C# library. It allows one to input expressions into the Google Search Engine and get all the results of the search into structured objects, which can be used by different applications.

Our seed is transformed into an URL link, after which an *HttpWebRequest* is performed for that link. The request goes to Google Search Engine, which returns an html page containing results corresponding to a user input for the expression, with search parameters embedded in the link. An *HttpWebResponse* gets the html results page. An *HtmlParser* parses the page and builds an object containing all the info in the page: the html source code, the URL of the page, number of occurrences and list of items. An item corresponds to a hit of the Google Engine. It contains: the title of the hit document, the snippet (the object of our interest), the type of the document (html, pdf, etc.) and the links to the cached document and similar pages.

6 Snippets Processing

For improving the results, we decided to process the snippets extracted by Google from the Internet. Two important sources of noise in these snippets are homonymy and disregard of sentence boundary. Google does not morphologically disambiguate and segment the texts in which it searches. Thus, it returns snippets that are sometimes useless: graphical identity of different words (homography or even homonymy), words in vicinity but belonging to different sentences, so that they cannot be considered as belonging to the patterns we are interested in. Cases of homography are very numerous on Internet pages in Romanian: besides homonyms such as *mare* "big" and *mare* "sea", the lack of diacritics increases in a large extent the number of homographs: for instance, *fata* may have 8 different values.

In order to solve these problems, we first introduced diacritics in these snippets using DIAC[+] (Tufiş and Ceauşu, 2008) and then we segmented, tokenized and PoS-tagged the snippets using the TTL module (Ion, 2007). We preserved only the snippets containing NPs.

As the geographical instances we are interested in are correctly written with capital letters, we further selected only those snippets in which the seed is followed by an NP with capital initial letter.

7 Results

We manually inspected the snippets containing our seeds and, although the websites in Romanian are quite numerous, we notice that most of our seeds are not frequent. Moreover, most of the patterns considered in the experiment have a good precision. The most useful one is *NP precum NP*, which is both frequent and very productive.

Pattern	Occurrences	Precision (%)
NP chiar şi NP ("even")	19	57.89
NP de obicei NP ("usually")	1	100
NP în special NP ("especially")	112	85.71
NP precum NP ("such as")	518	95.37
NP cum ar fi NP ("such as")	7	100

Table 3. Seeds evaluation.

In Table 4 we present the list of literals found on the web occurring in the seeds we created. For each of them we give the number of instances (NEs) found on the web that are already in the RoWN and the number of the instances (NEs) that are not in RoWN, but can be introduced (and defined by a lexicographer).

Literal	NEs already in RoWN	NEs not in RoWN
stat "state"	23	6
ţară europeană "European country"	12	2
ţară balcanică "Balkan country"	4	4
ţară africană "African country"	15	1
ţară asiatică "Asian country"	8	1
arhipelag "archipelago"	0	1
câmpie "plain"	0	2
insulă "island"	11	17
oraş "town"	36	13
fluviu "river"	3	1
capitală "capital"	11	1
cascadă "waterfall"	0	6
centru "center"	0	23
continent "continent"	5	0
imperiu "empire"	4	5
ţară "country"	37	4
provincie "province"	4	14

Table 4. Seeds productivity

8 Related Work

Repositories of Named Entities are necessary for various tasks in computational linguistics. Thus, their creation can be considered a task in itself.

Toral et al. (2008) automatically extend PWN 2.1 with Named Entities using Wikipedia: the is-a hyerarchy in PWN is mapped onto the Wikipedia categories; the NEs in Wikipedia are recognized and introduced in a resource called Named Entity WordNet. De Loupy et al. (2004) enrich PWN with NEs without specifying the method they used. The work that is the closest to our experiment is Mann (2002) which extracts an ontology of NEs from a news wire text using textual co-occurrence patterns, namely: common noun immediately followed by a proper noun.

Our study stands alone among these works in that it makes use of patterns reported in the literature as identified and tested for the co-occurrence of a hyponym and its hypernym at short distance in texts, with the aim of extracting instances (more exactly NEs).

9 Conclusions and Further Work

Our paper presents a new method of extracting NEs from texts, using patterns originally identified and tested for hyponym-hypernym co-occurrence in corpora. Our main aim was to test the validity of the hyponymic patterns for the instance-class relation. The second aim of this research was to enrich the RoWN with instances that could be further used for various tasks undertaken by our team. Thus, we aim at continuing the experiment with NEs from other domains. Afterwards, remarks can be made on the productivity of hyponymic patterns in various domains and on the adaptation of the methodology to each domain (e.g., in chemistry, chemical elements are considered instances, but are not normally capitalized). From such experiments we can draw conclusions about the relevance of such patterns for the hyponymy and instance-class relations, about their similarity in the way they are "lexicalized" in corpora.

Acknowledgements

The work reported here is funded by the SIR-RESDEC project, financed by the Ministry of Education, Research and Innovation under the grant no 11-007.

References

Verginica Barbu Mititelu. 2008. Hyponymy Patterns. *Text, Speech and Dialogue, 11th International Conference, TSD 2008*:37-44.

Luisa Bentivogli, Pamela Forner, Bernardo Magnini, and Emanuele Pianta. 2004. Revising WordNet Domains Hierarchy: Semantics, Coverage, and Balancing. *Proceedings of COLING 2004*:101-108.

Andrea Esuli and Fabrizio Sebastiani. 2006. SentiWordNet: A Publicly Available Lexical Resource for Opinion Mining. *Proceedings of LREC 2006*: 417-422.

Christiane Fellbaum (ed.). 1998. *WordNet: An Electronical Lexical Database*. MIT Press.

Radu Ion and Dan Tufiş. 2007. Meaning Affinity Models. *Proceedings of the Fourth International Workshop on Semantic Evaluations*:282-287.

Radu Ion, Dan Ştefănescu, Alexandru Ceauşu, and Dan Tufiş. 2008. RACAI's QA System at the Romanian-Romanian Multiple Language Question Answering (QA@CLEF2008) Main Task. *Working Notes for CLEF 2008 Workshop*.

Radu Ion, Dan Ştefănescu, Alexandru Ceauşu, Dan Tufiş, Elena Irimia, Verginica Barbu Mititelu. 2009. A Trainable Multi-factored QA System. *Working Notes for CLEF 2009 Workshop*.

Claude de Loupy, Eric Crestan, Elise Lemaire. 2004. Proper Nouns Thesaurus for Document Retrieval and Question Answering. *Atelier Question-Réponse, Traitement Automatique des Langues Naturelles (TALN)*.

Gideon S. Mann. 2002. *Fine-Grained Proper Noun Ontologies for Question Answering*.

Ian Niles and Adam Pease. 2001. Towards a Standard Upper Ontology. *Proceedings of the 2nd International Conference on Formal Ontology in Information Systems*.

Georgiana Puşcaşu, Adrian Iftene, Ionuţ Pistol, Diana Trandabăţ, Dan Tufiş, Alexandru Ceauşu, Dan Ştefănescu, Radu Ion, Constantin Orăşan, Iustin Dornescu, Alex Moruz, and Dan Cristea. Developing a Question Answering System for the Romanian-English Track at CLEF 2006. *Working Notes for the CLEF 2006 Workshop*.

Jörg Tiedemann. 2009. News from OPUS – A collection of multilingual parallel corpora with tools and interfaces. *Recent Advances in Natural Language Processing: Selected Papers from RANLP 2007*. John Benjamins:237-248.

Antonio Toral, Rafael Munoz, Monica Monachini. 2008. Named Entity WordNet. *Proceedings of the 6th International Language Resources and Evaluation Conference.*

Dan Tufiş. 2009. Paradigmatic Morphology and Subjectivity Mark-up in the RO-WordNet Lexical Ontology. In H.N. Teodorescu, Junzo Watada, and L. Jain. *Intelligent Systems and Technologies - Methods and Applications. Studies in Computational Intelligence*: 161-179.

Dan Tufiş, Ana-Maria Barbu, Radu Ion. 2003. TREQ-AL: A Word-Alignment System with Limited Language Resources. *Proceedings of the HLT-NAACL 2003 Workshop: Building and Using Parallel Texts: Data Driven Machine Translation and Beyond*:36-39.

Dan Tufiş, Dan Cristea, and Sofia Stamou. 2004. BalkaNet: Aims, Methods, Results and Perspectives. A General Overview. *Romanian Journal of Information Science and Technology*, 7(2-3):9-44.

Dan Tufiş, Radu Ion, Alexandru Ceauşu, and Dan Ştefănescu. 2006a. Improved Lexical Alignment by Combining Multiple Reified Alignments. *Proceedings of the 11th Conference on the European Chapter of the Association for Computational Linguistics*: 153-160.

Dan Tufiş, Verginica Barbu Mititelu, Alexandru Ceauşu, Luigi Bozianu, Cătălin Mihăilă, Margareta Manu Magda. 2006b. Noi dezvoltări ale wordnetului românesc. In Corina Forăscu, Dan Tufiş, Dan Cristea (eds.), *Resurse Lingvistice şi Instrumente pentru prelucrarea Limbii Române*: 17-22.

Dan Tufiş and Alexandru Ceauşu. 2008. DIAC[+]: A Professional Diacritics Recovering System. *Proceedings of the 6th Language Resources and Evaluation Conference.*

Introducing Sanskrit WordNet

Malhar Kulkarni
Department of Humanities and Social Sciences,
Indian Institute of Technology Bombay
malhar@iitb.ac.in

Chaitali Dangarikar
Center for Indian Language Technology,
Indian Institute of Technology Bombay
chaitali.dangarikar@gmail.com

Irawati Kulkarni
Center for Indian Language Technology,
Indian Institute of Technology Bombay
irawatikulkarni@gmail.com

Abhishek Nanda
Center for Indian Language Technology,
Indian Institute of Technology Bombay
abhi.nanda@gmail.com

Pushpak Bhattacharyya
Center for Indian Language Technology,
Indian Institute of Technology Bombay
pb@cse.iitb.ac.in

Abstract

How does one build the wordnet of a language that has a rich lexical tradition spanning over millennia? The sheer volume of words and their nuances, the rich, deep and diverse grammatical tradition, the pressure of modern developments on the language- all these factors and more combine to pose unique challenges in creating lexical resources for such languages. This present paper describes the construction of Sanskrit wordnet, being built using the *expansion approach*. It presents the processes and challenges involved in this task that purports to uncover the intimate linkage that underlies Indian languages most of which have speaker population numbering 20 to 500 million.

1 Introduction

Sanskrit is historically an Indo-Aryan language (Deshpande, 1992) and one of the 22 official languages of India. It has a vast literature and the interest in analyzing and translating these texts is always on the rise, worldwide.

Specifically, our motivation for building Sanskrit wordnet arises from the following facts:

1. For all languages in the Indo European family in India, the roots can be traced to Sanskrit. A large part of the vocabulary of these languages is derived from Sanskrit which can, therefore, provide the pivot resource for many Indian languages. The speaker population for these languages range from 10 million (Konkani) to 500 million (Hindi/Urdu).

2. Being a heritage language, there is need to digitize and preserve ancient texts in Sanskrit. This activity is greatly helped by word lists. An Optical Character Recognition Device (OCR) for Sanskrit, for example, would need spell correction after scan, and this would need an exhaustive lexicon.

3. Simlarly, there exists real need for translating ancient texts to preserve traditional culture and knowledge. An online wordnet would no doubt be a great help to a translator.

4. Machine aided translation (MAT) is maturing fast, and automatic translation of Sanskrit text is a challenging problem needing wordnet.

5. There is an enormous amount of Sanskrit text which should be available in keyword based searchable form. Text search is greatly helped by wordnets.

6. The tradition of developing lexical resource is very old in Sanskrit. There are diverse *koshas* (traditional and rich monolingual dictionaries) in Sanskrit (see section 1.2 below). Sanskrit wordnet will serve as the **single reference** point representing and pointing to all these resources.

1.1 Sanskrit language

Indian subcontinent is inhabited by a very large population who speak languages belonging to 4 major families, Indo-Aryan (a sub-family of Indo-European), Dravidian, Tibeto-Burman and Austro-Asiatic. Sanskrit is the oldest member of the Indo-Aryan language family, a sub branch of Indo-Iranian, which in turn is a branch of Indo European language family.

There is a traditional fourfold division of lexical units of Indian languages into:

1. तत्सम *tatsama*[1]- words having their origin in Sanskrit and accepted in the modern Indo-Aryan languages without any change in their phonology.

2. तद्भव *tadbhava*[2]- words which have their origin in Sanskrit but their phonological forms are changed as per the rules of the modern Indo-Aryan languages.

3. देशी *desh•* –words which are the native words of the particular language and

4. विदेशी *videsh•* – words borrowed from foreign languages.

The links to तत्सम *tatsama* and तद्भव *tadbhava* words, in particular, will be a great pan-Indian linguistic resource for computational purposes. Table 1 below lists some examples of Sanskrit words in Hindi wordnet[3].

HWN Synset	Tatsam word	HWN synset	English meaning
{तुलसी, पावनी, बहुमंजरी, वृंदा, वृन्दा, वैष्णवी, भारवी, मंजरीक, विश्वपावन, विश्व-पूजिता, पुष्पसारा, त्रिदशमंजरी, त्रिदशमञ्जरी, तीव्रा, पत्रपुष्पा, श्रीमंजरी,श्रीमञ्जरी, अमृता}	तुलसी	तुलसी	basil
	वृन्दा	वृन्दा	
	वैष्णवी	वैष्णवी	
	पावनी	पावनी	
	पत्रपुष्पा	पत्रपुष्पा	
{भौंह,भौं,भ्रू,भृकुटी, तेवर,कोंडर,कोंडं,अबरू}	भ्रू	भ्रू	eyebrow, brow, supercilium
	भृकुटी	भृकुटी	
{पेशी,माँस-पेशी,मांस-पेशी,माँसपेशी,मांसपेशी.माँस पेशी,मांस पेशी,नस}	पेशी	पेशी	muscle, musculus
	मांसपेशी	मांसपेशी	
{बैंगन,बैंगन,भंटा,भाँटा, शाकबिल्व,शाकबिल्वक, वृंताक,वृन्ताक,नीलवृषा, शाकश्रेष्ठा,वृंताकी, वागुनी,वरा, चित्रफला,रक्तकंठ, रक्तकण्ठ,निद्रालु, नीलफला,नटपत्रिका}	शाकबिल्व	बैंगन	eggplant, aubergine, mad_apple
	शाकश्रेष्ठा	बैंगन	
	चित्रफला	बैंगन	
	वृन्ताक	बैंगन	
	निद्रालु	बैंगन	
	नीलफल	बैंगन	

Table 1: Tatsama words in the HWN

These representative examples show that the synsets in Hindi wordnet contain 60-70% tatsama (directly borrowed from Sanskrit) words.

---

[1] *Tatsama Shabda Kosha* (*Tatsama* words dictionary) is published by Kendriya Hindi Nideshalaya, Shiksha Vibhaga, Manava Samsadhana Vikasa Mantralaya, Bharata Sarakara in 1988.

[2] See *Hindi ki Tadbhava Shabdavali* (Sarma, 1968).

[3] www.cfilt.iitb.ac.in/wordnet/webhwn.

1.2 Rich lexical tradition of Sanskrit

Sanskrit has a rich tradition of creating léxica (Kulkarni, 2008). *Nighantu*[4] (700BC) on which Yaska is believed to have written a commentary called *Nirukta* is the oldest known treatise that arranged lexical material from the point of view of *synonymy* as well as *homonymy*, and this tradition continued to *Pali*[5] tradition as well. The first and the foremost popular name of lexicon work in classical Sanskrit is Amarasimha's ***Amarakosha*** (6th century AD) (Oka, 1913). The Catalogous Catalogorum lists at least 40 commentaries on *Amarkosha* alone, which shows how important and popular this synonyms dictionary in ancient India was.

There were many other léxica created more or less in the style of *Amarakosha* which are given in Appendix A (11 of them).

The first modern-day dictionary of Sanskrit was the Sanskrit-English Dictionary compiled by Professor H.H. Wilson and published in 1819 (Wilson, 1819)Two Indian dictionaries came out soon after, namely, the *Shabdakalpadruma*[6] (Deb, 1988) of Pt. Sir Raja Radhakanta Dev and *Vacasptyam*[7] (Bhattacharya, 2003) compiled by Pt Taranatha Tarkavacaspati.

So far the electronic lexical resources available for Sanskrit are mainly online dictionaries.[8] The linguistic resources like Śhabdakalpadruma

---

[4] *Nighantu* is Sanskrit term for the collection of words, grouped thematic categories with brief annotations

[5] Pali is a Middle Indo-Aryan language (or Prakrit) of India. It is best known as the language of the earliest extant Buddhist scriptures.

[6] *Shabdakalpadruma* is a first Sanskrit uni-lingual dictionary arranged in the modern alphabetical principles. It gives full quotations and definitions from the original *Koshas* which were unavailable in print at that time. Sets of synonymous words from the traditional *Koshas* are arranged under the headword, followed by the brief gloss. Each entry in the lexicon includes headword, its category, meaning, usages in the Sanskrit texts.

[7] *Vacasptyam* is a modern mono-lingual Sanskrit lexicon. It arranges words in the Sanskrit alphabetical order and gives grammatical information with word derivations as per the traditional Sanskrit grammar. It contains about 46970 unique words. Each entry in the lexicon includes headword, its category, meaning, set of synonymous words, usages and some other information.

[8] The online dictionaries available for Sanskrit are-(1) Monier Williams dictionary < http://webapps.uni-koeln.de/tamil/>, (2) Apte's Sanskrit-English Dictionary < http://www.aa.tufs.ac.jp/~tjun/sktdic/>, (3) Apte's English-Sanskrit Dictionary < http://www.sanskrit-lexicon.uni-koeln.de/aequery/index.html> and (4) Spoken Sanskrit Dictionary: an online hypertext dictionary for Sanskrit - English and English - Sanskrit.< http://spokensanskrit.de/>. Apart from that various scanned versions of the printed dictionaries prepared by European scholars are available at < http://www.sanskrit-lexicon.uni-koeln.de/>.

and *Vaacaspatyam* are vast. For example, a comparison of the entries for the word **war** in these electronic dictionaries with the synsets of the same word in the Sanskrit Wordnet is a good indicator of the richness of this lexical tradition in Sanskrit.

1. Spoken Sanskrit Dictionary: (7 words) युद्ध, युध्, संग्राम, समर, आयोधन, आहव , रण्य .

2. Apate's Sanskrit-English Dictionary: (7 words) विग्रहः, संग्रहारः, वैरारंभः, वैरं, संग्रामः, युद्धं, रणं

3. Monier Williams Dictionary: (56 words) अनीक ,अभ्यामर्द ,अम्बरीष ,अरर ,आजि ,आनर्त, आयोधन, आहव, आहाव, कण्ठाल, कन्दल, खज, न, नदनु, निग्रहण , पुष्कर ,प्रविदारण ,प्रसर ,बलज ,भण्डन ,भर ,भीमर ,युत्कार, युद ,योध ,योधन ,रण्य ,राटि ,रु ,वराक ,विदथ ,विदार, विदारण ,विमर्द ,विमर्दन ,शम्बर ,शिलीमुख ,संयत् ,संयुग , संस्फोट ,संस्फेट ,संक्रन्द ,संक्रन्दन ,संख्य ,संगथ ,समनीक , समाघात ,समुदय ,समुदाय ,समुदर्ष ,समोह ,समर ,समृति , सम्पराय ,हान्त्र ,हार and

4. Sanskrit Wordnet: (97 words) युद्धम् , संग्रामः, समरः, रणः, समरम्, आयोधनम्, आहवम्, रण्यम्, अनीकः, अनीकम्, अभिसम्पातः, अभ्यामर्दः, अररः, आक्रन्दः, योधनम्, जन्यम्, प्रधनम्, प्रविदारणम्, मृधम्, आस्कन्दनम्, संख्यम्, समीकम्, साम्परायिकम्, कलहः, विग्रहः, संप्रहारः, कलिः, संस्फोटः, संयुगः, समाघातः, अभ्यागमः, आहवः, समुदायः, संयत्, समितिः, आजिः, समित्, युत्, संरावः, आनाहः, सम्परायकः, विदारः, दारणम्, संवित्, सम्परायः, बलजम्, आनर्तः, अभिमरः, समुदयः, विवाक्, विखादः, नदनुः, भरः, आक्रन्दः, पृतनाज्यम्, अभीकम्, समीकम्, ममसत्यम्, नेमधिता, सङ्काः, समनम्, मीळ्हे, पृतनाः, स्पृत्, स्पृद्, मृत्, मृद्, पृत्, पृद्, समत्, समर्यः, समरणम्, समोहः, समिथः, सङ्खः, सङ्गः, संयुगम्, सङ्गथः, सङ्गमः, वृत्रत्र्यम्, पृक्षः, आणिः, शीरसातिः, वाजसातिः, समनीकम्, खलः, खजः, पौंस्यम्, महाधनः, वाजः, अजम्, सद्म, संयत्, संयद्, संवतः

1.3 The process of building the Sanskrit wordnet

There are two methods to develop a Wordnet: (1) Expand method and (2) Merge method (Vossen, 2002). In the first method, a wordnet is constructed based on an existing wordnet. In the second method, sub-Wordnets for specific domains are built and later merged. For Sanskrit Wordnet, the Hindi wordnet is considered as the source resource. Though *expanded* from Hindi wordnet, care was taken to ensure that Sanskrit wordnet captures the real lexical structure of Sanskrit language.

1.4 Expansion approach for Indian language wordnets

Wordnet construction activities in India started in 2000 and the Hindi wordnet[9] (Narayan *et al.*, 2002) is the first one which got released on the Web in 2006. It was built *ab initio* using words from available lexical resources of Hindi. The design of the Hindi wordnet follows the famous English WordNet[10].

While following the expand method, the Sanskrit wordnet follows the hierarchy preservation principle (HPP) (Tufis *et al.*, 2008). In the hierarchy of the Hindi wordnet, if synset H_2 is a hyponym of synset H_1, and the translation equivalents in the Sanskrit wordnet for H_1 and H_2 are S_1 and S_2 respectively, then in the hierarchy of Sanskrit wordnet S_2 should be a hyponym of synset S_1. Thus, in the expansion approach lexicographers are spared the task of establishing afresh semantic relations for the synsets of Sanskrit wordnet. Appendix 2 describes and shows the screenshots of lexicographers' interface for creating the Sanskrit wordnet.

1.5 Synset creation in Sanskrit wordnet

Domains: Initially the Sanskrit wordnet started creating synsets with random synsets from the Hindi Wordnet. Later on, lists of important Sanskrit words were acquired from different sources. University of Hyderabad provided a list of most frequent words in their Sanskrit corpus. It consisted of 8338 words. Another word list available on the indology forum[11] contains a list of 127796 unique words from two major epics of Sanskrit literature: *Ramayana*[12] and *Mahabharata*.[13] The third list is prepared based on the lexicon called *Bharatiya Vyavahara Kosha* (Naravane, 1961). Table 2 shows the part of speech distribution of Naravane's lexicon. It contains 2766 words which are used for 1969 concepts related to the day to day life. Table 3 shows a comparison between the lists of Sanskrit words gleaned from various sources mentioned above.

---

[9] www.cfilt.iitb.ac.in/wordnet/webhwn
[10] Wordnet.princetoon.edu
[11] <http://indology.info>
[12] *Ramayana* is an ancient Sanskrit epic. The Valmiki *Ramayana* is published in 7 volumes, *Baroda*: University of Baroda Oriental Institute, 1960-1975.
[13] Mahabharata is one of the two important epics of India. *The Critical Edition of the Mahabharata* is prepared by the Bhandarkar Oriental Institute, Pune from April 1919 to September 1966. It has 19 volumes consisting 18 Parvan-s; 89000+ verses in the Constituted Text, and an elaborate Critical Apparatus.

The above mentioned words are organized into **52 domains**.[14] Omitting function words, a core set of concepts was prepared and then by Sept. 2009 synsets for all these core concepts were created.[15]

Nouns	Verbs	Adjectives	Adverbs
1512	225	180	52

Table 2: POS distribution of the synsets created (core concepts)

Sanskrit List 1	Sanskrit List 2	Sanskrit List 3	Hindi List 1
Univ. of Hyderabad most frequent words in Sanskrit (Amba Kulkarni)	Sanskrit Word list (Based on Ramayana and Mahabharata)	Number of Sanskrit Words in Naravane's Bhasha Vyavahar Kosh	Hindi wordnet Total number of unique words
8338	127796	2766	105157

Table 3: Sanskrit word list

While creating synsets the following considerations are kept in mind:

Inserting concepts or glosses in the Sanskrit wordnet: A combination of the glosses given in dictionaries like *Shabdakalpadruma* and the translation of the gloss of the Hindi wordnet synset is used to create the Sanskrit synset glosses. While writing the gloss, complicated सन्धि*sandhis*[16] and समास*samAsas* (compounds) are avoided. Whenever lengthy compounds (having 5-6 members) became necessary, the members of the compounds were invariably joined with the hyphen symbol (-) as in: "अन्य-स्थान-संयोगानुकूल-व्यापार meaning *the activity that is helpful in reaching a place*" *anya-sthAna-saMyogAnu-kUla-vyApAraH* where the members of the compounds are अन्य (*anya*), स्थान (*sthAna*), संयोग (*saMyoga*), अनुकूल (*anukUla*), व्यापार (*vyApAra*)[17]. and they are indicated by inserting hyphen. For example- the gloss of a verb in Sanskrit is generally created using technical terms like व्यापार *vyApAra* 'action', जन्य *janya* 'produced,' अनुकूल *anukUla* 'helpful,' etc.[18]

2 Problems faced in the expansion approach

In this section we enumerate the challenges faced in creating the synsets of Sanskrit wordnet in consonance with those of Hindi.

---

[14] These domains are: 1) Grains and Cereals, 2) Limbs of Humans, 3) Medical treatment, 4) Tools & implements, 5) Worms & Insects, 6) Minerals, 7) Food and Drinks, 8)Games & sports, 9) Ornaments & Trinkets, 10) Household articles, 11) Limbs of animals, 12) Post office, 13) Vegetables, 14) Directions, 15) Country, 16) Religion, 17) Court, 18) Birds, 19) Trees & plants, 20) Dress, 21) Nature, 22) Animals, 23) Fruits, 24) Flowers, 25) Young-ones of animals, 26) Amusement, 27) Spices, 28) Weights & measures, 29) Colours, 30) Relatives, 31) Diseases, 32) Reptiles, 33) Conveyances, 34) Occupations, 35) Education, 36) Time, 37) Government, 38) Verbs, 39) Adverbs, 40) Abstract nouns, 41) Adjectives, 42) Prepositions, 43) Numerals, 44) Conjunctions, 45) Collective words, 46) Pronouns, 47) Ordinals, 48) Feminines, 49) Interjections, 50) War, 51) House, and 52) Miscellaneous.

[15] From this time Sanskrit Wordnet became a part of Indo-WordNet activity which provided a common platform for the lexicographers working on various Indian language Wordnets.

[16] Phonological conjoining

[17] This way of giving definitions is typical of Sanskritic tradition which used to strongly emphasise precision. The long compound simply defines the act of *going*.

[18] So using these expressions, Hindi Wordnet gloss is adapted in following ways- (1){रोना,रुदन करना,आँसू बहाना,क्रंदन करना *ronA, rudana karanA, AMsu bhAnA, krandana karanA*} HWN आंख से आँसू गिराना *AMkha se AMsu girAnA* → SWN सुख-दुःखयोः भावनावेगात् नेत्राभ्याम् अश्रुपतन-रूप: व्यापार:। *sukha-duHkhayoH bhAvanAvegAt netrAbhyAm aZrupatan-rUpaH vyApAraH*, (2){मारना,पीटना,प्रहार करना, ठोंकना,ठोकना,पिटाई करना, धुनना, धुनाई करना, ताड़ना,प्रताड़ना,रसीद करना *mAranA, pITanA, prahAra karanA, ThokanA, piTAI karanA, dhunanA, dhunAI karanA, tADanA, pratADanA, rasIda karanA*} HWN किसी पर किसी वस्तु आदि से आघात करना *kisi par kisI vastu Adi se AghAta karanA* → SWN कस्मिन् अपि केन अपि वस्तुना आहनन-पूर्वक: व्यापार:। *kasmin api kena api vastunA Ahanana-pUrvakaH vyApAraH* (3) {खरीदना,क्रय करना,मोल लेना,लेना *kharIdanA, kraya karanA, mola lenA, lenA*} HWN पैसे आदि देकर किसी दुकान,व्यक्ति आदि से कुछ सौदा मोल लेना *paise Adi dekar kisI dukAna, vyakti Adi se kuch saudA mol lenA* → SWN आपणे वस्तु तथा च तन्मूल्यम् एतयोः आदान-प्रदानात्मक: व्यापार:। *ApaNe vastu tathA cha tanmUlyam etayoH AdAna-pradAnAtmakaH vyApAraH*, (4) {रूठना, रुष्ट होना, अनखना, रूसना, रिसाना, फूलना, अनसाना, अनखाना, अनैसना *rUThanA, ruSTa honA, anakhanA, rUsanA, risAnA, phUlanA, anasAnA, anakhAnA*} HWN अप्रसन्न होकर उदासीन,चुप या अलग हो जाना *aprasanna hokara udAsIna, cupa yA alaga ho jAnA* → SWN अप्रसन्नताहेतुजन्य: वियोगरूप: औदासीन्यफलजनक: वा व्यापार:। *aprasannatAhetujanyaH viyogarUpaH audAsInyaphalajanakaH vA vyApAraH* (5) {आना:1, पहुँचना, पहुंचना, पधारना, अवना, आगमना *AnaA, pahuMcanA, pahucanA, padhAranA, avanA, AgamanA*} HWN एक स्थान से आकर दूसरे स्थान पर उपस्थित होना *eka stAna se Akara dUsare stAna para upasthita honA* → SWN अन्य-स्थान-वियोग-पूर्वक: अन्य-स्थान-संयोगानुकूल-व्यापार:। *anya-sthAna-viyoga-pUrvakaH anya-sthAna saMyogAnukUla-vyApAraH*.

Difficulty of finding equivalent words:

Sometimes it is difficult to find a Sanskrit equivalent for a Hindi word. For example; the word {चाय} *cAya* (tea) is very widely used. The concept of *tea* is explained as follows in the Hindi wordnet:

(1) चाय के पौधे की पत्तियों को पानी में डालकर चीनी, दूध आदि मिलाकर बनाया हुआ पेय पदार्थ
cAya ke paudhe kI pattiyon ko pAnI mein DAlkar cinI dUdha Adi milAkar banAyA huA peya padArtha
(A drink prepared by mixing the leaves of the Tea-plant with sugar, milk and water)

But Sanskrit does not have a word of its own for this concept. Monier Williams in his Sanskrit-English dictionary (MW hereafter) suggests that "चहा" *cahA* (which is actually a Marathi word) should be used as a borrowed word. In the dictionary of spoken Sanskrit we find two different regional words "चाय" *cAya* and "चाया" *cAyA* belonging to the North and South regions of India. The gloss field in the synset of {कषायपेयम्, चायः, चाया, चहा} {*kaSAyapeyaM, cAyaH, cAyA, cahA*} in the Sanskrit wordnet is modified as follows:

(2) चायः चहा एवंविधैः शब्दैः भारतीय-भाषासु प्रसिद्धस्य क्षुपस्य शुष्कपर्णानां चूर्णम् उष्णजले अभिपच्य तस्मिन् द्रवे शर्कराद्-दुग्धादीन् संमिश्र्य निर्मितम् उष्णपेयम्।
cAyaH cahA evaMvidhaiH shabdaiH bhAratIya-bhASAsu prasiddhasya kSupasya shuSka-parNAnAM cUrNam uSNajale abhipacya tasmin drave sharkarA-dugdhAdIn saMmishrya nirmitam uSNapeyam
(A hot drink which is prepared by first mixing the leaves of the a plant, which is famous by the names like चहा *cahA*, चाय *cAya*, etc. in the Indian languages, into hot water and then mixing it with sugar and milk)

This change is needed to translate the simple Hindi wordnet gloss. Similarly, for the tree plant, the Hindi wordnet gloss is:

(3) एक पौधा जिसकी पत्तियाँ उबलते हुए पानी में डालकर एक पेय बनाते हैं।
eka paudhA jisakI pattiyAn ubalate hue pAnI mein DAlkar eka peya banAte hein
(A plant- dry leaves of which are boiled in the hot water and a drink is prepared)

and this gloss was modified in SWN as:

(4) चायः चहा एवंविधैः शब्दैः भारतीय-भाषासु प्रसिद्धः क्षुपः:- यस्य शुष्क-पर्णानां चूर्णं उष्णजले अभिपच्य तस्मिन् द्रवे शर्करा-दुग्धादीन् संमिश्र्य उष्णपेयं निर्मीयते।
cAyaH cahA evaMvidhaH shabdaiH bhAratIya-bhASAsu prasiddhaH kSupaH yasya shuSk-parNAnAm cUrNaM uSNajals Abhipacya tasmin drave sharkarA-dugdhAdIn saMmIshrya uSNapeyaM nirmIyate
(A plant, which is famous by the names like चहा, चाय, etc. in the Indian languages- dry leaves of which are boiled in the hot water and a drink is prepared)

Difficulties with *examples*:

Generally, examples associated with Hindi synsets are translated only if they *read* sensible when translated into Sanskrit. In some cases, quotations from the Sanskrit texts are included in the example field. A special field has been created to record the source of the quotations. This citation field is incorporated in the lexicographer's interface:

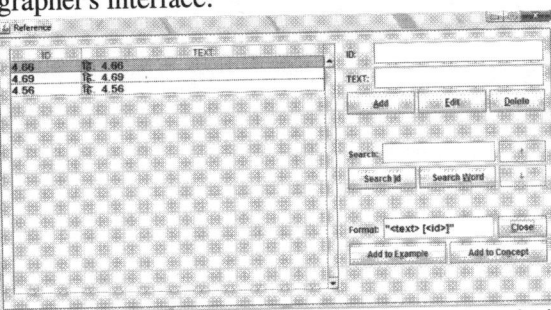

Figure 1. Lexicographer's interface to record citations

The example with the citation is inserted in this format:

(5) "शशि-दिवाकरयोर्ग्रहपीडनम्।"
[भर्तृ.2.91][19]

---

[19] Here, [भर्तृ.2.91] indicates the place of the quotation in the original Sanskrit text authored by Bhartrhari.

shashi-divAkarayor grahapIDanaM
[bhartR 2.91]
(the eclipse of Sun and Moon).

Sometimes, apart from the translation of Hindi example sentence, an alternative example from the Sanskrit text is provided. Multiple examples are separated with the "/" symbol. The sources of the examples are indicated in square brackets. In some cases the translation of the Hindi example sentence becomes problematic due to the unnaturalness of the sentence in Sanskrit.

Coverage of words in Sanskrit wordnet: Taking into consideration the linguistic change and time, it is possible to classify Sanskrit language into three periods- (1) Vedic period-beginning of Vedic Sanskrit can be traced as early as around 1500 BCE and Vedas are written using literals of that time, (2) Classical Sanskrit- A significant form of post-Vedic Sanskrit is found in the Sanskrit beginning with the Hindu Epics—the Ramayana and the Mahabharata. (3) Modern Sanskrit. The usage of the words changed during these periods. The general policy adopted for synset making is to start with the most frequent words of modern Sanskrit and to close the synset with the least frequent word of Vedic Sanskrit. The example of the synset of युद्ध (yuddha) *war*- shown below- is an illustrative case in point. The words in the synset of *war* are arranged from the most common modern Sanskrit words to least used Vedic Sanskrit words.

{ युद्धम्, संग्रामः, समरः, रणः, समरम्, आयोधनम्, आहवम्, रण्यम्, अनीकः, अनीकम्, अभिसम्पातः, अभ्यार्मदः, अररः, आक्रन्दः, योधनम्, जम्यम्, प्रधनम्, प्रविदारणम्, मृधम्, आस्कन्दनम्, संख्यम्, समीकम्, साम्यरायिकम्, कलहः, विग्रहः, संप्रहारः, कलिः, संस्फोटः, संयुगः, समाघातः, अभ्यागमः, आहवः, समुदायः, संयत्, समितिः, आजिः, समित्, युत्, संरावः, आनाहः, सम्परायकः, विदारः, दारणम्, संवित्, सम्परायः, बलजम्, आनर्त्तः, अभिमरः, समुदयः, विवाक्, विखादः, नदनुः, भरः, आक्रन्दः, पृतनाज्यम्, अभीकम्, समीकम्, ममसत्यम्, नेमधिता, सङ्काः, समनम्, मीळ्_हे, पृतनाः, स्पृत्, स्पृद्, मृत्, मृद्, पृत्, पृद्, समत्, समर्यः, समरणम्, समोहः, समिथः, सङ्खः, सङ्गः, संयुगम्, सङ्गथः, सङ्गमः, वृत्रतूर्यम्, पृक्षः, आणिः, शीरसातिः, वाजसातिः, समनीकम्, खलः, खजः, पौंस्यम्, महाधनः, वाजः, अजम्, सद्म, संयत्, संयद्, संवतः } {yuddham, saMgramaH, raNaH, samaraH, samaram, Ayodhanam, Ahavam, raNyam, anIkaH, anIkam, abhisampAtaH, abhyAmardaH, araraH, AkrandaH, yodhanam, jamyam, pradhanam, pravidAraNam, mRdham, Askandanam, saMkhyam, samIkam, sAmyarAyikam, kalahaH, vigrahaH, saMprahAraH, kaliH, saMsphoTaH, saMyugaH, samAghataH, abhyAgamaH, AhavaH, samudAyaH, saMyat, samitiH, AjiH, samit, yut, saMrAvaH, AnAhaH, saMparAyakaH, vidAraH, dAraNacd, saMvit, saMparAyaH, balajam, AnartaH, abhimaraH, samudayaH, vivAk, vikhAdaH, nadanuH, bharaH, AkrandaH, pRtanAjyam, abhIkam, samIkam, mamasatyam, nemadhitA, saGkAH, samanam, mIL_he, pRtanAH, spRt, spRd, mRt, mRd, pRt, pRd, samat, samaryaH, samaraNam, samohaH, samithaH, saGkhaH, saGgaH, saMyugacd, saGgathaH, saGgamaH, vRtratUryam. pRkSaH, ANiH, ZIrsAtiH, vAjasAtiH, samanIkam, khalaH, khajaH, pauMsyam, mahAdhanaH, vAjaH, ajaM, sadma, saMyat, saMyad, saMvataH }

The problem of meaning attestation: Sanskrit has a rich tradition of lexical resources. But the downside of this fact is that the lexicographer has to verify the consistency of word definitions at every step from multiple sources. For example, following words are mentioned in *Shabdakalpadruma*, but other dictionaries prepared by modern scholars like Monier Williams (MW) make the following remarks in the gloss of these words. All of them are used in the Vedic literature for the concept of "war".

सङ्खे	MW- सङ्ख -not found in MW and शब्दकल्पद्रुम
सङ्गे	MW- सङ्ग is not found in sense of युद्ध in MW and शब्दकल्पद्रुम
संयुगे	MW- संयुग n. conflict, battle, war MBh. Ka1v. &c (cf. Naigh. ii , 17)
सङ्गथे	MW- सङ्गथ m. conflict, war Naigh.
सङ्गमे	MW- सङ्गम does not have the sense of युद्ध
वृत्रतूर्ये	MW- वृत्रतूर्य n. conquest of enemies or वृत्र , battle , victory RV.
पृक्षे	MW- पृक्ष m. = संग्राम Naigh. ii , 57.
आणौ	MW- आणि m. (cf. अणि (the pin of the axle of a cart RV. i , 35 , 6 ; 63 , 3 ([" battle " Naigh. ii , 17]) and v , 43 , 8
शीरसातौ	शीरसाति is not found in MW and शब्दकल्पद्रुम
समनीके	MW- समनीक n. battle, war RV. (Naigh. ii , 17) Ballar. Vii , 60÷61.
खले	MW- खल m. contest, battle Naigh. Nir.
खजे	MW- खज m. contest, war (cf. -क्/ऋत् &c) Naigh. ii , 1
पौंस्ये	MW- पौंस्य is not mentioned in the sense of युद्ध
महाधने	MW- महाधन m. a great contest, great battle ib. Naigh.
वाजे	MW- वाज m. the prize of a race or of battle, booty , gain , reward , any precious or valuable possession , wealth , treasure RV. VS. AV. Pan5cavBr.
अजम्	MW- अजम is not found in the sense of युद्ध
सद्म	MW- सद्म n. war , battle (= सं-ग्राम (ib.ii , 17
संयत् संयद्	MW- संयत् संयद् f. contest, strife, battle, war (generally found in loc. or comp.) MBh. Ka1v. &c
संवतः	MW- not found in the sense of युद्ध

Table 4. Verification of meaning of words standing for *war*.

3 Special features of Sanskrit wordnet

Verbal concepts: In Hindi wordnet, verbs are not inserted in their root forms. Instead, their dictionary forms like होना *honA* (to be) , करना *karanA* (to do) , खाना *khAnA* (to eat) , पीना *pInA* (to drink) etc. are included in the synset. The last ना *nA* is dropped through suffix stripping in verb morphology and the verb forms are generated using only the initial parts like हो *ho* , कर *kara* , खा *khA* , पी *pI* . Sanskrit lexicographers have not conformed to this practice and have inserted the root forms of verbs like भू *bhU* (to be) , कृ *kR* (to do), खाद् *khAd* (to eat), पा *pA* (to drink), in verbal synsets.

Gender: Sanskrit has grammatical gender. The following practice is followed for tackling the issue of gender in Sanskrit wordnet: (1) In case of nouns all gender variations are included in the synset. (2) Adjectives in Sanskrit have no gender of their own. They take the gender of the nouns which they qualify. Hence in the synset of adjectives only root forms are included. (3) Adverbs-Technically adverbs in Sanskrit do not get conjugated as nouns and adjectives. But, we find that some adverbs have विभक्ति (case ending) suffixes attached to them indicating the closed form of the word in that particular विभक्ति. (case ending). In such cases, they are included as they are, i.e., in the closed विभक्ति form. For example-

```
(6) सन्निधौ sannidhau 'near'
(which is actually a locative
form of सन्निधि sannidhi),
निकटे nikaTe 'near' (which is ac-
tually a locative form of निकट
nikaTa), and
अदूरे adUre 'near' (which is ac-
tually a locative form of अदूर
adUra).
```

4 Conclusions and future work

One of main challenges in creating the Sanskrit wordnet is dealing with the sheer volume of lexical knowledge accumulated over at least 2000 years. The synsets tend to become long to accommodate coverage of words for a concept. The other challenge is the extremely rich morphology of Sanskrit which produces new words from simple elements. The question of trade-off between a complex morphological interface to the lexical data and the amount of lexicalization needs to be investigated.

The future work is proposed to be carried out in the following directions:

Use of ontology of नव्य-न्याय (Navya-NyAya)

The traditional Sanskrit Texts on Philosophy as well as Medicine contain various discussions on ontological categories and hierarchies. These texts are closely related to the grammar of the Sanskrit Language. The comparison of these ontological structures and hierarchies to the existing one coming from the Hindi wordnet may shed light on new Indowordnet specific issues.

धातु (dhAtu) based WN

There are theories in Sanksrit texts which adhere to the view that all nouns are derived from verbal roots. It is the actions denoted by the verbal roots that can be considered as the base of various objects denoted by nouns. There is a need to test this theory and build a lexical structure where all the verbal roots will be at the nodal level with connected nouns at the leaf level. A brief introduction of this is available in (Kulkarni and Bhattacharyya, 2009).

References

Abhishek G. Nanda. 2009. Tools and interfaces for wordnet construction, linking and maintenance. B. tech project report, Indian Institute of Technology Bombay, Mumbai.

Dan Tufis, Radu Ion, Luigi Bozianu, Alexandru Ceusu, and Dan Stefaescu. 2008. Romanian wordnet: Cirrent state, new applications and proposals. In Attila Tanáces, Dóra Csendes, Vernoika Vincze, Christaine Fellbaum, and Piek Vossen, editors, *Proceedings of the Foruth Global WordNet Conference*:441–445.

H. H. Wilson, editor. 1819. *A Dictionary in Sanskrit and English*. Calcutta.

Krsnaji Govinda Oka, editor. 1913. *Amarakosha of Amarasinha*. Law Printing Press.

Malhar Kulkarni and Pushpak Bhattacharyya. 2009. Verbal roots in the Sanskrit wordnet. In G. Huet, Amba Kulkarni, and Peter Scharf, editors, *Sanskrit Computational Linguistics*, Lecture Notes in Computer Science:328–338, Berlin/Heidelberg. Springer-Verlag.

Malhar Kulkarni. 2008. Lexicographic traditions in India and Sanskrit. *Journal of Language Technology*, (1):160–165.

P. Vossen. 2002. Euro WordNet: General Document. University of Amsterdam.

Raja Radhakanta Deb, editor. 1988. *Shabdakalpadruma*, volume 1-5. Nag Publishers, 2003 edition. Delhi.

Saranamasimha Sarma. 1968. *Hindi ki Tadbhava Shabdavali*. College Book Depo.

Taranatha Tarkavacaspati Bhattacharya, editor. 2003. *Vacaspatyam*, volume 1-6 of *Chaukhamba Sanskrit Book Series*. Chaukhamba, Banares.

Vishwanath Dinkar Naravane. 1961. *Bharatiya Vyavahara Kosha: Solah Bhasao ka kosha*. Triveni Samgama. [In HIndi.].

Appendix A: Early works on Sanskrit lexical knowledge bases (besides *Amarakosha*)

1. *Naamamaalikaa* of Bhoja (11 C)
2. *SiddhashabdaarNava* of Sahajakirti- (17th C)
3. *Shaaradiiyaakhyaanaamamaalaa* of Harsakirti- (17th C)
4. *Paryaayashabdaratna* of Dhananjaya-Bhatta.
5. *Koshakalpataru*
6. *Naanaartharatnamaalaa* of Irugapa Dandadhinatha (14th C)
7. *Naanaarthamañjarii* of Raghava
8. *DharaNiikosha* of Dharanidas a (12th C)
9. *Shivakosa* of Sivadatta-Misra
10. *Ekaarthanaamamaalaa-vyaksharanamamaalaa* of Saubhari
11. *Paramaanandiiyanaamamaalaa* of Makrandadasa

Appendix 2: Lexicographer's Interface for Sanskrit wordnet building

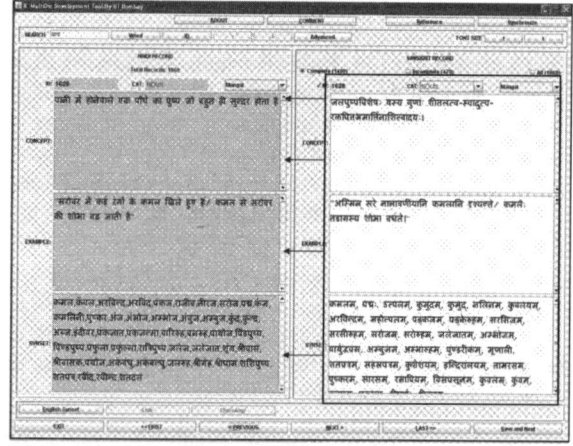

Figure A. 1 Lexicographer's interface.

To create a lexical resource like wordnet, one needs a user friendly tool. Sanskrit wordnet team uses the MultiDict tool developed at the Center for Indian Language Technology, Computer Science Department, IIT Bombay (Figure A. 1). The tool provides an interface for linking the synsets that express the same meaning in different language (Nanda, 2009).

The linker tool (Figure A. 2) is integrated in the interface for cross-linkage between the literals of source and target synsets. It allows a lexicographer to link a literal of the source language to one or more literals in the corresponding target language synset.

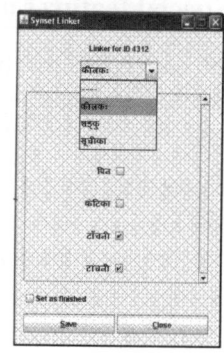

Figure A. 2 Linker

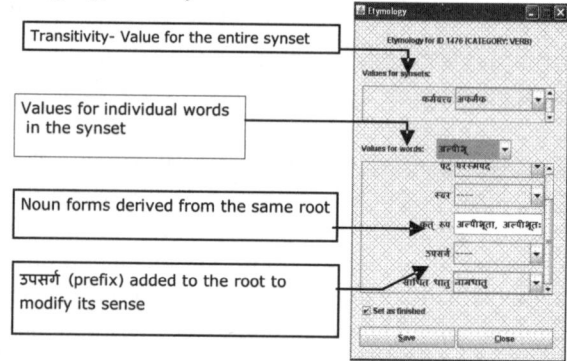

Figure A.3 Morphological elements in the SWN

A WordNet for Bodo Language: Structure and Development

Shikhar Kr. Sarma
Department of Computer Science
Gauhati University
Guwahati 781014: Assam, India
sks001@gmail.com; sks@gauhati.ac.in

Biswajit Brahma
Department of Computer Science
Gauhati University
Guwahati 781014: Assam, India
bswjtbrahma@gmail.com

Moromi Gogoi
Department of Computer Science
Gauhati University
Guwahati 781014: Assam, India
moromi_gogoi@yahoo.com

Mane Bala Ramchiary
Department of Computer Science
Gauhati University
Guwahati 781014: Assam, India
maner@gmail.com

Abstract

This paper discusses the linguistics foundations for developing a Bodo Wordnet, describing the Bodo language characteristics and properties specific to the development of Wordnet. The characteristics of the Bodo language in terms of its morphological and syntactic structure are outlined. Important characteristics related to building of Wordnet are discussed with examples. As the Bodo Wordnet is being developed as an expansion of the Hindi-English Wordnet, the experience gathered during the initial startup works are very important in carrying out the whole work. Such experiences during the building of core 2000 synsets are discussed in the paper, alongwith the challenges faced during linking.

1 Introduction

Wordnet building in relatively newly developed languages has been a challenge for the linguists, researchers and computing professionals. This is mainly because of the technologically immature language scenario, as well as lack of properly structured linguistics resources. Bodo language is also falls in this category. The language is in its developing state, and in recent years only proper linguistics and literal emphasizes have been started. The Bodo language is a scheduled language of India, mainly spoken by the Bodo Community of the state of Assam. The first generation researchers in the field of Bodo Linguistics are just coming up, and technological developments have just started. The bodo language uses the Devnagiri scripts with additional symbols. UNICODE compliant font sets, keyboard drivers, corpus, word-processors, spelling checkers, CLDR etc are being developed with Government of India initiative very recently. Work has also started simultaneously for developing the Bodo Wordnet as part of the North East Indo Wordnet development, which will ultimately be linked to the composite Indo Wordnet.

1.1 Bodo Language

The Bodo language has its written record from the last part of the 19th century. This language was introduced in the primary level of education in Assam from the year 1963 and presently is the medium of instruction upto 10th standard in the state of Assam. It was recognized by the government of Assam as official language in the Kokrajhar district and Udalguri sub-division from the year 1984. The language also got Indian govt. recognition as scheduled language from 2003. According to the census of 1991 it has a total of 11, 84,569 speakers.

The Bodo population has basic concentration in the northern part of the Brahmaputra valley of Assam. They have also thin concentration in the southern part of the valley. Besides that they have also concentration in small number in the border areas of Meghalaya, Nagaland, North Bengal, Nepal, and Bhutan adjoining Assam.

1.2 Origin and History

The Bodo language belongs to the Tibeto-Burman branch of the Sino-Tibetan language family. It is a major language of the North-Eastern part of India and has very close resemblance with the Rabha, Garo, Dimasa, Kokborok, Tiwa, Hajong and other allied languages of N-E India. It is thought that this language speakers have migrated through two different routes into Assam: one by the western route adjoining Himalayas and the other by the stream of the Brahmaputra river by eastern side of Assam. It is thought that the origin of this language is the headwaters of the Huang-Ho and Yang-Tsze-Kiang rivers in China. According to the scholars it is considered that this language presently has three distinct different dialect groups.

2 Characteristics of Bodo Language

This language has a total of 22 phonemes: 6 vowels and 16 consonants. Use of the high back unrounded vowel phoneme /w/ is very frequent in Bodo language. The Bodo language has different special characteristics such as: It has intonation pattern, juncture and two types of tones. The words in Bodo are highly mono-syllabic. It has agglutinative features also.

2.1 Morphological characteristics

a) The morphological feature of this language is discussed under two basic heads: primary and secondary grammatical categories. Primary consists of Noun, Pronoun, Verb, Adjective, Adverb, Conjunction and Interjection. Secondary consists of Number, Gender, Person, Case and Case-Endings, Numerals and Numeral Classifiers and Tense.
b) Noun has basic, derived as well as compound form composed of noun and verb, verb and noun as well as noun and noun.
c) Pronoun has five different categories.
d) Verb has simple, complex and compound as well as transitive, intransitive, causative, finite and infinite based on structure and function.
e) Adjective has basic and derived form and its basic foundation is verb.
f) Adverbs are basically derived from the adjectives by using derivational suffixes.
g) Numbers are two in this language and are inflected basically with nouns, pronouns also with adjectives.
h) It is basically a natural gender language having two genders i.e. masculine and feminine. Traditionally common and neuter are also used. It has three different phases of gender formation.
i) It has three persons: 1st, 2nd, 3rd and is discussed with the personal pronouns.
j) It has seven cases including ablative and genitive.
k) Numerals have basic and derived forms. Classifiers are prefixed with the numerals.
l) Traditionally tense has three different forms: past, present and future, but are very difficult to completely differentiate in some cases.
m) It has two affixes: prefix and suffix. In comparison to suffix the number of prefix is relatively small. Suffixes are inflectional and derivational as well as class maintaining and changing.
n) Kinship terms are discussed only with the personal pronouns.

2.2 Syntactic structure

a) Structurally syntax has three forms: simple, complex and compound.
b) General syntactic structure is of S-O-V pattern.
c) It has no concord relation.
d) Its word order is flexible and is based on the context and mood of the speaker.
e) It has idiomatic and non-idiomatic use of sentences.
f) It has the use of verb and verb less sentences.

2.3 Bodo Synonyms and Antonyms

Few Examples of Bodo Synsets:

[World, English]: [पृथ्वी,हिन्दी]: बुहुम, मुलुग, भुम, संसार, हालुर, बैसोमाथा, बिलाथलाथा [Bodo]।

[Jungle, English]: [जंगल,हिन्दी]: हाग्रामा, अरन, हाग्रा, हाग्राबारि, जाहार, आरंगा [Bodo] ।

[Body, English]: [शरीर,हिन्दी] : देहा, मोदोम, सोलेर, सावसि [Bodo] ।

[God, English]: [भगवान,हिन्दी]: इसोर, गसाइ, आनान_गसाइ, अबंलावरि, अबं [Bodo] ।

Few Examples of Bodo Antonyms are:

[Big-small, English]: [बड़ा-छोटा, हिन्दी]: गिदिर-फिसा [Bodo]

[Good-Bad, English]: [अच्छा-बुरा, हिन्दी] : मोजां - गाज्रि [Bodo]

[High-Low, English]:[ऊँचा-नाटा, हिन्दी] : गोजौ – गाहाय [Bodo]

2.4 Bodo Hyponymy and Hypernyms

Examples:

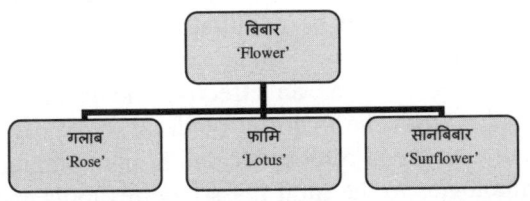

Here, गलाब, 'rose', फामि 'lotus', सानबिबार 'sunflower' are hyponyms of the superordinate term or hypernym of बिबार 'flower'.

Another Example:

Thaijwubilai; a leaf of a tree named *Thaijwu*
=>*bilai*; leaf

Here, *Thaijwubilai*, a leaf of a tree named *Thaijwu* is a kind of *bilai*; *bilai* means leaf; *bilai* is a hypernym and *Thaijwubilai* is the hyponym. Similar case with the example of *phakhribilai* also.

2.5 Meronymy and Holonymy

आसि : Finger
=>आखाय : Hand

बिथराय : Petal
=>बिबार : Flower

Here, आसि 'finger' and बिथराय 'petal' are meronymy and आखाय 'hand' and 'बिबार'flower' are holonymy.

2.6 Entailment

हंख्रदनाय : To snore
=>उन्दु : To sleep

2.7 Troponymy:

मिनिखैरो : *smiling*
=> मिनि : *laughing*

2.8 Antonymy

gwjwu ;High
=>*gahai*; Low
geder ;Big
=>*undwi*; Small

2.9 Inter-language Element

There are inter-language elements in Bodo and these elements are from the same language family. Few of these are shown below-

Bodo	Garo	Rabha	Dimasa	Kok-Borok	Hindi
न(house)	नक	नक	नक	न	घर
हा(land)	हा	हा	हा	हा	जमीन
लामा(road)	---	----	लामा	लामा	रास्ता

3 The Plan for Building Bodo Wordnet

Bodo Wordnet building is part of the North East Indian language Wordnet. This is in turn a sub part of the composite Indo Wordnet. As a policy, the Wordnet of Bodo language is planned as an expansion of the existing Hindi Wordnet. The work has been started with building of a prototype wordnet with 2000 core synset taken out of the Hindi Wordnet. The synset entries are done against concepts of those core Hindi synsets. A common interface has been used for data entry. Entries are started based on the corresponding Hindi Synset ID. The interface provides facilities for displaying already existing synsets with ID, Concept, Gloss, and the complete synset. For new entry, it provides the blank spaces and facilitates saving into the existing text file updating it on every saving attempt. The interface also provides display of corresponding English synset with examples and concepts, in a popup screen.

Expansion approach is followed to build the Bodo Wordnet. As the Bodo Wordnet is ultimately a part of the Indo Wordnet, this facilitates the creation of the composite Wordnet. This has also drastically reduced the preliminary work of generating and compiling concepts. For a developing language like Bodo, it has significantly accelerated the entire workflow.

Few general principles adopted for constructing the Bodo Wordnet are:

- Concepts are borrowed from the Hindi Wordnet. All Hindi concepts will have corresponding Bodo concepts, to the maximum extent possible.
- Direct translation of the concepts are encouraged. Whenever direct translation is not possible, conceptual translation is done.
- Examples are also direct translation of the Hindi examples. When it does not provide the proper meaning, or if a more language specific example prevails, translation is avoided.
- Synsets are created language specific, not looking at the Hind synset, but looking at the just created Bodo concept.

- When the concept or example could not be completed with the existing vocabulary of Bodo language, transliteration is done.
- English concept and example are referred for removing ambiguities.
- Validating with experts before finalization.

4 Challenges in Expansion

Bodo is a developing language. It does not have a very strong linguistic resource. Also literature resource is very limited. The language does not have enough vocabulary, and new and new words are being discovered, coined and added. As a result, the development of Bodo Wordnet faces typical and frequent problems, and overcoming the problems to accommodate expansion of the Hindi Wordnet with one to one mapping has been a big challenge. Out of the 2000 core synsets mapped from Hindi to Bodo till now, in around 20 Hindi synsets, there could not be found Bodo sysnsets corresponding to the exact Hindi concept. A very interesting observation is that sometimes to represent a particular concept of Hindi, Bodo language requires a complete sentence or long phrase as the synset, rather than one single word or combination of two words. In such exceptional cases, the synset entries are done with underscore as the linking between words. Some of the frequently encountered challenges during the initial exercises are:

i. Lack of proper vocabulary/set of vocabulary to mean the concept, or the example.
ii. For certain concepts in Hindi/English, there is no such vocabulary as member of the synset
iii. In many cases, the synset is very small. Two members/three members synsets are very common
iv. Sometimes the synset contains members containing multiple words. In case of multiple words, they are joined by an underscore.
v. In many cases, the synset entry itself appears in the concept.

5 Conclusions

Building of Bodo Wordnet is aimed in developing a comprehensive and rich computational linguistics resources for the language. As the language itself is developing in terms of linguistics and literature, the Wordnet building of Bodo language is with lots of challenges. The demand and requirements of digital technologies in local languages have been felt among the users and policy makers, including at government and academics. As a result efforts have been initiated to developing tools, applications, and technologies for developing Bodo as an effective media of the digital world. The majority of the Bodo spoken population are in rural areas, and bringing digital technologies to the rural mass requires tools and technologies in the language. Wordnet development in Bodo language is an ambitious project, but we visualize its potential impact integrating with other digital technologies and applications. This will certainly add newer dimensions to the Bodo language in its journey towards its success, spreading, expansion, and in becoming an effective and efficient media of knowledge society.

Acknowledgements

The Bodo Wordnet Development Project is sponsored by the Department of Information Technology, Ministry of Communication and Information Technology, Government of India.

References

Chakrabarti Debasri, Narayan Dipak Kumar, Pandey Prabhakar, Bhattacharyya Pushpak. 2002. *Experiences in Building the Indo WordNet: A WordNet for Hindi*, Proceedings of the First Global WordNet Conference.

Dave Shachi and Bhattacharyya Pushpak. 2001. *Knowledge Extraction from Hindi Texts*, Journal of Institution of Electronic and Telecommunication Engineers, vol. 18, no. 4.

E. Pianta, L. Bentivogli, C. Girardi. 2002. *MultiWordNet: Developing an Aligned Multilingual Database*, Proceedings of the First International Conference on Global WordNet Mysore, India.

Fellbaum, C. (ed.), 1998. *WordNet: An Electronic Lexical Database,*. The MIT Press.

Miller,G., Beckwith,R., Fellbaum,C., Gross,D., and Miller,K, 1990. *Five Papers on WordNet.* CSL Report 43, Cognitive Science Laboratory, Princeton University, Princeton.

Mintu Narzary. 2009. *Standard Anglo Bodo Dictionary,* Nilima Prakashani, Baganpara, Nalbari, India

Promod Chandra Brahma. 2003. *Bodo-Engraji-Hindi Swdwb Bihung,* Bodo Sahitya Sabha, Kokrajhar, India

Ramchiary and Daimary. 2009. *Hindi-Bodo Swdwb Bakhri,* Bina Library, Guwahati, India.

Surendra Goyari. 2000. *Hindi-Bodo Swdwb Bihung,* Ganesh Prakashan, Guwahati, India.

Experiences in Building the Konkani WordNet using the Expansion Approach

Shantaram Walawalikar
ILCI - Konkani Team
Goa University
goembab@yahoo.co.in

Shilpa Desai
Dept. of Computer Science
and Tech., Goa University
sndesai@gmail.com

Ramdas Karmali
Dept. of Computer Science
and Tech., Goa University
rnk@unigoa.ac.in

Sushant Naik
ILCI - Konkani Team
Goa University

Damodar Ghanekar
ILCI - Konkani Team
Goa University

Chandralekha D'Souza
Dept. of Konkani
Goa University
chanda@unigoa.ac.in

Jyoti Pawar
Dept. of Computer Science
and Tech., Goa University
jdp@unigoa.ac.in

Abstract

WordNet can be described as an electronic lexical database available on-line as a powerful resource to the researchers in the area of computational linguistics, text processing and many other related areas. Currently, the necessity of building WordNets has been felt for all the Indian Languages to aid in multi lingual machine translation and cross lingual information retrieval to promote tourism, farming, education and other related areas for overall growth and development of the nation. IIT Bombay, India has developed a number of tools, resources and facilities by which WordNet of any language can be constructed through what is known as the expansion approach. Projects to create WordNet in most of the Indian languages using this approach with Hindi WordNet as the base are currently in progress.

In this paper we report our experiences of creating a WordNet for Konkani language using the expansion approach with Hindi as the source language and Konkani as the target language. The Konkani WordNet is in the initial stage of development. The 1969 Hindi core synsets have been incorporated in the Konkani WordNet. The Offline Synset Linking Tool developed by IIT Bombay is being used for this task.

1. Introduction

WordNet can be described in short as a massive structure of words in a graph like form. It is an electronic lexical database available as a powerful resource to the researchers in the area of computational linguistics, text processing and many other related areas. Since 1987 when WordNet first appeared globally, it has come a long way, getting itself moulded as per the ongoing requirements of the users and making use of the advancement of technology viz. Computer Science and Communications. Indo WordNet is India's contribution to this global effort and the steps towards the development of Konkani WordNet शब्दमाळें shabdamAleM is a part of this initiative.

The layout of this paper is as follows – Section 2 discusses the characteristics of Konkani language. A brief description of the Hindi WordNet, the expansion approach used to create Konkani WordNet, observations made during the WordNet creation process and challenges faced are given in section 3. Section 4 concludes the paper with a discussion on the future work plan.

2. Characteristics of Konkani Language

Konkani language is one of the twenty two languages included in the eighth schedule of the constitution of India. It is also the official language of the State of Goa. Konkani is an Indo-European (Indo-Aryan) language derived from Sanskrit through Prakrit and is influenced and enriched by various other languages like Marathi, Kannada, Malayalam, Hindi, Portuguese and English. Though Devanagari script is recognised as official script of Konkani, it is also written in Roman and Kannada scripts. Old Konkani literature is also found written in Malayalam and Urdu scripts.

The first edition of Konkani grammar titled 'Arte da Lingua Canarin' was written somewhere in 1617 A.D. by Fr. Thomas Stephens (Asmitai, 2008; Cunha, 1958). It was enlarged by Fr. Diogo Ribeiro and revised by four priests of the Society of Jesus, and printed in 1640. This is considered to be the first published grammar not only of Konkani but of any Indian language. Monsignor Sebastiao Rudolpho Dalgado was the first known Indian lexicographer of Konkani as those preceded him were all European missionaries. He contributed to the development of Konkani with his three important works 'Konkani – Portuguese Dictionary' (1893), 'Portuguese – Konkani Dictionary' (1905), and 'Bouquet of Konkani Proverbs' consisting of 2177 proverbs.

2.1 Pronunciation

Shennoi Goembab (1949) in his book, 'Konkanichi Vyakarani Bandavol' discusses pronunciation in detail.

Konkani pronunciation for अ, ए, ओ, औ have additional pronunciations besides the original Sanskrit pronunciations. अ in पणस paNasa 'jackfruit' is known as स्वरित svarita in Vedic Sanskrit. ए and ओ also have open pronunciations. These open pronunciations must have been influenced by Pali language. These are found in other Indian languages like Bengali, Bihari, Gujarati, Kannada, Telugu, Tamil, Malayalam, etc, but it is not found in Marathi.

In Konkani, according to the pronunciation of a vowel in the same word, the meaning changes e.g. पेर pera '*guava fruit or guava tree*', मोर mora '*peacock, sl. or peacock, pl.*), वोंवळ voMvaLa;a '*kind of flower – mimusops elengi flower* or *its tree*'.

2.2 Number

Konkani has two numbers - singular and plural (Sardesai, 1986). The derivation of plural form from singular form is dependent on gender and phonetic characteristic of singular form.

In some cases the change in pronunciation of the vowel denotes change in number, e.g. दोतोर dotora '*doctor or doctors*', फातर phAtara '*stone or stones*', देर dera '*brother-in-law or brothers-in-law*', ओंठ oMTha '*lip or lips*'.

2.3 Gender

Konkani has three genders - masculine, feminine and neuter. However, in some cases feminine nouns are also addressed as neuter e.g., कमला आंगणांत खेळटालें kamalA AMgaNAMta kheLatAleM '*Kamala was playing in the courtyard*'. Here, the verb खेळटालें refers to the neuter gender whereas Kamala is otherwise a feminine noun.

It is also interesting to note that two synonymous nouns may have two different genders, e.g., रूख rUkha '*tree*, masculine' and झाड jhADa '*tree*, neuter'.

2.4 Word Structure

Konkani is a highly inflected language (Almeida, 1989). Nouns and pronouns are inflected for number and case. Verbs are inflected for person, number, gender, tense and aspect. Adjectives are inflected for gender and number.

The Structure of Konkani word (Goembab, 1949; Borkar, 1986) can be depicted as under:

Nominal Base (N.B.) + Nominal Inflection (N.I.)

पुस्तकाचें pustakAcheM '*of the book*'

(N.B.) + postposition

रामाकडल्यान rAmAkaDalyAna '*from Ram*'

(N.B.) + (N. I.) + (N. I.)

पुस्तकांतलें pustakAMtaleM '*from the book*'

(N.B.) + (N. I.) + postposition

पुस्तकांतल्यान pustakAMtalyAna '*from inside the book*'

(N.B.) + (N. I.) + postposition + (N. I.)
पुस्तकापेल्यानचें pustakApelyAnacheM 'from beyond the book'

(N.B.) + (N. I.) + clitic
पुस्तकाचेंच pustakAcheMcha 'of the book itself'

(N.B.) + postposition + clitic
रामाकडल्यानय rAmAkaDalyAnaya 'also from Ram'

(N.B.) + (N. I.) + (N. I.) + clitic
पुस्तकांतलेंच pustakAMtaleMcha 'from the book itself'

(N.B.) + (N. I.) + postposition + clitic
जेवचेपासतच jevachepAsatacha 'only for meals'

(N.B.) + (N. I.) + postposition + (N. I.) + clitic
पुस्तकापेल्यानचेय pustakApelyAnacheMya 'also from beyond the book'.

2.5 Verb Base

The verbal base of Konkani has three sources (Goembab, 1949), present active base, present passive base and past passive participles. The roots are either active or passive in sense, the passive being intransitive and the active being transitive. The following is a sample of these forms separated with base form of verb:

Non Perfective
Intransitive
The verb: धांवप dhAMvapa 'to run'

	Singular	Plural
Present		
1st person	धांवतां	धांवतात
2nd	धांवता	धांवतात
3rd	धांवता	धांवतात

In the present tense, gender has no effect. But the verb endings change as we go to all other cases and are differentiated below with the respective affixes in the sequence of masculine, feminine and neuter.

Imperfect						
1st	धांवतालों	लीं	लें	धांवताले	ल्यों	लीं
2nd	धांवतालो	ली	लें	धांवताले	ल्यो	लीं
3rd	धांवतालो	ली	लें	धांवताले	ल्यो	लीं

Future						
1st	धांवतलों	लीं	लें	धांवतले	ल्यों	लीं
2nd	धांवतलो	ली	लें	धांवतले	ल्यो	लीं
3rd	धांवतलो	ली	लें	धांवतले	ल्यो	लीं

Transitive
Verb खावप khAvapa 'to eat'

	Singular	Plural
Present		
1st person	खातां	खातात
2nd	खाता	खातात
3rd	खाता	खातात

Imperfect						
1st	खातालों	लीं	लें	खाताले	ल्यों	लीं
2nd	खातालो	ली	लें	खाताले	ल्यो	लीं
3rd	खातालो	ली	लें	खाताले	ल्यो	लीं

Future						
1st	खातलों	लीं	लें	खातले	ल्यों	लीं
2nd	खातलो	ली	लें	खातले	ल्यो	लीं
3rd	खातलो	ली	लें	खातले	ल्यो	लीं

Perfective
Intransitive

	Singular			Plural		
Present Perfect						
1st	धांवलां	ल्यां	लां	धांवल्यात	ल्यांत	ल्यांत
2nd	धांवला	ल्या	ला	धांवल्यात	ल्यांत	ल्यांत
3rd	धांवला	ल्या	ला	धांवल्यात	ल्यांत	ल्यांत

Past						
1st	धांवलों	लीं	लें	धांवले	ल्यों	लीं
2nd	धांवलो	ली	लें	धांवले	ल्यो	लीं
3rd	धांवलो	ली	लें	धांवले	ल्यो	लीं

Past Perfect						
1st	धांविल्लों	ल्लीं	ल्लें	धांविल्ले	ल्ल्यों	ल्लीं
2nd	धांविल्लो	ल्ली	ल्लें	धांविल्ले	ल्ल्यो	ल्लीं
3rd	धांविल्लो	ल्ली	ल्लें	धांविल्ले	ल्ल्यो	ल्लीं

Transitive

	Singular	Plural
Present Perfect		
1st person	खाला	खाल्यात
2nd	खाला	खाल्यात
3rd	खाला	खाल्यात

Past		
1st person	खालो	खाले

2nd	खालो	खाले
3rd	खालो	खाले

Past Perfect
1st person	खाल्लो	खाल्ले
2nd	खाल्लो	खाल्ले
3rd	खाल्लो	खाल्ले

2.6 Contextual Word Usage

There are different Konkani words for the similar sense denoting variety of shades.

Example 2.6.1: An example of this is the meaning of the noun 'stink' in Konkani being गुठ्ठाण guTh.hThANa *'stink'*. It is used in the following variations -

पोंवसाण poMvasANa *'smell of spoilt fish'*.

हिंवसाण hiMvasANa *'natural smell of fish'*.

खातसाण khAtasANa *'smell of urine'*.

घामसाण ghAmasANa *'smell of sweat'*.

कानुट्टाण kAnuT.hTANa *'smell of utensil in which food preparation of onion is made'*.

भातसाण bhAtasANa *'smell of paddy crop'*.

दर्बटाण darbaTANa *'smell of burning of dry chillies'*.

धुंवट्टाण dhuMvaT.hTANa *'smell of smoke'*.

Example 2.6.2: There are verbs which depict many shades of the word 'beating'.

मारप, बडोवप mArapa, baDovapa *'to beat'*.

थापटावप thApaTAvapa *'to beat by slapping more than once'*.

धुमकावप, कुमकावप dhumakAvapa, kumakAvapa *'to beat with blows'*.

चिमटावप chimaTAvapa *'to beat by series of pinching'*.

खोंटावप, गुडडावप khoMTAvapa, guD.hDAvapa *'to beat by kicking continuously'*.

बुडडप buD.hDapa *'to wound with claws or nails'*.

चेंचप cheMchapa *'to smash someone with stone etc.'*.

धोंगसप dhoMgasapa *'to forcibly push someone with the edge of a stick'*.

माडडप, चिडडप mAD.hDapa, chiD.hDapa *'to beat someone by putting under one's feet'*.

2.7 Homographic Words:

In Konkani, we also come across homographic words i.e. two words written alike but have different meanings.

Example 2.7.1: पेर pera pronounced as *'pair'* as in English the meanings are 1. guava fruit 2. joint of finger 3. part between two nodes of a stem.

Example 2.7.2: The word for mango tree is आंबो AMbo and the mango fruit (sl.) is also आंबो with same pronunciation and both are masculine. Further, the same word is used to denote that fruit as a group. e.g. अंदूं बाजारांत चड आंबो आयलोना aMduM bAjArAMta chaDa Ambo AyalonA *'This year there was not much mango fruit in the market'*.

3. Expansion from Hindi to Konkani

3.1 Hindi Wordnet(HWN)

The Hindi WordNet (Narayan. et. al., 2002; Miller, 1995) on which our expanded model is based has currently 32950 synsets covering 77800 unique words. Out of these synsets, 13830 synsets are linked with the synsets of the Princeton WordNet. The synsets are constructed abiding by the following three principles -
(i) Minimality - use the minimal set of words to make the concept unique
(ii) Coverage - The maximal set of words- ordered by frequency in the corpus - to include all possible words standing for the sense.
(iii) Replaceability - The example sentence should be such that the most frequent words in the synset can replace one another in the sentence without altering the sense

3.2 Konkani Wordnet(KWN) Creation Process

Konkani WordNet is created by using Expansion Approach. In this approach, instead of reinventing the wheel, the readily available Hindi WordNet synsets developed by IIT Bombay, are referred to. They are, one by one, understood by the lexicographer and the corresponding synsets in Konkani, expressing the same sense are created. Thus the HWN and KWN have identical glosses and examples as far as possible. This is being followed by many other Indian languages so that the resultant WordNet will take a shape of IndoWordNet.

According to Vossen (1996), the MultiWordNet Model seems less complex and guarantees the highest degree of compatibility across different WordNets. In the development of any WordNet a large number of subjective and sometimes far from accurate decisions are involved. Hence, building two different WordNets independently for two different languages, will display differences. Expand model tends to reduce these subjective choices and resultant discrepancies. It also to some extent helps in highlighting potential inconsistencies existing in the WordNet of the source language.

But this does not mean that expansion model is without any drawbacks. As Vossen (1996) points out it forces "an excessive dependency on the lexical and conceptual structure of one of the languages involved".

In Konkani at present (at the time of writing of this paper) all the core synsets are linked covering around 3500 unique words. These synsets are classified according to parts of speech (nouns, verbs, adverbs and adjectives).

3.3 Observations:

Hindi and Konkani being close languages and with the sentence structure of both being 'Subject Object Verb' (SOV), there was not much problem in maintaining identical concepts.

Our observations during the WordNet creation process can be subdivided under the following 8 broad categories –

Hindi English incorrect linkage
Some of the details are presented below –

Example 3.3.1: Id. 2897- छिपकली ChipakalI - एक रेंगनेवाला जंतु जो प्रायः दीवारों पर दिखाई देता है eka reMganevAlA jaMtu jo prAyaH dIvAroM para dikhA_I detA hai '*a crawling creature mostly seen on walls*'. Hindi and English synsets have wrong linkage. English should have been *House Lizard* instead of *Gecko*.

Example 3.3.2: Id. 3016- व्यवहार की वह प्रकृति जो लगातार दोहराव से प्राप्त होती है vyavahAra kI vaha prakRRiti jo lagAtAra doharAva se prApta hotI hai '*behavioral characteristic aquired due to constant repeatation*'. Hindi concept is understood as "habit" by us while it has been linked to "custom" in English.

Example 3.3.3: Id. 3464- जिसे ख्याति मिली हो jise khyAti milI ho '*one who is famous*'. Hindi concept suggests that the concept is "famous" while English synset is "popular".

Hindi concept/gloss definition not clear
Synset details of two such examples falling in this category are given below –

Example 3.3.4: Id. 231 concept in Hindi reads as किसी देशका वह विभाग जिसके निवासियोंकी शासन पद्धती, भाशा, रहन सहन, व्यवहार आदी औरोंसे भिन्न और स्वतंत्र हो kisI deshakA vaha vibhAga jisake nivAsiyoMkI shAsana padhdatI, bhAshA, rahana sahana, vyavahAra AdI auroMse bhinna aura svataMtra ho '*that territory of any nation, of which the residents have administrative system, language, customs, tradition, etc. different and independent from others*'.

For this the synsets are प्रदेश pradesha, राज्य rAjya, प्रांत prAMta. Here the mention of 'administrative system, language, customs, traditions etc. different and independent from others' is superfluous. Since linkage to English synsets was available this was referred to. The English concept reads as '*the territory occupied by one of the constituent administrative district of a nation*', with synsets as state, province. This is more appropriate concept.

Example 3.3.5: In Id. 882 the Hindi concept reads as संध्या का वह समय जब चरकर लौटनेवाली गौओंके खुरोंसे धूल उडती है saMdhyA kA vaha samaya jaba charakara lauTanevAlI gau_oMke khuroMse dhUla uDatI hai '*that time of the evening when the dust from the legs of cattle returning after grazing spreads in the air*'.

The synset for the same is गोधूलि बेला godhUli belA. The synset literally translates as '*the time of dust from cattle*'. Etymologically this word '*godhuli*' (*go* = cow; *dhuli* = dust) may have a origin of coinciding this time with the return of grazing cattle who come running through the dusty lands and the red dust gets mingled in the whole atmosphere around. But this description need not be a part of concept. Simple definition like 'a short span of time before and after the sunset' will meet the true sense of the concept and also abide by the principle of minimality. English synset was not available for this.

English concept/gloss definition not clear
Although our source language is Hindi, we had referred to English synset to get a better idea of the concept during which we made these observations. Following is an example

Example 3.3.6: Id. 3052 कोई वस्तु खरीदने या बेचने पर उसके बदले में दिया जानेवाला धन ko_I vastu kharIdane yA bechane para usake badale meM diyA jAnevAlA dhana *'Money paid when any goods are bought or sold'*. English concept given as *'cost of bribing someone'* not appropriate to convey the meaning of price.

English synset missing
As stated earlier in section 3.1, only 13830 synsets are linked with the synsets of the Princeton WordNet. Hence we found many synsets falling in this category.

English example missing
In some of the cases where the English synset was linked the examples were found missing.

Hindi example could have been better
We felt that more examples that would overall enrich the WordNet and improve the accuracy of the applications using the WordNet can be used.

English example could have been better
Same observation as above can be made with respect to the English examples.

Recursive definition of concepts
It was also observed that in certain concepts the definition was recursive, i.e. the synset itself was referred to in the concept.

3.4 Challenges Faced:

Linking culture specific concepts
The customs and culture played a challenging role. We have experienced in this exercise that very culture specific concepts do not have their parallels in other languages. The linking of such synsets to other languages remains a question.

In Hindi region chhapati vendor possibly comes door to door selling his chhapatis (a thinly made bread like eatable prepared from wheat flour). Konkani speaking populace is not familiar with this scene but they have met a vendor popularly known as पदेर padera *'bread seller'* visiting residential areas.

There was another such example of a type of saree of length nine yards popularly known as णववारी NavavArI (or नउवारी na_uvArI in Marathi) which women from Goa, Maharashtra and other parts of India wear. Major part of the population may not be aware of this concept.

Linking of contextual words
Using the expansion approach, certain synsets may totally get omitted because of the variety of shades of meanings of different words as mentioned in section 2.6 above.

Coverage of synsets
The question also arises with respect to the coverage for some of the synsets.
Many words though the meaning of them is known to the people, are not in parlance or common in literature; one may find them possibly in poetry. The glaring example could be of सूर्य sUrya *'the sun'*. Many people know that रवि ravi, आदित्य Aditya are other names of the sun. Likewise there are many words which are used for the sun in Puranas (ancient literature). Whether we have to cover these is a question.
The role of metaphorical usage of words – Should they be included in the synset? E.g. सुंगट suMgaTa *'prawn'* is commonly used metaphor in Konkani to mean a slim girl.

Linking a concept not present in the source language
The concept of a nine yard saree - Synset of this concept is not available in HWN. Hence Marathi WordNet has already created synset for this concept. Id number has also been assigned by MWN of its own. Since the other member languages would not know the existence of this synset, they would duplicate this under different IDs. Hence, centrally controlled system for issuing Ids will have to be established.

Coining of new words

Another issue that remains to be resolved is how far the lexicographer can be given liberty to coin new words. This issue comes up if a language does not have a word for a concept (typically happens for culture specific situations). This question will come after the other alternatives like transliteration and multiword expression (short phrases) are explored.

Computational concerns: Interface, efficiency of access and storage

Interface of Offline Synset Linking Tool could also show the relations like hypernymy, hyponymy, antonymy already defined for source language synsets so that if the same does not correspond in the target language it could be changed.

4. Conclusion and Future Work

WordNet has been a very essential constituent for any linguistic study. Hence creation of WordNet for Konkani language has been started. The expansion approach has been found most convenient to speed up the exercise. The software tool provided was also found adequate for the purpose. Though only the core synsets have been linked for the time being, the project is taking momentum and the rest of the synsets will also be linked with greater speed than earlier.

The Konkani WordNet शब्दमालें shabdamAleM is at the initial stage of creation. Currently only the concepts, synsets and examples have been dealt with. However, it is required to check all the semantic relations like synonymy, hypernymy, hyponymy, meronymy, holonymy, troponymy, entailment etc. Even the concept of gradations will have to be introduced as in Hindi WordNet. It is felt that the existing examples from the HWN should also be strengthened with our own additional examples. These examples could be taken from any of the existing Konkani Corpora. When the project gets completed it will be a useful tool for the computational studies of the Indian Languages and a valuable asset of the Konkani language in particular.

Acknowledgements

We wish to express our gratitude to the Indian Institute of Technology, Bombay (IITB) Hindi WordNet Team for providing the tools and guiding us in our process of creating the Konkani WordNet. We thank the Indian Language Corpora Initiative (ILCI) 11(12)/2008 – HCC (TDIL) project Team members for giving inputs and support to this Konkani WordNet creation process. We also acknowledge that we were able to carry out the work using some of the equipments that were purchased from the AICTE funding under RPS scheme 8023/BOR/RPS/091/06/07.

5. References

Almeida Matthew 1989. *A description of Konkani*. Thomas Stephens Konkani Kendr.

Asmitai Pratishthan 2008. *Dalgado on Konkani*.

Borkar S. J. 1986. *Konkani Vyakaran*, Konkani Bhasha Mandal, Margao.

Cunha Rivara.J.H. 1958. *An Historical Essay on the Konkani Language*.

Dipak Narayan, Debasri Chakrabarty, Prabhakar Pande and P. Bhattacharyya *An Experience in Building the Indo WordNet- a WordNet for Hindi*, in First International Conference on Global WordNet, Mysore, India, January, 2002.

Goembab Shennoi 1949. *Konkanichi Vyakarani Bandavol*, Gomantak Chhapkhano Girgaum Mumbai.

Miller, G. A. 1995. *"WordNet: a Lexical Database for English"*. Communications of the ACM 38, (November 1995): 39 – 41.

Miller, G. A., Fellbaum, C., and Miller K. J. (1993) *Five Papers on WordNet*[Computer file] [2006, November 2].

Sardesai Madhavi 1986. *Some aspects of Konkani grammar*. Department of Linguistics, Deccan College

Vossen P. 1996. *Right or wrong: combining lexical resources in the EuroWordNet project*. Proceedings of Euralex-96 International Congress.

Introducing Filipino WordNet

Allan Borra
Center for Language Technologies
College of Computer Studies
De La Salle University,
Manila, Philippines
borgz.borra
@delasalle.ph

Adam Pease
Articulate Software
Angwin, CA, USA
apease@articulatesoftware.com

Rachel Edita. O. Roxas
Center for Language Technologies
College of Computer Studies
De La Salle University,
Manila, Philippines
rachel.roxas
@delasalle.ph

Shirley Dita
Department of English and Applied Linguistics
College of Education
De La Salle University,
Manila Philippines
shirley.dita@dlsu.edu.ph

Abstract

In this paper, we introduce the Filipino wordnet project (FilWordNet). Filipino is the national language of the Philippines spoken by some 90 million people as their first or second language. However, it has historically had a limited number of computational linguistics resources. Creating the Filipino wordnet can be seen as the first step to enable a wide range of research projects. We describe our process of building a wordnet, including issues with the Filipino language itself, its morphology and structure.

1 Introduction

We discuss the construction of a WordNet for Filipino. Morphology is discussed to establish the need for analyzers and generators to support root word entries in the Wordnet as well as sysnset entries in root word form. Other aspects are investigated such as idiosyncratic and culturally unique words in Filipino.

2 Background

The motivation for the creation of Filipino Wordnet is to provide a solid base of formal linguistic information that could subsequently be used for pertinent language technology applications as outlined by (Morato et al., 2004) . These include information retrieval and extraction, particularly in concept identification in natural language and in query expansion, language teaching, translation applications, and in parameterizable information systems which allowed personal searching of documents based on users' interests. While there has been at least one earlier proposal for a Filipino WordNet (Tan&Lin, 2007), the proposed work was not performed.

2.1 Filipino Language

Tagalog is a language in the Austronesian group of languages, and is, de facto, the basis for the national language of the Philippines, called Filipino. Tagalog is a free word order language, and is somewhat agglutinative with a rich set of affixes, and as such, so is Filipino. The interested reader is referred to (Schacter&Otanes, 1972) for more information about Tagalog grammar..

As in many wordnet projects, the first step is to determine what words deserve to be synsets and which are morphological extensions of the root.

To take cases in English to illustrate this, 'walked' is simply the past tense of 'walk', and does not have additional meaning. In contrast, while 'catfish' is a fish that looks somewhat like a cat, there is no automatic way to know that is the case, and not that it is a cat that looks like a fish, or a cat that likes fish. These facts would encourage an English wordnet to include 'walk' but not 'walked', and to include 'cat', 'fish' and 'catfish' all as separate synsets.

The following examples illustrate morphological phenomena in Filipino. In each case, we illustrate different affixes that affect the focus of the verb, as well as enumerating the different tenses or aspect for each verb with a given focus. Verb focus has no direct analog in English, other than possibly a prosodic emphasis (Szwedek, 1986). Verb focus indicates to the listener where to place the focus of attention in a sentence

Take for example the case of the root word *bili* 'to buy' in actor focus. This focus indicates to the listener that the attention should be on the performer of the action. For actor focus, Filipino uses the infix –um-

Bumili = 'bought' – perfective (*Bumili ang bata ng kendi.* 'The child bought a candy.')

Bumibili = 'is/are buying' – the -um- focus marker + consonant-vowel reduplication yield progressive aspect (*Bumibili ang bata ng kendi.* 'The child is buying a candy.').

Bibili = 'will buy' – consonant-vowel

reduplication yields imperfective (or contemplated, unrealized) aspect (*Bibili ang bata ng kendi.* 'The child will buy a candy.') Note that rather confusingly for the non-native speaker, the infix disappears in this aspect.

In each case, one can imagine an English speaker placing an emphasis through loudness or pitch on 'child'.

For benefactive focus Filipino uses a prefix i- + infix -in-. Note that the future tense shifts the affix to the end of the word. Benefactive focus indicates that the focus of attention of the listener should be on the entity that benefits from the action.

Ibinili = 'bought' - perfective (*Ibinili ng bata ng kendi ang beybi.* 'The child bought a candy for the baby.')

Ibinibili = 'is/are buying' – progressive/on-going – (*Ibinibili ng bata ng kendi ang beybi.* 'The child is buying a candy for the baby.')

Ibibili = 'will buy' – imperfective – (*Ibibili ng bata ng kendi ang beybi.* 'The child will buy candy for the baby.')

In each case, one can imagine an English speaker placing an emphasis through loudness or pitch on 'baby'.

From here, we can complicate the morphology a bit by adding other morphemes, with the example *maipabibili* (I will be able to have him buy (something))

ma- = abilitative prefix (to be able to)
i- = benefactive topic marker (beneficiary of the action is the focus)
pa- = causative marker
bi = aspect marker (imperfective) - consonant-vowel reduplication form
bili = root

These examples provide an insight as to the effect of different affixes when applied to a particular root. We believe that a morphological analyzer is a better approach in modeling Filipino words than storing all of the inflections of a root word in the wordnet as different synsets.

Our initial approach is to be strict in only allowing root forms in the wordnet, unless the word has gained some meaning that cannot be automatically deduced from the root and any affixes.

Uniquely Filipino words

It is very often the case that each new wordnet will have synsets that do not appear in most or even any other existing wordnet (Elkateb et al, 2007). This is also true with Filipino. Let us take a few examples.

tinikling – a cultural dance that originated in the Visayas region utilizing two moving bamboo sticks over which the dancers perform
bayanihan – the spirit of communal unity
bilas – spouse of the brother or sister of one's own spouse
hilamos – to wash one's face

Words such as these form part of the motivation for using a formal ontology. While some wordnets have used English as an interlingua and created phrases to stand in the place of otherwise unlexicalized concepts, in our work, we use SUMO as an interlingua which can contain concepts which stand for the lexicalized concepts of any particular language. For example, rather than add a new English synset corresponding to "spouse of the brother or sister of one's own spouse", we create a concept in SUMO with that definition and relate the Filipino synset to it. This avoid creating synsets in a given language that are "artificial" and not actually lexicalized units. To use the example above of "hilamos", consider Figure 1

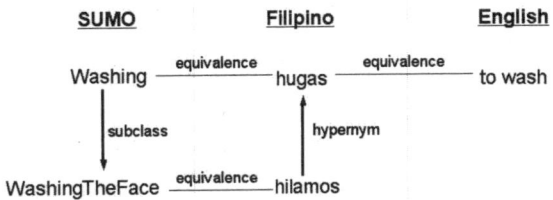

Figure 1: Relation among FilWordNet, SUMO and Princeton's English WordNet

"Hilamos" is a word not lexicalized in English, so above we show it as a term only linked to SUMO.

We should note that the equivalence relation is an informal one. It is neither wordnet semantic link nor a formal logical link as would be found in SUMO, rather it is a relationship without strict definition but denoting intuitively very close similarity to the point of equivalence. We also show the relationship subclass in SUMO which is a formal and truth-preserving relationship, and the hypernym relationship which is one of wordnet's semantic links.

3 Wordnets

Since Princeton's WordNet (PWN) is well-known, it may be sufficient simply to refer the reader to (Fellbaum, 1998). For the purposes of this paper, it bears mentioning that there are several features of WordNet that make it an ideal model for our work with FilWordNet, and an important product to link to.

- PWN is a mature product, having been started over two decades ago (Miller, 1985)
- It is very comprehensive, with over 115,000 word senses, making it the largest wordnet in existence
- It has been free since the project's inception
- It is richly interconnected as a semantic network
- Many other languages have linked their wordnet projects to it manually

4 Suggested Upper Merged Ontology

The FilWordNet project will provide a deep semantic underpinning for each psycholinguistic concept. We take the same approach that was previously used in mapping all of PWN to a formal ontology (Niles & Pease, 2003), the Suggested Upper Merged Ontology (Niles & Pease, 2001), as well as more recently using SUMO as the formal underpinning for Arabic WordNet (Elkateb et al 2007)

Synsets map to a general SUMO term or a term that is directly equivalent to the given synset (Figure 1). New formal terms will be defined to cover a greater number of equivalence mappings, and the definitions of the new terms will in turn depend upon existing fundamental concepts in SUMO. The process of formalizing definitions will generate feedback as to whether word senses in WN need to be divided or combined and how the glosses may be clarified. Since many wordnets in other languages are already linked by synset number, this work will benefit wordnets in other languages as well.

The Suggested Upper Merged Ontology (SUMO) (Pease&Niles, 2002),(Niles&Pease, 2001) is a freely available, formal ontology of about 1000 terms and 4000 definitional statements. It is provided in a first order logic language called Standard Upper Ontology Knowledge Interchange format (SUO-KIF) (Pease, 2000), and also has a necessarily lossy translation into the OWL semantic web language. It has undergone nine years of development, review by a community of hundreds of people, and application in expert reasoning and linguistics. SUMO has been subjected to formal verification with an automated theorem prover. SUMO has been extended with a number of domain ontologies, which are also public, that together number some 20,000 terms and 70,000 axioms. SUMO has been mapped by hand to the WN lexicon of over 115,000 noun, verb, adjective and adverb senses, which not only acts as a check on coverage and completeness, but also provides a basis for application to natural language understanding tasks. SUMO covers areas of knowledge such as temporal and spatial representation, units and measures, processes, events, actions, and obligations. Domain specific ontologies extend and re-use SUMO in the areas of finance and investment, country almanac information, terrain modeling, distributed computing, endangered languages description, biological viruses, engineering devices, weather and a number of military applications. It is important to note that each of these ontologies employs rules. These formal descriptions make explicit the meaning of each of the terms in the ontology, unlike a simple taxonomy, or controlled keyword list. SUMO is the only formal ontology that has been mapped to all of WN, and the only formal upper ontology that has been extended with a number of domain ontologies that are also open source. SUMO has natural language generation templates and a multi-lingual lexicon that allows statements in SUMO-KIF and SUMO to be expressed in multiple natural languages. These include English, German, Arabic, Czech, Italian, Hindi (Western character set) and Chinese (traditional characters and pinyin).

The ontology as a structured ILI

The comprehensive mapping and definition of synsets in FilWordNet to SUMO concepts reinforces a new perspective on the role of an Interlingual Index (ILI) in connecting wordnets (Vossen, 2004, Vossen et al 1999, Vossen 1998).

In the FilWordNet project, we want to take this idea a step further, as was done with Arabic. If both FilWordNet and English WN synsets are exhaustively defined in terms of SUMO concepts, SUMO can in effect become the ILI for wordnets. This means that SUMO not only maps word meanings and synonyms across languages but also provides a formal semantic framework for all these languages.

The development of FilWordNet will include a transition phase where FilWordNet synsets are both linked to the English WN serving as an ILI and exhaustively defined with SUMO.

5 Project Description

FilWordNet began an introductory set of lectures to students and faculty at De La Salle University, Manila, on wordnets, linguistics semantics and formal semantics. Six students volunteered to be the actual creators of the synsets with an intensive two-week process to complete the project. The objective was to create 40 synsets a day per person with each student present for roughly three hours a day. We were able to achieve an initial set of 1,000 synsets, although full completion took a few weeks longer than anticipated due to external unrelated events. The students are expected to continue work in order in a few months to cover the approximately 4,600 base concepts (Pease et al, 2008). Additionally, a small cash prize was announced for the creators of the most synsets in hopes of creating a mature wordnet of greater than 10,000 synsets at the end of the academic year 2009-2010.

We created an initial seed list of Princeton's English WordNet synsets for students to get started. This consisted of some synsets chosen from intuition as being semantically distant from one another. Each student was expected to translate synset word names and definitions into Filipino. They were assisted in this task by the use of Calderon's Tagalog-English-Spanish dictionary (Calderon, 1915). After some collaborative work on this initial set, they expanded their set to hypernyms and hyponyms of the seed word and continued in this fashion.

We have used Princeton WordNet semantic links and assumed them to be correct in Filipino subject to manual verification later on. Similarly, we reuse the links from Princeton WordNet to SUMO also subject to later manual verification as to whether it is also valid for Filipino.

We treat the links to SUMO and semantic links within wordnet to be an important part of the quality assurance process for wordnet construction. Considering the semantic links between different synsets helps the lexicographer to determine whether the definition and synset grouping is valid. For example, a critical test is to look amongst sibling synsets and consider whether the definition of a given synset fully distinguishes it from its siblings.

Initially, we had the students create their translations simply in spreadsheets tracking the link to English via each synsets WordNet 3.0 synset number. We have installed DebVisDic (Horak et al, 2006) and will be migrating to that tool as our construction environment shortly. We expect that this will help considerably especially with respect to group coordination.

We plan an open source release of FilWordNet for early in 2010, once we are close to covering the base concepts.

6 Conclusions and Future Work

FilWordNet is an enabling resource for computational linguistics on Filipino. We are currently conducting linguistics research on the evolution of Tagalog grammar among metropolitan residents of the Philippines in which we plan to use FilWordNet in performing manual markup of Filipino corpora. FilWordNet will be a basis for a stemmer/lemmatizer that will use FilWordNet to prevent overly "greedy" removal of affixes from words. FilWordNet will also provide a basis for work in developing a named entity recognition system. With a series of projects that all leverage the work on FilWordNet, we hope that will create motivation to continue expanding and improving this product. Additionally, we hope to involve other universities in the Philippines in this effort to improve linguistic resources for the national language.

Acknowledgments

We would like to thank our students, Alvin Garcia, Hun Ping Yu, Bryan Lacaden, Jeremy Bondoc, Darren So and Jhovee Yap who have created the actual synsets. We are grateful for their efforts. We acknowledge De La Salle University, Manila for hosting Adam Pease as a visiting scholar, and the Philippine Council for Advanced Science and Technology Research and Development (PCASTRD) of the Department of Science and Technology (Philippines) and Commission on Higher Education (Philippines) for partial funding of his visit.

References

Calderón, S., (1915) Diccionario Ingles-Español-Tagalog, Con partes de la oracion y pronunciacion figurada. Primera Edición, Manila, Libreria y Papeleria de J. Martinez, Plaza P. Moraga 34/36, Plaza Calderón 108 y Real 153/155, Intramuros. See also http://www.gutenberg.org/etext/20738

Elkateb, S., Black, W., Rodriguez, H, Alkhalifa, M., Vossen, P., Pease, A. and Fellbaum, C., (2006). Building a WordNet for Arabic, in Proceedings of The fifth international conference on Language Resources and Evaluation (LREC 2006).

Fellbaum, C., (1998, ed.) WordNet: An Electronic Lexical Database. Cambridge, MA: MIT Press.

Horak, A., Pala, K., Rambousek, A., and Povolny, M. (2006) DEBVisDic - First Version of New Client-Server Wordnet Browsing and Editing Tool. In Proceedings of the Third International WordNet Conference - GWC 2006. Brno, Czech Republic: Masaryk University, pp. 325-328. ISBN 80-210-3915-9.

Miller, G., (1985) "WordNet: a dictionary browser." In Proceedings of the First International Conference on Information in Data, University of Waterloo, Waterloo.

Morato, J., Marzal, M.A., Llorens, J., & Moreiro, J (2004). WordNet Applications. In Proceedings of the Second Global WordNet Conference (GWC-2004). Brno, Czech Republic.

Niles, I., and Pease, A., (2003). Linking Lexicons and Ontologies: Mapping WordNet to the Suggested Upper Merged Ontology, Proceedings of the IEEE International Conference on Information and Knowledge Engineering, pp 412-416.

Niles, I., and Pease, A. (2001). Towards a Standard Upper Ontology. In: Proceedings of FOIS 2001, Ogunquit, Maine, pp. 2-9. See also http://www.ontologyportal.org

Pease, A., (2000). Standard Upper Ontology Knowledge Interchange Format. Web document http://suo.ieee.org/suo-kif.html. This is largely a condensed version of the language described in (Genesereth, 1991)

Pease, A., (2003). The Sigma Ontology Development Environment, in Working Notes of the IJCAI-2003 Workshop on Ontology and Distributed Systems. Volume 71 of CEUR Workshop Proceeding series.

Pease, A., Fellbaum, C., and Vossen, P., (2008) Building the Global WordNet Grid. Proceedings of the CIL-18 Workshop on Linguistic Studies of Ontology, Seoul, South Korea.

Schachter, P., and Otanes, F., (1972) Tagalog reference grammar. ISBN: 0520017765, Berkeley : University of California Press

Szwedek, A (1986). A linguistic analysis of sentence stress, Gunter Narr Verlag: Tubingen, ISBN: 3-87808-298-3

Tan, P., and Lim, N., (2007) FilWordNet: Towards a Filipino WordNet. 4th National Natural Language Processing Research Symposium Proceedings, CSB Hotel, June 14-16, 2007, ISSN 1908-3092

Vossen, P. (ed) (1998) EuroWordNet: A Multilingual Database with Lexical Semantic Networks, Kluwer Academic Publishers, Dordrecht.

Vossen, P. Peters, W., J. Gonzalo. (1999). 'Towards a Universal Index of Meaning'. Proceedings of the ACL-99 Siglex workshop, University of Maryland, 81-90

Vossen P. (2004) EuroWordNet: a multilingual database of autonomous and language-specific wordnets connected via an Inter-Lingual-Index. International Journal of Lexicography, Vol. 17 No. 2, OUP, pp 161-173

Foundation and Structure of Developing an Assamese WordNet

Shikhar Kr. Sarma
Department of Computer Science
Gauhati University
Guwahati 781014: Assam, India
sks001@gmail.com; sks@gauhati.ac.in

Rakesh Medhi
Department of Computer Science
Gauhati University
Guwahati 781014: Assam, India
rakesh.medhi@gmail.com

Moromi Gogoi
Department of Computer Science
Gauhati University
Guwahati 781014: Assam, India
Moromi_gogoi@yahoo.com

Utpal Saikia
Department of Computer Science
Gauhati University
Guwahati 781014: Assam, India
utpal.sk@gmail.com

Abstract

Development of Wordnets of regional languages has been of great concern in recent years. This is mainly due to the ever increasing demands and requirements of putting those languages as effective media of the digital world, including the internet. As the technologies for putting regional languages in the digital media are being developed, research and development works related to Wordnets in those languages are also starting. Efforts have been taken at different level, including academic researchers and at government level for developing language technologies for the Assamese language, a scheduled language in India mainly spoken by the people in the state of Assam. Basic technologies like, UNICODE compliant fonts and keyboards, CLDR, Corpus, Spelling Checker etc. have been developed. As a part of the Government of India efforts on Technology Development of Indian Languages, creation of Assamese Wordnets has been started. This paper focuses on the foundations of the Assamese Wordnet, and describes the complete background concepts, language specifications, properties and characteristics, as well as the plan and challenges of creating such a Wordnet of Assamese language. The details of the structure, workflow are outlined. Considerable contents are included on the experience of handling developing the Assamese Wordnet with linkage to the Hindi and English Wordnets. The paper also focuses on the challenges faced on mapping to the Hindi and English Wordnets. The qualitative and quantitative achievements on structuring the core preliminary part of the Assamese Wordnet are also presented.

1 Introduction

Assamese language is the main spoken language of the state of Assam. This language is recognized as regional language in the eighth schedule of Indian constitution. This is one of the official languages of Assam. This language is also used as interstate communication language in many north eastern states specially Arunachal Pradesh and Nagaland. Apart from the states in Indian Territory, Assamese spoken people are found in Bhutan and Bangladesh also. There is a huge population of Assamese spoken people in different parts of India, who originated from Assam, but professionally settled in other states. There is also a considerable number of Assamese speakers in different other countries specially in UK and US. The tentative number of people speaking Assamese in the state of Assam and neighboring states of North East India, is 14 million, and the all India tentative counting is about 14.3 million.

While tracing the origin of Assamese language its relation is found to the Indo-Aryan language group and also a little bit to Sino-Tibetan language group. In 1870 linguist Ascoli divided Indo-European language in two main groups viz Satam and Centum. Satam group of language is again divided in four groups. One of which is Indo-Iranian group from where Indo-Aryan group is derived. Indo-Aryan language group is again divided into three parts[1], they are-

1. Old Indo Aryan (1500 BC to 600 BC)
2. Middle Indo Aryan(600 BC to 1000 AD)
3. New Indo Aryan(1000 AD to till now)

In Indo Aryan Languages, Assamese, Bangla, Oriya etc are derived from Modern Apabhransha. These languages are originally derived from the Magadhi-Prakrit. Presence of Assamese language dated back to the literatures of *Charyapadas*, written by Budhist scholars. The

Assamese language present in *charyapadas* reflects its evolutionary stages in initial state. Literatures with distinct Assamese language are found from the *Kavyas* of the pre Sankari era. This was in 13th century AD. From that time onwards pure Assamese language with its structured forms evolved.

Assamese script is derived from Brahmi script. It played a vital role in the evolution of the Indian script. The rock inscription and copper plate from 5th to 9th century showed the evolution of Assamese script. There are eight vowel phonemes in Assamese. There are twenty-one consonant and two semi-vowel phonemes in the Standard Colloquial Assamese.

2 Characteristics of the language

2.1 Morphological Characteristics:

The Assamese language has many special morphological characteristics [6]. Out of which few are outlined below:

i. Numbers are not grammatically marked in Assamese Language. There are two types of Numbers in Assamese Language, Singular and Plural.
ii. Gender is also not grammatically marked in Assamese. Linguistically, there are two types of Gender in this Language, Masculine and Feminine. But traditionally common and neuter genders are also used.
iii. Kinship nouns are inflected for personal pronominal possession.
iv. There are two types of affixes in Assamese Language, Prefix and Suffix. Both Prefix and Suffix are very commonly found in Assamese language. Suffix included derivational, Inflectional and conjugational forms.
v. There are six types of Cases in Assamese language, Nominative, Accusative, Instrumental, Dative, Ablative, and Locative.

There are six parts of speech (POS) in Assamese language [6]. They are :-

- Noun (Common, Proper, Collective, Material, Abstract.)
- Pronoun (Personal, Demonstrative, Inclusive, Relative, Indefinite, Interrogative, Reflexive)
- Verb (Transitive, Intransitive)
- Adverb (Manner, Place, Time)
- adjective (Nominal, Qualifying)
- Indeclinable (Conjunction, Interjection etc.)

2.2 Syntactic Characteristics

Few general syntactic characteristics of Assamese language are mentioned below [6]:

i. The general syntactic structure of Assamese language is Subject+Object+Verb (SOV).
ii. Syntactically Assamese sentence structure is mainly divided into three types - Simple, Complex and Compound.
iii. Assamese sentence structure is flexible. Depending on the context or mood of the speaker it might vary.
iv. Assamese sentence structure is of different kinds. Very short sentences are found frequently. Sometimes long expressions are made by adding indeclinables.
v. In Assamese, there are subject-verb agreements. The verbs in Assamese agree with the subjects in person. There is no agreement in number or gender like some other languages, English or Spanish etc.
vi. Verb-less sentences are also very frequent in Assamese language.
vii. Idiomatic expressions are also found in Assamese Language.

2.3 Assamese Synonyms/ Antonyms

There are large numbers of synonyms and antonyms used in Assamese language. Few examples are given below:

Assamese Synonyms

[English: Sun (सूर्य)]: সূৰ্য (*xurja*), বেলি (*beli*), ৰবি (*ravi*), ভানু (*bhanu*), তপন (*tapan*), মিহিৰ (*mihir*), দিবাকৰ (*dibakar*), সূৰুয (*xuruj*), সবিতা (*xabita*), চাকা (*saka*)...

[English: Moon (चन्द्र)]: চন্দ্ৰ (*sandra*), জোন (*jon*), জোনবাই (*jonbai*), শশী (*sasi*), চন্দ্ৰমা (*sandrama*), শশাংক (*sasanka*), মৃগাংক (*mrigangka*), নিশাকৰ (*nisakar*)...

[English: Earth (पृथ्वी)]: পৃথিৱী (*prithiwi*), জগত (*jagat*), ধৰণী (*dharani*), ধৰা (*dhara*), ধৰিত্ৰী (*dharatri*), মেদিনী (*medini*), বিশ্ব (*biswa*), বসুমতী (*baxumati*), অৱনী (*awani*), জাহান (*jahan*)...

[English: Sky (आकाश)]: আকাশ (*akash*), গগন (*gagan*), অম্বৰ (*ambar*), আছমান (*asman*), অভ্র (*abhra*), নীলিমা (*nilima*), অন্তৰীক্ষ (*antariksha*)...

Assamese Antonyms

[English: Day-Night (दिन-रात)]: দিন-ৰাতি (*din-rati*)

[English : Black-White(काला-चाफ)]: ক'লা-বগা (*kola-baga*)

[English : Good-Bad (अच्छा-बुरा)]: ভাল-বেয়া (*bhal-beya*)

[English: Dark-Light (अँधेरा-उजाला)]: আন্ধাৰ-পোহৰ (*andhar-pohar*)

[English : Warm-Cold (गर्म-ठंढ)]: গৰম-ঠাণ্ডা (*garam-thanda*)

[English : Birth-Death (जन्म-मरण)]: জন্ম-মৃত্যু (*janma-mrityu*)

[English : Win-Defeat (जीत-हार)] : জয়-পৰাজয় (*jay-parajay*)

2.4 Hyponymy and Hypernyms

Hyponymy involves in the notion of inclusion. Hyponymy is the relationship which obtains between specific and general lexical items, such the former is 'included' in the latter (i.e. 'is a hyponym of' the latter). In each case, there is a superordinate term, sometimes called a 'hypernym', with reference to which the subordinate term can be defined.
For instance,
Belpat ; a leaf of a tree named *Bel*
=>*pat*; leaf
Here, *Belpat*; a leaf of a tree named *Bel* is a kind of *pat*; *pat* means leaf; *pat* is a hypernym and *belpat* is the hyponym. Similar case is with the example of *kolpat* also.

2.5 Meronymy and Holonymy

anguli ;Finger
=>*hat*;Hand
pahi ; Petal
=> *phul*; Flower.

2.6 Entailment

usup ; To sob
=> *kand*; To cry, To weep

2.7 Troponymy:

misikiya; To smile
=>*hah*; to laugh
dour; To run
=>*za*; to go

2.8 Antonymy

suti ; Short
=>*dighol*; Long
din; Day
=>*rati;* Night

2.9 Inter-language element in Assamese synset/synonym

Assamese is rich in synonymous words. In fact, we can find many inter-language elements in Assamese synset. For instance, Hindi and Bangla elements are commonly found in Assamese synset, few of which are shown below:

Assamese	**Bengali**	**Hindi**
নদী (River)	নদী	नदी
বৰষুণ (Rain)	বৃষ্টি	वृष्टि
বিবাহ, বিয়া (Marriage)	বিয়া, বিবাহ	विवाह
স্বামী, পতি (Husband)	স্বামী, পতি	स्वामी, पति
কিতাপ, পুস্তক, গ্রন্থ (Book)	পুস্তক, গ্রন্থ	पुस्तक, ग्रन्थ

3 The developing plan

The Assamese Wordnet is being developed as a sub part of the North East Wordnet Development effort, which is a part of the Indo Wordnet. The basic principles adopted have been uniform for all the North Eastern Language Wordnet developments. A common interface for creation of Wordnet is being used. The interface has simultaneous multiple active spaces. One is for the Hindi Synset display. And the other is for the Assamese entry and display. The Hindi space includes the Hindi Synset ID, Category, Concept, gloss, and the synset. The corresponding Assamese space is on the right hand. The ID is same for the same concept. Part of Speech category could be changed. This is because, sometimes the corresponding concepts in Hindi and Assamese might have part of speech ambiguities. This space either displays the already entered contents, or facilitates the content entry. The interface has a third space, which is normally hidden, and could be made active on clicking button. This third space contains the corresponding English synsets.

As the whole idea is to create an integrated Indo Wordnet, we have adopted the expansion approach. The framework guidelines adopted for creating the Assamese Wordnet as an expansion of existing Hindi and English Wordnets are as follows:

- For Concepts:
  - Understanding using the Hindi one. For clarification, refer to the English one, if and only if it is required
  - Direct translation from Hindi in all possible cases
  - In case the translation is extremely difficult, not meaningful, or could not be represented with available set of vocabulary, create concept in local language style.

- For Examples:
  - Translation from Hindi Examples
  - If it is ambiguous/not fully meaningful in local language, create new one

- Building the synsets:
  - Standardisation
    - Use of official dictionaries
    - No new coining of Words
    - Rather Coining of proposals for new required words
  - Creating a reporting interface
    - Printing the entries in a tabular format
    - Distributing to the expert linguists and feedback
    - Putting in public domain and feedback

- Referring to the English entries, concepts and examples for any clarifications, or to resolving any ambiguities

4 Expansion from Hindi/English

The main challenge in expansion approach is in one to one mapping. Although initially in most of the cases, Hindi-Assamese mapping has shown one to one correspondence, but as we progressed, we started encountering many problems. The problem ranges from word meaning ambiguities to concept mismatch. Few important challenges faced during initial 2000 core synset creation are outlined below:

i. There is no equivalent concept in Assamese language against a Hindi concept. This has been found particularly in meaning corresponding to human relations
ii. There is no Assamese synset against a Hindi concept. The synset overlaps with another Hindi concept
iii. The Hindi concept itself sometimes differ from the English concept in meaning
iv. Direct translation of Hindi examples result in awkward/less-meaningful sentences in Assamese
v. In many cases in the Hindi Wordnet, the Synset entries are found in the Concept itself. This result in similar overlapping in the Assamese entries. This could have been resolved provided the flexibility to modifying the concept would have been there. But as a principle of Indo Wordnet, at present this flexibility is not allowed.
vi. In few cases, the Hindi and English concepts conflict within them.

5 System Architecture

The computational infrastructure for creating the Assamese Wordnet has been built in a Client Server Architecture. Although the standalone tool for creating the Wordnet is used at desktop node, the backup, replication and updating has been automated in the client-server configuration. The default text file where the entries are stored has been used to structure a database of the Wordnet entities against fields. A Web based interface has been developed integrating the main database, feedback forms, feedback database, and the corrected database of different levels. The block diagram of the integrated system is depicted below:

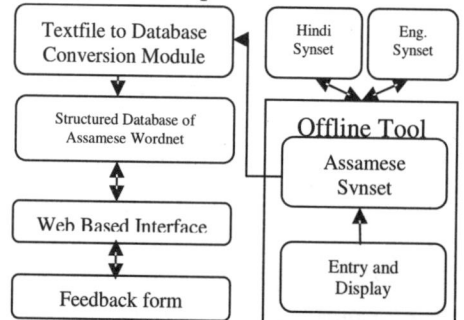

Figure 1. System Architecture for Development of Assamese Wordnet

6 Conclusions and Future work

Development of Wordnet is a collaborative work. Equal participation of academicians, researchers in fields like linguistics and computations are important to the building of a successful Wordnet. Such a structured and well-built Wordnet in a particular language carries the language to new heights. Attempt has been given in the present work to look at this angle so that a piece of well structured and valued finished product could be delivered. Language technology development in Assamese language signifies a lot, as Assamese is the most spoken language in the state of Assam, and also this is the official language of majority of the state population. Technology development in the language is the backbone for effective utilization and spreading of digital tools, appliances and applications to the mass people. An Assamese Wordnet will definitely openup the scope and opportunities for the language as an effective media for digital processing and communications. The work has been started with an integrated team comprising of lexicographers, computer professionals, and overseen by experienced linguistics, and language technologists. Although this is a part of the composite Indo Wordnet, but linguistically its a complete new work. The work has been integrated with fresh computational facilities like web-based feedback system, structured database, and also an automated rectification and correction system, with provision of different levels of modified and indexed databases. The target is to develop the complete Wordnet with 100% mapping of the present Hindi Wordnet with 12282 synsets, and also to add new concepts in the language specific space. The Assamese Wordnet so developed will definitely be a piece of technological importance which will lead to an extremely rich and useful lexical base facilitating automatic bi-lingual dictionary construction, machine translation between the Assamese and English, Hindi, and other Indian languages, Cross lingual information retrieval etc. The work will also produce user manuals and software in modules, which will ultimately have impact on social empowerment by IT, economic benefits, language learning, crossing of language barrier etc. An important secondary output of the whole exercise is in regards of manpower training and generation. Through this Wordnet development exercise a new breed of researchers in language technologies will be trained for proper skills and knowledge sets. As in Assamese, the linguistic and literature studies in formal education are with 0% computational linkage, and with no training/exposure for interlinking of linguistics and computing, the work will facilitate in developing a team of interdisciplinary researchers.

Acknowledgements

The Assamese Wordnet Development Project is sponsored by the Department of Information Technology, Ministry of Communication and Information Technology, Government of India.

References

1. Banikanta Kakati. 2008. *Assamese: Its Formation and Development*, Lawyers Book Stall, Guwahati, Assam.
2. Chakrabarti Debasri, Narayan Dipak Kumar, Pandey Prabhakar, Bhattacharyya Pushpak. 2002. *Experiences in Building the Indo WordNet: A WordNet for Hindi*, Proceedings of the First Global WordNet Conference.
3. Dave Shachi and Bhattacharyya Pushpak. 2001. *Knowledge Extraction from Hindi Texts*, Journal of Institution of Electronic and Telecommunication Engineers, vol. 18, no. 4.
4. E. Pianta, L. Bentivogli, C. Girardi. 2002. *MultiWordNet: Developing an Aligned Multilingual Database*, Proceedings of the First International Conference on Global WordNet Mysore, India.
5. Fellbaum, C. (ed.), 1998. *WordNet: An Electronic Lexical Database,*. The MIT Press.
6. Golock C Goswami. 1983. *Structure of Assamese*, Gauhati University, Assam.
7. Miller,G., Beckwith,R., Fellbaum,C., Gross,D., and Miller,K, 1990. *Five Papers on WordNet.* CSL Report 43, Cognitive Science Laboratory, Princeton University, Princeton.

Collaborative Management of KYOTO Multilingual Knowledge Base: The Wikyoto Knowledge Editor

**Francesco Ronzano, Maurizio Tesconi, Salvatore Minutoli
and Andrea Marchetti**

Institute of Informatics and Telematics (IIT) - CNR
Via G. Moruzzi, 1 – Pisa, Italy
{francesco.ronzano,maurizio.tesconi,salvatore.minutoli,
andrea.marchetti}@iit.cnr.it

Abstract

In this paper we introduce the Wikyoto Knowledge Editor, the wiki Web-based environment where the multilingual and multicultural community of KYOTO users interacts to maintain and extend, with respect to their particular domain of interest, the background knowledge resources of the KYOTO system, constituting the Multilingual Knowledge Base. KYOTO is a knowledge-driven system for fact mining from a multilingual collection of information sources concerning a specific domain of interest. Facts are mined from relevant documents that are linguistically and semantically annotated exploiting the Multilingual Knowledge Base, made of several language-specific WordNets all referred to a common Central Ontology.

1 Managing knowledge resources: the online collaboration paradigm

Nowadays, knowledge-intensive tasks like text mining, information extraction, semantic grounding of data as well as semantic integration of distinct datasets rely more and more on the background knowledge provided by properly structured knowledge resources such as ontologies or, in general, any semantic or linguistic network. Moreover, as a consequence of the great diffusion experimented by the Semantic Web along with all its related standards and methodologies, ontologies have also gained a central role as the preferred mean to provide shared conceptualizations over the Web in order to exchange and integrate knowledge among different communities of users.

In this context, knowledge resources need *to be properly structured and maintained so as to adequately and correctly model the required information.*

They often have to be tailored to a particular domain and kept up to date to reflect changes in the knowledge they describe; they need to be shared in one or among different communities of users that should reach consensus on the formalized knowledge.

Considering the process of creation and maintenance of knowledge resources, two distinct and often complementary categories of actors have to be actively involved: *knowledge engineers* and *domain experts*. The former ones are usually experienced in knowledge representation and formalization, but often they have little or no expertise in the domain being described. On the contrary, domain experts have a strong knowledge of the domain of interest, but they usually are not able to correctly deal with all the issues related to knowledge formalization.

During the last few years, to allow both of them to take part in the maintenance of a knowledge resource, the **online collaboration paradigm**, also referred to as the wiki paradigm, has been more and more adopted. Thanks to properly structured interfaces, many methodologies and tools, in the majority Web-based, have been proposed so as to collaboratively gather and harmonize all the contributions of the distinct involved actors.

In the remaining part of this Section we briefly describe some relevant example of tools and methodologies to collaboratively manage knowledge resources, summarizing, at the end, the core issues they deal with as well as the features they usually implement. The considered tools can be divided into two great categories:

- *Wiki tools to semantically structure information*: easily exploitable by users with little or no expertise in knowledge formalization, these tools usually help them to explicit structured knowledge starting from unstructured texts. As a consequence, the formalized knowledge can be exploited to improve information navigation and search. In order to be easily accessed by distributed user communities, these tools usually are provided with a Web interface. Three relevant examples are: Semantic *MediaWiki*, *OntoWiki* and *IkeWiki*.

- *Complex knowledge management environments*: they are usually exploited by experts in knowledge formalization in order to fully model information according to a specific and well known representational schema. Due to their usually complex knowledge editing patterns, these tools are mainly realized as standalone desktop applications, even if some of them can be accessed through a Web interface. Among them relevant examples are *Protégé*, the *NeOn Toolkit*, *SWOOP*, *UbisEditor* and *Ontoverse*.

A *Wiki tool to semantically structure information* is **Semantic MediaWiki**[1] (Kroetzsch et al., 2006): it represents a semantic extension of MdiaWiki[2], the wiki engine supporting the most important wiki projects like Wikipedia: it aims at extending Wikipedia contents with more structure and semantics so as to increase their consistency, their reuse and to facilitate their access exploiting semantic search patterns.

OntoWiki[3] (Auer et al., 2006) is a tool for collaborative knowledge editing. It is a Web-based ontology editor and a collaborative knowledge acquisition tool: it provides a graphic user interface for an easy and visual editing of RDF knowledge bases. OntoWiki allows defining instances with respect to ontology classes and properties, visualizing particular kinds of data through custom views, avoiding repetition of information and allowing also non expert users to easily understand knowledge organization.

IkeWiki[4] (Shaffert, 2006) is another semantic wiki that allows users to describe pages and links between pages with semantic annotations, in a way compatible with MediaWiki. IkeWiki implements Semantic Web standards like RDF and OWL and supports different levels of knowledge formalization and different users expertise. The KiWi (Knowledge In a Wiki) Project[5], co-founded by the European Commission, starting also from the background provided by the IkeWiki experience, aims at analyzing the most adequate way to define and make semantic wikis usable by huge communities of users, in a user-centric environment.

Taking into account the examples of *Complex knowledge management environments*, we consider **Protégé**[6] (Tudorache and Noy, 2007; Abraham et al., 2008), mainly devoted to knowledge engineers. It is an open-source extensible Java frame work to edit ontologies that can be expressed also in RDF(S) and OWL. It is one of the most widely adopted ontology editing environments supported by a huge community of users. Based on a client-server architecture, it allows to the collaboratively edit ontologies. Moreover, recently *Web Protégé* (Tudorache et al., 2008), a Web Interface for Protégé has been developed for editing ontolgies through a Web browser.

Also the **NeOn Toolkit**[7], developed in the context of the NeOn (Networked Ontologies) Project[8], co-founded by the European Commission, is a rich ontology editing environment. It allows to edit F-logic, RDF(S) and OWL ontologies, thanks to different visualization facilities, supporting also the definition of rules. It is easily extensible exploiting a plug-in mechanism and currently a large number of plug-ins have been developed; they provide support to collaborative Web-based ontology editing as well as to other important tasks like ontology-related argumentation.

SWOOP[9] (Kalyanpur et al., 2005) is an ontology browser and editor based on OWL, developed at the Maryland Information and Network Dynamics Laboratory of the University of Maryland. It supports full editing features of OWL ontologies, multiple ontology usage and collaborative annotation over the same ontologies. It has

---

[1] http://semantic-mediawiki.org/wiki/Semantic_MediaWiki
[2] http://www.mediawiki.org/
[3] http://ontowiki.net/Projects/OntoWiki
[4] http: http://ikewiki.salzburgresearch.at/
[5] http://www.kiwi-project.eu/
[6] http://protege.stanford.edu/
[7] http://neon-toolkit.org/
[8] http://www.neon-project.org/
[9] http://www.mindswap.org/2004/SWOOP/

been realized exploiting the Java Webstart technology in order to be accessed by a common Web browser and includes the possibility to rely upon a reasoner to validate the formalized knowledge.

UbisEditor[10] (Losky et al., 2009) is a collaborative Web ontology editing environment, developed in the context of the UbisWorld Project at the German Research Center for Artificial Intelligence. It allows users, through their Web browser, to navigate and edit hierarchies of ontological classes as well as to define instances or labels in different languages. Users can also exploit ontology ranking as well as define personalized ontology views.

Other examples of *Complex knowledge management environments* to build and enrich knowledge resources are **AceWiki**[11] (Khun, 2008) or the **CLOnE system** (Funk et al., 2007), both exploiting a controlled language to easily edit and refine ontologies and **Ontoverse**[12] (Bai and Zaloufa, 2007), allowing different actors to collaborate and concurrently build an ontology with a great focus on collaboration aspects and group awareness.

All the described tools underline how many issues need to be faced when we have to provide users with a useful environment to browse and edit knowledge resources: besides the *ease of interaction for the different kinds of users* with different levels of expertise, we have also to consider the *ease of accessing* to such a kind of environments, sometimes provided exploiting a client-server architecture and a browser-based Web interface. *Argumentation facilities* are needed as well as *concurrency controls* and *consistency checks* over the edited knowledge. *User-specific editing permissions* and *versioning support* are two other relevant features.

Starting from all the considerations, examples and analysis done, in the rest of this paper we present the Wikyoto Knowledge Editor, the wiki Web environment useful for editing and enriching the set of linguistic and ontological knowledge resources collected in the KYOTO Multilingual Knowledge Base: it constitutes the semantic reference to carry out the knowledge processing tasks of the KYOTO system, a complex knowledge mining architecture realized in the context of the homonym European FP7 Project. The description of the Knowledge Editor is based on and extends the presentation of the first developed prototype of the Knowledge Editor reported in (Marchetti et al., 2009).

2 Wikyoto Knowledge Editor, the wiki for the KYOTO Multilingual Knowledge Base

The Wikyoto Knowledge Editor represents the collaborative environment useful to edit and enrich the multilingual knowledge resources of the KYOTO system, referred to as the KYOTO Multilingual Knowledge Base. KYOTO is a complex knowledge-driven cross-language environment enabling communities of users to mine information form textual documents, sharing the collected facts: it is currently under development in the context of the homonym European FP7 Project[13], carried out also jointly with Asian partners. In KYOTO, most of the knowledge-based tasks are carried out by exploiting the background knowledge collected in the KYOTO Multilingual Knowledge Base: it is the core knowledge reference of the whole system. It is made of a set of linguistic and ontological resources. **The richer the Knowledge Base, the deeper and more effective KYOTO semantic analysis of data can be**.

Thanks to the support of the Wikyoto Knowledge Editor, the Multilingual Knowledge Base can be collaboratively maintained and enriched involving users with different levels of expertise, all belonging to the same community of interest. In particular, by accessing the Web interface of the Wikyoto Knowledge Editor, users can *create, as part of the Multilingual Knowledge Base, a set of customized domain-specific knowledge resources, referring to and extending the generic ones available in KYOTO*. Users can also browse different kinds of external resources like terminologies and thesauri getting useful hints to extend or refine the Multilingual Knowledge Base or defining mappings between these external resources and the same Multilingual Knowledge Base.

All the knowledge formalization activities carried out through the Knowledge Editor immediately affect the text mining and semantic processing capabilities and effectiveness of the whole KYOTO system that relies upon them.

---

[10] http://ubisworld.ai.cs.uni-sb.de/ontology/
[11] http://www.ontoverse.org/
[12] http://www.ontoverse.org/

[13] http://www.kyoto-project.eu/

In this paragraph, first of all we provide a global overview of the whole KYOTO system, so as to contextualize the Wikyoto Knowledge Editor (Section 2.1). Then we go deeper into details: in particular we describe the first release of the Wikyoto Knowledge Editor. It is useful to show many relevant core features of the wiki way to manage knowledge resources adopted in KYOTO. We present its Web-based architecture as well as the set of external resources it interacts with (Section 2.2). We describe its Web interface (Section 2.3) also by a simple example of usage (Section 2.4).

2.1 KYOTO: mining documents and sharing facts by means of the Multilingual Knowledge Base

In this Section we provide a brief overview of how the KYOTO system works. This description doesn't claim to be exhaustive since the main focus of this Section is to introduce the general context where the Wikyoto Knowledge Editor comes into play: to get further information about KYOTO, as well as more technical details about the different parts of the system, you can access the KYOTO Project Official Web Site, *http://www.kyoto-project.eu/*.

KYOTO architecture involves different interacting modules and data repositories so as to realize a complex set of knowledge-driven tasks and activities ranging from *text mining* to *terminology and facts extraction*, *semantic search* and *collaborative editing of knowledge resources* (see Figure 1).

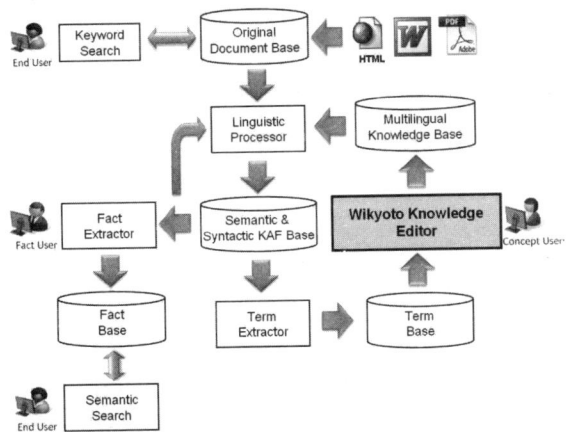

Figure 1. Global architecture of the KYOTO System: knowledge processing activities

The users of KYOTO are grouped by specific roles, depending on the purpose of their interaction with the system. In particular, as we can see from Figure 1, *End Users* mainly access KYOTO to search for information. On the contrary *Fact Users* and *Concept Users* have a stronger interaction with the system: the former ones support the definition of patterns to mine relevant facts from parsed documents, the latter ones directly deal with the Wikyoto Knowledge Editor.

All the documents of interest for KYOTO users (whatever is their format: HTML pages, MSWord or PDF, expressed in all the languages involved in the Project) are collected and indexed in the *Original Document Base*: End Users can perform keyword-based searches on their contents.

All those documents are linguistically and semantically annotated by language-specific *Linguistic Processors*. Semantic annotation is performed by accessing the language-specific knowledge retrieved from the *Multilingual Knowledge Base*. The annotation results are represented, in a language-independent way, thanks to the KYOTO Annotation Format (KAF) and stored in the *Syntactic & Semantic KAF Base*. Semantic annotation of documents can be repeated over time since the background knowledge exploited to perform this task, contained in the *Multilingual Knowledge Base*, is continuously updated by KYOTO Concept Users, by mean of the **Wikyoto Knowledge Editor**.

As previously said, the *Multilingual Knowledge Base* (see Figure 2) represents the semantic backbone for all the information mining and extraction tasks of the KYOTO system: it includes language-specific words and expressions, encoded in different WordNets[14], one for each language. Currently KYOTO includes the WordNets of seven European and Asian languages: English, Dutch, Italian, Spanish, Basque, Simplified Mandarin Chinese and Japanese. Those lexical resources are represented in a custom data format: KYOTO-LMF, derived from the Lexical Markup Framework (LMF, ISO/TC37). Proper mappings between the corresponding language-specific information contained in the WordNets are provided so as to support multilingualism. Moreover, all the WordNets are also mapped to a shared language-neutral ontology, the KYOTO Central Ontology: it is mainly intended to define a frame of reference to semantically characterize the entities described in the WordNets so as to strengthen the possibility to unify the particular and cultural-specific lexical patterns of each language. The Central Ontology, currently under refinement and extension, is mainly intended to

---

[14] http://wordnet.princeton.edu/

describe processes, relations and states in order to semantically specify the entities described in the WordNets.

WordNets are divided into a *fixed generic part* and one or more *domain specific extensions*.

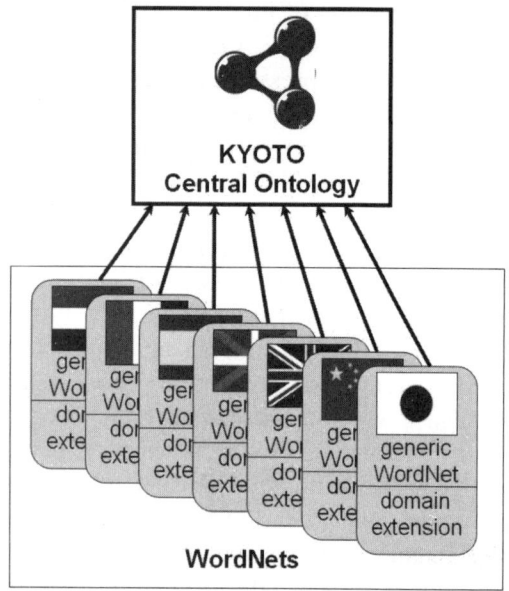

Figure 2. Structure of the KYOTO Multilingual Knowledge Base

The users of KYOTO are grouped Thanks to the **Wikyoto Knowledge Editor**, WordNets Domain extensions, that usually encode knowledge related to a specific domain of interest, can be created, maintained and enriched by KYOTO Concept Users, both domain experts and knowledge engineers; moreover proper mappings of WordNets to the KYOTO Central Ontology can be defined. These tasks are carried out also by exploiting the suggestions of new terms provided by the KYOTO terminological collection, contained in the *Term Base* as well as by accessing external resources like domain specific thesauri and DBpedia. All these issues will be better detailed in the following Sections of this Paragraph.

All KYOTO annotated documents collected in the *Syntactic & Semantic KAF Base* are processed by the *Fact Extractor*, called also Knowledge Yielding Robot or Kybot, storing and indexing the gathered knowledge in the *Fact Base*. Fact Users can define, by mean of the *Wikyoto Kybot Editor*, language-indipendent fact extraction patterns, referred to as Kybot Profiles.

End Users can perform semantic searches in the knowledge collected in the *Fact Base*, on the basis of natural language queries; they can retrieve facts of interest as well as relevant document excerpts.

2.2 The architecture of the Wikyoto Knowledge Editor

The Wikyoto Knowledge Editor has been realized as a *Web application* exploitable through a common Web browser, relying upon universally adopted Web technologies and standards like *(X)HTML*, *CSS* and *JavaScript*. To properly work the Wikyoto Knowledge Editor heavily interacts, through AJAX Web APIs, with a set of resources both internal and external to the system, as shown in Figure 3.

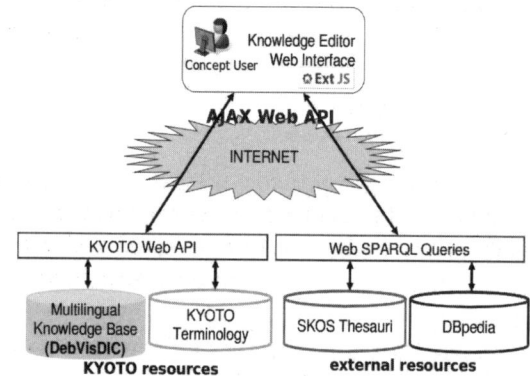

Figure 3. Architecture of the Wikyoto Knowledge Editor

In particular, the resources internal to KYOTO are:

- the **Multilingual Knowledge Base**: it is constituted by the Generic and Domain parts of the WordNets as well as by the KYOTO Central Ontology, all stored in and managed by the DebVisDic Server, a storage environment for semantic resources. *Domain WordNets represent the set of resources collaboratively edited by Concept Users through the Wikyoto Knoeldge Editor.*

- the **Term Base** or KYOTO terminology: it collects the terminology mined by the tybot from the set of KYOTO parsed documents (see Figure 1).

Both have been provided with a customized Web Application Programming Interface (Web API).

The Knowledge Editor exploits a set of external resources to provide useful suggestions to enrich or refine the Domain WordNets or simply to map the domain WordNets to. They include:

- **SKOS thesauri**: they are compliant to the model defined in the Simple Knowledge Organization System Specifications [15] of the World Wide Web Consortium (W3C). They are memo-

---

[15] http://www.w3.org/2004/02/skos/

rized in and accessed through the VIRTUOSO RDF triplestore[16]. In particular, they are queried through SPARQL[17], the W3C Query Language for RDF. Concept Users can browse these thesauri in order to search for useful suggestions to extend or refine Domain WordNets.

- **DBpedia**[18]: it is the Semantic Web version of Wikipedia. It can be queried through SPARQL and is mainly exploited in order to grasp and suggest textual definitions of synsets.

Also the set of external resources just listed is accessed by the Web Interface of the Knowledge Editor through SPARQL queries performed by REST Web API calls. In this context, the Ext.js[19] JavaScript library has been adopted as the main client-side programming facility and a set of custom JavaScript objects has been defined so as to realize a highly interactive and modular Web Interface in order to make easier knowledge editing tasks for Concept Users.

2.3 The Web Interface of the Wikyoto Knowledge Editor

By accessing the Web Interface of the Wikyoto Knowledge Editor, Concept Users can browse and edit the Domain WordNets of the seven languages of KYOTO. They can also navigate, integrate in and map to Domain WordNets, the set of knowledge structures belonging to the KYOTO Terminology as well as to external resources like SKOS thesauri and DBpedia. For the time being, the mappings of Domain WordNets to the KYOTO Central Ontology are still under definition and refinement: they will be integrated in the upcoming versions of the Knowledge Editor.

The interface, shown in Figure 4, is divided into two parts: on the left side there is the *Knowledge Resource Browser* while on the right side there is the *Domain WordNet Browser and Editor*.

The *Domain WordNet Browser and Editor* allows Concept Users to browse the Domain WordNet of a particular language and to extend it by encoding new lexical information relevant to the domain of interest. In the upper part of the *Domain WordNet Browser and Editor* box we can search for a synset typing a particular lemma and choosing among all the synsets referred through it (see the *Lemma Disambiguation Box* in Figure 4). Once a synset is chosen, the hierarchy of all its hyponyms is graphically shown in a tree view in the *Synset Hierarchy Box*. If we click over a node of this tree, corresponding to a specific Domain WordNet synset, all the information related to that particular synset are shown in the *Synset InfoBox*. In particular the definition of the synset is shown on the top of this box. The lower part of the *Synset InfoBox* is made of three tabs useful respectively to list the lemmas associated to a synset, deleting or adding new ones (*Lemma Tab*); to navigate or modify the synset-to synset relations, called internal relations, for instance hypernymy, holonymy, etc. (*Internal relations Tab*); to browse and navigate the set of external relations characterizing the specific synset (*External relations Tab*): external relations are for instance mappings of Domain WordNet synsets to Generic WordNet ones or to equivalent KYOTO terms, to concepts taken from SKOS thesauri and so on. On the top-right corner of the *Synset InfoBox* there is a set of *Synset Editing Buttons*; they are useful to modify the definition of the synset, to add a new synset from scratch or to delete the considered synset.

The *Knowledge Resource Browser*, visualized in the left side of the Interface provides a browsing interface to a set of read-only knowledge resources that can be exploited to enrich Domain WordNets or to simply define proper mapping relations from Domain WordNets synsets to entities belonging to these resources. In particular it is possible to browse and interact with three kinds of resources shown into three distinct tabs.

The **KYOTO Terms Tab** is useful to browse KYOTO term collections, representing a source of suggestions to create domain extensions of the WordNets: terms are extracted by the Tybot by mining the collection of KAF annotated documents. Terms are organized in specialization hierarchies; for instance, if we consider the English term 'bear' we can access the following hierarchy where 'bear' is the root:

bear
|— polar bear
|— grizzly bear
|— brown bears
|— sun bear
|— ancient bears

Each term can be characterized by:
- one or more possible ways to refer to it, called *term forms* (plurals, particular spelling or punctuation, etc.);
- one or more *document occurrences*;
- one or more *associated senses*, represented by synsets.

---

[16] http://virtuoso.openlinksw.com/dataspace/dav/wiki/Main/
[17] http://www.w3.org/TR/rdf-sparql-query/
[18] http://dbpedia.org/
[19] http://www.extjs.com/

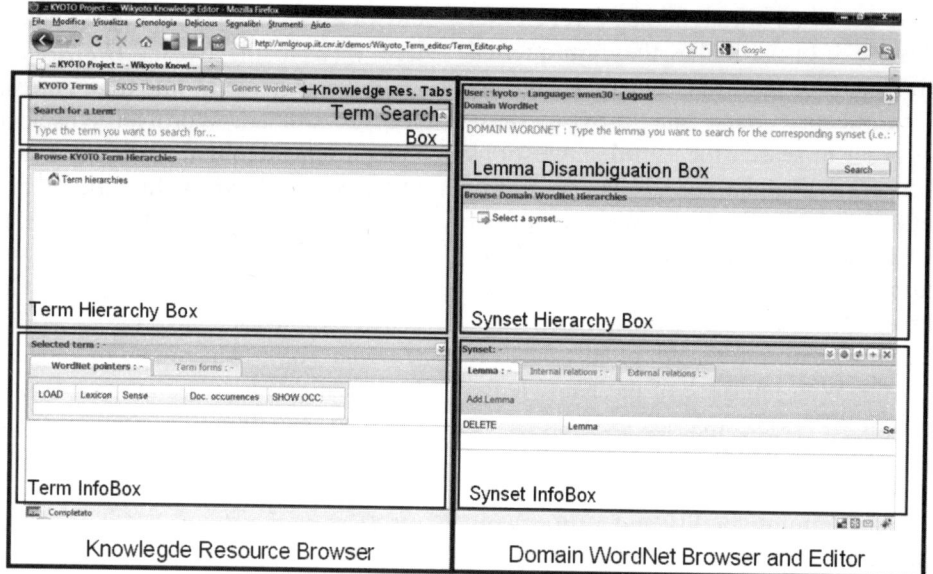

Figure 4. The Web Interface of the Wikyoto Knowledge Editor

As we can see from Figure 4, in the upper part of the KYOTO Terms Tab there is the *Term Search Box*, used to search for a term in the Term Base. Once a term is selected, it, along with the other terms of hierarchy it belongs to, if any, is visualized in a tree-view in the *Term Hierarchy Box*. Every time a term is selected from the opened hierarchies, all the information describing it is loaded in the *Term InfoBox* of the lower part of the interface: all the term forms as well as the WordNet synsets associated to a term are shown along with all its document occurrences.

Through the **SKOS Thesauri Tab**, Concept Users can search for a a particular concept in the set of SKOS thesauri available in KYOTO and browse, through a tree view, the related hierarchies of broader and narrower concepts, as well as the set of related concepts.

The **Generic WordNet Tab** allows Concept Users to browse the Generic WordNet of the language they have chosen once they authenticated to the Knowledge Editor, in a way similar to the *Domain WordNet Browser and Editor* just described, but without editing capabilities. By browsing the three knowledge resources just described, Concept Users can search for specific knowledge structures related to the information they want to express and formalize in the Domain WordNet. In particular, by simply dragging a node from tree of KYOTO terms, of concepts from SKOS thesauri or of Generic WordNet synset and dropping it over the intended Domain WordNet synset visualized in the *Synset Hierarchy Box*, Concept Users can easily:

- create a Domain WordNet synset from a KYOTO term or from a concept of a SKOS thesaurus (or create a hierarchy of Domain WordNet synsets from an entire terms/concepts hierarchy);
- define proper mapping relations between a Domain WordNet synset and one entity among a KYOTO term, a concept of a SKOS thesaurus or a Generic WordNet synset ('equivalence' and 'subsumption' relations are considered).

A practical example of usage of the Wikyoto Knowledge Editor is described in the following Section of this Paragraph. The current prototype of the Knowledge Editor is accessible at: *http://xmlgroup.iit.cnr.it/demos/Wikyoto_Term_Editor/*.

2.4 Enrich Domain WordNet: a practical Knowledge Editor usage example

In order to show a possible WordNet extension example by exploiting the Wikyoto Knowledge Editor, we consider the English language and the environmental domain, since the environment is the test-domain chosen for the KYOTO Project. Indeed two important environmental organizations are involved: the WWF[20] and the ECNC[21].

Let's suppose that we are environmentalist KYOTO Concept Users and we are interested in bears and, in particular, in bear species. After having accessed the Wikyoto Knowledge Editor, we can search for the term '*bear*' in the English Domain WordNet in order to see if the related synset has been added to and how it is

---

[20] http://www.wwf.org/
[21] http://www.ecnc.org/

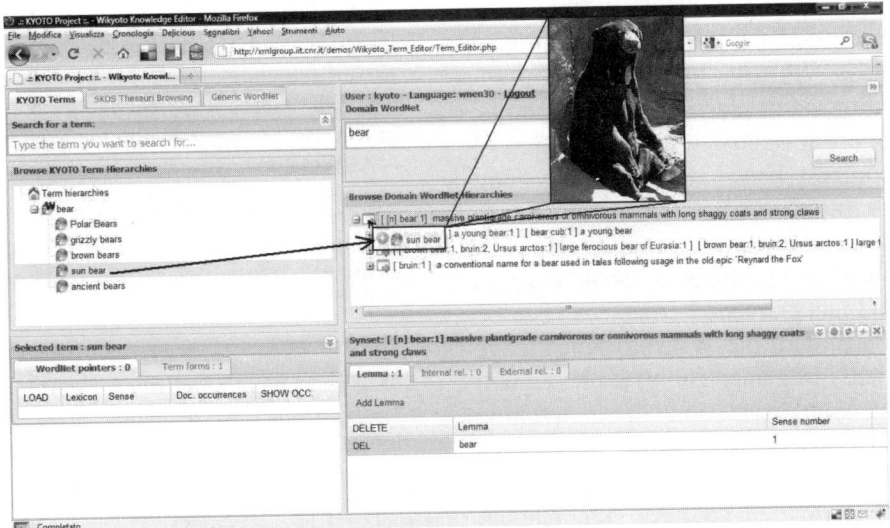

Figure 5. An example of Domain WordNet extension

semantically contextualized. Among all the different meanings, or better all the synsets associated to the word 'bear', we load the one referring to a '*massive plantigrade carnivorous or omnivorous mammals with long shaggy coats and strong claws*'. As shown in the right side of Figure 5, we visualize the list of all the hyponyms of the bear synset, that are all the more specific concepts present in Domain WordNet usually referring to particular specie of bears like the '*brown bear*' or to other particular meanings.

We would like to check if there are other relevant species of bear that have still not been added to the Domain WordNet. To get new suggestions about other possible kinds of bears we search for the term '*bear*' in the KYOTO Terms Tab and load the related term hierarchy (see the left side of Figure 5). As we can notice, there are five terms that are '*bear*' descendants, probably representing different kinds of bears: they have been extracted by the Tybot from the collection of KYOTO parsed documents. We can immediately see that only the root term '*bear*' has been associated to at least one synset because of the little '*W*' shown on the icon on the left of this term.

We can notice that the term '*sun bear*' is a kind of bear that is not present as a synset in WordNet, but it could be relevant to describe environment related contents and to mine environmental information, thus we decide **to extend the English domain WordNet creating a new '*sun bear*' synset**.

We can simply drag the term '*sun bear*' from the related term hierarchy and drop it over the more general synset (the '*bear*' one) in the hyponymy hierarchy visualized in the *Synset Hierarchy Box*. Thus we can choose if we want simply to define a mapping from the '*bear*' synset to the term '*sun bear*' or to create, starting from the term '*sun bear*', a new child (hyponym) synset of the '*bear*' one; this new synset will be mapped to the term '*sun bear*'.

In this case we choose the latter option and we edit the core information describing the new domain synset we want to create. We can refine its lemma, specify its part of speech and provide a descriptive gloss for '*sun bear*'.

In order to search for the gloss of the synset to be refined or to access other descriptive data, from the Knowledge Editor we can query relevant external resources like, for instance, DBpedia, the Semantic Web version of Wikipedia. We thus can easily retrieve all the meanings for the word '*sun bear*'. We can read the short description (abstract) of each of them, choose and import the correct one to easily provide the gloss for our '*sun bear*' synset. Once completed all the operations, we can confirm the creation of the new domain synset that is added to the English domain WordNet: it is immediately visualized among all the other hyponyms of the '*bear*' synset.

Switching from the *KYOTO Terms Tab* to the *SKOS Thesauri Tab* we can also search for SKOS concepts having '*sun bear*' as label so as to further enrich Domain WordNets with new lemmas or mapping relations.

3 Conclusion and future work

Starting from a general overview of the main features of collaborative knowledge editing environments also by providing some real example of such a kind of tools, in this paper we have described the Wikyoto Knowledge Editor, the wiki Web environment for the KYOTO Multilingual Knowledge Base. We have introduced its architecture, providing also a practical usage example. The Knowledge Editor constitutes a core part of KYOTO, a complex knowledge mining system: it allows users to experiment right away the outcome of the collaborative modifications of KYOTO knowledge resources as far as concern text mining and fact extraction processes.

The development of the Wikyoto Knowledge Editor is currently ongoing. The next phases will focus on the implementation of a tracking mechanism for users' modifications to the Knowledge Base as well as the related possibility to manage versioning of changes. We plan to realize more fine-grained concurrency control mechanisms as well as the possibility to define and to properly manage mappings of Domain WordNets to the KYOTO Central Ontology.

In conclusion, we can say that the Wikyoto Knowledge Editor represents an important example of Web-based wiki tool to collaboratively manage a complex set of interlinked knowledge resources, in the context of a complex knowledge processing system like KYOTO: the Knowledge Editor faces many of the fundamental problems that we have pointed out analyzing the tools to collaboratively manage knowledge resources.

References

Abraham S., Tudorache T., Noy N., and Musen M. A. 2008. *Customizable Workflow Support for Collaborative Ontology Development*. In proc. of the 4th International Workshop on Semantic Web Enabled Software Engineering in the 7th International Semantic Web Conference (ISWC08), Karlsruhe, Germany.

Auer S., Dietzold S., Lehmann J., and Riechert T. 2006. *Ontowiki - a tool forsocial, semantic collaboration*. In proc. of 5th International Semantic Web Conference (ISWC06), Athens, USA.

Bai F. and Zaoulfa E. J. 2007. *Interactive and collaborative ontology development*.

Funk A., Tablan V., Bontcheva K., Cunningham H., Davis B., and Handschuh S. 2007. *CLOnE: Controlled Language for Ontology Editing*. In proc. of The 6th International Semantic Web Conference, 2nd Asian Semantic Web Conference, ISWC 2007 + ASWC 2007, Busan, Korea.

Kalyanpur A., Parsia B., Sirin E., Cuenca Grau B., Hendler J. 2005. *Swoop: A 'Web' Ontology Editing Browser*. Journal of Web Semantics Vol 4(2), 2005.

Khun T. 2008. *AceWiki: Collaborative Ontology Management in Controlled Natural Language*. In proc. of the 3rd Semantic Wiki Workshop colocated with the 5th European Semantic Web Conference (ESWC07), Tenerife, Spain.

Kroetzsch M., Vrandecic D. and Voelkel D. 2006. Semantic MediaWiki. In proc. of the 5th International Semantic Web Conference (ISWC06), Athens.

Losky M., Heckmann D. and Kobayashi I. 2005. *UbisEditor 3.0: Collaborative Ontology Development on the Web*. In proc. of Web 3.0: Merging Semantic Web and Social Web, Workshop at Hypertext 2009, Torino, Italy.

Marchetti A., Minutoli S., Ronzano F. and Tesconi M. 2009. *Wikyoto Knoledge Editor: the collaborative environment to manage Kyoto Multilingual Knowledge Base*. In proc. Of the 6th International Conference on Knowledge Management (ICKM 09), Hong Kong, China.

Schaffert S. 2006. Ikewiki: A semanticwiki for collaborative knowledge management. In proc. of the 1st International Workshop on Semantic Technologies in Collaborative Applications (STICA 06), Manchester, U.K.

Tudorache T. and Noy N. 2007. *Collaborative Protégé*. In proc. of the Social and Collaborative Construction of Structured Knowledge Workshop at World Wide Web Conference (WWW2007), Banff, Canada.

Tudorache T., Venditti J. and Noy N. 2008. *Web-Protégé: A lightweight owl ontology editor for the web*. In proc. of the OWL experiences and directions, first International Workshop in the 7th International Semantic Web Conference (ISWC08), Karlsruhe, Germany.

Resources for Extending the PolNet – Polish WordNet with a Verbal Component

Zygmunt Vetulani
Adam Mickiewicz University
Faculty of Mathematics and Computer
Science, 61-614 Poznań,
ul. Umultowska 87
`vetulani@amu.edu.pl`

Tomasz Obrębski
Adam Mickiewicz University
Faculty of Mathematics and Computer
Science, 61-614 Poznań,
ul. Umultowska 87
`obrebski@amu.edu.pl`

Abstract

The paper presents the initial, basic step in extension of PolNet (Polish WordNet) with verbs. This step consists in formatting the source data necessary for final computer-assisted creation of verbal synsets including valency information. An algorithm for compiling verb descriptions contained in two human-oriented dictionaries into a computer tractable electronic resource is presented.

1 Credits

The research presented in this paper was partially covered by the on-going Polish Government research grant R00 028 02 "Text processing technologies for Polish in application for public security purposes" (2006-2009) within the framework of Polish Platform for Homeland Security.

2 PolNet – Polish WordNet Project

The long term PolNet project started in December 2006 and reached the maturity stage one year later with the core set of nominal synsets and the main hierarchical relation ISA corresponding to the hyponymy/hyperonymy between words (over 10600 synsets covering env. 18600 different word senses). This work was accomplished in 3 phases. The first phase consisted in elaboration of an algorithm for constructing synsets and relations, as well as in selection of the base concepts to be considered, cf. (Vetulani et al., 2009). The second and the third phases were those of creating synsets and relations. These phases appeared very efficient due to the tools provided by the Czech partners of the PolNet project: the VisDic system used during the second phase and the DEBVisDic used during the third one (Horák et al., 2007).

The algorithm, being highly language independent, allows for building a wordnet from scratch on the basis of a monolingual lexicon with well distinguished word senses and complete lexical and semantic coverage. It is clear that quality of the reference lexicon has direct impact on the quality of the output. In case of Polish, we were in good position due to the existence of high quality multimedia lexicons (cf. e.g. Dubisz, 2006).

In this paper we present the initial, basic step in extending PolNet with verbs. This step consists in proper (manual) formatting of source data necessary for final (software-assisted) synset creation. As initial lexical resource we have chosen two complementary human-user-oriented dictionaries (cf. Sections 3.1 and 3.2 below).

3 Initial Lexical Resources

The two source dictionaries selected as *initial resources* for PolNet are *Uniwersalny Słownik Języka Polskiego (Universal Dictionary of Polish (UDP))* (Dubisz, 2006) and *Słownik syntaktyczno-generatywny czasowników polskich (Generative Syntactic Lexicon of Polish Verbs (GSL))* (Polański, 2009).

3.1 UDP

UDP is a typical monolingual dictionary available for on-line consultation. For a given word it provides the description of its inflectional properties as well as the possible senses of this word. For each sense a definition and one or more examples are provided. The dictionary contains approximately 100,000 words. The structure of dictionary entries is as follows (Fig. 1.).

lemma register.
   a) «definition1; synonyms»:
      example(s).
   b) «definition2; synonyms»:
      example(s).
   c) ...
inflectional_information (aspect, inflection_class, endings, derivates...)

Fig. 1. UDP entry structure

For the Polish verb *mamić (to delude, to mislead)* we find the following entry in the UDP (Fig.2.).

mamić *książk.*
a) «rozbudzać w kimś próżne nadzieje, zwodzić kogoś fałszywymi pozorami; łudzić, tumanić, manić»:
   Mamili ludzi obietnicami.
b) «działać przyciągająco; wabić, nęcić, manić»:
   Oczy mami mnogość towarów.
   Ameryka mamiła dobrobytem.
ndk • VIa, mamię, ~isz, mam, ~ił, mamiony; *rzecz.* mamienie *n I.*

to delude *liter.*
a) «to cause sb to believe sth that is false, to waken futile hopes in sb, to decieve»:
   They deluded people with promises.
b) «to entice, to lure, to tempt»:
   The abundance of goods deludes people's eyes.
   America deluded people with welfare.
imperf • VIa, I delude, you delude, delude, deluded, *n* deluding *neut I.*

Fig. 2. The UDP entry for *mamić* (*to delude*) and its approximate English translation

Unfortunately, the UDP is addressed to a human reader. In particular, it is not well suited to feed the language processing software. Also, as it is the case for quasi totality of dictionaries for Polish, it does not contain complete description of verb arguments.

3.2 GSL

At present, the only publicly available dictionary with detailed information concerning the verb valency is the Generative Syntactic Lexicon of Polish Verbs (GSL).[1] This resource, the result of over 25-years project involving a very experienced team of lexicographers, is also addressed to a human user and automatic processing of its entries is practically impossible. The main objective of this lexicon was to characterize the syntactic and semantic connectivity of Polish verbs. For this purpose, over 10,000 verbs forming the core of Polish verbal system were selected on the basis of a corpus of 50,000 sentences representing literary, scientific and newspaper texts.

The GSL entries are organized as follows:
a) entry identifier (verb in infinitive) (lemma)
b) optional meaning description (informal), if necessary for meaning differentiation,
c) formula (or formulae), called by Polański a *sentential scheme*, showing the syntactic structure and syntactic requirements of the verb with respect to obligatory and facultative arguments (here called *syntactic frame*),
d) specification of semantic requirements (*semantic class*) of the verb with respect to the obligatory and facultative arguments (*syntactic_frame_slot*),
e) examples of use (natural language).

The typical entry structure may thus be presented as follows (Fig. 3.).

lemma
  1. *syntactic_frame1*
  2. *syntactic_frame2*
  3. ...
syntactic_frame_slot → semantic_class
syntactic_frame_slot → semantic_class
examples_of_use

Fig. 3. GSL entry structure

As a simple example, let us take the entry MAMIĆ. It has several meanings, one of them is represented by the lexicon entry given in Fig. 4.

Syntactic frame is an expression describing arguments of the verb on syntactic level. It may contain operators of alternative (disjunction) and optionality (round brackets in Fig.4.), so several sentence patterns may be encoded by one such expression. This notation is very compact but at the same time computationally very inconvenient. For the purpose of including syntactic information in the WordNet without making the processing too hard, we decided to expand these expressions into a list of simple patterns with no additional operators.

For each *syntactic frame* the *syntactic_frame_slots* are associated with feature-based/descriptor-based *semantic classes* characterizing the semantic requirement of the verb with respect its arguments.

---

[1] More detailed description may be found in (Vetulani, 2004)

MAMIĆ
I. 'działać łudząco, bałamucić, zawodzić, tumanić'
   1. NP^1_N __ NP^1_{ACC} + (NP_I)
   2. NP^2_N __ NP^2_{ACC}
NP^1_N → [+Hum]
NP^1_{ACC} → [+Hum]
NP_I → [-Abstr, -Anim][+Abstr]
NP^2_N → [-Abstr, -Anim][+Abstr]
NP^2_{ACC} → [oczy][wzrok][+Hum]
/examples of use omitted/

TO DELUDE
I. 'to deceive, to mislead (on purpose), to lead astray'
   1. NP^1_N __ NP^1_{ACC} + (NP_I)
   2. NP^2_N __ NP^2_{ACC}
NP^1_N → [+Hum]
NP^1_{ACC} → [+Hum]
NP_I → [-Abstr, -Anim][+Abstr]
NP^2_N → [-Abstr, -Anim][+Abstr]
NP^2_{ACC} → [eyes][glance][+Hum]
/examples of use omitted/

Fig. 4. The GSL entry for *mamić* (*to delude*) and its approximate English translation

For each *syntactic frame* the *syntactic_frame_slots* are associated with feature-based/descriptor-based *semantic classes* characterizing the semantic requirement of the verb with respect its arguments.

In order to express semantic requirements, Polański uses semantic classes of two types:

- feature-based classes e.g. [+Hum], [-Abstr,-Anim]
- descriptor-based classes e.g. [oczy], [wzrok]

Feature-based classes are defined using the following basic semantic features:

[+Abstr] – abstract
[-Abstr] – concrete
[+Anim] – animate
[-Anim] – non-animate
[+Hum] – human
[-Hum] – non-human
[Coll] – collective
[Elm] – element
[Fl] – plant
[Inf] – information
[Instit] – institution
[Instr] – instrument
[Liqu] – liquid
[Mach] – machine
[Mat] – material
[Pars] – part

These features and a number of their combinations are enough to express semantic requirements for the major part of verbs, nevertheless, the necessity to use more detailed specifications is quite common. This was the reason for Polański to complete the short list of semantic features with 1600 concepts expressed by common nouns (simple or compound). These nouns will be henceforth called *semantic descriptors* (for more details cf. (Vetulani 2003)). Semantic descriptors are used to define descriptor-based classes.

It is important to notice that the semantic descriptors proposed by Polański refer either to:

- "concrete entities perceivable by senses and located at any point in time in a three-dimentional space", e.g. *roślina (plant), zwierzę (animal),* and therefore belong to the category of 1stOrderEntities in the terminology of EuroWordNet (Vossen 2003), or to

- "unobservable propositions that exist independently of time and space", e.g. *myśl (thought), pamięć (memory),* and therefore belong to the category of 3rdOrderEntities in the terminology of EuroWordNet (Vossen 2003).

All the semantic descriptors used in GSL were included into PolNet. This means that PolNet is sufficiently reach to serve as reference ontology for semantic description of verbs contained in the GSL.

4 Algorithm 1: the algorithm for verb encoding

Access to the initial project resources described in Section 3 permits to benefit from a huge amount of manual work done by lexicographers and language engineers to gather the essential syntactic and semantic knowledge about words. The next step involving important investment of manual work was bringing the linguistic data to the format appropriate for further automatic processing and precise enough to obtain a high quality final product (extension of PolNet with verbs).

The Algorithm 1 compiles information from the two source dictionaries into a data structures formally simplified with respect to GSL entries (no optionality, no alternatives) but extended by addition of semantic roles and exhaustive/systematic usage examples. In order to ease further processing, the categorial symbols used in the output forms are simplified with respect to the human-addressed notation of the input data (GSL in particular): no indices, no stratified notation.

Algorithm 1

1. **Find** the entry for V in UDP dictionary
2. On the basis of the UDP **make** a list [V:1, V:2, ...] **of all** meanings for V

2a) **if** GSL includes meanings not present in UDP, **then** add them to the list
2b) **if** one sense in UDP corresponds to two or more senses in GSL (GSL presents a more fine-grained distinction),
then apply GSL sense classification
3. **For each** V:i
   3a) **copy** the definition from the dictionary in which the meaning was found (see 2.)
   3b) **indicate** the source reference (the dictionary identification+sense number)
   3c) **find** the matching meaning M in GSL
   3d) **for all** syntactic frames F listed for M in GSL
      i) **label** the frame with consecutive number
      i) **rewrite** the frame as a list of simple patterns (enumerate all combinations resulting from removing optionality and alternative operators from the original frame description)
      ii) **for each** pattern **provide** a usage example (preferably from a well documented corpus)
      iii) **indicate** the reference to GSL frame
      iv) **for all** elements E in the patterns obtained by expanding the frame F
         - **determine** the semantic role of E
         - **determine** its semantic class: **copy** the class from GSL (if given) **or add** according to your own linguistic competence
4. **For a** V' which differs from V only with respect to the grammatical aspect, **if** V and V' do not have separate entries in both UDP and GSL, **then associate** with V' the same description as for V

In the present extension of PolNet we use semantic roles proposed in the VerbNet project (Palmer, 2009), with however several minor modifications. These roles are: Action, Agent, Asset, Beneficient, Cause, Destination, Experiencer, Giver, Goal, Information, Instrument, Location, Manner, Material, Patient, Predicate, Product, Proposition, Recipient, Source, State, Theme, Time, Topic, Value.

What follows (Fig. 5.) is the format of the output data.

```
lemma:sense_index
ref dictionary_reference
frame 1
      fref frame_reference_number
      pat (syncat) _ syncat ... syncat
      pat (syncat) _ syncat ... syncat
      ...
      sem syncat → role semantic_class(es)
      sem syncat → role semantic_class(es)
      ...
frame 2
      ...
```

Fig. 5. Algorithm 1 output data format

The algorithm applied to the GSL entry from Fig. 3. (MAMIĆ) will result with the structure presented in Fig. 6. The new structure for MAMIĆ is:

```
MAMIĆ:1
ref Ua
def "książk. rozbudzać w kimś próżne
  nadzieje, zwodzić kogoś fałszywymi
  pozorami; łudzić, tumanić, manić"
frame1
   fref Pl1
   pat 1 n _ a "Oszukiwał i mamił nas, żeby
               osiągnąć swój cel"
   pat 2 n _ a i "Mamili ludzi
               obietnicami(UDP)"
   sem n -> Agent [+Hum]
   sem a -> Experiencer [+Hum]
   sem i -> Instrument [-Abstr,-Anim][+Abstr]
frame2
   fref Pl2
   pat 1 n _ a "Mamiły nas jego obietnice"
   sem n -> Cause [-Abstr,-Anim][+Abstr]
   sem a -> Experiencer [oczy][wzrok][+Hum]

TO DELUDE:1
ref Ua
def "liter. to cause sb to sb to believe sth
  that is false, to waken futile hopes in sb,
  to decieve"
frame1
   fref Pl1
   pat 1 n _ a "He cheated and deluded us in
               order to reach his aim."
   pat 2 n _ a i "They deluded people with
               promises.(UDP)"
   sem n -> Agent [+Hum]
   sem a -> Experiencer [+Hum]
   sem i -> Instrument [-Abstr,-Anim][+Abstr]
frame2
   fref Pl2
   pat 1 n _ a "His promises deluded us."
   sem n -> Cause [-Abstr,-Anim][+Abstr]
   sem a -> Experiencer [eyes][glance][+Hum]
```

Fig. 6. Algorithm 1 output for MAMIĆ (with English translation)

5 Application of the Algorithm 1

The Algorithm 1 have been applied by an experienced lexicographer[2].

At the present stage, the algorithm was applied to 350 verbs. In this number are in particular the most frequent verbs of general Polish (Przepiórkowski, 2004) as well as verbs selected among the most frequent in the field of public security (Walkowska, 2009) within the project "Text processing technologies for Polish in application for public security purposes" (cf. Section 1). PolNet is used in this project as ontology supporting reasoning in the POLINT-112-SMS system with emulated language competence (Ve-

---
[2] Beata Nadzieja, Faculty of Modern Languages, UAM.

tulani et al. 2008). From this list of 421 verbs we obtained ca. 1572 entries (verb senses) in the format shown in Fig. 5. The average number of frames per entry was 1,13 and the average number of patterns per frame was 3,12.

6 Algorithm 2: from set of Structures to a Verb Network

The Algorithm 1 described above resulted in an electronic, fully computer processable lexicon. The Algorithm 2 transforms the lexicon into a network:

- a verbal synset (initially containing a single item) is created for each verb meaning
- each verbal synset is connected with nominal synsets corresponding to semantic restrictions on arguments with relations labelled with roles
- all syntactic patterns and semantic constraints constitute a part of the synset description

It is a step towards full integration of verbs into PolNet. The initial requirement is that all descriptors are included in PolNet. This is already done. Next, correspondence between feature-based classes and nominal synsets has to be established.

A version of the algorithm for building verbal synsets is presented below.

Algorithm 2

For each verb sense V:i
1. **Create** a synset S with V:i as its unique lexical element
2. **Copy** the definition of V:i to S
3. **Copy** all patterns of V:i to S
4. **For each** semantic constraint of the form
   "sem $e \rightarrow$ role classes" **consider** classes;
   for each class **in** classes **create** an Intralingual Relation whose type is role and the target is set as follows (depending on class):
   - if class is a feature-based class then make the corresponding synset the target of the relation
   - if class is a descriptor based class then choose appropriate sense for the descriptor and make the synset containing this sense the target synset of the relation

An example of a verbal sysnset created in accordance with Algorithm 2 for the verb MAMIĆ (to delude) is shown in Fig 7.

```
word-senses: {mamić:1}
definition: "książk. rozbudzać w kimś próżne
   nadzieje, zwodzić kogoś fałszywymi
   pozorami; łudzić, tumanić, manić"
pat 1 n1 _ a1 "Oszukiwał i mamił
   łatwowiernych, żeby osiągnąć swój cel."
pat 2 n1 _ a1 i "Mamili ludzi
   obietnicami.(UDP)"
pat 3 n2 _ a2 "Mamiły nas jego obietnice."
sem n1 -> Agent1
sem a1 -> Experiencer1
sem i -> Instrument
sem n2 -> Cause
sem a2 -> Experiencer2
ilr type=Agent1 target=człowiek:1
ilr type=Experiencer target=człowiek:1
ilr type=Instrument target=przedmiot:1
ilr type=Instrument target=byt abstrakcyjny:1
ilr type=Cause target=przedmiot:1
ilr type=Cause target=byt abstrakcyjny:1
ilr type=Experiencer2 target=człowiek:1
ilr type=Experiencer2 target=oczy:1
ilr type=Experiencer2 target=wzrok:1

word-senses: {delude:1}
definition: "liter. to cause sb to sb to
   believe sth that is false, to waken futile
   hopes in sb, to decieve"
pat 1 n1 _ a1 "He cheated and deluded us in
   order to reach his aim."
pat 2 n1 _ a1 i "They deluded people with
   promises.(UDP)"
pat 3 n2 _ a2 "His promises deluded us."
sem n1 -> Agent1
sem a1 -> Experiencer1
sem i -> Instrument
sem n2 -> Cause
sem a2 -> Experiencer2
ilr type=Agent1 target=man:4
ilr type=Experiencer target=man:4
ilr type=Instrument target=physical object:1
ilr type=Instrument target=abstract entity:1
ilr type=Cause target=physical object:1
ilr type=Cause target=abstract entity:1
ilr type=Experiencer2 target=man:4
ilr type=Experiencer2 target=eyes:1
ilr type=Experiencer2 target=glance:1
```

Fig. 7. A sysnet for the verb MAMIĆ and its English translation

7 Conclusion

Creation of a real size application requires always an important effort. Language processing applications involving the modeling of human language competence are an example of practical problems where the final success of a computer system depends on mainly manual work invested in preparation of language data for being computer tractable. The work reported in this paper serves this objective. The data tools we have obtained so far will be used shortly in the POLINT-112-SMS application to be applied in the PolNet-based ontology, and first of all as main tool in the process of extending PolNet with the verbal component.

References

Stanisław Dubisz (ed.). 2006. *Uniwersalny słownik języka polskiego PWN*, (*Universal dictionary of Polish*, in Polish), 2nd edition, Warszawa: Wydawnictwo Naukowe PWN.

Aleš Horák, Karel Pala, Adam Rambousek, Zygmunt Vetulani, Paweł Konieczka, Jacek Marciniak, Tomasz Obrębski, Przemysław Rzepecki, Justyna Walkowska. 2007. DEB Platform tools for effective development of WordNets in application to PolNet. In: Z. Vetulani (ed.). *Proceedings of the 3rd Language and Technology Conference: Human Language Technologies as a Challenge for Computer Science and Linguistics, October 5-7, 2005, Poznań, Poland.* Wyd. Poznańskie, Poznań, pp. 514-518.

Martha Palmer. 2009. http://verbs.colorado.edu/~mpalmer/projects/verbnet.html (Access date: 04.10.2009)

Kazimierz Polański (ed.) 1992. *Słownik syntaktyczno-generatywny czasowników polskich (Generative Syntactic Lexicon of Polish Verbs*, in Polish), vol. I-IV, Ossolineum, Wrocław,1980-1990, vol. V, Kraków: Instytut Języka Polskiego PAN.

Adam Przcpiórkowski. 2004. *The IPI PAN Corpus*, IPIPAN, Warszawa.

Zygmunt Vetulani. 2003. Linguistically Motivated Ontological Systems. In: Callaos, N. et al. eds. *Proceedings of the 7th World Multiconference on Systemics, Cybernetics and Informatics.* Vol. XII (Information Systems, Technologies and Applications: II). Int. Inst. of Informatics and Systemics, pp. 395-400.

Zygmunt Vetulani. 2004. Towards a Linguistically Motivated Ontology of Motion: Situation Based Synsets of Motion Verbs. In: Barr, V., Markov, Z. (eds.) *Proceedings of the Seventheens International Florida Artificial Intelligence Research Society Conference (FLAIRS-04)*, AAAI Press (2004), Menlo Park, California, pp. 813-817.

Zygmunt Vetulani, Jacek Marciniak, Paweł Konieczka, Justyna Walkowska. 2008. An SMS-based System Architecture (Logical Model) to Support Management of Information Exchange in Emergency Stuations. POLINT-112-SMS. In IFIP International Federation for Information Processing, Volume 288; *Intelligent Information Processing IV*; Zhongshi Shi, E Mecier-Laurent, D. Lake (eds.); Boston: Springer, pp.240-253.

Zygmunt Vetulani, Justyna Walkowska, Tomasz Obrębski, Jacek Marciniak, Paweł Konieczka, Przemysław Rzepecki. 2009. An Algorithm for Building Lexical Semantic Network and Its Application to PolNet – Polish WordNet Project. In: Z. Vetulani and H. Uszkoreit (Eds.): *Human Language Technology. Challenges of the Information Society*, LNAI 5603, Springer-Verlag Berlin-Heidelberg, pp. 369-381.

Justyna Walkowska. 2009. Gathering and Analysing of a Corpus of Polish SMS Dialogues, In: M.A. Kłopotek, et al. (Eds.) *Recent advances in Intelligent Information Systems*, Academic Publishing House EXIT, Warsaw, pp. 145-157.

Rejuvenating the Italian WordNet: Upgrading, Standardising, Extending

Antonio Toral Stefania Bracale Monica Monachini Claudia Soria

Istituto di Linguistica Computazionale
Consiglio Nazionale delle Ricerche
Pisa, Italy

`{antonio.toral, stefania.bracale, monica.monachini, claudia.soria}@ilc.cnr.it`

Abstract

This paper reports on recent activities carried out within the KYOTO project aimed at enhancing the Italian WordNet Language Resource. On the one hand we study the formalisation of this lexicon according to the LMF ISO standard and explore its application into a real-world scenario by means of representing it in the WN-LMF dialect. On the other hand, we report on a semiautomatic procedure to upgrade the connections of the lexicon to WordNet, which obtains over 98% accuracy.

1 Introduction

The goal of the KYOTO project[1] (Vossen et al., 2008) is the construction of a system for facilitating the exchange of information across cultures, domains and languages. This system is expected to allow people in communities to define the meaning of their words and terms in a shared Wiki platform so that it becomes anchored across languages and cultures but also so that a computer can use this knowledge to detect knowledge and facts in text. Whereas the current Wikipedia uses free text to share knowledge, KYOTO will represent this knowledge so that a computer can understand it. The system is being developed for the domain of environment. For example, the notion of environmental footprint will become defined in the same way in all these languages but also in such a way that the computer knows what information is necessary to calculate a footprint. With these definitions it will be possible to find information on footprints in documents, websites and reports so that users can directly ask the computer for actual information in their environment.

This endeavour presupposes the sharing of lexical databases and knowledge bases, both general and domain-related, under the form of lexical repositories and ontologies. The lexical resources that will be integrated in KYOTO are wordnets for the English, Dutch, Italian, Basque, Spanish, Chinese and Japanese languages. Special-domain wordnets and ontology will be developed: they are to be seen as a plugin extension of the generic wordnet and ontology. These extensions contribute to the development of the Global Wordnet Grid[2], which is an initiative to anchor many wordnets for different languages and cultures to a shared ontology backbone.

As in KYOTO the integration of resources is viewed as a need, the use of formats that facilitates interoperability is essential. Interoperability allows an easier integration among general domain lexicons sharing the same structure (i.e other wordnets) and domain lexicons, but, more importantly, eases the integration of resources with different theoretical and implementation approaches, such as the ones being used within the project: Web 2.0 sources (DbPedia), species taxonomies (Species2000) and ontologies (DOLCE, SUMO, SIMPLE). There is no means to speak about interoperability if not paired with standards: they are bound to be the communicative channel by means of which diverse data, resources, formats, and models can interact on a common ground, in a controlled way.

This paper reports on recent activities aimed at enhancing the Italian WordNet (IWN) (Alonge et al., 1999), according to the needs posed by the KYOTO project. On the one hand we study the formalisation of this lexicon according to a standard and explore its application into a real-world scenario by means of tailoring the standard to the practical requirements. The adoption of a standard will allow IWN to communicate with the other resources available in the KYOTO architecture. On the other, we upgrade the connections of IWN to the Inter-lingual Index (ILI) (Vossen, 1998) to the

---

[1] http://www.kyoto-project.eu

[2] http://www.globalwordnet.org

latest version of the English WordNet (Fellbaum, 1998). This will allow a better interaction of IWN with the rest of wordnets of the project because it will be able to get corresponding senses by means of two different versions of the ILI.

The rest of the paper is organised as follows. Next section discusses the standardisation process followed to convert IWN to the LMF standard and to its dialect WN-LMF. After that, we report on the upgrade of IWN's connections to the ILI from WN 1.5 to the last version available, 3.0. Finally, we draw some general conclusions.

2 Standardisation

2.1 LMF

The Lexical Markup Framework (LMF) (Francopoulo et al., 2008) (ISO 24613, 2008) is an ISO standard for the representation of LRs. The goals of LMF are to provide a common model for the creation and use of LRs, to manage the exchange of data between and among them, and to enable the merging of a large number of individual resources to form extensive global electronic resources.

LMF has been chosen as representation format because it gathers experiences and harmonization efforts started by the interested community in the '90s. This format for lexical resource representation has now reached a high level of sophistication, theoretical consensus, and official international standard status, being ratified as an ISO standard (ISO 24613, 2008). LMF was specifically designed to accommodate as many models of lexical representations as possible. Purposefully, it is designed as a meta-model, i.e. a high-level specification for lexical resources defining the structural constraints of a lexicon. It is organised around two main components:

- The core package, i.e. a structural skeleton to represent the basic hierarchy of information in a lexicon, under the form of core classes of objects and relations.

- A set of modular extensions to the core package, i.e. additional classes and relations required for the description of specific types of lexical resources. Available extensions include morphology, syntax, semantics, multilingual notations, paradigm classes, multiword expression patterns and constraint expressions. Mutual dependencies among the various extensions hold.

Before being issued as an official ISO standard, LMF has passed a range of officially needed stages and has been extensively discussed and commented in a wide community comprising both academia and industry. LMF is thus mature enough to be taken as "the" choice when coming to selecting a standardised format for the representation and encoding of computational lexicons. Time is ripe now to start assessing LMF, providing the community with real examples of use.

A procedural routine has been developed in order to convert from the IWN specific XML format to LMF. The main difference found between both formats is that while in the specific one the information regarding the sense, synset and ILI relations are hold from a common ancestor ("WORD_MEANING"), in LMF they belong to different elements.

Let us present a sample from the specific IWN format:

```
<WORD_MEANING ID="AG#44455" PART_OF_SPEECH="AG">
 <GLOSS>che si può abbassare</GLOSS>
 <VARIANTS>
  <LITERAL LEMMA="abbassabile" SENSE="1"/>
 </VARIANTS>
 <INTERNAL_LINKS>
  <RELATION TYPE="liable_to" ID="75" INV_ID="75">
   <TARGET_WM ID="34802" PART_OF_SPEECH="V"/>
  </RELATION>
 </INTERNAL_LINKS>
 <EQ_LINKS>
  <RELATION TYPE="eq_synonym" ID="1" INV_ID="1">
   <TARGET_WM ID="r#345085"/>
  </RELATION>
 </EQ_LINKS>
</WORD_MEANING>
```

It follows the corresponding LMF code, separated in three blocks (lemma and sense, synset and ILI):

```
<LexicalEntry id="LE_abbassabile_a">
 <Lemma>
  <feat att="partOfSpeech" val="a"/>
  <feat att="writtenForm" val=
   "abbassabile"/>
 </Lemma>
 <Sense id="abbassabile_1"
  synset="ita-15-44455-a"/>
</LexicalEntry>

<Synset id="ita-15-44455-a">
 <Definition>
  <feat att="gloss" val="che si può
   abbassare"/>
 </Definition>
 <SynsetRelation targets="ita-15-34802-v">
  <feat att="relType" val="liable_to"/>
 </SynsetRelation>
</Synset>

<SenseAxis id="sa_0" synsets=
 "ita-15-44455-a eng-15-345085-r">
 <feat att="relType" val="eq_synonym"/>
</SenseAxis>
```

2.2 WN-LMF

Wordnet-LMF (WN-LMF) is an LMF dialect tailored to encoding of lexical resources adhering to the WordNet model of lexical knowledge representation. No real attempt has been made so far in order to fully apply LMF to wordnet-like lexicons: WN-LMF is an example of the practical use of LMF in a real-world application (Soria et al., 2009). The KYOTO project represents an ideal test case for this format: going beyond the level of toy examples it allows to make a crash test, as the various resources need to be fully integrated. This will put us in the position to both have a preview on any problems we might encounter and make LMF standard easy to adopt. More importantly, we will be able to convince people that there is a good reason to convert their legacy formats, by showing its usefulness and efficiency.

WN-LMF fully complies with the standard LMF as for its general framework. It builds on the representational devices made available by LMF and tailors them to the specific content requirements of the WordNet model of lexical knowledge representation. LMF library provides the hierarchy of lexical objects with structural relations among them. The Data Category library provides the elementary descriptors to be used in combination with the structural elements, necessary to represent lexical information (Francopoulo et al., 2006). Figure 1 shows a general diagram of WN-LMF.

2.2.1 WN-LMF overall design

The main conceptual components of WordNet-like lexicons that need to be represented in LMF are the following:

- Synsets, variants and synset relations, including information about synset identifiers and sense-keys;
- Domain attribution, linking to ontologies, administrative information;
- Interlingual information, i.e. mapping of synsets in a given language to Interlingual Index (ILI).

The LMF semantic package naturally lends itself to the representation of wordnet-like resources, since it already contains lexical objects devised for the representation of synsets, their associated gloss and examples, variants, and synset relations.

Expression of WordNet-related types of information (such as synset relations, external sources linked to wordnets) falls into the realm of LMF Data Categories, which are by definition either selectable from the pre-defined standard registry or custom-defined. The WN-LMF format, accordingly, has defined a Data Category Selection, necessary to fully represent the various wordnets to be integrated in KYOTO. Examples of custom Data Categories are values for describing synset relations, inter-lingual relations, for identifying external resources and their associated nodes, etc. For the sake of better parsing efficiency, in WN-LMF, Data Categories are represented by means of XML attributes and values instead of nested lexical objects. As an example consider the following sample of LMF code:

```
<Lemma>
  <feat att="partOfSpeech" val="n"/>
  <feat att="writtenForm" val="abbadia"/>
</Lemma>
```

and its equivalent in WN-LMF:

```
<Lemma partOfSpeech="n"
  writtenForm="abbadia"/>
```

By explicitly naming the attributes, we also make a stronger claim about the features and properties of the structure of a wordnet. This will enforce better compatibility and interoperability across the many wordnets for different languages that are available. In this respect, the WN-LMF DTD implementation has to be seen as a dialectal variant of the LMF DTD. Motivation behind this choice is to reach efficiency, while keeping adherence to standards.

2.2.2 The WN-LMF core component

The WN-LMF core package component provides the structural skeleton to represent the basic hierarchies of the lexicon.

KYOTO WordNets are represented as a grid of lexicons: *LexicalResource* is the container for all of them. A specific set of lexical objects is devoted to record general information about the lexical resource.

The lexical resource, besides the monolingual lexicons, contains the interlingual correspondences which are grouped in a section *SenseAxes* which is separated from the lexicons proper and contains inter-lexicon correspondences only.

Lexicon contains a monolingual resource, instantiated as a set of *LexicalEntry* instances. This element is a container for representing a lexeme in a lexicon. A *LexicalEntry* element contains the

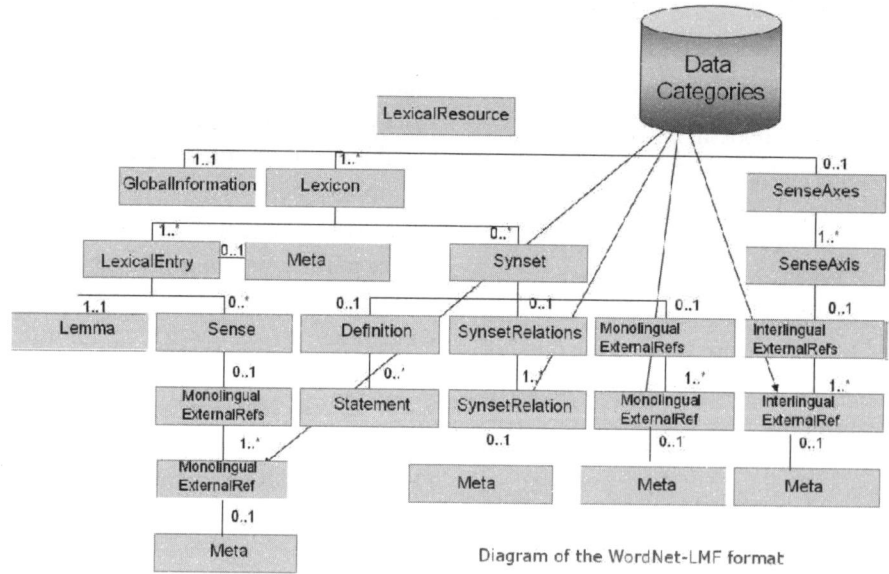

Figure 1: WNLMF diagram

basic building blocks: lemma and senses. *Lemma* represents a word form chosen by convention to designate the lexical entry, whereas *Sense* represents one meaning of a lexical entry. For wordnet representation, this triplet is used to represent the variant(s), or literal(s) of a synset.

MonolingualExternalRef represents linking between a *Sense* or *Synset* and another resource, be it a knowledge organisation system, a database, or another lexical resource. Mapping among different versions of the same resource, reference to external information, such as mapping onto entries of another lexical database and or referencing additional sources can be dealt with by the *MonolingualExternalRef* object.

When linked to a *Sense* element, it can be used to express mapping between the sense and its correspondent in another lexical resource (such as in the Dutch Cornetto database). In the particular case of the representation of English Princeton WordNet, *MonolingualExternalRef* serves as a representational device to express the Sense Key. When linked to the *Synset* element, then *MonolingualExternalRef* allows to encode reference to the domain and/or one or more links to an ontological system.

2.2.3 The WN-LMF semantic component

The Semantic component is in charge of describing information about a wordnet synset by means of the *Synset* element. A *Synset* clusters senses of different *LexicalEntry* instances within the same part of speech. The element *Definition* allows to represent the gloss associated with each synset. Relations between synsets are codified by means of *SynsetRelation* elements (represented by means of XML attributes), one per relation.

A set of harmonized KYOTO Data Categories has been defined. This is to be used in conjunction with the *SynsetRelation* elements for representing the various relations holding between synset. This Data Category library, for the sake of coherence, is being maintained as a centralized repository. This option has been followed in order to enforce better compatibility and interoperability across the many monolingual wordnets.

MonolingualExternalRef, which is used to represent linking between the lexical resource and another resource, when linked to the *Synset* element, allows to encode reference to the domain and/or one or more links to an ontological system.

2.2.4 The WN-LMF multilingual component

The Multilingual notation component is used in KYOTO for expressing interlingual correspondences. This component is designed as an independent package in order not to overload the representation of monolingual lexicons. The model is based on the notion of "Axes" that link synsets pertaining to different languages. For the purposes of creating a grid of WordNets linked via Interlingual Index, the *SenseAxis* device is specifically suited to implement approaches based on an interlingual pivot. Any *SenseAxis* element groups together monolingual synsets that correspond one to another by means of a particular type of relation.

The *SenseAxis* element is a means for grouping together synsets belonging to different monolingual wordnets that correspond one to another and share the same equivalence relation (e.g. a synonymy or near synonymy relation) to a pivot synset, which by convention is an English one. This is a compact way of encoding correspondences among wordnets, avoiding to have several LanguageX-English single correspondences.

InterlingualExternalRef is used in WN-LMF to express a linking between a *SenseAxis* instance and an external system such as an ontology, and represents the means to anchor a multilingual group of synsets to an ontological node. Its intended use, thus, is to provide a representational device to link a group of synsets from different wordnets to the same ontological concept.

3 Upgrading

IWN was originally linked to version 1.5 of the ILI. In this section we report on a semiautomatic procedure carried out in order to update these links to the last version of WN at the time being, 3.0.

We take advantage of the automatic mapping sets between pairs of WN versions[3] (Daudé et al., 2000). These mapping sets connect every combination of WN version pairs in both directions. E.g. for the version pair 1.5. and 3.0. there are two mapping sets, one from 1.5. to 3.0. and another one from 3.0. to 1.5. For each synset in the source version, the mapping sets provide the equivalent synset(s) in the target version together with a confidence score. Each mapping follows the following format:

```
synset_source [synset_target weight]+
```

An example taken from the WN 1.5 to 3.0 mappings is:

```
2728-n 4258-n 0.222 4475-n 0.778
```

which means that the synset "2728-n" of WN 1.5 is mapped to two synsets of WN 3.0, "4258-n" with confidence 22.2% and to "4475-n" with confidence 77.8%.

From the two directional mapping sets for our version pair (1.5. and 3.0.) we have created a bidirectional mapping set which follows the following format:

[3] http://www.lsi.upc.es/~nlp/tools/mapping.html

```
synset15 synset30 weight15->30 weight30->15
```

If a mapping is not present in one of the two directions we mark its weight as -1. These are the mappings for the source synset "2728-n":

```
2728-n      4258-n       0.222    1
2728-n      4475-n       0.778    1
2728-n      5217061-n    -1       1
```

An advantage of using this bidirectional mapping over using a directional one can be seen in this example. If the directional mapping would be used to upgrade the ILI connections, for the synset "2728-n" there are two target candidates, whilst taking into consideration the bidirectional mapping, a third additional candidate is found.

When using these mappings to upgrade the links to ILI three cases can arise:

- There is a one to one equivalence. We select a subset randomly and check it manually to calculate the accuracy of the automatic mappings.

- There is no equivalence. We analyse why no equivalence is found and create a connection manually.

- There is a one to n equivalence (where n>1). These mappings need to be manually disambiguated.

IWN contains 50,308 synsets. From these, 106 are not connected to ILI while the rest are mapped to a total of 57,164 ILI synsets. From these, table 1 shows the number of synsets that fall into each of the aforementioned cases when using different mappings schemes. These are a directional (Dir) scheme and two bidirectional, one following an union (Bidu) and the other following an intersection pattern (Bidi).

ILI synsets	Dir	Bidu	Bidi
Total		57,164	
No equivalence	1,897	1,897	2,021
1-to-1 equivalence	54,817	42,614	53,133
1-to-1 equiv. (dir)	-	-	1,800
1-to-n equivalence	450	12,653	210

Table 1: Distribution of synsets with different mapping schemes

The next subsections report in more detail for the different cases. We have chosen the *Bidi* mapping scheme because it is the one that requires us to disambiguate less 1-to-n equivalences.

3.1 One-to-one equivalences

We have randomly selected a subset of 100 mappings of this type for each Part-of-Speech, i.e. adjectives (a), adverbs (r), nouns (n) and verbs (v). These mappings have been manually checked in order to evaluate the accuracy of the automatic mapping procedure. Results are shown in tables 2 and 3. The "total" scores in both tables normalise the score obtained for each Part-of-Speech by the number of occurrences for each PoS, see equation 3.1.

$$\frac{\sum_{pos \in (a,r,n,v)} num_{pos} * acc_{pos}}{num_a + num_r + num_n + num_v} \quad (1)$$

Part-of-Speech	Accuracy
Adjective	96%
Adverb	98%
Noun	99%
Verb	99%
Total	98.77%

Table 2: Results of 1-to-1 bidirectinal mappings

Part-of-Speech	Accuracy
Adjective	97%
Adverb	100%
Noun	99%
Verb	99%
Total	98.68%

Table 3: Results of 1-to-1 directinal mappings

The accuracy obtained for the 1-to-1 mappings is therefore very high, above 98% in average for both types of mappings. The performance for adjectives is slightly lower than for the others Part-of-Speech.

Errors occur seldom and regard very fine grained distinctions. Consider the example of WN 1.5 synset "35605-a" (quiet) which has not gloss but is connected through a "similar to" relation to synset "35448-a" (dormant, inactive) with gloss "of e.g. volcanos; temporarily inactive". The synset is mapped to WN 3.0 synset "43615-a" (quiet) with gloss "of the sun characterized by a low level of surface phenomena like sunspots", instead, the correct mapping would be "40909-a" (quiescent) with gloss "being quiet or still or inactive".

3.2 Ambiguous and empty equivalences

Both the ambiguous and empty equivalences have been manually resolved. Regarding the disambiguation task, we have applied the following disambiguation pattern: for each ambiguous concept we have selected the most appropriate one. This choice has been carried out in different steps. If the meaning of the term was unknown then we have looked it up in the IWN web interface[4]. Using the MCR interface[5], we have looked for the WN 1.5 and the WN 3.0 corresponding synsets. The most similar WN 3.0 synset has been selected by consulting different types of information related to each synset such as, its variants, its hyperonymy chain, etc.

The empty equivalences have been resolved with a different methodology: in the first step, for each empty entry, we have found its English correspondent by using various English dictionaries. In a second step, we have searched the WN 3.0 synsets that contain as a variant the translation obtained. If this entry has been found in WN 3.0 and it corresponded to the same Italian semantic concept expressed in IWN, then the code of this synset has been linked. If the meaning corresponded exactly, the type of relation chosen was EQ_SYNONYM, while if the meaning was similar but presented slight differences, then the type of relation chosen was EQ_NEAR_SYNONYM. Otherwise, if no unique correspondence has been found, then no connection has been created. We note that the most complex disambiguation task concerns some Part-of-Speech entries, such as adjectives and adverbs. There are adjectives in IWN that only exist as nouns in English (e.g. accusato/accused), and some adjectives that in English are only found as verbs (past participle) e.g. illustrato/illustrated. There are also cases of adverbs for which no correspondence was found in English.

4 Conclusions

This paper has reported on two recent activities that regard the extension, standardisation and upgrade of IWN.

With respect to the standardisation, we have studied and developed the conversion of this lexicon into the LMF ISO format. Furthermore, we

---
[4] http://wordnet.ilc.cnr.it/
[5] http://www.lsi.upc.es/~nlp/meaning/demo/demo.html

have discussed the implications of using the resulting resource in a real-world NLP scenario. We have devised the creation of a LMF dialect, WN-LMF, in order to increase efficiency while keeping adherence to the standard.

On the other hand, we have carried out an upgrade of the ILI links of IWN. We have followed a semiautomatic approach that takes advantage of existing automatic mappings between pairs of WN versions and checks manually only those mappings which are ambiguous or whose confidence scores are low. A contribution of this paper is an empirical evaluation of the automatic mappings, which obtain accuracy values higher than 98%.

An indirect yet useful contribution is the availability of manually disambiguated mappings between WN1.5 and WN3.0[6]. These could be exploited by WNs for other languages that are linked to WN1.5 (e.g. those developed in the framework of EuroWordNet) in order to upgrade their connections.

Acknowledgements

This work has been partially funded by the EU Commission under the project KYOTO (ICT-2007-211423). We thank German Rigau for his valuable advice regarding the automatic WordNet mappings.

References

Antonietta Alonge, Francesca Bertagna, Nicoletta Calzolari, and Adriana Roventini. 1999. The Italian Wordnet, EuroWordNet Deliverable D032D033 part B5. Technical report.

Jordi Daudé, Lluís Padró, and German Rigau. 2000. Mapping wordnets using structural information. In *38th Annual Meeting of the Association for Computational Linguistics (ACL'2000).*, Hong Kong.

Christiane Fellbaum. 1998. *WordNet: An Electronic Lexical Database (Language, Speech, and Communication)*. The MIT Press, May.

Gil Francopoulo, Monica Monachini, Thierry Declerck, and Laurent Romary. 2006. The relevance of standards for research infrastructure. In *LREC 2006, Workshop Towards Research Infrastructures for Language Resources*. European Language Resources Association (ELRA).

Gil Francopoulo, Nuria Bel, Monte George, Nicoletta Calzolari, Monica Monachini, Mandy Pet, and Claudia Soria. 2008. (forthcoming) Multilingual resources for NLP in the Lexical Markup Framework (LMF). *Language Resources and Evaluation Journal*.

ISO 24613. 2008. Languages Resources Management – Lexical Markup Framework (LMF), rev.15 ISOTC37SC4 FDIS. [Online; accessed 25-March-2008].

Claudia Soria, Monica Monachini, and Piek Vossen. 2009. Wordnet-lmf: fleshing out a standardized format for wordnet interoperability. In *IWIC '09: Proceeding of the 2009 international workshop on Intercultural collaboration*, pages 139–146, New York, NY, USA. ACM.

Piek Vossen, Eneko Agirre, Nicoletta Calzolari, Christiane Fellbaum, Shu kai Hsieh, Chu-Ren Huang, Hitoshi Isahara, Kyoko Kanzaki, Andrea Marchetti, Monica Monachini, Federico Neri, Remo Raffaelli, German Rigau, Maurizio Tesconi, and Joop VanGent. 2008. Kyoto: a system for mining, structuring and distributing knowledge across languages and cultures. In Nicoletta Calzolari, Khalid Choukri, Bente Maegaard, Joseph Mariani, Jan Odjik, Stelios Piperidis, and Daniel Tapias, editors, *Proceedings of the Sixth International Language Resources and Evaluation (LREC'08)*, Marrakech, Morocco, may. European Language Resources Association (ELRA). http://www.lrec-conf.org/proceedings/lrec2008/.

Piek Vossen. 1998. Eurowordnet a multilingual database with lexical semantic networks.

---

[6]Freely available at http://www.dlsi.ua.es/~atoral/#Resources

The Need for Amharic WordNet

Tessema Mindaye
Computer Science Department
Addis Ababa University
tessemin@cs.aau.edu.et

Meron Sahlemariam
IS&T Division
UN ECA
nahmmer@gmail.com

Teshome Kassie
Ministry Finance and Economic
Development, Ethiopia
tkheran@yahoo.com

Abstract

WordNet has been recognized as a valuable resource in the human language technology and knowledge processing communities. Due to the success of Princeton WordNet, many language specific WordNets have been developed and are still in development. In this paper the need for Amharic WordNet is discussed and a way forward is also suggested.

1 Introduction

WordNet is a lexical database for the English language. It groups English words into sets of synonyms called *synsets*, provides short, general definitions, and records the various semantic relations between these synsets. WordNet has become one of the most valuable resources for a wide range of Natural Language Processing (NLP) research and applications, such as automatic word-sense disambiguation, information retrieval and document summarization and clustering. Due to the success of Princeton WordNet (PWN), many language specific WordNets have been developed and are still in development. Despite its application, there is no Amharic WordNet so far.

This paper is organized as follows; section 2 discusses the Amharic language, the script it uses and typical features of the language. Section 3 discusses different Amharic tools and the applications of Amharic WordNet for those tools. Section 4 discuses future work and gives conclusions.

2 The Amharic Language

Ethiopia is a linguistically diverse country where more than 80 languages are used in day-to-day communication. Although many languages are spoken in Ethiopia, Amharic is dominant in that it is spoken as a mother tongue by a substantial segment of the population and it is the most commonly learned second language throughout the country (Marvin et al., 1976). The language is the official language of the federal government of the country. According to the 1998 census of the country (ECSA, 1998), Amharic is the first language of more than 17 million people and second language for more than 5 million people.

2.1 The Amharic Writing System

According to Marvin et al. (1976), three writing systems are in use in Ethiopia, the Amharic syllabary, the Roman alphabet, and Arabic script. The Amharic syllabry, which is derived from the writing system of ancient South Arabian inscriptions, is used for Ge'ez, Amharic, and Tigrigna, with slight modification. The Amharic syllabry is uniquely Ethiopian writing system. The writing system has a similarity with some Semitic languages like Arabic in having vowel marks added to basically consonant letters. The present writing system of Amharic is taken from Ge'ez. Ge'ez in turn took its script from the ancient Arabian language mainly attested in inscriptions in the Sabean dialect (Marvin et al., 1976). The original Sabaean alphabet is said to have had 29 symbols. When Ge'ez became the spoken and written language in common use in northern Ethiopia, it took only 24 of the 29 Sabaean symbols, modify most of them and add two new symbols to represent sounds of Greek and Latin loanwords not found in Ge'ez. The style of the writing was also modified to left to right. By the time Ge'ez ceased to be a living spoken and written language and replaced by Amharic and other languages, further changes took place. Amharic did not discriminate in adopting the Ge'ez fidel; it took all of the symbols (Yemam, 1987) and added some new ones that represent sounds not found in Ge'ez. These added alphabetic characters are ቸ, ጬ, ጀ, ኘ, ቭ, ሽ, ኽ, and ዥ.

Currently, the language's writing system contains 34 base characters each of which occurs in a basic form and six other forms known as orders. The seven orders represent syllable combinations consisting of a consonant following vowel. This is why the Amharic writing system is often called syllabic rather than alphabetic, even if there is some opposition (Yemam, 1987). The 34 basic characters and their orders give 238 distinct symbols. In addition, there are forty others that contain a special feature usually representing labialization e.g. ጯ, ቷ. In Amharic there is no Capital-Lower case distinction. There are also punctuation marks and numeration system.

2.2 Typical Characteristics of Amharic Language

There is a process of change in any language in many of its aspects: change of meaning, change of syntax, phonetic change, etc (Haile, 1967). The case for Amharic is not different; especially the script underwent changes when it was borrowed from Ge'ez. Through the adaptation process and other factors the Amharic writing system got some problems.

The first problem is the presence of "unnecessary" alphabets (fidels) in the language's writing system. These fidels (alphabets) have the same pronunciation but different symbols. These different fidels can be used interchangeably without meaning change. The fidels are አ and ዐ, ጸ and ፀ, ሰ and ሠ and ሀ, ሐ, and ኀ. For example, the word "sun" can be written as, ጸሀይ, ጸሃይ, ፀሀይ, ፀሃይ, etc … all mean the same, although they are written differently.

The other problem is in the formation of compound words. Compound words are sometimes written as two separate words and sometimes as a single word. For example, the word "kitchen" can be written as "ወጥቤት" or "ወጥ ቤት". There are many such compound words, which need some effort to have a standard way of forming them.

Amharic is morphologically rich language where up to 120 words can be conflated to a single stem (Alemayehu and Willet, 2002). The word units of Amharic are phoneme, morpheme, root, stem, and word. The 34 base characters are a phoneme. A collection of phonemes forms morphemes, which is the smallest meaningful unit in a word (Yemam, 1987). An Amharic root is a sequence of base characters. A collection of phonemes or sounds creates a word, which can be as simple as a single morpheme or contain several of them.

In Amharic language, it is common to write some words in shorter form using "/" (forward slash) or "." (dot). The short form of words can be expanded as single or a combination of words. አ/አ, which is expanded as አዲስ አበባ (means Addis Ababa), is an example for the latter. መ/ር is a short form of the single word መምህር (means teacher).

Another problem of the language is, there are different ways of writing a single word due to different reasons. One reason for this can be regional dialects that can impact word formation in the basic level where the words are more likely to be written following their spoken form; "ሂጃ" vs. "ሂጅ", "አይደለም" vs. "አይደሰም", "ዓጡ" vs. "ዓጤ", etc (Yacob, 2006). Another one is, in Amharic there are many ways of writing loan words, i.e words that are taken from foreign languages. For example, the word Computer can be written as ኮምፒዩተር, ኮምፒውተር, ኮምፒዉተር, etc.

3 Application of Amharic WordNet

Tools that are developed for Amharic language need to consider the above-mentioned characteristics of the language in one way or another. Some of these tools are discussed below together with how the use of Amharic WordNet can increase their performance. The tools are developed without the use of Amharic WordNet.

3.1 Amharic Search Engine

The Web is a huge repository of information in the form text, image, audio, and video. Search engines, such as Google, Yahoo!, etc, are the first port of call for the discovery of resources from this huge repository. According to Internet World Stats, usage and Population (2009) Ethiopia took 0.4 % of Internet users out of Africa's share in 2009. The statistics also shows that there was an increase of users of Internet in Ethiopia by 3500% during the years 2000-2009. Due to this increase in Internet population within the country and large number of population that speaks the language in Diaspora, the number of web documents that are written in Amharic language and Ethiopic script is increasing. In order to search these documents we need a search engine that can handle Amharic queries, written in Ethiopic script, well.

As described earlier, Amharic has many unique features that affect the retrieval of the language's documents from the Web. ሐበሻ search engine (Mindaye, 2007) is a complete language specific search engine that is developed for Amharic web documents. The search engine has three components: the Amharic Crawler, The Amharic Indexer and the Amharic Query Engine. The crawler (Language Specific Crawler) crawls the Web and collects Amharic web documents and stores them in a repository. The Indexer processes the documents and stores them in a structure that is efficient for searching. Some of the processing in this component are: tokenization, stop word removal, stemming, etc. The Query Engine component gives an interface that the user can enter his/her information need in Amharic language using Ethiopic script. It returns the relevant documents according to their rank.

The application of Amharic WordNet is many folds in ሐበሻ search engine. Queries can be expanded using Amharic WordNet that will increase the recall of the search engine. Interchangeable alphabets (repetitive alphabets) can also handled easily by Amharic WordNet by considering all the different forms of a word as a synonym. The same applies for the regional dialects, Loan words and short form of a compound word, which are all different ways of writing a same word as discussed in section 2.

3.2 Amharic Automatic Text Categorization

The process of automatic text categorization involves calculating similarities between documents and categories using the information extracted from the document. In recent years, ontology-based document categorization method is introduced to solve the problem of document classifier. In order to resolve the problem of not considering semantic relationships between words, one study (Sahelemariam et al., 2009) proposes a framework that automatically categorizes Amharic documents into predefined categories using knowledge represented in the News ontology. At the heart of its classification system is the knowledge base that enables the representation of different domain concepts. With the help of News domain ontology, this study categorizes a given Amharic document (news) into a specific predefined category. The study shows that the use of concepts for Amharic document categorizer obtained a promising outcome. However, the study also recommend for further research and developmental effort in the area of external knowledge base such as Amharic WordNet. In the study, for the process of extracting concepts from the knowledge base, index terms are mapped on the corresponding concepts of the ontology. However, there is a possibility that the term may not exist because of the limited number of concepts available in the News ontology. This situation requires an alternative way of mapping onto the external knowledge base concept. The alternative way is to use the extended concept in order to map between the external concept and the existing knowledge base. In the linguistic knowledge base, we can find words semantically related with the other words in many ways. Using various semantics relationships, we can take the advantage to establish links between the words of the ontology concepts and WordNet vocabulary. These retrieved words from WordNet will be treated as the external knowledge base to enhance the result of the study.

3.3 Amharic Word Sense Disambiguation

Ambiguity is defined as the property of being ambiguous, where a word, term, notation, sign, symbol, phrase, sentence, or any other form used for communication, is called ambiguous if it can be interpreted in more than one way (Mihalcea and Pedersen, 2005). When language is capable of being understood in more than one way by a reasonable person, ambiguity exists. Ambiguity is inherent to human language. Successful solutions for automatic resolution of ambiguity in natural language often require large amounts of annotated data/knowledge resources to achieve good levels of accuracy. One study tries to develop a tool for Amharic word sense disambiguation (Kassie, 2009). In the study, Amharic Penal Code document was used for experimentation by applying Semantic Vectors of words of dimension 200. The term vectors are built from index of terms using lucene IR library. Using those term vectors thesaurus can be constructed by calculating the k nearest neighborhood from the word space by applying the distance measure between points of term representation according to the usage of terms in documents. In other words, a query that is one word is run using the prototype where the system retrieves words by applying the similarity calculation of nearest neighborhoods from documents according to their usage. The neighborhood is calculated from the co-occurrence frequency of words in documents. The average precision and recall of the system is 58% and 82% respectively. The author argued that if there was an Amharic WordNet the performance of the tool definitely would improve.

4 Conclusion and Future Work

WordNet has been recognized as a valuable resource in the human language technology and knowledge processing communities. From the above sections we can clearly see the application of Amharic WordNet. Developing the WordNet will enhance the performance of many information retrieval and natural language processing tools for the language. It will also give the language a chance to be integrated with other languages for cross-language processing.

Princeton WordNet is a great inspiration for the development of WordNet in different languages. There have been many efforts o develop a WordNet for different languages such as Arabic (Elkateb et al., 2006), different European languages (Vossen, 1997), etc. There are two approaches of developing a WordNet: the *merge* approach and *extended* approach. In order to develop Amharic WordNet, an extended approach seems appropriate due to the following reasons:

- It reduces the cost and time of developing Amharic WordNet from scratch.
- It gives an opportunity to integrate the language WordNet with other languages WordNet.
- It is wise to use the information in the Princeton WordNet for such under-resourced languages like Amharic.

However we may need to modify the PWN in order to incorporate some unique futures of Amharic language. This indicates the need for a coordinated effort from a linguist, Computer Science professionals and other stakeholders to develop Amharic WordNet (AmWN).

References

Baye Yemam. 1987 ዓ.ም. የአማርኛ፤ ሰዋስው፡፡ ት.መ.ማ.ማ.ድ. ፡፡

Daniel Yacob. 2006. "*Application of the Double Metaphone Algorithm to Amharic Orthography*", International Conference of Ethiopian Studies.

Elkateb, S., Back, W., Vossen, P., Farwell, D., Rodrigue, H., Pease, A., Alkhalifa, M. and Fellbaum, C. 2006. *Arabic WordNet and the Challenges of Arabic. The Challenges of Arabic for NLP/MT*. International Conference at the British Computer Society (BSC), London.,

Ethiopian Central Statistical Authority (ECSA). 1998. *The 1994 Population and Housing Census of Ethiopia: Results at Country Level*. Vol.1, Statistical Report 44, AddisAbaba, Ethiopia.

Getachew Haile. 1967. *The Problems of AmharicWriting System*. Unpublished.

Internet World Stats, Usage and Population Statistics. 2009. Available at:
http://www.InternetworldStats.com/stats.htm

Marvin L. Bender, Head W. Sydeny, andRoger Cowley. 1976. *The Ethiopian Writing System*. In Bender et al (Eds.) Language in Ethiopia. London, Oxford University press.

Meron Sahlemariam, Mulugeta Libsie, and Yacob, Daniel. 2009. "*Concept-Based Automatic Amharic Document Categorization*". AMCIS 2009 Proceedings. Paper 116. http://aisel.aisnet.org/amcis2009/116

Nega Alemaehu and Willet P. 2002. *Stemming of Amharic Words for Information Retrieval*. In Literary and Linguistic Computing. Oxford, Oxford University press, Vol. 17, No.1, pp 1-17.

Rada Mihalcea and Ted Pedersen. 2005. .*Advances in Word Sense Disambiguation Tutorial* at AAAI-

Teshome Kassie. 2009. *Word Sense disambiguation for Amharic Text Retrieval: A Case Study for Legal Documents*. Thesis ,Addis Ababa University.

Tessema Mindaye. 2007. *Design and implementation of Amharic Search Engine* .Masters Thesis ,Addis Ababa University.

Vossen P. 1997. *EuroWordNet: a multilingual database for information retrieval*. In: Proc. of the DELOS workshop on Cross-language Information Retrieval, Zurich, Switzerland.

Wordventure – Developing WordNet in Wikipedia-like Style

Julian Szymański
Gdańsk University of Technology
Narutowicza 11/12, 80-952 Gdańsk, Poland
`julian.szymanski@eti.pg.gda.pl`

Abstract

The article describes an approach for building WordNet semantic dictionary in a collaborative way. The idea of gathering lexical data has been proposed, as well as the system for linguistic data acquisition and management.

1 Introduction

WordNet (Fellbaum and others, 1998) is one of the most popular digital semantic lexicons of English. Its main advantage is that it is made by hand, so data stored within its semantic network are high quality. On the other hand these data cover only a small part of the relations between lexical elements, so there is a need to scale-up the project. Creating a large scale semantic dictionary in a manual way is labor-consuming and relatively slow. Alternative approaches for building semantic networks have been proposed, eg: Microsoft MindNet (Vanderwende et al., 2005), built from text documents parsing, or MIT ConceptNet (Liu and Singh, 2004) built from parsing simple sentences contained common sense knowledge, aquisited through web page. Methodology used in this projects allows to build large scale semantic networks, although their quality isn't as high as hand crafted data. The other issue is that they operate only on words, not as WordNet on word meanings (synsets).

WordNet is being built as a research project in Princeton by a group of linguists. The WordNet team has been working on a semantic dictionary for over 22 years. Because of the limited human resources the speed of development of the project is limited. Our goal is to deliver a generally available tools for cooperative development of semantic networks. Building semantic dictionaries by hand requires a large amount of human resources, generally grouped in one place. In our approach we would like to exploit the power of the Internet and give open community a set of tools which would allow a cooperative modification of WordNet.

The rest of this paper is organized as follows. The next section presents the idea of cooperative editing paradigm, which was applied to WordNet dictionary development. Section 3 describes the architecture and technical details of the Wordventure system. The subsections of this paragraph provide insight into server and client application features of the system. The concluding section presents the future plans regarding the presented approach and application.

2 Cooperative approach for editing WordNet

The best known application of a cooperative approach to gathering textual data is Wikipedia. The project received a great interest from the Internet community, which brought many positive results. Wikipedia has been developed since 2001 by volunteers from all over the world. Currently, the Wikipedia initiative is supported by almost 75000 people, working on over nine million articles written in 125 languages. The largest set of articles is available in English, and contains over 2 million articles.

Current implementations of WordNet web based applications are limited to database exploration, moreover they resemble the standard, dictionary-like, web interface for WordNet. Lack of tools for cooperative editing of semantic dictionary databases is the main barrier for rapid WordNet development. Our aim is to deliver a tool enabling a cooperative editing approach for many users placed in distributed Internet environment (Szymański et al., 2007).

Cooperative approach to editing content on the Internet is gaining increasing recognition in many IT fields. The main goal of our project is to create a system that would enable Web users free access and easy-to-use interface for WordNet content navigation and editing in an interactive, dynamic way. Moreover, the functionalities and the look and feel of the system should encourage web users to feed WordNet database with data.

The editing process in presented scheme consists of the following steps:

1. Users input data on their clients, which communicate changes to the server.

2. Server logs the operation and executes suitable procedures on the database.

3. Periodically, a moderator that has direct access to the server log and the database analyses logs and decides whether any of the user's modifications should be rolled back.

After several editing steps the original database is enriched with the content chosen from users contributions. This procedure is supported with regular database backups. Described editing process is similar to Wikipedia procedures which include regular content checks for vandalism and disrupting activities. If our approach proves successful in presented scenario it could be extended for building semantic databases in general. The example of Wikipedia gives reason for hope that with a proper system design we could achieve satisfactory results in this field at least.

Cooperative editing is connected with publishing the WordNet database and making it open to the Internet community. This might bring advantages for faster WordNet development. However some problems may arise:

- **Vandalism** – may cause loss of important data, kept in current release of lexical database. It can also affect the data structure e.g. creation of pointless connections between words and synsets. Because of that, it is important to deliver tools for moderating the users activities, which will reduce the risk of the above-mentioned.

- **Simultaneous** work on the same part of the database by many users may case some conflicts resulting from concurrent work of many users at the same time. In the worst case one user can add the connection to an element of the WordNet dictionary that was deleted by another.

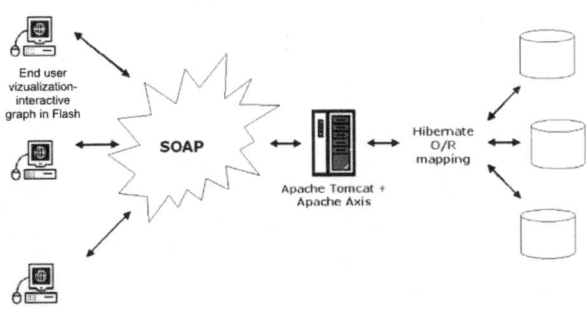

Figure 1: Basic concept of the WordVenture architecture and its elements.

3 System architecture

A WordVenture portal[1] has been developed at the Gdansk University of Technology at the Faculty of Electronics, Telecommunications and Informatics. It provides mechanisms for simultaneous work on lexical dictionaries for distributed groups of people and enables cooperative work on a WordNet lexical database. The Princeton Cognitive Science Laboratory approach to WordNet development requires a huge amount of resources: e.g people, time, money (Miller et al., 1990). With WordVenture lexical databases development becomes common and cheap. Our system offers functionalities to browse a WordNet dictionary and display its content on the screen with a graphical user interface based on an interactive graph. (The example is in Figure 3). It gives a user-friendly way for visualizing very large sets of contextual data.

The system supports cooperative editing approach for the WordNet database development. It has been implemented in a standard client-server architecture presented in Figure 1: with database and WordNet logic tier residing on the server and the visualization engine querying the server as a client application.

The success of a platform for cooperative editing depends on effective and easy-to-use graphical user interface. In order to achieve that we decided to use an interactive visualization engine that would be able to render graph-like structures and allow to implement editing features. In our implementation light-weight component for graph visualization enables convenient navigation in graph-like structures and provides basic support for graph editing.

---

[1]http://wordventure.eti.pg.gda.pl

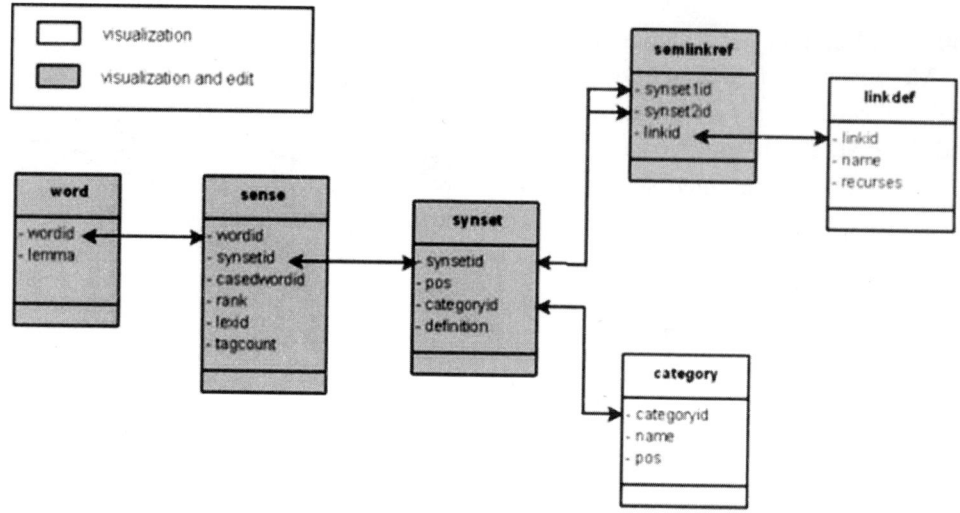

Figure 2: WordNet entities supported by the tool. Grayed out entities have support for both visualization and editing, white entities have only visualization support. Arrows represent relationships between entities.

3.1 Server side and Database

The server-side of the WordVenture application makes its functionalities available through web services. According to communication interoperability requirement it is possible to connect different client applications that can be implemented in different technologies.

Implemented functionalities allow a user to perform four different groups of actions depending on the role that the user has:

- **Functionalities for browsing WordNet lexical database**. Are available to every user (anonymous and logged-in) and gives an opportunity to look trough WordNet with interactive interface.

- **Functionalities that allow a user to edit WordNet lexical database**. Are only available to registered users. After performing an edit action on the client-side of an application the proper change proposition is created. Subsequently, this proposition is sent to the server to be added to the database.

- **Functionalities for managing the new data**. A privileged user (moderator) can view all change propositions and select data to commit or cancel. After committing, a proposition is permanently added to database and can be seen by other users.

- **Administrative functionalities connected with user management**. Are available only for privileged users – administrators. They allow to perform user deletion or user rights editing in WordVenture system. Every administrator can give administrative rights to another user.

The original implementation of a WordNet database uses text files. Because of their structure, modification is available only with dedicated tools. This type of storage doesn't support synchronous access for modification, nor allows to perform efficiently large amount of queries.

It was required to create special mechanisms for editing, including synchronization and file structure refactoring after any operation. To enable editing a WordNet lexical database through web we had to perform mappings between WordNet text files and a relational database. Transformation from text files to its relational representation was performed by the WordNet SQL Builder tool[2]. Data access routines were implemented with Hibernate ORM engine[3]. Manipulating the database content is made via implemented server API exposed as Web Services, which fulfills requirements of Service Oriented Architecture (SOA) (Erl, 2005) paradigm. The Web Services has been deployed on Apache Log4j on a Tomcat server. All the server components reside on a Debian Linux OS.

The elements of the original WordNet like a word position or morphological definitions are not

---
[2] http://wnsqlbuilder.sourceforge.net
[3] http://www.hibernate.org

as necessary as lemmas and synsets. To simplify the editing process it was decided to allow only for modification of the semantic network structure. The database structure for handling data provided by WordVenture is presented in Figure 2, where editable and dictionary tables of the system are shown.

3.2 Client side and visualization

WordVenture has been developed in rich-client architecture (Boudreau et al., 2007). Because of that, some logic connected with data visualization can be executed on the client-side of application. Because of ease-of-use requirement it was decided that the client application will be developed as a flash rich client application. The client is a modified gossamer component[4] for interactive graph visualization, where graph elements represent WordNet entities. The vizualization allows a user to:

- **Browse WordNet lexical database**. It enables the user to navigate over the WordNet semantic network in a user-friendly way. Words and synsets are visualized as graph nodes, connections between them are presented as graph edges. Additionally, the user can filter graph nodes and edges to obtain required content (according to a selected relation or pat of speech type), which makes user interface clean and readable.

- **Perform modifications on WordNet lexical database** – the tool enables a user to change graph content by adding, editing, or deleting its elements: nodes and edges. Modification of above-mentioned elements of WordNet lexicon (see Figure 2) does not cover all the components of WordNet. It includes only the four most desired, from the user point of view, elements of the semantic network: words, synsets, senses and relations.

Furthermore, the application offers additional features: manipulating the visible plane via zoom, rotating and moving, hiding selected nodes, etc. Currently, the application editing capabilities are as follows:

- adding new words and synsets,
- adding new links by dragging an edge between two nodes,

---
[4]http://gossamer.eti.pg.gda.pl/

- editing existing relations, words, synsets.

Described tool functionalities allow WordNet database to edit according to the approach presented in section 2. Our team has tested the tool in scenarios of extending the existing WordNet database and building a semantic network from scratch (only schema with no data). User's feedback on the approach and the support provided by the tool has been positive. Some users pointed out that using the tool for WordNet dictionary browsing actually supports extending English vocabulary. This is achieved by the eye-catching visualization of database exploration in the client and discovering word synonyms and other related words.

Graph-based visualization in a WordVenture system depicted in Figure 3 allows a user to work efficiently, and keep clean and readable a large amount of lexical data. In every moment a user can enable or disable required elements of the visualization, which makes his workspace personalized. Additionally, it is possible to zoom in or zoom out a view of graph, so a user is able to keep a lot of graph nodes on his workspace.

4 Conclusions and future work

The system for cooperative WordNet editing has reached the end of its third iteration. Since deployment, we have received positive feedback and feature proposals for extending the application. In general, future improvements in the system can be classified in one of the following categories:

- server-side API extensions (allow more types of WordNet data to be visualized and edited),
- UI improvements (tabbed viewing, more filtering capabilities, improved rendering, etc.)
- miscellaneous (server administration console, client-side action history, etc.).

At present we are evaluating future proposals for the system, gathering more feedback from users via our web-based forum system, prioritizing future goals, and evaluating the applied solution as a base for generic approach to semantic data editing tasks. We believe that our approach and the system can be used for effective management of WordNet-based dictionaries and that it is important to support ontology-based systems with editors similar to the one presented in this paper.

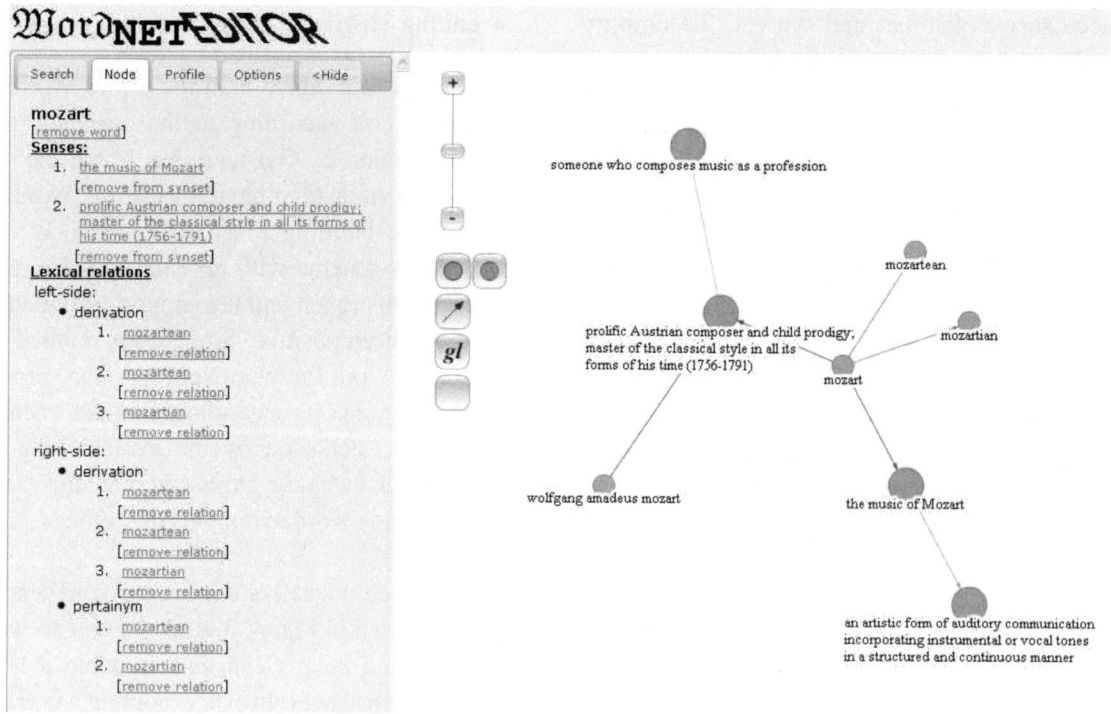

Figure 3: WordVenture visualization interface for WordNet

Wordventure can also be used as an interface for the correction of data obtained in an automated way, as it was in projects MindNet and ConceptNet. We plan mining Wikipedia to obtain new relations between synsets, it is also possible to enrich WordNet with data imported form other ontologies mentioned earlier: MindNet, ConceptNet or Sumo/Milo ontology (Niles and Pease, 2001). One of the most important things is synsets stratification, which will allow to filter data in terms of data importance.

In a few months we plan to integrate Wordventure with the second of our projects for visualization knowledge in Wikipedia[5] where WordNet stands as ontology for articles categorization system. Long term goal is to join WordNet synsets with Wikipedia articles (Szymaski and Kilanowski, 2009), which will allow to look through Wikipedia knowledge effectively.

References

T. Boudreau, J. Tulach, and G. Wielenga. 2007. Rich client programming: plugging into the netbeans platform.

T. Erl. 2005. *Service-oriented architecture: concepts, technology, and design.* Prentice Hall PTR Upper Saddle River, NJ, USA.

[5]http://swn.eti.pg.gda.pl

C. Fellbaum et al. 1998. WordNet: An electronic lexical database.

H. Liu and P. Singh. 2004. ConceptNet – a practical commonsense reasoning tool-kit. *BT Technology Journal*, 22(4):211–226.

G.A. Miller, R. Beckwith, C. Fellbaum, D. Gross, and K.J. Miller. 1990. Introduction to wordnet: An online lexical database. *International Journal of lexicography*, 3(4):235–244.

I. Niles and A. Pease. 2001. Towards a standard upper ontology. *Proceedings of the international conference on Formal Ontology in Information Systems-Volume 2001*, pages 2–9.

J. Szymański, K. Dusza, and Ł. Byczkowski. 2007. Cooperative Editing Approach for Building Wordnet Database. *Proceedings of the XVI International conference on system science*, pages 448–457.

J. Szymaski and D. Kilanowski. 2009. Wikipedia and wordnet integration based on words co-occurrences. *Proceedings of International conference on system science and technology.*

L. Vanderwende, G. Kacmarcik, H. Suzuki, and A. Menezes. 2005. MindNet: an automatically-created lexical resource. *HLT/EMNLP. The Association for Computational Linguistics.*

Adding Information to a Terminological Database by Means of Image Files

Rita Marinelli
Istituto di Linguistica
Computazionale C.N.R.
Via Moruzzi 1 Pisa, Italy
rita.marinelli@ilc.cnr.it

Giovanni Spadoni
S. Spadoni s.r.l. Shipping
Agency Via delle Cateratte
90 Livorno, Italy
g.spadoni@saurospadoni.it

Sebastiana Cucurullo
Istituto di Linguistica
Computazionale C.N.R.
Via Moruzzi 1 Pisa, Italy
nella.cucurullo@ilc.cnr.it

Abstract

A lexical semantic database containing terms belonging to the specialized lexicon of the maritime navigation and maritime transport was built according to WordNet/EuroWordNet model. Our paper present a project planning the enrichment of the terminological database by means of a set of images. A short description is given about a) the structure of the terminological database and the domain conceptual modelling; b) the various features of the database management tool, and, among all, the possibility of visualizing, on demand, the image which is associated with the term being sought, contributing to clarify and refine the meaning of the term, increasing its information and communication effectiveness.

1 Introduction

MariTerm is a database structured according to the EuroWordNet/ItalWordNet model, in the frame of the WordNet philosophy: the relational structure of the database is of lexical semantic type. An approximate 4000 lemmas are codified, which belong to the specialized lexicon of the technical-nautical and maritime transport domain (Marinelli and Roventini, 2006).

The objective of this project was to create a terminological resource that could be a support for management of the terms belonging to this domain that are used with an increasing frequency in spoken and written texts and, in general, in everyday life. Our study was guided by the need for a useful instrument for work and didactic activities and, in general, for various types of communication contexts. This paper presents a research recently undertaken and still in progress, which focuses on the improvement of the maritime database by providing visual information by means of a set of images.

In the following sections we describe: a) the structure of the terminological database and the domain conceptual modelling; b) the database management tool which allows consultation of the terminological database, updating of the set of data and, among the various features, visualization on demand of the image which is associated with the term being sought; c) final remarks and conclusions.

2 The Database Structure

The relational structure of the database provided by the model is represented in terms of:

a) Internal relations: which link synsets (sets of synonyms [1]) in hierarchical relationship (vertical relations), by means of hyperonymy/hyponymy relations, or in meronymy, entailment, role, etc. relationship (orizontal relations): the use of vertical (hyperonymy/hyponymy) relations leads to the definition of the most basic level of categorization namely "the most inclusive (abstract) level at which the categories can mirror the structure of attributes perceived in the world" (Rosch, 1988), while the use of the horizontal dimension for categorization implies the improvement of the distinctiveness and flexibility of categories.

Each synset is ontologically classified, on the basis of its hyperonym, in terms of the IWN Top Ontology (TO), i.e. a hierarchy of language-

---

[1] In the latest version of WordNet, (WN 3.0), "synset" is defined as "a set of one or more 'synonyms' or 'variants'", e.g.: *imbarcazione, natante* (vessel), *naufragare, colare a picco, affondare* (to sink).

independent concepts reflecting essential semantic distinctions, e.g.: *navigazione* (navigation) → Agentive, Dynamic, Purpose.

b) Equivalence relations: connect the Italian synsets with the closest concepts (synonyms, near synonyms, hyperonyms, etc.) of the Inter Lingual Index (ILI [2]). When possible an eq_synonym or eq_near_synonym relation is used, otherwise an eq_has_hyperonym relation is coded, e.g.:

nolo eq_synonym *freight*
nolo prepagato eq_has_hyperonym *freight*

by these links to the ILI, the terms are also connected to the Top Ontology (TO).

c) Plug-in relations: allow the linking of a synset of the specialized wordnet to the generic (IWN), (e.g.: "*porto*" is present in both the databases); in such a way a terminological sub-hierarchy (represented by its root node) is connected to a node of the generic wordnet. By means of the plug-in relations the tool we are using to manage the terminological database and the specific ontology also allows an "integrated" consultation of the database; it shows that if a synset is found in both databases (and is plugged-in), the synset belonging to the specific domain partially "obscures" the generic one: downward (hyponymy) and horizontal relations (part_of relations, role relations, etc.) are taken from the terminological wordnet, while upward (hyperonymy) relations are taken from the generic one.

3 Domain Structuring

In the integrated consultation a term is plugged in its hyperonym or synonym in the generic lexicon and the link with the upper part of the taxonomic chain can be shown visualized by the tool. Since the top ontology of a concept in the database is fully defined through its hyperonym, it is possible to see the highest concepts (TO) of the generic network to which the term is connected.

We deemed necessary to provide the terms with a specific ontology to better complete and support the functional value of terms as means of knowledge information. Following Cabré (2000), the terminological units have a double function: the specialized knowledge representation and its conveyance. The importance of a term is assessed according to the place it has in the conceptual structure of a domain following precise criteria.

The domain structure was outlined designating a "core" set of concepts which represent the two main sub-domains specified in maritime terminology: technical/nautical (nautics) and maritime transport (transport) domain and the various disciplines embraced by maritime domain. They range from astronomy to geography, from transport logistics to meteorology.

A comprehensive set of basic concepts was worked out and organized by the suggestions of ontological engineers and domain experts (Marinelli et al., 2006) so as to constitute the hook up points of the domain modelling, admitting the existence of different possible pathways among sub-domains under a common conceptual framework (Gangemi, 2005).

Two different criteria were followed to distinguish the most relevant concepts: i) for the technical/nautical terminology, we used the Glossary edited by the Harbour Master of Livorno (Tuscany) and the Italian Navigation Code, as a starting point for choosing the most frequently recurring and significant concepts and laying down a first categorization: the most interesting and representative patterns e.g. *attrezzatura* (equipment), *governo* (direction), *conduzione* (steering), etc., each incorporating a set of related concepts into which it is divided, were highlighted; ii) for maritime transport, the various stages of the "import/export" operation process were singled out, e.g. *operazioni di carico* (loading), *stivaggio* (stowage), *tassazione* (freight rating), etc., which are the main phases of the path necessary to follow so that a cargo (goods or passengers) can actually be transported to its destination. A representative concept was designated for each of these phases and perspectives and it was considered as a node to be fleshed out and developed within its own framework. When it was possible, we exploited official reference criteria or standards for high level classification, namely the criteria used by the Leghorn Port Authority and the codes used by ISTAT, *Istituto Nazionale di Statistica* (National Statistics Institute) for the classification of goods.

The definition of the criteria for classification is a crucial issue: the concept "*porto*" (harbour/port), for example, has many hyponyms but they can be classified from different points of view: with reference to harbour location (lake, sea, river), or to the specific use (commercial, industrial,

---

[2] An unstructured version of WordNet 1.5, containing all its synsets but not the relations among them.

military), or to the logistic services offered (*rifornimento/* bunkering, *immatricolazione/* registry) (Marinelli and Spadoni, 2007).

Each term is connected to one or more domain dependent concepts belonging to this "core" set; at the same time, the plug in relations described above bridge the term to the TO of IWN. The knowledge of a term is assured from both a general, foundation perspective and a specialized point of view, directly connected with the specific knowledge field. In the "integrated" consultation of the terminological database, the tool shows that every term can "inherit" the IWN Top Ontology definitions thus becoming an integral part of the structure; while codifying a term in the maritime database, reference to the concepts of the domain ontology is allowed, embedding the term in the terminological network. The example of "*porto*" (harbour) is shown hereafter as it appears in the integrated consultation of the tool:

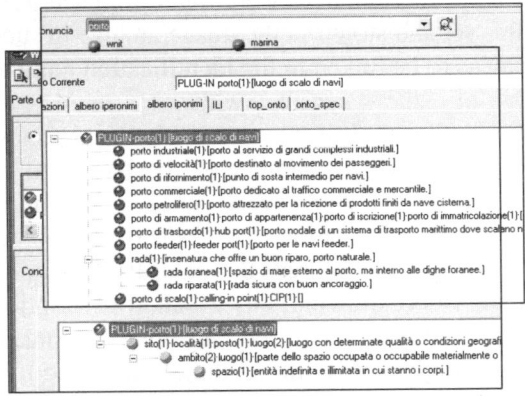

Figure 1. Downward and upward relations

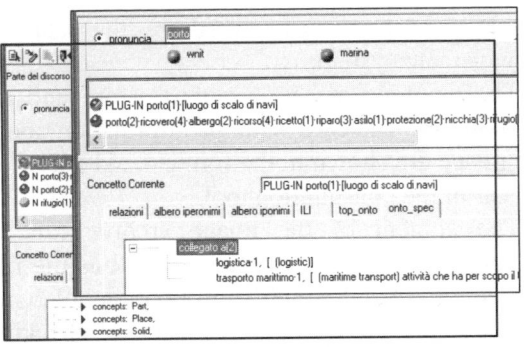

Figure 2. The links to the Domain Ontology and IWN TO

4 Increasing Lexical Coverage

The database has been enriched increasing its lexical coverage with a set of acronyms and abbreviations used in particular work environments (research, medicine, and, especially, transport) where the English language is very much used or even prevails. We mean acronyms like ASAP (As Soon As Possible), AGW (All Going Well), or WP (Weather Permitting), SHEX (Sunday Holidays Excluded). They hardly ever appear in literary texts, in newspapers, or in spoken language, but are included in the jargon of every day conversation belonging to the import/ export world and in maritime terminology in general. Universally recognized, they are fundamental and necessary for informal e-mail communications, for actual effective economy purposes. A set of proper names has also been added to the database, representing the most important ports and well known national and international Transport organizations. A group of terms belonging to maritime meteorology has also been codified: among the knowledge fields that are included in the maritime domain, Meteorology has a particular relevance. In fact, weather forecasts' accuracy makes it possible to plan the most "economical" and safest routes, in order to maintain the scheduled "transit time" between ports, to program cargo operations minimizing idle time and consequent costs, due to bad weather conditions. The weather component plays a significant role in maritime contracts as, e.g., the Expected Time of Arrival (ETA) for a ship into a port is always computed "Weather Permitting" (WP) and the calculation of the "lay time", the maximum time that the maritime contract assigns to perform the cargo operations, is always based on a fixed number of "Weather Working Days" (WWD) (Marinelli and Spadoni, 2007).

5 Enriching the Database with Images

In the last months, also the tool for the system management has been improved with new capabilities: it is possible to visualize the image illustrating the term being sought. An archive contains a set of images stored in such a way that a link can be created between each term of the database and the corresponding image. The archive can be updated by adding new files or replacing the old images with more recent ones. In this way, the information potential of the synset visualized by the database management tool is enriched and the imagery of the user is "guided" to the yielding of a more adequate knowledge of the term, abreast with the times:

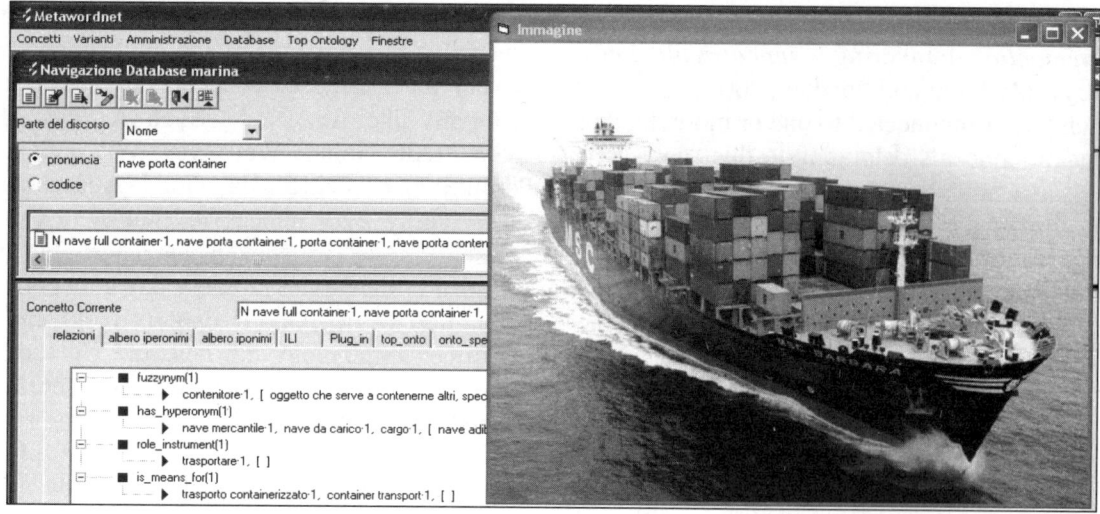

Figure 3. Example for "*nave porta-container*" (full container ship)

The database management tool allows connection on demand of the image selected to the term required: the image is activated by clicking on a button in the tool interface and can be substituted or even erased if not useful.

The new tool potential can be exploited for the sub-domain of "maritime transport" as well- which already includes a section "documentation"- inserting images of the standard documents that are used in the various phases of the logistic chain (standard charter-parties and bill of lading forms, documents of transport, international custom forms, etc.). The capability of the system can be boosted by making available to the users the immediate reference to the templates of the documents, whose definition is normally considered not sufficient for a full understanding of the processes involved.

A set of terms (about 150) that are the most frequent in the Maritime Corpus available in the Institute of Computational Linguistics [3] was considered the starting point of our research. They are representative of this domain and images could be easily obtained. These terms belong either to the generic or to the specialized lexicon and have a large number of hyponyms which are relevant to this knowledge field.

The images collected up to now were retrieved from different sources (on the basis of the domain expert's suggestions) [4] : web sites, personal photos, private archives, books and specialized publications, etc. They were also supplied by the Naval Academy of Livorno (Italy), by the CoMMA–Med Laboratory of the Institute of Biometeorology (C.N.R.) and by the Porto Livorno 2000, a passenger terminal managing company.

One or more images were found for each term of this set and stored in the image archive in such a way as to be linked to the identification number (id) of the synset with a one-to-one correspondence. It is possible to choose the most suitable image as example of the term and to compile a file for every image containing organized information: subject (the object represented), the source, the date, the type/kind (photo, video, drawing, etc.), a short description of the object represented, plus technical characteristics (resolution, dimensions, etc.), a field recording an inventory number; some fields will also be provided containing the reference to other related images and a field with one or more words to be used as keywords by the database management system.

The example of "*vela aurica*" (fore and aft sail) and the file/card with all information about the image are shown in the figure 4 and 5 as they appear in the consultation tool.

The content of the image archive can be visualized, saved and printed, as well as the file that contains catalographic information, allowing to determine the accuracy of data by checking them with various sources. In the near future a database including these descriptive catalographic files will be designed so as to be able to support our project. In such a way the set of images, chosen and structured on the basis of precise technical criteria, correspond to the set of terms and to a catalographic database of catalogued descriptive files.

---

[3] The corpus of maritime terminology, in progress at the ILC, consists of nearly 140,000 occurrences.
[4] A kind of evaluation is also planned.

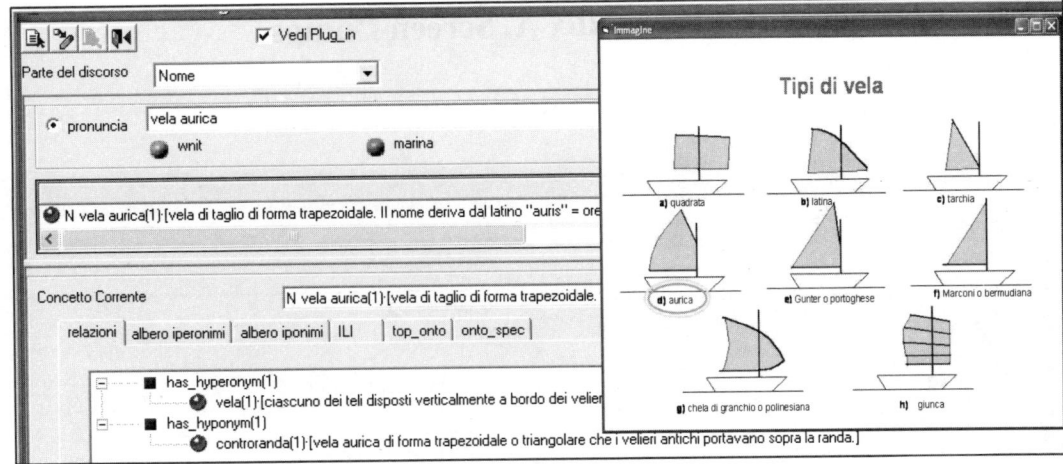

Figure 4. *Vela aurica* (fore and aft sail)

Figure 5. Catalographic file of "*vela aurica*"

The initial set of terms to be illustrated, used as a prototype set of samples, will be improved, including terms which are at lower level in the taxonomic chains which will be given a higher degree of specialization, and will, therefore, be more useful. Interesting points to be investigated in the future will concern methods able to: i) make this resource available to answer the needs of various kind of communities: professionals and non-professionals alike, ii) to interact with illustrated semantic networks namely PicNet (Borman et al., 2005) and large scale image ontologies such as ImageNet (Deng et al., 2009).

6 Conclusion

The terminological resource Mariterm was enhanced increasing its lexical coverage, designing a domain modelling and improving the tool for the database management with the possibility of giving visual information showing an image of each term. In such a way the meaning of a term can be clarified and more exhaustively represented.

Image classification and selection criteria were delineated together with the use of a set of files that contain catalographic information. In this framework, a system is planned for image cataloguing with more accuracy, based on user friendly tools and effective indexing strategies. In this way, the delivery of more complete description and useful information is performed from different points of view; the system, enlarged and provided with new details, becomes a flexible dynamic structure where there is a connection with applicative and pragmatic processes.

References

Borman A., Mihalcea R., Tarau P. 2005. PicNet: Pictorial Representations for Illustrated Semantic Networks, *Proceedings of the AAAI Spring Symposium on Knowledge Collection from Volunteer Contributors,* Stanford, CA.

Cabré Castelvì M. T. 2000. *La terminologia: representacion y comunicacion,* Barcelona: IULA.

Deng J., Li K., Do M., Su H., Fei-Fei L. 2009. Construction and Analysis of a Large Scale Image Ontology. *Vision Sciences Society (VSS).*

Gangemi, A. 2005. *Development of an Integrated Formal Ontology and an Ontology Service for Semantic Interoperability in the Fishery Domain,* CNR – ICST, OCM Group.

Marinelli R., Roventini A., Spadoni G. 2006. Using core ontology for domain lexicon structuring. *Proceedings of LREC 2006.* Paris, ELRA.

Marinelli R., Roventini A.. 2006. The Italian Maritime Lexicon and the ItalWordNet Semantic Database. In E. Miyares Bermúdez and L. Ruiz Miyares (Eds.), *Linguistics in the Twenty First Century,* Cambridge.

Marinelli R., Spadoni G. 2007. Modelling a Maritime Domain Ontology. *Proceedings of the X International Symposium on Social Communication.* Santiago de Cuba.

Rosch, E. Principles of Categorization. 1988. *Readings in Cognitive Science, a Perspective from Psychology and Artificial Intelligence,* Morgan Kaufmann, San Mateo-California.

Appendix A. Screen Dumps

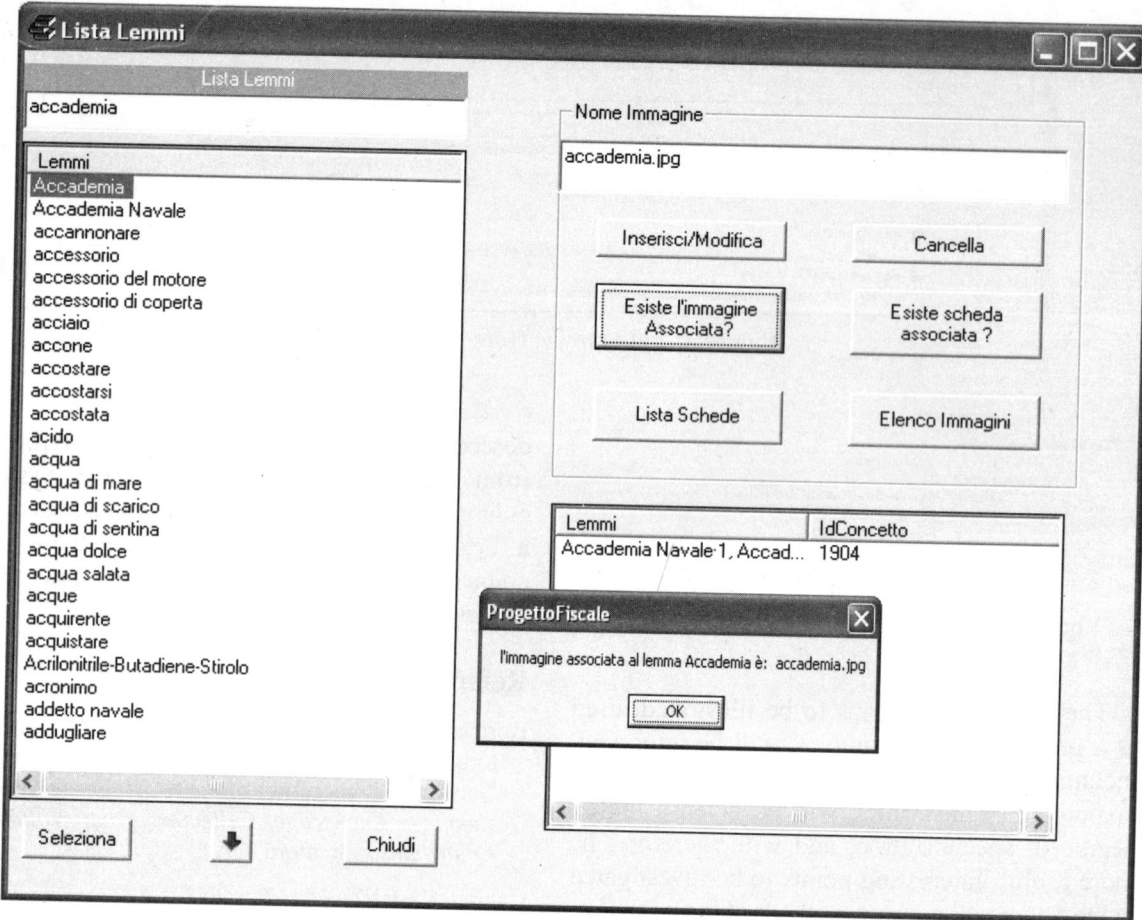

Figure 6. Screen Dump "Lista Lemmi".

The tool allows visualization of the image already inserted, e.g.:"*Accademia Navale*"(Naval Academy) is the lemma required; the name of the image and the identification number (id) of the concept are linked in a one-to-one correspondence.

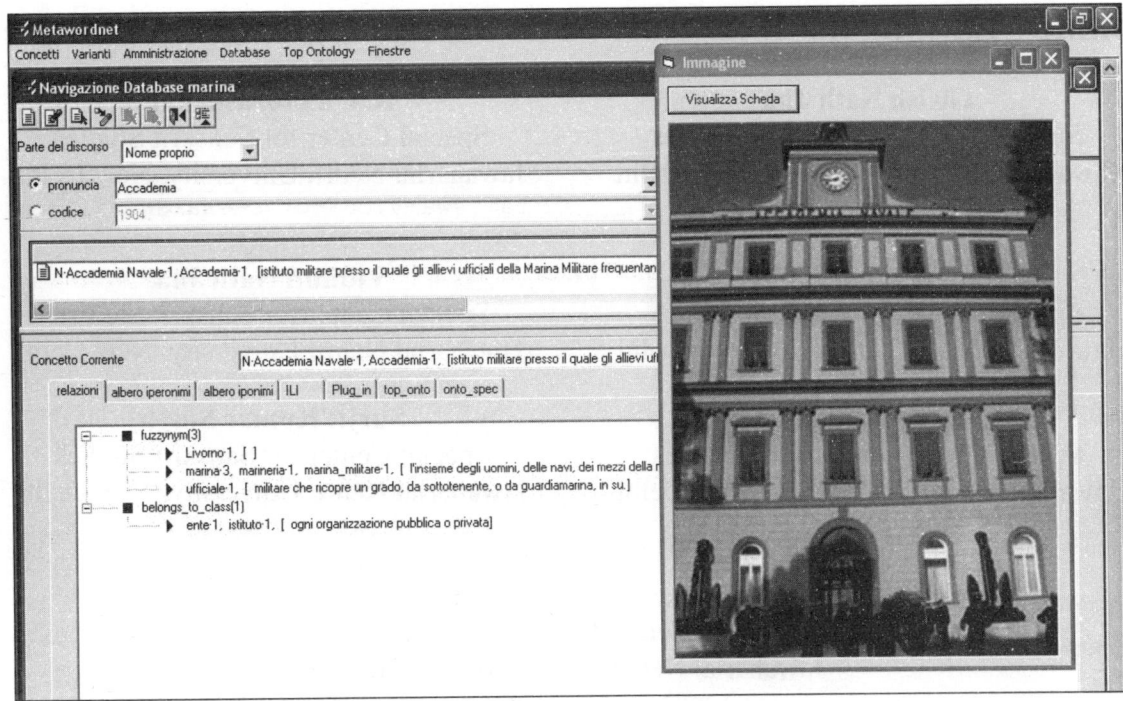

Figure 7. Screen Dump "Accademia"

The synset "*Accademia Navale*" (Naval Academy) is visualized together with the semantic relations and the image.

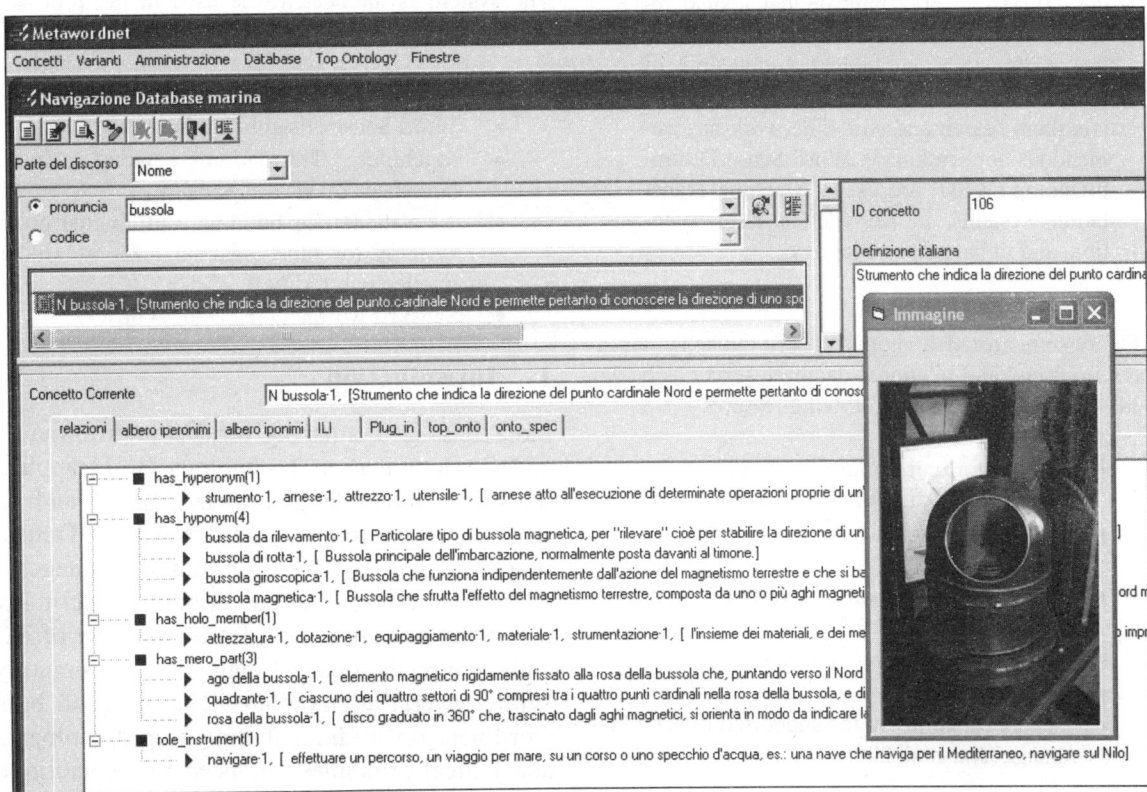

Figure 8. Screen Dump "Bussola"

The synset "*bussola*" (compass) as it appears with the semantic relations and the image.

Online Multilingual *Amarakośa*: The Relational Lexical Database

Girish Nath Jha
Special Center for Sanskrit Studies
Jawaharlal Nehru University, New Delhi
girishjha@gmail.com

R. Chandrashekar
Special Center for Sanskrit Studies
Jawaharlal Nehru University, New Delhi
ramaswamy.chandrashekar@gmail.com

Umesh Kumar Singh
Special Center for Sanskrit Studies
Jawaharlal Nehru University, New Delhi
umeshvaidik@gmail.com

Vibhuti Nath Jha
Special Center for Sanskrit Studies
Jawaharlal Nehru University, New Delhi
vibhutijha158@gmail.com

Satyendra Pandey
Special Center for Sanskrit Studies
Jawaharlal Nehru University, New Delhi
pandeysatyendra80@gmail.com

Surjit Kumar Singh
Special Center for Sanskrit Studies
Jawaharlal Nehru University, New Delhi
surjit.jnu@gmail.com

Mukesh Kumar Mishra
Special Center for Sanskrit Studies
Jawaharlal Nehru University, New Delhi
mukeshscssjnu@gmail.com

Abstract

This paper outlines the ongoing research project called "Online Multilingual Amarakośa (OMA)" for a multilingual lexical resource for Amarakośa (AK) which not only lets users store ontological equivalents of Sanskrit concepts in their languages, but also lets them search and edit. The work has tremendous applications in Word Sense Disambiguation (WSD) process of Machine Translation Systems, in Knowledge Representation, and in language pedagogy.

This system hosted at http://sanskrit.jnu.ac.in has a Java front-end and relational database server as back-end. At present, it has the following features –

- facility for online multilingual data entry in Sanskrit, Hindi, Kannada and English.
- data storage in multi-scriptural Indian langauge unicode
- stores up to 50 synonyms with grammatical information and detailed glosses
- cross-referencing among synonyms
- ontology display
- search capability in the supported Indian language (Jha et al, 2005)

Near future enhancements include
- selective data export in the user defined format
- display of the scanned imges of the pages from authorative text
- smarter search engine
- text processing based on AK

The system is intended to be used in the following domains –

- Multilingual concept acquisition
- Word Sense Disambiguation
- Machine Translation among Indian languages by way of Sanskrit
- As a model for building multilingual online systems for other seminal texts of Indian intellectual tradition
- Sanskrit wordnet (Jha et al, 2006)

1 Introduction

India has seen amazing strides in Information and Communication Technology (ICT) applications for Indian languages in general and for Sanskrit in particular. Since Machine Translation from Sanskrit to other Indian languages is often the desired goal, traditional Sanskrit lexicography has attracted a lot of attention of ICT and Computational Linguistics community. While several attempts are being made to build word-nets on traditional Indian epistemological and logical principles, the need for generating a multilingual lexical resource for AK, the Sanskrit lexicon built on ontological principles, has been largely ignored. AK, the 4th CE lexicon developed by Amarasimha has influenced modern lexicographic techniques in quite the same way as Pāṇini and Chomsky have done to generative linguistics. There have been some efforts in building a bilingual Sanskrit electronic dictionary. Huet (2004) is working on creating a Sanskrit – French electronic dictionary. Bontes (2005) had built a standalone system of Monier Williams dictionary. The Cologne Digital Sanskrit Lexicon contains Monier-Williams Sanskrit-English Dictionary has approximately 1,60,000 main entries. It has an online search facility in both Sanskrit and English. Capeller's Sanskrit-English Dictionary has been converted to a digital format similar to the Cologne project and has online search facility in both Sanskrit and English. It has only 50,000 entries. Apte Sanskrit Dictionary Search is a web Sanskrit dictionary based on the famous work of V. S. Apte - *The Practical Sanskrit-English Dictionary*. Andre Signoret's French-Sanskrit dictionary is freely downloadable from the net. The BhāratīyaBhāṣā multilingual dictionary built by Central Hindi Directorate, New Delhi under TDIL, Govt. of India funding consists of nearly 5000 common words in 14 different languages. It is available for download from the TDIL site. The Sanskrit Dictionary-Database being prepared by Jong-cheol Lee (2005), Academy of Korean Studies, Seoul, Korea will include mappings among Sanskrit, Tibetan, Chinese and Korean. Mohanty et. Al. (2004) has done some work on representing ontologies of Sanskrit words using Navya Nyāya methodology. As we can see, none of these works focuses on the AK and its rich semantic ontologies. In terms of search, the Cologne and Capeller's works are comparable.

As a text, AK has three *kāṇḍa* (chapters), each subdivided into *varga* (classes). The first and second *kāṇḍa* have 10 *vargas* each. The third *kāṇḍa* has 5 *vargas*. *Figure1* illustrates the structure of AK

There have been attempts to put the text of AK online or in digital formats. But there has been no attempt to create a version of this work which not only allows the users interactively build a database of AK but also search and test.

2 The AK system

The online system is being developed using Java servlets as front-end hosted on Apache-Tomcat platform and MS SQL server with multilingual Unicode data as backend.

The system has the following components –
- the relational database
- the data entry component
- search component
- detail search component
- data editing component

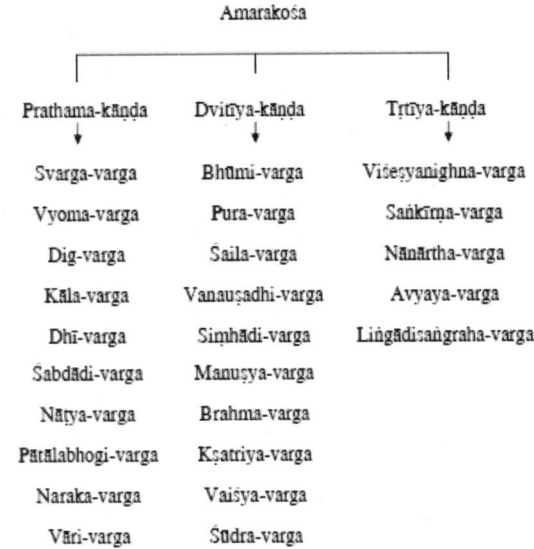

Figure 1: Structure of AK

2.1 The AK Database

The AK database is a relational database designed using MS SQL server objects and procedures. The database includes intricate relationships between the base words, synonyms and multilingual glosses.

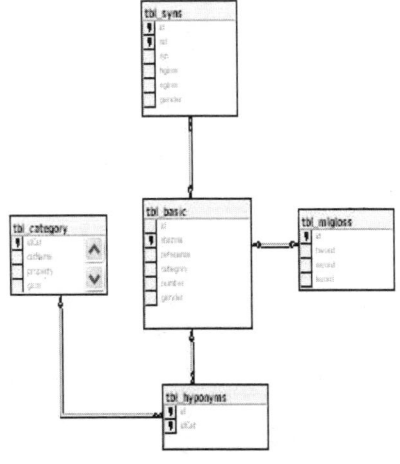

Figure 2: AK database-diagram

2.2 Data entry component

This component allows users to enter data in their language by way of user validation by password checking. Users can select the basic Sanskrit entry and provide information in their language (at present 8 Indian languages including English are supported). The screen capture for this page is given below -

Figure 3: Basic data entry page

After the basic data, the synonyms (up to a maximum of 50) can be entered with other relevant information.

2.3 Data Search

The search facility procided is of three kinds – direct search, alphabetical search and search by AK structure. Search can be done in the base word (Sanskrit), multilingual glosses and synonyms. There is scope for more languages in future. For example, the alphabet search of 'छ' displays all the words starting with this letter as:

Figure 4: Direct-search page

The direct search can be done by typing the word in Devnagari (using an inbuilt Unicode keyboard for the iTrans scheme) or by clicking on the word list obtained by alphabet search.

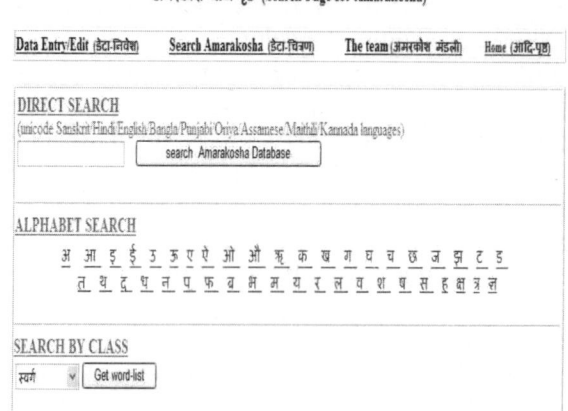

Figure 5: Alphabet-search page

A successful direct search displays the basic information including the multilingual glosses and all the synonyms associated with the search string –

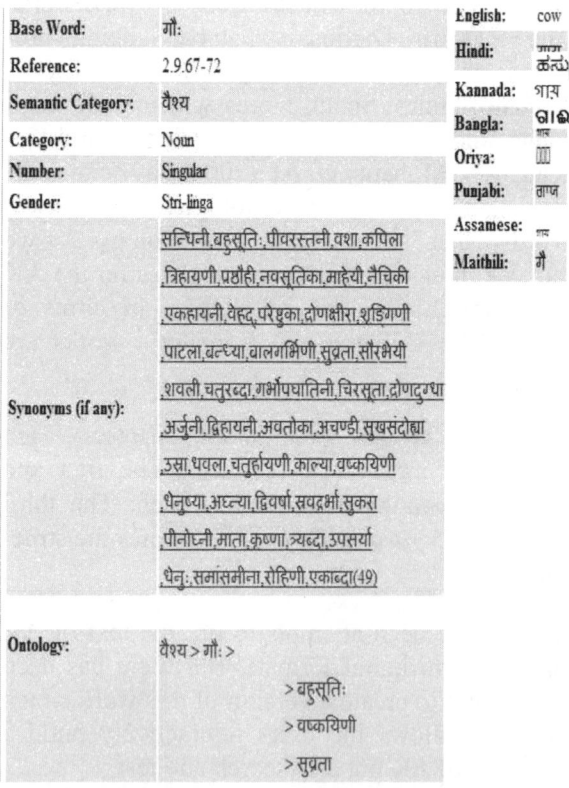

Figure 6: Search-result page

The search by structure (semantic classes) can be done by selecting a semantic class from the drop down box as follows –

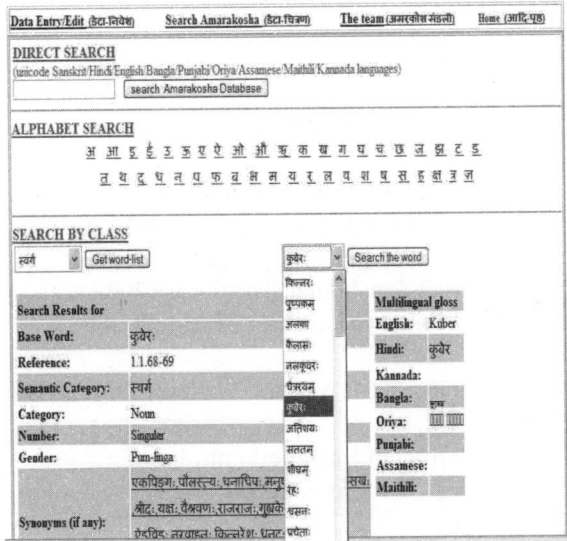

Figure 7: Search by semantic class

Clicking on the synonym link takes to the details page where each synonym entry is explained according to AK. The image that follows shows the synonym details for the English search string 'cow' –

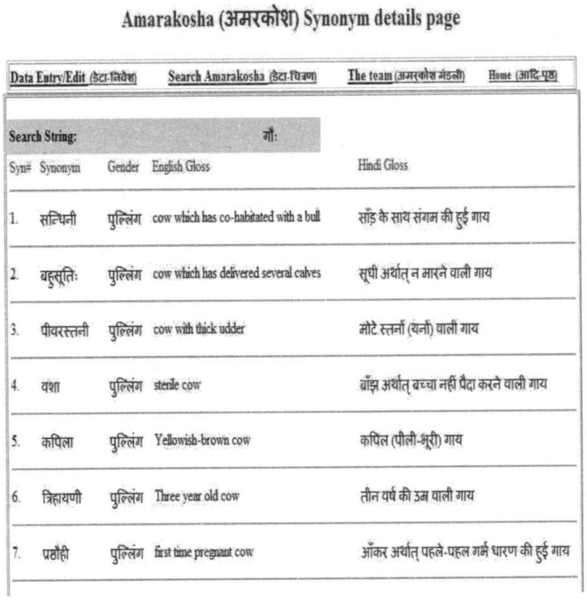

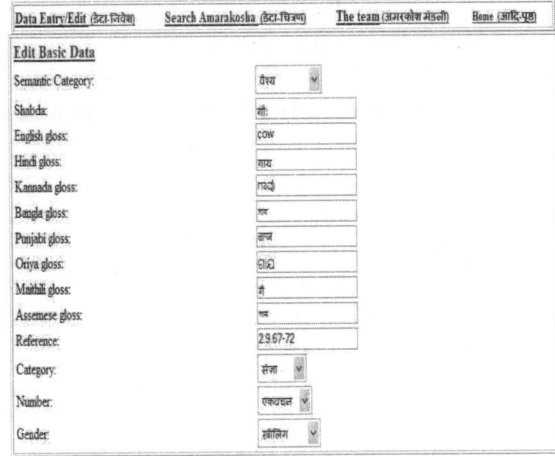

Figure 8: Search-result-detail page

3.4 Data Edit

This module lets language experts (by login only) to edit a wrongly entered data. The experts are sought through a registration module connected to the OMA website at http://sanskrit.jnu.ac.in/user/register.jsp which stores the user information in a database and determines who to give access for editing AK database directly on the server. The following screen allows the logged-in experts to edit AK data on the server -

Figure 9: Data edit page

4 Structure of lexical data

The current structure of AK is a change from the earlier database structure mentioned above. While the text edition being followed is the same (*Rāmāśramī ṭīkā (RT)*), the data organization has undergone significant changes. We have also allowed POS annotation with two tagsets – the JNU tagset (Chandrashekar, 2007), and the Sanskrit Consortia tag-set (2009). The abstract data structure in the base table is as follows –

- *kāṇḍa>varga>śloka*
- reference of AK according to *RT*
- Word id
- Word in the AK according to *RT*
- Nominal base
- Word type
- Gender
- Number
- JNU POS Tag
- Sanskrit Consortium POS Tag
- AK gloss
- RT / Amarapadavivṛti gloss
- Interpolation
- Variant reading
- Other reading
- Inferred reading
- Pāṇini sūtra

The relations table stores the relations of the words with only the ids of the words related as follows –

- id of the first word
- id of the second word
- relation between the two words

Currently, we have stored the lexical items obtained from AK verses as per the RT, but later on we may also display respective *śloka* (verse) corresponding to the searched word.

5 Limitations and future enhancements

We would like to include as many langauges as possible depending on the resources at our hand. A Sanskrit textual analysis based on AK database is being carried out at the level of Ph.D. research. An analytical research (at the level of M. Phil.) is being carried out on the homonyms used in AK. These components will be added in future. The system presented here is the first Sanskrit *śāstra* made available in this format. We aim to include more and more texts in future. Other enhancements include improved display of information in terms of showing the *ślokas* with scanned image of the page where the word occurs. We are also developing a data download module where data export in customized formats will be supported.

6 Credits

The OMA project was started with the first batch (2002) of Ph.D. students–Sudhir, Chandrashekar, Sharda, Nagesh, Asha Shahi, Manju Pandit, Ashok Tiwari, Devendra Singh, Uma. The idea of an online interactive multilingual Sanskrit dictionary was liked by the BBC when they interviewed Dr. Girish Nath Jha in their *aaj ke din* Hindi program. Subsequently the project got funded under a generous grant from J.N.U. under the UPOE scheme. Currently, the editing and formatting of data is in process under a funding from Dept. of Information Technology for the Sanskrit Consortium. The authors of the paper would like to thank the above mentioned students and institutions as well as the following students and staff who contributed data and gave valuable suggestions – Sangeeta, Priti Bhowmick, Subash, Manji Bhadra, Muktanand Agrawal, Sachin Kumar, Diwakar Mani, Diwakar Mishra, Surjit Kumar Singh, Sureshwar Meher, Debashis Ghosh, Satyamudita Snehi and Vishav Bandhu.

References

Andre Signoret's French-Sanskrit dictionary (2005), http://asignoret.free.fr/index.html (accessed : 23 March 2005)

Apte Sanskrit Dictionary Search, 2009 http://aa2411s.aa.tufs.ac.jp/~tjun/sktdic/

BhāratiyaBhāṣā multilingual dictionary,2005, TDIL website (accessed : 23 March 2005)

Bontes Louis, 2005, Monier William Digital Dictionary
http://members.ams.chello.nl/l.bontes/. (accessed : 23 March 2005)

Capeller's Sanskrit-English Dictionary,2005 http://www.uni-koeln.de/phil-fak/indologie/tamil/cap_search.html (accessed: 23 March 2005)

Chandrashekar R., 2007, *POS tagging for Sanskrit*, Ph.D. thesis, JNU

Cologne Digital Sanskrit Lexicon,2005, http://www.uni-koeln.de/phil-fak/indologie/tamil/mwd_search.html (accessed : 23 March 2005)

Dadhimatha, Pandita Sivadatta, 1929, The *Nāmaliṅgānuśāsana (Amarakośa)* of Amarasimha with the commentary (*Vyākhyāsudhā* or *Rāmāśramī*) of Bhanuji Dikshit, Nirṇaya Sāgar, Bombay

Huet Gerard, 2005, Sanskrit –French dictionary, http://pauillac.inria.fr/~huet/SKT/indo.html (accessed : 23 March 2005)

Jha Girish Nath et al, 2005, *Information technology applications for Sanskrit lexicography: case of Amarakośa*, procs of the 4th AsiaLex conference organized by NUS, Singapore

Jha Girish Nath et al, 2006, *Computational lexicography and Amarakośa : an online RDBMS approach*, Presented at the *National Seminar of Language and Interface*, Deptt of Linguistics, Delhi University

Lee Jong-cheol, 2005, Sanskrit Dictionary-Database, Academy of Korean Studies, Seoul, Korea
http://www.hm.tyg.jp/~acmuller/ebti/dictionaries/sanskritdb.htm (accessed : 23 March 2005)

Mohanty et al, 2004, *Ontological analysis in Sanskrit wordnet, Procs of ICSLT-O-COCOSDA*, New Delhi, 2004

Ramanathan, A.A. 1978, Amarakosa with the unpublished South Indian commentaries, Vol. 1- 3, The Adyar Library and Research Centre.

Eurown: An Euro WordNet Module for Python

Neeme Kahusk
Institute of Computer Science
University of Tartu, Liivi 2, 50409 Tartu, Estonia
neeme.kahusk@ut.ee

Abstract

The subject of this demo is a Python module for editing and managing EuroWordNet database files. Python is a programming language that is dynamic, object-oriented, and has shallow learning curve. In this paper we give a short overview of the eurown module for managing EuroWordNet export files. This tool run on broad range of hardware platforms, including Windows, MacOS, Linux, and Unix.

1 Introduction

In this paper we present a Python module for developing EuroWordNet.

The subject of this demo are open-source tools for editing and managing EuroWordNet database files. The Python module serves as API and Graphic User Interface is implemented in Qt. These tools run on broad range of hardware platforms, including Windows, MacOS, Linux, and Unix.

The Python programming language is dynamic, object-oriented, and interpreted. It offers strong support for integration with other languages and tools, and comes with extensive standard libraries. Python has a very shallow learning curve and great online learning resource (Python Tutorial, 2009). It can be used for many kinds of software development, Natural Language Processing among them.

The EWN module enables a programmer to handle EuroWordNet synsets and semantic relations easily. Synsets are implemented as objects, operations on them as methods. Calculations on synsets can be used both in interactive Python sessions and by importing into other modules, like word sense disambiguation.

There are already two tools that make use of the eurown module. These are Kykap, a tool for lexicographers to help manual word sense disambiguation, and OpenPolaris, the open-source program that has roughly the same functionality as Polaris by Novel once had. Both of these applications are built using Qt and PyQt.

2 Python programming language

Python was created in the early 1990s by Guido van Rossum at Stichting Mathematisch Centrum in the Netherlands. Van Rossum is considered Python's principal author, although there have been many other contributors. The main development team has resided in many places, including CNRI and Zope Corporation. Nowadays the Python-related intellectual property is owned by the Python Software Foundation, a non-profit organization created specifically for this purpose. All Python releases are Open Source, most Python releases have been GPL-compatible. (Python 2.6.2 license, 2009).

Although Python is a flexible answer in programmer's choice of styles, its bright side come out with object-oriented approach. Most of its library programs, called modules in Pythonic, are designed bearing object-oriented usage in mind. They contain classes of objects, and methods and attributes to use with objects. All recent versions of Python make it possible to use even more flexible tools — properties. They are closely related to attributes, but use get, set, and delete functions to manage. We have used mostly properties instead of attributes, so there are no attributes in the section of class descriptions (see Section 3).

Python can be used for many kinds of software development, Natural Language Processing among them. There are NLP modules for Python developed since 2002, making up the Natural Language Toolkit package. The package has several subpackages for accessing text corpora and lexical resources, processing raw text, analyzing sentence structure, and other tasks. (Bird et al., 2009; Loper and Bird, 2002)

There are tools and resources for browsing wordnet data, but they concern Princeton Word-

Net only, not EuroWordNet. According to NLTK Guides[1], WordNet Interface is accessed like corpus reader, and can be used for finding words, synsets, lemmas, and three types of similarities based on hyperonym hierarchy.

There is a Python module for parsing EuroWordNet data developed by Marsi (2009), but the development of this code seems to be stopped in 2004.

3 Synset structure in EuroWordNet export file and eurown module contents

EuroWordNet import-export format follows Gedcom standard and is defined by Louw (1998). The main structure of the file format reflects the buildup of the database itself. A record in the database consists of level number, field name, and optional value. Level 0 records can have optional record number, enclosed between '@'-tokens.

```
0 WORD_MEANING
  1 PART_OF_SPEECH "n"
  1 VARIANTS
    # futher details of
    the variants go here
  1 INTERNAL_LINKS
    # futher details of
    the internal links go here
  1 EQ_LINKS
    # futher details of
    the equivalence links go here
  1 PROPERTIES
    # futher details of
    the properties go here
```

Figure 1: Main structure of the WORD_MEANING record (for a noun synset). The records for WORD_INSTANCE have PROPERTY_VALUES section instead of PROPERTY, and PART_OF_SPEECH "pn". Adopted from (Louw, 1998)

Classes in the `eurown` module follow the main data structure of the EuroWordNet database. The most used class is Synset representing word meaning objects. On the same level, WordInstance is also defined, it derives from the Synset class. There is also a class for wordnet — this makes it

```
0 @234@ WORD_MEANING
  1 PART_OF_SPEECH "n"
  1 VARIANTS
    2 LITERAL "amazona"
      3 SENSE 1
      3 STATUS "New"
      3 USAGE_LABELS
        4 USAGE_LABEL "sub"
          5 USAGE_LABEL_VALUE
                      "Medicine"
      3 FEATURES
        4 FEATURE "number"
  5 FEATURE_VALUE "singular"
      3 EXTERNAL_INFO
```

Figure 2: A nonsensical example of a synset record. Adopted from (Louw, 1998).

easy to use multiple wordnets in one application. There are classes for Level 1 records as well — namely Literal, InternalRelations, and ILI Relations. For an overview of classes in `eurown`, and their content, see Figure 3. Main classes and their properties and methods are listed in the following subsections.

3.1 Class WordNet()

Methods:

make_indexes() Makes all necessary indexes. This procedure takes time, thatswhy the indexes are made all at once and pickled[2] into files.

Properties:

synsetFileOffsetIndex Dict keys are synset numbers and values file offsets. Read only.

synsetTupleFileOffsetIndex Dict keys are synset tuples[3] (literal, pos, senseNo) and values file offsets. Read only.

literalIndex Dict keys are literals, values lists[4] of synset numbers. Read only.

synsetObjectIndex Dict keys are synset numbers and values Synset objects. Read only.

---
[1]http://nltk.googlecode.com/svn/trunk/doc/howto/wordnet.html

[2]Python uses its own method to write objects into text files. It is called *pickling*.

[3]Henceforward 'tuple' is meant as Python data structure, immutable sequence type.

[4]Henceforward 'list' is meant as Python data structure, mutable sequence type.

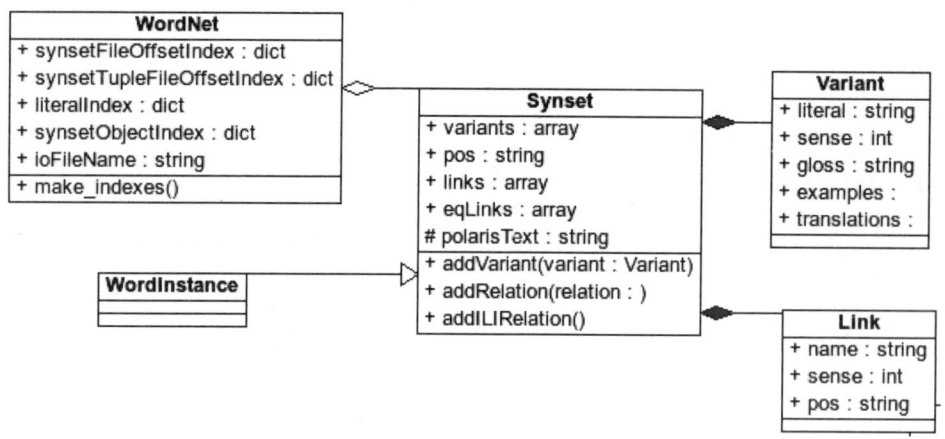

Figure 3: Class diagram of `eurown` module.

3.2 Class Synset()

Properties:

ident – synset identification number

pos – Part of Speech. One of [n, v, a, b]

variants – member of Variants class: list with Variant class members

links – member of Links class: list with Link class members

eqLinks – member of EqLinks class: list with EqLink members

properties – list of properties

firstLiteral – first literal and its sense number. Read-only. Computed by first member of Variants list.

literals – list of literals in Synset (without sense numbers). Read-only.

polarisText – output of Synset in Polaris format. Read-only

Methods:

addVariant(variant) adds a variant to Synset, *variant* must be an instance of Variant class.

addRelation(relation, relSynset) adds a synset to Synset, *relSynset* must be an instance of Synset class.

addILIRelation(relation, relSynset) adds a synset to Synset, *relSynset* must be an instance of Synset class (from ILI synsets file).

3.3 Class Variant()

literal Literal of the current variant

sense Sense of the current variant. Int type.

gloss Gloss (explanation) of current sense.

examples Examples of usage. List of strings (sentences).

3.4 Class Link()

name link name ('has_hyperonym', 'has_hyponym' etc.)

literal literal of the target concept

sense sense number of the target concept

pos part of speech of the target concept

There are also planned properties for adding and reading external info, but they are not implementeid into the module yet.

3.5 Other classes

There is also class EqLink() for managing ILI relations. Class WordInstance()] is mostly the same as Synset class, only pos is limited to "pn".

3.6 Functions

Functions defined in `eurown` module:

read_synset(fn, milestone) reads synset from file *fn* starting from byte *milestone*, returns tuple of (synset, new_milestone). This function is also useful for reading whole file into list of synsets.

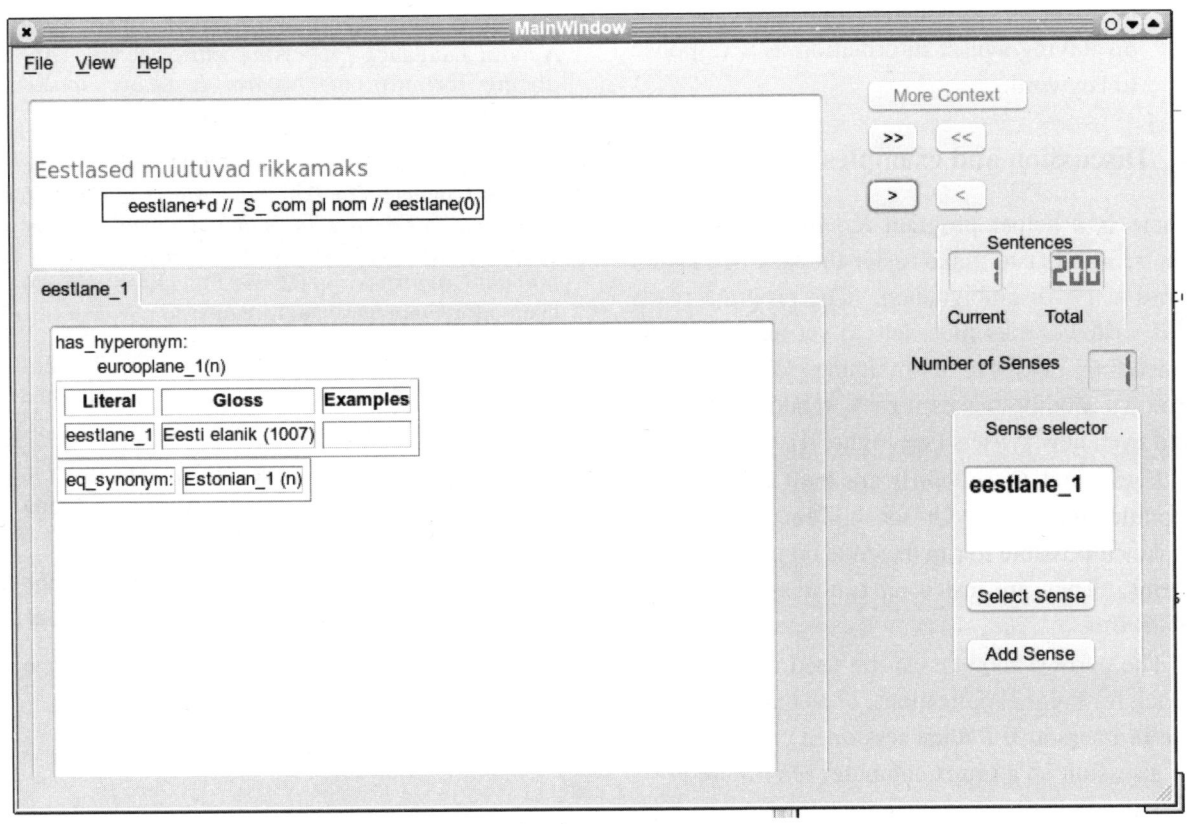

Figure 4: Screenshot of *Kykap* program. This application is built using the eurown module.

```
 Python 2.6 (r26:66714, Feb  3 2009, 20:52:03)
[GCC 4.3.2 [gcc-4_3-branch revision 141291]] on linux2
Type "help", "copyright", "credits" or "license" for more information.
>>> from eurown import *
>>> a = Synset(pos='n')
>>> print a.polarisText
0 WORD_MEANING
  1 PART_OF_SPEECH "n"
>>> b=Variant(literal='test',sense=1,gloss="just testing")
>>> a.addVariant(b)
>>> print a.polarisText
0 WORD_MEANING
  1 PART_OF_SPEECH "n"
  1 VARIANTS
    2 LITERAL "test"
      3 SENSE 1
      3 DEFINITION "just testing"
>>>
```

Figure 5: Screen dump of an interactive Python session using eurown module.

def ask_for_keyword Mostly for testing purposes, serves as a model of an application for displaying synset information as a response to keyword.

4 Discussion and examples

There is a helper program *Kykap* for lexicographers, in order to make easier the task of manual word sense disambiguation. The program reads and writes corpus files, lets to set many options (encoding, POSes to disambiguate, WordNet file). Eurown module makes it easy to add new senses and even new synsets (see Figure 4).

Kykap and *OpenPolaris* are built on `eurown` module and use PyQt for building GUI. This makes it possible to run the code on multiple platforms. They are tested on Linux and Windows platforms.

The eurown module can be used as a building block for bigger applications, or as imported module in interactive Python session. For an example of a session on a Linux computer see Figure 5.

The `eurown` module makes it easy to add, edit and remove synsets, variants, variant details, and links to EuroWordNet database. It is possible to use more than one Polaris export file at a time, so one can work with databases coming from different languages. Although we have tested it with ILI coming from WordNet 1.5, it would be possible to use newer versions as well. Output as `polarisText` makes it easy to compare the added or edited synsets to these that are made with Polaris, and import to it.

5 License and availability

The Python module and helper programs are licensed under GPL license and freely downloadable as Python source files at `http://www.cl.ut.ee/inimesed/nkahusk/tarkvara/ewnpy/`.

Acknowledgments

This project is supported by grants SF0180078s08 "Development and implementation of formalisms and efficient algorithms of natural language processing for the Estonian language" and EKKTT09-62 "Resources and tools for Estonian Semantics".

References

Steven Bird, Ewan Klein, and Edward Loper 2009 *Natural Language Processing with Python — Analyzing Text with the Natural Language Toolkit* O'Reilly Media http://www.nltk.org/book

Edward Loper and Steven Bird 2002 NLTK: The Natural Language Toolkit *Proceedings of the ACL Workshop on Effective Tools and Methodologies for Teaching Natural Language Processing and Computational Linguistics*, pp 62–69, Philadelphia, Association for Computational Linguistics.

Michael Louw 1998 *Polaris User's Guide: The EuroWordNet Database Editor* Lernout & Hauspie Antwerp, Belgium

Erwin Marsi 2009 Retrieved October 5, 2009 Homepage of Erwin Marsi: ewnpy http://ilk.uvt.nl/emarsi/software/ewnpy.html

Python 2.6.2 License 2009 http://www.python.org/download/releases/2.6.2/license/

The Python Tutorial 2009 http://docs.python.org/tutorial/